THE FREDERICKSBURG CAMPAIGN

THE
FREDERICKSBURG
CAMPAIGN

Winter War on the Rappahannock

Francis Augustín O'Reilly

Louisiana State University Press

Baton Rouge

Copyright © 2003 by Louisiana State University Press
All rights reserved.
Manufactured in the United States of America
First printing
12   11   10   09   08   07   06   05   04   03
5   4   3   2   1

Designer: Melanie O'Quinn Samaha
Typeface: AGaramond
Typesetter: Coghill Composition Co. Inc.
Printer and binder: Thomson-Shore, Inc.

ISBN 0-8071-2809-0

In loving memory of Thomas J. O'Reilly, Ph.D.

Scholar, Teacher, Friend

1930–1998

Tá sé faoi suimhneas le Críost ar rí

CONTENTS

ILLUSTRATIONS

PICTURES

following page 275

Confederate Washington Artillery on Marye's Heights

The stone wall and the Sunken Road

Confederates defending the stone wall

The Union assault against Marye's Heights

A. A. Humphreys' attack against the stone wall

Burnside's Mud March

MAPS

ACKNOWLEDGMENTS

I undertook this study five years ago at the behest of the historian William D. Matter. I wish to thank Bill Matter above all people for this opportunity. This book was Bill's dream, and he personally scoured the country, from New England to California, collecting manuscript sources for it. He amassed the largest collection of Fredericksburg material in private hands. He has made countless pilgrimages to the battlefield to walk the site, pinpoint critical landmarks, and wrestle with my nagging questions on remote points. I particularly enjoyed discovering the Mud March routes with him. I see a little piece of Bill in every page of this book. I am deeply touched by his generous spirit and consummate historical skill; and I am honored that he trusted me with his book.

I am also deeply indebted to Robert K. Krick, Chief Historian of the Fredericksburg and Spotsylvania National Military Park. His unrivaled knowledge of Robert E. Lee's Army of Northern Virginia is only matched by his indisputable command of the English language. I have for years been awestruck by his uncanny ability to know always what I want to say. His editorial genius has proved to me that great editors make great writers. This work has improved in every way under his careful guidance and suggestions. Any shortcomings are purely my own.

My closest friends and associates rallied repeatedly to my whims and demands, providing a level of detail that surprises even me. I appreciate the efforts of all of them, particularly those of "Colonel" Keith S. Bohannon, a gypsy-historian and foremost authority on Georgia in the war; Robert E. Lee Krick—"Krick the Slender"—of the Richmond National Battlefield Park, who sent me obscure tidbits and manuscripts from his many research junkets; and John J. Hennessy, historian, oracle of Manassas, and the keeper of the most thorough collection of information on the Army of the Potomac. Eric J. Mink, historian at Richmond National Battlefields, gladly shared information on the Pennsylvania Reserves and gave me many useful leads.

Terrain often holds the key to understanding the past. Noel G. Harrison, historian and author, and Erik Nelson, Fredericksburg City Planner and worldy philosopher, taught me the value of battlefield terrain in tying critical events to the ground. My historical colleagues at the National Park Service offered constant perspective and input. I am particularly indebted to Gregory A. "Papa" Mertz, Donald C. Pfanz, Janice M. Frye, Mac Wyckoff (master of South Carolina troops), Elsa L. Lohman, Keith Alexander, and Kelly O'Grady (of the Confederate Irish O'Gradys). I am also indebted to "Uncle" Ford Maune, whose wit and willingness to keep me in cocoa strengthened my understanding of obstacles and approaches.

During my years of researching and writing, I made the acquaintance of many valuable contacts, who generously shared their knowledge and insight. I am wiser for working with Don Cearley of Fredericksburg; Dr. George C. Rable of the University of Alabama; Lieutenant Colonel Kenneth Powers (retired)—*the* historian of the Irish Brigade; Southern scion at large John Bass of North Carolina; lawyer-scholar Gordon C. Rhea; U.S. Marine Corps historian J. Michael Miller; Barksdale aficionado Major Steven Hawley of the U.S. Army; and the industrious historical duo Toni and Terri Jeski of Minnesota.

Numerous institutions graciously allowed me access to and use of their treasured collections. I owe a great deal to the Civil War Library and Museum in Philadelphia, particularly to Director Steven Wright and Patrick Purcell; the U.S. Army Military History Institute and its assistant director of archives, the encyclopedic Dr. Richard J. Sommers; and the National Archives and its choice archivist, Michael P. Musick. Also helpful were the Historical Society of Pennsylvania; the Pennsylvania State Library; the Library of Congress; the Virginia State Library; the Virginia Historical Society; Duke University; the University of North Carolina at Chapel Hill; the University of Georgia;

the University of Michigan; and the Huntington Library of San Marino, California.

I wish to give a special acknowledgment to Sylvia Frank Rodrigue, acquisitions editor at Louisiana State University Press, who believed in my book and whose enthusiasm and guidance have been an endless source of encouragement. I also want to thank my lifelong friend and nemesis, Edward P. "Seagull" Coleman, the fecund genius of Coleman Computers Woodworking, Inc., who translated my flights of fancy into a magnificent set of battle maps. His mother is a saint (and a much better Flyers fan, too).

Lastly, and most importantly, I wish to thank my wife, Amy, whose poise and grace—sprinkled with a little hockey mischief—cheerfully supported me throughout this project, and remind me daily of why I adore her.

THE FREDERICKSBURG CAMPAIGN

"POOR BURN FEELS DREADFULLY"

The Winter Campaign of 1862

Foul weather blasted through Washington, D.C., accentuating the mood of the capital. The old general Catharinus P. Buckingham finished his supper and relaxed by a crackling fire. An emphatic rap on the door startled him to attention. A War Department messenger announced that the secretary of war wished to see him at once. The fifty-four-year-old general bundled up and headed for the War Department. Entering the offices of Secretary Edwin M. Stanton, Buckingham stepped out of one storm and into another.

Edwin Stanton and General-in-Chief Henry W. Halleck wanted him to deliver two unsealed envelopes to the Army of the Potomac. Buckingham thought peevishly "that it was a singular proceeding to make a mere messenger of a Brig. General when a corporal would have done the duty just as well." Stanton encouraged the general to read the contents before he left for the front.[1]

The officer returned home and opened the envelopes. The first contained General Orders 182, relieving Major General George B. McClellan from command of the army. The second gave the army to Major General Ambrose E. Burnside with the injunction: "Immediately on assuming command of the Army of the Potomac, you will report the position of your troops, and what you purpose doing with them." Catharinus Buckingham carried the full weight of the president's authority on his shoulders, something no corporal could convey. Stanton hoped the brigadier general would use his stature, guile, and persuasiveness to make sure that Burnside accepted the appointment.[2]

Buckingham commandeered a railroad engine in Alexandria on November 7, 1862, and started for the army. The wheezing locomotive, he was told, "had but one good quality . . . it was always *lucky*" (emphasis in original). Its good fortune carried him through treacherous snow squalls and guerrilla-infested country. Buckingham sat cooped up in the cab with the engineer and stoker until they reached Salem (modern-day Marshall) at sundown. Procuring a horse and an escort, the War Department general rode fifteen miles south to the town of Orleans.[3]

Buckingham interrupted Ambrose Burnside's supper and handed over the orders. Burnside balked, arguing that no one, including himself, was competent to command the Army of the Potomac. Besides, he was "under very great personal obligation" to McClellan. Little Mac had rescued him from financial ruin before the war. Buckingham coerced Burnside to accept. He pointed out that McClellan could not be saved, and if Burnside refused to do his duty, then his rival and nemesis, Major General Joseph Hooker, would get the command. Burnside consulted his staff. They encouraged him to accept, and he reluctantly acquiesced.[4]

Burnside, Buckingham, and a small retinue (which included an English observer looking for a ride to Washington) set out to see McClellan at once. The party got lost in the snow, but eventually found its way to Salem by 9:00 P.M. They took a train five miles up the Manassas Gap Railroad, and rode through Rectortown to McClellan's headquarters tent.[5]

McClellan sat up late, awaiting their arrival. He knew a high-ranking War Department official had come from Washington, and guessed the reason when he had gone straight to Burnside's headquarters. At 11:00 P.M., McClellan was writing a letter to his wife when Burnside arrived.[6]

McClellan received his guests cordially. He invited everyone to have a seat and offered General Buckingham a cigar. Uncomfortably, Buckingham came right to the point. "General," he said, coughing, "I might as well tell you at once what my business is." He handed the order to McClellan, who glanced at it. George McClellan informed Buckingham, "Gen. If you will permit Burnside and myself to consult together I will turn over the command to him." The rest withdrew for ten minutes while the two generals conferred. As the officers returned to the tent, McClellan asked Buckingham if he (McClellan) could stay a couple of days so he could familiarize Burnside with his plans and troop positions. The War Department emissary agreed, and the meeting broke up. Burnside returned to Orleans, Buckingham to Washington with his English charge, and McClellan to his letter, informing his wife: "Poor Burn feels dreadfully, almost crazy—I am sorry for him & he never showed himself a better man or truer friend than now."[7]

Abraham Lincoln had relied on McClellan to restore the Union, but after eighteen months of turmoil the president saw no end in sight. Lincoln looked anxiously to Burnside to provide a quicker route to success. He needed a victory before the end of 1862. He had spent much of the year reassuring the Northern populace that the war was going according to plan and ultimate success was guaranteed. Lincoln only reluctantly called for large drafts of men to fill his armies in times of genuine crisis. Confederate victories during the summer of 1862 led to incursions into Maryland and Kentucky. Popular opinion throughout the North suddenly questioned Lincoln's ability to handle the war. The contest appeared closer than the government in Washington had intimated. And while the North did not panic, it reflected its concern in rising economic inflation and fluctuations in the gold standard. A Northern observer remembered, "Wall Street was making itself *felt* as it never had before."[8]

The administration had further alienated the populace with the introduction of a billowing national debt, high taxes (including the first national income tax), suspension of habeas corpus, and numerous arrests. The most overt show of Northern dissatisfaction came in the fall congressional and gubernatorial elections. Lincoln attempted to avert disaster to his party and administration by prodding the nation's principal army—George B. McClellan's Army of the Potomac—to action.[9]

McClellan reluctantly and languidly plodded across the Potomac River into Virginia on October 26. A couple of weeks later, his army stalled at Warrenton without a showdown with its opponent, General Robert E. Lee's Confederate Army of Northern Virginia. The elections passed without a political respite for Lincoln's party, and the Democrats made significant gains. The key states of New York and New Jersey elected new anti-administration governors (Horatio Seymour and Joel Parker, respectively); and even Republican bastions like Pennsylvania replaced half of their representatives to Congress with Democrats. Democrats from the chief executive's home state of Illinois outnumbered Republicans in the House almost two to one. The election was a serious setback, and Lincoln understood that "the ill success of the war had much to do with this."[10]

In a broader sphere, Europe viewed Lincoln's war with aloof contempt. England had divided sympathies. The upper class rooted for the South and the expanding middle class leaned toward the North. Military reverses and Lincoln's radical abolitionist reforms, however, muted the middle class. The rest of Europe disdained the United States' excessive bloodshed, yet they refrained from intervention, at least for the moment. France had already taken advantage of Federal weakness to invade Mexico and attempt to establish a permanent aggrandizement with the puppet Archduke Maximilian on the Mexican throne.[11]

Lincoln's aims became more specific after the elections. He needed a victory to stave off his opponents and silence his detractors. He mobilized all of his field armies, hoping they would revitalize his war policies and sustain his administration. Lincoln had urged George McClellan to move into Virginia, while Don Carlos Buell took his Army of the Cumberland deeper into Tennessee. He encouraged Ulysses S. Grant and William T. Sherman to seize Vicksburg, Mississippi. The forces converging on the Mississippi hub could combine or work independently. Where Lincoln perceived indolence he acted swiftly. He removed Buell from command and replaced him with the seemingly more animated William S. Rosecrans. The president soon realized that sacking Buell had made little impression on his benefactor, McClellan; and on November 5, the president cut the orders giving the army to Burnside.

Confederate war aims focused on maintaining the strategic defensive. After failed attempts to "liberate" the slave states of Maryland and Kentucky, the Confederacy replenished its armies and planned to recoup lost territory. President Lincoln had isolated the South from potential allies and international recognition by late 1862, when he issued the preliminary Emancipation Proclamation. The document redefined the war in some European eyes from one of internal discord to a crusade for human rights. Refusing to aid openly a slavery-perpetuating state, Europe kept a distance from the American conflict despite all of her rumblings to the contrary. The South had to rely on itself to achieve independence. The year had started badly with the loss of Confederate armies and territory, primarily in the western theater and the Trans-Mississippi. The Confederacy stood in danger of being severed in two, with Union forces driving north and south along the Mississippi River. A manpower shortage in Southern armies led to the first instituted conscription, or compulsory draft, in American history. Most Southerners abided by the law, but some armed dissidents resisted, primarily in the Appalachian regions. States' rights governors, like Joseph Brown of Georgia, openly criticized Confederate president Jefferson Davis' strong central government. Davis, he said, trod heavily on the authority of state sovereignty. Conscription among other things compelled the secretary of war, George Wythe Randolph, to resign, discredited. James A. Seddon replaced him in November 1862, becoming the fourth secretary of war in thirteen months.[12]

A brilliant string of victories in Virginia sustained the Confederacy through the bleak year. Southern nationalism became associated with—and later, synonymous with—the ascendancy of the South's most successful commander, General Robert E. Lee. His exploits compensated emotionally for the losses of New Orleans, Forts Henry and Donelson, Shiloh, and the Carolina coastal regions. The apparent unity of command in Lee's Army of Northern Virginia muted the divisiveness of militant states' rights factions and rifts in Jeff Davis' centralized government.[13]

Robert E. Lee's objective was to finish out 1862 without a Union triumph in Virginia. If the advanced season forced the Yankee army into winter quarters without success, then discontent would fester throughout the North. A growing faction of Northern "Peace Democrats"—called "Copperheads" by their opponents—was gaining a ground swell of support. The Copperheads raged against the war they believed could not be won. The Confederates had based their war aims largely on a quick and decisive war, but for once, Lee saw time as an ally to frustrate the North.

The Civil War entered a unique, new phase in the fall of 1862. Lincoln's need for victory demanded an unprecedented winter campaign. Typically, nineteenth-century armies rested and refitted during the bad-weather months and campaigned during the spring and summer, when nature became more amenable, or at least more predictable. Armies relied primarily on dirt roads for moving men and matériel and for communications. Winter often turned those avenues into quagmires. Streams and rivers habitually flooded, threatening to cut off and isolate armies from their bases. Lincoln also promoted, for the first time, a "coordinated" offensive for the Union war effort. All of the individual Federal armies moved at the same time and with fairly well defined objectives. To date, the Northern armies had operated in a vacuum, defining their own goals and timetables without reference to one another. They did not communicate or synchronize their operations under Lincoln's new call either, but the president had them striking at the Confederacy at roughly the same time. (All four Union armies climaxed their campaigns within twenty days of each other.) Political necessity dictated immediate action and overrode all military considerations for timetables, justifications, and planning. The Union armies started their campaigns ill prepared and poorly equipped to handle a winter expedition for some tenuous political capital. Lincoln, too, entered into a winter of discontent, which was best exemplified by his largest and most newsworthy army, Burnside's Army of the Potomac.

Confederate armies had to endure the rigors of a winter campaign as well. Lee's army would experience the novelty of fighting on the defensive and the innovation of using cover to protect front-line troops. The remarkable encounter at Fredericksburg made the storied "stone wall" and Marye's Heights legendary, and the doctrine of fortifications for combat troops a necessity.

The opposing forces in the Fredericksburg campaign used the same basic structure for command and drill. Both sides relied on an expanded model of the pre-war U.S. Regular Army's organization of regiments, brigades, divisions, and corps. The largest unit of maneuver was the corps (composed of two to five divisions), and the fundamental unit for combat was the brigade. Brigades might be composed of two to seven regiments. The full complement of a brigade numbered 4,000 to 8,000 men, but campaign attrition, detachments, and disease more often left brigades with just 1,500 to 3,000 effective troops.

General Ambrose E. Burnside's Army of the Potomac consisted of men from eighteen Northern states. The general was thirty-eight years old when he assumed command. Burnside came from Indiana, but his family had once owned slaves in South Carolina. He was a tailor's apprentice before graduating from the U.S. Military Academy at West Point in 1847. He saw little action in the army (though he was slightly wounded in an Indian fracas in 1849) and quickly resigned. Burnside failed in several private enterprises before he accepted a position in George B. McClellan's Illinois Central Railroad. In 1861, Burnside returned to the army as the colonel of the 1st Rhode Island Infantry. Steadily rising, he commanded an amphibious, multiservice expedition against the Carolina coast in early 1862. By late 1862, Burnside had earned a reputation for action, which Lincoln dearly hoped to capitalize on.[14]

General Robert E. Lee commanded the Confederate Army of Northern Virginia, made up of soldiers from twelve states (with both sides claiming Maryland as their own). The general was the fifty-five-year-old son of a Revolutionary War general and past governor of Virginia. He had graduated second in his class at West Point in 1829, and excelled in a number of ventures in the old army, from serving on General Winfield Scott's staff—and ensuring victory during the war with Mexico—to capturing John Brown at Harpers Ferry. He turned down offers to command the Union armies in 1861 and cast his lot with his native Virginia—and the Confederacy. Lee struggled early in the war with failures in western Virginia and the Carolina coastal forts. He left the field to become an advisor to President Jefferson Davis, only to re-emerge in June 1862, with a series of victories that drove the war from the doorstep of Richmond to the doorstep of the Union. His training as an engineer gave him an unequivocal eye for terrain. He would make Fredericksburg a model of defensive efficiency.[15]

The Northern army, divided into 68 brigades and 8 corps, mustering 135,000 men. Burnside commanded the largest army yet assembled on the continent. Lee's forces, composed of 43 brigades in 2 corps, amounted to 78,000 troops. His army would never be this strong again.

Small arms had been varied and numerous in the early part of the war, with men using everything from flintlocks to shotguns. By late 1862, both armies had fairly well standardized their weapons. Most of the soldiers carried .58 caliber Springfield rifled muskets or the imported English .577 caliber Enfield rifled musket, though some still carried antiquated Belgian and Austrian rifles during the winter campaign. Soldiers were trained to load and fire the muzzle-loading weapons as rapidly as three times a minute—though that was achieved only under ideal circumstances.

The addition of rifling, or spiral grooving, to the bore of muskets revolutionized warfare. Prior to the Civil War, military leaders had been inculcated with Napoleonic tactics, which were based on smoothbore musket fire. Smoothbore muskets had proven notoriously inaccurate and rarely damaged a target beyond a hundred yards. Rifling, however, made shoulder weapons accurate at ranges exceeding four hundred yards. Massed fire practice—or close-order tactics—planted men shoulder to shoulder firing in unison, to compensate for the inaccuracy of smoothbore muskets by creating a dense concentration of fire. But close-order tactics for attacking forces had become a liability in the face of superior firearms. Military practice had failed to evolve past massed formations, so weaponry decidedly favored the defender over the attacker. Fredericksburg would prove that better than anywhere else.[16]

Artillery had undergone a dramatic change as well. Ordnance had been heavy and bulky, and primarily relegated to fixed support roles. In Europe, these unwieldy guns had been retained, and on European battlefields they were kept largely stationary. But Americans experimented with lighter, mobile guns to exploit maneuverability. Mobility generated an element of offensive capability. Guns also improved during the years leading up to the Civil War. The old, smoothbore cannons, primarily the 12-pounder Napoleons, remained the workhorses for the artillery because of their ability to fire shot, shell, or canister. But newer, rifled pieces—the 3-inch rifles and 12-pounder Parrotts—had become highly sought after. The Napoleon gun weighed 1,200 pounds and fired a shell up to 1,500 yards. The 3-inch rifle weighed only 820 pounds and extended the range of a shell to 2,800 yards. The Parrott had a comparable 890-pound weight and 3,000-yard range. Burnside's army had approximately 410 guns in 83 batteries; a battery typically comprised of 6 guns. Lee's artillery counted 240 guns in 55 batteries, averaging four guns per battery.[17]

Logistically, Lee's and Burnside's armies relied on railroads and hard-surfaced highways to provide for their needs. Foul weather in the winter months limited the use of many roads and placed a heavier reliance on sturdy railroads. Few rail lines ran north and south to benefit a Union advance. McClellan had banked on the single-track Orange and Alexandria (O&A) Railroad to supply his army up to Warrenton, but that line continued southwest, away from the Federal goal of Richmond. The only other track that could service a move south was the Richmond, Fredericksburg and Potomac (RF&P) Railroad. As the line proceeded south it crossed the Virginia Central Railroad at Hanover Junction (modern Doswell), and then both lines ran roughly parallel to Richmond. Limited to these two options, the Union commander regarded the rail line through Fredericksburg with especial interest.

CHAPTER ONE

"TO CRIPPLE THE REBEL CAUSE"

The Road to Fredericksburg

Robert E. Lee's army needed time to rest and refit after its return from Maryland. A South Carolinian in Gregg's Brigade wrote, "It is difficult to describe the condition of the troops at this time, so great and various was their wretchedness." A member of the 3rd Arkansas revealed, "We were sorely in need of clothing and shoes, and there was not a blanket in the command." Manpower had dwindled to barely 30,000 men in ranks. Logistics had snarled terribly, and battle-hardened veterans bordered on the brink of collapse. A North Carolina soldier confessed, "The condition of our troops [is] now demanding repose."[1]

The short campaign in Maryland had taken its toll on the exhausted army. Men collapsed along the floor of the lower Shenandoah Valley. The momentum that had led the army over the Potomac River a few weeks before seemed completely spent upon its return. Western Maryland's cold reception of the liberating Southrons left many in Lee's forces with dismal sentiments of the foray. When an army band struck up the tune "Maryland, My Maryland," it was shouted down with "groans & hisses" by the soldiers.[2]

Financially, the Southern Confederacy felt the first pangs of ruin. Unsecured paper currency gave rise to rampant inflation and foreboding commercial disaster. An early Confederate biographer of Lee lamented that financial deterioration threw "greater obstacles in the way of Lee's success than all the Federal armies in the field."[3]

Personal tragedy left Robert E. Lee grief stricken. He received notice that his daughter, Annie, had died unexpectedly on October 20. A staff officer accidentally caught the general sobbing in his tent. Lee wrote to his wife, "I cannot express the anguish I feel at the death of my sweet Annie." Lee's head of cavalry, Major General James Ewell Brown "Jeb" Stuart, lost his five-year-old daughter, Flora, two weeks later. Unable to leave the army, Stuart notified his wife, "I shall have to leave my child in the hands of God; my duty requires me here." A month later, Major General Ambrose Powell Hill—commander of the largest division in the army—lost his firstborn, Henrietta, to diphtheria. Lee consoled his subordinates in their darkest hour.[4]

Lee and his commanders immersed themselves in rebuilding the army. Confederates herded stragglers from across Virginia to the Valley. Wounded men from earlier campaigns returned, and Lee further enhanced his strength with heavy recruitment and a general reorganization of the army. Lincoln's preliminary Emancipation Proclamation sparked an influx of new volunteers. Others enlisted to avoid conscription. An early Confederate writer averred that "in the course of a fortnight the army was increased by the arrival of about thirty thousand fresh troops." Soon that number burgeoned to 78,000. A division staff officer rejoiced: "The Army is filling up rapidly." A South Carolina private wrote: "Our brigade is becoming stronger every day. . . . it is very cheering to see our ranks beginning to fill up."[5]

Lee, by a special act of Congress, organized his army into two corps. On November 6, the army officially divided into the First Corps, under command of Lieutenant General James Longstreet, and the Second Corps, under Lieutenant General Thomas J. "Stonewall" Jackson. The new organization created a means for efficient growth, discipline, and supply. But as the army expanded, supplies did become a problem. A Confederate confided to his diary: "The men are for the most part destitute of blankets. . . . Our fare is very poor . . . no beef." A staff officer cautioned, "though we have done wonders, we can't perform miracles." The army was still largely naked, even as another campaign appeared imminent.[6]

Lee's army drilled endlessly, and supplies trickled in for most of its needs. A proud South Carolina soldier wrote, "We are drilling with considerable energy, and old soldiers tho we be . . . it is certainly wisdom to prepare ourselves." Pride returned with the transformation of the ragged force. "Our army is very different from the naked, barefooted handful of gallant men who held the field of Sharpsburg," applauded one of Lee's men. "Our Regiment would carry into battle tomorrow more men than were in the Brigade at Sharpsburg." An artilleryman agreed: "This army is in the best condition I have ever known it; the men are cheerful almost to recklessness." Major General John Bell Hood's division grew from 5,759 to 7,312 in just two months. An Alabama soldier reported that the Confederates "are ready for anything." Anything came in the final week of October, when George B. McClellan's Army of the Potomac returned to Virginia.[7]

McClellan's army loped through the piedmont of Virginia, skirting the eastern face of the Blue Ridge Mountains. Jeb Stuart's cavalry monitored the Union advance. Stuart was an engaging, energetic officer. Thirty-one years of age, he served as Robert E. Lee's intelligence officer and cavalry commander. One of Lee's staff members claimed that "Stuart was unequaled as an outpost officer." A trooper under Stuart recalled the end of October and the beginning of November as "an endless series of skirmishes." Federal cavalry fought with a newfound tenacity, keeping Stuart's prying eyes at a distance. James McCabe, an intimate biographer of Robert E. Lee, admitted that the unexpected Union challenge, combined with epidemics of sore tongue and rotting hooves among the horses, gave Stuart only "varied success." Nevertheless Stuart ascertained enough information to report that McClellan's entire force was heading down the O&A Railroad toward Culpeper Court House.[8]

Lee needed to block the Federal advance. If McClellan reached Culpeper, he could plant his army between Lee and Richmond. "The orders came so suddenly to prepare for a march," mused a Confederate, "that some of us were first led to believe that a fight was in contemplation." James Longstreet's soon-to-be First Corps started for Culpeper by October 31. Two divisions, under Major Generals Henry T. Walker and Lafayette McLaws, slipped through Chester Gap and hurried ahead. Once they had barred McClellan's path, Longstreet's three remaining divisions, under John B. Hood, Richard H. Anderson, and George E. Pickett, took a more leisurely route over the mountains. One soldier recalled, "Our movement was unhurried." An artilleryman fondly remembered the "delightful march through [a] country of good things and kind people in harvest and fruit." Lee and the army's reserve artillery joined Longstreet at Culpeper, all arriving by November 2. Longstreet had Hood guard the upper Rappahannock River, near the Robertson River, while Walker's division—now under the command of Brigadier General Robert Ransom—kept watch at Madison Court House. The rest of the corps camped around Culpeper Court House. Despite its relaxed appearance,

Longstreet's command needed the time to recuperate from the move. A worn-out Confederate admitted: "We were on the march about three or four days; the men having been lying about in camp, without any exercise, did not stand it very well." The most common complaint was sore feet.[9]

Lee intended Jackson's corps would follow Longstreet's, but he canceled the order at the last minute, because Jackson appealed to stay in the Valley. Stonewall Jackson hoped that he could swoop down from the mountain gaps and strike McClellan's susceptible supply lines. Lee gave his assent but cautioned his subordinate to stay in touch, in case Lee needed to concentrate the army in short order. When Longstreet left the Valley, Jackson occupied the Blue Ridge gaps—looking for a way "to threaten the enemy's flank and rear, and thus prevent his advance southward." A. P. Hill's division covered Snicker's Gap. Major General Daniel Harvey Hill, brother-in-law to Stonewall, moved his division to the forks of the Shenandoah River, and furnished parties to guard the adjacent passes. Jackson concentrated the rest of his forces at Berryville and Winchester.[10]

After blocking McClellan's advance at Culpeper, Lee went to Richmond on October 30 to consult the president, Jefferson Davis. A provost at Gordonsville station noted that Lee "is much younger than I expected." Lee had grown his beard longer than normal, which enhanced his athletic build. The general met with Davis and Major General Samuel G. French on November 1 to discuss reinforcements. French volunteered that he could hold southern Virginia and North Carolina briefly with 6,000 troops. Lee agreed and asked that the rest of French's force be shipped to him. The Virginian returned to the army on November 5 and established camp "near Orange Court House, on a wooded hill, just east of the village."[11]

A couple of days later, Robert E. Lee learned that Ambrose E. Burnside had replaced George B. McClellan. He worried that the change portended immediate action. Lee warned Jackson that if the First Corps retired under pressure, "you will fall back upon General Longstreet by the most advantageous route open to you." On November 6, he wanted Jackson to move through Swift Run Gap and join him as soon as possible. Another reason to reunite the army came when Stuart's cavalry unearthed a way to strike the Union supply base at Warrenton Junction. Stuart pitched the idea on November 7, but Lee refrained. The Confederates could not strike the Army of the Potomac with Longstreet's corps alone, as he was not strong enough and Lee feared provoking a general engagement while his own forces were so widely separated. Later that day, Lee gave Stuart his evacuation plans in case the Federals attacked. "Should we be pressed back from here," he explained, "my design is to retire through Madison, while Jackson ascends the Valley, so that a junction can be made through Swift Run Gap." Lee wired Jackson to hurry before the Federals could close the gap. The next day, Lee thought the Union army might be targeting Jackson rather than Longstreet. In that case, Lee planned to advance his First Corps once the Federals entered the passes, and cut Burnside's line of communications—in essence, reversing the roles between his two corps. Jackson's answers have been lost, but his actions appear to suggest that Lee always deferred to his Second Corps commander. Jackson continued to sit tight and wait for the Northerners to let down their guard.[12]

The Federal army, meanwhile, had not moved since it arrived at Warrenton. Stalemate seemed to rule the upper Rappahannock River, with Federals and Confederates glaring at each other from opposite banks. A Mississippian wrote in his diary: "no serious demonstrations made by the Federals." Stuart enlivened the scene briefly on November 10 with a skirmish along the Hazel River, a tributary of the Rappahannock. A bullet clipped off half of Stuart's mustache in a cavalry brush at Amissville. Aside from these brief forays, the armies remained at an impasse; neither side was certain what the Federal high command intended to do next.[13]

Ambrose E. Burnside inherited a strategic situation that had befuddled George McClellan. When Lee blocked the O&A Railroad at Culpeper, McClellan cast his eye toward Fredericksburg as the logical route to Richmond. He had ordered the army to concentrate at Warrenton for resupply, but snow hampered the movement, and along with inclement weather came Catharinus Buckingham. Burnside allowed McClellan's directive to stand, and most of the army moved to Warrenton on November 8 and 9. The Union First, Second, and Fifth Corps, along with the army's reserve artillery, gathered near the small courthouse town. The Sixth Corps massed at New Baltimore. The Ninth Corps combined with Brigadier Generals George Stoneman's and Amiel W. Whipple's divisions near the hamlet of Waterloo. Major General Franz Sigel's Eleventh Corps stretched across Burnside's rear from New Baltimore to Gainesville and Thoroughfare Gap. Brigadier General Daniel E. Sickles' division guarded the O&A from Manassas Junction to Warrenton Junction; and the Union Twelfth Corps watched the Potomac at Harpers Ferry. Brigadier General Alfred Pleasonton's Union cavalry screened the front around Amissville and Jeffersonton (or simply Jefferson, as many called it). Brigadier General George D. Bayard covered the army's left flank near Rappahannock Station. Morale appeared to be fragile, as Brigadier General William T. H. Brooks noted in an October letter: "Our army . . . is not in condition to take the field at present. Our men are tired out, and they are out of clothing, discipline, [and] everything that goes to make efficient soldiers."[14]

Five hours before he was relieved of command, McClellan ordered both Sigel's Eleventh Corps and Bayard's cavalry brigade to reconnoiter Fredericksburg and ascertain the condition of the RF&P Railroad. Bayard did not participate, owing to his duties at Rappahannock Station. Sigel confessed that his cavalry was too busy watching Jackson's forces through the Blue Ridge passes. The German sent instead his headquarters escort. Captain Ulric Dahlgren, son of the famous naval ordnance expert, Captain John A. Dahlgren, and aide to Sigel took 60 men from Captain Abram Sharra's 1st Indiana Cavalry, and another 100 horsemen from the 6th Ohio Cavalry. With that force he set out from Gainesville in the middle of the night, hoping to reach Fredericksburg before dawn.[15]

Bad weather and poor roads delayed Dahlgren's arrival until 7:30 A.M. on November 10. Fortunately for him, the Confederate defenders lacked numbers and discipline. Three companies of the 15th Battalion Virginia Cavalry had garrisoned the city since September. Lieutenant Colonel John Critcher patrolled the lower end of the Rappahannock, which left 80 cavalrymen in Fredericksburg at any given time. On November 8, Captain James Simpson and a small contingent of the Chesapeake Light Cavalry came to town, bolstering Critcher's force to approximately 200 troopers. The Southerners had neglected to picket the river above Fredericksburg, which allowed Dahlgren to approach the city undetected.[16]

The Confederates may have relaxed their vigilance when the river rose and fords became impassable. Dahlgren, however, discovered a shallow point upriver, near the village of Falmouth. Horsemen splashed across the river in single file. The 1st Indiana Cavalry crossed while the 6th Ohio covered the ford in case Dahlgren needed to beat a hasty retreat. The Indiana cavalry spotted a group of "rebels gathering to meet us" at the northern fringe of the city. Dahlgren and Captain Sharra charged and routed the group and pursued it into the city.[17]

Lieutenant Colonel Critcher quartered his Confederates in a tobacco factory near the RF&P Railroad; and Captain Simpson's Chesapeake Cavalry rested in Citizens' Hall, several blocks away, on Princess Anne Street. Many of the men had wandered downtown looking for better food and quarters. The Confederates had chosen their barracks out of convenience, rather than for defense. None of them managed to get to the perimeter of the city before the enemy was upon them.[18]

Ulric Dahlgren detached a small force under Lieutenant James H. Carr to ride ahead and locate the main Confederate force. At 8:30 A.M., Carr's troopers galloped down Caroline Street, followed by Dahlgren and the rest of the 1st Indiana Cavalry. Carr brushed aside several small groups before he located Critcher's command in the tobacco factory. The Federals formed in line opposite the factory. Critcher's Confederates inside panicked when they saw the Yankees swarming outside, and fled. Lieutenant Colonel Critcher could not rally his forces until they were a mile south of the city. Dahlgren's men, however, netted 20 or 30 of the Rebels before they escaped.[19]

Commotion, shooting, and a stampede of soldiers awoke Simpson's command from its repose at Citizens' Hall. Some of the frightened Confederates warned the Chesapeake Light Cavalry, "Run for your lives! The Yankees are coming!" Simpson tried to cordon off Princess Anne Street with mounted men, but the narrow passage to the horse lot behind the hall choked traffic to an unseemly crawl. Nine troopers blocked the street, but the Federals easily burst through, leaving one dead, another unconscious from a saber blow, and taking the remaining seven as prisoners. The Federals little realized that they had left the bulk of Captain Simpson's command mounting in the lot behind them. Simpson charged into the street in time to engage another party of Dahlgren's raiders. A general melee broke loose in the crowded street, punctuated by saber strokes and the reports of six-shooters. Simpson put the Northerners to flight and liberated six of his men.[20]

Captain Dahlgren's force had splintered by now, chasing prisoners in all directions. When the captain heard an erroneous report that the Confederates had cut off his retreat, he ordered Captain Sharra to break off the fight. Sharra brought away thirty prisoners, the colors of the 15th Virginia Battalion Cavalry, which he found in the tobacco factory, and two wagonloads of gray cloth.[21]

The Federals retraced their steps to the ford above Falmouth, Simpson's Confederates in pursuit. A number of individual encounters slowed the Union retreat. Oney Brock, a member of Simpson's company, spotted Critcher's captured colors and demanded that the Federals surrender it. When they ignored him, he killed the Yankee carrying the flag, and disappeared with the colors. Another Federal, escorting two prisoners up Caroline Street, found his path blocked by an angry young maiden wielding a pistol. Quick talking disarmed the girl, but the delay allowed other Confederates to overtake the Northerner and liberate his charges. Union cavalrymen complained that the civilians of Fredericksburg attacked them with stones. One Northerner ended up a captive when a well-aimed rock unhorsed him. Some of the ladies refrained from combat, but bravely stood on their porches, waving handkerchiefs and cheering their gray-clad heroes. Simpson broke off the pursuit at the north end of Caroline Street when he heard that a regiment waited ahead to ambush him.[22]

Dahlgren safely recrossed the river and divided his forces. The captain took twelve hand-picked men and set off to reconnoiter the railroad line to Aquia, while the rest of the raiders headed back to the Union lines with their prisoners and prizes. The two wagons stalled a couple of miles out of Falmouth, and the Federals burned them.[23]

Captain Dahlgren's party ventured up the railroad and surprised Rebel pickets at Accokeek Creek bridge. The youthful aide discovered that the rail line was in tolerable condition, but for some unknown reason, he exceeded his orders and torched the bridge. The captain's indiscretion would cause serious headaches for the U.S. Military Railroads later on. Dahlgren backtracked from Aquia and re-joined Sigel later that evening. Franz Sigel sent a second scouting party to Fredericksburg and informed Burnside that his scouts had found the Confederates still in small force. "No train of cars has been there since the attack," Sigel reported, implying that the Confederates had neither evacuated nor reinforced the city—things had returned to normal in Fredericksburg. The road to Richmond via Fredericksburg appeared to be open.[24]

The people of Fredericksburg denigrated John Critcher for allowing himself to be surprised. One inhabitant wrote, "Col. Critcher's pickets must have been extremely negligent of their duty, or our men could not have been so completely surprised." A more combative Fredericksburg native declared ruefully: "It seemed a pity that we could not have captured the forces that came over, as they did not exceed 75 in number, and ours numbered in all upward of 200." Captain Simpson's command, on the other hand, received the heartfelt thanks of the people. The ladies of Fredericksburg presented the Chesapeake battalion with a new battle flag as a token of their appreciation. Colonel William B. Ball, commander of the 15th Virginia Cavalry, arrived soon after to supplant Critcher in command. Major General Gustavus W. Smith, head of the Richmond defenses, strengthened Ball's Confederates with Captain John W. Lewis' Virginia battery.[25]

Burnside, in the meantime, had assumed command of an army, which was angry about losing its favorite commander. The provost marshal of the army confided in his diary, "The Army is in mourning & this is a blue day for us all." Word of McClellan's removal traveled fast. The general remained with the army for several days to arrange his affairs, which fueled speculation that he might stay. The sacking of the army's beloved leader only exacerbated the army's discontent. Recently, the army seemed to be at cross-purposes with the government. Like their commander, many in the army bristled at the preliminary Emancipation Proclamation. Lincoln had postulated that on January 1, 1863, all slaves in areas "in rebellion" would be free men. The measure infuriated Southerners because they construed some passages as inciting Negro insurrection. Northerners also abhorred the act for being, as they perceived, too radical. In a decided minority, one Lincoln supporter lamented that the soldiers were "too conservative" to support abolition. Changing the status quo made it more difficult to restore the Union in their eyes. Others mocked the idea that a proclamation would succeed where armies had failed. "I suppose no more fighting will be necessary to terminate the war," mused a Sixth Corps general, "only several more proclamations of the president and peace will spread her wings over the whole country." Some felt betrayed by Lincoln because he had changed his war aims. "I was never a negro worshiper," groused a Maine soldier. "I believe the principal [*sic*] of slavery is wrong, but it was none of our business to meddle with slavery in the state[s] w[h]ere the constitution planted it. . . . Let the North look after her own affairs and she has enough to attend to." Others feared that the proclamation was an idle threat and would cause further trouble and embarrassment. "I suppose you are all in high glee because Abe had set 3 million Niggers free (on paper)," wrote a member of the 96th Pennsylvania. "I care not if the Niggers eat the Whites or the Whites kill the Niggers, just so the War is ended. But alas . . . the Proclamation will not go even as far as our bullets go."[26]

Emotions peaked on November 9 and 10, when George B. McClellan bade farewell to the army. Officers crowded McClellan's headquarters at 9:00 P.M. on November 9 to shake their general's hand one last time. "A feeling as deep as I have ever known," General Marsena Patrick recalled, overcame many. Officers embraced their commander and bawled like children. A number of junior officers, perhaps fortified with liquor, grumbled that McClellan ought to march on Washington. Prudently, the others ignored such dangerous talk, and McClellan admonished them never to speak that way again.[27]

The next morning, troops lined the roads around Warrenton to catch a final glimpse of the heroic Little Mac. A signal officer remembered what followed as "one of the most affecting scenes and indeed most exciting . . . that I ever witnessed." McClellan emerged from his headquarters at 8:00 A.M., and joined by Burnside, proceeded to review the infantry and cavalry of his bodyguard. "His appearance was the signal for a general outburst from all on the ground," recalled a witness. "The men cheered, threw up their hats and waved their swords and gave vent to their feelings in every conceivable way." The general passed through a gauntlet of cheers from the Second and Fifth Corps, which drew up on both sides of the road. A signal flag announced McClellan's arrival and once more, "The men were wild with excitement," according to a 27th New York soldier. "They threw their hats into the air and cheered their old commander as long as his escort was in sight . . . the soldiers have always idolized him." Some units rippled with more or less enthusiasm, but generals quickly whipped them into a frenzy. Even the pasty puritan Brigadier General Marsena R. Patrick encouraged them. The general called for a cheer: "Once more & All Together." "It was magical in its effect," he scribbled in his diary, "and the result was splendid." McClellan's caravan grew, as numerous generals left their commands to join the "Young Napoleon" on his last ride. "The heavy tread of many flying feet, from his mounted guards," marveled the soldiers of a new regiment, "shook the earth under our feet as he passed." McClellan rode the entire way with his head uncovered, acknowledging the cheers and salutes. He rounded the two corps and returned to Warrenton by way of the Sixth and First Corps, meeting with more shouting, more hat tossing, and more crying. "Many of his brave veterans shed tears," a diarist recorded. "They all cry come back to McClellan." A telegraph officer recalled, "The whole army[,] from major generals down to foot orderlies, cried like babies when he left."[28]

The coterie of well-braided officers reconvened that evening at the headquarters of Fifth Corps commander Major General Fitz John Porter. The officers ringed McClellan "sobbing and crying like children." The general stood in the center of the tent "with tears in his eyes and sobs choking his utterance." Provost Marshal Marsena Patrick confided that the party became emotional. "We had a rough time last night," he wrote. "Officers and men had been drinking . . . but in their cups men spoke their minds." Some of the party blamed their hero's demise on Radical Republicans and newspaper pressure to strike at the Confederacy before the army was ready. A group of drunken "young, rattlebrain" turks assaulted a New York *Tribune* correspondent. Lieutenant George A. Custer appeared to be the chief instigator. The harried newspaperman appeared the next morning armed with a pistol and fearing for his life, but the anger had subsided with hangovers—and a stern lecture from McClellan. The general admonished, "Gentlemen please remember that we are here to serve the interests of no one man. We are here to serve our country."[29]

McClellan's train arrived at Warrenton Junction on November 11. Marsena Patrick notified the general, who quickly packed and left the Warrenton Hotel, bound for New Jersey. His eyes still moist and puffy, McClellan saluted the throng outside his hotel. He rode quietly past an honor guard at the station and boarded his train. As he disappeared inside, the honor guard broke formation and pleaded with him not to go. Some of the men uncoupled the train from the locomotive. The general returned to the platform and soothed the crowd, "Boys, you have fought with me on the Peninsula and I know your worth. All I can ask of you is to fight as well with Genl. Burnside as you have done with me." Choking back tears, the general retreated into the car. The engineers recoupled the locomotive and lurched down the track for Washington. McClellan returned to the rear platform to wave good-bye. Soldiers ran after the cars cheering as long as they could see him. And then McClellan was gone.[30]

The army mourned sullenly. "We will follow our beloved Gen McClellan to the Death anytime he calls upon us," reiterated a New York soldier. The troops felt misunderstood and exploited. "The army begins to feel that they are only the tools of designing political demagogues," one Northerner complained. A Fifth Corps soldier seethed, "This move at this time particularly is suicidal—our men care for nothing now—& will not fight worth .05 if at all." He added, "We feel now just like a large family, who has lost its father. . . . if we have another heavy engagement we are certain to be defeated." A New York correspondent reported that "many and loud are the curses uttered against the authors of this change in the command of our army." Another soldier wrote, "The troops are all discouraged and don't care whether the Union is saved or not."[31]

Burnside inherited an army in turmoil. Officers tendered their resignations. Even Northern civilians condemned him. One correspondent went so far as to notify Burnside: "Dear Sir: god has spoken to me through a funnel from heaven." Providence wanted the general to know that "You are now fighten against god and man." Several hours after McClellan departed, Burnside held a reception to meet his new subordinates. The generals congregated from 4:00 to 4:30 P.M., and welcomed their new leader "handsomely—but not enthusiastically." Burnside's private secretary, Daniel R. Larned, wrote to Mrs. Burnside that her husband's promotion "increases my hopes of a vigorous & speedy termination of the war," but acknowledged that the change "comes at a very unfortunate time." Burnside would have to prove himself to the Army of the Potomac, the administration, the North, and apparently, God.[32]

Secretary of War Edwin Stanton demanded Burnside's plans immediately. The new commander adopted a plan already fermenting in the Warrenton camp—a move to Fredericksburg. Burnside believed he first introduced the subject to George McClellan, telling an investigative committee, "I said to him . . . that if he proposed to go to Richmond by land, he would have to go by way of Fredericksburg." He claimed that McClellan "partially agreed with me," and considered the idea. McClellan, however, had already given up on the O&A Railroad and had turned his attention to the RF&P Railroad. Herman Haupt, civilian superintendent of military railroad construction, informed McClellan that the single-track O&A could ship only 700 to 900 tons per day, whereas the army daily required 1,500 tons of supplies. Little Mac responded by asking Quartermaster General Montgomery C. Meigs to "put in repair" the RF&P Railroad. McClellan also had his chief engineer, Captain James C. Duane, request that the engineers at Harpers Ferry transfer their pontoon trains to Washington in preparation for a move to Fredericksburg. Duane telegraphed the War Department on November 6. The engineers, however, would not receive the communiqué for another six days. McClellan no longer had direct communications with Harpers Ferry, and the War Department forwarded Duane's message on a Chesapeake and Ohio Canal packet, rather than risk guerrillas intercepting a telegraphic message. Burnside thought that Duane's request resulted from his conversation with McClellan that very day. But when Burnside took command, his secretary said the general had inherited a "campaign planned & begun by another person & carried on, not as the General would have done perhaps, had he *begun* it" (emphasis in original).[33]

Herman Haupt, a railroad genius, reiterated to Ambrose E. Burnside that the O&A Railroad could not supply the army adequately. The railroad lacked vital water and wood resources. "Its protection against raids," Haupt continued, "will be almost impossible, and the breaks of connection will become frequent." Haupt judged that the O&A could not handle Burnside's needs because its "ordinary working capacity . . . [was] not equal to the half of your requirements." In Haupt's opinion, the RF&P had become "a military necessity."[34]

Burnside told the War Department on November 9 that he intended to "concentrate all the forces near this place [Warrenton], and impress upon the enemy a belief that we are to attack Culpeper or Gordonsville." He hoped that would tie Lee to the upper Rappahannock. Then, Burnside would "make a rapid move of the whole force to Fredericksburg." He envisioned Fredericksburg would be the springboard for a short and decisive campaign against Richmond. He asked for thirty days of supplies be forwarded to "the neighborhood of Aquia creek." He also requested a pontoon train with enough bridging material to span the Rappahannock River twice.[35]

Burnside suspected that Lee would refuse battle on his current front until he could reunite his forces. With Jackson hovering "on the right flank, it would render the pursuit very precarious," Burnside surmised. Even if he could bring Lee to bay, the wily Confederate chieftain would have "many lines of retreat." At best, Burnside would be compelled to "simply follow a retreating army well supplied," while his own supply line became overextended and unreliable in hostile country.[36]

Burnside stated that his objective was to capture Richmond: "the taking of which, I think, should be the great object of the campaign." He believed the fall of the Confederate capital would "tend more to cripple the rebel cause than almost any other military event." To that end, Fredericksburg provided the "shortest road to Richmond," complete with a direct efficient railroad that linked into the Federal-held waters of the Chesapeake Bay. As Burnside pressed closer to Richmond, he could redirect his supplies into any one of several rivers that flowed into the bay, thus protecting his line of communications. The Fredericksburg route also provided a haven for the army in case the winter weather bogged down the offensive. An army stranded in the piedmont might not survive on scant, uncertain supplies, but Fredericksburg almost guaranteed a constant flow of material to the army.[37]

Burnside also proposed to combine his army corps with artillery and cavalry to create "grand divisions." He eliminated the adjutant-general's office attached to general headquarters, and disseminated its responsibility to the wing and corps commanders, who would deal directly with the Washington offices regarding furloughs, resignations, discharges, and recruiting. Burnside cleared his headquarters to focus on weightier matters. He grumbled to Halleck, "The General-in-Chief will readily comprehend the embarrassments which surround me in taking command of this army, at this place, and at this season of the year." Under the circumstances, he kept his plan simple. "A telegram from you approving my plans," Burnside promised, "will put us to work at once."[38]

Burnside sent his plan to Washington on November 10. Anticipating approval, he notified Herman Haupt to "get ready for the work on that road." The railroad facilitator assembled a work crew, under William W. Wright, and outfitted it with a number of Schuylkill barges, pile drivers, piles, scows, boats, and anchors. Haupt asked the War Department for "several regiments of infantry, some cavalry, and a couple of gunboats" to protect Wright's workers. The War Department ordered Burnside to send "small detachments of cavalry" instead.[39]

General Henry W. Halleck, an enigmatically bureaucratic soldier, delayed Burnside's operations. Neither Lincoln nor Halleck cared for Burnside's plan, and consequently they withheld their approval. As soon as the president criticized the proposal, Halleck asked Burnside for a meeting the next day. The general-in-chief begged Burnside to "carefully consider the views of the President." Lincoln had urged McClellan to take the route "*nearest* the enemy, so as to operate on his communications." Lincoln hoped that Burnside would do the same, forcing Lee to either fight or retreat from Culpeper. If Lee did neither—and Lee habitually failed to do what was scripted for him by Northern strategists—then the Union army could threaten his ties to Richmond. Lincoln saw an opportunity to isolate a portion of Lee's army in the piedmont and did not relish the idea of marching away from it. Burnside might have guessed the degree of the president's displeasure when Halleck demanded a meeting. The general-in-chief rarely left Washington to consult with field commanders. Halleck, joined by Herman Haupt and Quartermaster General Montgomery Meigs, hopped a train on November 12, set on convincing Burnside to attack Lee at Culpeper.[40]

The generals met at Warrenton and conferred well into the night. Records are sketchy on what was discussed or promised, and we are left with conflicting testimony given after the fact, and colored by the outcome of the campaign. An excellent case in point arose when Burnside did not specify in his proposal the route he would take to get to Fredericksburg. He discussed the route during the meeting, but Halleck, and apparently Haupt, misunderstood him. In light of the presidential directive to stick close to the enemy and threaten his communications, Haupt thought, "This plan, if followed, would have taken the army to Fredericksburg on the south side of the Rappahannock instead of to Falmouth on the north side." Halleck also used this logic to diffuse criticisms aimed at him for not rushing pontoon trains to the Army of the Potomac. Burnside may have confused his guests when he offered to put "a *small force*" (emphasis in original) across the river during the operation. Burnside wanted to tie Lee to the Culpeper area by crossing the upper Rappahannock with a diversionary force. Burnside's lieutenants, Edwin V. Sumner and William B. Franklin, both agreed that Burnside never intended to move to Fredericksburg by the south side of the Rappahannock. In fact, none of Burnside's subordinates considered the south side idea until Major General Joseph Hooker arrived. Hooker, the overly ambitious self-promoter, jumped on it much later to build a case against Burnside's ability.[41]

Halleck tried to dissuade Burnside from going to Fredericksburg at all. The president desired a strike down the O&A Railroad. The Army of the Potomac could cross the upper Rappahannock easily, and the open country of the piedmont provided an opportunity to maneuver his full force in a classic Napoleonic setting. Moving east to Fredericksburg, the Rappahannock River, and all the rivers below it, became major obstacles to the offensive. Burnside countered that Lee would never allow himself to be cornered in the piedmont, and following the O&A took the army away from its primary objective of Richmond. Pontoon bridges, Burnside insisted, would eliminate delays on the wider eastern stretches of the Rappahannock, leaving his maneuvering unimpaired.[42]

Halleck had brought Herman Haupt to the meeting for support, but the railroad engineer sided with Burnside. "Never before, perhaps," he mused, "has a single-track railroad, of such limited capacity, been so severely taxed." He estimated that the line needed to double its tonnage and required 550 cars. Currently, the line operated with fewer than 300 cars, 200 of which he had borrowed from other lines. The only way the O&A could possibly continue to supply an offensive campaign would be, according to Haupt, "by the most extraordinary good management and good luck combined." Haupt believed Burnside's plans made more sense from a logistical standpoint. Burnside's second in command, Major General Edwin Sumner, concurred that a move to Fredericksburg "was the wisest plan."[43]

Outnumbered and unable to sway the meeting, Halleck withdrew. He promised to re-evaluate the matter with the president. The general-in-chief cautioned Burnside that nothing had been approved and that the army should wait until he talked to Lincoln. Burnside asked Halleck to outfit a pontoon train to meet him at Aquia Landing, in case Lincoln approved the plan. Halleck promised to have Brigadier General Daniel P. Woodbury, commander of the volunteer engineer brigade, get ready. Quartermaster General Montgomery Meigs wired Woodbury from Warrenton to outfit a pontoon train at once. Little did Burnside—or anyone present—realize that there were only twelve serviceable pontoon boats in Washington. Burnside assumed that McClellan's November 6 order had shuttled the bridge trains from the upper Potomac to Washington. No one in Warrenton dreamed that the engineers would receive the stale order only that day. Burnside could not track the pontoons himself because communications from Harpers Ferry extended only to Lovettsville, Virginia—and couriers were out of the question, as the country between Lovettsville and Warrenton "was infested with bush whackers." All of the army's communications had to be relayed through Washington.[44]

Ambrose Burnside reorganized his army while waiting for Lincoln's approval. He combined two army corps into a "Grand Division" and then added some cavalry and artillery, allowing grand divisions to function independently, like small-scale armies. On November 16, Burnside divided the Army of the Potomac's six corps into the Right, Left, and Center Grand Divisions.

Major General Edwin Vose Sumner commanded the Right Grand Division. Sumner had been in the army since 1819, making him the oldest corps commander in the army. Burnside relied on Sumner as his confidant. Unfortunately, Sumner had a limited mental capacity and an overwhelming desire to accommodate his superior. Sumner commanded the Second and Ninth Corps as well as a cavalry division led by Brigadier General Alfred Pleasonton. The Left Grand Division, composed of the First and Sixth Corps, and Bayard's cavalry, came under Major General William Buel Franklin. The general was a meticulous engineer, with a tendency to overthink any situation. Yet he had been closely allied with George McClellan, and his opinion still held sway with Burnside. The army leader assigned the Center Grand Division to Major General Joseph Hooker. He commanded the Third and Fifth Corps, and a brigade of cavalry under Brigadier General William W. Averell. Fitz John Porter, of the Fifth Corps, should have had the Center Grand Division command, but the War Department arrested him to stand trial for his actions at Second Manassas. Hooker joined the army on November 10, and gained instant seniority for the post. He had an outstanding record for action and bravery in battle, but Burnside despised his unabashed ambition for higher command. Burnside formed a Reserve Grand Division under Major General Franz Sigel, a petulant German exile who had gained rank while unifying German support for the Union. He had seen only limited action in the

West and in the Shenandoah Valley, but his close association with Lincoln kept him in the field. Sigel's Eleventh Corps joined Major General Henry W. Slocum's Twelfth Corps (which was then at Harpers Ferry) and Julius Stahel's cavalry brigade.[45]

Armies often operated in wings; but Burnside's organization differed in that he set precise parameters for command. This rigidity made overlapping jurisdictions on the battlefield chaotic when elements of different grand divisions attempted to coordinate under fire. McClellan, and later Hooker and Meade, found the movement and supply of their troops best handled with combined elements of the army, but they dissolved the wings in battle for better cooperation.

Back in Washington, Lincoln listened to Halleck's synopsis of the Warrenton meeting and deferred to Burnside. Perhaps he relented because of the commander's conviction and aggressiveness. Confidence like that needed to be encouraged, and Burnside's zealousness differed refreshingly from the always-whining McClellan. Yet the president still had reservations. "The plans of General Burnside," wrote Herman Haupt, "did not meet with the cordial approval of the President and General Halleck, and their assent was given with reluctance." At 11:00 A.M. on November 14, Henry Halleck wired Burnside: "The President has just assented to your plan," adding for emphasis: "He thinks that it will succeed if you move rapidly; otherwise not." Burnside had the power to act at last. Lincoln and the War Department would learn quickly that Burnside did not need prodding like his predecessor. Decisive action was Burnside's strength, but it was also a liability, which led to tragedy.[46]

Burnside acted as soon as the orders arrived. He concentrated the army at Warrenton. He withdrew his right flank from the Rappahannock, and anchored it outside of Warrenton. Sumner, Hooker, and Franklin received their marching orders in the afternoon. The next day, Burnside started his campaign.[47]

Artillery shook the Confederates from their slumber on the morning of November 15. An irate diarist noted, "Brisk cannonading all the morning." Elements of the Union Ninth Corps struck the Rappahannock River at Fauquier White Sulphur Springs (also known as Warrenton Springs). The First Corps demonstrated at the fords to the east, focusing on Freeman's and Beverly's fords. Bayard's cavalry, joined by Brigadier General Nelson Taylor's First Corps brigade, attacked the Confederates at Rappahannock Station and captured the bridge there intact. The sudden action on a wide front surprised the Confederates. Colonel John R. Chambliss commanded a cavalry brigade on Longstreet's right at Rappahannock Station. The Federals drove his small force, composed of the 13th Virginia, 15th Virginia, and 2nd North Carolina Cavalry, out of their camp with shellfire. The horse soldiers watched the 11th Pennsylvania Infantry cross the river and confiscate their camp equipage. Upriver, Confederates forwarded some of the their heavy guns to duel with the Yankee attackers. Georgia Captain John Lane's Battery E, Sumter Artillery, engaged the Federals near Fauquier White Sulphur Springs with 20-pounder Parrotts. A staff officer noted in his diary: "Heard our battery got the worst of it. . . . [The Federals] opened 8 batteries on our one."[48]

Lee and Longstreet evacuated the Rappahannock line without much of a fight. Longstreet concentrated his First Corps at Culpeper Court House. The corps commander issued what one officer called "a very startling order" to the rearguard. The general cautioned his troops "to be ready for battle at a moment's notice," and instructed: "Officers to take care of your men! Soldiers obey—take good aim! Keep steady in your ranks."[49]

Robert E. Lee reacted just as Burnside had hoped. He had fallen back from the river and broke most of his contact with the Federals. But Burnside did not react as Lee had expected. The new "On to Richmond" campaign had struck with vigor at all the crossing points from Waterloo to Rappahannock Station, yet the Federals stopped dead in their tracks. Outside of the 11th Pennsylvania's dash into Chambliss' camp for pots and pans, no one in the Army of the Potomac had ventured south of the river. In a sense, Burnside's demonstration had worked too well. Lee could not dispute the Federals' passage—but the lack of follow-up activity betrayed their feint. Lee held his ground for the moment, and warned Fredericksburg to be on the lookout for a Union attack.

Burnside knew his ruse would be discovered soon enough, but he hoped that he had gained enough time to reach Fredericksburg before the Confederates. He started the race on November 15. Sumner's Right Grand Division took the direct road from Warrenton to Falmouth, the Second Corps leading the column. Hooker's Center Grand Division and Franklin's Left Grand Division departed the next day. Franklin marched to Stafford Court House, and Hooker followed Sumner's route. Pleasonton's cavalry covered the rear, while Bayard and Averell screened the flanks and front. Rain soaked the marchers for the next two days. The Union soldiers approved of their new commander's decisiveness. "Everything seems to be working well," wrote a New York soldier, "and as all have faith in Burnside nothing is any longer said of the removal of Little Mac."[50]

A hitch developed in Burnside's plans almost immediately that threatened to upset his timetable. The army commander inquired about his pontoon train before cutting his communications with Washington. "Receiving no information of its departure," Burnside later told an investigative committee, he asked his chief engineer, Lieutenant Cyrus B. Comstock, to query the War Department for an update. Comstock received nothing in reply, and Burnside started "feeling uneasy with reference to the pontoons." He directed Comstock to "telegraph again," but it would be two days before he received an answer.[51]

In Washington, engineer General Daniel P. Woodbury wrestled with an answer. Woodbury responded that the 50th New York Engineers had arrived in Washington on November 14 with thirty-six pontoons from Berlin and Harpers Ferry; another forty boats were expected the next day. The engineer guessed he could outfit an overland train by November 16 or 17, depending on when the Quartermaster Department could furnish horses and transportation. It would take several more days for them to reach the army. Burnside had reached Fredericksburg before Woodbury's note arrived. By then, the Union army had broadcast its intentions to the enemy. Burnside could only pray that the engineers would catch up in a timely manner.[52]

The three grand divisions covered fifteen miles of marching each day over muddy and rutted highways. The army set a brutal pace, and a number of horses died along the way. "The whole Country through which we passed," Burnside admitted, had been "completely devastated." High morale kept the army buoyant. "The troops have made a rapid march," wrote an amazed signal officer, "& scarcely a straggler could be seen." They were closing in on the prize and there was seemingly nothing Lee could do about it.[53]

Robert E. Lee suspected the Union army might strike Fredericksburg. As early as November 12, Lee warned Colonel Ball's garrison to be alert. He also ordered Ball to destroy the RF&P Railway north of Fredericksburg as a precaution. Two days later, while Burnside demonstrated near Culpeper, Ball telegraphed Richmond that "the enemy are moving upon him in some force and asks help." General Gustavus W. Smith, temporary head of the War Department, alerted Lee and Samuel French in southside Virginia. Lee still confronted the bulk of Burnside's army in front, so he declined to overcommit reinforcements to Fredericksburg. Only the 61st Virginia and the Norfolk Blues Virginia artillery went to Ball. French sent four companies of the 42nd

Mississippi from Richmond. Major William A. Feeney's Mississippians arrived in Fredericksburg by train, and the people of the city welcomed them with grateful enthusiasm. "We were joyfully received by the women and children, who thronged the streets," wrote a Mississippian, "and saluted us with miniture [*sic*] Flags, and audible prayers for our safety and success."[54]

Colonel Ball told the reinforcements "to prepare for a fight." Cavalry scouts "were continually returning to town with news that the Yankees were advancing," recorded a Mississippi infantryman. News became more detailed and urgent during November 16 and 17. Confederates quickly dismantled the railroad north of the Rappahannock and burned all of the bridges across the river. Ball apprised Lee of developments, but Lee lingered at Culpeper. William B. Ball prepared to meet the Army of the Potomac with approximately 1,000 to 1,500 defenders.[55]

On November 17, Robert E. Lee informed President Jefferson Davis: "There is a general movement of the enemy from Warrenton," yet he could not be certain of its destination. He thought Fredericksburg could be a logical target, but the lack of activity at Aquia Creek or neighboring Belle Plain troubled Lee. The Confederate discounted a major offensive on that line largely because Burnside had not established a supply base. The Southern commander wrote, "I should think some provision would be made for subsisting a large army if a movement upon Fredericksburg was designed." In this case, the Northern War Department's delays actually helped Burnside's deception. True, Ball reported daily contact with Federals, but his scouts had encountered only William W. Averell's cavalry. Failing to penetrate Averell's screen, Ball had not located the main body of the Union army. "There is nothing to show his purpose in that direction," Lee told the president, "beyond the guards established on the roads leading to Fredericksburg." Averell's Federal cavalry might be masking an advance, but conceivably, it could also be covering a retreat. A cavalry buffer between Fredericksburg and Washington would "naturally . . . cut off information of his movements toward Alexandria." Lee needed more information.[56]

General Lee asked Jeb Stuart to find where Burnside's army was going. He wanted Stuart to identify the Federal strength based around Warrenton and confirm whether Fredericksburg was in danger. The cavalier crossed the Rappahannock at Fauquier White Sulphur Springs on November 18. Two brigades under Brigadier Generals Fitzhugh Lee and Wade Hampton stampeded a regiment of Union cavalry heading for Warrenton. Confederates entered from the south just as Alfred Pleasonton's rearguard evacuated the town to

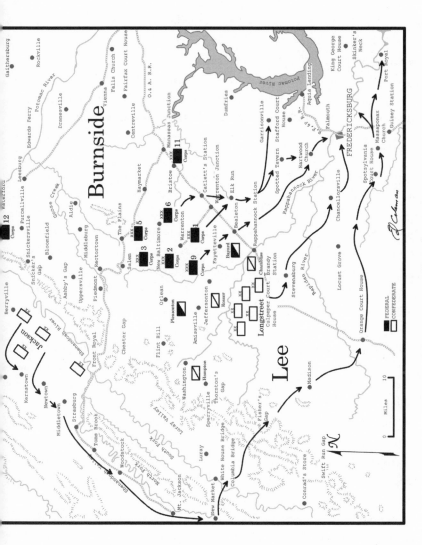

Movements in November 1862

the east. A brief skirmish ensued with trifling losses before Pleasonton yielded the area to Stuart. The Southerners sent back a bevy of prisoners to Lee, along with the observation that the Union rearguard had retreated toward Fredericksburg. Stuart reconnoitered for another two days to be certain that Burnside had not retired up the O&A. Confederate cavalry learned that the Federals had abandoned Fauquier and Loudoun Counties, destroyed all of the railroad bridges from the Rappahannock back to Bull Run, and burned the stores at Warrenton Junction and Manassas Junction. Both Stuart and Lee deduced that the Federals had abandoned the O&A Railroad without retreating, so they must be heading for the RF&P out of necessity. Lee began to believe Ball's reports, but by then the Union commander was way ahead of him.[57]

Fredericksburg stood at the midpoint between Washington and Richmond and straddled the main road between them. Inevitably, the war would have an impact on the city. The colonial city, founded in 1727, had once been the home of George Washington, James Monroe, John Paul Jones, and Matthew Fontaine Maury. Census records show 5,020 inhabitants in the city in 1860. Up to now, residents had endured quiet military camps crowding their pastures; bawdy houses downtown; and crass drunks attacking the Presbyterian church's gas lanterns with rocks. Even Dahlgren's raid seemed remote and nostalgic for its brevity and excitement.[58]

Fredericksburg appeared like a vestige of a bygone era. One visitor called it "an ancient city . . . noted for the refinement of its inhabitants, their aristocratic characteristics and the beauty of its women." The city nestled on the fall line of the Rappahannock and retained a quaint charm when newly constructed railroads diverted trade and development to Washington and Richmond. In recent years, the city had revitalized its commercial interests. A western canal linked the city to the interior of Virginia. The unsullied city of Fredericksburg became the forefront of war on November 17 when the armies earmarked it as the new frontier.[59]

Sumner's Right Grand Division arrived opposite Fredericksburg on the afternoon of November 17. Colonel William Ball's Confederates had tracked the Yankees' advance and prepared to contest them at the river. Ball placed a company of the 42nd Mississippi in ambush at the Falmouth ford with instructions to "hold it at all hazards." The colonel instructed the men "to wait until the Yanks had gotten about midway [across] the river" before firing. Lewis' Virginia battery covered the ford from a knoll adjacent to the town.

The rest of the 42nd Mississippi stood close by in support. Ball's cavalry roamed north of the river, shadowing the approach of Sumner's column.[60]

The Federal Second Corps led the Right Grand Division to Falmouth. Two regiments—the 57th New York and 53rd Pennsylvania—marched in the van. Three batteries followed them. Lewis' battery sighted the Yankees silhouetted on the hills above Falmouth and opened fire. "A battery," Sumner reported, "opened on us the moment a portion of my troops appeared on the ridge."[61]

Colonel Samuel K. Zook hurried forward Captain Rufus D. Pettit's Battery B, 1st New York Light Artillery. The battery of 10-pounder Parrotts took a commanding position that dominated the river valley. Federal guns answered Lewis' battery at 3:00 P.M. Despite Lewis' best effort, Rufus Pettit silenced him within fifteen minutes.[62]

"They drove every man on the other side from the guns," Edwin Sumner related. "They ran off and left four guns on the field." A Confederate infantryman complained, "The men of this artillery company were not accustomed to such sport, and the majority of them stampeded with the horses." Reports of fire, and fleeing cannoneers, terrified some of the citizens of Fredericksburg. Jane Howison Beale, proprietress of a school for young ladies, watched the fight from her home on Lewis Street. In the street below she witnessed "The poor people from the upper part of the town [fleeing] from their homes and . . . running wildly along with children in their arms." An errant shot struck the nearby paper mill "and frightened the poor girls who were at work there terribly.[63]

Colonel Ball rallied the artillerymen and returned them to their guns. The Virginian ordered a special detachment of the 42nd Mississippi "to keep the artillery men at their post with instructions to shoot all men who should attempt to run." Having been run over by the rout, the infantry took grim pleasure in keeping the gunners squirming under fire. Later, the Mississippi men rued how the newspapers painted the gun crew as heroes. "The brave artillerists," complained a diarist, "were Virginians, and from this fact the Richmond papers lauded them very highly—the Mississippians . . . were not known in the newspaper."[64]

Unable to stop the Federals from crossing, Ball decided to evacuate Fredericksburg. He ordered stockpiles of cotton and tobacco destroyed. Confederate authorities recently had seized 150,000 pounds of tobacco from speculators waiting for the Federals to occupy the city and pay top dollar for the commodity. Ball lined the streets with bales of cotton and torched them. Fearing the tobacco would not burn fast enough, Ball had it dumped into the river.[65]

Sumner reported some resistance at Fredericksburg, hoping Burnside would allow him to cross the river before the Confederates escaped. Sumner had discovered a passable "rough cavalry ford" below the fall line of the river and thought mounted troops could negotiate it at low tide. Burnside rejected the idea, explaining "that he did not think it advisable to occupy Fredericksburg until his line of communications were [*sic*] established." Sumner later commented that "on reflection, I myself thought that he was right." The Federals planted artillery on Stafford Heights overlooking the city and waited for Burnside's next instructions.[66]

The next day Burnside received the disturbing news that the pontoons would be delayed. A courier found the general at Falmouth, and handed him Engineer General Woodbury's telegram. The note informed Burnside that Captain (soon to be Major) Ira Spaulding would "start on Nov. 16 or 17." Until then, Burnside had to sit tight and hope the pontoons would arrive before Lee thoroughly blocked the direct route to Richmond.[67]

Burnside's army concentrated near the RF&P Railroad over the next few days. Franklin's Left Grand Division marched into Stafford Court House on November 19. Hooker's Center Grand Division halted at Hartwood Church above United States Ford and Richards' Ford on the Rappahannock. Pleasonton's and Bayard's cavalry covered the fords and guarded the road back to Warrenton at Deep Run. Hooker proposed that his Center Grand Division should cross the Rappahannock "at the ford nearest to him," and cut across country to Bowling Green and Hanover Junction (which Hooker's maps identified as Saxton's Junction). Hooker sent his idea to Burnside and then mailed a second copy covertly to the secretary of war, along with a letter criticizing Burnside's campaign. Burnside told Hooker on November 21 that he "could not approve of the move he had suggested." Whether Hooker crossed the river at Richards' Ford or U.S. Ford, Burnside feared that the Federals would have to march thirty-six miles and cross two rivers before reaching Hanover Junction. Rain had fallen for two days and the river was high. The army commander could not risk getting his headstrong lieutenant trapped on the wrong side of the river with no means of reinforcing him. Burnside's intuition was correct. He reported later that "after the 19th of November the weather and the roads were particularly bad."[68]

Union scouts examined all of the fords on the lower Rappahannock to see if the army could cross and maintain its tie to the north bank. They reported that incessant rain had made the river virtually impassable. Even if the storm relented, the army had no guarantee that it would not resume once they were on the other side. Burnside notified the War Department on November 19 that "examination of the fords here today demonstrated that the Infantry and Artillery cannot pass." The Army of the Potomac had no choice but to wait for the pontoons. With much anxiety, Burnside complained to the War Department, "I cannot make the promise of probable success with the faith that I did when I supposed all parts of the plan would be carried out."[69]

Confederate colonel William Ball wondered why the Federals did not take Fredericksburg. The garrison commander calmed down and decided to hold the city as long as possible. He spread his small force along the riverfront. For five days and nights, the Southerners kept watch. "We suffered from cold, rain and want of food," griped one sentinel. The ladies of Fredericksburg tried to alleviate their hunger pangs. "They swung their well filled baskets on their arms," marveled a famished Mississippian, "and brought them to us at night. Never was such a patriotic and noble heroism displayed by women." Even with such chivalric acts, the garrison teetered on the brink of exhaustion. They needed help soon or they would collapse under the stress and strain of incessant duty.[70]

Robert E. Lee learned the Union army had reached Fredericksburg and set out to block the road to Richmond. Lee expected Burnside would cross the Rappahannock without delay. Unable to stop him, Lee planned to make a stand on the next defensible ground south of the Rappahannock, the North Anna River. An early historian of the war called it "a small but difficult stream," which offered "peculiar advantages to the defence." Lee sent two of Longstreet's divisions toward Fredericksburg to retard the Union advance while the rest of the First Corps headed for the North Anna. Meanwhile, Lee encouraged Stonewall Jackson to hurry across the mountains. Lee must have expected tremendous effort from his rearguard to think that Jackson would cover close to 200 miles in the time Burnside traversed 36. More likely, Lee counted on Longstreet to defend the North Anna alone while Jackson struck at Burnside's line of communications. One of Lee's staff officers, Colonel Armistead L. Long, said that Lee "moved in such a manner as might enable him to fall upon the flank and rear of the Federal army," which hints at Jackson's roll in Lee's scheme. Longstreet did not have the strength to handle Burnside alone, much less attack him, so Lee relied on Jackson to attack. Under those circumstances, Jackson did not have to go as far to get into Burnside's rear, and conceivably, Longstreet could handle the Federals until Stonewall arrived.[71]

Major General Lafayette McLaws' division started for Fredericksburg on November 18. Brigadier General Robert Ransom's division followed briefly before diverging southeast on "the most direct route to Hanover Jct." The rest of Longstreet's command prepared to move as soon as Jeb Stuart's cavalry determined that all of Burnside's army had left. Soon after, Major General Richard H. Anderson's division started for Spotsylvania Court House. Two divisions, under Major Generals George E. Pickett and John B. Hood, headed for the North Anna the same day. To help McLaws, Longstreet redirected Ransom's division to Guiney Station on the RF&P, twelve miles south of Fredericksburg.[72]

McLaws knew little about his mission. Privately, he complained that "further orders will be given me on the march. What I am to do or where to go, I know not." Soldiers tramped across Orange and Spotsylvania Counties in what one officer called "a very disagreeable march." Wind and rain beat on the bone-weary Confederates, who splashed through the bracing waters of the Rapidan River at Raccoon Ford. Soldiers spent several days on "a forced march in a continuous downpour of rain." A Mississippian in Anderson's division recalled, "The wind was blowing so hard that we could scarcely hear anything." Pickett's division, at the tail of Longstreet's column, suffered all of this plus a road badly mauled by traffic that had preceded it. A South Carolinian wrote, "the roads . . . are in the most deplorable condition imaginable." Another soldier agreed: "The roads were in a very bad condition, very slippery." Men toughed the long hours under brutal conditions to close the miles between them and the Yankees. By the end of the second day, a chronicler in the 5th South Carolina said ruefully, "I thought that I had experienced a rough time of it last winter, but that was nothing in comparison to what we have had to endure lately." Barefoot men wallowed in mud and hoarfrost. Mud coated everyone and everything until one soldier proclaimed that the army was "the most muddy and worst looking set you ever saw."[73]

In mid-stride to the North Anna, Lee discovered that Burnside had not crossed the Rappahannock River after all. This startling news made the Confederate leader alter his plans immediately. He halted the move to the North Anna and redirected all of Longstreet's columns to Fredericksburg. Lee remembered some impressive defensive features at Fredericksburg and knew "these heights afforded a stronger defensive line than the North Anna." The army commander told the War Department: "The longer we can delay him and throw him into winter, the more difficult will be his undertaking. It is for this reason that I have determined to resist him at the outset and to throw every obstacle in the way of his advance."[74]

Fredericksburg offered other advantages for Lee to consider. Strategically, Lee could buy more time for Jackson to play a role on the North Anna. Longstreet's 40,000 troops probably could not stop Burnside at the Rappahannock, but they could significantly delay the Union advance. Politically, Jefferson Davis encouraged Lee not to yield any more territory than absolutely necessary. Economically, the Richmond government put a premium on protecting crops in unspoiled Spotsylvania and Caroline Counties. A biographer of Lee attested, "the Confederate Government held the corn crops between the Rappahannock and North Anna rivers to be of more importance than the strategic advantage of luring Burnside as far as the Anna." Lee yielded to these considerations and surrendered a vital tactical concern—the only way to destroy Burnside was to draw him away from his supply base at Aquia Landing. Southern chief of artillery William N. Pendleton confided to his wife that Lee still intended to fall back to the North Anna River when the time came. As late as December 13—the day of battle at Fredericksburg—Pendleton wrote, "He long ago resolved that for a desperate battle it would be best to get Burnside farther away from the river." The test would start at Fredericksburg, but the climax of the campaign would ideally come at the North Anna River.[75]

The van of Longstreet's corps arrived at Fredericksburg on the evening of November 20. McLaws and then Ransom concealed their divisions in the hills behind the city. Hood's and Anderson's divisions reached Spotsylvania Court House before angling toward the city. They re-joined Longstreet on November 22. Pickett and the reserve artillery plodded into camp the next day. Longstreet left Colonel Ball's overtaxed pickets on the river to keep Burnside ignorant of his presence.[76]

Burnside assumed that Lee was on his way to Fredericksburg, but without bridges or supplies, there was nothing he could do about it. The Union commander tried to secure bridging sites near the city by bluffing Fredericksburg to surrender before Lee arrived. Provost Marshal Marsena Patrick delivered Burnside's ultimatum to the mayor of Fredericksburg.[77]

Burnside demanded that the city surrender at once, complaining that Sumner's troops "had been fired on from the city"; mills and manufacturers "were furnishing food and clothing to troops in rebellion"; and the RF&P Railroad had evacuated stores from the Confederate depots. "Such a state of affairs," the Federal general blustered, "could not be allowed to exist any longer." If the Confederates persisted, Sumner would shell the city. The Rebels had until 5:00 P.M. to agree, and if they failed, civilians had sixteen hours to evacuate before the guns commenced. Marsena Patrick parleyed with the Confederates on November 21, explaining that he had a communication for the mayor. Colonel Ball insisted that Patrick go through proper military channels. The Confederate colonel dispatched a courier while Patrick chatted with the Rebels at the river. Three and a half hours later, Longstreet's chief of staff, Major Gilbert Moxley Sorrel, arrived to take the message to his commander. At least one bystander thought "The Yankee General was surprised to learn that General Longstreet would return an answer soon." Burnside was too late—Lee had arrived.[78]

Robert E. Lee had been sitting in his tent with James Longstreet and Lafayette McLaws when Burnside's ultimatum arrived. Lee sent the two generals to see Mayor Montgomery Slaughter. The head of the Army of Northern Virginia promised that he would not use the city for military purposes. "The State of affairs complained of, as existing in the city, should no longer exist," Lee pledged, and "his troops should no longer occupy the city." But he also warned that he would resist any attempt by the enemy to occupy it. Montgomery Slaughter trusted Lee and abided by his suggestions.[79]

Montgomery Slaughter convened an emergency meeting of the city council, which approved General Lee's provisos. Mayor Slaughter met General Patrick at 7:30 P.M. and gave him written assurances that all military activities and transgressions would cease. The Union general returned to his side of the river and briefed Burnside. Demanding the surrender of a city that the Federals could not occupy rang hollow, and the results surprised no one.

The contending armies placed the population of Fredericksburg in an ambiguous and frightening predicament. The Confederates had seemingly defused the surrender by withdrawing from the town. But the Federals had not rescinded the threat to shell Fredericksburg after sixteen hours. Early on the morning of November 22, Mayor Slaughter, with several civil and military leaders, crossed the river to clarify Marsena Patrick's position. The provost marshal declined to meet them, since he had no leeway to treat with military authorities. Slaughter's group then returned to Fredericksburg, but not before the mayor pleaded for an extension of time. Patrick promised to withhold the bombardment until the women and children had gone. The next day, protocol appeared straightened out. Patrick welcomed the mayor's group and two Confederate officers, Brigadier General Joseph B. Kershaw and Colonel Elbert Bland, of the 7th South Carolina. The conference lasted for close to an hour at J. Horace Lacy's stately mansion, Chatham. Patrick assured the group that "the town will not be shelled until *she* fires" first. The Southerners returned to Fredericksburg relieved.[80]

Even with Patrick's promise, most of the civilians fled Fredericksburg. "The citizens are all leaving as fast as possible," a diarist in Pickett's division noted. Women, children, the old, and the infirm made a pathetic procession heading they knew not where. Some hiked for miles, seeking shelter in remote farms and churches. Some stayed close to the front, partly out of curiosity and partly to keep watch over their homes. Some of the residents left town via the railroad. Families packed cattle cars when the passenger cars had filled up. A young woman wrote that her mother and two children rode in cattle cars to Milford Station with five hundred other refugees. Confederates tried to help. Lafayette McLaws wrote, "Our ambulances have been running all day, and are now going back and forth, carrying out the families." Weeks passed before the armies stirred again. In the interim, the natives of Fredericksburg began to discount Burnside's threats, and quite a few returned to their homes.[81]

As Robert E. Lee learned more about Burnside's difficulties regarding pontoons and supplies, the general reconsidered the pact between Mayor Slaughter and Ambrose Burnside. Over the next few weeks, Rebels reoccupied Fredericksburg and surreptitiously fortified it. Longstreet's corps spread across the landscape, establishing camps and erecting breastworks on the ridges behind the city. At night, Longstreet's campfires loomed as large as the Federals'. "Our camp fires shine up & light the air so far and wide as those of the enemy," wrote General McLaws, "and we no longer care for any attempt they may make to cross the river." Longstreet's First Corps bristled like a substantial host, but in truth, Lee and Longstreet opposed Burnside's 120,000 with only 40,000 men. The Union army had been stalled, not by the Confederates' efforts, but by its own lack of supplies and pontoons. Eventually, Burnside would get his supplies and pontoons, and Lee knew he would need help then to stop him. Lee had scrambled to get ahead of Burnside and had won. But as the threat of battle amplified, it became imperative to bring Stonewall Jackson from the Valley.[82]

CHAPTER TWO

"THE ENEMY WILL BE MORE SURPRISED"

Countdown to Crossing

The same day that Fredericksburg refused to surrender, Thomas J. Jackson's Second Corps started marching to join Lee. Jackson had resisted leaving the Valley until the last moment, hoping that McClellan, and then Burnside, might let his guard down. By the middle of November, the Second Corps commander gave up the notion, yet he remained in place because he affected the Union army's dispositions. The constant threat posed by Stonewall's legions had as much to do with the stalemate on the upper Rappahannock as Longstreet's forces at Culpeper. Toward the end of the month, the armies marched farther east, and everyone in the Valley expected Jackson to follow. Even the staff officers anticipated Jackson's movement across the Blue Ridge.

Lieutenant James Power Smith, an impressionable aide, begged his secretive commander, "General, as we are going across the mountains to-morrow, I wish to go to Winchester early in the morning." Jackson smiled and asked, "Are you going over the mountains to-morrow?" Eventually, the general gave the aide a pass with the injunction, "*don't tell* any one that we are going over the mountains." Smith treasured Jackson's confidence. The young lieutenant completed his business in Winchester only to discover Jackson and the Second Corps marching *to* Winchester. Jackson chuckled as he rode by, "Are you going over the mountains, Mr. Smith?" No one second-guessed Stonewall Jackson, not even his staff.[1]

Jackson received Lee's November 18 dispatch at Winchester, which stated: "it would be advisable to put some of your divisions in motion across the mountains, and advance them at least as far as Sperryville or Madison Court House." The commander wanted the army reunited, but he deferred to Jackson if "it is advantageous for you to continue longer in the Valley, or can accomplish the retention and division of the enemy's forces." Jackson had not held the Union army in check or forced it to split its strength, so he took up the march to Fredericksburg. Jackson's old Valley army trudged through the streets of Winchester on the evening of November 21 heading south. The retreat presented "a melancholy spectacle" to the people of the town. James P. Smith—so anxious to see Winchester one last time—now was anxious to leave the Valley. The aide had rebuffed the legendary spy-heroine Belle Boyd's request to have an unannounced audience with Jackson. She left in a huff and a few days later threatened to lop off Smith's ears if she ever caught him near Martinsburg.[2]

Jackson tarried one last night in Winchester. The general seemed edgy and uncomfortable. He waited uneasily for news from his wife, Mary Anna—or as Smith teasingly called her, the "Lieutenant Generaless." Anna Jackson was due to give birth to the couples' second child at any time. Jackson dined with the Reverend James R. Graham and his family. The Jacksons had spent the previous winter with the Grahams, and the general felt at ease with them. He romped and played with their children. "It did seem so much like old times—those good old times of last winter," Mrs. Graham wrote to Anna, "we are all so cozy in our dining room, and around the table we did wish for you in your seat between us." Mrs. Graham prepared a lunch for the general's journey, and the night concluded with Jackson and the whole family "bowing before the family altar."[3]

Jackson disappeared before dawn. The wily commander left a small contingent of defenders behind under Brigadier Generals George H. Steuart and William E. "Grumble" Jones to deceive the Federals, while his columns marched south along the old Valley Pike. Because both branches of the Shenandoah River flowed north, Valley residents referred to heading south as going "up" the Valley. This unique parlance entertained and confused many of the Confederates. A lieutenant in Gregg's South Carolina brigade playfully wrote, "this is a curious world here. Up is down and down is up."[4]

Jackson marched with his men, camping along the Pike. On November 24, Stonewall's corps crossed Massanutten Mountain at New Market Gap. Rain and sleet soaked the tired marchers. The troops waded across the South

Fork of the Shenandoah River at Columbia Bridge ford. Jackson sat on a log watching the column slog through the river. The pouring rain caused his wide-brimmed hat to droop over his face. The corps jogged south for a few miles and picked up the road east to Madison Court House. The men bivouacked one last night in the Valley, shivering around Hawksbill.[5]

Jackson rose early the next morning and donned a brilliant new uniform—a gift from his friend Jeb Stuart. The staff stared in utter amazement until the general explained, "Young gentlemen, this is no longer the headquarters of the Army of the Valley, but the Second Corps of the Army of Northern Virginia." Apparently the new era with Lee required more style than his own no-nonsense days of the Valley Army—or more likely, his normal uniform was still too drenched to wear. For the religious youths of the staff, the picture of Jackson, a Presbyterian deacon in his own right, crossing the Blue Ridge in glittering attire reminded them of scriptural passages of messianic transfigurations. Many recalled the day with a smile and a certain sense of mysticism. Stonewall Jackson left the Valley of Virginia for the last time on November 24, his career as an independent commander at an end. Six months later, he came back to Lexington in a casket.[6]

Jackson's Confederates found the trip through Fisher's Gap, or as some called it, Milam's Gap, icy, cold, and treacherous. The command wound up the mountain on a series of ice-glazed switchbacks. Ragged Southerners dropped down the other side through Criglersville to Madison Court House. Soldiers warmed themselves en route by several stills on the mountain, and in some cases, the local residents set up stands to sell their homemade liquor. An officer in the 15th Alabama recalled, "While passing through . . . whiskey was obtained from some of the mountaineers and several officers and men got drunk." Cantankerous Brigadier General Jubal A. Early posted guards to keep the troops away from the stills. When sentinels turned away a party from the 21st Georgia, the whole regiment surrounded them. The men learned upon questioning the guard that Old Jube Early "had his canteen filled and the keg [placed] behind his ambulance." Riotous Georgians overwhelmed the guard, and everyone enjoyed a forbidden drink. A member of the 21st Georgia later remarked, "It was a cool November afternoon, [but] the brandy warmed the boys up and made them hilarious." Brigadier General Harry T. Hays' Louisiana Brigade also ferreted out liquor, leaving the road lined with drunken men. "Nearly everybody in the Louisiana brigade, and many in other brigades, had taken a drink too many," admitted one soldier. Early appeared oblivious, as one witness recounted: "old Jubal was merry and a-grinning" with brandy. Jackson knew the situation intimately. The besotted 21st Georgia encountered the austere general and regaled him with bawdy corn-shucking songs and "some very risqué couplets." Deacon Jackson sternly noted the situation for later.[7]

Jackson came down from the Blue Ridge and camped a mile beyond Madison Court House. Angry with Early's poor showing, the corps commander sent his chief of staff, Major Alexander S. Pendleton, to demand an explanation. Early, still under the influence, quipped that the reason Jackson had seen so many stragglers from his division must be because he *had followed* his column. Jackson was not amused, and ordered Early arrested. Sandie Pendleton dissuaded Jackson from pressing charges that night, hoping Early would sober up and make amends.[8]

Jackson spent the next two days at Madison Court House before moving to Orange. Before Jackson brought Early to heel, good news arrived from North Carolina, which may have rescued him. Stonewall received a letter on November 27 announcing that his wife had given birth to a daughter. Mrs. Harriet Irwin, Anna's sister, assumed the persona of Jackson's newborn, writing: "My own dear Father—As my mother's letter has been cut short by my arrival, I think it but justice that I should continue it." Anna's sister described the child as "a very tiny little thing" and "the express image of my darling papa." Jackson responded with overwhelming joy, "Oh! How thankful I am to our Heavenly Father for having spared my precious wife and given us a little daughter!" Jackson beamed with pride; and old accounts with Jubal Early were suddenly forgotten. Mrs. Jackson had spared him.[9]

Jackson had halted at Madison Court House, since Lee no longer needed to fall back to the North Anna and have him cut Burnside's supply line. The Second Corps had closed the gap to within three days' march of Longstreet's command. Jackson explored the possibility of striking the Union line of communications from his present location. Lee wrote to Jackson on November 25: "I have thought . . . that if we could take a threatening position on his [Burnside's] right flank, as a basis from which Stuart with his cavalry could operate energetically, he would be afraid to advance." Jackson shifted his command closer to Culpeper and Rappahannock Station. Wade Hampton's cavalry reconnoitered in front, but Jackson found no opening for him to strike.[10]

Lee and Jackson both concluded it was necessary to reunite the army. Unpredictable weather and the threat of winter-damaged roads compelled Lee to ask Jackson to join him. The army commander had learned that Burnside was building a supply base at Aquia. "I anticipate no forward movement," Lee assured Jackson, "until the wharves on the Potomac are constructed and the railroad to the Rappahannock repaired." Union construction, however, had progressed rapidly, and Burnside would be ready soon. Jackson's men started for Fredericksburg on November 29.[11]

Jackson went ahead to see Lee. He arrived at army headquarters after dark. Lee came out and greeted his subordinate amid joyous commotion. "There was quite a stir," Jackson's orderly recalled, "now that Jackson had come back again." Stonewall Jackson appeared more radiant to onlookers. A London newspaper correspondent reported, "I never saw him looking better." During the meeting, Jackson's aide, James Power Smith, went to find lodgings for the night. The affable lieutenant inquired at Muscoe Garnett's residence, but the owner snarled through the door, "I have no room for anyone; my house is full!" When Smith mentioned Jackson, Garnett flung open the door and asked, "What! General Jackson? Is he here? Go and tell him to come at once. All my home is his, sir!" Smith had done well.[12]

Robert E. Lee conferred with his reunited corps commanders the next morning. Jackson and Longstreet studied a large map of Virginia while Lee explained his defenses and those that needed to be added. An observer noted that Longstreet and Jackson listened "in attentive consideration of his remarks." A reporter for the London *Times* wrote, "With such a stormy petrel as General Jackson, of course, there are rumours of immediately imminent battle." Jackson, for his part, left the meeting disappointed. He had hoped that Lee would fall back to the North Anna now that the army was reunited, but Lee had overruled him. After the council, Jackson complained to his brother-in-law Daniel Harvey Hill, "I am opposed to fighting here." He argued, "We will whip the enemy but gain no fruits of victory."[13]

The head of Jackson's Second Corps marched into Fredericksburg on the afternoon of December 1. The tail of the column arrived two days later. Jackson's forces had trekked 175 miles in just twelve days (including two days' rest around Madison Court House and Orange). Jackson's forces spread across the landscape south of Longstreet's lines. Lee stretched his defenses along the river for thirty miles. W. H. F. Lee's cavalry brigade guarded the lower Rappahannock near Port Royal. Wade Hampton and Fitzhugh Lee picketed around the confluence of the Rappahannock and Rapidan Rivers. Longstreet guarded the high ground from Fredericksburg west, and Jackson watched the river south to Port Royal. The river conveniently limited Burnside's actions to a narrow window of thirty-two miles of riverfront.[14]

The Confederates erected breastworks above and below Fredericksburg. Richard H. Anderson's division fortified Banks Ford. Lafayette McLaws and Robert Ransom guarded the hills behind Fredericksburg, while George E. Pickett and John B. Hood extended the line south down the spine of a commanding ridge known as Spotsylvania Heights. McLaws remembered, "my whole division were actively employed in fortifying their several positions." The division commander toured the ground with his brigade and regimental commanders and familiarized himself with "all the details." McLaws in fact went beyond his duty and studied Richard Anderson's works upriver. He discovered "that the defenses and preparations to resist an attack were, in my opinion, inconsiderable and incomplete." The Confederates had never constructed an elaborate river defense before. Their work lacked cohesion or uniformity, but they had no precedent to draw from. "Looking back on the situation," Longstreet's chief of staff marveled, "it seems surprising that we did so little in the way of defensive fieldworks."[15]

A. P. Hill's division of Jackson's corps joined Longstreet's right, near Thomas Yerby's home, "Belvoir." Brigadier General William B. Taliaferro (from an ancient FFV lineage who pronounced their name "Toliver") extended the line south along the RF&P Railroad. Major General D. H. Hill's division guarded Port Royal against either army or naval incursions. Snide Jubal A. Early—sober but unrepentant—acted as a reserve at Guiney Station. None of Jackson's corps fortified their positions.[16]

Longstreet had ordered Lieutenant Colonel Edward Porter Alexander on November 22 to "select positions at once for all of our Batteries." Alexander laid out an elaborate network of gun pits. Engineers tried to put the pits well behind the summit of the ridge, but Alexander insisted that they place them on the crest. Robert E. Lee fussed at Alexander's placement. Captain Samuel R. Johnston, the engineer in charge, complained to Alexander that Lee "was blaming him for not having located the pits further back on the hill." "You made me put them here," Johnston argued. "Now you come along & help me take the cussin." General Lee told Longstreet's young artillerist, "Ah, Col. Alexander, just see what a mistake Captain Johnston has made here!" Porter Alexander explained, "Gen., I told him to put the pits there, where they could see all this canister & short range ground this side [of] the town. Back on the hill they can see nothing this side [of] the river." Alexander later admitted that Lee "rather sat on me & had the last word." After Lee left, however, the artillerist ordered Captain Johnston to keep the pits where they were. "I knew I was right," Alexander wrote, "& did not give it up."[17]

While Lee's army entrenched, Jeb Stuart's cavalry gathered information and harassed Burnside's line of communications. The Federals had been dormant for a long time and then withdrew from sight. Lee needed to know whether Burnside, against logic, was transferring the Army of the Potomac down the Chesapeake Bay. Wade Hampton's cavalry splashed across the river at Kelly's Ford on November 27 and tested the Union outposts. Hampton and 208 cavalrymen captured an entire Federal picket reserve at Hartwood Church. The cavalier launched another foray against Dumfries, where he bagged two squadrons of cavalry and a number of wagons in the next few days. On December 10, Hampton led a third expedition into the Union rear. At the same time, local lads in the 9th Virginia Cavalry made a daring raid across the river below Fredericksburg. Major Thomas C. Waller surrounded a Federal outpost at Leedstown on December 1, capturing 60 members of the 8th Pennsylvania Cavalry and 48 horses. Hampton's and Waller's reports confirmed that Burnside was in force around Aquia Landing.[18]

Union morale slumped when the days passed and the pontoons did not arrive. Major General Erasmus D. Keyes wrote, "I am almost heart-sick at the disappointment—upon the non-arrival of the pontoon train." Marsena Patrick noted in his diary, "Burnside feels very blue—Lee & the whole Secesh Army are, or will be, in our front." Burnside had won the race to Fredericksburg, but that had been erased by the concentration of Lee's army. Everyone blamed the errant engineers for the missed opportunity.[19]

Major Ira Spaulding's 50th New York Engineers remained isolated at Berlin and Point of Rocks, Maryland, for a long time. Some engineers suspected they had been forgotten. On the afternoon of November 12, Spaulding received McClellan's November 6 order to move to Washington immediately. The War Department injudiciously sent the message up the C&O Canal on a slow packet to avoid bushwhackers wiretapping the telegraph. Engineers disassembled the bridges on the upper Potomac, hauled the boats into the canal, and towed them to Washington.[20]

The same day that Spaulding moved, Halleck notified Engineer General Woodbury that Burnside needed a bridge train. Woodbury warned the War Department that the engineers would need five or six days to get equipped. According to the engineers, Halleck refused to delay the army's move, but at the same time, he failed to alert Burnside of the engineers' predicament. Ira Spaulding reached Washington late on November 14, and he reported to General Woodbury the next day. Woodbury went to the War Department, where Halleck gave him Comstock's inquiry: "Is that train ready to move, with horses and everything needed supplied? If not, how long before it will be ready?" For some unknown reason, Woodbury ordered Spaulding to put his equipment into depot. Spaulding "considered this as countermanding his order to make up the overland pontoon train," inferring that Burnside did not need him. Woodbury, on the other hand, telegraphed Burnside that the pontoons would start in the next couple of days. Perhaps the general wanted to amass the command first, but he erred in not sharing that with Spaulding.[21]

Daniel Woodbury waited until the morning of November 16 before telling Spaulding to prepare a pontoon train for the Army of the Potomac. The general ordered two trains—one to go by water to Aquia Landing, and the other to move overland. Woodbury promised Burnside that Spaulding would start on the 16th or 17th. The old Navy Yard bustled with activity. One captain thought his men were "fitting up as rapidly as possible." Spaulding requisitioned horses from Quartermaster General Montgomery Meigs. The quartermaster department delivered 270 horses and 500 unbroken "greene, wild mules."[22]

Spaulding wasted November 17 haggling with the quartermaster department for more equipment. Woodbury informed Burnside, that the engineers "had not been able to get off," but guaranteed they would start the next day. "Night and day we labored to get our trains in marching order," groaned an engineer. Five hundred mules had to be subdued and harnessed. The mules confounded the engineers, and Spaulding spent the 18th looking for teamsters. "Our men," laughed an officer, "knew little of the ways of the mule."[23]

Major Ira Spaulding's 50th New York Engineers started on November 19—two days after Sumner had shelled Fredericksburg. The caravan crossed Long Bridge and plodded over the Virginia roads like a huge serpent. A pontoon train consisted of 40 pontoon wagons, each toting a boat 31 feet long and 5$^2/_3$ feet wide. The engineers packed them with tools and gear. Every wagon carried 27-foot-long timber balks, cable lashings, rack sticks, oars, boat hooks, pumps, and spring lines. Under the rear axle, they lashed an anchor. A train typically contained 15 chess wagons (each carrying 60 floorboards for the bridge), 4 trestle wagons (jammed with trestle caps, legs, shoes, chains, and claw-balks), 4 abutment wagons (two abutment sills, and more trestle caps, legs, shoes, chains, and 14 short balks), 4 tool wagons (containing carpenters' and entrenching tools as well as spare cordage), and 2 traveling forges. Each wagon required six horses or mules. Men accompanied each wagon, lest it get stuck in the mud, "as it frequently does," reported one soldier.[24]

The engineers started in a gentle rain, which "made the way difficult." It poured in the afternoon and turned to sleet. The column passed along Hunter's Run as the creek rose out of its banks. "We could not tell whether we were in the road or in the Stream," admitted a frustrated engineer. The train struggled to make eight miles before 11:00 P.M.[25]

The 50th New York Engineers awoke early the next morning and labored through another dreary day of rain. The downpour made the men cold and miserable. They halted at Occoquan Creek at 10:00 P.M., when they found their path blocked by a raging torrent. Messengers from Burnside pestered Spaulding to hurry, but nothing could be done until daylight.[26]

The rain subsided on November 22 and temperatures dropped, as engineers tried to cross the swollen Occoquan. "Obstacles seemed to accumulate as they had never done before," mused an engineer. "The situation was *extremely* unpleasant." Major Spaulding unpacked his train and bridged the flooded stream. "We had strained every nerve," wrote one of the laborers, but success came slowly. Burnside's couriers harangued them to hurry, but they did not finish the bridge until 10:00 P.M. Below the stream, Spaulding discovered the roads in even worse shape. "South of the Occoquan," reported General Woodbury, "the roads become impassable to pontoon trains." The major decided to float the pontoons down to Aquia Landing.[27]

Spaulding sent Captain James H. McDonald back to Alexandria to fetch a tugboat while the mud-caked caravan trudged into the "notorious Secession hole" of Dumfries on the Potomac. Major Spaulding divided his train, taking "all that would float" to the Potomac and leaving Captain Wesley Brainerd to haul the empty wagons and animals overland. Spaulding's pontooniers fashioned their boats into rafts. McDonald returned with a steamer and towed them downstream. Meanwhile, Captain Brainerd plodded south with a small escort from the 1st Maine Cavalry. Brainerd navigated through unfamiliar territory with nothing but a pocket map. The men dropped in their tracks after they covered sixteen miles on November 24. Brainerd started again at 2:00 A.M. the next day. The 50th New York Engineers reached Burnside's army late on November 25. A downpour marked their arrival.[28]

Major Spaulding's waterborne expedition disembarked at Belle Plain earlier. But they had no transportation, so the pontoons sat unused on the shore. Burnside little dreamed that his overland train would arrive by steamer at Belle Plain, so he had nothing waiting for them. The army commander blamed both the War Department and the engineers for the foul-up. He complained that someone should have told Spaulding to bring his own wagons, or at the very least inform the Army of the Potomac to dispatch wagons to Belle Plain.[29]

When Burnside grumbled to Halleck, the empiric general-in-chief quipped, "If there has been any unnecessary delay, call [Woodbury] to an account. There has been no delay at these headquarters in ordering as you requested." On November 23, Burnside ordered Woodbury arrested for "unnecessary delay." General Erasmus Keyes wrote, "I was very sorry to have to arrest Woodbury and I sincerely hope he will be able to purge himself of all blame." The initial impression in Burnside's army was that Woodbury "should have started the train when [Quartermaster Meigs] telegraphed him . . . on the night of the 12th." They did not know the pontoons were still far upriver. General Keyes thought, "had he even started by the 16th he could have come right through before the storm." But the 50th New York could not get the necessary equipment before November 19; and bad weather already dogged Burnside by November 16 and 17. When the army commander calmed down, he released Woodbury.[30]

Burnside thought Spaulding had been slow, but not criminally negligent. "He was not impressed with the importance of speed," Burnside concluded, "neither was he empowered with any special authority that would hasten the issuing of the necessary transportation." Blame lay elsewhere.[31]

The Army of the Potomac ultimately blamed General-in-Chief Halleck and Quartermaster General Meigs for the delay. Without direct contact to Spaulding, Burnside relied on the War Department to expedite the pontoons. Burnside testified before the Committee on the Conduct of the War: "I understood that General Halleck was to give the necessary orders." The army leader depended on Washington for help. "I expected, that all parts of the plan which were to be executed in Washington would be attended to by the officers at that place." Later he asserted, "I never imagined for a moment that I had to carry out anything that required to be done in Washington." Halleck and Meigs could have handled the logistics easily. Even Burnside's antagonist Joseph Hooker agreed. A master of left-handed compliments, Hooker noted that the failure "rested upon Gen. Halleck and Gen. Meigs, because it was beyond the control of Gen. Burnside."[32]

Halleck deflected the guilt back to Burnside, telling the army commander that he "ought not to have trusted them in Washington for the details." Burnside manfully assumed part of the blame. In a conciliatory gesture, he informed the Committee on the Conduct of the War, "I could have sent officers of my own there to attend to those matters and perhaps I made a mistake in not doing so." Halleck and Meigs were not so magnanimous, and the matter rested on Burnside's luckless shoulders. "We would have been in Fredericksburg," imagined a Union general, "but it can't be helped now."[33]

Burnside faced another problem before he could proceed with his campaign. He needed to secure a reliable supply base. Union forces had used Aquia Landing as a base prior to Second Manassas, but Lee's offensive compelled the Northerners to burn it and retreat. The railroad engineers smartly recorded the dimensions of the bridges and tracks before they demolished them. Herman Haupt appointed William W. Wright to reconstruct the Aquia wharves and the RF&P Railroad based on those plans.[34]

Steamers filled with engineers and carpenters chugged down the Potomac on November 14, accompanied by two gunboats. The ships anchored off Aquia Creek "just at nightfall" on November 16. The transports had hoped their arrival would coincide with Burnside's, so troops could be forwarded for their protection. Burnside, however, refused to send help to guard his rear.[35]

Federal parties landed the next morning at Aquia Creek and Belle Plain near the mouth of Potomac Creek. The 15th New York Engineers found the area remote and "dreary." "Every thing here was burned by Burnside when he left here on the big retreat," recorded an engineer. "Our Reg were the first U.S. forces here." The carpenters started building docks and wharves, while a contingent of the 15th New York Engineers surveyed the railroad. "We had to moove cautious as very soon [we] found it was swarming with Gorelas," wrote a New Yorker. The 15th New York Engineers netted nine assumed partisans, who "were armed to the teeth & the most veratious cutthrote looking pack" the soldiers had ever seen. The engineers reported that the railroad bridges had been destroyed (not realizing that Ulric Dahlgren had burned them). This unforeseen problem increased their workload dramatically.[36]

Teams worked around the clock to rebuild the base at Aquia and Belle Plain. William Wright extemporized a machine shop at Aquia, with a lathe planer, portable engine, small tools, and shafting. He furnished his blacksmith shops with army forges. Men slept on the winter ground between shifts, since Herman Haupt dictated, "Put up no buildings until the wharf is finished." The dock proved to be a special problem. The old wharf had "limited accommodations." As a result, the new dock extended 1,000 feet into a deep channel, allowing heavier-draft ships to land their freight. Built with "superhuman exertions," the landing "sprung up as if buy [*sic*] magic," according to a 15th New York soldier. Shipping started to unload "with considerable rapidity" at Belle Plain and Aquia Creek, but the railroad could not move it until Wright rebuilt the RF&P. In the interim, Burnside's supplies trickled to the front in wagons, while his soldiers suffered from shortages of food and clothing. Some of the troops christened their camp "Starvation Hollow." The Pennsylvania Reserves protested their hunger by howling for "Crackers and Hardtack!" Major General George Gordon Meade squelched the revolt by ordering the entire division to stand at attention in the rain until it cooled down.[37]

Wright started construction on the RF&P Railroad on November 21. Haupt promised Burnside that "when we commence we will do the best we can to get trains to Falmouth in the shortest possible time." Superintendent Wright procured eight small lighters, which he filled with tents, tools, and rations. Railroad parties pushed the lighters down the tracks as they rebuilt them. The machine shops hummed around the clock, sawing lumber for the bridges over Accokeek and Potomac Creeks. Wright replaced the Accokeek bridge by November 21, and the Potomac Creek span shortly afterward. The first train engine landed on November 21 and ran as far as Potomac Creek. The rest of the line opened on November 27.[38]

Soldiers celebrated when the train rolled into Falmouth. One soldier wrote that "a wild hurrah broke from the thousands of troops. . . . Cheer after cheer went up in joyous welcome as that pioneer train passed the successive camps." Herman Haupt organized a fleet of Schuylkill barges to form the nucleus of what he called "a new era in Military Railroad transportation." The railroader shuttled hundreds of loaded cars from the O&A Railroad to the docks at Washington. There he transferred them onto the barges. Steamboats towed the barges down the Potomac to Aquia, and six hours later, dockworkers unloaded the trains onto the RF&P rail line ready to roll. Incredibly, Haupt reported that "no accident ever occurred" between the transfers.[39]

The Union base completed, the railroad finished, and the pontoons arrived, Burnside now hunted for a new plan of operations. His initial plan had relied on speed and surprise to secure Fredericksburg before Lee blocked the road leading south. "I deem it my duty," Burnside informed the War Department, "to say that I cannot make the promise of probable success with the faith that I did." The Washington government, however, insisted that Burnside must continue the winter campaign. The general-in-chief allegedly prodded Burnside to "fight a battle *now*, even if he is to lose it."[40]

Burnside groped for ideas. He spent several days reconnoitering the Rappahannock for crossing and fording points. Winter weather showed the river and the roads at their worst. "Rain was falling; the river began to rise; supplies were short; and the roads were in bad condition," according to an engineer officer. Burnside probed the river from Port Royal to the confluence of the Rappahannock and Rapidan, just as the Confederates had predicted. The roads became unreliable upriver, and Burnside was loath to stray away from the railroad. The general sent a reconnaissance party to U.S. Ford on November 20, with the idea of drawing Lee away from the more palpable fords. The Federals scrapped the expedition when R. H. Anderson's Confederates blocked U.S. Ford.[41]

Burnside could not cross above Fredericksburg because of a "slack-water navigation" canal. The extra watercourse made crossing too complicated. Edwin Sumner sent "a private note" warning Burnside not to cross at Fredericksburg. He worried that "throwing our bridges directly over to the town might be attended with great loss, not only from their artillery, but every house within musket range could be filled with Infantry." He wrote, "I would rather undertake to carry a line of rifle pits than such a position." Sumner proposed that they look downriver and "by a determined march turn their right flank."[42]

The commander took Sumner's advice and studied the river below Fredericksburg. The Rappahannock widened from a 400-foot width at the city, to almost 1,000 feet just five miles below. Crossing points were few and far between, and the Confederates had a considerable force in the neighborhood. Daniel P. Woodbury and the 4th U.S. Cavalry tested several likely crossing points. Military crossings required solid and easy approaches to support heavy traffic. Several times, engineers stole across the river at night to test the ground on the other side but came back disappointed. An engineer captain wrote in frustration, "It was evident that General Burnside was at a loss *where* to cross."[43]

Lincoln came to the same conclusion. Two days after Sumner suggested a crossing below Fredericksburg, the president wired Burnside for a meeting. The Chief Executive inquired, "If I should be in a boat off Aquia Creek, at dark tomorrow evening, could you . . . pass an hour or two with me?" Burnside met the president on November 27. The general explained his dilemma in getting across the Rappahannock and volunteered to "cross the river in [the] face of the enemy and drive him away." But under close questioning, Burnside admitted that the venture would be "somewhat risky." Burnside intimated that he was under incredible pressure to move from the general-in-chief. The president assured him that Henry Halleck was "not to be the authority," and that "the country will wait until he . . . is ready."[44]

Lincoln consulted Halleck the next day. He disapproved of Burnside's plan to launch a "risky" crossing in Lee's front. "I wish the case to stand more favorably than this," he said. He raised two points he thought imperative to success. First, the president wanted Burnside's crossing to be "nearly free of risk." Secondly, he wished the enemy to "be prevented from falling back, accumulating strength as he goes, into his intrenchments at Richmond." Burnside's plan, at best, would only drive the Confederates before him. Lincoln wanted more.[45]

Burnside turned his attention to a bend in the river known as Skinker's Neck. A scout confirmed that the ground could handle a large-scale movement, and the Confederates had neglected to guard it. Burnside visited the president covertly in Washington on November 28. He briefed his generals next on December 3, little dreaming that Stonewall Jackson's legions were arriving even as they spoke. The general notified his subordinates that the army would descend on Skinker's Neck in two days. He wanted to strike with speed and surprise, hoping to isolate a portion of Lee's army and destroy it before the Confederates could react. Commodore Andrew A. Harwood, commanding the U.S. Navy's Potomac flotilla, agreed to cover the crossing with his gunboats.[46]

Captain Samuel Magaw sent four light-draft gunboats up the Rappahannock to help. Acting Master William F. Shankland commanded the USS *Currituck, Anacostia, Jacob Bell,* and *Coeur de Lion* and started upriver on December 4. Stonewall Jackson's newly situated Southerners harried the navy with a couple of rifled cannon on the bluffs overlooking the river. Jeb Stuart added his elite Stuart Horse Artillery, under the command of the boyish Major John Pelham. Several shots below Port Royal hurried the squat rivercraft upstream. The flotilla steamed to Rappahannock Academy, where more Confederates lay in wait. The 1st Rockbridge Artillery set up a pair of 20-pounder Parrotts just as Shankland's expedition chugged into view. The Confederates pummeled the navy with solid shot. Though the mariners reported no damage, Master Shankland's ships dropped back past Port Royal. The gunboats anchored peacefully off Pratt's Landing, where D. H. Hill ambushed them with a full complement of batteries, including a rare breech-loading Whitworth rifle. The navy clung to its anchorage, trading shots with the Rebels. Both sides fired blindly, as Commodore Harwood reported: "it was dark and the effect could not be ascertained." D. H. Hill's guns managed to score a hit on the USS *Jacob Bell*, but no one was hurt. Confederate sharpshooters crowded the bank, compelling the navy to drag anchor and drift downriver.[47]

Unaware the navy had tipped his hand, Burnside began to move on December 5. Union infantrymen each collected sixty rounds of ammunition and several days' rations. Burnside's grand divisions marched at dawn. Ominous thunderheads stole over the columns. Rain commenced during the night and continued into the next day as the Northern men headed for King George Court House. "It was raining very smartly," recalled a soldier. The roads became mucky and troublesome. A signal officer reported, "the roads are awful." At midday, the rain turned to ice and snow. Rutted roads froze, making a bumpy ride for caissons, wagons, and ambulances. Soldiers slipped on the icy sheen. "Oh how cold!" a Sixth Corps officer noted in his diary. "Our clothes were frozen," a New Jersey combatant told his hometown newspaper.[48]

Before the column reached Skinker's Neck, scouts notified Burnside that the Rebels had appeared in force across the river. The naval escapades of the previous day had drawn Jackson's attention to the undefended stretch of river. He sent Jubal Early's division to guard Skinker's Neck. Edwin Sumner told an investigative committee, "You could scarcely cross a river in the face of an enemy, except by surprise." Without surprise, Burnside had no chance of success. The Confederates had spoiled Burnside's second offensive. The Federal commander ordered his troops to camp on the road. Three or four inches of snow buried their bivouac before morning. A Sixth Corps veteran insisted that no one "will ever forget the 5th of December and its hard experiences, which tested patience and physical endurance to the extremest tension." Franklin and Hooker's grand divisions brushed the snow off their blankets and started back to camp on December 6. A Confederate picket announced confidently, "I think myself the campaign is over."[49]

Burnside refused to give up just yet. He cast around for another plan, but found the Confederates swarming at every bend in the river from Port Royal to the Rapidan. Burnside accordingly gave up on an extended campaign against Richmond to focus instead on defeating Lee swiftly. A quick victory would secure a short-term crossing and open the road to Richmond. Burnside thought that "we could break up the whole of their army here, which I think is now the most desirable thing, not even second to the taking of Richmond." Burnside assumed that Lee's army was stretched rather thin to guard thirty-two miles of river. The Union commander wanted to strike where Lee was most vulnerable, so he determined to launch his next offensive in the center at Fredericksburg itself.[50]

Burnside notified Lincoln, "I think now that the enemy will be more surprised by a crossing immediately in our front than in any other part of the river." This was contrary to Sumner's advice and Lincoln's wish for a secure crossing with no means of Confederate escape. Yet Burnside believed he had run out of options. The general later told a confidant, "when once convinced of the correctness of my course, all the influence on the face of the earth cannot swerve me from pursuing it." The army head convened a council of war at noon on December 9. He informed the generals that Fredericksburg could be taken because "they did not expect us to cross here." This seemed confirmed by the immense concentration of Confederates at Skinker's Neck. He planned a quick lunge across the river, which would catch the Southerners divided and unprepared for "the most decisive battle" of the war. A lightning thrust would cut off the Confederates above Fredericksburg from those below. The weakest point in any defensive scheme is the seam where two units join together. Fredericksburg conveniently marked the seam between James Longstreet's First Corps and Stonewall Jackson's Second Corps. Sour-faced generals left the meeting at 5:00 P.M., unhappy with Burnside's third offensive. Union strategists and gainsayers balked at Burnside's idea, but at least one Confederate conceded, "Many advantages seemed to favor the enterprise."[51]

Burnside's grand division commanders disseminated the information to their corps, division, and brigade leaders. Meetings in the Left and Center Grand Divisions went smoothly, if not complacently. Sumner's Right Grand Division, however, raised some serious objections. Sumner tried to quell the furor, but his generals persisted. Second Corps chief Darius N. Couch thought "Sumner seemed to feel badly that the officers did not agree to Burnside's mode of advance." Couch and the new division commander, Winfield S. Hancock, led the opposition. Burnside was "irritated" when he learned of it. For some reason, Burnside was particularly hurt by Hancock's remarks. Burnside allegedly told the courier carrying Couch's objections to "Say to General Couch that he is mistaken."[52]

Ambrose Burnside ordered another meeting the next day. The Union chief berated his subordinates for their lack of loyalty. "He seemed to be rather severe on Hancock," one general noted. Burnside told them that "he had formed his plans, and all he wanted was the devotion of his men." Couch immediately professed to the group, "That if I had ever done anything in any battle, in this one I intended to do twice as much." The chastened group "discussed & talked & discussed again the plan of Battle." General William H. French, arriving in the midst of the debate, exclaimed, "Is this a Methodist camp-meeting?" The generals yielded to Burnside.[53]

Burnside set the wheels in motion on December 10. The army's provost marshal reported that "Citizen prisoners are being taken up by the pickets throughout the country," so no one could raise an alarm. Marsena Patrick processed the civilians and provided them with shelter. "I have been overrun by that kind of business," he fussed in his diary. Meanwhile, engineers plotted where to place bridges, and artillery officers scanned Stafford Heights for the best positions to cover them. Officers reissued 60 rounds of ammunition to their infantrymen along with three-days' rations.[54]

General Daniel Woodbury briefed the army's engineers at the Lacy house. He told them that the army would cross the next morning. The general had selected three different points for bridges along a two-mile stretch of the river. Woodbury chose Major Ira Spaulding's 50th New York to build two bridges at the northern end of Fredericksburg. Another contingent of the 50th New York Engineers would erect a third span at the lower end of the city. Major James A. Magruder's 15th New York Engineers would construct a bridge one mile south of the city, below Deep Run; and the U.S. Engineer Battalion under Lieutenant Charles E. Cross would build another bridge right next to it. The general estimated the bridges would measure 400 feet by the city, to 420 or 440 feet below Deep Run. "Under favorable circumstances," noted an officer, "[the river] could be bridged in two hours."[55]

Engineers reconnoitered the crossing sites after the meeting. Lieutenant Cross and the Regulars liked the spot chosen for their span. One engineer called it "altogether a favorable location for a bridge." In contrast, the New York volunteers detested their locations. "For us to attempt to lay a Ponton Bridge right in their very faces," noted a captain, "seemed like madness." One of the bridge commanders scribbled, "we all came to the conclusion that we might now return to our quarters and with great propriety execute our last Wills & Testaments."[56]

Engineers spent the afternoon packing in light marching order. The 50th New York Engineers left everything behind, including their blankets. Wagons were ready, teams hitched, and the men in line by 3:00 P.M.[57]

Burnside initiated a number of feints and deceptions to confuse the Confederates. He worked with the navy and other military departments to generate ruses on a wide front. A large wagon train rumbled down to the Federal camp opposite Skinker's Neck specifically to catch the Confederates' eye. Federal pickets engaged in speculative conversations with D. H. Hill's sentries at Rappahannock Academy. The 4th Maine spent the next two days building a corduroy road in plain view of the Rebels at Skinker's Neck. The road led nowhere, connecting one treeline to another, but the Confederates duly noted the effort.[58]

The navy's Rappahannock squadron churned upriver again on December 10. Acting Master T. J. Linnekin sailed the USS *Currituck* up to an anchorage three miles below Port Conway. Confederate artillery ambushed him a mile below his destination, at Brandywine Hill. The ship immediately returned the fire, exchanging thirty rounds. The Southerners struck the ship at 2:25 P.M., and then disappeared. The wounded *Currituck* limped upstream to join the *Yankee, Anacostia, Jacob Bell,* and *Teaser.* The Confederates reappeared at 3:00 P.M. and attacked the flotilla. "The object of the enemy," Captain Magaw surmised, "was to drive us down the river." The navy acted as if it needed to stay, and all five ships blasted the shore "with much elevation." The *Yankee* opened with an 8-inch rifle, a 32-pounder howitzer, and a 12-pounder rifle. The *Anacostia* fired a 50-pounder rifle and 9-inch shells. The *Jacob Bell* relied on its 50-pounder rifle and 8-inch shells. The *Teaser* used a 50-pounder Dahlgren rifle and a 12-pounder Dahlgren. The *Currituck's* armament is unknown.[59]

The *Jacob Bell* got under way quickly to cover some nearby coal schooners. Before it could intercede, a shell burst through the stern of the schooner *Sarah Minge,* mortally wounding Captain S. A. Simmons. The dying captain was the master of the neighboring coal vessel, the *Kadosh,* a private ship "which was seized and brought here through necessity," according to Samuel Magaw. The navy deeply regretted the civilian's death. "He leaves an indigent family," Commodore Harwood lamented, "for which the flotilla has raised a liberal subscription."[60]

Fighting continued for an hour. Most of the shells flew high on both sides. The Confederates eventually scored a hit on the *Currituck,* putting a Parrott shell through her starboard side twenty inches below the water line. Navy tars braved flooding waters to hammer a shot plug into the hole. Thirty-five minutes later, another Parrott shell struck the *Currituck,* aft of the main rigging. The round breached the fire room and exploded, wounding three men, including the forecastle captain, John McClusky. Fire tapered off with the advent of night. The Federals maintained a defiant profile through the night, even though the *Currituck*, by all accounts, was "still leaking badly."[61]

Lieutenant Commander Samuel Magaw sailed upriver the next morning "at the request of General Burnside." Leaving his anchorage at Oaken Brow, the ships attacked D. H. Hill's artillery at Pratt's Bluff. The flotilla divided, with a part shelling the Confederate gun emplacement from the previous day. Magaw took the rest of the command and fired into the hills behind Port Royal. Magaw was surprised when he failed to provoke a response. "I think they had gotten intelligence of the feint to be made by a portion of Franklin's grand division at Skinker's Neck," the captain reported. The tars continued to pound the southwest bank, if for no other reason than to make enough noise to mask the sound of artillery resonating from Fredericksburg. They did not venture farther north for fear of the banks closing in and the Confederates ambushing them at pointblank range. Magaw acknowledged that Burnside "may wish us to come to Fredericksburg, and we are ready at five minutes' notice," but he thought it unlikely that his ships could materially aid the Army of the Potomac. Burnside agreed, and let the navy continue its ruckus at Port Royal. "The general wished us to make a noise," Magaw wrote, "and we did."[62]

Other military departments fielded expeditions to divert attention away from Burnside's offensive. Major General John G. Foster, commander of the Department of North Carolina, sent a force inland from the coast. Foster's Federals advanced on December 11 and skirmished up to Goldsborough before dropping back to New Berne on December 20. Major General John A. Dix, head of the Department of Virginia, commanded all of the Union forces on the Virginia peninsula, Norfolk, and Suffolk. He sent Brigadier General Henry M. Naglee across the York River to Gloucester Point on December 11. Accompanied by a brigade of infantry, a battery, and some cavalry, Naglee occupied Gloucester Court House. The cavalry dashed northward and came within a couple of miles of Lee's rear on the Rappahannock. Naglee threatened Lee's communications for several days and withdrew on December 14 without doing any genuine damage. The Confederates stood powerless to stop these incursions, but Lee refused to be distracted from the Army of the Potomac.[63]

The Confederates grew increasingly wary with each new diversion. "The stir and excitement about the enemy's camps on the 10th of December, as well as the reports of scouts, gave notice that important movements were pending," noted General Longstreet. Confederate batteries were ordered to be harnessed an hour before dawn and be ready to move at a moment's notice. Lee knew that Burnside would strike on December 11. The question was, where?[64]

CHAPTER THREE

"A SCENE OF WILDEST CONFUSION"

The Pontoon Crossings on December 11

Night spread over the Rappahannock Valley on December 10 before Woodbury's engineers stole out of camp. Major Magruder and the 15th New York
Engineers started at 8:00 P.M. The U.S. Regulars followed at 10:00 P.M., and
the 50th New York set out an hour later. The engineers stopped briefly at the
pontoon park and outfitted their trains for the night's assignment. The teams
started for their assigned bridge sites by 11:50 P.M. As soon as the engineers
stirred, the army "knew that the moment for action had arrived for the *Pon-
tons* were moving for the river." The 50th New York left the pontoon park
first, followed by the U.S. Engineers and the 15th New York. For some unknown reason, the 50th New York started its march first even though the
other engineers had farther to go to get into position.[1]

The 50th New York Engineers rumbled along heavily rutted dirt roads
with three bulky pontoon trains. Each caravan toted 34 pontoon boats on
wheels accompanied by 29 support vehicles laden with lumber, tools, and
forges. One hundred eighty-nine wagons lurched into a ravine behind the
Lacy house. The 50th divided into three sections. Captains Wesley Brainerd
and George W. Ford kept two trains behind the Lacy house, while Captain
James H. McDonald led the third train south to the lower end of the city.
Major Spaulding accompanied McDonald's crew to a point below the burned

trestle of the RF&P Railroad. Surgeons set up hospitals on Claiborne Run, while assistants selected forward aid stations closer to Stafford Heights.[2]

The engineers settled down for a nap before building the bridges. "All was quiet, peaceful, calm," remembered an officer. "Who would have dreamed that a *terrible tragedy* was soon to be enacted there?" The surgeon's assistant, Clark A. Baum, wrote in contrast: "We shall probably have some surgical practice. . . . But let it come." He believed anything was better than "this *killing* inactivity."[3]

Captain Wesley Brainerd rested in the parlor of the Lacy house, listening to the bell toll solemnly from Fredericksburg's Saint George's Episcopal Church. "Dear Father," the captain wrote hastily, "To night the grand tragedy comes off." With the peel of the church bell still resonating in his ears, Brainerd readied his command to move.[4]

The moon set at 1:00 A.M., blotting out the landscape and giving the engineers their best chance to work on the river undetected. Four companies of the 50th New York Engineers moved to a ravine north of the Lacy house. A wagon train met them there. The men stealthily unloaded the pontoons and dragged them down the ravine. They manhandled the boats down the steep gorge for 200 yards. Stafford Heights drops quickly, and some of the workers found it easier to slide the pontoons down the precipice. At the foot of the hill, engineers carted the boats over a wide floodplain to the river's edge. "We marched as quietley [sic] as possible," Captain Brainerd noted, "so as not to disturb the enemy." The men dashed up and down the hill until they had transferred all of their equipment to the riverbank.[5]

Engineers complained about the wintry morning chill. One remembered the morning as "bitter cold." Another recalled how the dampness and fog "penetrated to the bones." A weather observer in Georgetown recorded the temperature as twenty-four degrees in the District of Columbia at 7:00 A.M. However, the temperature rose through the day, reaching into the fifties by afternoon. The dramatic fluctuation in temperature buried the Rappahannock Valley in an unremitting fog, which aided the Northern workmen in their clandestine operations.[6]

Barely visible figures flared across the slopes of Stafford Heights while the engineers struggled with their gear. Colonel Samuel K. Zook of the Union Second Corps sent the 57th and 66th New York regiments to protect the upper crossing. The 57th New York covered the right flank, while the 66th New York watched the left. The 46th and 89th New York regiments of the

Ninth Corps guarded the middle pontoon crossing. The 2nd U.S. Sharpshooters and the 10th Pennsylvania Reserves watched the lower pontoon site. The infantrymen formed near the riverbank and stood "at ease," while the engineers worked.[7]

Colonel Zook despaired of success. He had spent the night in his Falmouth headquarters scribbling hopeless messages to friends. "Tomorrow we commence the crossing of the Rappahannock & will be sure to have a fearful fight," he wrote. "In fact I expect we will be licked." To another, he admitted, "I expect to be sacrificed tomorrow." The brigade commander ended one note: "Goodbye old Boy & if tomorrow night finds me dead remember me kindly as a soldier who meant to do his whole duty."[8]

Federal artillery unlimbered on the heights above the bridges. Burnside expected his cannon to dominate the ground around the pontoon crossings. He made his chief of artillery, Brigadier General Henry J. Hunt, responsible for (1) checking enemy movements on the plains below Fredericksburg, (2) silencing any Confederate artillery that came into play, (3) commanding the city, (4) protecting the engineers throwing the bridges and the infantry who would cross the spans, and (5) guarding the army's left flank against attack. Hunt needed guns planted along the entire length of Stafford Heights before he could fulfill Burnside's directive, but his reserve artillery lacked sufficient cannon. The army commander boosted Hunt's force with a rifled battery from each division in the army. The division commanders complied only after they received assurances that their guns would be returned once the infantry crossed the river.[9]

Hunt divided the heights into four sectors. The chief of artillery put Lieutenant Colonel William Hays in charge of the right end of the line—the space north of the Lacy house to Falmouth. Colonel Charles H. Tompkins took command of the right center, from the Lacy house south to a point below the burnt railroad bridge. Colonel Robert O. Tyler commanded the left center from Tompkins' left to the mouth of Deep Run. Hunt's brother-in-law, Captain Gustavus A. DeRussy, headed the far left from Tyler's left to a point below Pollock's Mill.[10]

Hunt controlled the river crossings with 147 guns. Hays, on the "Right," used seven batteries with forty guns—six 20-pounder Parrotts, eighteen 10-pounder Parrotts, and sixteen 3-inch ordnance rifles. Tompkins' "Right Center" had seven batteries, with 38 pieces—fourteen 12-pounder Parrotts and the rest 3-inch rifles. Tyler's "Left Center" stood farther back from the river because it had the heaviest-calibered weapons. Tyler's seven batteries contained only 27 guns—eight 20-pounder Parrotts, twelve 10-pounder Parrotts, and seven massive 4½-inch siege rifles. DeRussy commanded nine batteries on the "Left," with 42 cannon. All of his guns were 3-inch rifles, with the exception of eight 20-pounder Parrotts.[11]

The artillery gathered at four different rendezvous points. Hays' Right group met "about a mile behind Falmouth" and started for their positions. At the same time, Tompkins' Right Center concentrated at the Alexander K. Phillips house. Tyler's Left Center gathered by General Burnside's headquarters' camp near Gustavus B. Wallace's home, Little Whim. DeRussy met the left artillery group at the rustic chapel called White Oak Church.[12]

Hays moved onto the hills above Falmouth. His right rested above Beck's, or Winchester, Island. Lieutenant Samuel N. Benjamin's Battery E, 2nd U.S. Artillery, covered the flank with 20-pounder Parrotts. Lieutenant Rufus King's Battery A, 4th U.S.; Captain Charles D. Owen's Battery G, 1st Rhode Island Artillery; Captain Jacob Roemer's 2nd New York Battery; Captain Rufus D. Pettit's Battery B, 1st New York Artillery; Captain George W. Durell's 2nd Pennsylvania Battery; and Lieutenant Charles E. Hazlett's Battery D, 5th U.S. Artillery, extended the guns to the left.[13]

Tompkins joined Hays' left with Captain James E. Smith's 4th New York Battery. Captain William M. Graham's Battery K, 1st U.S., formed next, just to the right of the Lacy house. Lieutenant Marcus P. Miller's Battery G, 4th U.S., sidled south of the house, followed by Lieutenant David H. Kinzie's Battery K, 5th U.S. Captain Charles Kusserow's Battery D, 1st Battalion New York Light Artillery, ended up below the railroad with Captain Richard Waterman's Battery C, 1st Rhode Island Artillery. Lieutenant George W. Norton's Battery H, 1st Ohio Artillery, held the far left. Before dawn, Tompkins added Lieutenant Francis W. Seeley's Battery K, 4th U.S., between Waterman's and Norton's guns.[14]

Captain Otto Diederichs placed his Battery A, 1st Battalion New York Light Artillery, on the right of Tyler's Left Center group. Two batteries of mammoth siege guns, left over from McClellan's days on the Peninsula, set up next to the New Yorkers. Major Thomas S. Trumbull commanded both batteries and arranged them with Captain Albert F. Brooker's Battery B, 1st Connecticut Artillery, on the right and Captain Franklin A. Pratt's Battery M, 1st Connecticut Artillery, on the left. The 1st Connecticut Artillery's siege guns were the largest guns in either army at Fredericksburg. Tyler completed his line with Captain Adolph Voegelee's Battery B, 1st Battalion New York Light Artillery, Lieutenant William A. Harn's 3rd New York Battery, Captain

Jeremiah McCarthy's Battery C, 1st Pennsylvania Light Artillery, and Captain Michael Hall's Battery D, 1st Pennsylvania Light Artillery. Voegelee's battery had been on the river bluffs since November 20, and enjoyed the unique advantage of earthworks.[15]

DeRussy's Left artillery group sprawled to the left of Tyler's position. Captain James A. Hall's 2nd Maine Battery lined up on the right. Next came Captain John W. Wolcott's Battery A, 1st Maryland Artillery; Lieutenant Bernhard Wever's Battery C, 1st New York Artillery; and Captain Elijah D. Taft's 5th New York Battery. On the next ridge to the south, DeRussy placed Captain John A. Reynolds' Battery L, 1st New York Artillery; Captain Andrew Cowan's 1st New York Battery; Lieutenant R. Bruce Ricketts' Battery F, 1st Pennsylvania Light Artillery; Captain James Thompson's 4th Pennsylvania Battery; and Lieutenant Frank P. Amsden's Battery G, 1st Pennsylvania Light Artillery.[16]

Henry Hunt had the cannon in position before 2:00 A.M. To one artillerist it seemed that "The whole riverside thus became one vast battery." Hunt's gunners expected to quash anything the Confederates threw at them. "The order was to be watchful," reported Captain Roemer of the 2nd New York Battery, "and, if necessity demanded, to open fire at once without waiting for further orders." Keen eyes searched the darkness for any sign of trouble.[17]

Engineers gathered below them at the river's edge and started shoving pontoon boats into the water "at a lively rate." Captain Brainerd took Companies C and H and commenced work on one bridge, while Captains Ford and Perkins led Companies A and I upriver 100 feet for a second bridge. Each battalion divided the men into eight sections and started construction.[18]

The first section, known as the abutment party, anchored a pontoon at the point where they intended to build. Engineers ran a long beam back to shore. Another crew held the beam level with the top of the pontoon and fastened it in place with stakes. The abutment party graded the bank to make an easy approach to the level of the beam. Some low areas leading to the bridge required filling. A second group, called the trestle party, constructed log cribs to support traffic through the marshy approaches to the bridge.[19]

While these engineers prepared the entrance to the bridge, two more parties—dubbed boat parties—maneuvered the unwieldy thirty-one-foot pontoons into position. A six-man team controlled each rectangular hulk. One group hovered above the axis of the bridge and the other stood below. The group to the north cast an anchor upstream and then lowered the boat into place, using a wench and cable system. The downstream parties placed their boats into position the same way with downstream anchors, these anchors being needed when the tide came in; and both parties alternated during construction. The pontoons anchored thirteen feet apart. The men found the work difficult and noisy. An annoying sheet of ice coated the river's edge and cracked underfoot. Some of the ice measured more than an inch thick.[20]

While the pontoons were anchored in position, the next group, the balk party, hauled long beams—or balks—out to the end of the bridge. The balks measured twenty-seven feet in length and five inches square on end, and required two men to carry. Seven teams laid their balks between the pontoons. The space from the center of one pontoon to the center of the next was called a bay. Balks spanned exactly one bay.[21]

The sixth group, referred to as lashers, fastened the balks to the pontoon gunwales. While the lashers tied the boats together, the seventh team—the chess carriers—laid wide plank floorboards called chesses onto the bridge. Chesses typically measured fourteen feet long and one foot wide, with a thickness of an inch and a half. The chess carriers did not plank the last six inches of the balks so the engineers could add another bay.[22]

The final group of engineers, called the side-rail party, secured the chesses to the structure with rack-lashing. All eight groups of engineers worked with a synchronization that ensured "every thing went smoothly and quietly as clock work." Engineer Arthur T. Williams recalled, "All went 'merry as a marriage bell'" with the work groups.[23]

While the bridges took shape, wary engineers eyed the Confederate pickets on the distant shore. Rebels huddled around small fires "burning brightly on the bank." The fires dimmed by 4:30 A.M. and "one after another began to go out," until only two remained. The Confederates had extinguished their campfires when they heard the bridge builders. The 50th New York jumped when two cannon erupted at 5:00 A.M., summoning Lee's Army of Northern Virginia to the hills behind Fredericksburg. Many of the New Yorkers worried about what might come next. "I was in a terrible anxiety and dread," admitted an engineer. "Such a feeling of anxiety and suspense I never experienced. I could scarcely breathe."[24]

Meanwhile, Major Spaulding and Captain McDonald started the middle pontoon crossing below the burnt trestle of the RF&P Railroad. The pontoon train had parked at the boyhood home of George Washington and the alleged site of the fabled dollar toss across the river. The workmen immediately went to work, unloading pontoons and unpacking chesses and balks.

Engineers hauled the boats down an old colonial rut that led to a defunct ferry. Colonel Harrison S. Fairchild's 89th New York, of the Ninth Corps, formed in support. Lieutenant Colonel Joseph Gerhardt's 46th New York joined them and covered the river above the wrecked trestle.[25]

On McDonald's orders, workers from Companies F and K, 50th New York Engineers, plunged the wooden pontoons into the black water and poled them into place. The impenetrable fog hid the construction, but it also concealed the enemy-held wharves. About the time the engineers glimpsed the Rebels at the upper crossing, Captain James McDonald spotted the far shore only eighty feet away. The men worked with calculated silence to ensure surprise as long as possible. Work accelerated when the Northerners realized they had been spotted. The 50th New York Engineers little guessed that they had had the undivided attention of the Confederates for quite a while. The lower pontoon crossing had hit a snag and had not materialized yet. The Southerners, unaware of the third crossing, focused on the two locations opposite the city.[26]

The 50th New York abandoned caution and quiet in the interest of speed. Captain Brainerd's team spanned almost half the river, and Captains Ford and Perkins' second bridge stretched a quarter of the way across. "Our men sprang to their work as if their lives depended upon their efforts," Brainerd reported. Boats rushed through the icy water, while engineers raced back and forth, banging chesses and balks into place. Their loud splashes and heavy footfalls seemed to be magnified on the heavy morning air.[27]

The engineers noted, even amid their scramble, that the Confederate-held city remained ominously quiet. One New Yorker wrote, "not a sound could be heard in the city." Another thought that everything was "*still as death*." A surgeon's assistant admitted, "Dreadful suspense is felt by all. Every one expecting the next moment would '*open the ball.*'" The young soldier wrote, "Expectation and *dread* mixed with *hopes* that the Rebs had evacuated."[28]

General Robert E. Lee never considered evacuating Fredericksburg without a show of force. He had scattered troops along the Rappahannock to alert him when Burnside moved. Mississippi brigadier general William Barksdale occupied Fredericksburg and the fields below the city. Brigadier General Jerome B. Robertson—nicknamed "Aunt Polly" by his soldiers—extended the picket line south of Deep Run. The Confederates had constructed rifle pits and knocked loopholes in riverfront houses. Barksdale's Mississippians even dug a rifle pit behind a high board fence, through which they pierced "port holes." They cut zigzag trenches to reinforce their fortifications without being seen.[29]

Barksdale's Brigade fortified Sophia Street, which skirted the Rappahannock, and also the next two streets back from the river, named Caroline and Princess Anne, respectively. Several key streets bisected these Confederate strongholds, particularly in the northern half of Fredericksburg, where troops reinforced the river by way of Hawke, Fauquier, William, and George Streets. Barksdale sent a company of the 17th Mississippi under Captain Andrew J. Pulliam to guard the rope ferry at the foot of Hawke Street. Another company of the 17th Mississippi, under Captain Andrew R. Govan, watched the southern end of Fredericksburg. Lieutenant Colonel William M. Luse's 18th Mississippi strung across the plain below the city, and the 13th and 21st Mississippi regiments formed a reserve to reinforce any part of the river above Deep Run.[30]

Barksdale had anticipated the Federal crossing. He had observed an unusual amount of activity among the Northerners on December 10. The general surmised that the Yankees probably would move that night. Barksdale alerted McLaws of the impending strike and reinforced Captain Pulliam's group at Hawke Street with two more companies. These reinforcements arrived around 11:00 P.M. The Mississippi brigadier kept his division commander informed of events. McLaws, in turn, notified Robert E. Lee and James Longstreet. McLaws advised Barksdale at 2:00 A.M. "to let the bridge building go on until the enemy were committed to it and the construction parties were within easy range."[31]

Barksdale listened to the Yankees opposite Hawke Street, and ordered Colonel John C. Fiser to take four more companies there at 4:00 A.M. An hour later, Barksdale received a small reinforcement from Major General Richard H. Anderson's division. Barksdale divided Captain David Lang's 8th Florida, sending three companies under Captain William Baya to Captain Govan's Mississippians at the city docks. The remaining 150 Floridians joined Fiser's 17th Mississippi at Hawke Street.[32]

Colonel Fiser examined the upper crossing, and quietly evacuated the slumbering citizens. "I deemed it proper to notify all the women and children of their danger," explained Fiser, "and give them time to get from under range of the enemy's guns." Most of the civilians fled from the city swiftly. Some, however, failed to escape in time. They hid in basements and cellars, trapped in their houses. Meanwhile, Barksdale confirmed the Yankee crossing for Lafayette McLaws sometime after 4:30 A.M. At 5:00 A.M., McLaws ordered Captain John P. W. Read's Pulaski Artillery, from Georgia, to fire two cannon as the signal for Lee's army to concentrate. These were the reports the engineers had heard with such concern. As the echo of the guns disseminated over the misty river valley, Barksdale summoned his reserves. The sleepy 13th and 21st Mississippi regiments trudged into the dark city and halted at Barksdale's headquarters in the Market House on Princess Anne Street. William Barksdale had fulfilled his mission of alerting Lee to the crossing in a timely manner so he could prepare for battle. The Mississippian next undertook to delay Burnside's crossing so Lee could gather his forces together. Barksdale sent a succession of couriers to update Robert E. Lee every fifteen minutes. An orderly returned one time with the army commander's injunction "to hold the enemy in check until ordered to retire."[33]

The 50th New York Engineers spliced their bridges together as rapidly as possible at the upper crossing. Captain Wesley Brainerd's bridge passed the halfway mark of the river while Captains Ford and Perkins' span lagged behind. Brainerd paced nervously at the end of his bridge. He peered into the fog for some hint of the Confederates. The mist parted for a moment and Brainerd shuddered. "What I saw almost chilled my blood," he wrote. A long line of men's arms bounded furiously up and down. Instantly, he knew that the Confederates were massing in his front and loading their muzzle-loading rifles. The captain quietly told General Woodbury. The general instructed, "Captain, do the best you can and when they open fire upon you, as they probably will in a few moments, retire to the shore in as good order as possible." The need to finish the bridge should have precluded interruption, but Woodbury believed that the Federal artillery would minimize any delays. The general never considered preempting the Confederates with Hunt's cannon. Perhaps he wished to keep the charade of secrecy to the very last minute.[34]

Colonel John Fiser of the 17th Mississippi watched the last refugees escape into the darkness even as the noise of the signal guns lingered on the cold morning air. The Mississippi colonel distinguished the vague outline of a pontoon bridge about halfway across the river. Fiser gave the order to fire. A volley roared from the clapboard dwellings, stone fences, and the rifle pits at the upper end of Fredericksburg. Captain Govan's party at the middle crossing echoed the fire with a volley of its own.[35]

Wesley Brainerd had waited for this inevitable moment. Ten minutes after Saint George's clock tolled 5:00 A.M., all hell broke loose. An engineer standing 200 feet from the Confederate shore heard the Rebel order to "Fire!" A nearby infantryman wrote, "out from the opposite bank, flashed a long line of light followed by the report of musketry." A sheet of fire exploded across the riverfront and the engineers panicked. One engineer recalled the hateful sound of bullets as they "went whizzing and spitting by and around me, pattering the bridge." The lead slugs scythed through the workmen, splashed the water, or slammed into the boats. "Many of the pontoons were riddled with musket balls," reported the army's chief engineer. Pandemonium reigned as the men fled "one of the most murderous fires you can imagine." Some engineers fell in the river or tumbled into the pontoons. Horses and mules pitched onshore and collapsed with ghastly wounds. A Union officer wrote, "It was simple murder, that was all."[36]

Captain Augustus S. Perkins stood on the bank, guiding one of the pontoons into the stream when the musketry exploded. A bullet pierced his neck; Perkins died almost instantly. The captain had had a premonition of his death. After the battle, engineers sent his body home in a handcrafted wooden box. Sergeant Thomas J. Owen accompanied the remains to Pennsylvania, where bereaved family and friends unsettled him. "Up to this time I had not fully realized what war was," the sergeant confessed. "This was the first time I witnessed the great sorrow of friends at home over the loss of their sons and brothers killed in war, and it left an impression on my mind that I shall never forget."[37]

The construction teams scrambled to safety without orders, and their officers fled with them. Engineers took cover behind grounded boats and piles of lumber. Some sprawled flat on the ground. Bullets hummed along the shore, suggesting to one soldier music "not at all pleasant or harmonious." Taking stock at the upper crossing, Major Spaulding counted three killed (Perkins being the only officer), and several wounded, including one of the bridge foremen. Captain George Ford, however, ignored his wound and stuck close to his bridge. The same scenario unfolded at the middle crossing.[38]

Captain James McDonald finished two-thirds of the middle pontoon bridge by 5:00 A.M. The fire upriver suddenly triggered an eruption from the Fredericksburg wharves. Andrew Govan's 17th Mississippi contingent rushed down the "Rocky Lane," a cobbled thoroughfare with high stone walls, which connected Caroline Street to the boat landing. Dashing across the wharves, the Confederates fired pointblank into the engineers. They then dispersed amid the warehouses, walls, and cellars before the Union supports could respond. Two engineers fell on the bridge. The rest fled for their lives. Workers cowered behind the riverbank for safety. Burnside's plan for a swift and efficient crossing had ground to a calamitous halt.[39]

Colonel Charles Tompkins' Federal artillery responded to the Confederates at both the upper and middle pontoon crossings. An artillerist recalled that the guns answered at once with "a most tremendous cannonade upon the city." Several batteries opened on the buildings where they had spotted Confederate fire. Tompkins coached his batteries to fire in short bursts—three to six shots per gun—and then allow the smoke to dissipate so they could judge the effect. Darkness and fog conspired to make this impractical. Some of the batteries, like Lieutenant Francis Seeley's, chose to fire at a steady rate. Seeley discharged one round every five minutes.[40]

Artillery chief Henry Hunt expanded the artillery fire at 9:00 A.M. He ordered William Hays' command to assist Tompkins. Hazlett's Battery D, 5th U.S., responded immediately. The rest of Hays' command, however, offered little support. At the same time, Robert Tyler's Left Center and Gustavus DeRussy's Left battalions started to heat up to the south. Hunt turned to the Right and Center Grand Divisions for reinforcements to bolster Tompkins' batteries. The artillery chief took five batteries of light guns from the Second, Third, and Ninth Corps. Captain Charles H. Morgan, the Second Corps artillery chief, gave him Captain John G. Hazard's Battery B, 1st Rhode Island Artillery; Captain John D. Frank's Battery G, 1st New York Light Artillery; and Lieutenant Edmund Kirby's Battery I, 1st U.S. Artillery. The Third Corps released Lieutenant John G. Turnbull's Batteries F and K, 3rd U.S., and the Ninth Corps sent Lieutenant James Gilliss' Battery A, 5th U.S. Hunt assumed that Seeley's Battery K, 4th U.S. Artillery, came forward at the same time, making a total thirty-six guns.[41]

Tompkins dispatched Turnbull's Batteries F and K, 3rd U.S., to the middle crossing, while the other batteries headed to the Lacy house and the upper pontoon crossing. Gilliss' U.S. Regulars replaced Kinzie's battery. Kinzie had lost two guns when their stock trails snapped. Kinzie's remaining cannon shifted left and joined Marcus Miller's Battery G, 4th U.S. Kirby went into battery between Gilliss and Kinzie. Frank took a position to the right of Gilliss, and Hazard formed on his right. All of the new batteries had 12-pounder smoothbore Napoleons. Hunt now had 183 guns.[42]

Hunt's batteries intensified their effort between 9:30 and 10:00 A.M. A soldier in Seeley's battery wrote, "We could see the boards and brick fly as the shells went dashing through the buildings which soon began to present a sorry look." Confederate General Barksdale sent a detachment of the 21st Mississippi to the river, but Miller's Union battery shredded it before it reached the foot of William Street. A Second Corps staff officer recounted, "It was a magnificent sight to see the bombardment of the sleepy old town, and we expected to see it quickly reduced to ashes." "Oh! It was terrific!" rejoiced a man in the 50th New York Engineers. "From the time the fire opened until about 11 A.M., it was one continuous roar." One soldier called the barrage "a spectacle never, never to be forgotten," and believed that "every shot told." An infantryman at the upper crossing said, "It was a great amusement to us to watch a solid shot tear through a building, beat down a wall, topple over a chimney or root out a nest of sharpshooters." Each explosion reverberated with an intensity that startled even the Federals. A New Yorker recalled, "The 11th was a day of bombardment such as even soldiers rarely see." But Tompkins' gunners lacked the wherewithal to drive the Confederates away.[43]

Some Union commanders became critical as the artillery "did not appear to do much good." Every time the Confederates appeared subdued, the guns fell silent and the Rebels' fire sizzled the returning engineers. The cannon repeated the cycle several times in a feeble attempt to drive away the Southerners. A member of Zook's brigade wrote bitterly, "Thursday was spent in wasting ammunition from about 100 guns." A staff officer noted, "the effect was ridiculously out of proportion to the noise and weight of metal thrown into the place." Gunners blamed their poor execution on the darkness before dawn, and then the fog until it disappeared. General Hunt explained to Burnside that his guns made the city unfit for large bodies of troops, but Barksdale's Confederates had divided into small cells, which were difficult to pinpoint and destroy. A battery commander reported that he knew where the Rebels were hiding, but "found it quite impossible to drive them from the buildings, as the cellars underneath afforded a secure refuge from our shots." Impatient engineers grumbled, "Our artillery were very inefficient or they could have blown the buildings that sheltered the devils to atoms." Whatever the cause, the effect created an impasse, which disrupted Burnside's plans predicated on speed and surprise.[44]

Union infantry jumped into the action at dawn. The 57th and 66th New York blazed unenthusiastically from the upper crossing, but made little impact. A member of the 57th New York said the fog obscured the other side of the river. Foot soldiers advanced to the riverbank to get a better view, but this recklessly exposed them to Confederate sharpshooters. Some took the opposite tack, and moved up the hillside to more-commanding positions, but Colonel Samuel K. Zook shooed them back to the river. A New York soldier complained, "We could have done some execution, perhaps, if stationed higher up."[45]

The Confederates savaged the Federal infantry. A New York sharpshooter noted how the Rebel soldiers "worked their will with little danger to themselves." The Federals made easy targets on the bank, and the Rebels raised "fearful havoc" with them. A New Yorker stated that "a man did not have half a chance for his life." With every Confederate shot, the Federals "wondered whose turn had come." Casualties accumulated at a significant rate. A Second Corps officer recalled that "many in each regiment fell as this bloody farce was being played."[46]

Lieutenant Colonel Alford B. Chapman stood by his horse, directing the fire of the 57th New York. After several close calls, an orderly appealed to Chapman, "Colonel, please don't expose yourself unnecessarily." A bullet punctuated the moment by clipping the orderly's suspenders. Chapman remarked, "That was a providential escape," when he suddenly clasped his chest and sank to the ground. A ball had struck the colonel in the chest, but a package of letters and a blank book deflected the blow and saved his life. The men carried Chapman to the hospital, and Major N. Garrow Throop assumed command. The 66th New York lost its commander at the same time. A Southern bullet killed Lieutenant Colonel James Bull instantly. Captain Julius Wehle took charge of the regiment. After two hours, Zook's regiments lost 8 officers and men killed and 60 wounded. The 57th New York bore the brunt of the loss and had to be replaced by the 7th Michigan of Colonel Norman J. Hall's brigade. Hall's men filed into position at 8:00 A.M.[47]

General William Barksdale reinforced his river defenses when the shooting redoubled at dawn. The brigadier hurried Colonel James W. Carter's 13th Mississippi to the left to back up John Fiser's 17th Mississippi at the upper crossing. Carter formed his regiment along Princess Anne Street immediately behind the 17th Mississippi. At the same time, Colonel Benjamin G. Humphreys dispatched Major Daniel N. Moody with half of the 21st Mississippi to support Captain Govan's defenders at the city docks. This left only half of Humphreys' 21st Mississippi at the Market House as a reserve for Barksdale. A small contingent of the 18th Mississippi also joined Govan at dawn. Meanwhile, the rest of the 18th, under Lieutenant Colonel William M. Luse, prepared for a crossing below Fredericksburg.[48]

* * *

After considerable delay, Union engineers at last had made their presence known at the lower crossing. Lieutenant Charles E. Cross took the U.S. Army Engineer Battalion to a point on Stafford Heights approximately a mile below the city crossing sites. Major James A. Magruder's 15th New York Engineers accompanied the Regulars. Together they would build two bridges at the lower crossing site.[49]

The engineers reached their destination at 3:00 A.M. Men started unloading their boats and equipment while the officers went ahead to examine the ground. Cross could not find an easy way to get to the river from Stafford Heights. It appears that the Regulars did not reconnoiter the site thoroughly beforehand. The gruff Regulars forged ahead, wrestling the ungainly 1,300-pound, box-shaped pontoons across a plowed field and down the steep slope of Stafford Heights. The extra work delayed construction until almost 7:00 A.M. The 15th New York Engineers saw the Regulars' dilemma and scouted farther upriver. Magruder located a point 250 yards upstream that provided access to the river. The New Yorkers cast their pontoons into the freezing water and poled downstream to the bridge site. Unknown to Magruder, he had entered the river directly in front of William Luse's 18th Mississippi.[50]

Luse had doubled the pickets along the river and kept the rest of the 18th Mississippi by the widow Eliza Ferneyhough's home, Sligo. Barksdale met with Luse and his subordinates before dawn, and listened to their excited reports about the Yankees splashing in the river in front. The colonel reported hearing wagons creaking to the river and Northerners unloading lumber. Luse imagined the Federals had started bridging just above Deep Run. Barksdale detached three companies of the 18th Mississippi to reinforce the city docks, and Luse took the rest of the regiment to the bank near Deep Run. The commander spread his sharpshooters along the riverbank and waited for first light. The Mississippian was so certain of the crossing site that neither he nor Barksdale bothered to warn the Confederates south of Deep Run of the impending strike. The Southerners never dreamed that the Northerners had floated silently downstream. Meanwhile, the Confederates below Deep Run knew nothing of the blue-clad forces marshaling on the opposite bank.[51]

The 15th New York commenced lashing their bridge together well before the U.S. Regulars could drag their boats to the river. A crust of ice hindered the swift flow of operations, but the soaking engineers shivered through the ordeal as they aligned their boats. Southern pickets from Robertson's Texas Brigade walked their beats below Deep Run and listened to the staccato bursts of fire coming from Fredericksburg. The Union engineers used the noise upriver to mask their construction. Well after the Federals had begun their tasks, Robertson's pickets heard the ice cracking on the river and detected the dim outline of a pontoon bridge. A Confederate flared a torch to signal the picket reserve that the Yankees were crossing. The alarm brought sleepy and startled soldiers to attention as they took their positions along the banked thoroughfare called the Richmond Stage Road or the Bowling Green Road.[52]

The engineers quickly banged the lower pontoon bridges into shape. They knew their cover had been blown when they saw the waving firebrand. The Federals abandoned all attempts at secrecy and rushed their construction. An admiring artillerist wrote, "the pontooniers worked like beavers" to finish the bridges. The 15th New York's bridge neared completion by 8:15 A.M., requiring only one more section to finish. The tardy and tired U.S. Regulars had beaten a path to their construction site and had finished half of their bridge. The Confederates offered no resistance, which stood in marked contrast to the dispute at the upper and middle crossings. The U.S. battalion became so accustomed to free reign of the river that they sent a small party to the other side to work on an exit abutment. Lieutenant Cross watched the men land and realized that they were "undoubtedly the first of the Federals to gain the opposite shore."[53]

Chief engineer Cyrus Comstock knew his workers had been blessed with good luck at the lower crossing, but he ordered up more artillery for insurance. The lieutenant asked the Left Grand Division commander William B. Franklin for the guns. Franklin had DeRussy shift Cowan's 1st New York Battery, Ricketts' Battery F, 1st Pennsylvania, and Amsden's Battery G, 1st Pennsylvania, to the bridge site. The First Corps chief of artillery, Colonel Charles S. Wainwright, added Captain Dunbar R. Ransom's Battery C, 5th U.S., and Lieutenant John G. Simpson's Battery A, 1st Pennsylvania Light Artillery. DeRussy's fourteen 3-inch rifles and Wainwright's eight 12-pounder Napoleon smoothbores bristled over the worksite. Two Napoleon batteries stood directly above the bridge; DeRussy's rifles spread to their left.[54]

General Jerome B. Robertson, meanwhile, had gathered his Confederate troops on the sunken Bowling Green Road and waited for dawn to investigate the Union activity. As morning began to thin the mist, both Lieutenant Colonel Luse of the 18th Mississippi and General Robertson ventured forth independently to reconnoiter. Luse was dumbfounded to find the river empty in front of the Ferneyhough farm. The Yankees had laid their bridges too far downstream for him even to annoy. "Aunt Polly" Robertson, however, faced the problem head-on. Union artillery dominated the river and kept the Rebels at bay. Several of Robertson's scouts made it to the frame home of Alfred Bernard near the bow in the river. Bernard's house was known as "The Bend." The Confederates saw the bridges from the bluff behind the house. They noted that Robertson could not hope to stop the Federals without being destroyed by their artillery.[55]

Robertson tested the lower pontoon crossing with a small sortie at 8:15 A.M. Texas soldiers crept down the Deep Run ravine to the Bernard house. At a signal, the Southerners rushed out of the ravine and charged the bridges. The Confederates startled the Federals. The engineers fled the bridges "in some confusion" and hid behind wagons and bullet-riddled pontoons. Some of the lashers cowered in the bottom of the boats. The 15th New York Engineers lost six men in the first volley, while the U.S. Regulars apparently lost only one man wounded. The U.S. Engineers' abutment party made a sensational dash from the Rebel side of the Rappahannock while others hid under the embankment. A small boat party volunteered to rescue them. They saved all except two—Allen McDonald and J. A. Curtis. The Southerners had captured the duo before they knew what had happened.[56]

Federal artillery and the 10th Pennsylvania Reserves blasted the Rebels. Some of the engineers grabbed their rifles and joined the fight. Ransom's and Simpson's light 12-pounder Napoleons proved to be the mainstay of Union execution. The smoothbore guns riddled the Southerners with canister. The Rebels were too exposed and suffered terribly. Robertson's Confederates exchanged a few feeble volleys and then scattered for cover. Most of the command hastened back to the Bowling Green Road, but some took shelter in The Bend. A covey of sharpshooters sniped at the work parties from the windows. Federal engineers later testified that they "annoyed us a great deal." Union artillery concentrated on the Bernard house and eventually drove the Confederates from their stronghold. The engineers resumed their duties at once.[57]

The overwhelming cover fire discouraged the Confederates from any more forays. Robertson's Texans could not stop the bridge from completion, so they focused on preventing the engineers from cutting an exit route through the west embankment. Sharpshooters directed a solid fire at the crest behind the Bernard house. Robertson could delay the work parties from grading the slope, but he could not halt their construction.[58]

The 15th New York completed its bridge and the approaches forty-five minutes after Robertson's attack. By 10:30 A.M., the U.S. Engineer Battalion had finished its span and started working on the approaches. At 11:00 A.M., the lower pontoon crossing was ready for Franklin's Left Grand Division. Robertson's Confederate brigade had yielded all the ground between the river and the Bowling Green Road, and Colonel Luse's 18th Mississippi faced the ominous prospect of being flanked as soon as the Federals crossed. Seeing this danger, Confederate general Lafayette McLaws forwarded two regiments to reinforce Luse's precarious line. Colonel William D. DeSaussure's 15th South Carolina and Colonel Goode Bryan's 16th Georgia hurried down a farm lane from John Howison's house, Braehead, to the Ferneyhough house.[59]

DeSaussure's South Carolinians formed on the right of Luse's 18th Mississippi and rested their flank on the Bowling Green Road at Deep Run. Bryan moved the 16th Georgia to the left of the Mississippians and extended their line along Deep Run to the river. The 15th South Carolina sent three companies to skirmish in front. Bryan's Georgians, on the other hand, concentrated and suffered a severe artillery fire. A Georgia soldier recalled, "We had a pretty rough experience." Major James S. Gholston asked Lieutenant Colonel Henry P. Thomas, "Colonel, what will we do in a case of this kind?" Thomas replied, "Well, I don't see we are hurt so very much as yet." The men disagreed and jumped into the Deep Run ravine for cover. General Joseph Kershaw visited the position and agreed with the men. He ordered all three regiments to the Bowling Green Road for protection. General Barksdale heard of the withdrawal and flew to the site. The general demanded that the 18th Mississippi "must not recede another inch." Barksdale and Kershaw agreed to hold the road, but no one could stop the Union Left Grand Division from crossing. Burnside, however, refused to let William Franklin advance until the upper and middle bridges could be finished; but the Confederates in Fredericksburg frustrated Burnside's plans tremendously.[60]

Morning fog burned away and the day became spring-like. Rebel sharpshooters also heated up. Northerners peppered the city without effect. For some unknown reason, Burnside thought the Confederates were weakening. He ordered General Woodbury to finish the bridges "whatever the cost." The engineer general relayed the orders to Major Spaulding, but the 50th New York Engineers had very little inclination to obey. "The officers and some of the men showed a willingness" to try, according to the general, but the majority refused to budge, believing "their task a hopeless one." Woodbury confessed, "I was greatly mortified." The general drew his pistol and tried to force the laborers back to work. Some still refused, according to Woodbury, and "would not continue at work until actually shot down." The engineer refused to say whether he actually shot anybody, but later conceded, "Perhaps I was unreasonable." The army banished Woodbury to an effete assignment at the Dry Tortugas after Fredericksburg.[61]

Ira Spaulding pooled enough men to finish one span at the upper crossing. Wounded Captain Ford joined Brainerd on his half-completed bridge. Enemy fire had slackened somewhat, but no one believed the Federal guns had silenced the Rebels permanently. Shortly before 7:00 A.M., the 50th New York Engineers returned to the bridge. The men reached the end of the structure before the Confederates resumed their fire. "Our situation was dreadful in the extreme," opined the bridge leader. Engineers stampeded for cover.[62]

Few Federals understood or sympathized with the engineers' plight. None of them fathomed the intricacies or technical aspects of the engineers' work, so no one could help or replace them. Lost men amounted to lost skills in the Engineer Corps. Soldiers, untrained in engineering, construction, or landscaping, could perform only peripheral tasks. The skilled work crews needed trained reinforcements, otherwise the same engineers had to suffer the same ordeal over and over again. One captain wrote caustically, "there was nothing left for us but to die."[63]

A little after 7:00 A.M., the 50th New York Engineers tried again. Captain Brainerd led a team of lashers to secure the pontoons bobbing loosely at the end of the bridge. On Brainerd's signal, Captain Ford forwarded a group of chess carriers and Major Spaulding prepared to follow with ten men carrying balks. Federal artillery above the bridge laid down a covering barrage.[64]

Brainerd lost half of his crew before he reached the end of the bridge. Another three fell before they could lash the boats together. The last man standing beside Brainerd fell dead at his feet. The captain continued to fasten the pontoons with a little help from the wounded. Spaulding and Ford shouted for him to get off the bridge, but a bullet broke Wesley Brainerd's left arm before he escaped. The captain collapsed in Spaulding's arms. Officers bandaged Brainerd's wound and sent him to the hospital. The captain confessed that he felt "a little more than a lifeless lump of lead . . . more dead than alive." Spaulding had lost his second bridge foreman. Lieutenant George W. Folley succeeded to Brainerd's command, perhaps because Ford had become too incapacitated to take over.[65]

Moments after Spaulding's third attempt failed at the upper pontoon crossing, Captain James McDonald led a sortie at the middle crossing. Artillery had forced the Confederates under cover, and McDonald hurried his men onto the bridge. The engineers had barely reached the end of the pontoons when Confederates emerged from the rubble and blistered them anew. One Northern officer wrote, "The range being so short and the fire so heavy, it was impossible for the men to work." Losses mounted and the men melted back to the shore. The 50th New York Engineers lost another four men and Captain McDonald. The bridge commander took a ball in his left arm near the elbow. Lieutenant Michael H. McGrath assumed command of the middle pontoon crossing. Spaulding now had lost all three of his bridge commanders.[66]

Arthur T. Williams of the 50th New York Engineers thought, "It seemed like murder to ask them to go out on the bridge." But orders demanded that they try again at 9:00 A.M. Men dutifully grabbed their gear and started onto the exposed bridge one more time. "I tell you it takes a man of *strong* nerve," declared one engineer, "to take up a bridge plank and march out onto the bridge under such fire . . . takes pluck I tell you." The men sprinted 200 feet with their heavy loads before they felt the Confederate fire. One man stooped over just as a bullet crushed his jaw, passed through his neck, and exited out his shoulder blade. Men worked frantically to save his life as immediate swelling around the soldier's throat threatened to suffocate him. The officers had lost too many men to make any progress and ordered the survivors back to cover.[67]

Lieutenant McGrath took advantage of a lull in the fighting to rekindle efforts at the middle bridge at 10:00 A.M. A couple of volunteers sculled across the river to rescue some pontoons that went adrift. Minutes later, Rebel fire swept McGrath's workers off the bridge deck for the third time. The lieutenant reported that this fire was "much heavier than either of the others." The middle bridge team counted eleven more casualties—two killed and nine wounded. One engineer guessed another attempt like the last would ensure "there would not have been men enough in our battalion to complete the task."[68]

The 50th New York Engineers needed reinforcements, skilled or otherwise, if they were to continue. Lieutenant McGrath's party was paralyzed for the rest of the morning and early afternoon because it lacked sufficient manpower. Daniel Woodbury secured some assistance from Colonel Edward Harland's brigade of the Ninth Corps. Harland gave Woodbury 80 men from the 8th Connecticut to help the engineers. The general guided the Connecticut troops, under Captain Wolcott P. Marsh, to the upper pontoon crossing between 10:00 and 11:00 A.M. Woodbury put half of the 8th Connecticut contingent under cover, while the rest joined Major Spaulding. Spaulding led the newcomers to the bridge, but several Connecticut men fell wounded before they reached the span. The rest faltered. The New York engineers cajoled them to help, but the 8th Connecticut refused to go near the pontoons or the bridge deck. Captain Marsh's 8th Connecticut company ultimately fled, leaving the 50th New York Engineers to handle the problem alone. Captain Brainerd once observed that "there were no troops in the Army that understood our duties or that could relieve us." The sophisticated level of specialization doomed the 50th New York Engineers to suffer alone. Their only compensation, according to one level-headed analyst, was that their casualties should have been much worse. "That the loss was not greater seemed miraculous," wrote John T. Davidson, who thought the Rebels fired too low, and more often hit the boats than the pontooniers. "Most of the pontoons were thickly pierced with balls, and before the battle was over some of the boats had to be taken out of the bridge and replaced by others to prevent the structure from sinking."[69]

Franklin's bridges at the lower pontoon crossing stood in contrasting quiet, and unused, even though Union troops anxiously awaited orders to move. Franklin, with uncharacteristic boldness, appealed to Burnside to let him cross. The Left Grand Division commander, supposedly playing a support role, provided an alternative means for taking Fredericksburg. Northern troops could cross at the lower bridges and outflank Barksdale's defenders from the south. The grand division general anticipated approval and started his men forward. Burnside entertained the thought, but rejected it. He feared that Franklin's flanking movement would get trapped between two streams—Deep Run and Hazel Run—before it could reach Fredericksburg. If the Confederates cornered Franklin, he would be completely cut off from reinforcements. Burnside lacked the daring or the vision to take the risk. Incredulous, Franklin recalled the vanguard of the Sixth Corps from the bridge spans.[70]

Burnside relied on his artillery to break the impasse at the upper two crossing sites. Hunt's cannon intensified their efforts against the houses opposite the bridges. Burnside, in a more desperate mood, ordered Henry Hunt to smother the city in a general bombardment. Hunt remonstrated but Burnside insisted, and Hunt issued the command. Since the Confederate resistance had quieted around the lower crossing, Robert Tyler's Left center artillery group assisted Tompkins' right center. Hunt reported, "All the batteries that could be brought to bear were now, by order of General Burnside, turned upon the town" at 12:30 P.M. Hunt hated the idea of destroying the city beyond the necessity of combating the hidden sharpshooters. His conservative view limited war and its consequences to armies, and not civilians. But the war was changing and conservatives like Hunt were slow to realize it.[71]

The cannon concentrated on "the doomed city" for an hour. After 1:30 P.M., the artillery slowed its rate of fire, and selected targets more meticulously. Tompkins and Tyler punished the city thoroughly. A member of Hazard's Battery B, 1st Rhode Island, described the barrage: "The roar of the cannon, the bursting of shells, the falling of walls and chimneys; added to the fire of the infantry on both sides, the smoke of burning houses, made a scene of wildest confusion, terrific enough to appall the stoutest hearts."[72]

Hunt's results, however, were disappointing, even laughable. Colonel Charles S. Wainwright, chief of the First Corps artillery, observed Tompkins' fire. To his chagrin, he watched solid shot pass through wooden buildings without effect. Brick and stone structures crumbled under fire, but the wooden structures absorbed the solid shot. Every time they poked a hole through a clapboard house, they made another firing portal for the Rebels. Hazard's battery targeted "any objective point where a shot would prove effective," which meant firing "through the gable of a house, the steeple of a church, or the top of a tree." None of these conquests materially aided the engineers.[73]

Hunt lost several guns during the bombardment. Kinzie's battery already had lost two guns to broken carriages and it soon lost a third. Trails cracked on five 12-pounder Napoleons in Tompkins' right center group. The cannon recoiled through mud and pounded into a frozen subsurface, which snapped their trails. Hunt also cited defective craftsmanship. Greedy contractors, like the Wood brothers of New York, built carriages out of "very bad material, part of the wood being completely rotten." Ammunition proved another problem. Rounds burst unpredictably, and fuses continuously failed. "Although every precaution was taken," Colonel Robert O. Tyler lamented, "the ammunition generally behaved badly."[74]

Across the river, Barksdale's Confederates weathered the storm under cover. Though relatively safe in their impromptu shelters, the Mississippians endured hours of shelling. A thirsty member of the 17th Mississippi recalled plaintively, "All day we could not go out to get water." Another Rebel remembered that Sophia Street "was ploughed by shot and shell, as though a disk plough had run over it." By the end of the day, wrote one soldier, "The town could not boast of a whole window."[75]

A number of near misses undermined the Rebels' resolve. A shell collapsed a chimney, which collapsed an entire house. Everything fell on the startled victims in the basement. Debris trapped half a dozen men with the shell spinning like a top between them. Mercifully, the fuse fizzled. Another shell tumbled a chimney on top of Captain David Lang, commander of the 8th Florida. The Floridians dug the wounded Lang out of the rubble and evacuated him. Without a commander, the 8th Florida became demoralized. At the same time, fires erupted downtown, burning whole blocks and endangering the Confederate position.[76]

William Barksdale sat on the sidewalk outside of the Market House, eating lunch with his staff. While the officers ate hardtack and honey, a Union shell glanced off a nearby roof and "dropped directly in the center of the party and spun around upon the brick pavement." A witness wrote, "The hearts stood still," but the fuse sputtered. Barksdale escaped with only a bad bruise from a piece of roofing tile.[77]

Unable to drive Barksdale away from the river, Ambrose Burnside searched for another solution. By 2:30 P.M., his plans were in turmoil. His bridges floated only half way across the Rappahannock and his surprise attack had been paralyzed for close to ten hours. The commander seethed aloud, "The army is held by the throat by a few sharpshooters!" Engineer Woodbury offered no consolation, but Burnside's chief of artillery, Henry Hunt, volunteered a novel idea to break the deadlock. He proposed something that Major Ira Spaulding of the 50th New York Engineers had advocated earlier that morning. The major reckoned that they should ferry some infantry across the river and establish a protective bridgehead. Forcing the Confederates away from the river would allow the engineers to complete the bridges. Both Captain Brainerd and Arthur Williams agreed that the idea had originated with the engineers and that Spaulding proposed it to Woodbury. It appears that Hunt showed more interest in it than Woodbury did. The engineer officer never mentioned it to the army's commander. Burnside leapt at the idea. "Let us do that," he agreed, but then he wavered, refusing to take responsibility for ordering such a risky, unprecedented venture. Burnside finally conceded that if Hunt found volunteers to undertake the operation, he would allow it. Hunt headed for the nearest troops at hand.[78]

CHAPTER FOUR

"A FIERCE AND DEADLY CONTEST"

Fighting in the Streets

Colonel Norman J. Hall's brigade was lounging on the grass behind the Lacy house when Henry Hunt came looking for volunteers to lead his experimental assault across the river and establish a bridgehead. Hall immediately offered his men. A few minutes later, Ambrose Burnside rode up, and Colonel Hall reiterated that his brigade could make the crossing, but then hedged, saying he had a regiment ready to cross. Burnside inquired, "What regiment?" Hall specified his own 7th Michigan. The army commander hesitated to give the order, telling Hall that "the effort meant death to most of those who should undertake the voyage." At the same time, he conceded that "if any should cross under the conditions it would be one of the greatest military feats of the war." Hall asked for the chance to try. The colonel turned to his troops and proposed crossing the river. The men responded with three loud cheers. Hall turned to Burnside and affirmed, "My soldiers are ready to cross the river and drive out the Confederates." Burnside relented.[1]

At the middle crossing, Colonel Harrison S. Fairchild's 89th New York and Lieutenant Colonel Joseph Gerhardt's 46th New York tangled with Captain Andrew R. Govan's Confederates. Govan's men, a conglomeration of detachments from the 17th Mississippi, 18th Mississippi, 21st Mississippi, and 8th Florida, eluded the New Yorkers' fire, but reappeared every time the engineers set foot on the bridge. Encouraged by Norman Hall's fervency,

Burnside sent a peremptory order to Colonel Fairchild to force a landing as well. Burnside instructed the 89th New York at 3:15 P.M. to detail 4 officers and 100 men to make a river assault in four boats. Fairchild readied the left half of his regiment; however, "some of the officers of the left wing did not want to go," stated a witness, and conversely, some of the officers on the right did. The colonel compromised and took a cross section of volunteers from both wings. Gerhardt's 46th New York closed on Fairchild's right to provide cover fire for the assault.[2]

General Hunt instructed his cannoneers to bombard the riverfront with a renewed vigor and force the Confederates to take shelter again. At a specific time, the artillery would stop. That would be the signal for the infantry to jump in the boats, where engineers would ferry them across the river. As Hall's men funneled down a ravine by the Lacy house, they noted that the engineers "came down in fear and trembling."[3]

General Woodbury alerted the 50th New York Engineers that there would be a riverine crossing because "the Artillery could do nothing." The general reinforced his engineers for the big push. Lieutenant McGrath, the engineer in charge of the middle pontoon crossing, had warned Woodbury that he lacked the manpower to build a bridge and row the infantry across the river. General Woodbury accordingly ordered Major James A. Magruder to bring the 15th New York Engineers to the upper crossings. Magruder left one company under Lieutenant Henry V. Slosson to guard the lower bridges while the rest of the regiment headed for the upper sites. The 15th New York passed general headquarters on the way, where Burnside told Major Magruder that "he wanted that bridge over at all hazards." The engineer promised to do his best.[4]

Woodbury went over the attack with Majors Spaulding and Magruder "in accordance with the advice of General Hunt." Spaulding would handle the operation at the upper pontoon crossing and select a team to ferry the 7th Michigan over the river. Woodbury asked, for some unknown reason, that Lieutenant James L. Robbins take charge of the first boat. Robbins dutifully organized the boat crews and showed Lieutenant Colonel Baxter where to put his 7th Michigan. The infantry rested out of sight in the ravine north of the Lacy house.[5]

Major Magruder would lead the assault at the middle crossing. Woodbury's assistant adjutant general, Captain Henry W. Bowers, quickly explained the situation to Lieutenant McGrath. The lieutenant yielded his command to Magruder. The major needed four pontoon boats for the 15th New York

Engineers to row the assault party across the river. He put one company in charge of the boats and prepared the 89th New York to move. With everything set, the engineers and infantry waited for the signal from the artillery.[6]

General Hunt ordered Colonel Tompkins to cover the assault, and authorized other batteries to join in where practicable. Hazlett's Battery D, 5th U.S., switched from William Hays' command to Tompkins'. Colonel Robert O. Tyler released Major Trumbull's behemoth Connecticut siege guns and the German batteries of Captains Voegelee and Diederichs to help. Hunt gave Tompkins control of all the guns covering the upper pontoon crossing. The artillery chief put Major Alexander Doull, inspector of artillery, in charge of the guns around the middle pontoon crossing. Hunt instructed his batteries to concentrate on the bridgeheads and drive the Rebels underground. At his signal, the artillery would cease, which would be the cue for the engineers to start across the stream. The guns opened fire at 3:00 P.M. with an unprecedented fury.[7]

Hunt's cannon raked the town with a violence theretofore unknown. Confederate general Lafayette McLaws claimed the Yankee guns transformed the city into "a scene of indescribable confusion, enough to appall the stoutest hearts!" Union artillery rooted through the Confederates' hiding places and completely demoralized the leaderless 8th Florida. The Deep South detachment at the city docks had declined to fight from the very beginning. Captain William Baya refused to open fire, arguing "that his position was too much exposed, and firing would draw the fire of the artillery." Baya's Floridians reasoned that they would be left alone if they did not bother the Federals. At the height of the artillery barrage, Captain Baya feared his command was still too exposed. He notified the Mississippian Govan that he was pulling out. Just when the Southerners needed everybody in place, the 17th Mississippi lost the unit guarding its right flank. A disgusted Govan wrote in his report, "I am convinced that if any [of the 8th Florida] were captured it was from inefficiency and from fear of being killed in the retreat."[8]

Floridians at the upper crossing also began to crack under the strain. Colonel John Fiser of the 17th Mississippi noted that they "seemed troubled and in want of a commander." The colonel reinforced them with ten sharpshooters from the 13th Mississippi. Fiser later reported that "a certain lieutenant" became so unnerved at this time "and so far forgot himself as to draw his pistol and threaten to kill some of my sharpshooters if they fired again, as it would draw the enemy's fire on his position." A Federal engineer remembered hearing the Mississippians scream at the Florida men: "Why in hell don't you fire!" At that moment, Colonel Fiser fell unconscious when a shot toppled a brick wall on top of him. Soldiers quickly freed the colonel from the rubble. The shaken commander revived somewhat and retained tenuous command. With morale weakening among the Confederates, the Federals chose the opportune time to launch their attack.[9]

The Federal guns, after half an hour's constant roar, suddenly fell silent. Norman Hall's 7th Michigan scampered across the mud flats and piled into the first six boats. As the infantrymen, some 135 strong, tumbled into position, some of the engineers panicked and fled the boats, leaving the infantry alone on the riverbank. Major Ira Spaulding admitted with embarrassment that some of his men "showed the effects which are usually produced upon unarmed men placed for the first time under a heavy fire." In his report, the major said that many of his men were "panic-stricken." The timely arrival of the chief engineer of the army, Lieutenant Cyrus Comstock, kept the rout from getting out of hand. Comstock led quite a few of the 50th New York back to work. Lieutenant James L. Robbins stayed with his boat and shoved off with his crew of four, poling into the current. Other boats, filled with Michigan infantrymen, followed Robbins' lead. Lieutenant Colonel Henry Baxter led the 7th Michigan's sortie. Baxter had advised his men not to waste time shooting during the crossing. He wanted them to focus on poling or paddling their boats instead. When they landed, Baxter's soldiers were to surround the Confederate positions without waiting to form a proper line of battle. At the same time, Baxter warned his troops to stick close together after they reached the other side.[10]

"As soon as their hands touch the gunwales, the crack of scores of rifles were heard, and over fell our gallant fellows," remarked one engineer. The men muscled the bulky thirty-one-foot pontoons into the river; and then struggled to drive them through the water. Confederates blistered the boats, which were crammed with 20 to 25 men apiece. The Michigan soldiers crouched low in the boats "and paddled away the best they could." Several men fell dead or wounded in the first few minutes. Near mid-stream, Lieutenant Robbins lost one of his oarsmen and his boat stalled. About the same time, Lieutenant Colonel Baxter of the 7th Michigan fell seriously wounded, shot through the lung. Command devolved upon Major Thomas J. Hunt (no relation to artillery chief Hunt). Robbins replaced his bloody oarsman and his pontoon lurched forward again. A Michigan sergeant remembered that his boat "made for the opposite shore with all possible speed." Another infantryman wrote, "We were not long in crossing." When the boats reached two-thirds of the way across the Rappahannock, the Confederate fire slackened. The bank between Sophia Street and the river blocked the Southerners' fire. This allowed the bluecoats to land in relative safety. The bows of the boats grounded on the riverbank and the men closest to the front leapt onto shore. Those in the back slid over the sides and waded ashore. "The water was cold," recalled a Michigan soldier, "but it was no time for ceremony." Union soldiers atop Stafford Heights grew "almost wild with excitement, cheering and yelling like Comanche Indians."[11]

The first 60 or 70 soldiers to land clawed their way up the steep bank and surged across the intersection of Sophia Street and Hawke Street. The Federals "formed a skirmish line and went for these sharp shooters in a hurry." Excitement reached a fevered pitch. Major Hunt ordered the 7th Michigan to give "no quarter"—to take no prisoners. Most of the soldiers ignored the order. As one private remarked later, "for humanity's sake, we did not obey." But not everyone disobeyed. According to one Northern onlooker, "Our men bayoneted a great many but some begged so hard for mercy that they saved them." The Federals divided into small groups of 5 to 10 men and surrounded the houses filled with Mississippians, who were still shooting from the windows and doorways. One group of Michigan soldiers allegedly burst into a house and bayoneted or shot every man they could find "whether he threw down his arms or not." An engineer thought: "It was fiendish work," but he allowed that "the provocation was a strong one." Within twenty minutes, the 7th Michigan had captured some 30 prisoners and drove the rest of the gray-uniformed foe away from Sophia Street. The Union army had established a tenuous bridgehead in Fredericksburg. Few of the Michiganders realized that the last few minutes had made history. Henry Hunt's desperate riverine crossing had been the first bridgehead landing secured under fire in the annals of the United States armed forces.[12]

Colonel John Fiser tried to defend Sophia Street, but the Federals had swarmed around his fortified positions before he could assemble his men. "Being deprived of all protection," Fiser wrote, "we were compelled to fall back to Caroline street." The Confederates took up new positions in the backyards between Sophia and Caroline Streets. The 17th Mississippi concentrated their fire on the head of Hawke Street, and kept the 7th Michigan away from the crown of the hill. Fiser hoped he could prevent the Yankees from crossing Sophia Street again. The 7th Michigan's Major Hunt bided his time on the slope and waited for the pontoons to bring the rest of his regiment. The pontoons left with the wounded Lieutenant Colonel Baxter and the captured Confederate sharpshooters and returned a few minutes later with the rest of the 7th Michigan.[13]

Fiser's 17th Mississippi and Hunt's 7th Michigan were deadlocked. Fiser could not force the Federals to retreat; in fact, he could not get close enough to shoot them, but he had discouraged them from advancing again. The 7th Michigan held its ground, waiting for the engineers to splice the last section of the bridge together. Half an hour after the 7th Michigan landed, Norman Hall reinforced it with Captain Harrison G. O. Weymouth's 19th Massachusetts. Weymouth required three trips to ferry his regiment across the Rappahannock. The 19th Massachusetts held the embankment to the right of the 7th Michigan. Among the Massachusetts men was the Reverend Arthur B. Fuller. The chaplain had resigned the previous day due to poor health, but when he stopped to say good-bye to the 19th Massachusetts, he found it marching to Fredericksburg. Caught up in the moment, the chaplain volunteered to join the troops for one last action. The Reverend Mr. Fuller found a rifle and took his place with the regiment.[14]

Burnside's soldiers cheered Hall's landing party and then cried, "Hurrah for the bridge!" as the engineers jogged onto the span one final time. Spaulding's 50th New York Engineers, supplemented by two companies of the 15th New York Engineers, pieced the final stretch of the upper bridge together. Work progressed sluggishly at first, as "many of the boats were so much damaged by the shot of the enemy that it was difficult to keep them afloat." Workers corked the holes adroitly with wooden plugs or replaced the sinking pontoons with new ones. The pontooniers soon found their rhythm and completed the work. One of the engineers confessed that the men "worked in a manner that is surprising even to ourselves." Spaulding had made the upper bridge passable thirty minutes after Hall had crossed.[15]

Abutment parties graded the city waterfront for traffic, while the 15th New York Engineers went to work on the second bridge at the upper crossing. Originally, this had been Captain George W. Ford's bridge when it was abandoned half finished. Spaulding rushed the first bridge to completion without realizing its impact on finishing the latter. The 15th New York Engineers wrestled with a quandary as a result. The incomplete bridge stood upstream, while most of the pontoons were downstream of the completed bridge. Major Spaulding ordered the 15th New York Engineers to start over again on the downstream side, but the engineers manhandled the pontoons upriver and resumed work at the original, upstream bridge site. The 15th completed four bays in short order before a fatigued party of the 50th New York Engineers reinforced it.[16]

While the engineers finished the bridges, Colonel Hall encouraged some very unhappy soldiers. Many of the men in the bridgehead had experienced disaster under similar circumstances the previous year at Ball's Bluff, near Leesburg, where Confederates had trapped them against the Potomac River with no means of escape. The similar circumstances fostered a certain degree of edginess among the Yankees. Hall also dealt with disappointed men on the Stafford side of the river. Hall had promised Captain George N. Macy's 20th Massachusetts—called the "Harvard Regiment" because of the number of scholars within its ranks—the honor of leading the brigade and the army into Fredericksburg. Now two regiments had usurped that honor. Captain Macy sulked and Hall told him to cheer up. Macy remembered Hall telling him, "I *need not look so disappointed* about it." The brigade commander promised the 20th Massachusetts would cross as soon as the engineers completed the bridge. Either the verbal order was garbled or the impatient captain ignored it. Macy commandeered some of the pontoon boats and ferried his regiment across. The 20th Massachusetts, 307 strong, took cover behind the 7th Michigan and 19th Massachusetts just as the engineers finished the first bridge. As the last of the Union soldiers waded ashore, space along the crowded bank became a problem. The muddy rise could not accommodate the rest of Hall's brigade. The Union officers saw that the bridgehead needed to be expanded—so the troops prepared to cross Sophia Street again.[17]

In the meantime, Colonel Harrison Fairchild's 89th New York had mounted a successful assault against the southern end of the city. "It looked like a forlorn hope," said one participant. Charles Graham admitted, "We expected to be badly cut up before we got across." As soon as General Hunt's artillery ceased firing, the men piled into the pontoons, along with boat crews from Major Magruder's 15th New York Engineers. The men paddled furiously under a storm of lead. Lieutenant Colonel Gerhardt's 46th New York opened a cover fire over their heads. Suddenly the shooting stopped as the men churned past mid-stream. A small lip of ground hid the Federals from Captain Andrew Govan's Mississippi sharpshooters. The 89th New York landed with ease and sprang across the city wharves toward the nearest buildings. Govan's men, combined with elements of the 18th Mississippi and 21st Mississippi, fell back to Caroline Street. No one thought to notify the 8th Florida contingent, since they had announced their departure an hour before. Unfortunately, as much as Captain Baya had wanted to leave, he had decided to stay. Within moments, the 89th New York surrounded his tiny command and forced them to surrender. The Federals secured the dockside and finished the middle pontoon bridge. Fairchild ferried the rest of his regiment over the river in support. The reconstituted 89th New York sat tight for the rest of the afternoon and never tested Govan's defenses on Caroline Street. The Mississippians clung to the southern end of Caroline because it ran along the spine of a commanding ridge. Nearby, John Slaughter's three-story mansion, Hazel Hill, provided a cupola that offered Confederates a distant view of the docks. The ridge and its houses discouraged the Federals from moving off the wharves, but the warehouses along Sophia Street also offered protection and allowed the engineers to work without hindrance.[18]

Lieutenant Michael McGrath's detachment of the 50th New York joined two companies of the 15th New York Engineers to finish the middle pontoon bridge. The bridge builders worked at first "under a scorching fire," according to engineer John Smart, but the 89th New York soon forced the Confederates out of range. This allowed the work parties to function with "spunk," according to one, as they rapidly lashed their span together. Naturally, both the 15th and 50th New York Engineers claimed the lion's share of the credit for the work. Either way, engineer Bartholomen Dailey believed that both regiments had generated "plenty of honor for one day." The bridge parties tied into the Fredericksburg wharves an hour after restarting. Federal troops on Stafford Heights hailed the moment with cheers and hearty congratulations for the fearless bridge team. Infantry officers applauded the engineers' valor over the next few days as they tried to inspire their men for battle. A delighted member of the 15th New York Engineers enthused, "We are known everywhere we go."[19]

Brigadier General Orlando B. Willcox, commander of the Ninth Corps, rushed the 46th New York over the middle bridge "as fast as the planks were laid down." These two commands—the 46th and 89th New York—constituted the only defenders at the middle pontoon crossing. Strangely, they came from different divisions and had no history of working together. The Federals clung passively to the waterfront and proved right away that they had no intention of driving beyond their bridgehead. Govan's Confederates surmised the danger had passed and slipped away to re-join Barksdale at the Market House.[20]

The crossings under fire marked a new chapter in America's fighting experience, but as the men prepared to expand the upper bridgehead, they entered another, more direful sort of military endeavor—urban combat, or street fighting. Colonel Norman Hall needed to enlarge the bridgehead before any more troops could cross the Rappahannock. With the bridge down, Union Second Corps commander Major General Darius N. Couch ordered the pious but vapid Brigadier General Oliver Otis Howard to take his entire division and clear the Confederates out of Fredericksburg. Howard crammed the rest of Hall's brigade—the 42nd New York, 59th New York, and 127th Pennsylvania—onto the bridge. Behind them Colonel Joshua T. Owen's "Philadelphia Brigade" waited with Brigadier General Alfred Sully's brigade. To make room, Howard wanted Hall to push into the city.[21]

Norman Hall directed the 7th Michigan to advance through the block to the left of Hawke Street, while the 19th Massachusetts kept pace on the right. Skirmishers bounded across Sophia Street. The 7th Michigan gained half a block before Confederate fire sapped its momentum. Most of the regiment hid in a blind alley, which opened onto Hawke Street. Others sought cover behind neighboring houses. Major Thomas Hunt could not advance so he sat tight in the alleyway. On the other side of Hawke Street, the 19th Massachusetts met a similar fire. Northern soldiers were hit from all sides, but they never saw the enemy. Fiser's Confederates hid in attics, chambers, and cellars of the houses along the east side of Caroline Street. A Massachusetts veteran recalled that the fire was "not only novel but a great strain upon the moral and physical courage" of the men. Unable to see their adversaries, the bluecoats pushed ahead blindly. They climbed a rise between the houses on Sophia Street and Caroline, and scurried across fenced backyards. The 17th Mississippi allowed the Federals to enter the yards leading to Caroline Street before they loosed a volley in their faces. Southerners stole out of every corner and even from buildings behind the Yankees to trap them in a crossfire. Confederate James Dinkins remembered, "It was a dreadful slaughter, which might have been considered a retaliation for the dreadful bombardment of two hours before." "The most dangerous and trying part," a Federal stated, was that "the enemy could fire a volley at such close range without being seen."[22]

Unlike the 7th Michigan, the 19th Massachusetts elected to go forward. The Federals drove the Confederates "from street to street, from house to house, from yard to yard," inflicting and suffering damaging losses. At one point, Massachusetts soldiers cornered and captured 5 Southerners in one house. In the next instant, Company B, 19th Massachusetts, ran into a crossfire that dropped 10 of its 30 men in less than five minutes. Shortly before dusk, the Northerners infiltrated Caroline Street. The tired Yankees were too

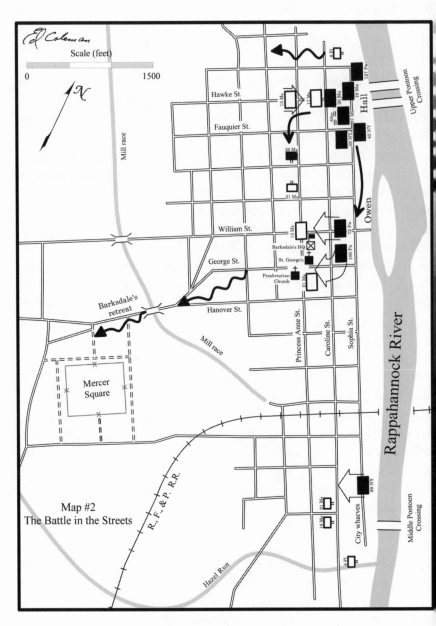

The Battle for the City

few and disorganized to advance any farther. Officers stopped and re-formed the regiment on Fredericksburg's main thoroughfare.[23]

Colonel John Fiser withstood the Federal attack as best he could. His Mississippians stopped the 7th Michigan cold, but the 19th Massachusetts turned the Rebels' left flank and penetrated Caroline Street. Fiser asked for help from Colonel James W. Carter's 13th Mississippi. He requested two companies to reinforce his line, but before they arrived, Fiser's line collapsed and his troops evacuated Caroline Street. At the same time, Fiser notified Captain Govan of his retreat and directed him to fall back from the middle crossing to avoid being turned or captured. The colonel knew nothing of Govan's new defense along the lower portion of Caroline Street. As Fiser's 17th Mississippi yielded Caroline Street, it passed the 13th Mississippi heading to the front. Fiser told Colonel James Carter that his men had done everything they could to stop the Yankees. Carter agreed and suggested: "Fall back, colonel, and reform. We will take your place." Fiser started his men for Princess Anne Street and the Market House. Carter's 13th Mississippi went ahead and charged into Caroline Street.[24]

The 19th Massachusetts had barely caught its breath before the Rebels counterattacked. Captain Moncena Dunn was realigning his men when he ran into the ex-chaplain, Arthur Fuller. The minister asked Dunn, "Captain, I must do something for my country. What shall I do?" The officer put Fuller on his left flank. The clergyman took a position at the corner of Hawke Street just before the 13th Mississippi stormed into the intersection. He was one of the first to fall, shot through the chest and side. The Confederates thronged the left flank of the 19th Massachusetts, driving it back toward the river. Carter's Southerners chased the Yankees down Hawke until they blundered into the 7th Michigan holed up in the alleyway. A quick burst of fire caused the graycoats to back away. Other Confederates fired up Caroline Street, forcing the Massachusetts men to retreat into the houses and backyards for protection. One company of the 19th Massachusetts ducked behind a fenced corner lot, but the Southerners swarmed around them. A stunned Federal reported that the Rebels "were thick as bees." As the Unionists ran away, Michael Redding of the 19th fell wounded. Friends tried to drag him to safety, but he refused, saying, "No, you'll be back again shortly and I'll sit here and wait for you." Carter's 13th Mississippi collapsed the expanding bridgehead in a matter of minutes and closed to within a couple of hundred yards of the bridges.[25]

Yankee captain Weymouth confirmed what Colonel Norman Hall feared:

his line had crumbled. Hall requested artillery support for his shrinking front. Charles Tompkins' and William Hays' artillery opened on the streets beyond Hall's flanks. Tompkins' guns provided negligible support, as they could not see anything in the gathering darkness. Hays' gunners meanwhile opened a smart duel with Southern artillery behind the city. The dormant Rebel guns had suddenly come to life, sparking some encouragement for Barksdale's defenders at the upper crossing. Lieutenant Colonel William Hays ordered Roemer's 2nd New York Battery and Owen's Battery G, 1st Rhode Island, to enfilade the Confederate cannon. The two batteries moved to a peach orchard at the Bryant house above Falmouth. King's Battery A, 4th U.S., joined their right. The Federal batteries fired across Beck's, or Winchester, Island at Confederate guns on Stansbury and Taylor's hills. The artillerists exchanged approximately twenty-five rounds before the Southern guns yielded. Roemer retired his battery and the Confederates flared up again. The New Yorker returned to the Bryant farm and the Federals squelched the Rebels again. Darkness probably limited the contest more than the accuracy of either side's artillery at that late hour.[26]

Meanwhile, Norman Hall had sent several "urgent requests" begging General O. O. Howard to halt his reinforcements on the other side of the river until he untangled the mess in the deteriorating bridgehead. Howard ignored Hall and forwarded Colonel Joshua T. Owen's brigade over the bridge. Howard crossed to sort the mess himself. Finding Hall, Howard blandly told him "to push ahead." Owen's Philadelphians crowded the swaying ribbon of boats, trapped under a shower of Confederate artillery. "The hostile guns had found the range, so the shells burst uncomfortably near the moving column," General Howard recorded. Second Corps commander Darius Couch stood exposed on Stafford Heights trying to hurry forward more troops. Shellfire inundated the general's entourage of staff officers and orderlies, but "no damage was done beyond spattering horses and men with mud thrown up by the plunging shot." Couch expedited the flow of troops down the ravine leading to the upper crossing.[27]

Colonel William W. Jennings led the 127th Pennsylvania to the river. The commander noted some trepidation in the brand-new regiment. He ordered a band to play for the column. The bandsmen stood by the bridge and played "Yankee Doodle." General Howard reviewed the passing troops. Several missiles abruptly plunged into their midst, throwing mud spouts ten feet into the air. Bandmembers scattered, except for a musician with the huge bass drum. "With ludicrous precipitancy," related one of Couch's staff officers, "he ensconced himself behind his drum, where . . . he cuddled up with the apparent feeling of relief and security." O. O. Howard cajoled the green soldiers: "Don't dodge, men," he called; "the shells are not half as dangerous as they seem." Just then a round shrieked past the general's ear and he jumped. One of the soldiers chaffed him, "Don't dodge, General, that shell is not half as dangerous as it seems." The general replied sheepishly, "Dodging appears to be natural." Howard later joked, "After that, our music was confined to cannon."[28]

Howard returned to the bridgehead and prodded his brigadiers—Norman Hall and Joshua Owen—to expand the bridgehead again. Hall relied on the slighted 20th Massachusetts to retake the lost ground. He told Captain Macy that the 7th Michigan held a forward position in the alley and the 19th Massachusetts defended some of the fences to the right of Hawke Street. Hall wanted the 20th Massachusetts to advance directly between them and "clear the street leading from the bridge at all hazards." He promised that the 7th Michigan would skirmish ahead of Macy's column. The brigade commander told Macy to "bayonet every armed man firing from a house." The captain remembered the order even more dramatically. In a letter home, Macy quoted Hall as saying, "Bayonet every male found—take no prisoners." Hall gave Macy a reluctant civilian to guide him through the city. The brigade commander would support the 20th Massachusetts with Lieutenant Colonel George N. Bomford's 42nd New York. Bomford's command would advance up a parallel street to the left—Fauquier Street. Hall canceled the New Yorkers' advance at the last minute, afraid they might collide with the 20th Massachusetts in Caroline Street. Hall thus unleashed the 20th Massachusetts to attack alone. While Hall readied the 20th Massachusetts, Joshua Owen ordered his Philadelphia Brigade to break out of the bridgehead, heading south. He instructed his skirmishers to cover Hall's left flank. Companies from all of his regiments—the 69th, 71st, 72nd, and 106th Pennsylvania—infiltrated the city and stretched to the left, down Sophia Street.[29]

George Macy's 20th Massachusetts charged over the embankment in column of fours. Reaching Sophia Street, it took fire from Confederates to the south, probably several companies of the 21st Mississippi stationed at the foot of William Street. Sophia Street undulated over several ridges that ran perpendicular to the river. Southerners on one hill at William Street could easily see the Federals advance on the next ridge at Hawke Street. Captain Macy's guide hesitated. The commander shoved the old man and the guide dropped dead at his feet—killed by a Mississippi bullet. Macy and his column shuffled past the unknown civilian and stormed into Hawke Street.[30]

Much controversy surrounds the question of which street the 20th Massachusetts attacked up. The old veterans of the 20th regiment in their twilight years repeatedly named Fauquier Street as the avenue of attack, but contemporary accounts and maps clearly identify the street used as the one with the bridge at its end—making it Hawke Street. This is further substantiated by the 20th Massachusetts' encounter with the 7th Michigan in an alleyway. Hawke Street has a blind alley, which is still evident in 2000, whereas Fauquier Street never had one at all.

At the head of Hawke Street, the Massachusetts commander doubled up his column and closed on the 7th Michigan's alleyway. Much to Macy's surprise and annoyance, he discovered the Michigan soldiers stalled halfway to Caroline Street. The commander of the 20th Massachusetts signaled the 7th Michigan to push ahead, but the troops refused to budge. The captain asked the Michigan commander to move, but Major Thomas Hunt declined. Hunt insisted that he had no orders to advance his skirmishers. Macy requested Hall and Howard to reiterate the orders, but Hall merely replied: "Push forward—drive them [the Confederates] out." Macy begged Hunt one more time to move, but the Michigander held back, insisting that "the Rebels were there in force." Macy turned to the head of his own column, Captain Henry L. Abbott, and shouted, "Mr. Abbott you will take your first platoon forward." As Abbott marched ahead, Major Hunt called after him, "No man could live beyond that corner." Captain Macy glowered back, "Go to Hell with your regiment then," and joined Abbott's men. The exchange had lasted only a couple of minutes, but it gave the Confederates plenty of warning to prepare for the attack on Hawke Street.[31]

Colonel James Carter's 13th Mississippi stood poised along Caroline Street, watching the 20th Massachusetts approach with "a pretty line." Confederate James Dinkins later admitted: "They moved forward in splendid style. . . . It was a magnificent sight, which won the admiration of the Mississippians. . . . They were a fine body of men." The Southerners hid behind walls and between houses waiting for the column to reach the intersection at Caroline Street. Seconds later, the Yankee regiment barreled into the dark cross street and everything exploded in fire, "the street lighted up by the flash of muskets." Confederates sprang from every direction, from doorways, windows, and around corners, to fire on the Yankees from all sides. "A sheet of flame brought into clearest outline the two battalions at the crossing" of the streets. Carter's volleys seemed "almost literally to wipe out the leading platoon." Captain Macy was taken by surprise. He later confessed, "I [had] hardly the least idea what to do." Lieutenant Henry C. Ropes wrote that the fire "staggered the column but in a moment they pressed on, led by Abbott in his usual fearless manner." Abbott pushed straight through the intersection, running a gauntlet of fire.[32]

The second and third battalions of the 20th Massachusetts filled the intersection behind Abbott. The second group swung into Caroline Street and faced south. They met the heaviest Confederate fire. Union officers shouted at the men to charge the Rebels, and the waiting Confederates goaded them to "Come on!" The third battalion entered Caroline and wheeled to the north. In a matter of minutes, the 20th Massachusetts cordoned off the intersection of Hawke and Caroline Streets.[33]

Darkness hid the Confederates, making it nearly impossible for the Federals to return an accurate fire. "Hold your fire, boys, until you see something to fire at," Captain Henry Abbott cautioned his men. Union soldiers discovered the Rebels "could not be seen except by the flash of the guns." The heavy concentration of musket flashes in the intersection made it elementary for the Southerners to hit the Yankees massed in the open. The 13th Mississippi picked their targets easily and fired with near impunity. At the same time, the Confederates spread out to keep the Northerners from concentrating their fire. Yankees shot in every direction at the elusive flashes. George Macy reported, "we could see no one and were simply murdered." More than a dozen soldiers fell killed or wounded next to the regimental commander. "How I escaped I cannot say," Macy confessed. The 20th Massachusetts later counted a staggering ninety-seven casualties in a fifty-yard space. The regiment lost a third of its strength. One of the wounded, Josiah Murphey, recollected, "In no battle of the war in which we were afterwards engaged did we lose so many men in so short a time."[34]

Macy hesitated to return the fire against his left because he feared it might be his promised supports. He reported the problem to Colonel Hall. The brigade commander immediately informed Macy that the New Yorkers had never advanced; the fire he faced came from the Rebels. The 20th Massachusetts responded by spattering the street with gunfire. The Confederates took cover and continued the fight.[35]

While the 20th Massachusetts was caught in the crossfire, the 19th Massachusetts crept through the backyards to reclaim its hold on Caroline Street. Fighting remained tight and desperate. Weymouth's Bay State regiment slipped into Caroline Street by "climbing fences and filing back through back gardens" and breaking into the backdoors of houses. Unlike Macy's dense mass of men charging in column and getting butchered on Hawke Street, the 19th Massachusetts spread out in small clusters of skirmishers. Bunching up drew fire, so the men instinctively avoided crowding. Returning Massachusetts men discovered Michael Redding's body where they had left him. The wounded man had been pierced seven times and killed. It was alleged that Redding had sustained seven bayonet wounds. Although this may be an exaggeration, it may also be the case that Confederates had indeed bayoneted him in retaliation for the Federal "black flag" order to take no prisoners. William Davis of the 13th Mississippi wrote unabashedly, "We killed lots of them in backyards."[36]

Captain H. G. O. Weymouth's 19th Massachusetts obliqued to the right to avoid clashing with the 20th Massachusetts. Hall's fear of the 42nd New York shooting the 20th Massachusetts apparently did not extend to the 19th Massachusetts. The 7th Michigan's inertia more likely compelled Hall to redeploy the 19th Massachusetts as a support for Macy. Weymouth moved through the backyards "urging his men forward." At one point, the regimental commander joined a small detachment under Lieutenant John G. B. Adams pinned down near a gate fronting Caroline Street. Weymouth cajoled Adams, "Can't you go forward, Lieutenant Adams?" The subordinate ventured, "It is a might hot, captain." Unconvinced, the commander pushed through the gate just as "a barrel of bullets came at him." Weymouth dove for cover. "It is quite warm lieutenant," he conceded. Pointing to a nearby dwelling, Weymouth ordered the party to "go up through the house." The Yankees forced the backdoor, and Gilman Nicholls rushed up to the second story. As he kicked in a locked door, a Confederate sharpshooter killed him from across the street.[37]

Most of the 19th Massachusetts infiltrated the houses on the east side of Caroline Street. "Up went the windows. The blinds were thrown open, the first door smashed into fragments and the men posted up stairs and down," according to one Union soldier. Northern riflemen crammed the windows and peppered the other side of the street, where the 13th Mississippi also took cover in the houses. The fiery streaks of light from hundreds of rifles laced back and forth across the darkened avenue. The brick and clapboard structures provided protection from a myriad of bullets, which smacked against the facades. Some men, however, learned their defenses were really deathtraps. Confederate Albert Henly wrote that "Splinters caused by balls passing through chimneys, fences and framed houses were more dangerous than the balls and shells themselves and many were killed and wounded by them." The battle raged for another hour before the Mississippi troops vanished into the night. The 19th Massachusetts slipped across Caroline Street and cautiously entered the houses on the street's west side. Convinced the Confederates had gone, they halted for the night. Meanwhile, the battle continued and redoubled to their left.[38]

Carter's 13th Mississippi kept the 20th Massachusetts pinned down in the intersection at Hawke Street. Southerners decimated the bluecoats and killed or wounded most of their officers. Captain Henry Abbott was one of the few still standing. A bullet clanged off of his sword scabbard but left him untouched. Captain Macy admired his subordinate's trademark calm, but confessed to his wife, "I trembled for Abbott." Abbott led his men up Hawke Street toward Princess Anne Street. They covered only thirty yards before overwhelming casualties stopped their progress. Abbott lost nearly half of his command in the block beyond Caroline Street. The rest of Macy's Federals split up, looking for cover and a way to get around the Rebel-held houses. Small groups of Yankees weaved through a maze of unknown backstreets and dark alleyways. The 20th Massachusetts bypassed certain houses and backyards, only to find their way blocked by barricades of stacked boxes and barrels filled with rocks and dirt. The close nature of the combat and fighting in the dark demoralized many of the participants, including Captain Macy. He wrote simply, "It was awful." By 6:00 P.M., the impenetrable darkness brought a lull to the fighting. Hall replaced the 20th Massachusetts with Lieutenant Colonel William Northedge's 59th New York. Most of the Massachusetts men fell back to the river to regroup. Captain Abbott, however, had strayed beyond recall and continued to press toward Princess Anne Street.[39]

Fighting erupted again when Northedge's 59th New York stumbled into the Mississippians. The 59th New York's fire quickly tapered off, and Carter's 13th Mississippi slipped away to the Market House. By this time, General Barksdale had recalled everyone to the Market House. Joshua Owen's Philadelphia Brigade had penetrated the center of the city and threatened to sever Barksdale's line of retreat. The 13th Mississippi raced south on Princess Anne Street. Carter found Colonel Benjamin G. Humphreys' 21st Mississippi at Barksdale's headquarters.[40]

Barksdale had sent several contingents of Colonel Humphreys' Mississippians to the river on parallel streets. One company held the foot of William

Street, while another moved down George Street to the right. A third company held Sophia Street between them. The Confederates on William Street had fired on the 20th Massachusetts when it crossed Sophia Street. This drew Norman Hall's and Joshua Owen's attention. Owen's Federals probed south from the bridgehead at sunset. His Philadelphia Brigade filtered down the riverfront, looking for the Rebels who had fired on Macy's 20th Massachusetts. The antagonists collided at William Street, and a brief firefight broke out. Both sides recoiled in the darkness and quiet resumed.[41]

Barksdale's soldiers thought they had routed the Yankees, but the Federals were regrouping for another attack. The Mississippians at William Street retired, exposing the other companies on Sophia Street. Colonel Turner G. Morehead's 106th Pennsylvania drove straight down the street and plunged into the unsuspecting Rebels. Confederate captain Robert C. Green spotted the attackers at the last second and deflected their thrust, but the Pennsylvanians rallied and struck again. Green tried to organize his two companies of the 21st Mississippi, but he was killed in the middle of the gun battle, and his men fell back to the Market House. Colonel Benjamin Humphreys commended Green's defenders for "contesting each foot of ground" before retreating two blocks to Princess Anne Street. The pursuing Yankees clambered after them. Colonel Humphreys led three fresh companies of the 21st Mississippi in a counterattack down George Street. The quick parry from the Market House drove the bluecoats back to the river and bought time for General Barksdale to collect the rest of his forces at the Market House.[42]

Colonel James Carter's 13th Mississippi arrived shortly afterward. Barksdale flung his troops into line on Humphreys' left. The general told Carter that Humphreys' regiment held Caroline Street and covered several of the streets leading to the river. Barksdale wanted the 13th Mississippi to extend Humphreys' left and clear Caroline Street of Yankees. The 13th Mississippi formed one block above, on Princess Anne Street. Colonel Carter in the meantime reconnoitered toward Caroline Street. Much to his astonishment, as he advanced a block, he found the street filled with Federal troops.[43]

Feisty Joshua Owen had reinforced his Union skirmishers and sent them forward again. The Philadelphia Brigade slipped into Caroline Street about the same time Colonel Carter spotted it. The Northern commander pushed his men quietly through the darkened business district. The Yankees had trouble seeing in the dark. Owen conceded that "much time was therefore expended, and but little progress made." Unaware of the 13th Mississippi's close proximity, the Pennsylvanians stormed into Humphreys' 21st Mississippi's vulnerable left flank. Owen had sent the 72nd Pennsylvania to attack the Rebels in front. "There was considerable fire for some time," reported one Union soldier. While Humphreys'—and possibly some of Carter's—Confederates focused on the Yankee regiment, Owen's 106th Pennsylvania surprised the Rebels in flank. The 106th Pennsylvania trapped 21 prisoners and forced the rest of Humphreys' command to flee to Princess Anne Street. The Yankees also unearthed a large cache of mail. They presented ten bags of Confederate parcels to General O. O. Howard along with their Mississippi prisoners. As one prisoner passed Union colonel Turner Morehead, he mused aloud, "Old man, I see you are alive yet. I had four good shots at you, and don't see how it is I did not hit you." Morehead shot back, "You scoundrel, you."[44]

The ground in Fredericksburg rises from the river to a pronounced ridge neatly delineated by Princess Anne Street. It extended from Fauquier Street, three blocks north of William Street, to the RF&P Railroad on the south side of town. This formidable crest commanded most of the streets leading from the river, and William Barksdale relied on it for his final defense. He anchored his line on the Market House. Mississippians entered houses and fired from windows commanding William and George Streets. Some of the Confederates took over Saint George's Episcopal Church and probably the Presbyterian church across the street for a clear shot down George Street. Their plunging fire slowed the Federals to a crawl. Colonel Joshua Owen reported, "The houses and churches contiguous to my route were filled with sharpshooters, which rendered great caution necessary." This "great caution" provided Barksdale with time to make his final move.[45]

The Confederates had held the city much longer than anyone had anticipated. Barksdale provided Lee with ample time to start concentrating his army on the heights behind the city. Barksdale's division commander, Lafayette McLaws, listened to the ebb and flow of the fighting downtown, and believed the time had come for the Mississippi brigade to fall back. Longstreet wanted to keep a foothold in Fredericksburg, but yielded when McLaws insisted that the city was untenable. McLaws sent his aide, Captain Henry L. P. King, to order Barksdale out of Fredericksburg.[46]

Barksdale pocketed McLaws' order and continued battling the Federals around the Market House. Some speculated that his fighting blood refused to yield the contest. Others argued that the Yankees made it too difficult for him to disengage. Colonel Benjamin Humphreys more astutely stated that Barksdale waited for complete darkness before retiring. Humphreys explained that McLaws had "ordered us to fall back to the hills, which we could not safely attempt until dark." If that was the case, then Barksdale needed to hold the ridge by the Market House until night completely blotted out the landscape. The Confederates' losing the ridge would allow the Federals to pour infantry and artillery fire into them as they retreated. Barksdale unfortunately failed to make his intentions known to McLaws. When McLaws realized that Barksdale had not moved, he sent a second order, demanding compliance. In the interim, Barksdale had won his point. Shortly after 7:00 P.M., Owen's Federals relented and withdrew to the houses along Caroline Street. Barksdale seized the opportunity to withdraw his troops. He started the 17th Mississippi and portions of the 18th Mississippi to the rear and directed the 13th Mississippi to follow. He sent a message to Colonel Luse's 18th Mississippi to fall back from Deep Run, leaving the 15th South Carolina and 16th Georgia to hold the line below the city. Barksdale left the 21st Mississippi to cover the withdrawal while he regrouped his scattered regiments at the base of Marye's Heights.[47]

The 21st Mississippi spread out along Princess Anne Street while the rest of the Confederates quietly withdrew to safety. The retreat went flawlessly until gunfire exploded in the northern part of the city. Mississippi lieutenant Lane Brandon had extended Humphreys' left flank and brushed against a small band of Federals on Princess Anne Street. Lieutenant Brandon learned from prisoners that he confronted Captain Henry L. Abbott's isolated command of the 20th Massachusetts. Brandon and Abbott had been inseparable friends during their school days at Harvard—and now they faced each other in battle. According to one old Confederate, Brandon "lost his head completely." He impulsively ordered his men to attack. The schoolmates clashed near the northern end of the ridge at Fauquier Street, though Abbott probably never knew the personal nature of the attack until later. Colonel Benjamin Humphreys heard the fire and sent an order to Lieutenant Brandon to disengage. The 21st Mississippi officer ignored the order and pressed Abbott's squad back to Hawke Street. Humphreys found the renegade commander there and placed him under arrest. A subaltern withdrew Brandon's men. After the campaign, Brandon and Abbott exchanged notes, probably illuminating the whole episode for the Massachusetts officer. After Brandon's Mississippians fell back, silence settled over the city.[48]

The Confederates disappeared and the Federals bedded down along Caroline and Sophia Streets. The city of Fredericksburg took on an eerie new aspect. Civilians who had been trapped in their homes quietly emerged from their cellars to see their world torn apart. "It was a large and beautiful city when we arrived here," wrote John Smart of the 15th New York Engineers. "It now presents a sad spectacle of the desolation of war." "At midnight . . . the town . . . exhibited all the destruction to private property, customary to a place taken by storm," recorded another soldier. To the inhabitants, this type of destruction defied understanding. Some of them had waved white handkerchiefs from their windows during the day to stop the bombardment. Federal provost marshal Marsena Patrick saw their flags and scoffed, "Utterly impossible!" Hours later, the "Yards and gardens that had been the pride of families were scenes of destruction and ruin." Dead soldiers cluttered their streets, and wounded filled their beds. Amid the carnage lay the innocuous pets and animals of the townspeople. Cats and dogs lay dead beside cold corpses, and lifeless hens and chickens littered their coops. A couple of Union soldiers discovered an unoffending milk cow that had lost one of its legs. Members of the 20th Massachusetts shot the animal, and later, the 19th Massachusetts turned it "into steaks which were greatly enjoyed."[49]

Some of the Federal soldiers resorted to former occupations to contain the fires blazing through downtown Fredericksburg. The "fire-boys" of the 72nd Pennsylvania battled blazes up and down Caroline Street. Other Union soldiers rooted through destroyed homes to claim "some memento of Fredericksburg." Many of the common soldiers indulged their palates and ate lavishly from the city's larders. Officers sought something more substantial. Even the ostensibly aristocratic Captain Henry Abbott admitted, "I went into nearly every house to get some nice little silver thing for mamma . . . but was too late." Many of the Northerners felt they had earned the right to take whatever they wanted simply because of the determined struggle to take the city. Others exacted vengeance on the city that had sheltered their enemies and abetted the slaughter in the streets. Some assumed the houses had been compromised when the Rebels used them, so nothing downtown was inviolate. General Oliver O. Howard wrote, "There was some rioting" that evening. Things would get much worse before the Union army left Fredericksburg.[50]

Federal troops stirred near the lower pontoon crossing at sunset. Burnside ordered Franklin to cross his Left Grand Division when the upper crossings had been secured. Thousands of excited Unionists crowded toward the bridges. Brigadier General Charles Devens led the way with his brigade from Major General William F. Smith's Union Sixth Corps. Devens' regiments— the 7th Massachusetts, 10th Massachusetts, 37th Massachusetts, 36th New

York, and 2nd Rhode Island—halted briefly behind the artillery on Stafford Heights.[51]

In the twilight, Captain Andrew Cowan's 1st New York Battery fired a few rounds at the Bernard house to clear away the Rebel sharpshooters. A few minutes later, Devens' troops dashed over the bridges. Devens sent Colonel Frank Wheaton's 2nd Rhode Island across first. The regiment debouched from the bridge and ballooned out in skirmish order. Climbing the embankment, the Northerners received a few scattered shots from Robertson's pickets, who promptly fell back to the Bowling Green Road. The Rhode Islanders pursued a short distance, but darkness made it hard to see the Confederates. Wheaton halted the 2nd Rhode Island, while the rest of Devens' brigade crossed "with great enthusiasm." The new arrivals shouted joyfully, "Three cheers for the Regiment first over!" Devens ordered Wheaton to form his regiment in a large semicircle around the bridgehead, resting both of its flanks on the river. As Wheaton evacuated his wounded, Devens complimented them: "Boys, you have had a hard time, but Rhode Island did well." Before the rest of the army crossed, Burnside changed his mind. He worried about confusion if they tried to cross during the night. General William F. Smith's Sixth Corps had started onto the bridges, only to be turned back and herded into bivouac. Charles Devens' brigade alone guarded the lower bridgehead. He reinforced the 2nd Rhode Island and waited for morning.[52]

Burnside halted the rest of the army too, and ordered it to camp. Thousands of troops, their enthusiasm temporarily dulled, shuffled into bivouacs. On the other side of the river, O. O. Howard reinforced the bridgehead around the upper pontoon crossing. He posted his men on the first two streets from the river and left the rest of the city to the Confederates. The next day, he would clear the city according to Darius Couch's orders. At 8:00 P.M., the men rested easier when the engineers completed the second bridge at the upper pontoon crossing.[53]

On the lower end of Fredericksburg, Ninth Corps leader Orlando B. Willcox buttressed the middle-crossing bridgehead with Colonel Rush C. Hawkins' brigade. The 46th and 89th New York had cordoned off the docks with skirmishers, but Hawkins' arrival allowed them to probe carefully into Caroline Street. O. O. Howard's men, probably Owen's Philadelphians, contacted the Ninth Corps troops sometime after 11:00 P.M. Though Howard never intended it, the two bridgeheads had finally connected.[54]

When the armies separated on the evening of December 11, both sides had had the first taste of street fighting ever known on the North American continent. Yet two great feats had been accomplished, one of them a milestone in American military tactics. William Barksdale's defense of the Rappahannock River, and later, the city of Fredericksburg, exceeded all expectations. His Mississippi brigade had sustained 242 casualties out of 1,500 men, but it had also secured time for Robert E. Lee to marshal his forces behind the city. Barksdale had thoroughly disrupted Ambrose Burnside's plans for a swift strike, which led directly to the disastrous Union assaults two days later. The Confederate First Corps commander, James Longstreet, attributed Lee's ultimate success to Barksdale's men. "A more gallant and worthy service," he wrote, "is rarely accomplished by so small a force." Another Confederate officer called the Mississippians' defense "one of the finest acts of heroism and stubborn resistance in our military annals." Only Barksdale's division commander Lafayette McLaws was chary with his praise. In all likelihood, he still disagreed with his subordinate's decision to hold the city against his orders.[55]

The Federals had established the first bridgehead landing under fire in American history. The price for such notoriety sobered most of the participants. Major Ira Spaulding's 50th New York Engineers had lost 9 engineers killed on the bridges and another 40 wounded in the futile attempts to force the bridge crossings. The Federals used close to 3,000 infantrymen in the bridgeheads and lost 10 percent of them in a very inequitable distribution. The 20th Massachusetts had been bled white in a matter of fifty yards on Hawke Street. One witness categorized this single day in Fredericksburg as "one of the hardest fought battles of the war." The historian for the 20th Massachusetts summarized, "This is the first and proved to be the only instance in the war of a fierce and deadly contest for the control of a populous town."[56]

Fredericksburg had been reduced to ruins as a silent punishment for lying on the Rubicon of two warring nations and on the threshold of modern military history. Events on December 11 had destroyed the city of Fredericksburg and, at the same time, set the stage for the way modern armies would fight from then on.

CHAPTER FIVE

"THE MOST GOTHIC OF GOTHS"

The Sacking of Fredericksburg

Robert E. Lee's Confederates hurried to Fredericksburg as soon as the signal guns boomed on December 11. James Longstreet's First Corps sprawled across the hills behind Fredericksburg. Richard H. Anderson's division anchored the Confederate left on the Rappahannock at Taylor's Hill. Robert Ransom's small division of two North Carolina brigades covered Marye's Heights, which was really two hills melded together by a saddle. The southern crest was called Willis Hill, and its northern and larger neighbor bore the resident family's name—Marye's Hill, but the whole area became known as Marye's Heights. A fence traversed the cleft between the hills and neatly delineated Willis' from Marye's hill. McLaws' division extended south of the Telegraph Road, and Pickett's command stretched the line to Deep Run. Hood's division held the right at Prospect Hill, near Hamilton's Crossing. Lee's front extended for nearly eight miles. Artillery filled earthworks as prescribed by E. P. Alexander. Deep Run bisected the defenses. The hills bowed around the stream, forming a concave line with both ends closer to the river. The left end formed a salient nine hundred yards outside of Fredericksburg at Marye's Heights; and Prospect Hill formed the other salient one and one-quarter miles from the river. Lee secured his flanks with Anderson's division hugging the river and Hood's division abutting a swampy stream called Massaponax Creek.

Robert E. Lee alerted Stonewall Jackson to the crossing at 8:00 A.M., but issued no further updates. Jackson bided his time, ordering his troops to cook two days' rations and fill their cartridge boxes. The corps waited through the day for Lee to ascertain Burnside's true motives. Jackson moved his headquarters closer to Fredericksburg, spending the night at John Ewing's farmstead near Hamilton's Crossing.

As Barksdale's battle dissipated, Longstreet ordered McLaws to reinforce the salient opposite Fredericksburg. Brigadier General Thomas R. R. Cobb's Georgia brigade occupied a sunken lane that skirted the base of Marye's Heights at 8:00 P.M. Cobb placed three regiments in the road where years of traffic had cut into the hillside. The lane became known as Sunken Road and was reinforced by four-foot stone retaining walls. The stone wall facing the city made an ideal breastwork, which one Confederate proclaimed as a "very good protection." When Barksdale's rear guard passed through Cobb's position, the Mississippians warned the Georgians, "You will see sights at daylight!"[1]

Confederates stirred before dawn on December 12, a day that proved to be as balmy as the last. Morning fog gave way to hazy skies, and the temperature climbed to fifty-six degrees. Confederates continued to file into line and shift positions. Thomas R. R. Cobb rearranged his Georgia brigade behind the stone wall, placing the Phillips Legion on the left, near the Martha Stephens house, and the 18th Georgia on the right, with the 24th Georgia in between. He kept the 16th Georgia in reserve behind Willis Hill. The regiment relaxed "near the Old Rock Mill" operated by the Howison family. For some reason, Cobb left one of his regiments, Cobb's Legion, in camp. The rest of Lafayette McLaws' division completed their dispositions south of the Telegraph Road. General Robert Ransom's division started the day straddling the Plank Road six hundred yards behind Marye's Heights. Longstreet ordered it below Telegraph Road but then returned it to the heights— immediately behind the Washington Artillery.[2]

General Lee excused all of his barefoot and ill-clad troops from duty, leaving them to guard the camps. Seeing the first genuine benefit to his nakedness, a shoeless North Carolinian wrote, "I was glad then that my shoes did not come because I would rather loose a hundred dollars than go in a battle." No statistics enumerate the number of troops Lee excused, but there is some evidence that suggests that Confederates embellished their after-battle casualty reports to furlough shoeless troops home to re-equip themselves.[3]

Lee came to the front at dawn to watch Burnside's movements. James

Longstreet, Jeb Stuart, and "many other smaller fish" joined the army chief as he reconnoitered the front. General Lee sat on a stump atop Marye's Hill and studied the terrain with his field glasses. An onlooker noted that Lee was "dressed quite plainly . . . like a plain old farmer." Longstreet, bundled in a small blanket that reminded one of a shawl, mustered even less martial aplomb. An irreverent Carolinian thought that the First Corps commander looked "like a large hog drover." Only Jeb Stuart, clad in a "roundabout jacket and a feather in his hat," struck the nearby Confederates as an ideal "young dashing looking officer." Satisfied that Burnside had committed his army to Fredericksburg, Lee summoned Jackson and two of his divisions.[4]

General Thomas J. Jackson had risen early at Ewing's farm. Receiving Lee's orders to come to Fredericksburg, he started A. P. Hill's division from the Thomas Yerby estate, Belvoir, at 6:30 A.M. William B. Taliaferro's division broke camp at Guiney Station and traveled "in much haste" along backroads to Hamilton's Crossing. For the moment, Jackson left Jubal Early's and D. H. Hill's divisions on the lower Rappahannock in case Burnside's crossing proved to be a ruse. With his troops in motion, Jackson rode ahead to see Lee. Ordered to assume command of the right, Jackson reconnoitered the woods and fields around Prospect Hill. Lee joined him, and together they scouted the Federal positions below Deep Run. Accounting for almost all of Burnside's forces, Lee instructed Jackson to bring up his last two divisions. The subordinate complied. Jackson appeared to be well pleased with his positions, almost to the point of uncharacteristic whimsy. Jedediah Hotchkiss, Jackson's longtime topographer and mapmaker, noted with incredulity that his acerbic chieftain passed the time "whistling as we went along."[5]

Major General A. P. Hill's "Light Division," ironically the largest in the army, relieved John B. Hood's troops at Hamilton's Crossing by 8:00 A.M. Hood's division sidled to the left, shortening Longstreet's front. "Little Powell" Hill's troops took over their makeshift trenches, eventually filling 3,300 yards of front line from Hood's right flank to the rounded ridge cap called Prospect Hill. Hood's men had excavated a shallow line of works out of the thawing soil, but Hill's men referred to them as "ditches" because of their dubious depth and protection. Part of the line may have been a genuine ditch running along a logging road atop Prospect Hill. William Taliaferro's division arrived sometime later and moved into the woods behind Hill's men. Jackson's troops held two miles of an eight-mile front, leaving Longstreet to cover the remaining six. Since Longstreet had the benefit of stronger natural features for his defense, the First Corps could afford to cover more frontage

Jackson, on the other hand, had to compensate for weaker terrain by stacking his forces on a narrow front. He relied on a defense in depth, which would get deeper when his last two divisions arrived.[6]

Jackson's Second Corps marched to Fredericksburg "in fine spirits," according to one of its number. Archer's Brigade teased Captain Junius Kimble unmercifully because he wore a dazzling new uniform coat. Many of the soldiers speculated aloud how he would make an splendid corpse in his finery. Everyone, including the captain, laughed at the gibes. A man in Hood's command, however, thought A. P. Hill's troops looked particularly glum. They reminded him more of "a funeral cortege than a column of soldiers."[7]

Stonewall Jackson sent for his last two divisions as soon as Lee asked for them. Unfortunately, the order went astray. Late in the afternoon, Jackson dispatched Lieutenant James Power Smith to check Early's and D. H. Hill's progress. Smith was surprised to find Early's troops still at Rappahannock Academy and their general at dinner. The division commander claimed that he had no knowledge that he was expected at Fredericksburg. Early hastily ordered his men to march. Smith left to see D. H. Hill at once. The aide reached Port Royal at sunset and relayed the orders. Both divisions undertook a difficult night march to reach Lee's army before dawn on December 13. Early's division covered fifteen miles, and D. H. Hill's traveled closer to twenty that night. Unseasonable warmth had drawn the frost out of the ground, making normally dirt roads slick with mud. The Confederates churned the thoroughfares into a virtually impassable bog. Men struggled to keep on their feet, slipping and falling in the dark, only to be mocked with laughter and frustrated imprecations. Hours passed and men struggled to stay awake, much less to keep their place "over the worst kind of road (without resting)." A Carolina soldier recalled the night march to Fredericksburg as "one of the hardest I ever saw."[8]

Early's division reached Brooke's farm two miles below Hamilton's Crossing by midnight. D. H. Hill's men closed up by 3:00 A.M. The generals rested their commands before assuming their positions at sunrise. Robert E. Lee's army had concentrated successfully before Burnside could make his next move. Lee had won another race against his opponent and doomed Burnside's operation to failure.[9]

The Confederates at Fredericksburg spent December 12 improving their positions. Longstreet assigned the elite Washington Artillery of Louisiana to the Marye's Heights salient. Three companies of the renowned artillery battalion, under Colonel James B. Walton, had taken position on December 11 and strengthened their gun pits on the 12th. "For the first time our army will fight behind dirt," chronicled a young cannoneer. The Louisiana gunners had inherited shallow works that barely covered a man to his chest. They raised the walls higher and fashioned embrasures for their cannon. The artillery adjutant Lieutenant William Owen noted, "Without delay the men made the redoubts as snug as possible." The engineers protested that the artillerists had "spoiled their work," but the gunners retorted, "We have to fight here, not you; we will arrange them to suit ourselves." The engineers appealed to the corps commander, but James Longstreet sided with the Washington Artillery. "If we only save the finger of a man, that's good enough," the general replied.[10]

Walton placed his companies on either side of John Marye's mansion, Brompton. The 1st Company, under Captain Charles W. Squires, held the left, occupying two gun pits adjacent to Brompton. The captain moved Lieutenant John M. Galbraith's 10-pounder Parrott to a point just north of Hanover Street and in line with the mansion. The captain personally commanded a 3-inch rifle and a 10-pounder Parrott on the northern fringe of Willis Hill. The brick-enclosed Willis cemetery stood immediately behind him. Captain Merritt B. Miller's 3rd Company unlimbered on Squires' right with two 12-pounder Napoleons. Holding the far right, Captain Benjamin F. Eshleman's 4th Company guarded the southern approach to Willis Hill with a couple of 12-pounder Napoleons in one pit and two 12-pounder howitzers in another.[11]

Thomas R. R. Cobb improved the defenses along the Sunken Road below Walton's guns. Men shoveled dirt from the road to lower the ground behind the stone wall and reinforce the bank in front of it. Cobb sent others in front to clear a field of fire. Work details tore down the board fence from Martha Stephens' garden and the west wall of the neighboring Fredericksburg agricultural fairground. The ten-acre fairground was commonly known as Mercer Square. Some of the Confederates stole Mrs. Stephens' beets surreptitiously while rummaging around her garden.[12]

On Jackson's front, A. P. Hill also cleared a field of fire. He noted a number of outbuildings and obstructions on the Mannsfield and Smithfield plantations that he feared Northern sharpshooters would use against him. The general selected a party of North Carolinians to eradicate the problem. Major Christopher Columbus Cole of the 22nd North Carolina spent the day examining the cover. At the same time, Southern artillerists traipsed across the fields, familiarizing themselves with landmarks and distances. It is hard to determine how much communication they had with A. P. Hill or Major Cole, or if Cole unwittingly removed some of their reference points. Rebels watched the Yankees fill the plains: "their bayonets glistened in the setting sun." One thought the scene "was beautiful and awful to contemplate." After dark, Cole's detail slipped past the picket line. North Carolinians fanned across the blackened fields. The major waited for everyone to reach his place, then he snapped a pistol cap as the signal to begin. Fires erupted across the front. Flames engulfed barns and outbuildings. The incendiaries disappeared into the night and returned to A. P. Hill's lines. Astonished soldiers on both sides gazed at the conflagration between the lines.[13]

Another fire along the Sunken Road bathed Marye's Heights in a dull glow. Cobb's Georgians lit small fires to keep warm and to roast Mrs. Stephens' beets. Their reflection on Marye's Heights provoked an artillery salvo from Union guns on Stafford Heights. Cobb ordered the fires doused, and the spirited shelling ebbed into silence.[14]

Despite elaborate preparations for action on December 12, the Northern army frittered away the day getting ready for battle on December 13. After consulting Burnside, William Franklin ordered a third bridge to be laid at the lower pontoon site to expedite crossing. Unfortunately, work crews started late and did not finish until the next night. Some time after midnight, December 12, Burnside notified Franklin to be ready to cross at an unspecified time and "as soon as he and Sumner are over, attack simultaneously." The endorsement, in Burnside's hand, hints at the army commander's intentions for December 12, but he failed to issue the necessary orders or a timetable.[15]

General O. O. Howard inspected the bridgehead at the upper end of the city at 3:00 A.M. The general encouraged Sully's and Owens' brigades to push farther into the city and "enlarge our space." At the same time, Colonel Rush Hawkins' Ninth Corps brigade would expand the middle-crossing bridgehead. Sully's brigade relieved Norman Hall's pickets at dawn. Companies from several regiments scouted the northern part of the city. Yankees secured "the built-up section of the city" and reconnoitered the western suburbs. Confederate pickets met them with "considerable resistance." Southern artillery fired as soon as Howard's troops appeared at the Gordon house, Kenmore, and the unfinished monument to George Washington's mother. Southern guns curtailed Howard's advance and allowed the Confederate pickets to retreat. As soon as the Southern artillery opened fire, Union guns responded. "The shells have been flying both ways for some 15 minutes," noted an expectant bluecoat, "and their music is anything but *sweet*."[16]

Sully's men stopped at the Mary Washington monument and watched the gray-clad skirmishers retire across a piece of low ground, known locally as Gordon's Marsh. The 82nd New York Infantry reinforced Sully's pickets. The general placed the New Yorkers on the overlook by the monument. Hawkins, meanwhile, had cleared the lower city easily because the Rebels had evacuated that portion of the city during the night. A small group of Confederates clung to the western outskirts of Fredericksburg, but the Federals ignored them. Burnside's army focused more on securing the city and making room for the influx of reinforcements.[17]

The Right Grand Division commander, Edwin Sumner, rose at 5:00 A.M., ready to cross the river. His expected orders, however, did not arrive until Sumner finished his breakfast. Burnside allowed his senior officer to cross at his discretion. Sumner notified Franklin and Hooker and then started Darius Couch's Second Corps across the river. Couch moved at 8:00 A.M. Brigadier General William French's division tramped over the upstream bridge at the upper crossing. Brigadier General Winfield S. Hancock's division marched on the bridge beside it. "The first views that greeted us," recalled a Pennsylvania soldier, "were those of the newly-made graves of the brave boys belonging to the 19ᵗʰ Massachusetts." French filed into Caroline Street. Hancock's column turned down Sophia Street to the Ninth Corps bridgehead.[18]

Hancock's lead unit—Meagher's Irish Brigade—reached the city docks, allowing General Orlando Willcox to cross the rest of the Ninth Corps over the middle pontoon bridge. Brigadier General William W. Burns' division led the Ninth Corps' column. Brigadier General Samuel D. Sturgis' command and Brigadier General George Washington Getty's last brigade followed at 11:00 A.M. Sturgis halted on the south end of Sophia Street, extending Hancock's line. George Getty put his division behind Sturgis' force; and Burns' division moved to the Ferneyhough farm downstream.[19]

Soldiers entered the city in a steady stream. "Troops are pouring over as fast as possible," noted a signal officer. A New Hampshire soldier thought that "the whole scene and surroundings on all hands wear an air very romantic and theatrical, shading down the awful grimness of war, and making its affairs an interesting study for the impressionable and active." Officers and orderlies admired the march from the Phillips house. One exclaimed, "My God was there ever anything like this?" An officer on Sumner's staff recalled breathlessly, "The pen of an angel could not do justice to the awful sublimity of the hour & the scene." Small hitches occasionally jeopardized the panoply. Quite a few men had fortified themselves with a dram of whiskey. Several of them came close to falling off the bridges. Others nearly nudged their comrades into the water. Officers lectured their troops to march out of step to keep the bridges from swaying. Sometimes that was difficult, especially when well-meaning regimental bands serenaded the troops. Music naturally encouraged the men to march in cadence. A number of embalmers hawked business cards on Stafford Heights. They promised to recover clients' bodies and ship them home presentably. Soldiers generally shunned them and pressed on.[20]

Brigadier General George Stoneman, commander of the Third Corps of Hooker's grand division, reinforced Couch with a division at the upper crossing. Brigadier General Amiel W. Whipple's two brigades started at 11:00 A.M. with the intention of securing Couch's right flank. Brigadier General A. Sanders Piatt's brigade led the column across the upper bridge at 2:00 P.M. The head of Piatt's brigade crossed "as speedily as possible," but halted when it found the city too crowded to enter. The rest of the brigade stopped on the bridge. Colonel Samuel Sprigg Carroll's brigade came up behind them, stretching the column all the way back to the top of Stafford Heights. The 12th New Hampshire, a large new regiment, had headed Carroll's advance. Colonel Robert B. Potter tried to go around the troops clogging in the ravine. He took a shortcut over the crest. With great fanfare, officers rode in front while a brass band played "Yankee Doodle," which drew everyone's attention. "The regiment made a grand display," wrote a spectator. At the foot of the bridge, the band switched to the tune "Bully for You." Then a Confederate shell landed in its midst, demolishing the bass drum. A deluge of shells followed. The frightened 12th New Hampshire broke and fled, much to the delight and derision of the troops in the city. "The regiment disappeared as if by magic," gibed one witness. A second thought the New Englanders presented a "ludicrous and really amusing scene." A member of another New Hampshire unit admitted that it was a "seriously hazardous affair" that cost several lives, but he could not resist the "feeling of levity," when he saw "the men skulk and seek shelter in such a hurried and frantic manner." The demoralized soldiers reminded him of a "brood of chickens when the old hen raised her cry of warning against a hawk." Later, he mused, "Not a chicken could be seen a moment later."[21]

Piatt's men tried to stay calm while shells rippled the water on either side of the bridge. "The range was accurate enough," reckoned a bystander, "but fortunately the missiles fell into the water . . . or struck the opposite bank.' A soldier remembered the sight of shells plunking in the river and "throwing up the water as if big stones were being dropped in." A nervous New Yorker cried out, "The next time, they will fetch us." Piatt crammed his first regiment, the 122nd Pennsylvania, into the city. With no room to form, the men took cover along the riverbank. The rest of the brigade, meanwhile, retreated to Stafford Heights. Their rapid exit caused the bridges to sway uncontrollably, and the pontoons threatened to break free. General Alfred Sully watched Piatt's flight and announced, "There goes a lot of brave Soldiers to *hell*, that is providing that is their destination."[22]

A small contingent of horsemen, perhaps the 8th Illinois Cavalry, approached the upper pontoon bridge next, and offered a remarkable contrast to Whipple's division. They moved at a slow trot under a heavy cannonade. Three artillery rounds burst in the ranks, but instead of hurrying, the horsemen slowed to a walk before crossing the bridge "in perfect order." An admiring Massachusetts soldier recalled: "The contrast was magnificent."[23]

Confederates shelled the middle pontoon crossing as well. Their fire caught Colonel Edward Harland's brigade of Getty's division coming over Stafford Heights like "an immense blue ribbon from the river up the slope." Several rounds struck the column while it was trapped in a narrow lane. One shell landed in a new regiment, the 15th Connecticut. "Suddenly I am thrown flat on the ground, covered with dirt and stunned by an explosion," remembered a survivor. The shell exploded on the bank beside him, killing one man, tearing a limb off another, and otherwise critically injuring a third. The explosion filled the air with stones and gravel. The concussion knocked over dozens of men. Those still standing broke and ran. A Union soldier admitted: "There was some scattering at first." A man from another regiment empathized, "I must confess I was frightened as well as were all the rest. . . O! if you could have seen the men knocked down by the concussion & then the bodies being carried away then you would have felt as I did." Men struggled to free themselves from the heap of soldiers. "What a howling mob," proclaimed a bystander. Soldiers spit out dirt, rubbed their eyes, and cursed as they shook the gravel from their clothes. "As for swearing," one participant mused, "the proverbial trooper was left far behind." Harland's brigade quickly retreated behind Stafford Heights. Once their targets were out of sight, the Confederates stopped firing and Harland's brigade regrouped. "We had scarcely got seated when Gen. Burnside came along," wrote a haggard ew recruit, "and ordered the brigade over the river." Harland's troops marched over the crest again without further mishap. "This was our first introduction to actual war," reflected a newly indoctrinated veteran.[24]

Union artillery also proved to be a problem for the Federal infantry. Regiments crammed like sardines in "battalion mass" on the city wharves. Northern guns on Stafford Heights fired over their heads. Defective ammunition and fuses resulted in "very many" rounds exploding over the densely packed Yankees. Some blamed Benjamin's U.S. Regular battery, while others named Thomas Trumbull's 1st Connecticut Heavy Artillery as the culprits. "We watched it," recalled a New England soldier, "certain that with every discharge some one was either to be killed or dangerously wounded." To him, it seemed "every shell exploded over us." One shell struck the 4th Rhode Island infantry. Another detonated in the 9th New York, Hawkins' Zouave regiment, killing a man. A witness said the victim's head was "nearly torn off." An irate diarist noted, "As yet no one today has been hit by rebel shells while our own guns are killing us by the wholesale!" Another writer observed, "Human life was cheap that day!" Darkness provided the only reprieve for the trapped infantry.[25]

Franklin's Left Grand Division began crossing the lower pontoon bridges shortly after Sumner started into the city. The large influx of troops jammed the spans. Some of the commands became jumbled and separated, but officers maintained discipline and kept the bluecoats slowly sifting over the river. Many of the soldiers discarded well-worn playing cards and other damning paraphernalia that could be shipped home in the event of their death. A sanctimonious New Yorker noted that he crossed on a "bridge covered thickly with playing cards." Novice soldiers in the 13th New Hampshire threw away hundreds of steel bulletproof vests. The men had paid exorbitant prices for the armor but now "one can pick up any quantity of them," because they were "too heavy to carry" and probably did not work anyway.[26]

Major General William F. Smith—good-naturedly called "Baldy" for his sleek pate—watched his Sixth Corps cross the higher of the two spans at the lower crossing. At the same time, artillery filed across the bridge beside him. Smith commanded the largest corps on the battlefield but would see the least amount of action and suffer the strongest repercussions. Smith had a profound influence over the Left Grand Division commander, William Franklin. Joseph Hooker, in an unguarded moment of hypocrisy, once dubbed Smith "the evil genius" behind Franklin. Smith's first division, under Brigadier General William T. H. "Bully" Brooks, led the procession over the river.

Brooks relieved Charles Devens' brigade from guarding the bridgehead. Brig
adier General Albion P. Howe's division crossed next, and Brigadier General
John Newton's division brought up the rear.[27]

After Brooks crossed, corps commander Smith forwarded all of his rifled
batteries to secure the bridgehead. He aligned them in a grand battery to
cover the *tete-de-pont*. Baldy Smith kept Brooks' division close to the river in
reserve until Howe finished crossing. With Brooks on the right and Howe's
division on the left, Smith advanced the Sixth Corps cautiously up the rise
past The Bend, and one-quarter of a mile to the Bowling Green Road. Smith
held Newton's division in reserve near the bridges as a precaution.[28]

After Smith's Sixth Corps came Brigadier General George D. Bayard's cav
alry brigade. The horsemen prodded their less-than-sure-footed mounts over
the swaying pontoons. Bayard was one of the North's most promising caval
rymen, even though he had grown secretly disillusioned with the war. He
remained with the army purely out of personal loyalty. He had rushed to join
his command for the Fredericksburg campaign, postponing his marriage to
Miss Sallie Bowman—daughter of the superintendent of West Point—for the
third time. Once across the river, the cavalry slowly trotted into the fog to
make room in the bridgehead for others to cross.[29]

The Union First Corps, under the highly esteemed and polished Major
General John F. Reynolds, followed Bayard's brigade over the bridges. Reyn
olds, and much of his command, had been in Fredericksburg before. They
had trained there during the spring of 1862, and they knew the ground per
haps better than anyone in either army. Reynolds had endeared himself to
the local population as a judicious and benevolent provost. When the Con
federates captured him at Gaines' Mill during the Seven Days' battle, Freder
icksburg residents petitioned for his release.[30]

Brigadier General John Gibbon's 1st Division crossed the pontoon bridge
first, followed by the 2nd Division under Brigadier General Abner Double
day, and the 3rd Division under recently promoted Major General George
Gordon Meade. All three commanders each appeared to be something of a
enigma. Gibbon was a North Carolinian who stayed with the Union. He
had earned promotion to division command after forming the famed "Iron
Brigade"—a collection of feisty midwesterners—but he was still largely un
known. With no representatives in Congress to herald him, he seemed des
tined to remain so. Gibbon had commanded his division for little more than
a month before Fredericksburg. The vainglorious New Yorker Abner Double
day struck many as a caustic and volatile officer. He had distinguished himself

by firing the first Yankee shot from Fort Sumter in 1861, but modern memory has enshrined him (erroneously) as the father of baseball. George Meade outranked three corps commanders in the army at Fredericksburg, but the modest general refused to press his case during active operations. Meade and Reynolds were close friends even though they competed constantly for promotion. Neither man showed much sentimentality, but both harbored a quiet affinity for the other. The knotty-faced Meade had a notorious hair-trigger temper that exploded under the slightest provocation. If nothing else, this made Meade a marvel to be behold.[31]

The lower pontoon bridges groaned under the constant tread of the Left Grand Division until 1:00 P.M. Once across, the Yankees swarmed the bottomland near The Bend while officers figured out where to put them. Brooks' division of the Sixth Corps shuffled north across Deep Run while Howe's division covered the Bowling Green Road south of the stream. John Newton's reserves backed Howe's line. Baldy Smith directed Brooks' division to send feelers up the Bowling Green Road to contact the troops in the city. Colonel Henry L. Cake dispatched two companies of the 27th New York to scout the road. Captain H. Seymour Hall encountered Rush Hawkins' brigade at a blockhouse on Hazel Run. Hall extended Hawkins' picket line and relayed the news back to the lower pontoon crossing. When the fog lifted, Brooks' soldiers discovered they had threaded a corridor between Burns' division of the Ninth Corps and the Confederates—who were only two hundred yards away—without seeing either one of them.[32]

With his right established, Franklin ordered Reynolds to secure the army's left flank. Gibbon's division moved south and joined the Sixth Corps's left. Meade linked with Gibbon's left flank and re-fused his line to the Rappahannock River. Doubleday's division formed a reserve behind Gibbon's and Meade's commands. Doubleday left Colonel James Gavins' brigade to guard the pontoon bridges for the night. He posted the 7th Indiana and 76th New York on the right bank, while the 56th Pennsylvania and 96th New York held the Stafford side. Meade used a precipitous ravine that ran across his front to strengthen his position. The gorge sliced into the Rappahannock near the "Smithfield" plantation of Dr. Thomas Pratt, so the soldiers called it the Smithfield ravine. Meade's pickets plunged across the deep cleft and took position around the Pratt house. The doctor had fled, leaving his overseer to defend the estate. The attendant dutifully locked the front door, but incautiously left a window open for Yankee intruders to climb in. They arrested the overseer and sent him across the river for safety.[33]

Another Southerner uprooted from his home and arrested was Arthur Bernard, the owner of the elegant stone mansion Mannsfield. He lived on an immense estate that stood adjacent to his brother Alfred's home at The Bend. A bit of a curmudgeon, and what one Yankee called "an old secesh bachelor, very aristocratic in his notions," Arthur Bernard objected loudly to the Yankees vandalizing his precious gardens and ruining his estate. He set upon a group of generals headquartered beside his driveway. John F. Reynolds listened impatiently and then ordered the fulminating civilian removed. Guards trundled the startled old gentleman across the river and incarcerated him at Aquia Landing. Union officers took advantage of Bernard's hasty departure to move into his luxurious manor. A bevy of generals slept comfortably at the owner's expense, enjoying his larder and his wine cellar.[34]

After the Sixth Corps' skirmishers contacted the Ninth Corps, William Franklin sent Bayard's cavalry to reconnoiter the ground in front of the lower crossing. Bayard selected two regiments, the 1st Pennsylvania Cavalry and 1st New Jersey Cavalry—known as the "twin regiments"—to scout the ground on either side of Deep Run. The Pennsylvanians headed north of the stream to see what lay beyond the 27th New York. The 1st New Jersey Cavalry moved south of Deep Run to look for the Confederates. As the Northern troopers pushed blindly through the dense fog, the 1st Pennsylvania eased up the Lansdowne Valley to the RF&P Railroad. Troopers clopped across the tracks and ran headlong into Jerome B. Robertson's Texas brigade. Robertson's soldiers, along with Brigadier General George T. Anderson's Georgia brigade, had just entered the valley from the opposite direction when they saw the bluecoats approaching through the fog. The atmosphere distorted the horsemen's appearance to larger-than-life proportions. A nearby artillerist thought the Yankees looked as large as haystacks. A Confederate volley jolted the troopers and sent them reeling in confusion. Bayard ordered the regiment to take cover behind the railroad. Several companies of Texans charged, and Bayard's cavalry broke and fled.[35]

The 1st New Jersey halted at the first sound of gunfire and tried to fathom what Bayard's right had encountered. Glimpses through the mist revealed Union cavalry stampeding to the rear with Texans in pursuit. Lieutenant Colonel Virgil Broderick found Deep Run prevented his New Jersey regiment from aiding Bayard. The steep banks and heavy foliage prohibited mounted troops from getting across the stream. Deep Run also disrupted communications between the two wings. Without Bayard's directions, Broderick worried that the Rebel infantry might cross Deep Run and cut his line of retreat. The

1st New Jersey Cavalry fell back rapidly to the cover of Howe's division on the Bowling Green Road. After losing a part of the 1st Pennsylvania Cavalry, General Bayard checked the attacking Confederates with Captain Horatio G. Gibson's Battery C, 3rd U.S. Artillery, and a portion of the 1st Maine Cavalry. Robertson's Southerners broke off the engagement and retired to their lines without further incident. Bayard reported the mishap in the fog to Franklin and admitted that the mission had yielded nothing. Franklin decided to wait until the fog lifted before he tried another reconnaissance.[36]

Railroader Herman Haupt arrived during the crossing to take charge of rebuilding the RF&P Railroad south of the Rappahannock. His civilian work crew, supplemented by 200 soldiers, started to rebuild the burnt railroad trestle over the river. Confederate cannon opened fire just as the work began. "As soon as the fight commenced the soldiers all deserted," Haupt complained. He reported the incident to Burnside and begged for replacements. Burnside shrugged his shoulders, saying "no more could be spared." Crestfallen, Haupt returned to the bridge, only to discover that his civilians had deserted also. "Not a human being was in sight in that vicinity," the normally efficient head of the U.S. Military Railroad complained. His project was scrapped.[37]

In another unprecedented move, Burnside ordered Captain Samuel T. Cushing, his chief signal officer, to establish a telegraph across the upper and lower pontoon bridges "with the advance guards of each grand division" and find "suitable positions" for communicating with general headquarters. Lieutenants James B. Brooks and Charles F. Stone went with Couch's Second Corps. They selected the steeple of the Fredericksburg courthouse for a signal station. Lieutenants Edward C. Pierce, John C. Wiggins, and George J. Clarke used a small field telegraph train to patch Franklin's headquarters into Burnside's. A wagon traversed the route between the headquarters, while engineers spooled out insulated wire from a reel (each reel held five miles of cable). Signalmen draped the line over trees or suspended it from poles and fences. By afternoon Cushing's men had attached batteries to both ends of the cable, which animated a pointer that jumped from letter to letter on a dial, spelling out messages. Cushing claimed that his telegraph wire was vulnerable to artillery fire, but his admission that shirkers and malingerers congregated along his line intimated that the location was safe. Riding one portion of the line, Cushing found a line of those men spaced ten feet apart on both sides of his telegraph line. He asked what they were doing, and an authoritative spokesman responded, "they were watching that telegraph wire." Cushing left them to continue their "guard" duty unmolested. The line worked flawlessly. "It is claimed for the Signal Corps of the Army of the Potomac," the captain reported, "that it was the first to introduce on this continent as a medium of communication upon the field of battle the magnetic telegraph." He had revolutionized battlefield communications.[38]

The fog diminished during the afternoon, and Franklin personally reconnoitered the ground in front of the Left Grand Division. He studied the Confederate heights from afar, and learned nothing of the Southern defenses, because Lee kept his troops hidden in the woods. Union artillery probed the ridge for more information. A member of Lane's North Carolina brigade recorded, "Friday we had [an] Artillery duel, but no musketry engagement." Toward sunset, Union skirmishers charged the Confederate picket line "trying to learn the exact locality of the enemy." Fire bristled through the gloaming without yielding any new information for the Northerners. Franklin assumed the Confederates had distributed their strength along the western face of the Rappahannock Valley, which formed a concave wall with salients at Marye's Heights and Prospect Hill.[39]

While Franklin analyzed the Confederate right, Burnside and Sumner looked at the left. Sumner crossed the upper pontoon bridge at 4:30 P.M., just as the Confederates opened another flurry of artillery fire to hurry him along. Burnside probably crossed the middle pontoon bridge and spent some time with Sumner's troops before examining the salient at Marye's Heights. The general may have attended a wedding near the prominence many years before, but if so the happy occasion had left little martial impression on him.[40]

Provost Marshal Marsena Patrick—a familiar member of the Fredericksburg garrison from the previous spring—immediately set out to eliminate one of the roadblocks that hindered a breakout from Fredericksburg. The millrace around the city was fifteen feet wide with sheer walls, sometimes seven feet high. Five feet of standing water made it an imposing obstacle. At noon Patrick approached Sully's brigade to "turn off the water from the upper canal, by raising the mill sluice." Sully sent part of the 82nd New York, under Captain Thomas Cummings, to clear the Confederate pickets from a paper mill overlooking the juncture of the millrace and the canal. The Federals charged across a hollow north of the Mary Washington monument and drove away the Rebels. They secured the paper mill under fire and turned off the water by closing the gates to the canal. Patrick opened the other end of the millrace at Heston's Mill to let the water drain out. The water dropped to three feet, but then it leveled out.[41]

Burnside wanted to improve communications between his wings, so he ordered Darius Couch to bridge Hazel Run. Even though the Ninth Corps straddled the stream, Burnside gave the assignment to the Second Corps. The Second Corps commander understood that the project portended a move to mass the army on Franklin's front, yet Burnside did very little with the bridge once it was done. Zook's brigade detailed the brand new 27th Connecticut to construct the bridge. The large regiment started work near the Fredericksburg gas works and soon caught the attention of Confederates on Marye's Heights. The Washington Artillery fired a few rounds into the workers. The shells exploded among the new recruits and routed the entire command. "Our new regiment," mused one of Zook's staff officers, "had its equanimity sadly disturbed by a shell bursting in its ranks killing several men." The Confederates howled delightedly as they watched the Yankees scatter. Most of the Connecticut men hid beneath the steep bank of Hazel Run. Lieutenant Josiah Favill tried to roust them back to work, but they refused to budge. Favill reported that the cannonfire had "almost paralyzed them." Because of the delay, Couch did not complete the bridge until well after dark; by then Burnside had changed his mind about his next move.[42]

General Burnside left Fredericksburg as soon as he was satisfied with the Right Grand Division's dispositions and went to see Franklin. The commander rode down the Bowling Green Road amid enthusiastic cheers from his old Ninth Corps. "Gen. Burnsides and staff rode past us and as usual we greeted him with thousands of huzzas," wrote a Connecticut soldier. "He dropped his hat as usual and rode smilingly on." Crossing Deep Run, Burnside stopped briefly at Franklin's headquarters. Burnside arrived at twilight and took a cursory glance at the ground with Franklin. The army chief then returned to the Bernard house, where he conferred with Franklin and his generals.

Cloistered in an opulent study, the Left Grand Division leaders pressed Burnside to attack on their front. Franklin and his lieutenants argued that the Confederates around Prospect Hill appeared to be much less imposing than those in the fortified lines Burnside had seen on Marye's Heights. Assuming the Southerners had divided the front evenly between their two corps and all things being equal, then logically, Prospect Hill would be easier to assail than Marye's Heights. No one suspected the inequitable distribution of the Confederates along Lee's front. Franklin, however, attached several caveats to an attack on Prospect Hill. He wanted the offensive to start before dawn so the Union forces could cross the plain under cover of darkness; and the Left Grand Division needed substantial reinforcements from Hooker's Center Grand Division to guard the lower pontoon crossing in case the attack failed and the Rebels counterattacked. Burnside left Franklin and his retinue convinced of their plan's merit. He promised that orders would be forthcoming. The army commander sped away into the darkness, and the generals of the Left Grand Division celebrated their anticipated orders with dinner. They settled into Mannsfield's posh splendor and waited. Burnside headed north to communicate with some of his other generals, perhaps in light of his decision to attack with Franklin's men. But he may have gotten lost in the darkness and rising river fog. There is a chance that he was looking for his confidant Sumner in Fredericksburg, not realizing that the Right Grand Division commander had retired to the Lacy house "to the surprise of every one." Whatever the reason, Burnside lost several critical hours before he returned to the Phillips house. He started drafting orders well after his subordinates expected to have them in hand.[43]

Meanwhile, an endless procession of Yankees filed through the smoldering rubble of Fredericksburg amid chilling scenes of destruction and callousness. "It was a weird sight that met our gaze," recalled a member of the 34th New York. "Piles of dead" littered the street corners, and "every doorstep was a tombstone" for discarded corpses. "It was a scene which no man desires to behold but once," a Northerner confessed. Massachusetts soldiers gawked passively as hogs gnawed on the body of a dead Confederate. "Such is war," shrugged a bystander. Large sections of Fredericksburg lay in ruins; and most houses bore telltale scars from the bombardment. Soldiers sifted through the desolation, mesmerized by the "great, gaping holes [which] stared at us from every dwelling," according to one young man. A Connecticut man admitted, "I expected to see some Shattered houses, but was not prepared to witness such *general ruin* as Fredericksburg presented" (emphasis in original). A New Hampshire soldier thought the city looked "as if a huge shell had burst on almost every square rod in all Fredericksburg." A Rhode Islander proclaimed, "Fred[e]ricksburg is now in ashes, a heap of ruins."[44]

Residents had fled at the first fire, leaving most of their property behind. Union officers availed themselves of the opportunity to outfit or replenish their commands with necessities. They allowed men to tear down fences for fuel. Junior officers supervised the removal of foodstuffs, blankets, and bedding. The 15th Massachusetts laid approximately one hundred mattresses in the street so 300 soldiers could avoid sleeping in the mud. A 15th Connecticut man averred, "We could go into the houses and get all the flour we wanted." New Hampshire men slaughtered stray pigs. Officers stretched the rules regarding necessities, and permitted their men to commandeer ladies' dresses and gowns, as well as chairs, sofas, and silverware. The commander of the bloodied 20th Massachusetts informed friends back home, "I saw men cleaning their guns with ladies silk gowns." Another remembered: "Such sights were never witnessed. Soldiers making coffee in silver pitchers, cleaning guns with lace undersleeves." Soldiers in the 16th Connecticut "with a lot of others" received orders from brigade and division surgeons to "go foraging for the Hospital." A member of the detail said that the doctors "told us to take any thing we could find."[45]

General officers took advantage of their exalted positions to establish their headquarters in some of the more genteel homes. Brigadier General Alfred Sully carefully selected Douglas H. Gordon's home on Princess Anne Street. The general banged on the door but no one answered. Trying one or two windows, the general eventually found a way in. A house servant peeped through the door just as the general entered a window. Grinning onlookers hooted, "Look out, there, Sam, somebody's going to break in there." The servant sized up the situation and answered, "Well, I suppose dey will. Some of dese chaps is privilege characters." Sully's persistence earned him a head-quarters "finely furnished . . . [with] a large and well stocked library; an elegant piano and the walls of the room were hung with beautiful paintings and engravings and large and costly mirrors." A rumor spread that Sully had selected the house because it was the residence of his sister and her "d——rebel" husband. Despite their ideological differences, Sully appears to have spared the house from outlandish mischief. Some generals took residence in houses to "protect" them, but only for their own comfort. Common soldiers invaded a myriad of unoccupied houses, noting "the men had free access except where General officers took up their head quarters & placed guards for their own convenience." As a result, the men obtained "all the flour they wanted, and a number of other things besides."[46]

The destruction downtown, combined with the methodical confiscation of private property and the casual access to the homes, led many Union soldiers to assume that Fredericksburg was already a violated city. That opened the door for further depredations. "We had all we could wish for," wrote a Pennsylvanian in the Second Corps. "Oh we lived like kings while we were over there." A soldier in the Philadelphia Brigade confessed that his men simply could not resist the temptation to pillage. "The old troopers had not spent a night in so civilized a place as a city in a long while," he explained, "and they felt like making the most of their rare opportunity." Men rediscovered the joy of cooking with refined culinary utensils, eating off of bone china, and resting tired bodies on comfortable sofas. "We kind of hated to leave the city for I tell you we had a good time there," professed a new soldier. "I tell you we lived high." Some fared better than others, but most lived better than they had in private life. "We went into stores or houses & took just what we were a mind to," a New Hampshireman recalled with pride. The chaplain of the 145th Pennsylvania, the Reverend John H. W. Stuckenberg, condemned his men's wanton behavior, but admitted, "The men lived well, better perhaps, than at any time since they were in service."[47]

A member of Owen's brigade thought the absence of the residents and "the effect of liquor" contributed to the escalation of looting. Almost all of the civilians had gone, except for some of the poorer classes and a few free blacks, who clung to the northern end of the city. An Union apologist who trivialized the widespread theft of property as mere "irregularities" claimed that they "were confined almost exclusively to houses that had been abandoned." Since the entire population with few exceptions had fled, the point is narrowly valid but fails to acknowledge the vast scale of the criminal spree. Drinking inflamed passions to wreak still greater havoc. Soldiers broke into a wholesale store on Caroline Street, stocked with casks of liquor. Men turned on dozens of spigots and filled their canteens with a variety of expensive brandies and bourbons. They left the alcohol running until it flooded the store and spilled into the street. An observer noticed that the "men drank what they wanted, filled their canteens" and stumbled off in search of booty. Soldiers carried whole cases of assorted wines. A frustrated teetotaler in Kimball's brigade wrote in disgust, "Nearly all the men were drunk" by the evening of December 12. Surrounded by temptations and fired with alcohol, normally inhibited men felt free to scour the city for sybaritic pleasures.[48]

Even disciplined soldiers succumbed to the allure of pilfering articles great and small. Officers, many with ostensibly aristocratic bloodlines and incomes, vied with one another in a fevered search for souvenirs to send home. The Harvard Regiment's officers plundered heartily through the upper end of the city. The well-to-do Captain Henry Abbott stole a writing desk, which the provost marshal later confiscated. He then purloined several volumes from a private library, sending one of them to the governor of Massachusetts as a prize. Captain George N. Macy, commander of the blue-blooded 20th Massachusetts, rummaged through the houses one step ahead of Abbott, pilfering "a little bed lamp of solid silver," among other things. A captain in another Massachusetts regiment stole a silver fruit dish. He wrote home, "I have got a little relic if I can get it home." Even chaplains could not resist gathering trophies and spoils from their sojourn in Fredericksburg. A Pennsylvania recruit gave his chaplain several books he had stolen from an elegant family library. The minister, in turn, gave a copy of *The Life of Washington* to his colonel, no doubt for inspiration, and kept a biography on the marquis de Lafayette. This blatant disregard for private property by the officers quickly encouraged the common soldiers to engage in an extravagant rampage of looting and pillaging.[49]

The iron discipline of the Army of the Potomac melted in the carnival-bacchanal atmosphere of Fredericksburg. Normally sane men acted irrationally. Subdued, upright citizens became maniacal plunderers. The accepted rules of civilization and the common code of ethics were trampled in the heat of the moment. Men lost themselves in a psychotic dream-state that allowed them free rein to do as they pleased. This is not to suggest that rapine or salacious misconduct should be added to their crimes, but that an insatiable lust for the finer things in life, or simply a reminder of former happiness, induced men to carry off everything and anything they coveted. This debauchery failed to bring satisfaction, which frustrated the Union vandals and spawned a vicious cycle of even more destructive behavior.

Frustration, fear, and anger fueled the plunderers' aberrant greed. The Confederates had gained an unfair advantage by exploiting the city to delay the pontoon crossings, they rationalized smugly. Rebels had hidden in the houses and alleyways and fought with unconventional tactics. Union dead testified to its effectiveness. Soldiers wanted revenge for this unprecedented form of warfare. Anger easily mixed with frustration, as the Northerners realized the Rebels were immune to punishment and, in fact, stood poised to inflict even greater havoc. A pensive Irish Brigade soldier confided to his chaplain, "Father, they are going to lead us over in front of those guns which we have seen them placing, unhindered, for the past three weeks." The priest scoffed, "Do not trouble yourself, your Generals know better than that." But apprehension pervaded the ranks. Maybe their generals did not know better. They sought diversion to avoid dwelling on their terrible predicament. When pious General O. O. Howard reprimanded a "very hilarious group" of besotted soldiers for their "unusual preparations for battle," one of them responded, "Ah, general, let us sing and dance tonight; we will fight better for it to-morrow." The fact that so many Yankees tried to smuggle their prizes back across the bridges before the battle belies their truthfulness. Few believed they could win at Fredericksburg, so it behooved them to secure their treasures before the opportunity disappeared. Nonetheless, the phenomenon of rampant looting "was curious to observe," wrote a Second Corps staff officer. Lieutenant Josiah Favill thought the troops "rid themselves of all anxiety by plunging into this boisterous sport." Officers on the whole appeared content to let them have their diversion, provided they stayed within earshot of their commands.[50]

Men looted according to their inclinations and opportunities. Tobacco was the most sought after commodity in the city. "There was quite a jubilee over tobacco," a New Jersey soldier revealed. Sutlers in camp had charged two dollars a pound, forcing the impoverished soldiers to do without "that luxury, or rather necessity," as one Massachusetts man grumbled. "I begin to think that I shall have to quit using it entirely," lamented a penniless man in Hancock's division. Confederates had sunk whole hogsheads of the prized weed in the Rappahannock. Soldiers fished them out and discovered the leaves unspoiled. Compacted cakes of the tobacco kept water from damaging the center of the disks. A flurry of men swarmed the riverfront, rescuing hundreds of crates filled with tobacco. Some of the more adventuresome—or desperate—dove into the river to recover cigars and chewing plugs. The 81st Pennsylvania alone retrieved thirty boxes, and the total haul of Virginian tobacco exceeded a thousand pounds by all accounts. Not since Stonewall Jackson's scarecrows had raided the Union supply base at Manassas Junction had soldiers experienced such a euphoric embarrassment of riches. "Those who had been paying exorbitant prices for it a few hours before," wrote a triumphant smoker, "now had more than they could dispose of."[51]

The most ambitious thieves desecrated houses and took whatever they pleased without consequence. They burglarized jewelry stores and banks, as well as lowly hovels and shacks. Soldiers stuffed their haversacks with wads of Confederate script, which they subsequently used to buy food while marching across Virginia. Others prized the letterhead of the Bank of Virginia because stationery was hard to come by. Greedy men carried off elegant furniture to sit in the street, or to fuel their fires.[52]

Marauders absconded with any amount of food. They carted off eggs, hams, flour, corn, molasses, potatoes, lard, and candy. A bystander witnessed a procession of men carrying jars of "pickles in one hand and preserves in the other." Proud recruits shared their bounty with the officers. "Lieutenant, have some honey," said a grinning a 15th Massachusetts soldier. "Free as water."

In this particular case, so were the bees that came with the hive, which caused a "general routing" of the robbers. Poorer houses lacked expensive relics but yielded "no scarcity of provision" for those content to just take food. The 13th New Hampshire broke into one shack that had nothing but a "bucket full of walnuts." They took them to garnish whatever else they found for dinner that night.[53]

Dye Davis, John Howells, and William Hill of the 48th Pennsylvania broke into a carpenter's storeroom, mistaking it for a pantry. Davis stole a sack of what he assumed was flour and exclaimed, "Now, lads, let's go down to the fire & we will have some Johnny Cakes." The trio mixed the batter, cooked it, and ate it, only to discover it was plaster of Paris![54]

A member of Joshua Owen's Philadelphia Brigade watched a stream of men going from house to house, carrying all manner of things, only to discard them at the next home for something better. Looters stole meaningless bric-a-brac without rhyme or reason. Items they no longer desired, they destroyed. Their nefarious behavior sank into an orgy of destruction. "The boys 'went in' for such things as they could carry off and *many* of the things they could *not*," admitted an 11th New Hampshire man. A Massachusetts soldier wrote, "The houses were turned upside down, or rather the articles in the houses." Plunderers filched flower vases, books, private letters, and, as one diarist noted, "even children's toys." Captain Abbott took two children's books that he thought his nephews might enjoy. One noteworthy plunderer somewhere purloined "a fine stuffed alligator," which he joyously paraded around town. Captain Lewis Leavens of the 7th Rhode Island instructed his servant Tom to "secure a piano." The youth managed to drag it all the way to the pontoon bridges before guards stopped him. In return for these extravagant acquisitions, lawless soldiers slashed oil paintings and portraits, and vandalized pianos, mirrors, furniture, and walls. They ripped open mattresses and chairs and threw the stuffing in the air. Musket butts shattered window sashes and broke gas fixtures. "Our men took what they chose, and destroyed any amount of property of all kinds," claimed a disgusted Ninth Corps soldier, "in fact made it worse than an utter waste." A brigade commander rebuked one of his regiments, telling the culprits that "the 19th Maine if let alone would steal the whole Southern Confederacy in three months."[55]

The revelry became even more absurd and unbelievable when looters broke into trousseaus and trunks, picking through ladies' clothes and anti-quated fashions—and not just for rags to clean their weapons. A New Yorker in Norman Hall's brigade traded his uniform for a vintage militia uniform that resembled something worn in the Revolutionary War, complete with cockaded tricorn hat. Others lampooned in women's garments, wearing hoopskirts "that were in fashion in the days of Mary Washington." Escorts for the "ladies" donned "high shirt collars & tall beaver hats." They formed an impromptu parade as they promenaded through the crowds, "walking arm and arm with a comrade." Two prized wenches were rewarded—one can only assume for their incongruous ugliness—with a jaunt down Caroline Street in an old gilded coach, "a relic of colonial days," replete with a somber driver, perched ceremoniously atop the cab and a ludicrously lop-eared old mule drawing the contraption. The "belles of a by-gone age" sat in the back "scattering smiles and kisses to an applauding crowd." A Minnesota youth found it hard to believe that "the boys [were] capering around as if no Enemy were in the vicinity," but the festive atmosphere temporarily distracted them from their plight.[56]

In another unprecedented aspect of the campaign, Fredericksburg became the first American city sacked since the British had burned Washington in the War of 1812. The unsavory specter of wanton destruction took on an even more grotesque significance when Fredericksburg became the first American city ransacked by Americans. The provost marshal of the Union army stood by, powerless to stop the mayhem. Designated provost units found their hands full with other matters. A sizable portion of the provost in the north end of the city came from the newly formed 127th Pennsylvania. Sergeant Solomon Cover and his patrol were gobbled up by Confederates, which left the upper part of the city virtually free of law enforcement. Civilians flocked to O. O. Howard's headquarters, begging for protection. Their numerous pleas exceeded the general's capacity, and most were turned away. Howard conscientiously evacuated the women and children to Falmouth for their own safety. Similarly, guards at the middle pontoon crossing rescued a lost child who searched the crowd, telling passersby, "I want to find mamma." But at the lowest levels, officers quietly condoned their men's frenzied rampage. "It seems to have been the intention of the generals," wrote an irate chaplain, "to give the city for pillage . . . at least no efforts were made to check them." Similarly, a wary staff officer observed, "No attempt was made by the officers to interfere." Colonel Rush Hawkins complained to Howard about the Second Corps' lawlessness to which the Bible-thumping commander allegedly quipped in uncharacteristic frustration, "Soldiers are not expected to be angels."[57]

Without cooperation from the units or their commanders, the provost marshal, Marsena Patrick, conceded the downtown to the marauding gangs. He relegated his guards to the pontoon bridges. The provost caught hundreds of looters who attempted to smuggle booty out of the city. Unable to detain so many rioters, Patrick merely confiscated their plunder and returned the soldiers to their commands. Thus Captain Leavens' servant Tom lost his piano after wrestling it all the way to the river, but the captain suffered no consequences. "The provost guard stopped the stragglers in their attempts to cross the river," reported a New York soldier, "and made them disgorge their plunder there." As a result, Patrick accumulated "great piles of goods" at the end of the bridges. When one looter refused to surrender his treasures, Patrick swatted him with his riding crop. More egregious offenders, such as officers sporting all sorts of trinkets and mantel ornaments, were remanded directly to Joseph Hooker for punishment, though little came of it. Later, Patrick was called away, and the piles vanished under the pillagers' deft hands.[58]

Some soldier-plunderers justified their malefaction as punishment for the many horrors of the war. They called Fredericksburg the "hot-bed of secession" and held the city responsible for all of their troubles "under the plea that 'secesh' has brought the country to its present unpleasant condition." Self-righteous hooligans felt that Fredericksburg should be "assessed" for the damage inflicted on the army. Other Union soldiers asserted that the city itself was a prize of war fairly won and to be disposed of without recrimination. While pillaging was widespread, witnesses pointed out that many soldiers abstained from the looting. At the same time, some civilians thoroughly immersed themselves in the riot. "Citizens that had remained in town, and the negroes," recalled a Philadelphia Brigade chronicler, "seemed to join in appropriating their neighbors' property." One resourceful old woman, who was "disposed to profit by these transactions," opened a pancake stand, trading food for "any article of personal property." She easily attracted "a lively throng of soldiers about her doors."[59]

While many argued that the city was a prize fairly won, most of them condemned the excessive and wanton destruction. A Pennsylvanian informed the newspapers back home that the Northerners plundered "in a manner worthy of the most Gothic of Goths or hungriest of Huns." Another soldier said the army "completely sacked" the city, adding, "we cannot express it by any other word." A 20th Massachusetts officer recalled that the despoliation "went far beyond anything of the kind I ever read of . . . every thing combined to make it horrible." A New York diarist wrote, "Fredericksburg, once a proud and wealthy city is now nothing but a sacked and ruined town."

Shame overtook legions of bluecoats when they realized the extent of the destruction. "In short, Everything is destroyed," a Minnesota man admitted sadly: "and the citizens of Fredericksburg are Houseless, Homeless and destitute. . . . It will be a hard winter of intense hardship for them." The war on civilians had taken on its most punitive definition to date.[60]

As things settled down for the night, pickets and skirmishers stopped shooting; looters and carousers, apparently satiated for the moment, ceased marauding; and soldiers shivered in the darkness reflecting on the events about to unfold. "We knew the next Day would see perhaps the greatest battle that was ever Known," recalled a soldier in the 57th New York. A staff officer admitted, "we all feel shaky about coming events and there was very little hilarity." The idea of attacking Lee's fortifications struck one soldier as "an enigma that no one can solve." "One thing is certain," Lieutenant Josiah Favill of Zook's staff recounted, "that by tomorrow at this time many of our old comrades will have fought their last fight, whatever may be the result." Another man dolefully agreed: "That night gave the last natural sleep of life to many a brave soldier." Mules brayed, wheels creaked, and Major C. C. Cole's fires crackled as two hundred thousand troops slowly fell asleep on the morrow's killing fields.[61]

CHAPTER SIX

"THE JAWS OF DEATH"

The Battle Begins

Fog blanketed Fredericksburg again on December 13, promising another day of unseasonable warmth. The weather observer in Georgetown recorded the temperature as thirty-four degrees at 7:00 A.M. By 2:00 P.M., the mercury rose to nearly sixty degrees. Frost on the battlefield quickly gave way to mud.[1]

Confederates in D. H. Hill's and Early's divisions broke camp reluctantly at the Brooke farm and set out to find their places in Jackson's line. Early's men wended along country lanes and logging trails to Hamilton's Crossing, and took position behind A. P. Hill's division. D. H. Hill followed and assumed a spot in the third line, behind Early's and Taliaferro's divisions. Jackson designated Harvey Hill's command as the general reserve for his right wing. Safely tucked away in the woods behind Prospect Hill, Early's and Hill's men flopped down on the ground and resumed their slumber.[2]

Robert E. Lee rose before dawn and went to his advance command post on Telegraph Hill. He listened to the sounds of movement through the fog. Soon James Longstreet and two of his division commanders, Lafayette McLaws and Robert Ransom, joined Lee. Longstreet had spent the morning reconnoitering his left flank, pleased with his dispositions. The officers huddled by a fire while Longstreet relied on his shawl-like blanket to keep warm. Jeb Stuart showed up later and took his place by the fire. Soon after his arrival, Stonewall Jackson and his staff loomed out of the fog. Jackson glistened in the new uniform that Stuart had given him, much to the delight and amusement of the gathering. Most of them had never seen the plain Virginian so adorned. The correspondent of the London *Times* understated the conviction that Jackson normally had "a great disregard of dress and appearance." Jackson completed his ensemble with an appropriately gilded kepi.[3]

The fog burned off somewhat to reveal a portion of the field to the assemblage. Longstreet jokingly baited the resplendent Stonewall. Gesturing to the Yankees, the First Corps commander asked if the Northern horde frightened him. Jackson answered tersely, "Perhaps I'll frighten them after awhile." He added that his troops may have failed to carry a position once in a while, but they never failed to hold one. Longstreet withdrew the question, leaving Jackson to his patented reticence. Lee asked Jackson and Stuart to inspect the right with him. The generals mounted and left Longstreet to mind the left. A coterie of generals and attendants rode along the line, passing through the woods from division to division. A civilian spectator recalled: "In their full regalia, with swords clanking, spurs clicking, with side-arms, it was a sight never to be forgotten." Cheers reverberated in their wake and electrified the line ahead. A wry Carolinian listening to the cascade of sound announced, "Boys, look out! Here comes 'old Stonewall' or an old hare, one or 'tother."[4]

Lee examined Major General George E. Pickett's division line and quickly moved on to Major General John B. Hood's division. Lee had placed these commands in the center, and in a sense in reserve. They would be spared from heavy action. Lee's cavalcade halted briefly to chat with Hood. The army commander wanted the lanky Kentuckian to serve as the link between Longstreet's First Corps and Jackson's Second Corps. Hood would support either wing—whichever needed him. John B. Hood, unlike any other officer on the field, would receive orders from Lee, Longstreet, and Jackson. Lee counseled Pickett to cooperate with Hood. Hood placed his division in two lines to assist either wing. Robertson's and G. T. Anderson's brigades had assumed the front (where they had battled Bayard's cavalry the day before), while Brigadier General Henry L. "Rock" Benning's Georgia brigade formed behind them. Hood's fourth brigade, under Brigadier General Evander McIvor Law, took position away from the rest of the division, separated by a branch of Deep Run. Law's Brigade was the only part of Hood's division to see serious action on December 13.[5]

Lee entered Stonewall Jackson's lines next, riding along the front held by fiery A. P. Hill. Hill's poisoned relationship with Jackson had reached an intolerable climax with both commanders poised to file court-martial grievances against each other. Hill, in anger, called Jackson a "crazy old Presbyterian fool," and added, "The Almighty will get tired of helping Jackson after awhile, and then he'll get the d——ndest thrashing." Though Hill was a favorite with his men and trusted by Lee as his most gifted division commander, the willful lieutenant could barely tolerate Jackson, and the stern Presbyterian reciprocated. A. P. Hill staggered his troops in two lines, placing Brigadier General James H. Lane's North Carolina brigade in front on the left. Brigadier General James J. Archer, a displaced Marylander, formed his brigade of Tennesseans, Georgians, and Alabamians in the center, and Colonel John M. Brockenbrough held the right with his Virginia brigade. Hill used three brigades to make a second line. Brigadier General Edward L. Thomas' Georgia brigade stood three hundred yards behind Lane's Brigade. Brigadier General William Dorsey Pender's Brigade of North Carolinians formed close to Lane's left rear, holding the woodline west of Bernard's Cabins and tying directly into Hood's line. The South Carolina brigade of the renowned fire-eater Brigadier General Maxcy Gregg took a position in the woods between Lane's and Archer's brigades.[6]

Gregg rested his command on the Military Road, behind a waterlogged marsh. The road was an improved logging path that ran along the ridgetop. The Confederate high command had determined that the six-hundred-yard-wide wetland between Archer and Lane was impassable to an organized force. Officers from Lane's and Archer's brigades objected, but A. P. Hill assured them that the "interval," a trivializing term used by Hill to describe the area, could not be breached. He placed Gregg's South Carolina brigade in reserve behind the gap just to be certain. The aging and somewhat deaf Gregg reassured both Lane and Archer that he would assist them and seal the gap if the Federals attacked.[7]

A. P. Hill had the most brilliant combination of subordinate officers in the army, even though their styles and habits widely differed. Gregg's outspoken candor balanced with Thomas' unassuming reticence. Archer's rough-hewn discipline balanced Pender's polished fearlessness. Lane and Brockenbrough had just risen to brigade commands. Lane would prove a valuable addition; Brockenbrough would not. Of all the officers, Archer was the last to arrive at Fredericksburg and had the least amount of time to prepare for action. He had left his sickbed in Richmond when he learned Lee's army was concentrating at Fredericksburg. The general traveled all night by train to Guiney Station and arrived at Prospect Hill shortly before Lee rode by. He had departed so hastily that he left several members of his staff behind because they were too drunk to travel.[8]

Jackson aligned two divisions behind A. P. Hill's line. Brigadier General William B. Taliaferro's four brigades backed Hill's left, while Early guarded his right. Taliaferro commanded Jackson's old division, much to the regret of the Second Corps leader. Jackson had clashed with a cabal of officers in the Valley, in which Taliaferro featured prominently. Taliaferro had drafted a petition against Jackson that the War Department approved. Jackson almost resigned over the incident. Since then, the unforgiving Stonewall had made the unexceptional division commander regret his actions. Taliaferro supported Gregg's Brigade and Thomas' Brigade with Brigadier General Elisha F. "Bull" Paxton's famed "Stonewall" Brigade and Colonel Edmund Pendleton's rowdy Louisiana brigade. Colonel Edward T. H. Warren's Brigade stood behind the Stonewall Brigade, and Brigadier John R. Jones' Brigade formed to their left, behind Pendleton's Louisianans.[9]

Early's division spread out in the woods south of Taliaferro's command. Colonel James A. Walker's Virginia brigade formed on the left, and Colonel Edmund N. Atkinson's Georgia brigade stood next to it. Brigadier General Harry T. Hays held Early's right flank with his Louisiana brigade, poised to cover A. P. Hill's right rear. Colonel Robert F. Hoke's brigade of North Carolinians and Alabamians marshaled behind Hays. Early's division had seen hard service and, outside of the indomitable Harry Hays, had all new brigade commanders. James Walker, who took over Early's old brigade, showed the most promise. He had been expelled from the Virginia Military Institute by then-professor Thomas J. Jackson. He even challenged Jackson to a duel. But he showed a remarkable aptitude for command that belied his dismissal. Edmund Atkinson was the third leader in as many engagements for the respectable Lawton-Gordon-Evans' Brigade. Robert Hoke had joined his brigade en route to Fredericksburg. His subordinates assured the colonel that they would get him promoted or killed. Harry Hays may have been the steadiest leader, but his brigade was also the most notorious in the army. A Virginian admitted coyly that the Lousianians terrorized the Union army in battle, but frightened everyone else the rest of the time. Their hardened courage made crusty Jube Early overlook their many transgressions.[10]

Major General Daniel Harvey Hill placed his division three hundred yards behind Early's troops. The dense forest hid it from sight. The vitriolic North Carolinian spread his five brigades in a thin line parallel to the Mine Road, with orders to act as a general reserve for Jackson's corps. Hill's troops experienced a good deal of maneuvering at Fredericksburg, but saw little fighting until the very end of the day.[11]

Robert E. Lee studied Jackson's defenses and the skirmish line in front. The 1st Tennessee and 7th North Carolina, from Archer's and Lane's brigades, respectively, formed across the field, including the six-hundred-yard wooded marsh. The RF&P Railroad wrapped around the base of Prospect Hill as it turned from southeast to southwest. The Confederate picket reserve lay behind the railroad's raised embankments. Lee left Prospect Hill and crossed the railroad at Hamilton's Crossing. Jeb Stuart showed him where he had placed two brigades of cavalry to protect the army's right flank. Lee's nephew, Brigadier General Fitzhugh Lee, guarded the flat ground between Hamilton's Crossing and the swampy bottoms of Massaponax Creek. A portion of Brigadier General William H. F. Lee's Brigade extended Stuart's right through a maze of hedgerows reminiscent of Normandy's bocage. He anchored his right flank on the Rappahannock River. "Rooney" Lee (R. E. Lee's son) not only guarded Jackson's flank, but also threatened the Yankee left flank.[12]

Robert E. Lee approved of Jackson's and Stuart's dispositions, including the gap left in A. P. Hill's front. The army commander also paid close attention to the placement of his artillery. Lee's chief of artillery, Brigadier General William N. Pendleton, had selected a favorable array of gun emplacements. Over the past few weeks he had plotted positions, erected gun pits, and cleared fields of fire for his guns. He received valuable assistance from Jackson's chief of artillery, Colonel Stapleton Crutchfield, and Major Thomas M. R. Talcott of Lee's staff. Together they identified several keys points for artillery to cover Jackson's front. When the Second Corps had assumed its positions on December 12, Jackson's artillery lumbered into these preordained locations.[13]

Artillerists and engineers puzzled over the problem of covering the gap in A. P. Hill's line. Pendleton and Crutchfield ultimately decided to place guns on either side of the opening and establish a crossfire across its front. Pendleton hoped their fire would discourage the Federals from penetrating the woods. Lieutenant Colonel Reuben Lindsay Walker, reputedly the handsomest man in the Confederacy, placed fourteen guns on the crest of Prospect Hill. The colonel packed as many guns as he could fit between Archer's and Brockenbrough's brigades. He spaced his guns twenty paces apart, but as room ran out, he halved the distance between guns, and then halved it again. Walker covered the south side of the gap. He enjoyed an open field of fire as

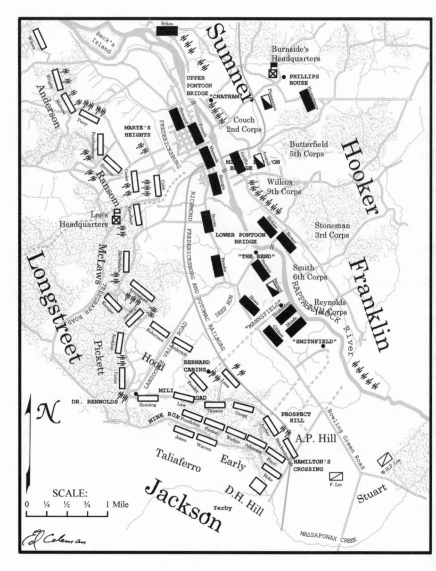

Positions on December 13, 1862

well as cover from a white oak forest that stood behind his guns and concealed his batteries from the Federals.[14]

Walker placed a two-gun section of Captain Alexander C. Latham's
Branch (North Carolina) Artillery on his left, under Lieutenant John R.
Potts. Another two-gun section from Captain Marmaduke Johnson's Virginia
battery, under Lieutenant Valentine J. Clutter, formed on Potts' right. Cap-

tain David Gregg McIntosh held the center with four guns from his South Carolina Pee Dee Artillery. Captain William J. Pegram's four guns of the Purcell (Virginia) Artillery formed next, while Walker crammed in two final guns from Captain William G. Crenshaw's Virginia battery, under Lieutenant James D. Ellett. Walker divided his guns into two ad hoc battalions, giving the eight guns on the left to David McIntosh, and the six on the right to Willie Pegram. The gunners appreciated the clear field of fire, but also noted several problems with their position. Heavy timber masking their position also retarded the redeployment of guns. The obstruction also made it difficult to evacuate the guns. Walker held the static line with the understanding that the Yankees would never get that close.[15]

Jackson's chief of artillery discovered the marshy gap extended across the railroad into a finger of woods. Crutchfield played with the idea of lining the interval with howitzers, but he found few suitable positions on the heavily wooded ridgetop. As an interim measure, Crutchfield sent Captain John B. Brockenbrough's battalion of twelve guns across the railroad tracks north of the swamp. Crutchfield advised Brockenbrough to place his guns during the night "so as not to attract attention." Jackson's chief of artillery told the battalion commander that his position "would be the center of the Army . . . and the point of attack by the enemy." Jackson hoped that Brockenbrough's guns would draw the Union attackers away from the gap and closer to the re-fused portion of Lee's defenses. Crutchfield went over the ground with Brockenbrough "very carefully," and ordered him to "*hold it to the last* extremity."[16]

John B. Brockenbrough (no relation to brigade commander Colonel John M. Brockenbrough) was a youthful Virginia lawyer. One soldier thought he was "a young man, not long from college." The Marylander quickly added, "but in that intellectual face you read more than the ordinary man." Brockenbrough waited until the foggy morning of December 13 before he took six 3-inch rifles, three Napoleons, and three 6-pounders across the railroad in front of Lane's Brigade. He placed his batteries in an open field two hundred yards to the right front of Bernard's Cabins. Brockenbrough's guns came from three batteries, Captain Joseph Carpenter's Virginia battery, Captain George W. Wooding's Danville (Virginia) Artillery, and a section of Lieutenant Edward A. Marye's Fredericksburg (Virginia) Artillery. Brockenbrough located them on a small rise, which provided a clear view of the finger of woods. Crutchfield hoped Brockenbrough's guns could cross their fire with Walker's battalion on Prospect Hill. Crutchfield—and Brockenbrough's whole battalion—must have known that any activity north of the finger of woods would compel Brockenbrough to retire, which would renew the difficulty of covering the gap.[17]

Crutchfield offset the problem somewhat by Captain Greenlee Davidson's small battalion of guns at the Bernard slave cabins to cover Brockenbrough's left rear. Crutchfield believed that an attack against Brockenbrough's battalion would expose its flank to a raking oblique fire from Davidson's guns. Davidson used elements of three batteries with a combination of six 3-inch rifles, two Napoleons, and one light 6-pounder. The artillerist posted Captain William H. Caskie's Hampden (Virginia) Artillery with another section of Ed Marye's Fredericksburg Artillery and Lieutenant Charles W. Statham's Lee (Virginia) Artillery. The batteries unlimbered behind a rise capped by Bernard's Cabins, three hundred yards behind Brockenbrough, and a thousand yards to R. Lindsay Walker's left. Some of Marye's Fredericksburg Artillery fought within sight of their homes. The gunners tore down the Bernard Cabins to clear their field of fire.[18]

Another cluster of guns guarded the Confederate right wing under Major John Pelham of the Stuart Horse Artillery. Pelham had eighteen guns to cover the hedgerows along the road from Hamilton's Crossing to the river. The willowy Alabamian, known as "Sallie" by his West Point classmates for his cherub-like features, had sparked Jeb Stuart's admiration with his aggressive use of artillery as an offensive weapon. Pelham conferred with Crutchfield before dawn and arranged for some additional guns from the artillery reserve to strengthen his force. Crutchfield dispatched two batteries to Pelham. Captains John Milledge's Georgia battery and John Lane's Battery E, Sumter (Georgia) Artillery, moved into position below Prospect Hill. Lane's battery had two important 20-pounder Parrotts, which were rare among the Confederates' relatively small-caliber ordnance. Captain Robert A. Hardaway's Alabama battery moved well south of the Confederate lines, going into battery below Massaponax Creek. His weapons included a much-touted Whitworth rifle. Hardaway's unique breech-loading cannon, imported from England through the blockade, had an effective range of three miles and could enfilade Burnside's entire left wing. Its small, rifled bolts emitted an eerily high pitched squeal when fired. News correspondent Murat Halstead distinguished the gun by its unique sound. He wrote that it "broke the monotony of sound by hurling a bolt that as it flew gave a long shrill whistle." It reminded him of "the high note of a whip, if one could cut the air for a mile." Hardaway's Whitworth had bedeviled the U.S. Navy on the lower Rappahannock prior to Fredericksburg, but during the battle it fired few rounds. At a time when most artillerists relied on direct firing at visible targets, the Whitworth's extreme range was superfluous and its small shells caused little real damage.[19]

Crutchfield kept the rest of Jackson's reserve artillery near the railroad by Forest Hall, the home of Miss Jane Hamilton and her sisters (of Hamilton's Crossing fame). Between William Pendleton, Stapleton Crutchfield, and John Pelham, the Confederates had sited fifty-four guns along the Confederate right wing. Robert E. Lee and Stonewall Jackson approved of the artillery's dispositions. Presumably, that included Brockenbrough's precarious placement beyond the RF&P Railroad tracks. If true, then Jackson's skill as an artillerist offered no better solution for covering the gap. Lee, Jackson, and Stuart returned to Prospect Hill and met with A. P. Hill. The time neared 8:30 A.M., and the Federals remained strangely docile.[20]

Major General William B. Franklin's enthusiasm to attack had waned. He had longed for orders during the night so he could assail the Confederates before dawn on December 13. Burnside had assured him the orders were forthcoming, but the Left Grand Division head began to worry after several hours of waiting. He allegedly dispatched an orderly after midnight to use the newfangled magnetic telegraph to find out about the orders. The attendant returned with a curt message from Burnside's headquarters that he would get his orders when they were ready. Franklin became disillusioned and irascible. He never forgave Burnside for keeping the left-wing generals "sitting up the whole night like fools." As Franklin's churlishness grew, the commander of the First Corps, John F. Reynolds, prudently excused himself to get some rest before the attack. Baldy Smith, Franklin's friend and confidant, also retired, leaving the Left Grand Division commander alone to puzzle over the missing orders. Rigidly methodical and precise, the old engineer Franklin fretted about a myriad of details that he needed to address before he could attack, yet he was powerless to act—in his mind—because he had no orders.[21]

John Reynolds was startled to awake in the fullness of morning on December 13. Surprised that Franklin had not called him, he quickly dressed and returned to headquarters, accompanied by General George G. Meade. William F. Smith also re-emerged, and Franklin astounded them with news that the orders had not yet come. All of their plans and provisos for a swift strike before dawn had vanished. Sunrise came at 7:10 A.M. (according to a meticulous staff officer's account), and the orders were nowhere to be had. Debate raged over what they should do. Franklin apparently refused to risk another rebuff via the telegraph, because he made no more inquiries to headquarters. At 7:30 A.M., Brigadier General James A. Hardie of Burnside's staff ended the debate as he clopped up the driveway with the belated orders.[22]

The delay in orders is difficult to understand and served as a point of contention between Franklin and Burnside—and between Burnside and Hardie. The army commander alleged that Hardie had delayed the order by stopping for breakfast along the way. Hardie, however, answered with a peevish memo detailing how he went to Burnside's tent twice that morning only to be informed "the order I was to take was not prepared." Burnside told Hardie that he had several orders yet to write, but he hoped to expedite matters by sending Hardie with an "interlined order in pencil." Burnside explained the nature of both Franklin's and Sumner's orders, and then dispatched the brigadier to the Left Grand Division with the unofficial pencil copy. Burnside intimated that formal orders would be transmitted by telegraph. Hardie left the Phillips house at 6:00 A.M. by his own reckoning, and immediately encountered an unforeseen obstacle. "The sidling roads from near Philips' to Franklin's bridges, were one glaze of frozen mud with smooth surface and so slippery," he recalled, "that with all my anxiety to get on . . . I could not move rapidly." His mount slipped on the icy road, and Hardie feared "the momentary risks of falling . . . when I dared beyond a walk." General Hardie assumed that the official telegraphic order would reach Franklin well before he did. The general arrived after a plodding adventure only to find Franklin still waiting and cross as a bear. "The delay, you observe," Hardie concluded, "was owing *not* to my want of alacrity, but to the frozen condition of the road." James Hardie cleared his name of any malfeasance. The War Department later trusted him to carry the orders putting George Gordon Meade in command of the Army of the Potomac just before Gettysburg. Regardless of the long-breakfast rumor, or the slick roads, Burnside's orders should have started well before 6:00 A.M. if he intended to attack before dawn. Ultimately, the blame resided with Burnside for not discharging the orders sooner.[23]

Franklin opened the penciled orders and scanned an astonishingly vague and rambling directive. He read little that resembled the generals' counsel from the night before. Burnside's orders directed Franklin to "keep your whole command in position for a rapid movement down the old Richmond Road and . . . send . . . a division at least . . . to seize, if possible, the height near Captain Hamilton's . . . taking care to keep it well supported and its line of retreat open." Franklin learned that it was not Hooker's Center Grand

Division that was coming to protect his rear, but only two understrength divisions from George Stoneman's Third Corps.[24]

The commander of the Left Grand Division had lost all of the qualifiers that he felt were necessary for making an attack. His confusing and evasive orders provided no pre-dawn cover or heavy reinforcements. The left wing marshaled 60,000 troops, but Franklin believed he needed more. Burnside, on the other hand, had directed him to engage as little as one division. The army commander later claimed that he did not give half of the army to Franklin to make an armed reconnaissance with a single division. Franklin may have felt constrained to use only a small force because Burnside had stipulated the rest of the grand division should be ready to make a rapid move down the old Richmond Road. The army chief's maps showed that the road to Bowling Green and Richmond ran parallel to the river until it passed one-half mile south of Dr. Pratt's Smithfield estate, then it veered west to Hamilton's Crossing. In essence, Burnside had ordered an attack against Prospect Hill to be supported by the rest of Franklin's command in force. Franklin knew nothing of the Richmond Road angling off toward the Confederate positions. In fact, Burnside's map—and other generals' as well—mislabeled the road, since the thoroughfare to Hamilton's Crossing did not go to Bowling Green or Richmond. The Left Grand Division commander thus concluded that Burnside wanted his main force ready to move in an illogical direction—away from Fredericksburg and the rest of the army.[25]

The precise William Franklin weighed these strange circumstances against the weakly written order to "seize" the heights. He expected a more forceful command to "carry" the position. He concluded that Burnside had changed his mind about launching the grand assault on the left. Franklin prepared his wing to make a demonstration, a diversion for someone else's benefit. If General Hardie had been less afraid of the obviously angry grand division commander, or less reticent, he might have explained the orders as Burnside conceived them. Hardie himself admitted that Burnside went over the orders with him so he understood Sumner's role as well as Franklin's. But Hardie apparently never spoke up, and Franklin continued to labor in dark bewilderment.[26]

Despite the mish-mash orders, Burnside still wanted Franklin to lead the main attack. The army commander intended the Left Grand Division to force Jackson's Confederates from their defenses. Once Franklin penetrated the Rebel lines, the rest of the left wing would move to Hamilton's Crossing by a road which misfortune labeled as the "old Richmond Road" on Burnside's map. The Federals would then sever Lee's line of communications to Richmond. At the same time, Sumner's Right Grand Division would force another lodgment on the Confederate left. Burnside hoped that Sumner's attack would keep Lee from sending Longstreet's reserves to contain Franklin's breakthrough. Trapped between two Union forces, Lee would be forced to retire. Franklin would be poised astride the RF&P Railroad to block a retreat to Richmond, and necessitate a Confederate withdrawal to the west. This left Burnside the option of chasing Lee in the open or taking the inside track to Richmond. Railroad kingpin Herman Haupt was busy repairing the railroad even as Burnside's army assembled for battle, which strongly suggests that Burnside would have headed for Richmond. Unfortunately, neither Franklin nor Sumner knew how they complemented each other. Burnside's orders simply did not reflect his intentions, and Hardie offered no help.[27]

William B. Franklin lacked the boldness or creativity to be a successful commander. Already agitated by the lateness of the hour, Franklin refused to take the time to ask Burnside to clarify his orders. In Franklin's rigidity, perhaps he thought the orders needed no clarification. Sending an inquiry to general headquarters by military telegraph should have been quick and easy. But waiting for the reply could have wasted the rest of the morning. Burnside had yet to send the official version of the order over the wire. Franklin might have mistrusted the untested telegraph. In any event, the army chief's quizzical orders obligated Franklin and his lieutenants to fulfill them as quickly as possible. Franklin therefore determined to execute the orders as literally as possible. The commander chose Reynolds' First Corps to make the demonstration. He advised John Reynolds to send one division and keep it well supported. Reynolds immediately picked George Meade to make the attack. The division commander objected that Burnside would squander his forces in a piecemeal effort, but Franklin snapped, "That is General Burnside's order." Meade excused himself to prepare his division. Reynolds also left Mannsfield to get the rest of the corps ready to support him. The long roll summoned the First Corps to attention on the fields between Mannsfield and Smithfield.[28]

Reynolds gave Burnside's orders to his three division commanders as he understood them. Reynolds explained that Meade's Pennsylvania Reserves would spearhead the attack. John Gibbon's division was to guard Meade's right flank. The Sixth Corps, in turn, would watch Gibbon's right from afar. Abner Doubleday's division would swing behind Meade's line and protect his left. Consequently, Doubleday also guarded the left flank of Burnside's entire army, which turned out to be a responsibility that overtaxed his abilities.

Reynolds chose Meade to play the primary role, which made perfect sense, even though he commanded one of the smallest divisions in the Union army. Meade outranked all of the other division commanders in the army (and several corps commanders) and had the most battle experience in the First Corps. His troops had seen more action than Gibbon's or Doubleday's and boasted more veteran regiments than either of the other divisions. Reynolds had once commanded the division, and he trusted it to open the climactic battle at the halfway mark between Washington and Richmond.[29]

The Pennsylvania Reserves, a state-fostered unit, had mustered into Federal service late in 1861 with 10,000 men. A year later and a half-dozen battles wiser, Meade's veterans numbered only about 3,800 troops. Two new regiments with full ranks—the 121st Pennsylvania and 142nd Pennsylvania—had joined the division that fall to augment the command. A Pennsylvania Bucktail noted that each of the new regiments had as many men as the smallest brigade. The experienced soldiers looked disfavorably on the raw recruits and often intimidated them. "The young men . . . were very anxious to gain the favor of the old soldiers," mused an unimpressed veteran. When ordered to march on Fredericksburg, one new officer coached his men to keep pace with the old Pennsylvania Reserves and not embarrass themselves in front of the seasoned soldiers. If they could not do that, Lieutenant Colonel Alfred B. McCalmont hoped his 142nd Pennsylvania could at least "Let the old regiments see that we are . . . equal to any new regiment." The untested additions brought Meade's strength up to 4,500 men, but no one knew how the new regiments would perform under fire.[30]

Meade put his troops in motion "immediately on receiving orders." His division crossed the Smithfield ravine, passed a burnt mill, and marched eight hundred yards downriver to Smithfield. Meade drew them into line south of the flooded gorge and arranged his command for the attack. Colonel William Sinclair's 1st Brigade formed in front of Smithfield. Colonel Albert L. Magilton's 2nd Brigade assembled a second line three hundred yards behind Sinclair's men. Meade kept his 3rd Brigade, under Brigadier General Conrad Feger Jackson, in column south of the other two brigades to protect his left flank. Several batteries rumbled across the ravine and parked between Sinclair's and Magilton's lines. Meade's division formed behind the Bowling Green Road, taking cover beneath a ridge topped by the highway. Meade was concerned about cover because the fog was burning off.[31]

Meade's brigade commanders formed a paradoxical cortege. Their troops had earned high praise under Reynolds, Meade, Truman Seymour, and Edward O. C. Ord, but now the latest brigadiers appeared to be unexceptional or indifferent leaders. Only one brigade had a general officer. General C. Feger Jackson elicited the strongest feelings—not in the army but at home—for being, incongruously, a member of the Society of Friends. His patriotism, penchant for adventure, or both, exceeded his conscientious objection to military service. Meade relied on him, but offered little acclaim for his abilities. Colonels commanded the other two brigades. William Sinclair had taken command of the 1st Brigade just a few weeks before the battle. Albert L. Magilton, a ruddy-faced classmate of Stonewall Jackson's from West Point, without the comparable rank, had assumed charge of the 2nd Brigade a month before Fredericksburg. Their lack of experience would play a crucial role in the upcoming assault. The strength of the division lay in the seasoned regimental commanders and the drive of the division head. Since Magilton's and Sinclair's brigades had suffered the most damaging losses over the past year, Meade gave each of them a new regiment to boost their numbers. Sinclair took Colonel Chapman Biddle's 121st Pennsylvania, and Magilton commanded Colonel Robert P. Cummins' 142nd Pennsylvania.[32]

General John Gibbon's division rolled into position on Meade's right. Gibbon aligned his command behind the Bowling Green Road, with his three brigades stacked one behind the other. Gibbon's command totaled 4,000 men, a little smaller than Meade's reinforced division. Gibbon placed Brigadier General Nelson Taylor, his most experienced brigade commander, in the front line. Behind Taylor came Colonel Peter Lyle's brigade and Colonel Adrian Root's brigade.[33]

Gibbon's division had new commanders from top to bottom. Gibbon himself had been with the division for only a month. Two of his three brigade leaders had even less experience. None of Gibbon's subalterns were professionally trained for military service, though Gibbon elevated Peter Lyle and Adrian Root over the objections of more senior colonels because they had some militia experience. Gibbon rearranged his regiments so that his chosen commanders had seniority in their respective brigades, which left the disaffected commanders to resign or mope in General Taylor's brigade. Taylor owed his rank largely to his political connections, which extended from Connecticut to California. Gibbon would have to rely on his iron discipline to meld the unit to his satisfaction.[34]

Abner Doubleday's division followed Meade's across the Smithfield ravine and passed farther south to protect Meade's left flank. He formed his troops at a right angle to Meade's and anchored his left on the river. Facing south,

Doubleday's four brigades stood from left to right under Brigadier General Solomon Meredith and Colonels William F. Rogers, James Gavins, and Walter Phelps, Jr. Meredith's Iron Brigade wore distinctive black Hardee hats to set them apart from the rest of the army. They eventually became as renowned as the Confederate Stonewall Brigade.[35]

William F. Smith's Sixth Corps protected the First Corps's right flank, but from a purely defensive posture. Smith nominally guarded Gibbon's flank against a turning movement, but he emphasized security for the bridgehead first. Franklin also worried about the river behind him and the three tiny bridges that provided his only means of escape. His fear underscored the belief that Reynolds' assault was already doomed to failure. Smith's large corps formed the vital safety net to keep Reynolds' line of retreat open, as per Burnside's instructions. Smith was also the only deterrent to keep the Confederates from overrunning the entire left wing with a counterattack. Despite Franklin's caution, Smith's Sixth Corps might have been inadequate to save the bridgehead if Reynolds' corps met disaster.[36]

Smith kept the line he had on December 12, with William T. H. Brooks and Albion P. Howe holding both sides of Deep Run and John Newton's division lying in reserve. Brooks' and Howe's divisions stacked their brigades one behind the other like Gibbon's command.[37]

Brooks' and Howe's lead brigades massed on the Bowling Green Road while skirmishers roamed in front. A narrow ridge shielded most of the Sixth Corps from direct fire. Only pickets ventured past the rise. The ridge, however, obstructed the Sixth's Corps's view of Reynolds' attack and negated much of its support. Smith worried about the ridge, but Deep Run concerned him more. The stream flowed through a wide ravine that split his forces in two. Smith did not want to advance too far from the Bowling Green Road lest he complicate his communications between the two divisions, especially since the pickets of both armies began to heat up around the Deep Run cut. A Yankee picket stationed by the stream wrote that skirmishers were trading bullets—"little lead fellows"—that swarmed through the air "like so many bumble bees." Even before Meade commenced his assault, Brigadier General Francis L. Vinton of Howe's division fell wounded while examining the skirmish line. Surgeons found the ball lodged in his abdomen and extracted it through his back.[38]

The First Corps paid little attention to the skirmish fire as it prepared to advance. Meade's and Gibbon's divisions stood one hundred yards behind the Bowling Green Road. Meade's Pennsylvania Reserves halted and unslung their knapsacks and excess gear. Gibbon's men kept their equipment with them. As the Reserves piled their gear, Reynolds conferred briefly with Meade and Gibbon. The First Corps commander and Meade rode across the Bowling Green thoroughfare and reconnoitered the Confederate defenses. Ditches topped with dense cedars flanked the highway, making it difficult to cross. It also hid most of the field from view. Reynolds and his subordinates studied the open plain that ran from the Bowling Green Road to the RF&P Railroad, a thousand yards away. Beyond the tracks the Confederates held a wooded ridge. The field of attack appeared to be flat and unobstructed, but unbeknownst to Reynolds, it held several small ridges, which strung across their front from north to south. Unusual Virginia "ditch-fences," or irrigation ditches, sliced across the fields, some of them four or five feet deep. Reynolds informed Meade that a dirt road ran along the spine of the wooded heights, connecting Longstreet's and Jackson's lines. Burnside had learned of the "Military Road" and the Confederate efforts to improve it from a recently captured contraband. Meade's primary objective was to cut the road and sever the Confederate communications. The two generals fixed on a coppice that jutted toward them in a thin belt. Meade proposed to guide his advance by the timber, and Reynolds agreed. The corps commander would precede the assault with an artillery barrage to soften the Rebel defenses. Once the cannon disrupted Jackson's line, Meade could storm the heights. Meade returned to his division, while Reynolds readied the artillery.[39]

Before he could advance, George Meade ordered Sinclair's brigade to clear the cedar hedges from the Bowling Green Road. Pennsylvania soldiers hacked down the bushes and stacked them in the ditches so artillery could cross the road and enter the field. William Sinclair forwarded the 6th Pennsylvania Reserves to serve as skirmishers. They dashed into the plain and opened a sputtering fire at their Southern counterparts. Major Wellington H. Ent's 6th Reserves allowed Sinclair's pioneers to finish filling the ditches without difficulty. The 13th Massachusetts acted as skirmishers on the right for Gibbon's division. Sinclair's brigade entered the field and so did Taylor's troops. C. Feger Jackson's Federal brigade kept pace with Sinclair, filing across the road in column. Three batteries trotted over the Bowling Green Road and set up behind Sinclair's line. Magilton's brigade followed the artillery, halting in the depressed roadbed.[40]

George Meade met briefly with Gibbon when he noticed Sinclair's troops march into the field. "Good God!" he allegedly blustered. "How came that brigade out here?!" Bystanders noted that Meade flew into a rage, incensed that his infantry had exposed themselves prematurely to the watching enemy. Meade stopped Sinclair three hundred yards beyond the road. Jackson's brigade halted on Sinclair's mark. Magilton idled near the road. Meade's operation had hit a snag before it had fairly begun. The general had little time to fulminate because the time approached 10:00 A.M. and a cannon boomed far to the left.[41]

Meanwhile, Gibbon had no qualms advancing Brigadier General Nelson Taylor's brigade on line with Sinclair's command. Taylor stopped 300 yards from the road with Lyle's brigade 100 yards behind him. Root's brigade formed a third line 100 yards behind Lyle, near the road. Lyle's and Root's brigades aligned parallel to the Bowling Green Road, but Taylor's command was slightly askew, with its left pushed ahead. The left regiments took advantage of one of the subtle wrinkles in the field for cover. Taylor seemed unconcerned and did not bother to adjust his line. John Gibbon left his brigades to take their cue from Meade's actions while he brought up more artillery to cover his front. Barking orders at his battery commanders, he was interrupted by a sudden report of a cannon downriver.[42]

Jeb Stuart's Confederate cavalry had crowded the Union picket line since dawn. Skirmishers attacked Meade's troops at Smithfield, causing the 13th Reserves—known as the Pennsylvania Bucktails for their sharpshooter prowess and their aggrandized headgear—to call for help. Several regiments responded and drove the Rebels back. Stuart and his lieutenants used these forays to study the terrain around the Yankee flank. Major John Pelham, the popular head of Stuart's horse artillery, found an ideal place to put a cannon squarely on the enemy's flank. He begged Stuart to let him try. Stuart approved and Pelham bounded down the road between Hamilton's Crossing and the Bowling Green Road, towing a 12-pounder Napoleon from Captain Mathis Henry's horse battery.[43]

Stuart left Lee and Jackson on Prospect Hill to join Pelham on his excursion. The cannon crew trotted down the lane to the Bowling Green Road (ironically where Burnside intended Franklin to march his main force), and Pelham ordered them to unlimber in the southwest corner of the intersection. "We came to a cross hedge row, of cedar," reminisced George W. Shreve of the gun crew, "behind which we noiselessly formed 'In Battery.'" Captain Henry placed the piece just behind W. H. F. Lee's cavalry pickets.[44]

Pelham examined the ground once more while Meade's division moved to Smithfield in force. The Southern artillerist positioned his cannon deliber-

ately on lower ground than Meade's troops at Smithfield. The mist had
begun to burn off, but the last wisps of fog clung to the bottoms where Pelham secreted his Napoleon. Cedars framed the intersection and helped conceal the Confederates. Pelham cleverly selected an unlikely position in the
bottom of a shallow basin to mask his gun and complete his surprise as unsuspecting Yankees exposed their flank on the rise above him.[45]

Pelham's artillerists waited anxiously for orders. Occasionally, some curious gunner would peer through the hedges to catch a glimpse of what one
called "a grand spectacle of marshaled soldiery." Meade's men halted four
hundred yards away, and the Confederates watched them stamp their feet for
warmth and listened to the Yankee commanders bellow orders. "We could
hear the Federal infantry," recalled an artilleryman, "distinguishing a medley
of voices." Pelham returned, satisfied that the Unionists knew nothing of his
presence. He gave the command to fire and his lone Napoleon broke the
morning calm, resonating down the Rappahannock River valley at 10:00
A.M.[46]

The Northerners recoiled in surprise, and Captain Henry's artillerists continued to shell the dumbfounded bluecoats as fast as they could load. Confusion marred the alignment of the densely packed Yankees. Pelham's men
imagined that they saw the Union soldiers fall down paralyzed with fear. Moments later, Northern artillery wheeled in front and challenged the Confederates. By Pelham's third round, the Union guns returned the fire. Yankee
batteries responded from Meade's front and from Stafford Heights across the
river. Meade's light artillery answered first, rumbling in front of Sinclair's and
Jackson's brigades. Captain Gustavus A. DeRussy's three batteries heard the
commotion and opened a menacing crossfire with Meade's pieces.[47]

Pelham clung to the low ground. The noise was deafening and the explosions unnerving, but Pelham suffered no real harm. His small gun and crew
proved too elusive for the Yankees to hit. Hidden in the mist and masked by
hedges, Pelham watched the Union light batteries fire over his head. DeRussy's cannon also fired long from a right angle to Meade's guns. The Union
gunners on Stafford Heights found it problematic to depress their heavy ordnance enough to strike a target so near the river as Pelham. Union shells thus
criss-crossed over the Confederates' heads, but few landed near the mark.[48]

Pelham pressed Henry's gunners to fire faster as he became both calculat-
ing and impassioned by their success. A member of the Stuart Horse Artillery
recalled that Pelham had the unique ability to be "dashing and at the same
time cautious." Stuart's chief of artillery ignored the retaliatory shellfire and

focused on the enemy's prostrate infantry. Lee and Jackson observed the fight from Prospect Hill. A. P. Hill joined them and together they admired Pelham's pluck. Lee spoke at one point, "It is glorious to see such courage in one so young." Conscious that he needed to be at his command post, Lee reluctantly left Prospect Hill before he knew the outcome of the singular battle.[49]

Thirty minutes into the contest, Pelham ordered his men to cease firing and lie down. Rooney Lee's cavalry had seen some activity in the Union lines and moved forward to investigate. Stuart feared the Federals might try to capture Pelham's cannon. Lee's troopers crept cautiously ahead, using the hedgerows along the Bowling Green Road for cover.[50]

The Federals, for their part, wondered what had hit them. The Pennsylvania Reserves halted in the field just as the sun broke through and the ground began to thaw. Batteries jangled ahead when one of Magilton's soldiers noted: "A cannon boomed out on our left, at close range, seemingly on the Bowling Green road, a shot whizzed high in the air passing over our heads from left to right along the line. Naturally supposing, from the position, 'twas one of our own batteries. We thought our gunners had had too much 'commissary' this morning and so remarked."[51]

Before their chuckles subsided, a second and then a third round struck closer, abruptly ending the mirthful speculation. The men then knew they were the target of a very purposeful fire from an enemy located on their flank.

C. Feger Jackson reacted swiftly, ordering his column into line by the left face. The brigade turned toward Pelham and connected with Sinclair's line at a right angle, forming a hinged line resembling the letter L. Meade's brigades lay down to avoid the fire. "The order was given 'down' when from the force of the custom we fell forward face downward," wrote one of Meade's veterans. A member of the 7th Reserves recalled lying in the muddy field, "pressing down hard, . . . and flattening out that I might not interfere with any of the flying iron." Officers alone remained mounted or on foot. The Federals suffered a number of casualties, including John A. Camp of the 11th Reserves, who was killed at the outset. Meade happened upon his mutilated body and "thru some queer fancy" ordered it buried at once. Soldiers dug a shallow grave with bayonets and covered Camp with mud.[52]

Meade's batteries, already passing Sinclair's brigade when the fire broke out, quickly trained their guns on the general area of Pelham's cannonade. Meade placed Lieutenant John G. Simpson's Battery A, 1st Pennsylvania Light Artillery, in front of Jackson's brigade. Captain James A. Cooper's Battery B, 1st Pennsylvania Light Artillery, and Captain Dunbar R. Ransom's Battery C, 5th U.S. Artillery, took position on a slight knoll near the hinge in Sinclair and Jackson's line. All three batteries rattled the hedges where Pelham lay hidden.[53]

The deeper tones of Gustavus DeRussy's heavy field guns echoed from Stafford Heights. DeRussy had sent several 20-pounder Parrotts downriver to discourage turning movements like Pelham's. DeRussy's close proximity to the Rebels embarrassed his efforts. He simply could not strike a target so close to his huge Parrotts. "Both their Field Batteries at close range, and also from their big guns on the north bank of the river shot too high," noted a Confederate, "and so we escaped." Six Union batteries opened on Pelham, and "the rain of shot and shell . . . was terrific." Yet Pelham not only eluded them, he punished them. Simpson's Pennsylvania battery lost a gun when a direct hit smashed its carriage. Pelham scored another hit on a limber chest.[54]

Doubleday's division hurriedly extended C. Feger Jackson's line from the road to the river while the Union artillery wrangled with Pelham. Shortly thereafter, Northern general Jackson spotted Stuart's cavalry approaching through the hedgerows along the Bowling Green Road. He informed Doubleday of the movement, and sent two companies of the 10th Reserves to investigate. Doubleday advanced his skirmish line in support. Jackson's and Doubleday's infantry met the dismounted cavalry, probably the 13th Virginia Cavalry, which guarded Rooney Lee's right flank. A burst of infantry rifles drowned out the lighter pop of carbines wielded by the cavalry, and the Confederates withdrew. Heavy riding boots and mud hampered Lee's retreat, but the Federals halted and allowed the Rebels to retire to a ravine beside Pelham's gun.[55]

Doubleday noted the wooded ravine and directed several batteries to fire on it. Captain George A. Gerrish's 1st Battery, New Hampshire Light Artillery, went into action on Doubleday's left, while Lieutenant James Stewart's Battery B, 4th U.S. Artillery, unlimbered on the right. The Union batteries focused their fire exclusively on the woods. Meade's guns could engage Pelham, but Doubleday wanted Rooney Lee's cavalry driven away. Union cannon combed the woods thoroughly before Doubleday advanced his skirmishers to clear the area. Lieutenant Colonel Samuel R. Beardsley led Doubleday's advance. The 24th New York and 2nd U.S. Sharpshooters forced the Confederates out of the forest. The Iron Brigade followed in close support. The 7th Wisconsin soldiers and the untried 24th Michigan led the way, seconded by the 2nd Wisconsin and 19th Indiana. The 6th Wisconsin formed a third line. The black-hatted Wisconsin soldiers and Michiganders helped flush the Rebels from the woods. Doubleday beamed with delight as he pointed them out to General Reynolds. The division commander also praised Beardsley's skirmishers for their effort.[56]

Stuart's Confederates abandoned the woods, leaving John Pelham to fend for himself. The forest ravines made pursuit difficult for the Yankees. But the gorges also trapped some of the Rebels before they could escape. Beardsley netted nine prisoners and five mounts, while killing another seven or eight horses. The skirmish commander personally captured a Southern lieutenant and kept his pistol as a prize. Even Colonel Charles Wainwright captured some prisoners, a novelty for an artilleryman. Once Meredith's Iron Brigade secured the woods, Doubleday advanced Captain John W. Wolcott's wayward Battery A, Maryland Light Artillery. Wolcott's artillery was a Sixth Corps unit that somehow had attached itself to Doubleday's division. Presumably Wainwright had sanctioned this, since he was there. Doubleday placed the battery on Pelham's flank. The Marylanders opened on the Rebels at a scant couple of hundred yards.[57]

Pelham had withheld his fire while Rooney Lee and Doubleday battled in front, even though the Federal guns had found his range. Once Lee's cavalry fell back, Doubleday's guns joined the fight against Pelham. The Federals intensified their barrage. Jeb Stuart sent a courier to ask Pelham "how he was getting on." The orderly found the major sitting on his horse with one leg draped over the saddle, quietly giving orders. Pelham replied cheerfully, "Go back and tell General Stuart [that] I am doing first rate." In actuality, Pelham thought he should retire, but Captain Mathis W. Henry begged to stay a while longer. The Rebel major yielded, keeping up the fight by shifting his position. The cannon crew fired, changed position, and fired again. Constant motion made it difficult for the Federals to pin them down. At the same time, Pelham showered the Federal skirmishers with fire to keep them back. "Part of the time we were under a terrific fire of grape and canister," complained Colonel Samuel Beardsley, "but by lying down we only had one man wounded." Many Yankees had close calls. Canister balls knocked rifles out of several soldiers' hands. A round even tore the skirt off Colonel Beardsley's overcoat and two other shells buried him in mud. Pelham's pointed salvos kept the Yankees at a respectful distance.[58]

Stuart watched Pelham's duel from Hamilton's Crossing. Encouraged by Pelham's courageous stand, the cavalry leader ordered Captain John Esten Cooke to add another gun to the fight. The staff officer hurried a Blakely rifle down the road to Pelham. Cooke halted the crew half way between Pelham's location and Hamilton's Crossing and brought his rifle into position. The captain hoped to converge his fire with Pelham's while at the same time forcing the Yankees to disperse their fire over a wider range. Cooke unfortunately selected a dangerous spot to unlimber. The Blakely fired only once before Wolcott's Maryland battery made a direct hit on its first try. The Union shot dismantled the Blakely and killed several of the crew. Once again, Pelham fought alone.[59]

Union fire started to tell on Pelham after a while. Captain Henry's team suffered several casualties, and eventually even Pelham had to help man the gun. Ammunition began to run low, and the Confederates could not expect to hold much longer. Stuart allegedly sent a couple of orders inviting Pelham to disengage. When the third order arrived at 11:00 A.M., Pelham and Henry obeyed. They limbered their Napoleon and fell back to Hamilton's Crossing.[60]

Major Pelham's gunners had attacked an entire wing of the Union army single-handedly and opened the Battle of Fredericksburg. Alone, they had endured a storm of shot and shell for close to an hour. The chief of Stuart's horse artillery earned the praises of both Lee and Jackson. Lee glorified the artillerist as "the gallant Pelham" in his official report. Captain Mathis Henry seemed to be overlooked in the accolades. According to a brother officer, Henry was "very disappointed" by the oversight. Pelham subsequently died in March 1863 without heralding Henry's heroics, though "he freely gave credit to Henry" if anyone bothered to ask. John Cheves Haskell, a South Carolina artillery officer, declared at the turn of the century, "It was he [Henry] who was entitled to the credit given Pelham at Fredericksburg for holding a section of the horse artillery for a long time under the fire of a large number of the enemy's guns."[61]

Lieutenant R. Channing Price, of Jeb Stuart's staff, noted that Lee was pleased, but not overly so, about Pelham's feat. Price overheard Lee express his "warm admiration" for the artillery major, but added "that the young major general (alluding to Gen. Stuart) had opened on them too soon." Stuart and Pelham had developed a superb plan, but they had sprung it prematurely. Lee wished they had waited until Meade's Federals had come a little closer so Jackson's artillery could have trapped them in a more destructive crossfire.[62]

Despite using only a single gun, Pelham had upset the Federals' plans and forced them to divulge their strength before they were ready. His cannon engaged Reynolds' full complement of artillery and delayed Meade's attack for an hour. Stonewall Jackson learned the extent of the Northern buildup in front and understood their intentions without having to feel their sting. Pelham also provided Jackson with time to prepare for the attack. Ambrose Burnside, on the other hand, assumed the barrage to the south heralded Franklin's assault and started making preparations to engage Sumner's Right Grand Division at Fredericksburg. The time approached 11:00 A.M., and events began to unfold rapidly.

John F. Reynolds readjusted his lines in the aftermath of Pelham's sortie. He hurried Doubleday's division to the intersection that the Rebels had abandoned. Meredith's Iron Brigade anchored his left on the river. Rogers' brigade joined his right. Phelps' and Gavins' brigades extended the line to the Bowling Green Road. Doubleday wrapped his line around the intersection, closely watching the Confederates south and west of the crossroads. Concerned about guarding the left flank of the Army of the Potomac, the division commander assumed a defensive posture from which he was loath to move.[63]

When Doubleday took his position, he uncovered George Meade's left flank. Meade adjusted his line by wheeling C. Feger Jackson's brigade into the gap. Pivoting on Sinclair's brigade, Jackson's troops extended Sinclair's line. Ransom's battery swung around on the knoll between Sinclair's and Jackson's brigades. He now faced toward Prospect Hill one thousand yards away. Cooper's battery also turned and shifted to the right. Meade planted Captain Frank P. Amsden's Battery G, 1st Pennsylvania Light Artillery, between them.[64]

Colonel Charles S. Wainwright, chief of the First Corps artillery, galloped to the lower pontoon crossing to hurry the rest of Reynolds' guns. Wainwright started the cannon forward and returned to the Bowling Green Road with Captain James A. Hall's 2nd Battery, Maine Light Artillery. The artillery chief placed Hall's battery in a corn stubble field on the left of Gibbon's division. It went into battery behind the rise protecting Taylor's brigade. Gibbon shifted Adrian Root's brigade to the left to support the battery. Captain James Thompson's Pennsylvania battery came forward later and took position on Gibbon's right. All of Wainwright's artillery trained on Stonewall Jackson's positions, with the exception of Simpson's battery. Simpson's three guns (having lost one to Pelham) faced south to guard against Pelham's return.[65]

When all was ready, Charles Wainwright commenced shelling the Confederate heights. The colonel divided the high ground into five sectors and instructed his batteries to target specific zones. A sudden roar echoed across the plain; gun carriages recoiled heavily and missiles shrieked into the Confederate lines. John Reynolds, an old artillerist himself, flitted between the batteries, admiring their fire. He even offered advice to Cooper's battery to improve its fire. The corps commander stuck close to the artillery for the rest of the day, even at the expense of more important duties.[66]

Union batteries across the river lent their support. Notified by telegraph from Franklin's headquarters, DeRussy added four batteries to the bombardment. Captain Elijah D. Taft's 5th New York Battery; Captain Andrew Cowan's 1st New York Battery, Lieutenant Bernhard Wever's Battery C, 1st New York Light Artillery, and Lieutenant R. Bruce Ricketts' Battery F, 1st Pennsylvania Light Artillery, combined for ten 3-inch rifles and eight 10-pounder Parrotts. DeRussy diminished their effectiveness by limiting them to only visible targets. With a murky atmosphere, and Stafford Heights looming two thousand yards from the action, DeRussy's gunners struggled to identify positive targets. The woods concealed Jackson's Confederates and made shooting a guessing game for the closest guns. The forest thoroughly mystified DeRussy's crews. Despite DeRussy's restrictions, most of his batteries blanketed the Confederate hills with a heavy barrage. On the other side of the Rappahannock, Wainwright gauged his fire, hoping he could destroy the Rebel artillery before Meade went forward. Reynolds relied on Wainwright to determine when the Confederates were crippled enough for the infantry to proceed.[67]

Federal artillery pounded the hills without provoking a response. Each cannon fired once every three minutes, according to a new directive from the army chief of artillery, Henry Hunt. Recoiling guns etched deep ruts in the soft, thawing sod. Mud coated the pieces and caked between the wheel spokes. Cannon trails glided through the liquid glaze only to shudder harshly against the frozen, rock-like ground underneath. Trails and axles snapped and splintered from the shock. Artillerists waded back and forth in their furrows, firing into the woods, and cursing the mud underfoot. The Rebels "preserved an ominous silence," which concerned some of the Union officers and quite a few veterans in the ranks. Without the Southerners revealing their location, Wainwright could only guess where to concentrate his fire.[68]

Confederate gunners weathered the storm as best they could. Stonewall Jackson strictly forbade his batteries from engaging the enemy. He knew the Federals enjoyed a vast superiority in ordnance, with guns of better quality, caliber, and reliability than he had. The Confederate light artillery was no match for the heavier Union guns. Jackson chose to save his guns for the likely infantry assault to follow. Until the Yankees attacked, the Southerners lay low in the woods and prayed for revenge. The nearby infantrymen of Stonewall Jackson's corps empathized, believing the one-sided barrage to be the most unnerving part of the battle. The soldiers felt powerless under the daunting deluge of explosives.[69]

Casualties accumulated randomly along the Confederate line. Captain David Gregg McIntosh discovered that his "gun redoubts offered little protection." His artillerists abandoned the pits and hid behind trees. Many of their injuries stemmed from falling tree limbs clipped by incoming rounds. Soldiers in the reserve lines also fell prey to the shelling, and the reserve artillery stampeded when it came under fire. Wagons and limbers caused a frightful rout from Hamilton's Crossing before officers brought them to heel.[70]

At noon, Charles Wainwright scoured the hills for some sign of weakness. His batteries had pummeled the Confederate positions for close to an hour, but without resistance, Wainwright could only conjecture how effective his guns had been. The Federal artillery chief notified General Reynolds that he had done a thorough job. In actuality, the Federal guns had done very little. Most of their shells had ranged long, missing the front line and its artillery (much to the discomfort and annoyance of Stonewall Jackson's reserves). Unaware of this, Wainwright recommended Meade advance. Reynolds notified Gibbon of the pending move and went to see Meade personally. The generals studied the heights again and agreed with Wainwright's assessment. Stonewall Jackson's stratagem had worked. Reynolds dashed away to arrange for some artillery cover, and Meade roused his division from the sopping mud.[71]

Stiff-limbed and numb, soldiers stood up slowly and stretched for the first time in two hours. A bemused Pennsylvania Reserve recalled that everyone was covered with filth, making them look as "dingy and muddy as turtles." His only consolation was that the officers had also "lost their shining qualities." Sinclair's brigade formed behind the artillery with the 2nd Reserves on the left, the 1st Reserves on the right, and the rookie 121st Pennsylvania sandwiched in between. C. Feger Jackson's brigade closed ranks beside Sinclair's troops with the 11th Reserves likely on the right, followed by the 5th Reserves, 12th Reserves, and 10th Reserves. Jackson advanced Lieutenant Colonel Robert Anderson's 9th Reserves to join Major Wellington Ent's 6th Reserves on the skirmish line. Magilton's brigade dressed its line directly behind Sinclair's troops. The 7th Reserves anchored the left, with the 3rd, 4th, and 8th Reserves extending the line to the right. For unknown reasons, Magilton gave the 142nd Pennsylvania regiment the place of honor on the right.[72]

Meade's and Gibbon's divisions spanned a thousand yards of Reynolds' front. Close to 8,000 men prepared to attack, with both of the divisions ostensibly two brigades deep. Reynolds' artillery opened again, laying down a steady cover fire. Meade's Pennsylvania Reserves lurched forward, Sinclair and Jackson side by side, Magilton keeping three hundred yards behind. As Meade's first line came abreast of Gibbon's front, Nelson Taylor's brigade latched onto Sinclair's right. Colonel Peter Lyle's brigade marched a hundred paces behind Taylor.[73]

Doubleday's command did not move. The Union general feared leaving the army's flank unprotected, so he held onto the intersection that Pelham had abandoned. Doubleday had overextended his line and could not cover Meade's flank once the Pennsylvania Reserves left the Bowling Green Road. Unable to guard both Meade's flank and the army's, Doubleday elected to protect the intersection from any more Rebel incursions. He watched the Confederates demonstrating south of Massaponax Creek and probably felt the effect of Hardaway's dreaded Whitworth rifle. Solomon Meredith added to Doubleday's worries by raising repeated alarms of attacks that never materialized. Doubleday notified Reynolds of his predicament and suggested that someone else should support Meade. Rather than halt the operation at the point of moving, Reynolds let Meade go ahead without anyone on his left. The First Corps commander begged Franklin's headquarters for another division to support Meade. The Left Grand Division leader immediately summoned one of Stoneman's Third Corps divisions from across the Rappahannock. At the same time, Bayard's cavalry brigade forwarded a regiment to Doubleday's assistance. The 1st Pennsylvania Cavalry buffered the flank. General Meredith, however, continued to howl about danger until he was arrested and his command given to Colonel Lysander Cutler of the 6th Wisconsin. Meade's new supports would take a while to arrive and all but missed the attack. As an unexpected benefit of Pelham's actions, the Confederates had neutralized Reynolds' largest division—6,000 strong—and practically halved the strength of Reynolds' force.[74]

Meade's and Gibbon's soldiers shuffled past Wainwright's batteries. The front line—C. Feger Jackson's, William Sinclair's, and Nelson Taylor's brigades—rolled over a slight rise and into a flattened hollow that extended to the RF&P Railroad. The front line descended into the muddy depression, followed by Magilton and Lyle. Wainwright's cannon shelled the woods ahead of them. Reynolds hovered near the batteries, alarmed to see several rounds explode prematurely over Meade's division. The corps commander halted all cover fire, afraid that it would cause more harm than good. Silence fell over the field except for the odd order and the steady tramp of 8,000 Northerners slogging through the muddy hollow.[75]

Confederate artillerists, once again at their posts, waited anxiously for the Yankees to draw closer. They gazed in fascination at the beauty and pageantry of the Federal corps arrayed for battle. "I could see fully half the whole Yankee army, reserves and all," wrote an excited youth in Jackson's command. "It was a grand sight seeing them come in[to] position." "We could see their guns and bayonets glittering in the sun," a breathless Tennessee soldier related, "oh! it looked *awful* and yet beautiful for it was the grandest sight I ever beheld." Another Confederate feared that the enemy's "greatly superior numbers and equipment gave promise of success to his advance." A comrade agreed: "it seemed that the host would eat us up." A less intimidated Rebel, however, came to a different conclusion. He wrote, "I felt sorry for those poor Yankee soldiers as they marched into the very jaws of death."[76]

Confederate batteries remained menacingly quiet even as the Federals marched across the broad stretch of field. Bluecoats hoped the silence reflected success for Wainwright's thorough cannonade. Southerners bided their time under Stonewall Jackson's strict orders to let the Union army approach to an ideal killing range. R. Lindsay Walker, for instance, waited for the Yankees to come within eight hundred yards before he engaged. Walker's battery commanders had walked the field prior to the battle and measured distances to various landmarks. David McIntosh found a lone tree standing eight hundred yards in front of his battery. The gunners waited impatiently for Meade's division to pass the tree.[77]

Meade's Pennsylvania Reserves surged past the nondescript sapling, and suddenly the Confederate lines exploded with cannon fire. Shells deluged the stunned Federals, and smoke roiled off of the hill and rolled heavily into the plain. Walker's guns fired as fast as the gunners could load them. About the same time, Northerners spotted Captain John B. Brockenbrough's Confederate artillery on the right. "The Rebs brought out ten pieces and planted them on a knoll," noted one of Meade's men. "This was a bold move on their part." Brockenbrough's guns fired into Gibbon's advance. Greenlee Davidson also joined the fight, directing his weapons obliquely across Brockenbrough's right rear from the dismantled Bernard Cabins. John Pelham opened again on Meade's advancing left flank. Shuttling several guns down the road from Hamilton's Crossing, Pelham placed his horse artillery in the flat ground south of the road. The artillerist did not venture too far beyond Hamilton's

Crossing because of the proximity of Doubleday's division. A charging Pennsylvanian thought the "Artillery fighting was grand" to see, but he particularly detested Pelham's cannon because his "concealed battery on our left" struck with a devastating enfilade fire.[78]

The scenario that Lee had hoped for when Pelham engaged the first time had come to pass. Between the four artillery groups of Walker, Brockenbrough, Davidson, and Pelham, the Confederates had trapped the Federals in a massive crossfire that encompassed between forty and fifty-three cannon. A Northern participant reported, "The enemy are visible at all points except our rear." They struck with such precision that one Northerner accused the Confederates of planting surveyor's stakes in the field as range markers.[79]

Shells ripped through the packed ranks, and the attack faltered. A Confederate shell snapped the flagstaff of the 2nd Pennsylvania Reserves in two. One of Pelham's rounds wiped out seven members of the 121st Pennsylvania in a single flash. Another shot tore a soldier in two. Gibbon quickly ordered his troops to lie down before they became too disorganized. Meade opted to retire his division one hundred yards behind his line of batteries. Brigade commanders placed the men under cover, and the muddy "turtles" sprawled again on the sloppy ground. Surprised Confederates marveled at the ease with which they had repulsed the Union attack. Walker's gunners grinned, hooted, and "were wild with joy," according to David McIntosh. "Oh! it did me good," gibed a South Carolina cannoneer, "to see the rascals run." They had unraveled all of Union colonel Charles Wainwright's work in a brief flash of fire.[80]

Meade and Gibbon waved the Federal artillery back into action. Time approached noon—five hours past dawn—and Reynolds' assault had yet to materialize. The would-be attackers returned to the first stage of their plan and commenced bombarding the heights again. Wainwright, however, had gained one advantage since the first barrage—the Confederates had unmasked their batteries and revealed their positions.

The First Corps artillery chief, shadowed by Meade and Gibbon, and presumably Reynolds, arranged the artillery for another bombardment. Hall's 2nd Maine Battery took a forward position on the left flank of Taylor's brigade, where it confronted Brockenbrough's Rebel artillery at short range. Thompson's Pennsylvania battery, and some of the Sixth Corps artillery, lent their support. Meade's batteries fixed their fire on Walker's Prospect Hill guns, while Simpson's battery engaged Pelham's horse artillery. Intense shelling erupted on both sides as the antagonists grappled for dominance of the field. A startled soldier noted that "the air was resonant with the savage music of shells and solid shot." A nearby Pennsylvania Reserve wrote, "cannon balls were flying over and among us all the time, killing men and horses and tearing up the ground all around us." The adjutant of the 2nd Reserves, Evan M. Woodward, recalled that many of the missiles "plowed up the earth in deep furrows, or went howling and bursting over our heads, filling the air with iron hail and sulphur." Some of the shots landed among the Pennsylvania Reserves and kicked up spigots of mud "higher than the tallest tree," while others bounded through the ranks like grotesque rubber balls.[81]

Wainwright had the customary Federal advantage of better, more reliable, and more numerous guns, but the Confederates had the calculated advantage of commanding ground. Stonewall Jackson exploited the lay of the land to unleash a plunging fire, while Pelham opened a telling enfilading fire. James Hall's Maine battery felt the immediate sting of the crossfire. He complained that the Southerners hit him from his right front (Brockenbrough) and his left (Pelham) at the same time. Hall wanted to strike Pelham first, since he posed the greatest threat, but Reynolds refused to let him. The general still feared shooting over the intervening Union infantry. Reynolds insisted that Hall engage Brockenbrough's guns, because no bluecoats intervened between the batteries; unreliable shells would burst in the no man's land between the lines. Unfortunately, Gibbon's skirmishers, the 13th Massachusetts, ranged in front and occasionally caught a blast intended for the Rebels.[82]

Prospect Hill quickly became the center of the storm. R. Lindsay Walker's guns blazed away amid a swirling cacophony of explosions and shrieking metal. Shrapnel filled the air and ripped apart the gun emplacements. A Southern artillerist claimed, "The trees around our guns were literally torn to pieces and the ground plowed up." Colonel Walker had sent his artillery horses and ammunition chests to the woods for protection. Most of the Union shells missed the crest and sailed into the ravine where the animals were packed together. Cannonfire destroyed numerous horses. David McIntosh thought it was ironic that he had spared his prized mount from coming to the front only to have it disemboweled while he stood untouched on a gun pit. The excessive loss of horseflesh led many veterans to give Prospect Hill the name "Dead Horse Hill."[83]

Confederate artillerymen, too, suffered their share of death and near misses. Some batteries stopped firing as frightened gunners fled for cover. Even Willie Pegram's vaunted Purcell Artillery—renowned for its fearlessness—suddenly buckled under the pressure. Battery men abandoned their pieces and scurried into the trees, despite Pegram's plaintive entreaties. The chagrined captain embarrassed his men back to work by draping himself in the colors and pacing angrily between the silent guns. A nearby artillerist confessed, "It was a time to test a man's courage." Pegram's men paid for their moral lapse. Later, when Jackson replaced Walker's guns, the captain insisted that his battery stay behind and redeem itself.[84]

The Pee Dee Artillery endured the same fire as Pegram's battery. One cannoneer wrote that evening that he considered Fredericksburg to be "the hottest fight I have ever heard of." He told his father that "all the other fights crowded into one would hardly make anything to be compared to today's fight." Shells splashed through the watery mud and struck the frozen soil underneath, exploding lethal chunks of icy dirt into the air. Artillerymen had to dodge shell fragments and shrapnel-like soil as well. Mud splattered the gun crews. A South Carolinian complained that he was "several times covered with dirt." He cleaned mud from his eyes, ears, nose, and mouth. Other close calls knocked a wheel off a cannon and cleaved the head off a ramrod that a gunner was holding.[85]

Walker's batteries struggled to stay in the contest. McIntosh's Pee Dee Artillery lost two guns to direct hits. A shot killed Lieutenant James D. Ellett, commander of the section from Crenshaw's Battery. Another round killed Lieutenant Valentine J. Clutter of Marmaduke Johnson's Virginia battery. Colonel Walker concentrated most of his fire on the prone infantry lines of dingy blue, but heavy losses diverted some of his fire to the enemy artillery. Walker's surviving guns lacked the strength to disrupt Meade's foot soldiers or destroy their artillery. Dividing his fire out of necessity only exacerbated the problem. Walker later calculated that "in weight of metal they much exceeded us."[86]

Greenlee Davidson's cannon by the Bernard Cabins and John B. Brockenbrough's battalion beyond the railroad tracks also experienced a ravaging fire and severe losses. Davidson discovered too late that some of his batteries had useless ammunition. Statham's Battery fired numerous shots that simply would not detonate. Davidson thought the battery's efforts were futile and ordered its three guns to the rear. William Caskie's Hampden Artillery soon after lost one of its guns when the axle snapped on the ice beneath the mud. Defective ammunition and frozen ground deprived Davidson of four of his nine cannon. His fire diminished appreciably, and Brockenbrough's artillery later criticized Davidson for not protecting their vulnerable right flank.[87]

John Brockenbrough's guns at the same time suffered a smothering fire from several Union batteries and needed all the help they could get. A watching Northerner estimated that twenty pieces concentrated on Brockenbrough's command. A short time into the fight, the commander of Carpenter's Battery, Lieutenant George McKendree, reported that his ammunition failed to explode properly. Like Statham's Battery, its fire proved pointless and Brockenbrough ordered the battery withdrawn. McKendree disengaged two guns but retained one, which fought creditably, even exploding a limber in Hall's 2nd Maine Battery. Hall, however, returned the favor, leaving McKendree the worse for it. George Wooding's Battery lost two rifles to broken axles. Wooding also suffered a number of casualties at the hands of Gibbon's pesky skirmishers. The captain even dismounted to help man the remaining cannon. This act cost him his life as he fell with a mortal wound in his thigh. Like Wooding, Brockenbrough toiled with the guns, pitching in where needed. While he was sighting a piece, a shell burst overhead, catching the young battalion commander in the arm. The shrapnel ended John B. Brockenbrough's military career. Several artillerists assisted Brockenbrough to his horse and implored him to go to the rear. The captain steadfastly refused until the next ranking officer assumed command. The senior surviving officer was Lieutenant McKendree, who found Brockenbrough walking his horse behind the guns. The captain turned over command to the lieutenant and rode slowly to the hospital.[88]

Brockenbrough's battalion had lost a third of its guns, a limber, and numerous personnel before George McKendree took charge. The lieutenant did not hesitate to withdraw the battalion, leaving one of his crippled guns behind. McKendree rode to General A. P. Hill and explained the situation. Hill ordered him to place his remaining guns in the field to Greenlee Davidson's left rear. McKendree would protect Davidson's flank as the captain once had protected Brockenbrough's. The lieutenant's eight guns retired to their new position within the first half-hour of the artillery duel.[89]

Stapleton Crutchfield, Stonewall Jackson's chief of artillery, reacted swiftly to the losses in Brockenbrough's and Davidson's commands. He hurried five rifled pieces to the front under the boyish Captain Joseph W. Latimer. The captain took two rifles from his own Courtney (Virginia) Artillery and three from Lieutenant John E. Plater's Chesapeake (Maryland) Artillery. The guns rumbled past McKendree's battalion and went into battery on a rise to the left of Greenlee Davidson's guns. Like Davidson, Latimer placed his guns on the reverse slope for protection.[90]

Crutchfield busily fed other batteries into the battle. He used the reserve artillery at Hamilton's Crossing to fill holes in the artillery defenses. As he toiled to make good on the artillery's losses, Crutchfield searched for another way to take advantage of the Yankees. The colonel turned his attention to Pelham's enfilading fire. Despite the fact that Stuart's artillerist appeared to be the least engaged and the least demanding of help, Crutchfield ordered two of his batteries to Pelham's assistance. Captain Louis D'Aquin's Louisiana Guard Artillery and Captain Asher W. Garber's Staunton (Virginia) Artillery rumbled across the railroad tracks and out the Hamilton's Crossing road to join Pelham's horse artillery. Crutchfield encouraged Pelham to use the extra guns to shift the momentum of the fight away from Prospect Hill and Bernard's Cabins. The escalating fire from Pelham's command did not go unnoticed, and Union commanders responded with additional batteries to the left to keep the balance of fire in their favor.[91]

Union guns from Meade's and Gibbon's divisions held their own against the Confederate heights, but they had little support from the rest of the Left Grand Division. Doubleday's artillery quietly guarded its new position on Pelham's former location. DeRussy's guns remained hamstrung by the extreme range and the lack of positive targets. Smith's Sixth Corps had massed a grand battery of seven artillery units near Alfred Bernard's house. Other Sixth Corps batteries spread out north of Deep Run. But fire from Lee's center and left interdicted Smith's guns and diverted most of their attention to Hood's and Pickett's Confederates. The Federals suffered a terrible barrage for their trouble. "After a short time they got our exact distance," wrote a New Jersey man in Vinton's brigade, "then the shells burst in front and right over us." At one point, an artillerist in Snow's Maryland battery cried, "This won't do; they will kill us all." Relief came when the Federals slackened their fire and the Confederates shifted their attention elsewhere. The Sixth Corps refused to provoke another Rebel retaliation.[92]

Along the entire Union left, the artillery was trapped in a tight spot. They stood exposed on an open plain and battled Confederates on all sides. Northern cannon made easy targets when compared to the Rebels hidden in the wooded hills. Exacerbating the problem, black powder smoke choked the field, obscuring the view. Confederate smoke billowed off the hills and mingled in the dead air of the bottoms. Union commanders became desperate to clear the air so they could sight their weapons. Captains ordered some of their men to run around the cannon to disperse the smoke.[93]

When they could see, the sight was anything but encouraging. James A.

Hall maintained his composure as he chatted with several officers, including the brigade commander, Adrian Root. A Confederate shot from Carpenter's Battery interrupted their conversation when it bounded through the gathering and exploded one of Hall's limbers. The commander of the 2nd Maine Battery dismounted and personally sighted the nearest gun. When he ordered it fired, a shell shrieked across the sky, and the ensuing blast revealed the captain had blown up a limber. Hall, with calculated sang froid, resumed his conversation. General Gibbon admired the captain's coolness but quietly suggested that he should withdraw his remaining ammunition chests to safer ground.[94]

While Hall traded limbers with the Rebels, Captain Frank Amsden's battery suffered painful attrition. The Pennsylvania battery waded back and forth through deep mud and chunks of ice. Two of the cannon cracked their axles when they recoiled through the slush. Walker's Confederate artillery struck a third gun, which shivered the wheels and axle. Amsden feared the piece had been damaged and ordered it to the rear with the other two. The rest of the battery, seeing half of the guns withdrawn, assumed the whole unit was to retire. As the cannoneers hitched up their guns to leave, Captain Amsden tried to stop them. Before he could make himself heard, a Confederate shot toppled the captain's horse, trapping Amsden underneath. Amid the noise, smoke, and confusion, no one noticed him, and the battery disengaged. Amsden eventually wriggled free of his dead mount and chased down his battery on the Bowling Green Road. The artillery commander, uncertain of what to do, sought Colonel Wainwright for orders. He found General Reynolds instead, still flitting among the batteries. The general told him to replenish his ammunition and return to action. Amsden searched in vain for the ammunition train and never did resume his position.[95]

Lieutenant John G. Simpson's Battery A, 1st Pennsylvania Light Artillery, held the most treacherous position of Wainwright's guns. Simpson singlehandedly engaged Pelham's batteries on the road to Hamilton's Crossing. R. L. Walker's Confederates had a clear shot at Simpson's right flank and bedeviled it unmercifully. Wainwright called the position "a very ugly place with more or less shots coming from three directions." Simpson ignored the flank fire, as his Pennsylvania battery required all of its strength to cope with Pelham's command. When Crutchfield's batteries came to Pelham's assistance, Simpson had his hands full. He gladly accepted belated help from Doubleday's suddenly reanimated guns. The Pennsylvania cannoneers had been the victims of a terrible crossfire, and now they coalesced their fire with

Doubleday's to do the same to Pelham. Louis D'Aquin's Louisiana Guard Artillery lost a gun as soon as it engaged. Another shot killed the captain. Union ordnance hounded Asher Garber's Staunton Artillery as well, knocking one of its guns off its trunions and eviscerating the captain's horse. When Pelham seemed subdued, Simpson turned his Union battery to the west and opened fire on Walker's Confederates atop Prospect Hill.[96]

Simpson's and Doubleday's cannon stymied Pelham only temporarily. Convinced that John Pelham's position held the key to gaining the upper hand over the mighty Union artillery, Stapleton Crutchfield sent reinforcements to make good Pelham's losses. Lieutenant Archibald Graham hurried forward a 10-pounder Parrott from Captain William T. Poague's Rockbridge (Virginia) Artillery. Lieutenant James S. Utz led a pair of 3-inch rifles from Captain Benjamin H. Smith's 3rd Company, Richmond Howitzers. Pelham took the replacements and again pitched into Simpson's Pennsylvania battery. According to a Confederate artillerist, Pelham seemed rejuvenated, "like a boy playing ball." Simpson's Federal battery continued to battle Walker's guns on Prospect Hill, but shifted position several times to avoid Pelham's barrage. Simpson calculated that his battery lost eleven men and sixteen horses while maneuvering between Walker's and Pelham's fire. Rebel shells scarred and battered every gun and caisson in the battery. A member of the Union command reported that Simpson's losses at Fredericksburg "exceeded that of any other engagement, so far as men and horses were concerned."[97]

The Union First Corps commander, John F. Reynolds, saw the Southerners smothering Simpson's battery and determined to eradicate Pelham. With that purpose, the artillery duel shifted its intensity from the Confederate front to the Confederate right. Reynolds and Wainwright reinforced the Union left to get better leverage against Jeb Stuart's spry cannoneer. The First Corps general and his artillery chief shifted Doubleday's batteries so they could concentrate on Pelham's impromptu battalion. Wainwright placed Captain George A. Gerrish's 1st Battery, New Hampshire Light Artillery, on the Bowling Green Road to Doubleday's left front. The battery opened on the Rebels 1,100 yards away. Meanwhile, Reynolds moved Stewart's Battery B, 4th U.S., to the mouth of the road leading to Hamilton's Crossing.[98]

Confederate colonel Crutchfield countered by forwarding two more artillery sections to Pelham. Captain David Watson advanced two 10-pounder Parrotts and a small brass gun from the 2nd Company, Richmond Howitzers. Lieutenant Willis J. Dance followed Watson with a 3-inch rifle from the Powhatan (Virginia) Artillery. As the new sections entered the battle, they passed the remains of Lieutenant James S. Utz being carried to the rear. The commander of the 3rd Company, Richmond Howitzers, had been killed almost as soon as he joined the action. Watson and Dance reported directly to Jeb Stuart, who had joined Pelham during the bombardment. The cavalry chief directed Colonel Thomas L. Rosser to place the four guns north of the Hamilton's Crossing Road. Colonel Rosser, leader of the 5th Virginia Cavalry and one-time artillery officer, knew just where to put them.[99]

Rosser had Watson's and Dance's men fill in the ditches along the road so their cannon could enter the field. Watson's gunners charged into the plain, only a couple of hundred yards from Simpson's Pennsylvania battery. The surprised Richmond Howitzers hurried their guns into battery as the Federal guns wheeled around to greet them with solid shot. The closeness of the action unnerved a few of the combatants not used to fighting at such short range. One of Watson's cannoneers tried to impart an aura of fearlessness to the battery. He intended to draw his pipe from his mouth and casually spit. But the fire distracted the youth, causing him to pull off his cap and spit out his pipe instead! The Howitzers guffawed at his ludicrous mistake.[100]

Jeb Stuart and Tom Rosser reined their horses behind Watson's guns to observe the contest. A bullet wounded Rosser's horse, and another slapped Stuart's saddle, beside the general's leg. Stuart dismissed it with a chuckle. Rosser remounted and rode over to the Rockbridge Artillery to check on Graham's Parrott. Steven Dandridge, a member of the battery, hailed his friend Rosser and inquired aloud when Pelham would relieve them. Rosser smilingly jested that Pelham had ordered them to remain until Dandridge had been killed. In fact, the gun remained in action through the rest of the battle. They lost numerous personnel, though Dandridge survived. Pelham later complimented Graham's gun crew, stating that the Rockbridge Artillery men "stand killing better than any I know."[101]

Both sides intensified their efforts to control the area along the road to Hamilton's Crossing. Union captain George Gerrish's New Hampshire artillery lost thirteen men and one of its limbers. Among the fallen lay Captain Gerrish. The acting chief of Doubleday's artillery relinquished command to Captain John A. Reynolds and left the field. Wolcott's Maryland battery lost one of its guns, dismounted by a solid shot. Another round knocked a cannon tube off a carriage in Stewart's Battery B, 4th U.S. Artillery. James Stewart responded by directing the rest of his guns against Watson's Richmond Howitzers. David Watson's exposed battery worried Rosser, and he returned to find Pelham guiding its fire. The two officers stood together, watching the fight, while shell fragments gashed the ground around them. Caught between Simpson's and Stewart's fire, the Confederates found their position untenable. When one shell sliced through the battery and exploded an ammunition chest, the Southern artillerists broke and fled for the ditches on the Hamilton's Crossing Road. Tom Rosser and John Pelham led the dash, reaching the road before the cannoneers.[102]

Watson collected some volunteers and retrieved his two Parrotts, but he left the small brass gun behind because it was too difficult to recover under fire. Union skirmishers advanced to claim Watson's cannon, but Colonel Rosser's dismounted cavalry drove them back with a surprise volley. Jeb Stuart happened upon Watson's teams withdrawing the Parrotts without his orders. The general appeared nettled until Rosser assured him that the artillerists had behaved nobly and were compelled to retire. Stuart accepted the colonel's explanation and calmed down.[103]

The artillery battle raged for close to an hour, engaging fully half of the battlefield, and testing the mettle of the cannoneers on both sides. The artillerists suffered terrible losses as a result. But the truly afflicted were the infantrymen, North and South, who shared the gunners' ordeal because of their proximity to the dueling cannon. Artillerymen thought little of the danger, keeping busy, concentrating on their drill, and knowing the satisfaction of fighting back. Infantrymen, on the other hand, did not participate in the bombardment. They huddled close to the ground and tried to stay out of harm's way. The infantry had no means of protecting themselves against the rain of bursting shells that saturated their positions. Almost universally, foot soldiers dread this more than any other part of the battle. A Pennsylvania soldier explained, "to remain quiet under such a fire was more trying than active conflict." Unable to fight, they weathered the trial as best they could, and prayed to be spared.[104]

Confederate leaders near Walker's guns saw the demoralizing effect the barrage had on their infantrymen. Most of Archer's Brigade abandoned its shallow earthworks and took cover behind trees, stumps, and logs along the wooded hilltop. Four members of the 1st Tennessee, including Major Felix Buchanan, vied for the protection of a lone sapling. A Union shell plowed under the tree and exploded, wounding three of them. Major Buchanan received five shrapnel wounds in his head and collapsed in a bloody heap. Observers assumed that he was dead, but he survived this, and four other wounds during the war, to return home in 1865. A lieutenant in the 19th Georgia tried to comfort his company amid such spectacles. He told the men that the bombardment was mere "child's play, compared with the sequel to come." The promise that their ordeal would only get worse probably undermined what little confidence still existed in his company.[105]

General James Archer rode down the line to steady his brigade's resolve. In a show of bravado, the general made a point of ignoring the bursting projectiles and shrapnel. He had earned the nickname "the Little Gamecock" for his poise under fire. An admiring soldier called him "the very God of War, and every inch a soldier." Staff officers trailed Archer, cheering the soldiers and encouraging them to emulate the general. Frank Wootten, a member of A. P. Hill's staff, misplaced his general and latched onto Archer's retinue. The whole brigade watched Wootten "most gallantly cheering the troops," when a Union shell practically decapitated him. That stifled any fervor Archer had generated.[106]

Another figure rode among Archer's men during the bombardment. He did not demand their attention, but he commanded it nonetheless. At first glance, the soldiers failed to recognize the sparkling equestrian in the lieutenant general's garb as their esteemed leader, Stonewall Jackson. Many of the onlookers noted a quiet serenity about him as he reined his horse and surveyed the field. Captain Junius Kimble of the 7th Tennessee, also regally attired, recalled that Jackson "sat there undisturbed, calm, deliberate, but alert, and seemingly unconscious of danger," even though the air around him crackled with shrapnel. The captain further noted that Jackson's horse had assumed the same demeanor as its master, and may have fallen asleep "dozing under the music of the guns," as Kimble put it! Another Tennessean, William H. Moore, recalled that "the first time I ever saw old Stonewall was the morning of the Battle." Under the worst fire, Moore noticed that Jackson was "a noble looking fellow, never flinches from a shell or ball." The reckless bravery of Archer and the sublime presence of Jackson encouraged the men to take heart. Southerners came out of the woods and returned to their works. They suffered complacently while the cannon continued to roar for more than an hour.[107]

Across the way, Union soldiers cowered in the mud and weathered the same storm of shot and shell. One of Gibbon's men reminisced, "the shells flew pretty thick over us." Another soldier recalled, "Surely such troops . . . were fitted for nobler work than standing upon an open plain, exposed to fierce artillery fire, without ever being turned upon the enemy." A novice in the 16th Maine confessed, "The rebs have their shells nearer than I liked it. It made us lay as snug to the ground as we could." Mud added to the soldiers' misery. One of Meade's Reserves wrote that the cannonballs were "throwing mud and dirt all over us."[108]

The supine Pennsylvania Reserves lay in a particularly exposed position and found it as terrifying as the Rebels on the hill. A member of the 8th Reserves admitted struggling with "an indefinable feeling" over whether "to stand or run." Frank Holsinger reflected, "I know of no horrors so terrible as that period just preceding the shock of battle." Seemingly a target for every conceivable type of projectile, a Maine soldier complained that the Confederates hurled "old gun barrels, railroad iron, and anything handy" at him. Another professed that the Rebels "threw over a whole blacksmith shop, anvil and all." Meade waded through the muddy ranks reassuring his officers and calming the troops. Notorious for his temper, Meade exhibited unusual gentleness and compassion during the cannonade. The general smiled at Colonel William McCandless of the 2nd Reserves, and pointing to his shoulder straps, suggested, "A star this morning, William?" McCandless glowered at the Confederate positions, churning with smoke and fire, and answered, "More likely a wooden overcoat," making the outline of a coffin with his hands. As if on cue, a Confederate shot gutted the colonel's horse, leaving him on foot for the rest of the day.[109]

General Reynolds also offered encouragement as he rode along the First Corps line. He paused briefly to steady the 142nd Pennsylvania. The First Corps commander must have wondered at the green troops who not only behaved well under fire but actually jumped up and cheered when their sickly colonel, Robert Cummins, hobbled onto the battlefield to resume command of the regiment. Moments later, a Confederate shell tore the head off Lieutenant Colonel Alfred McCalmont's mount. Reynolds advised the colonel to withdraw his regiment to better cover. John Reynolds left Meade's division when he spotted the Third Corps enter the field. Brigadier General David Bell Birney's division had double-quicked from the pontoon crossing and Reynolds placed it behind the heavy embankments of the Bowling Green Road, directly in the rear of Meade's Pennsylvania Reserves. Some of the new arrivals had ventured into the field but Reynolds shooed them back to the road.[110]

While Meade slogged through mud, patting soldiers on the shoulder, Union artillery ranged over the Confederate heights searching for a decisive mark. The Yankees found it in a limber and a caisson parked behind McIntosh's Pee Dee Artillery. Shells exploded the ammunition in a ball of flame that sent shells soaring and bursting across the crown of Prospect Hill. The

Pennsylvania Reserves cheered as they realized the impact on their enemies: "this made them run and leave several of there [*sic*] cannons." Meade seized the initiative. He personally dashed down the line shouting for the Pennsylvanians to charge. Northerners dressed ranks feverishly and rolled forward to the attack. It was now 1:00 P.M., and Jackson's artillery could no longer resist the swarming Federals as it had an hour before. The Southern ordnance had sustained crippling losses in their duel with the Union guns. Jackson had lost one of his battalion commanders to wounds and another five battery commanders killed or wounded. More importantly, the Confederates had lost twelve guns: eight dismounted, three disengaged because of faulty ammunition, and one abandoned. Finally, the Confederate artillery tallied the loss of three limbers and a caisson blown up during the bombardment. Some of Walker's, Davidson's, and Pelham's guns continued to hold their positions, but they offered only feeble resistance after 1:00 P.M. McKendree's (formerly Brockenbrough's) guns had been battered, and Latimer's guns were too far north to challenge Meade's assault. Confederate guns had easily rebuffed Meade's first assault, but Stonewall Jackson would have to rely on his infantry to stop the Yankees now.[111]

The Union artillerists celebrated their success, knowing they had subdued the Rebels this time. Wainwright had no guesswork now. As Meade's men shuffled past the grimy Federal batteries, the guns fell silent and a smiling artillerist sang out, "Boys, we have done our duty. Now go and do yours."[112]

CHAPTER SEVEN

"A TERRIBLE SLAUGHTER IN OUR RANKS"

The Federal Breakthrough

Mud-pasted Federals drove through no man's land in what one called "the most gallant charge of the war." The division surged across the fields in perfect alignment. A participant recalled, "the old Reserves went forward as steady and with as good a line as I ever saw. . . . Every rank was dressed." Stretcher-bearers followed behind to gather the wounded while the lines closed mechanically, filling holes left by fallen soldiers and striding ahead. The Northern ranks dressed snugly shoulder to shoulder, making an impenetrable wall of bluecoats. A hare, frightened from its warren, dashed frantically up and down the line before it made its escape. The greatly impaired Southern artillery continued to shell the oncoming division, and Meade's Pennsylvanians instinctively shied away. The shortened flanks crowded the center into a dense mass of muddy blue. A member of Magilton's brigade remarked that he saw little difference in the weakened Confederate cannonade. He thought "hell itself had broke loose." A Confederate shell caught "portly" Captain William Stewart of the 11th Reserves in the chest and cartwheeled his body through the ranks. A 7th Reserves soldier believed the barrage was "even worse than standing in front of the famous cornfield at Antietam." The compacted lines became suffocating. When a Pennsylvania Reserve soldier got turned around accidentally, he could not right himself again and went into the assault backwards![1]

George Meade started Sinclair's and Jackson's brigades forward, and then he turned to hurry up Magilton's brigade. The general galloped through his artillery and noted that Sinclair seemingly had forgotten one of his regiments. The crusty commander accosted Captain Charles F. Taylor of the 13th Reserves (Bucktails) and wanted to know why he had not advanced with his brigade. Taylor replied that Sinclair had ordered him to stay and support the artillery. Meade overruled the order and sent the Bucktails to re-join Sinclair's brigade. The Bucktail regiment re-formed and "started on the double-quick to the right of the brigade." Taylor's line rolled ahead with Magilton's brigade close behind. The blue lines broke ranks to pass through the artillery, then they closed formation and swept ahead in the wake of Sinclair's brigade.[2]

Waves of Union attackers swarmed over the stubble fields and plunged through three disruptive ditches that etched across their front. A Pennsylvanian described the "earthen fence" as "four or five feet in depth, with the earth usually thrown up in a ridge on one bank." Northern infantrymen tumbled into these unexpected recesses and clambered out the other side. Alignments became confused, and Meade's brigades started to drift apart. Taylor's Bucktails rushed to join their brigade, but noticed a gap developing between Sinclair's and C. Feger Jackson's brigades. On his own initiative, Taylor redirected his regiment "by the left oblique" into the hole while the line continued to roll ahead intact.[3]

Southern infantry quietly watched the closing throng, waiting for the signal to open fire. Just as the Confederate artillery had a specific distance before it could open fire, the Rebel foot soldiers also had an ideal target range. Southern officers cautioned their men to "Hold your fire, boys, until the command is given, be sure you make every shot count." Archer's Brigade designated the RF&P Railroad as their landmark. When the Northerners set foot on the railbed, the brigade would commence firing. Confederate skirmishers from the 1st Tennessee must have known that their picket reserve stood at the very point where Archer's Brigade would direct its fire. The skirmishers, caught between the lines, saw the Yankees closing fast and prepared to get out of the way. Before the pickets abandoned the banked railroad, however, the Union line surprised everyone.[4]

Dashing toward the railroad, the Federals "involuntarily made a momentary halt." Union soldiers stopped just as the Tennessee skirmishers gave them "spirited" fusillade "just along and in front" of the railroad. Archer's Brigade watched "in breathless silence" as Meade's division dressed its line. "Suddenly the bugles sounded a yankee blast," remembered a Georgia officer, and "down came these long lines of muskets, and how the enemy poured into our ranks, volley after volley." Northerners blasted the railroad grade with buck and ball—a musket ball wrapped in a cartridge with three buckshot.[5]

The Yankee volleys threw the Confederates into turmoil. Consternation rippled through the Southern ranks atop Prospect Hill. Soldiers questioned whether they should return the fire or wait. Archer demurred for the moment, anxious to see what the Yankees did next. He may have delayed because his pickets still clung to the railroad in front. Captain Aaron T. Alexander, commander of the pickets, had temporarily halted Meade's attack just by his presence, but now he had to find a way to escape. The railroad bank provided some cover, but to retreat up the hill would expose his men in a crossfire from both sides. Unwilling to mire his command in the boggy woods to his left, Alexander opted to slide his troops south under cover of the railroad. The Rebels sidled out of the trap and re-entered the Confederate lines through Brockenbrough's Virginia brigade or Hays' Louisiana brigade. Alexander's men avoided a tough situation, but their move had profound implications for the course of the battle. The decision to avoid the marsh unintentionally deprived Gregg's Brigade of any warning about events in front. Maxcy Gregg continued to act as if the Confederates still had a presence in front of him.[6]

C. Feger Jackson's Federals inched closer to the railroad embankment, laying down a terrific fire on the Confederates they assumed were on the other side. Once Alexander's Tennessee skirmishers evacuated the position, the rest of the Southerners waited for the Yankees to swell across the bank. Finding the railroad clear of Rebels (some Northerners assumed this was Jackson's first line), the Yankees scrambled over the tracks in pursuit. General Archer shouted the order, "Fire!" and the command echoed down the line, followed by a stabbing sheet of flame, a jaw-snapping explosion, and an opaque cloud of black-powder smoke. A soldier in the 14th Tennessee stated summarily, "The work of death began." Minié balls sleeted through the throng of startled bluecoats, who pitched and fell across the railroad. Survivors dove into the ditches. A Virginian wrote, "The conflict at once began with a great fury." James H. Wood of the 37th Virginia recalled, "Musketry and artillery continued to play upon his ranks with withering effect." A member of Archer's command thought "the enemy were falling like hay before the mower's blast." Some of the Southerners forsook the protective earthworks to get better shot at the Federals. "Our boys [were] standing up," boasted a Tennessee veteran, "and shooting at them like we were shooting at squirrels."[7]

Jackson's Union brigade hid in the ditches lining the RF&P Railroad while their wounded writhed underfoot or overhead on top of the railbed. Their return fire crackled without strength or order, which encouraged the Confederates to redouble their efforts. A Confederate soldier noted that Archer's volleys "caused them to melt away as did the mist of the morning before the sun." A Pennsylvanian agreed that the Rebels had "the exact range of the position." Southern fire riddled and pocked the railroad ditch, "literally filling it with shot and shell." Quaker General C. Feger Jackson calmed his nervous men by spurring his large gray mount along the ditch and repeatedly urging his troops, "Rally men, rally right here." The Pennsylvania Reserves reorganized loosely along the railroad and opened a better-directed, "desultory fire" from their cover. Several Union regiments attempted to charge across the railroad, "loading and firing as we ran," recalled a member of the 11th Reserves. They met fresh salvos of gunfire, which blew them back behind the grade.[8]

Regiments of Pennsylvania Reserves became inextricably entangled behind the railroad. The ditches overflowed with the shambles of C. F. Jackson's brigade. The 9th Reserves had relinquished its skirmish duties and stepped aside to re-form moments before the gunfire erupted. Startled by the fusillade, the regiment took cover behind a low stone fence fifty yards short of the railroad. Lieutenant Colonel Robert Anderson, commander of the 9th Reserves, lost contact with the rest of the brigade to his right and had to watch Meade's left flank from afar. The rest of C. Feger Jackson's command hied for the shelter of a three-foot-deep furrow. The 10th Reserves did not see the 9th Reserves behind the stone fence and assumed it guarded the brigade's flank. The 12th Reserves sprawled next to the 10th Regiment, followed by the 5th and 11th Reserves. C. Feger Jackson's brigade extended its right to the edge of the woods that Meade used to guide his attack. Unknown to Jackson, a gap had developed between the 5th and 11th Reserves. The regiments had deviated from each other during the advance, and Captain Charles Taylor plugged the hole with his Bucktail regiment. Though Jackson's line appeared to be intact, the brigade actually had fractured into three parts. One part, the 9th Reserves, lay beyond immediate control of C. F. Jackson, and the 11th Reserves formed a third group to the right of the necessary but intrusive Bucktails.[9]

While C. F. Jackson's brigade battled along the railroad, Colonel William Sinclair's brigade had fallen behind. The 1st Brigade entered the landmark finger of woods and slashed its way through the tough underbrush to the railroad. Sinclair's men eventually reached the railroad, but they lost contact

with C. Feger Jackson's command and the Confederates. The Federals heard
the crash of musketry to the left, but the dense vegetation hid the action and
protected them from involvement. Sinclair re-formed his ragged brigade at
the railroad. General Meade may have been on hand to help. After a brief
pause, the brigade commander sent his skirmishers across the tracks. The 6th
Reserves disappeared into the marsh, and the rest of the brigade prepared to
follow.[10]

Colonel Albert L. Magilton's 3rd Brigade, Pennsylvania Reserves, gained
some ground on Sinclair's brigade as it plunged into the copse. Magilton en
couraged his men to "press the First [Brigade] as closely as possible," and
led the advance in person. The three-hundred-yard interval between brigade
diminished to only one hundred yards. The brigades wallowed through the
bog, and Meade dashed back and forth to expedite their movement. Magil
ton's troops encountered some of Jackson's and Sinclair's men, who had
dropped out of ranks or lost their places during the advance. Magilton swept
them up and carried them forward with his command. Soon after, Magilton'
brigade stumbled into the units stalled at the railroad. The brigades jumbled
as Magilton's left piled into the railroad ditches with Jackson's troops o
meshed with Sinclair's line in the wetlands on the right. Meade managed to
keep a semblance of order between Magilton and Sinclair, but confusion
reigned elsewhere.[11]

George Meade alleviated some of the crowding in the woods. He ordered
Sinclair's brigade to press ahead; and after a suitable interval, he released
Magilton in support. Meade next tried to rectify C. Feger Jackson's dilemma
He saw Jackson's disjointed frontal assaults fail repeatedly against Prospec
Hill. The addition of Magilton's troops swelled the ranks beyond the cove
of the railroad embankment and casualties accumulated among the hind
most. The division commander dispatched his aide, Lieutenant Arthu
Dehon, to shift C. F. Jackson's hodgepodge units into the copse. Meade
hoped the woods would allow Jackson to turn the Confederate artillery posi
tion. Dehon darted down the railroad on horseback.[12]

Conrad Feger Jackson cantered along his confused line, rallying his men
for another attack. Confederates drew a bead on the conspicuous general, and
a volley brought down his mount. A Tennessee Confederate remarked, "
think every man in the 7th and 14th [Tennessee] fired at least one shot at him.'
The general rolled free of his horse and leapt onto the railbed with his swore
in hand. He called on the 5th Reserves to follow him in a desperate charge
(Rumors persisted later that the general was addled and disoriented.) Lieuten

ant Dehon interrupted the bruised and irate officer when he reined his horse and snapped a salute. A Confederate bullet, however, tore through the aide's chest and killed him before he could relay Meade's orders. C. Feger Jackson whirled around, only to fall victim to another Rebel salvo. A bullet pierced the general's skull, and he tumbled lifeless in the ditch next to Dehon. The general's adjutant, Captain T. Brent Swearingen, lost his horse in the same volley. The battered aide reflexively recovered some of Jackson's and Dehon's personal effects, only to lose them later when he fell wounded and captured.[13]

Despite the loss of their general, the right of C. Feger Jackson's brigade fulfilled Meade's orders intuitively and rushed for the woods. Command of Jackson's forces devolved upon Lieutenant Colonel Robert Anderson of the 9th Reserves. Unfortunately, Anderson knew nothing of the change. Trapped behind the rock fence on the left, the colonel could not communicate with the troops along the railroad, much less command them. As a result, the brigade fragmented further, with the 11th Reserves breaking contact with the other regiments when it entered the bog. The Bucktails and the 5th Reserves tried to follow, but found their path barred. A Bucktail recalled how "our ranks had been terribly thinned," holding what he termed the "valley of death." Major Harvey Larliner of the 5th Reserves called for volunteers to follow him as he charged over the tracks. The two regiments lunged over the bank with a cheer. "They made a noble effort," recalled a participant, "but were driven back with fearful loss." After Sinclair's brigade advanced on the right, the two regiments found it easier to rush forward in support.[14]

A member of Magilton's brigade named James McCauley exhorted the left of the 3rd Brigade to follow him. As he skipped across the railroad tracks, McCauley shouted at the 7th Reserves: "Wide awake fellows, let's give 'em hell!" The regiment charged after the reckless McCauley, losing its color-bearer, Reuben Schell, wounded on the railroad. A bullet had glanced off his belt plate as he crossed the railroad grade. Henry Dilman seized the colors and dropped dead a few steps farther. A third soldier took the flag and led the regiment into the woods. Men sprinted for the cover without order. A mad dash through a storm of canister and bullets caused many individuals to incline their heads "as though moving against a driving rain." To watching Confederates it appeared that "the Yankees [were] running for life." A 7th Tennessee soldier recounted: "Their front line was scattered and almost annihilated." Dry broomsedge caught fire, which spurred the Pennsylvanians to move faster.[15]

Meanwhile, the 10th and 12th Reserves remained pinned down along the railroad, and the 9th Reserves huddled behind its fence. Unable to move, the three regiments supported the others with cover fire. Their effort succeeded; most of the Rebels focused on them without concern for the Yankees piling into the woods. Archer's troops assumed that Maxcy Gregg's South Carolina brigade would take care of them.[16]

Sinclair's brigade stole silently across the railroad and climbed the hill under cover of scrubby oaks and pines. The Federals puzzled over the lack of Confederate resistance as they unknowingly penetrated the gap in A. P. Hill's line. The 6th Reserves skirmishers crept warily ahead, and Magilton's brigade trailed behind at a suitable distance. Since Magilton had five regiments in his command and Sinclair had only three, Magilton's line overlapped both of Sinclair's flanks. Thus, the 7th Reserves became entangled with C. F. Jackson's brigade on the left and lost its color-bearer, while Sinclair's brigade had no contact with Jackson at all. Another problem developed on the right. The untested 142nd Pennsylvania reached the railroad just north of the finger of woods. The novice soldiers marched over the tracks and right into the fire of the waiting Confederates. General James H. Lane's North Carolina brigade had watched the Northerners inch closer before rocking them with a close volley. The Yankees fled at the first fire and took cover in the railroad ditches.[17]

The experienced 8th Reserves stormed past the stunned 142nd Pennsylvania and crossed the railroad tracks farther south. Exposing their right flank to the hidden Confederates, the 8th Regiment staggered under a sudden and tremendous fire. The Federals, according to a participant, never had been "subjected to so terrible an ordeal." The veteran Reserves intuitively wheeled around and returned the fire. Lane's Rebel brigade yielded a portion of the railroad to re-fuse its flank and face the 8th Reserves head-on. Colonel Robert Cummins of the 142nd Pennsylvania took advantage of the shift to forward a couple of companies to the 8th Reserves. Despite their lodgment on the tracks, both Northern regiments had lost their momentum—and their contact with the advance—having their hands full with Lane's obstinate Confederates.[18]

Albert Magilton knew little of the fighting on the right and therefore compounded the problem. The colonel assumed that Sinclair's troops covered his entire front, which was a strange notion, since he had ridden well in front of his line and should have known his brigade overlapped Sinclair's flanks. But when he heard the green 142nd Pennsylvania shooting, he was horrorstruck. He ordered them to cease at once, lest they strike their comrades in the back.

There is no evidence that Magilton visited the right or ascertained the cause of the fight. In fact, Colonel Cummins appealed to the brigade commander, stating that the enemy was pouring a "most galling fire" into his command. Magilton refused to listen to him, and the 142nd Pennsylvania ended up "entirely at the mercy of the enemy . . . who took the best advantage of it." The new soldiers grumbled, but dutifully withheld their fire. The 8th Reserves, on the other hand, continued to fight without interference from the brigade head. Magilton may not have known of their involvement—or that they had wheeled out of line—or, the 8th Reserves simply ignored him. Either way, the 8th Reserves battled alone while the 142nd Pennsylvania sat exposed and discouraged.[19]

The introspective soldier Frank Holsinger, who had welled with terror at the start of the attack, had undergone a transformation. "The mind being engaged by a thousand circumstances," the 8th Reserves soldier reflected, "fear had been dissipated, and a sense of relief had taken its place." The young man admitted that he was "most comfortable under a most galling fire," simply because he was too busy to worry. The crescendo of fire from Lane's North Carolina brigade drowned the cries of the wounded and left the Federals with a focused desire "to get in your best licks" before the other side did.[20]

The isolated 142nd Pennsylvania huddled behind the railroad while the rest of Magilton's brigade vanished into the woods. The Confederates let the others go and concentrated on the exposed new regiment. The novices braved the fire stoically, but their losses mounted. A bullet killed Colonel Cummins' horse, and Lieutenant Colonel McCalmont lost his second mount at the railroad. Major John Bradley fell mortally wounded with a shattered leg, and the acting adjutant, Cyrus Campbell, hobbled to the rear with a bullet in his foot. The nearby 8th Reserves lost their commander, Major Silas M. Baily, who fell along with five of his captains. "We were mowed down like grass upon the field," reminisced a new enlistee. The losses deranged the right of Magilton's brigade and effectively stopped its advance.[21]

The rest of Magilton's brigade swept over the tracks unchallenged by the action on the left or right. It followed loosely in the path of Sinclair's brigade. The bog and foliage disrupted the battle line, and regiments drifted apart. Magilton's left regiment, Colonel Henry C. Bolinger's 7th Reserves, strayed through the forest alone. The regiment had lost contact with the brigade and inclined toward the sound of the heaviest fighting on the left. With his left and right regiments shorn from the advance, Magilton's center—composed of three regiments—thrust directly up the wooded slope toward the Confederates' military road.[22]

The majority of C. F. Jackson's brigade continued to battle along the railroad, while Sinclair's and Magilton's brigades hacked through the dense underbrush. Soon the attackers slowed to a crawl, obstructed by uneven ground and patches of swamp. The terrain concealed the Northerners from Confederate cannon and small-arms fire, which removed some of the urgency and allowed the Federals to advance at a more deliberate pace. Meade's division moved unseen through the unguarded opening in the Confederate lines. Unfortunately, the Union troops had penetrated the gap without leadership, understanding, or purpose. C. Feger Jackson was dead, and his brigade was virtually leaderless. The other brigades of Meade's command also lacked direction. During the advance, Colonel William Sinclair fell wounded with a mangled left foot and had to be carried from the field. His replacement, Colonel William McCandless of the 2nd Reserves, probably had disappeared into the woods and did not know Sinclair's fate until later. Colonel Albert Magilton lost control of his brigade in an ignoble way. A Confederate volley brought down the colonel's horse and left him trapped underneath. By the time he freed himself, the attack had dissolved. Incredibly, no one missed Magilton, and the right of his brigade probably benefited from his disappearance. No one could stop them from ignoring his meddlesome orders and resuming the contest with Lane's Brigade. Since Magilton technically never lost command, no one stepped forward to replace him.[23]

None of Meade's brigadiers crossed the railroad. As a result, the regiments lost guidance and functioned on their own accord. Units deviated from each other, making regimental commanders independent and uncertain of where to go and what to do. No one could see through the woods to determine how many—or few—Federals had entered the gap or what lay ahead. Caution seized some, while impulse prodded others to push forward. Units dissolved into small groups and clusters, a straining mob that battled terrain more than Rebels. The woods that Lee, Jackson, and Hill had proclaimed impassable to an organized unit had been breached by a force anything but organized. Incredibly, Archer's and Lane's Confederates had done their duty so well that they literally drove the Union troops into the gap. One side saw the finger of woods as an obstacle to advance, while the other side quickly learned that it made an ideal avenue of approach.

Throngs of Union soldiers clawed their way up the wooded hillside. A portion of the 1st Pennsylvania Reserves caught up with the skirmishers of the 6th Reserves, and together they pressed deeper into the forest, heading straight for General Maxcy Gregg's South Carolina brigade. Gregg's unsuspecting Confederates lounged in reserve along the Military Road. The general had ordered their weapons stacked to avoid potentially dangerous clashes with friendly units. Gregg knew nothing of the Yankees bearing down on him. He had no skirmishers out, since Archer and Lane had done that for him. He assumed they would keep him apprised of happenings in front. Little did Gregg know that the skirmishers had returned to their brigades without notifying him.[24]

Most of the Carolinians sat quietly listening to the combat to their left and right front. Gregg's Brigade formed a relaxed line on the crest of the ridge. The 1st South Carolina Rifles, or Orr's Rifles, held the right near a bend in the Military Road. The 1st South Carolina came next, followed by the 12th, 13th, and 14th South Carolina Regiments. General Gregg rested on horseback by the 14th South Carolina while his mount grazed. Some of Orr's Rifles spotted the ragtag Northerners creeping through the underbrush and seized their weapons from the stacks. At the first sound of gunfire, Gregg panicked. He dashed down the line, sure that his men had fired into their comrades. The mortified general could not see the Federals from his high perch in the saddle. He rode in front of the line to block his soldiers' fire, shouting, "You are firing on our friends!" He appealed to their logic: how could the enemy be at hand when they had not seen the Confederates in front retreat? Perhaps Gregg believed a Southern battle line stood arrayed somewhere in front, but more likely he looked for the 1st Tennessee pickets to fall back through his position. Either way, Gregg's expectations opened him to disaster. Incredibly, the Confederates restacked their weapons.[25]

The 1st and 6th Pennsylvania Reserves closed in, fumbling through vines and tangles to get a closer shot. A Keystone soldier, unaware of Gregg's orders to cease fire, attributed the Federals' success to "a low flat piece of ground grown up with blackberry and alder bushes," which hid the attackers until the last moment. Another Reserve wrote that the bluecoats approached quietly, which added to the surprise. The foliage disrupted alignments, but the 1st Reserves formed roughly on the left while the 6th Reserves took the right. Meade's soldiers struck Gregg's right flank. The somewhat deaf Maxcy Gregg turned around to see Orr's Rifles armed again and blazing into the woods. Little realizing the proximity of the foe, the brigade commander galloped in front, chastising his foolhardy ranks. Gregg saw and heard nothing of the Yankees in the thicket or the bullets whistling past his head. As he knocked

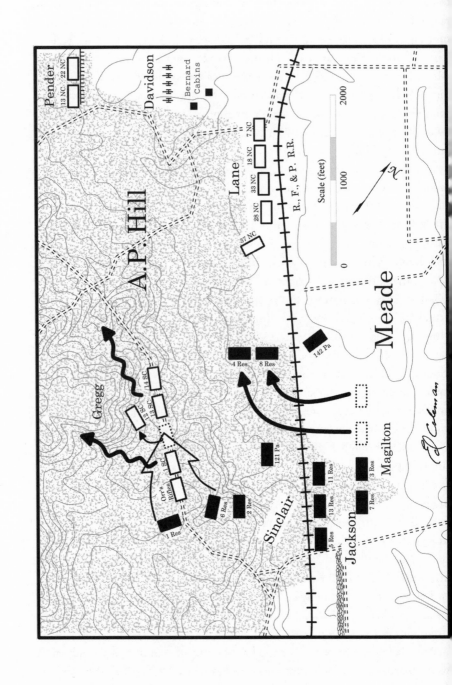

down rifles with his hand and cursed, a volley from the trees swept the general out of the saddle. A ball passed through Maxcy Gregg's side and severed his spinal cord. The paralyzed commander lay dazed while Orr's Rifles scrambled to defend themselves.[26]

Federals fell upon the Southerners "with wild yells." They swarmed out of the woods and around the exposed right flank of Captain Joseph J. Norton's company of Orr's Rifles. The beset South Carolinians found it difficult to hold the Military Road, especially when some of the men could not retrieve their rifles from the stacks because of the point-blank fire. Norton raised his sword over his head as a rallying point. A bullet passed through his arm and he dropped the sword. Picking it up with his other hand, another bullet pierced that arm, and the sword clattered to the ground again. Unable to use either limb, Norton had to be assisted from the battlefield. Orr's Rifles quickly fell apart. The Pennsylvania Reserves stormed into the rifle stacks and, after a brief "scramble and hand-to-hand fight," scattered the Rebels through the underbrush. Pursuing the fleeing Confederates, the 1st and 6th Reserves wheeled right and expanded the breakthrough northward. They struck the 1st South Carolina next, around the bend in the Military Road. Many of the startled Southerners retreated before they could reclaim their arms from the neat stacks strung along the road. They left behind their cof-feepots and even their colors, according to one Pennsylvanian, though the Yankees never reported the capture of a South Carolina flag. A nearby Virgin-ian discerned plainly that "the advantage was with the Federals," even though many of the Carolinians fought with "heroic desperation."[27]

The Pennsylvanians pressed their advantage. The 1st Reserves overlapped the Rebels' right flank and drove into the rear of the 12th South Carolina. The Southern battleline bent backward to meet the turning movement head-on. The 12th South Carolina, anchoring its left on the 13th South Carolina, swung around like a gate so that the two Confederate units fought back-to-back. Caught in a crossfire, the Rebels fired in every direction. "Here the action was close handed," wrote a member of the 6th Reserves, "and men fell on both sides like leaves in autumn." The precarious defenders soon collapsed and fled from the crushing Union vice. The 14th South Carolina also fell back before the Yankee attackers. Gregg's Brigade had been savaged and its commander stricken in a matter of minutes. The brigade historian admitted candidly that Gregg's command, "as a body, [was] broken, slaughtered and swept from the field." An inferior Union force had surprised the unprepared Confederates and unraveled their line with powerful efficiency. Gregg's successor, Colonel Daniel H. Hamilton of the 1st South Carolina, darted through the thicket, frantically trying to rally his disintegrating command. Despite his efforts, the brigade ceased to function for the remainder of December 13. Driven from their positions, the Carolinians left their wounded behind. "The dead and dying on both sides lay intermingled on the field with no hope of assistance to the wounded until the battle should end," a nearby Confederate observed with regret.[28]

The Pennsylvanians drove another three hundred yards through the forest before halting. They met only a "slight force," but feared, as one put it, "that we would get too far" ahead of the rest of Meade's division. The 1st Pennsylvania Reserves split from the 6th Reserves and wandered to the west. The foliage made it "impossible to keep the column unbroken." The 6th Regiment pursued the Confederates north but halted when its line "had grown weak and began to waver." The unit linked up with Magilton's 4th and 8th Reserves, which had penetrated the woods but could not bypass the obstinate Confederates of Lane's Brigade. Together, these Pennsylvania regiments still failed to drive away the Rebels pinning the 142nd Pennsylvania to the railroad. The rest of Sinclair's First Brigade, at the same time, passed deeper into the Confederate rear. The 2nd Reserves and the 121st Pennsylvania lost contact with the rest of the brigade, and before long, lost contact with each other. Meade declared, "regiments separated from brigades, and companies from regiments," as they muddled through the natural obstructions.[29]

Meanwhile, elements of the 1st Reserves rummaged through Gregg's abandoned stacks collecting prizes. As the Union troops lolled in disarray, they spread across the biggest prize of all—the Military Road—Meade's objective in severing Lee's communications. The tiny, confused Federal command had achieved its goal, but the lack of knowledgeable commanders left the clump of soldiers unaware of their success. George Meade, still at the railroad sorting out the confusion, probably learned of their achievement only much later.[30]

While the Union breakthrough expanded north and west, the rest of Meade's troops roved south and southwest, groping blindly for the Confederates. After losing contact with the 121st Pennsylvania, the 2nd Reserves ran into the 11th Reserves, and together they wandered through the gap without opposition. Reaching the summit of the ridge, a portion of the 2nd Reserves heard heavy gunfire to their left and went to investigate. The 11th Reserve headed in the same direction. The mixed group of Union soldiers eased to the edge of the woods and spotted Archer's Brigade sprawled before them on the crest. The adjutant of the 2nd Reserves, Evan M. Woodward, saw that the unsuspecting Confederates had left their left flank unguarded, 150 yards from his motley band. Woodward, on his own initiative, took thirty men and charged the Rebels.[31]

The 19th Georgia anchored the left of James Archer's Brigade. Its flank rested in a small saddle that straddled Prospect Hill. The Georgians had a clear view of the railroad, but the indentation on the ridge masked the Federals pouring out of the woods. Woodward's Pennsylvanians massed near the Confederate flank and rear. Archer's men had just repulsed another Union attack from the railroad when the Georgians raised "that wild yell so well known in those days." Suddenly they were assailed from the flank. A Union volley exploded in fire and smoke, hiding the attackers in an acrid cloud. Lieutenant John W. Keely of the 19th Georgia wrote that the Yankees struck "with the precision of a battering ram," wording that really imparts more a sense of force than precision.[32]

Union adjutant Woodward shifted his troops into the woods behind the Confederates to get a better shot at them. The Federals had crept to within fifty yards of the Rebel trench when they unleashed their fire. From his position atop the saddle, Woodward raked Archer's entire left flank. The Northerners had caught the 19th Georgia in a devastating crossfire. Other Union soldiers, independent of Woodward's group, spread across the face of Prospect Hill. Part of the 7th, 11th, and 5th Reserves blasted the 19th Georgia's earthwork in front. Between them and Woodward, the Confederates took fire from the front, flank, and rear.[33]

The commander of the Georgians, Lieutenant Colonel Andrew J. Hutchins, rushed a courier to Archer, telling him that the flank had been turned. James Archer sent his ordnance officer, Lieutenant George Lemmon, to notify Maxcy Gregg. He hoped the South Carolinian would seal the gap. As Lemmon disappeared into the woods, Archer had no idea that the Federals had already routed the South Carolina brigade. Lemmon later testified that he saw the last of Gregg's Brigade being driven from the Military Road. The staff officer reported that Gregg's "arms were stacked, and the enemy's bullets were rattling amongst his stacks of muskets." Archer hoped that Gregg would rally his brigade in time and drive the Yankees back. Unknown to Archer or Lemmon, Gregg had been mortally wounded and his brigade scattered beyond recall.[34]

The 19th Georgia clung desperately to its ditch while Federal fire swirled around it. Colonel Hutchins appealed to the men to keep their composure. Some of the soldiers panicked and fired wildly. Others failed to fire at all, too frightened to load their rifles. Officers crawled along the ditch, occasionally taking a rifle to show the men how to fire deliberately. The Georgians lasted for ten minutes before they caved in. Butternut-clothed Rebels abandoned their earthworks and stampeded for the woods. The 2nd Reserves fired point-blank into them as they flocked across the Pennsylvanians' front. Confederate dead and wounded piled up behind the trench. A Yankee soldier boasted that the Rebels "were slaughtered like sheep" as they attempted to flee. The second in command of the Georgians, Major James H. Neal, received a grazing wound but managed to escape with scores of other men. Some of the terrified Southerners dashed within a few feet of the Unionists, yet they ignored their entreaties to surrender. Some tried to protect themselves from the gunfire by holding their hands or canteens next to their heads. Many Northerners stopped shooting out of pity simply because they could not miss at such a short distance.[35]

Some of the Georgians feared to run the gauntlet and ended up trapped in the ditch straddling the swale in the hill. Union soldiers closed in on all sides, maintaining a brisk fire. The ubiquitous Adjutant Woodward noticed that his bluecoats had suffered numerous casualties but the Confederates were not shooting. He realized then that the 7th Reserves in front was firing too high and striking his men. Without realizing the irony, a Pennsylvanian called it, "the hardest fight that the Reserves was ever in." At the risk of his life, Woodward sheathed his sword and waved his kepi to stop the Union fire on the crest. The adjutant sprinted to the Confederate line and dove in. Surrounded by Georgians, he asked them if they wanted to surrender. The exasperated Rebels rejoined, "If you will let us." Woodward grabbed two prisoners and together they bounded down the hill "waving their hats." Explaining the situation to the 7th Reserves, Woodward quieted its fire and removed more than one hundred captured Georgians from the trench. Several Confederates, grateful to be alive, shook the hands of their captors, and one maudlin Rebel swore that he would take an oath of allegiance a foot long. Another Confederate congratulated the Pennsylvanians darkly, telling the 7th Reserves soldiers, "Yanks, you have done it nicely enough, but there are more of Jackson's men" still on Prospect Hill.[36]

Among his captures, Woodward wrested the flag of the 19th Georgia from a fleeing color-bearer. This was the only Confederate flag captured and retained by the Federals at Fredericksburg. Unable to leave his command, Woodward entrusted John Schalck, of the 2nd Reserves, to carry the colors to safety. Schalck got as far as the railroad before he fell wounded. Corporal

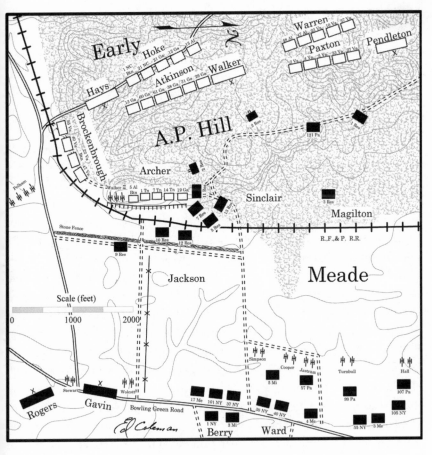

Meade's Assault: The Left

Jacob Cart of the 7th Reserves took the flag and headed for the rear. By the time he reached the river, he had concocted a story about how he had pummeled the gargantuan color-bearer into submission, who not only yielded his flag but also complimented his assailant by saying, "Bully for you." The Congress thanked Cart by awarding him the Medal of Honor. Thirty years later, the government issued a second medal to Evan M. Woodward (without retracting Jacob Cart's citation).[37]

Following the collapse of the 19th Georgia, the Pennsylvanians swarmed into their lines. Northerners quickly descended upon the 14th Tennessee, the next unit in James Archer's Confederate line. As the Union attack thronged across Prospect Hill, from north to south, pressure eased on some of the Union regiments pinned near the railroad. The Yankees took advantage of the break and piled forward to join the mix of commands on the summit and the slope. The majority of the 11th Reserves joined Woodward's band. Colonel Samuel M. Jackson, head of the 11th Reserves, probably superseded Woodward and took command of the hilltop. The colonel sat his horse on the crest, looking "as cool and unmoved as though he were the Sphinx itself." The 5th Reserves and the Bucktails bolstered the 7th Reserves below the crest.[38]

The 14th Tennessee battled to hold back the Yankees in front as best they could. The Confederates appeared to be keeping them at bay when they saw the 19th Georgia unaccountably break and riot across their rear. "Look yonder!" a disbelieving Southerner sputtered. "See those ——— cowardly Georgians running!" The biased Tennesseans assumed the Georgians were too excitable. Cooler heads could plainly see the Federals could not get up the slope in front. "Our men became furious," wrote a Tennessee man. The stalwart 14th Tennessee redoubled its effort to compensate for the unreliable Georgians. In essence, they fought with blinders on, unable and unwilling to see what was happening to their comrades. The Pennsylvanians exploited this prejudice and filed into the woods directly behind the Tennessee regiment. Bullets blasted the trench from the rear, which failed to alert the engrossed Confederates to their danger. When three balls narrowly missed Private T. D. "Dick" Johnson, the homespun soldier turned to offer his criticism. "Stop that shooting back there, you damn fools," he bawled, "or I'll shoot Hell out of a half dozen of you!" The piqued soldier gazed in astonishment as a rough legion of bluecoats stepped out of the timber. His surprise reflected that of his entire regiment.[39]

Archer tried to reinforce his left, unaware that the 19th Georgia had collapsed and the 14th Tennessee was hard beset. He sent a second appeal to Maxcy Gregg to plug the break in the line; but he suspected that Gregg would not act in time, so he dispatched another message to the rear for help. Pleas went to Colonel John M. Brockenbrough's Brigade and to Colonel Edmund N. Atkinson's Georgia brigade of Jubal Early's division. Before word returned, Archer pulled the 5th Alabama Battalion from his right flank and directed it to the left. Time became critical, as the 14th Tennessee started to waver.[40]

Alarmed by the sudden eruption of fire from behind, Lieutenant Colonel James W. Lockert tried to keep the Federals back from both his front and rear. Union soldiers stormed up the slope and crowded his vulnerable left flank. The 14th Tennessee started to crack under the strain, and that encouraged the Yankees to drive harder. Union officers exhorted their men: "Give 'em hell, boys, we've got them on the run. Give 'em hell!" The 14th Tennessee quickly succumbed. Hit from all sides and unable to see their tormenters in the piney forest behind them, the Tennessee regiment panicked and fled in the direction of the despised Georgians. The disorderly Confederates hung on until virtually surrounded. Many failed to escape the trap, and the Yankees herded quite a few to the rear as prisoners.[41]

The 7th Tennessee had witnessed the rout of the 19th Georgia and accepted it philosophically, but the unexpected flight of the 14th Tennessee struck them with horror. Still unaware of the closing Northerners, 7th Tennessee men leapt from their ditch and tried to rally their demoralized comrades. Members of the 7th Regiment could not comprehend their comrades' unseemly behavior. Their appeals to halt went unheeded, and the soldiers became "enraged at what seemed to them dastardly cowardice." They rushed among the shattered 14th Tennessee, begging them to stand. Lieutenant John H. Moore of the 7th Tennessee reported that "officers and privates stormed at, shouted and threatened them as base cowards." The 14th Tennessee refused to rally and continued its hasty retreat. According to Lieutenant Moore, some of the officers in the 7th Regiment "leveled their pistols and, with many privates, fired into these fleeing comrades and broken ranks." The provocative incident was short-lived because astute leaders soon spotted the approaching Federals coming down the trench. The bluecoats lunged after the stampeding 14th Tennessee and blundered into the 7th Tennessee. Confederate officers frantically ordered their men to re-form. A Tennessee soldier recalled how the regimental officers "rushed to and fro, wildly shouting 'Into line, into line!'" An avalanche of Northern soldiers rushed into their midst. The Tennesseans had only two or three rounds of ammunition left.[42]

The Confederates formed a ragged line and met the attackers head-on. General Archer ordered the 7th and 14th Tennessee to re-fuse their flank. The 14th Tennessee had vanished before the orders arrived, and the 7th Tennessee bore the full brunt of the Union onslaught. The Confederates lacked the cartridges to drive the Yankees back, but they quickly learned that the Northerners also had run low on ammunition, and neither side had time to reload. Both sides resorted to clubbed muskets and bayonets to force the other to yield. The 7th Tennessee held its own in the bludgeoning match, which allowed the 1st Tennessee—the "Hogdrivers"—to wheel out of the trench and assist. The leader of the 1st Regiment, Colonel Peter Turney, moved along the line, waving his sword and exclaiming, "Stand firm, you boys that never flicker." He repeatedly cajoled his men, "Stand firm and Victory will be ours." The lines rolled and receded, sometimes separated by only a few paces. Casualties escalated and collected underfoot.[43]

Colonel Peter Turney's fiery exhortations hid a dark premonition. The colonel suspected he would be killed at Fredericksburg, but no one had taken him seriously, since he had had the same feeling before *every* battle. Captain John A. Fite wagered Turney a gallon of whiskey that neither one of them would die at Fredericksburg. In the middle of the melee, Colonel Turney suddenly keeled over. A bullet had pierced his mouth and torn through his neck. Nearby soldiers ignored the immobile figure until later, when they evacuated him to the hospital. After the battle, Turney chided Captain Fite that he had nearly won the bet. Fite bit his tongue, knowing the colonel was right. Lieutenant Colonel Newton J. George assumed command of the 1st Tennessee. In the midst of the battle, he suffered several small wounds. A Federal bullet passed through his index finger and another nicked his ear. George ignored the pain and continued to lead his rapidly diminishing command.[44]

Across the way, Union troops also sustained serious losses. Colonel Henry C. Bolinger of the 7th Reserves hobbled off Prospect Hill with a painful ankle wound. Captain Charles F. Taylor, quick-thinking leader of the Pennsylvania Bucktails, rode into the melee until a volley killed his horse. The commander continued to fight on foot. Soon, Taylor was dragged away with a dangerous wound. His replacement, Captain Edward A. Irvin, was soon after wounded. Corporal John Looney, color-bearer for the Bucktail regiment, died in the close combat, splattering his blood across the flag. The 5th Reserves lost all of its commanders. Lieutenant Colonel George Dare fell seriously wounded and had to be carried away. Major Frank Zentmeyer, second-in-command, fell mortally wounded and was captured on the hill. His brother, David, the acting adjutant of the regiment, also died in the desperate action.[45]

The 11th Reserves suffered the highest casualties of C. F. Jackson's brigade, most particularly among its color-bearers. Every time the flag fell someone quickly picked it up, only to be sacrificed in turn. Lieutenant Daniel R. Coder rescued the colors three times during the battle and brought them safely back at the end of the engagement. The regimental flag revealed nineteen new bullet holes, and the staff had been shattered by another bullet. The regiment lost 211 out of 300 effectives. One company went into action with 30 men and counted only 6 "who escaped," at the end of the day. Though he had circulated through the ranks of the 11th Reserves, Evan Woodward of the 2nd Reserves somehow avoided getting hurt. After the action, the charmed adjutant counted thirteen bullet rents in his uniform, no bullet having drawn blood.[46]

Another officer as fortunate as Woodward was the division commander, George Gordon Meade. The general rode imperiously along the railroad, fashioning order out of chaos, and ignoring danger in all its guises. A Rebel musket ball tore through the peak of Meade's bell-crowned hat. Another struck the general's mount in the neck. The animal behaved so well that Meade did not know the horse had been hit until later. Meade also encountered danger from his own troops. The general saw an officer leave his post and dash for the rear. Meade personally corralled the frightened skulker and demanded explosively that he return to his command. Unthinking, the desperate lieutenant leveled his rifle at the general. Meade lashed back with the flat of his sword, bashing the subordinate over the head and snapping the steel blade clean down to the hilt. The enraged division commander ordered the man back to the battle line, and the staggered lieutenant meekly complied.[47]

Despite the efforts of Meade and his junior officers, the Pennsylvanians began to falter, and their impetus waned within sight of R. Lindsay Walker's trapped Confederate artillery. Men still hammered and stabbed at each other. "We had strewn that plateau with [our] dead and wounded," mused a disgruntled Bucktail, who concluded that it was a "fearful price to pay." But the disorganized bluecoats had run out of steam. The defenders, equally disorganized and without ammunition, had stopped the breakthrough from growing any larger. Both sides continued to slash and fire without an effective means of driving the other back. As Meade's momentum collapsed against stiffening resistance, fire erupted to the Federal right, heralding a renewal of the battle north of the breakthrough.[48]

General James Lane's North Carolina brigade was holding its own against Meade's right flank. His five regiments, starting on the right with the 37th North Carolina, followed by the 28th, 33rd, 18th, and 7th North Carolina, had repulsed several attacks on their positions along the railroad. Meade's Pennsylvania Reserves had threatened to turn the right when it entered the woods 250 yards from the Carolinians' flank. Lane's left also could be turned, and a small ridge blocked the center of his field of fire. A. P. Hill had placed Lane in this unlikely position with the idea that Gregg's and Pender's Brigades would support him. But the elevation in front proved to be bothersome. The ground swelled almost imperceptibly just fifty yards in front of the line. John B. Brockenbrough's cannon had held the rise during the artillery barrage, and many of the Yankee missiles overshot the mark, hitting the Carolinians along the railroad. Some of the 7th North Carolina volunteered to man the guns when casualties threatened to silence them. McKendree replaced Brockenbrough soon after and removed the guns. Lane forwarded companies of the 7th and 18th North Carolina to cover his retreat. Climbing the knoll, the Southern infantry came under heavy fire. The Rebels fell back to the railroad as soon as the guns withdrew. Lane's center remained obstructed. Only the Confederates on the flanks could see the Union movements on the field.[49]

Colonel William Barbour watched Meade's division penetrate the woods and cross the tracks a couple of hundred yards to his right. He ordered his 37th North Carolina to open an oblique fire, which effectively stopped the 142nd Pennsylvania cold. The North Carolina regiment drew fire from the 8th Pennsylvania Reserves, who crossed the tracks and filled the woods behind Lane's right. Colonel Barbour re-fused several companies on his right, and their fire successfully checked the bluecoats. As the Confederates exchanged volleys at 250 yards, Lane hurried a courier to A. P. Hill asking for Maxcy Gregg to join the fray. Lane, like Archer, had no way of knowing that Gregg's Brigade already had been routed. Until help arrived, Lane beseeched Barbour's 37th North Carolina "to hold as long as possible."[50]

Three companies of the 37th North Carolina wheeled out of the railroad ditch and formed at a right angle to the brigade battle line. Blazing into the woods, the 37th North Carolina kept the 8th Reserves at bay, then the 4th Reserves, and part of the 6th Reserves. The Confederates defied all comers and succeeded largely because of the thoroughly disorganized state of the attackers. Despite the Union repulse, losses accumulated among the Southerners at a considerable rate. Colonel William Barbour fell wounded and was carried to the rear. Major William Grove Morris assumed command. A Yankee ball smashed the major's canteen and another buried in a stale biscuit he carried in his haversack. A third bullet clipped the lobe off of Morris' ear. The major clasped his bloody ear but refused to have it treated. As he stormed up and down the line, Morris' blood discolored his uniform. The commander admitted that he was "bloody as a hog," and wanted desperately to avenge the scar—"ol' Abe's mark," he styled it. The 37th North Carolina prevailed against lengthening odds. A Carolinian called the fight "a bloody and gallant struggle." Major Morris thought it was "the hardest fight that I have ever been in." Federals gained little ground and the battle lapsed into a static exchange of musketry. Just as Lane stabilized his right flank, the rest of the line exploded in fire. After a considerable delay, Brigadier General John Gibbon's Union division had advanced to Meade's support.[51]

Gibbon's division had lain beside Meade's muddy Pennsylvania Reserves during the artillery bombardment. When two of Walker's ammunition chests exploded and the cheering Pennsylvanians charged, Gibbon was not ready. The sudden attack surprised him. He needed time to arrange his forces to go forward in support. General Nelson Taylor appealed to the methodical division commander to hurry, but Gibbon refused to move prematurely. Once he had everything set, he let Taylor's brigade advance. By then, enough time had elapsed that Meade begged John Reynolds to reinforce his weak right flank. The First Corps chief personally went to see Gibbon (something he should have done even before Meade's request). Since Taylor already had permission to go forward, Gibbon's prompt compliance appeared in marked contrast to his preceding desuetude.[52]

Nelson Taylor marshaled his brigade behind the rise next to Hall's Maine battery. The 11th Pennsylvania held the left, with the 83rd New York to its right, followed by the 97th New York and 88th Pennsylvania. Taylor paid close attention to the skittish 88th Pennsylvania. The regiment had reinforced his skirmish line when the Confederate artillery had opened fire. Across the smoke-laden field, Major David A. Griffith had advanced his Pennsylvanians fifty yards to a knoll. They had dressed ranks, had fired a volley, then had inexplicably broken and run. Major Griffith admitted sheepishly that the regiment had panicked at the sound of its own fire. Taylor helped the major rally his distraught command and put it back into line.[53]

In front of Taylor, Colonel Samuel Leonard's skirmishers ran out of ammunition just at the point of Gibbon's attack. Leonard ordered his 13th Massachusetts to lie down and let the brigade pass over them. Once Taylor swept by, Leonard sent four companies to support Hall's battery, and the rest returned to the Bowling Green Road. George E. Maynard of the 13th Massachusetts reached the road only to discover that his comrade, Charles Armstrong, was missing. Maynard returned to the field and found Armstrong badly wounded in the thigh. He tied a tourniquet around Armstrong's leg and carried him back to the Union lines. Maynard earned the Medal of Honor for risking his life for a friend. Unfortunately, Armstrong died that night in a field hospital.[54]

Gibbon watched Taylor's brigade advance and the 13th Massachusetts filter to the rear. Turning to his next brigade, Gibbon ordered Colonel Peter Lyle to follow Taylor. Lyle aligned his brigade, placing the neophyte soldiers of the 136th Pennsylvania on the left. The 90th Pennsylvania, 26th New York, and 12th Massachusetts filled out the line. The sodden troops scrambled into position and set off at an earnest pace. Gibbon withheld his third brigade, Colonel Adrian Root's, as a reserve for the division and a support for the artillery.[55]

Taylor's brigade fumbled and wallowed across the waterlogged plain. Mud caked on shoes and trousers, weighing down the already heavily encumbered troops. The ragged line tumbled through several ditches and gullies, which further disrupted the formation. When the bluecoats closed in on the railroad, James Lane's Brigade erupted with fire. Taylor's Northerners, stung by the wrenching volley, halted 150 yards from the Confederate line and returned the fire. Lane's left and right gave—and felt—a storm of shot and ball. Lane's center sat idle, hidden by the knoll that obstructed their view. Unable to see for themselves, they prepared for the worst. The commander of the 33rd North Carolina called his men to attention when the Yankees approached. One of his subordinates repeated his orders, adding excitedly, "Look out—the Yanks are coming!" A nervous conscript named Noah Lewis dropped to his knees, fired into the air, and ejaculated, "Oh Lordy!" at the top of his lungs. The regiment convulsed with laughter—one of them explained, "The whole thing looked so ridiculous." While the center guffawed, Lane's right—the 37th and 28th North Carolina—compensated for them with a smothering deluge of fire that jolted the Yankees.[56]

Nelson Taylor's brigade stalled under the fusillade. Caught in the open, Union soldiers lay down to return the fire. Taylor's right took minimal losses. The unsure 88th Pennsylvania, and the 97th New York, benefited from the obstructive knoll that hid the antagonists from each other. Taylor's exposed left, as a result, bore the brunt of the battle, the 11th Pennsylvania and 83rd New York absorbing a disproportionate number of casualties. Colonel Richard Coulter, commander of the 11th Pennsylvania regiment, bowed out of the fight early with a painful wound. Captain Christian Kuhn took his place. The regimental standard fell three times as Confederates shot the color-bearers one after another. The 83rd New York also lost its commander, Captain John Hendrickson, who received a crippling knee wound. Captain Joseph A. Moesch assumed command of the regiment. Hendrickson stayed with the regiment, lying in the mud behind the line and exhorting his New Yorkers, "On to glory!" Soon after, Captain Moesch fell wounded, but he retained

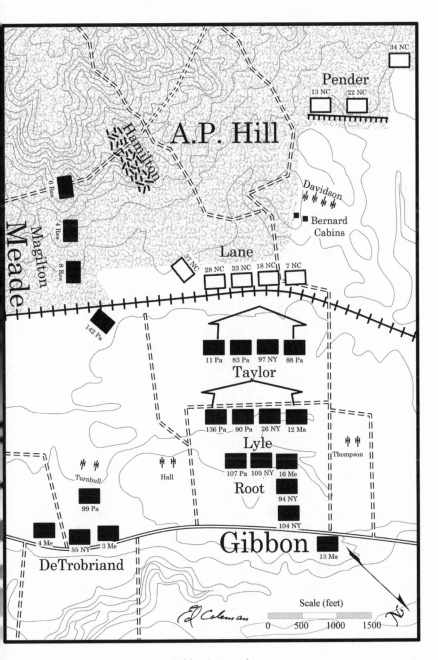

Gibbon's Assault

control until blood loss left him too faint. He reluctantly yielded his command to Lieutenant Isaac E. Hoagland. The two regiments endured for a short time, but the fire took its toll. The Rebels made "a terrible slaughter in our ranks," recorded one of Taylor's men. "It was impossible to advance as our boys fell as fast as they attempted it." Another wrote that the Union "men fell thick and fast." Taylor's left collapsed and soon fled the field, leaving only two regiments—the 88th Pennsylvania and 97th New York—to face Lane's Brigade.[57]

Fortunately for Taylor, Peter Lyle's brigade arrived just as his left gave way. The disorganized flight of the 11th Pennsylvania and 83rd New York blasted through Lyle's left and partially disrupted the brigade. Taylor gave up trying to rally his stalled regiments and quickly returned to his remaining units. He shifted the two regiments to the right to make room for Lyle's brigade. As Taylor moved, Lyle came into line and Gibbon's attack grew from a four-regiment front to a six-regiment line. Despite the encounter with the frightened and broken commands, Lyle's left easily regrouped and pressed on. The momentum of Lyle's brigade drove the entire line closer to the Rebel lines. As the Federals crested the rise fifty yards from the railroad, a whirlwind of fire and smoke enveloped the attackers with startling intensity. The Northerners, riddled by the murderous fire, fell back behind the knoll "in considerable confusion." The added Confederate might came from the 33rd North Carolina and 18th North Carolina, which had joined the battle at last. Lane's entire brigade loosed an explosive volume of fire. Seeing the Yankees shocked and reeling, Colonel Clark M. Avery begged Lane to counterattack. Avery offered to spearhead the assault with his 33rd North Carolina. Lane demurred, quietly telling his subordinate, "No, Colonel, hold your position at all hazards." A punitive attack might have swept Taylor and Lyle away, but Lane worried that the preponderance of Union artillery would wreak havoc with his Carolinians once they cleared the rise.[58]

Lyle's and Taylor's Federals re-formed behind the knoll. Sprawling on the ground, the bluecoats returned a heavy fusillade on the Confederates. The railroad bank and rolling ground prevented direct fire on any part of Lane's defenses except his right. As a result, the Northerners crossed their fire with the Pennsylvania Reserves and hit the 28th and 37th North Carolina from the front and flank. The fire weakened the Carolinians dramatically and they began to waver. Captain Edward F. Lovell heartened his hard-pressed command by standing defiantly on top of the railroad grade. Waving his cap and cheering boisterously, Captain Lovell riveted everyone's attention, yet he survived the battle untouched. Another show of bravery inspired the 28th North Carolina. Private William A. Martin rested on the railroad and picked off Union standard-bearers. His repeated success encouraged the Southerners, and the regiment cheered every time a Union flag went down. Nearby soldiers passed loaded rifles to Martin, who kept up his impressive show of marksmanship. But a new crisis developed to worry the Confederates—bullets started to become scarce. Lane's right bore the brunt of the fight and, correspondingly, expended more ammunition than the rest of the brigade. As rounds ran low, officers confiscated cartridges from the wounded and rifled the bodies of the dead for them. The 37th North Carolina had about used up its cache of ammunition, and the 28th North Carolina counted only one or two rounds left per man. Lieutenants divvied up the few bullets left.[59]

Beyond the tracks, Gibbon's troops suffered heavy casualties. Their exposed position under "a perfect shower of leaden hail" cost the Federals enormous numbers of men. One of Lyle's brigade members reported that the "men fell rapidly." The left of Gibbon's line sustained higher losses than the center or the right, doubtless because they had no knoll to interdict the fire. Lieutenant Colonel Gilbert C. Jennings, commander of the 26th New York, fell in the exchange, and Major Ezra F. Wetmore took over his regiment. Major Alfred J. Sellers of the 90th Pennsylvania also left the battlefield with a serious wound. A first-time warrior, S. Dean Canan of the 136th Pennsylvania, recalled the unnerving sensation of bullets and shells fanning his face. The color-bearer enjoyed it even less, especially with the likes of Rebel William Martin singling him out. Several close calls caused the standard-bearer to ditch his colors and run away. Private Philip Petty saw this shameful misconduct and took the flag himself. Pacing ahead of the line, Petty planted the colors in the soft ground and knelt beside them, shooting at the Rebels. The 136th Pennsylvania gave Petty three cheers, and Congress later gave him the Medal of Honor for his gallant gesture.[60]

Union fire diminished as the contest went on. Several regiments in Lyle's brigade reported that they had exhausted their sixty rounds of ammunition. Lyle turned to General Gibbon for help. Gibbon had seen Taylor's and Lyle's brigades stumble and had anticipated the crisis. Galloping to the rear, the general directed Colonel Adrian Root's brigade to prepare for action. Unlike their clumsy predecessors, Root's soldiers unslung their knapsacks and stacked their equipment before advancing. Once in line, the brigade fixed bayonets and waited for Gibbon's orders. Root placed three regiments in his front line: the 107th Pennsylvania, 105th New York, and the brand-new 16th

Maine. Behind the Maine unit, he stacked his two remaining regiments, the 94th New York and 104th New York. Fifteen yards separated the 94th New York from the first line. The 104th New York, in turn, formed fifteen yards behind the 94th. Some anxious soldiers noted that their nervousness dissipated as they started moving. A member of the 16th Maine explained this calm to his wife. "I want you to . . . bear in mind that our lives are not our own," he penned before the battle. "Death takes place in the State of Maine, even. We didn't all come here to be killed, many of us are going home, and I don't worry myself thinking that I may be one who cannot go home." The stoic brigade rolled forward, passing around Hall's Maine battery, and slogging across the muddy stubble field. Root started forward fifteen minutes after Taylor and Lyle had stalled.[61]

Federals trapped near the railroad saw the reinforcements lurching toward them and cheered. Colonel Lyle ordered his exhausted regiments—the 26th New York and 90th Pennsylvania—to let Root's line pass over them. Once relieved, the two units could retire to replenish their cartridge boxes. Root's brigade quickly gained the prostrate line and marched through without difficulty. The relieved Federals shouted to Root's men, "Give it to them, boys!" before passing to the rear. Near the center, the 16th Maine met the hardpressed 12th Massachusetts. The Massachusetts colors had been chewed to bits by bullets and threatened to fall apart completely. Colonel Charles W. Tilden's 16th Maine took over the 12th's front, breaking ranks and filing around the grimy Bay State soldiers. The tired veterans hailed the adept newcomers, yelling, "Three cheers for old Maine!" as the blue line glided past. The 94th and 104th New York followed Colonel Tilden's lead, and passed the 12th Massachusetts without as much fanfare.[62]

Lyle's attempt to bow out surprised and alarmed Adrian Root. The colonel assumed that Gibbon's men would join his attack, if not support it. Replacing Lyle's troops drained away the strength necessary to overrun the Confederate lines. When he saw Lyle's left pull back, Root grabbed Colonel James L. Bates of the 12th Massachusetts and pleaded, "Don't retire!" Bates explained that his regiment had no ammunition, but the brigadier cut him short. "Never mind," he snapped. "I am going to make a charge," and he pressed Bates to join him. The Massachusetts colonel relented and ordered his regiment to the right of Root's men. Nelson Taylor helped by urging his two regiments to unite with Root and Bates. Far to the left, the 136th Pennsylvania pressed forward on line with the 107th Pennsylvania and 105th New York; but without a firm connection to Root's brigade, the regiment functioned on its own. Only Lyle's 26th New York and 90th Pennsylvania quit the line and headed to the rear—an act that Root considered reprehensible.[63]

John Gibbon's mixed battle line, composed of elements from three different brigades, expanded to a seven-regiment front. The 16th Maine held the center, flanked on the left by the 136th Pennsylvania, 107th Pennsylvania, and 105th New York; and flanked on the right by the 12th Massachusetts, 97th New York, and 88th Pennsylvania. The Union attack pressed forward with the center outdistancing the flanks. The crescent-shaped line billowed over the knoll and charged the Confederate-held railroad. James Lane's Carolinians blasted the third assault with volleys of fire. Overwhelming losses robbed the Union attack of its momentum. Many of the bluecoats stopped reflexively and traded fire with the defenders. General Gibbon, however, was determined to drive home the assault. The division commander, joined by Nelson Taylor and Adrian Root, rode along the front, coaxing and cajoling the Federals onward. The attacking phalanx crept forward again, building speed with every step until the whole line cascaded down the rise, cheering and cursing at the top of their lungs. A First Corps writer commented later, "That was as grand a charge as was ever made." Gibbon's line plunged across the railroad "almost at a dead run." Despite the intense musketry, the Northerners pitched right into the midst of Lane's North Carolina brigade.[64]

The Union onslaught struck at the most inopportune moment for Lane's Confederates. Yankees burst into the Rebels' defenses just as they expended their last cartridges. The Union wedge lost some of its formation as it dashed down the slope. The center and left reached the railroad almost simultaneously. The head of the Union center, Tilden's 16th Maine, breached Lane's line between the 33rd North Carolina and 28th North Carolina. At the same time, Union troops swarmed around the exposed right flank of the 37th North Carolina.[65]

Union soldiers inundated the Confederates. The attack developed so rapidly that the enemies mixed before the Southerners could react. Defenders flailed their empty rifles at the multitude of Northerners. Federals, in turn, blistered the Confederates, by firing down the railroad ditch. A Maine soldier remembered the fire "was so rapid and constant that they could not stand it." Another rare encounter of hand-to-hand combat left dozens of wounded and dead trampled underfoot as the survivors grappled for possession of the railroad. Some of the Rebels hurled their bayonet-tipped weapons like spears at the attackers. Several Yankees fell pierced—one through the shoulder and another in the groin. "These were the first and only bayonet wounds that I ever saw during my service," reminisced a soldier in Gibbon's division. Many of the Federals had expended all of their ammunition and relied on their bayonets as well. Otis J. Libby of the 16th Maine staggered with pain when a Rebel clubbed him over the head with a rifle. He lashed back, bayoneting two Southerners before going to the rear for medical treatment. James M. Lyford of the same regiment saw his older brother, Charles, fall wounded. Charging his assailant, James drove a bayonet through the Rebel, shrieking, "Curse you, you killed my brother!" Noah Collins of the 37th North Carolina called the bloody battle "flagitious or grossly wicked." An officer of Root's staff agreed that "the fighting was savage." The 33rd North Carolina could not stop the Yankees from pouring into the ditch. Confederate James A. Watson recalled soldiers ducking and squirming on the ground because of the numerous "balls falling thick and fast around us." Captain Gold Griffin Holland had a similar experience to that of Major William Morris when a stale meal saved his life by deflecting a bullet. "I am indebted to a biscuit for my own life," he reflected after the war. Federal officers waded into the melee and encouraged their men. Since the 12th Massachusetts lacked ammunition, Colonel James Bates urged his men to use "the stock of the musket against the back of the neck." The spirited fight at close quarters took on a gruesome existence of its own.[66]

Outnumbered and swamped by Yankees, James Lane's Southerners abandoned the railroad line. The regiments on the right, the 37th North Carolina and 28th North Carolina, broke first and retreated into the marshy woods. Their thin ranks had been shattered and their duty for the day terminated. Union soldiers fired into the backs of the fleeing Rebels. "The boys made short work of those last retreating Confederates," a Yankee recalled. "I doubt whether any of them ever lived to rejoin their command." The 33rd North Carolina hung on a little longer, but overwhelming enemy numbers drove it from the ditch. The regiment rallied at the wood line west of the tracks in a defiant show of force. When the 33rd North Carolina left the ditch, Colonel Thomas J. Purdie re-fused the right of the 18th North Carolina to meet the attackers. An intense fire in front and flank propelled his regiment backward. Colonel Purdie sustained a slight wound, but continued to exercise command. The last Confederate regiment on the railroad, Lieutenant Colonel Junius L. Hill's 7th North Carolina, had been "left . . . to stand by herself" when the rest of Lane's Brigade had been forced to "give way and give back." The regiment fired across the tracks and down the ditch to keep the assailants back, but the Federals mobbed their line. Hill's Carolinians quickly withdrew. A forlorn Southerner noted that Lane's entire line had "caved in" by 2:00 P.M.[67]

Seeing his line collapsing, Lane hurried an aide to beg Maxcy Gregg to come forward. If Gregg could not be found, he instructed, then ask Edward L. Thomas' Brigade or any available unit for help. In the interim, Lane dashed through the woods, collecting broken fragments of his brigade and piecing them together in a new defense. The routed 28th and 37th North Carolina had gone beyond his reach and continued far to the rear. Lane managed to corral the 33rd North Carolina. Needing time to rally his other troops, Lane ordered the aggressive Colonel Clark Avery to launch a suicidal counterattack. Avery hurled his tiny command impulsively at the center of the Union line—where the Yankees were the thickest, and, conceivably, the most disorganized.[68]

The 33rd North Carolina blunted the advancing 16th Maine, stopping it cold at the railroad tracks. The 94th and 104th New York surged ahead to meet the Rebels, and trampled the 16th Maine in the process. The 94th New York locked with the 33rd North Carolina in a death grip, but could not budge the Southerners. The 104th New York cleared the 16th Maine and split in two. Part of the regiment pushed ahead and became tangled inextricably with the 94th New York. The other portion of the regiment angled to the right and plowed headlong into the Confederates. A brief face-to-face battle ensued, and Avery's Carolinians gave way. Clark Avery sacrificed his regiment to buy Lane a few precious minutes to regroup. Once Lane had formed the kernel of a new defensive line, he summoned Avery to fall back. The battered command retreated through the woods and found Lane's line standing one hundred yards west of the tracks. Lane had rallied the 7th North Carolina and ordered it to anchor his left. The 18th North Carolina stood beside it, and what was left of Avery's 33rd North Carolina assumed the right.[69]

Gibbon's division, flushed with success, charged into the forest after the retreating Confederates. They brushed against Lane's new line and readily retired to the railroad. Gibbon's troops had exploded in several different directions during the fight and pursuit. The units had become badly mixed and lacked any semblance of unity or command. The 136th Pennsylvania lost contact with the 107th Pennsylvania. The 107th Pennsylvania broke its tie to the 105th New York, which obliqued to the right and vanished into the trees. The 105th New York became isolated and unsupported on either flank. Three regiments in the middle of the line—the 16th Maine and 94th and 104th New York—were jumbled beyond use despite the efforts of harried commanders screaming themselves hoarse for their regiments to rally around them. The 12th Massachusetts decided not to venture beyond the tracks without ammunition and passively watched the chaos to its left. Nelson Taylor's two regiments, the 97th New York and 88th Pennsylvania, strayed farther to the right and broke contact with the 12th Massachusetts. Gibbon's division had carried its objective but became fractured beyond easy recall. As a result, Gibbon halted the advance and ordered everyone back to the railroad to redeploy. Root brought his left out of the woods, and the other commands more or less, complied.[70]

Gibbon secured his gains and tallied his losses. He held Lane's defenses and had captured a substantial number of Carolinians, particularly from the pernicious 33rd North Carolina. Among the captives was Avery's second-in-command, Lieutenant Colonel Robert V. Cowan. A Northern newspaperman, Murat Halstead, studied Gibbon's prisoners and reported, "It was pathetic to see their home-made outfits, their knapsacks of worn carpets . . . and ragged hats." Gibbon lost two more regimental commanders when he captured the railroad. Colonel Gilbert C. Prey of the 104th New York received a slight wound. Major Daniel A. Sharp took a much more serious injury, which required Captain Abraham Moore to replace him.[71]

Adrian Root took responsibility for reorganizing the troops on the railroad. While his staff extracted one unit from another, and strung regiments into line, Root sought Gibbon for instructions. The division commander commended Root for his accomplishments "so far," and encouraged him to resume the offensive as soon as possible. Gibbon snapped curtly, "Go on," and Root wheeled to get his brigade moving.[72]

Meade and Gibbon had succeeded in fulfilling their orders, and then some. Despite the paucity of their numbers, the First Corps troops had shattered and routed Maxcy Gregg's Brigade, battered James H. Lane's Brigade, and fairly dismembered James J. Archer's Brigade. Meade had control of the vital Military Road and was closing in on R. Lindsay Walker's stranded Confederate artillery battalion. Gibbon held a firm grip on the railroad, within supporting distance of Meade and striking distance of Greenlee Davidson's Southern cannon at the Bernard Cabins. Union attackers had taken a six-hundred-yard gap and burst it to twice its size. Eight thousand Union soldiers had attacked A. P. Hill's division of some 10,000 men and thrown it into fits.

Meade and Gibbon relied on very different methods of command to or-

chestrate their combined success. Meade, the wily old veteran, had breached
the Confederate defenses, whereas the fresh young Gibbon had bruised them
and driven them back. Meade's troops reactively exploited the breakthrough,
stabbing at Confederate flanks and expanding the gap far beyond what their
numbers warranted. They exceeded all expectations and occupied a wide ex-
panse of Prospect Hill. Gibbon, on the other hand, had wrested an important
position from the Confederates but left the Southerners intact and forming
another defensive cordon in his front. Meade's men had found the hole in
Stonewall Jackson's line and quickly seized the initiative. An improvised series
of attacks and sorties had netted the Pennsylvania Reserves numerous prizes,
prisoners, and valuable ground. But Meade's men flared across the landscape
without leaders or ammunition, and beyond retrieval or assistance. Gibbon
faced a similar dilemma developing on his front. As his troops scattered in
every direction, he opted to stop their progress and reorder their ranks along
the railroad. He intended to press his attack up the hill, but he believed that
further success could be attained only by orderly ranks and through discipline.

In both cases, the Union First Corps had achieved its objectives. A jubilant
Pennsylvania Bucktail wrote, "All that was expected of us had been fully accomplished." The key to Meade's and Gibbon's continued success depended
on their ability to consolidate their gains, obtain reinforcements, and capitalize on their efforts. Meade held the key to Stonewall Jackson's position, and
a terrible backlash was assured. If the Confederates could not destroy the
Union lodgment, Robert E. Lee might well have to abandon his defenses and
retreat. With victory tantalizingly close, Meade and Gibbon unfortunately
had their commands scattered and overextended; and reinforcements were
not immediately available.[73]

CHAPTER EIGHT

"GETTING HILL OUT O' TROUBLE"

The Confederate Counterattack

George Meade heard the fighting on Prospect Hill erupt with renewed intensity. Wounded Federals streamed to the rear in great numbers, and none of
them knew where to find his brigade. The Pennsylvania general had predicted
that he could take Prospect Hill, but he would need reinforcements to hold
it. As his splintered command clung to its far-flung gains, Meade sent an aide
to the rear to fetch some fresh troops. As time was critical, the staff officer
made a beeline for the closest troops. The force stationed directly behind the
Pennsylvania Reserves was the Union Third Corps division of Brigadier General David Bell Birney. The dour abolitionist soldier, who reminded at least
one soldier of a stone-faced sentinel from a tombstone, had positioned his
division just before Meade's attack. Brigadier General George Stoneman,
commander of the Third Corps, had sent Birney's troops over the Rappahannock River with orders to cooperate with Franklin's grand division. Though
officially part of Hooker's Center Grand Division, Birney entered the battlefield at 11:00 A.M. and reported to Franklin. The Left Grand Division chief
directed the division to bolster Reynolds' First Corps line. Stoneman's Third
Corps had been parceled across the battlefield with a division in Fredericksburg, another idling by the lower pontoon crossing, and Birney's command
heading for the hot spot on the field. Technically, Stoneman had no command, so he accompanied Birney to help place his troops.[1]

Despite Stoneman's assistance, Birney started his division so unexpectedly that he marched with only two of his three brigades. Brigadier General J. H. Hobart Ward's brigade led the column across the river, followed by Brigadier General Hiram G. Berry's brigade. Somehow orders miscarried and the division sped away without Brigadier General John C. Robinson's command. Robinson remained behind guarding the bridges with Brigadier General Daniel E. Sickles' division. Stoneman spurred ahead to see Franklin at the Bernard house, and Birney passed into the field at the height of the artillery barrage. John Reynolds intercepted Birney and ordered his division to take cover on the Bowling Green Road behind Meade. The Third Corps soldiers lay down along the highway ditches and watched the Pennsylvania Reserves charge the hills in front.[2]

Birney replaced some of the exhausted batteries in front with his own guns under Captain George F. Randolph. Lieutenant Pardon S. Jastram's Battery E, 1st Rhode Island Light Artillery, relieved Captain Dunbar R. Ransom's tired Pennsylvania battery. Lieutenant John G. Turnbull's Batteries F and K, 3rd U.S. Artillery, filled the gap to its right where Frank Amsden's artillery recently had been. Birney directed Ward and Berry to detach three regiments to support the cannon. Berry forwarded the 5th Michigan, while Ward sent the 57th and 99th Pennsylvania. The infantry advanced a couple of hundred yards and lay down behind the long row of guns. The rest of the troops sat comfortably covered by the roadbed, holding the critical link between Doubleday's division and Root's brigade of Gibbon's command.[3]

George Stoneman uselessly milled around Franklin's headquarters. With his corps broken up and scattered, he was a general without a command. He bridled at his lack of responsibility and left the Bernard house to join Birney's troops on the Bowling Green Road. The division offered little solace for the disillusioned general. Birney was under Reynolds' control now and had nothing to do but wait in reserve. Stoneman wandered to the right and met John Gibbon just as he stripped Root's brigade from reserve. Gibbon "begged" the Third Corps commander, according to Stoneman, to replace his supports for Hall's Maine battery. Though he had no authority to do so, Stoneman readily agreed and sped off to detail some of Birney's troops. Confused by the muddled chain of command, Birney complied with Stoneman's orders and directed Colonel Asher S. Leidy's 99th Pennsylvania to shift from Randolph's guns to Hall's 2nd Maine Battery. Birney reinforced Hall with the 55th New York and 3rd Maine, and placed all three regiments under the senior officer Colonel Philippe Régis de Keredern De Trobriand. The fussy Frenchman spread his troops behind the guns with the 99th Pennsylvania on the left, then the 55th New York, and the 3rd Maine on the right.[4]

Meade's urgent request for reinforcements came at the worst possible moment for David Birney. One of his brigades was missing and the other two had been parceled into several insignificant forces to protect the artillery. Furthermore, he was unprepared or unwilling to accept orders from one of Reynolds' subordinates. He shocked Meade's aide by declining to help. The incredulous staff officer returned empty-handed, explaining to Meade that Birney insisted that he was "under the orders of General Reynolds, sustaining General Stoneman, and could not move without their orders." And Reynolds was nowhere to be found.[5]

Meade listened to the improbable explanation and sent a second order to Birney to come forward at once. The battle hung in the balance, and the Pennsylvania Reserves grew weaker with each passing minute. He had no time to quibble over the niceties of protocol: he needed help and his peremptory order should have absolved Birney of all responsibility for obeying. The courier flew to Birney, but the adamant general refused to budge. The Third Corps officer allegedly directed Meade's emissary to find Reynolds, "who was on the field." Birney insisted that he "had just received an order from him to retire my command; but that on hearing from General Reynolds I would advance immediately." The staff officer could not locate Reynolds to mediate the impasse and returned unsuccessfully to Meade. The explosive Reserves commander flew into a rage and set out to see the uncooperative Third Corps general himself.[6]

General John Gibbon scrambled at the same time to find reinforcements for his division. His troops had suffered high casualties when they captured the railroad, and the survivors were in disarray. Gibbon encouraged his men to keep the attack alive. He pressed Colonel Adrian Root to "go on," but he knew the attackers were too weak to succeed without help. Once Gibbon ordered Root to go ahead, he started for the rear to get reinforcements. Having found Stoneman eager to help him once, perhaps he looked for the Third Corps leader to provide more substantial aid. If so, he was disappointed. He found little infantry available, and Stoneman was nowhere to be seen. Desperately, Gibbon forwarded James Hall's and James Thompson's batteries to guard both of his flanks against counterattacks. The cannoneers advanced well into the field, and Hall set up extraordinarily close to the woods. Régis De Trobriand's supporting regiments did not advance, because Gibbon's final battery, the 5th Battery, Maine Light Artillery, under division artillery chief

Captain George F. Leppien, moved up and took Hall's old position. De Trobriand opted to guard Leppien's guns rather than Hall's more advanced ones.[7]

While searching for reinforcements, Gibbon spotted two regiments, seemingly cowering in a ditch near the copse. He sent his acting inspector general, Captain Edward L. Lee, to guide them up to the railroad. Colonel Peter Lyle had directed the 26th New York and 90th Pennsylvania to fall back when Adrian Root's brigade had passed to the front. Lyle's regiments had refrained from charging the railroad with Root because they had no ammunition. Instead, they retired one hundred yards to scour the dead and wounded of Taylor's brigade for cartridges. Confederates infiltrated the woods, causing the Federals to expend whatever rounds they had gathered. This necessitated more gleaning and delayed their return to the division. Captain Lee, ordered to roust the assumed shirkers, charged into their midst, cursing and insulting the throng. He demanded that they return to the front immediately and threatened to shoot anyone who did not obey. The Northerners stood dumbfounded by the caustic young tyro. Lieutenant Colonel William Leech of the 90th Pennsylvania stormed up to the pistol-waving captain and told him that these men were seasoned veterans and knew "what they were about." Dressed down by the colonel, the staff captain scuttled away to find Gibbon. The acrimonious Colonel Leech duly reported that "the men that he threatened were, to say the least, much cooler than he appeared to be." Leech surmised that the captain would return as soon as he complained to Gibbon. To preempt the nettlesome staff officer, Leech gathered the 26th New York and 90th Pennsylvania and started back to the division. Most of Leech's soldiers still had no ammunition.[8]

While Meade and Birney wrangled over matters of propriety and Gibbon anguished over reinforcements, Stonewall Jackson's Confederates held their ground by a precarious margin. A. P. Hill's line had been ruptured and his division thrown into disarray. One brigade had been routed and two others badly hurt. One brigade commander lay dying as a result of the Union breakthrough. Jackson's artillery stood perilously close to being captured. Gibbon's men advanced to within yards of Greenlee Davidson's cannon, while Meade's men closed in on R. Lindsay Walker's fourteen guns. Walker could not rescue his guns because the woods allowed no exit, and legions of confused Confederates choked the Military Road, rendering it impassable.[9]

A. P. Hill and his lieutenants enjoyed one benefit over their enemies: they obtained reinforcements without delay. Confederates from the reserve line surged through the woods to contain the breakthrough and seal the breach. Troops in butternut and gray swarmed to Archer's and Lane's assistance. James Archer led the first reinforcements himself. He pulled the 5th Alabama Battalion from his right flank and circled it around to his left. The general rode at the head of the command. Moments before the 5th Alabama Battalion came into line, the 7th Tennessee collapsed. Amid the confused melee, Yankees asked Colonel John F. Goodner to surrender his Tennessee regiment, but the point became moot as the 7th Tennessee broke and fled, and so did the colonel. The men who had fired in anger at their comrades moments before, now followed them in flight. Goodner admitted that his regiment expended all of its ammunition and "made their escape by a hasty retreat." Lieutenant William A. McCall left in such a panic that he guessed he made "about thirty miles an hour" in speed.[10]

Archer arrived with the Alabamians just as the Tennesseans crumbled. The general parried the Union surge by flinging the tiny battalion into the Union flank. The fleet Lieutenant McCall recalled: "as I went out . . . I met Archer going in with that band of heroes." Some of the 7th Tennessee hung on and joined the 5th Alabama Battalion. The close nature of the fighting surprised some of the Alabamians, one of whom confessed, "for a time things looked squally." Archer appeared at the fulcrum of the storm, lashing in every direction as the Yankees surrounded his battalion. Confederates reported that the Little Gamecock general stood "like a rock" while men fell all around him. Major Albert S. Van de Graaff, commander of the 5th Alabama Battalion, fell wounded in the melee and turned over command to Captain S. D. Stewart. Nearby, General A. P. Hill encouraged the 1st Tennessee Hogdrivers to hold their ground "until hell froze over." Meanwhile, Archer's appeals for reinforcements, probably helped by A. P. Hill's imprimatur, started to produce results. Far to the rear, Confederates began to hurry forward to relieve the harried Light Division.[11]

A. P. Hill likely summoned Colonel John M. Brockenbrough's Brigade to help. Not engaged on his own front, Brockenbrough ordered his entire brigade to Archer's aid. Three Virginia regiments and a battalion left the railroad embankment south of Walker's artillery and marched to the sound of the fighting. The brigade pushed through the woods behind R. Lindsay Walker's guns, shouldering aside the flotsam of battle. The two leading units—the 47th Virginia and 22nd Virginia Battalion—lost contact with the rest of the brigade and disappeared into the crowded forest. The two trailing regiments—the 40th and 55th Virginia—endeavored to follow, but Colonel

Brockenbrough completely lost his way and wandered astray. He found the front only after the battle had abated. The lead units, unencumbered by Brockenbrough's absent sense of direction, threaded their way to Archer's beleaguered left flank. The Virginians arrived just as the Alabamians appeared on the brink of collapse. Some of the battalion had already broken, and the rest teetered under intense pressure. The newly arrived 47th Virginia and 22nd Virginia Battalion jumped into line beside Archer's Alabamians and shored up their flank. The Federals fell back slightly, which allowed the 5th Alabama Battalion to regroup.[12]

Deep in the forest behind A. P. Hill's line, Jubal Early's division spotted the first signs of a crisis in front. Early's men listened to the sound of battle spread across their front, but few guessed its magnitude. Small groups and individual soldiers straggled through the woods, recounting stories of disaster on Prospect Hill. Some of Archer's officers pleaded with Early's men to help them re-form their units. Lieutenant Colonel Andrew J. Hutchins, of the 19th Georgia, appealed to the Georgians in Robert Hoke's Brigade to assist him in rallying his troops. The 21st Georgia directed Hutchins' men to regroup behind it. Colonel Edmund N. Atkinson's Georgia brigade reorganized scores of soldiers from Georgia and Tennessee. Most of A. P. Hill's survivors, however, slipped through the cordon and kept going. Sifting across the Mine Road, Archer's soldiers regrouped in comparative safety beyond the Hamilton house.[13]

News from Archer heightened Early's anxiety and put him in a difficult bind. Archer had sent several staff officers to beg him for assistance. At the same time, a courier from Stonewall Jackson ordered the stooped general to be ready to move south of Hamilton's Crossing. Jackson had stripped D. H. Hill's division from reserve to counter Doubleday's shift down the Bowling Green Road. Assuming that Doubleday represented the main threat, Jackson went with Hill to bolster Jeb Stuart's front. He left word for Early to get ready to follow. Early listened uneasily to Archer's pleas, as he did not want to commit his troops against Jackson's wishes. Early had fallen afoul of the unbending Stonewall once during this campaign, when he struggled over Thornton's Gap. He had no intention of upsetting Jackson again, though impelling circumstances on Prospect Hill forced Early to admit, "This caused me to hesitate a moment." Early calculated his commander's displeasure and then manfully ordered Atkinson's Brigade to stand by to help A. P. Hill's troops.[14]

Moments later, a breathless artillery officer galloped up, panting about ca-

tastrophe. That snapped Early into action. The artillerist claimed that the
Yankees had burst "an awful gulf" in front and only Early could drive them
back. Early elected to err on the side of decisive action. He directed Atkinson
forward, despite Jackson's supposed wishes. Committing one brigade while
husbanding three hardly jeopardized Early's career, but any deviation from
Jackson's plans could be personally risky. Still, a sin of omission in a time of
crisis was unforgivable, especially with Stonewall Jackson.[15]

Atkinson's Georgia brigade dressed ranks in the dim, confining woods.
Broken terrain and watersheds divided the brigade and severed contact between regiments. The 13th Georgia stood in a deep recess on the right and
could not see the rest of the brigade. As a result, the regiment never noticed
Atkinson's command advance. Early happened upon the oblivious 13th

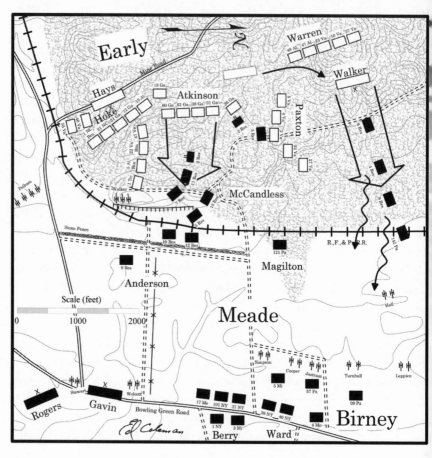

Early's Counterattack

Georgia well after Atkinson's Brigade had vanished into the forest. The vituperative general castigated the command and demanded that it find its brigade at once. Colonel James M. Smith hurried his chastened 13th Georgia into the woods, relieved to escape Early's vitriol as much as to rejoin Atkinson's Brigade.[16]

Atkinson advanced rapidly, probably without knowing he had lost the 13th Georgia. Within a few minutes, the woods erupted in gunfire as Atkinson's left blundered into a pocket of Union resistance 250 yards from Early's line. The 26th Georgia, under Captain Benjamin F. Grace, protected Atkinson's left flank. It ran headlong into a mass of bluecoats, most likely the 2nd Pennsylvania Reserves. Uncertain what they had hit, the Confederates recoiled in shock. The 26th Georgia quickly regained its composure and returned the fire, though one soldier wrote that the 26th "hardly saved its reputation." Grace's regiment sparked a close firefight, which checked its farther progress. His right missing and his left shorn off, Atkinson continued to drive ahead with the bulk of the brigade. The colonel found nothing to impede his path to Archer's Brigade, so he left Captain Grace's 26th Georgia to fend for itself. The Georgia regiment vanquished the Pennsylvanians a short time later, but by then Atkinson had driven well ahead and the regiment could not catch up.[17]

Atkinson's Brigade crashed through the underbrush, wary of Yankee ambushes in the thickets. A few minutes after the 26th Georgia became embroiled on the left, the rest of the brigade plowed headlong into Meade's main force. The Georgians unleashed a volley and charged. Screaming Confederates, howling the bone-shivering Rebel Yell, hacked into the overextended Union force at the edge of the woods and sent it reeling down the hill to the railroad. Small groups of Pennsylvanians disputed the Confederates on the slope and in the woods. Atkinson's Brigade clambered out of the woods and over the hilltop, fortuitously close to the left of Brockenbrough's 40th Virginia and 22nd Virginia Battalion. The Georgians shouted at A. P. Hill's men resentfully: "Here comes old Jubal!" "Let old Jubal straighten that fence!" "Jubal's boys are always getting Hill out o' trouble!" Early later cornered James Power Smith of Jackson's staff and complained that A. P. Hill's "Light Division" had been *too light* "to keep the Yankees from getting in on me." Archer's tired defenders bit their lips, happy to see Early's men stabilize their line. The Virginians joined the reinforcements as they drove the Yankees off of the hill. The crisis passed; Walker's guns were safe, and the tide of battle turned in favor of the Confederates.[18]

Meanwhile, Jubal Early received more calls for help from A. P. Hill's division. The wide range of messages made Early realize the immensity of the breakthrough and how Atkinson's Brigade could never seal it alone. Reluctantly, he detached Colonel James A. Walker's Brigade to assist in front. The Virginia command surged ahead "with a yell that would have scared the very devil himself." Early listened to the cheer reverberate in the woods and then reordered his line in anticipation of fulfilling Stonewall Jackson's orders. Colonel Robert Hoke's Brigade shifted from reserve to assume Atkinson's former position next to Harry Hays' Louisiana brigade. With half of his division committed to the fight on Prospect Hill, Early hoped that the other half would placate Jackson if he needed them below Hamilton's Crossing. When Brockenbrough's Brigade, however, left its works on the right, Early spread himself thinner. Hays' Brigade took over the empty sector of the railroad. Minutes later, word arrived that Archer's frayed right flank was collapsing. Jubal Early discarded Jackson's orders completely and released his final brigade.[19]

Hoke's Brigade had moved into line next to Hays' command, when Early ordered it to Archer's relief. Hoke started at once, only to run into the luckless 13th Georgia. Hoke's Brigade broke ranks and marched around the obstructing Georgians. Redressing ranks, the battle line hurried to the sound of fighting on Prospect Hill. Early dashed ahead, stumbling over the 13th Georgia again. He screamed at the regiment with even more anger than before. As Hoke approached the crest of Prospect Hill, he obliqued to the right, lest he collide with Archer's troops. The line swept into the clearing by R. L. Walker's guns and neatly tied into the right flank of Archer's 1st Tennessee. With the arrival of Atkinson, and then Hoke, Archer's flanks had been resecured.[20]

Early worried about Stonewall Jackson's wrath, but by this time, Jackson had seen the Federals atop Prospect Hill. He and D. H. Hill got an excellent view once they entered the bottomlands below Hamilton's Crossing. Jackson told Early to disregard his previous orders and support A. P. Hill. Early received the reassuring message after three of his four brigades had lunged into battle. Early was relieved. He summoned his final brigade, Hays' Louisianans, to back up Hoke. Jackson, meanwhile, started D. H. Hill back to Prospect Hill on the doublequick. The corps commander rode ahead to sort out the confusion in the Confederate line. In marked contrast to the Federal torpid response to Meade's success, Confederates flocked from all directions to save R. L. Walker's artillery and contain the breakthrough. Still, the battle hung in the balance, especially to the north, where Lane's Brigade struggled to re-group.[21]

General James Lane rallied his broken command in the woods and marshes north of the breakthrough. After losing two of his regiments, Lane re-formed the rest of his brigade on the next defensible line to the rear. Brigadier General William Dorsey Pender's North Carolina brigade held a defensive position nearby. Pender divided his command, putting two regiments—the 13th and 22nd North Carolina—in a trench behind Greenlee Davidson's guns. Two more regiments, 34th and 36th North Carolina, formed a separate line to their left rear. Pender's fifth regiment, the 16th North Carolina, ranged in front as skirmishers. Lane asked Pender to help him reassemble his disorganized brigade. Pender obliged, reinforcing the skirmishers in front to buy time for Lane to gather his brigade.[22]

The 22nd North Carolina, under the incendiary Major C. C. Cole, joined the 16th North Carolina and checked Gibbon's advance for the moment. The skirmishers locked in a heated battle that, one Carolinian reported, "was close, sharp, and continuous." Major Cole wrote, "Of all the battles I ever entered I never so much dreaded one" as he did Fredericksburg. While the 16th and 22nd North Carolina fired obliquely across the railroad, Greenlee Davidson's and Joseph Latimer's artillery sprayed the tracks with canister. Double-shotted cannon blasts carved huge swaths through the Union troops behind the railroad. "The head of the column," Davidson noted, "went down like wheat before the reaper." Latimer's guns played havoc with the Union right flank. General Pender admired Latimer's exploits, later remarking that the captain was "as brave a soldier as I ever saw." Greenlee Davidson also praised Latimer, saying that "he was one of the coolest and bravest boys I have ever met with." Latimer sat poised on his horse, looking "as if he had been at a holiday frolic." Union attackers withered under the voluminous fire.[23]

Dorsey Pender supported the guns at Bernard's Cabins until he saw Lane's men stream past his right flank. Greenlee Davidson remembered, "General Pender who was standing by at the time immediately leaped on his horse and accompanied by his aide attempted to rally" Lane's Carolinians. Federals stormed up the hill and split the air with a hail of bullets. Pender and Lane rallied the 7th and 18th North Carolina, and then the reformed 33rd North Carolina. The 7th North Carolina latched onto the right flank of Pender's 13th North Carolina. Moments later, the Yankees charged through the forest.

A brief exchange of shots—largely from Pender's Brigade, since everyone else had run out of ammunition—sent the Northerners tumbling backward. Colonel Alfred M. Scales, commander of the 13th North Carolina, intimated that his regiment handled the bulk of the fighting and "passed through a terrible ordeal." The colonel lost a number of casualties, which attests to the severity of the contest. Scales wrote: "I expected any moment to be my last." Pender drew up lame with a bullet in his forearm. The general shook off the blood and turned over the brigade to Scales, before heading to the hospital. Scales was somewhat embarrassed, as he had joined the brigade recently and did not know the command. The colonel maintained his line along the trench and assisted Lane in rebuilding his brigade.[24]

Out of view of Lane and Scales, Confederate reinforcements raced through the forest to provide relief. Early had dispatched James Walker's Brigade to fill the gap north of Atkinson's Brigade. Walker's Virginians shifted left to clear the Georgia brigade—and the battle between the 26th Georgia and 2nd Pennsylvania Reserves. In doing so, the brigade blundered right into Brigadier General Elisha F. "Bull" Paxton's Stonewall Brigade. Walker, finding his route blocked by Taliaferro's division, ordered his troops to muscle through the static line. Paxton objected and demanded that Walker go around his command. The Stonewall Brigade, far less perturbed than its new commander, opened ranks and allowed Walker's Virginians to pass ahead. The advancing troops laughed at Paxton's strictures and disappeared into the trees. A short distance beyond, James Walker encountered artillery fire and a vestige of Gregg's South Carolina brigade. The fire scattered the skittish South Carolinians. Walker's Virginians guyed one skulker, telling him that he would "be safer in the ranks," and "Fortune favors the brave." A Union shell struck the Carolinian, "and he was literally no more." Another soldier cowered behind an oak tree, where a random shot plowed through the root and exploded underneath him, "tearing him to bits."[25]

Walker's Virginia brigade left the South Carolinians and pressed toward the front. The Confederates suddenly ran into Yankees near the Military Road. Good fortune had led Walker directly to the flank of the Pennsylvania Reserves who had swung north during the breakthrough. The Virginians lashed into the end of the 1st Pennsylvania Reserves, and then the 6th Reserves. The Federals, surprised and without ammunition, panicked when they heard gunfire in the flank and rear. The Pennsylvanians broke and fled with the Virginians hot in pursuit. The rout carried away the 4th and 8th Reserves as the Yankees tumbled down the hill pell-mell to escape the trap. Pockets of resistance disputed the Confederates in the woods. A Rebel lieutenant claimed, "the fighting was terrible beyond description." A Pennsylvanian concurred that the Rebels "handled our Division pretty rough." Confederates surrounded a portion of the 1st Reserves. The Northerners hacked their way to freedom. "It was a nasty time thare for a bit," recalled a survivor, "the Rebs and our men were all mixed up together." Casualties ran high and "the ground was covered with dead and wounded," by one account. All of the momentum sided with the Confederates, who put the dazed and weary Federals to flight.[26]

Northern troops stampeded across the RF&P Railroad and through the copse. Walker chased them until he reached the finger of woods. Looking to his left, the brigade commander spotted Yankees massing in the field opposite his flank. In all likelihood, he brushed the 26th New York and 90th Pennsylvania while they were collecting ammunition. His troops fired a caustic warning from the treeline, and Peter Lyle's Federals reciprocated with a sputtering volley. Hall's battery laced the woods with canister, which mortally wounded Edward M. Dabney, the acting major of the 52nd Virginia. The Southerners prudently withdrew behind the railroad. Colonel Walker had difficulty getting some of his Virginians to fall back. He reported, "I had no trouble getting them to fight, but a good deal to get them to stop." Lyle's Federals did not pursue, as the excitable staff officer Lee rode up and distracted them with his pistol-wielding threats. The Confederate retreat passed tamely through the wetlands until Walker discovered Gibbon's division controlled the railroad embankment beside him. Apparently Gibbon never saw Walker. The Confederate commander detached his left regiment, the 13th Virginia, to develop Gibbon's strength while the rest of the brigade held the railroad.[27]

Colonel James B. Terrill's 13th Virginia moved stealthily through the marsh, feeling for the Union left flank. In the depth of the forest, the Virginia veterans—A. P. Hill's old regiment—struck an isolated Yankee command, apparently the novices of the 136th Pennsylvania. The Northerners had driven through the woods beyond Lane's right flank. Had Terrill not checked them, the Federals might have turned Lane's position. The woods erupted anew in gunfire. Greasy smoke filled the swamp and billowed above the trees. Pennsylvanians, uncertain what had hit them, halted and traded shots with their assailants. This halt allowed James Lane to solidify the grip on his new position.[28]

Reinforcements hurried to Lane's assistance from other directions. A. P. Hill's last brigade, Brigadier General Edward L. Thomas' Georgia brigade, rested several hundred yards behind Pender's Brigade, on the Military Road. Shortly before Gibbon's assault breached Lane's defenses, A. P. Hill had amended Thomas' orders so he could support any part of the line that needed it. Before the North Carolina brigade relinquished the railroad, Lane sent an orderly to General Thomas. The winded staff officer explained the situation in front and implored the Georgian for help. Thomas instantly agreed and rushed his brigade into battle line. Four Georgia regiments scrambled into formation and hurried down a wood path to Lane's assistance. The dense foliage and wetlands disrupted the brigade's advance and hindered its deployment. Thomas led the column with the 14th Georgia and the 49th Georgia. A break developed in the column, but the last two regiments, the 45th and 35th Georgia, somehow followed Thomas' trail to the front.[29]

Edward Thomas found Lane's right—and the Yankees at about the same time. The woods flashed with fire and the Georgians wheeled into line of battle. Thomas may have discovered the break in his column and sent an aide to hurry the other regiments along. Until they arrived, the general relied on two regiments to beat off the attack. The 14th Georgia took the right, under Colonel Robert W. Folsom. His troops called him "Cedar Run" Folsom because of his impressive role in the prelude battle to the Second Manassas campaign. Colonel Folsom formed his men in line of battle in a relatively open spot in the forest. The 49th Georgia formed to the left, hidden in a stand of old pines. The rest of Thomas' Brigade arrived and deployed out of sight as they came up.[30]

John Gibbon's division had re-formed on the RF&P Railroad by now, and renewed the advance into the woods. Greenlee Davidson wrote of the new attack: "The enemy are now on a line with the rear of my command. I expect every moment to see them dash out of the timber on my right." When the Federals drew closer to the guns, Thomas' Brigade whirled into action and mauled them with a stunning fusillade. A Georgian marveled at how the Confederates "poured volley after volley into the host of Yankees" until the Northerners broke and melted back into the timber. Folsom's 14th Georgia followed cautiously until it reached a field two hundred yards from the railroad. The Confederates redressed their formation along the tree line and waited for the Federals to try again. Folsom instructed his regiment to kneel down, keep quiet, and draw a careful bead on its targets.[31]

The colonel waited for the Union troops to advance to within fifty yards of his hidden line. A regal Northern officer rode temptingly in front of the blueclad legions. Anxious Confederates forgot their orders and fired at the horseman. The Northerners halted in their tracks and returned the fire, tearing up the trees with a storm of minié balls. A member of the 14th Georgia later admitted that the premature volley served as the "signal for the dire conflict which ensued." Yankees stormed the woods, and the 14th Georgia fell back a short distance before repelling the attackers. Gibbon's troops withdrew, regrouped, and tried again. The third assault surged through the forest only to be blunted by stiff resistance. Yankee fire ravaged the Georgia ranks. Feeling isolated and vulnerable, the 14th Georgia held its ground, but overwhelming casualties made it difficult to say how long the regiment could last. Little did the Southerners realize it, but the Federals felt the same way. A private in Gibbon's command recorded that his regiment expended all of its ammunition and the Rebels "all the time returning as good as they got."[32]

While the 14th Georgia battled, seemingly alone, the rest of Edward Thomas' Brigade came forward and engaged the Federals. Folsom's regiment did not know that the 49th Georgia stood right next to it because of the dense pine thicket. For their part, the 49th Georgia never saw or communicated with the regiments on either of its flanks. Folsom heard little fighting to his left. At one point, he wished petulantly the 49th Regiment would come up if only to divert some of the fire away from him. Unknown to the 14th Georgia, the bulk of Gibbon's division had advanced around its left flank and crashed into the 49th Georgia. Rifles crackled across the hillside and smoke obscured the enemies. In close combat, the 49th Georgia captured prisoners from a couple of New York regiments. Most likely, they encountered the 104th and 105th New York. Peals of gunfire paralyzed the Union advance and drew fire in return. A Confederate stated that Thomas' men "never occupied a more trying position, held it more firmly, fought more desperately, . . . or suffered so severely."[33]

Under the circumstances, the 49th Georgia also felt uncomfortably isolated. The Georgians had no contact with the 14th Georgia or with the other half of Thomas' Brigade to the left. Some of the soldiers blamed their predicament on "the delinquency of others," meaning the disappearance of the 35th and 45th Georgia. Others shared that conviction, but hoped the regiments had been delayed or misplaced "through a misconception of orders." The 14th Georgia and 49th Georgia presumed they endured the brunt of the attack (individually, of course) until the rest of Thomas' Brigade caught up. In fact, the supposedly wayward commands had arrived some time before. The 45th Georgia suffered several delays before finding the other half of Thomas' Brigade. Then the regiment struggled to establish a line in a dense grove of cedars. The 35th Georgia followed suit and formed on the left. Unlike their comrades on the right, the 45th and 35th Georgia had heard the battle going on beyond their flank and dressed their ranks accordingly. Unfortunately for the Southerners, the thicket obstructed direct contact, and the proximity of Gibbon's Yankees kept them from wandering too far afield. The latecomers, instead, sat tight and felt the incidental fire coming from the right, which was "thick and fast," according to one Georgian. Even on the left, Thomas' soldiers suffered numerous casualties from stray missiles. A 35th Georgia man complained afterward, "to tell you of the dangers which I have passed through . . . would be anything but pleasant." Fifteen minutes after the 14th and 49th Georgia regiments confronted Gibbon's attackers, the Northerners retreated into the forest. Edward Thomas had bought a critical respite during which the Confederates could regroup.[34]

Southern officers tried to re-form their jumbled commands. Men dressed their ranks and reloaded their weapons. In a few minutes, the Federals rolled forward again like a tidal wave in their fourth attempt to break the Confederate lines. Rebel fire halted the attackers in front, but Gibbon's line overlapped the right of Thomas' Georgia brigade. Union soldiers roared past the end of the Southern line and enfiladed the 14th Georgia. The Confederate flank began to yield, but Colonel Folsom ordered his men to hold—either to "conquer there or die." The regiment answered with a mighty cheer and drove the Federals back at the point of the bayonet. The Union host unexpectedly abandoned the attack and withdrew to the railroad. Robert Folsom's regiment had lost one-third of its force stopping the Yankees, but it could not account for the sudden retreat. Perhaps the appearance of Captain James Terrill's 13th Virginia on the flank upset the Northerners, or perhaps Gibbon or Root summoned them back to reorganize. Either way, the break in the fighting proved auspicious for the heavily beset Georgia brigade. The Federals had mauled Edward Thomas' right flank and more or less battered the rest of his command. But Thomas held his ground, repulsed four assaults, and blocked the widening breakthrough. The break in the action allowed Thomas to reconnect his loosely scattered regiments. The four brigades of Scales (Pender), Lane, Walker, and Thomas had repelled the Union tide and repaired much of the ruptured Confederate line.[35]

A. P. Hill and Jubal Early showed celerity and decisiveness in resecuring the line around the breach; but General William B. Taliaferro stayed remarkably aloof from the action. He held his division in reserve to the north of Early's position. Taliaferro allegedly had instructed his brigade commanders to stay alert and available to support A. P. Hill if he needed them. Taliaferro, however, maintained no communications with the front or with his own subordinates. The individual brigade leaders listened to the battle pitch and swell in front of them without knowing what was happening. Elisha Paxton, for example, had placed the Stonewall Brigade four hundred yards behind Maxcy Gregg's Brigade. Paxton knew that Gregg would govern his moves, so he detailed an orderly to serve as a liaison between the two commands. Though that preliminary measure showed initiative, the Pennsylvanians surprised Gregg's South Carolinians and the Stonewall Brigade sat idly by. Paxton waited naively for "official" word from his liaison before he moved. The brigade commander vacillated while most of his soldiers plainly heard Gregg's troops getting throttled. The soldiers could not understand why their general did not do something at once.[36]

Bull Paxton ultimately received a full report of the rout in front and readied the veteran Stonewall Brigade for battle. The general, with far less experience than his brigade, wasted an inordinate amount of time fretting over minor imperfections in the alignment. Just when he was satisfied that everything had been corrected, James Walker's Brigade plowed through his ranks and passed remorselessly to the front. Paxton glowered and threatened, but Walker's Virginians only laughed. The brigade commander returned to perfecting his line. Once again pleased with his alignment, Paxton slowly advanced his brigade to the Military Road. The Stonewall Brigade spotted the remnants of Maxcy Gregg's Brigade in the woods. Paxton expected the disheveled South Carolinians to join his brigade, but the Deep South units lacked leaders and cohesion. The Virginians cajoled the Carolinians without effect. Colonel James K. Edmondson, of the 27th Virginia, thought these men "seemed to be doubting as to their duty." Paxton also condemned Gregg's Brigade, now under the command of Colonel Daniel Hamilton, and started the Stonewall Brigade in motion again. Artillery fire blanketed the woods, annoying Walker's Brigade and thoroughly disrupting the Stonewall Brigade. Paxton perceived a blemish in his alignment, and halted his brigade to redress the ranks under fire. A captain in the 2nd Virginia mocked Paxton's baffling mania for taking the brigade "into action in perfect alignment." The soldiers stood patiently under fire while their unseasoned general arranged everything to his liking. In the interim, needless casualties multiplied, including the commander of the 4th Virginia, Lieutenant Colonel Robert D. Gardner, who suffered shrapnel wounds to his face and chest. Major William Terry assumed command of the regiment.[37]

While Paxton tinkered with parade-ground formations, Captain John Q. A. Nadenbousch noticed movement in the woods to his right. The commander of the 2nd Virginia spotted a sizable group of bluecoats pouring through the gap beyond his flank. Nadenbousch worried that the unchallenged Yankees might turn the Stonewall Brigade's flank. He tried to notify Paxton, but the general had disappeared, perhaps to scold Hamilton's South Carolinians. The 2nd Virginia captain decided on his own initiative to confront the Federals on the Military Road. Almost as soon as Nadenbousch wheeled out of line, he collided with the Northerners. The 2nd Virginia had met the 3rd Pennsylvania Reserves. Nadenbousch had difficulty in identifying the enemy because of the dense woods. This aspect of the encounter troubled the Confederates. They feared that they might have brushed against friendly units so far to the rear. When the woods rang with small arms fire, the acting lieutenant colonel, Raleigh T. Colston, objected, "We [are] firing on our own men!" The rank and file returned volley for volley, with the understanding that whoever stood in front deserved to be shot at, since "they are firing upon us mighty lively," or so Raleigh Colston's brother reasoned.[38]

Bull Paxton perked up as soon as he heard the crash of musketry to his right. The general yearned for a fight, and so far the lack of Yankees had discouraged him. Nadenbousch had revived his dream, as the general cryptically revealed in a letter home: "I made sure we should be in the battle." Paxton rushed the rest of the brigade to Nadenbousch's assistance. The excitement caused Paxton even to forgo precise regimented drill. He found the 2nd Virginia astride the Military Road, perpendicular to its former position. The general extended its flanks, sending the 4th and 5th Virginia to the right; and the 27th and 33rd Virginia to the left. Only the 4th Virginia and a portion of the 5th Virginia joined the battle. One Confederate characterized the action as "a fierce fight which only lasted a few moments" before the Federals retreated. The encounter ended so abruptly that the other Stonewall regiments did not get involved; but during that brief moment, the fighting had sparked with intensity. The 2nd Virginia suffered twice as many casualties as any of the other regiments in Paxton's Brigade. Captain William Colston, brother to the acting lieutenant colonel, described how a shell eviscerated one soldier, decapitated another, and then struck him in the stomach. Even though the 33rd Virginia reported no casualties, the unit in the aftermath of the struggle described it as "severe to us, but most terrible to them."[39]

The Stonewall Brigade claimed that the Yankee "slaughter was tremendous," which added further laurels to the unit's already remarkable combat record. No one dwelled on the fact that Paxton had mismanaged the brigade, caused needless casualties by halting under cannon fire, and missed an opportunity to surround and capture two Union regiments. Paxton, because of his inexperience, made numerous mistakes, but none so disappointing as misjudging his opponent. He assumed the Federals were part of a large attack force, when in fact they were two understrength units already contemplating retreat when John Nadenbousch struck. Paxton wasted important time trying to wheel his brigade into position without first pinning the enemy in place. Consequently, Paxton's Stonewall Brigade barely collided with the Northerners before the Pennsylvanians escaped from the trap.[40]

The rest of Taliaferro's division played an ancillary role in the battle. Colonel Edmund Pendleton's Louisiana brigade watched Thomas' Brigade leave the Military Road unexpectedly, but received no call to support it. Pendleton concluded independently to occupy Thomas' former position. He advanced to the road and no farther. Taliaferro's last two brigades tentatively followed Pendleton's movement. General Taliaferro hurried Brigadier General John R. Jones' Brigade to support Pendleton. Jones found the proximity of the battle unsettling and hid behind a tree. Colonel Edward T. H. Warren, commander of a mixed brigade of Virginians and Alabamians, filled the gap, between Daniel Hamilton's South Carolina brigade and the Stonewall Brigade on the Military Road. Following the contest in the woods, Paxton reassembled his brigade and halted on the road.[41]

On another part of the field, D. H. Hill's division raced back to Prospect Hill after its foray to Jeb Stuart's front. Stonewall Jackson rode in the van, driven by the sound of gunfire. Jackson had led D. H. Hill's division into the bottoms below Hamilton's Crossing, where he assumed the Federals would try to turn Prospect Hill. Now he reversed his decision and rushed troops to Jubal Early's old position in the second line. Until they arrived, Jackson's defense in depth had committed all of its troops to the front. The collapse of the front line meant the collapse of the entire position. Unknown to Jackson, Early's reinforcements had buttressed A. P. Hill's right. The fresh Confederates had worsted the disorganized Northerners with relative ease—and actually contemplated an offensive to retake the RF&P Railroad and beyond.[42]

George Meade flew into a towering rage. Once he found the troublesome David Birney on the Bowling Green Road near Dr. Pratt's house, Meade exploded in angry frustration. A bystander noted that "Meade was almost wild with rage as he saw the golden opportunity slipping away and the slaughter of his men going for naught." Meade had begged and ordered Birney twice to reinforce his division, but Birney twice had refused, arguing that he could not accept orders from John F. Reynolds' subalterns when Reynolds himself had told him to stay put. Reynolds, of course, could have solved the dilemma, but he was nowhere to be found. Meade refused to accept Birney's excuses. The Pennsylvania Reserves commander cursed the witless officer in such a manner that an onlooker wrote that Meade's tone was enough to "almost make the stones creep" underfoot. The abusive general calmed somewhat to explain that he was a major general, which obligated the inferior brigadier to obey his commands. "General," Meade snarled, "I assume the authority of ordering you up to the relief of my men." With that, Meade left to re-join his hard-pressed division; and the chastened Birney organized a hasty column of reinforcements. By this time, George Meade no longer aspired to holding the entire breakthrough. Waves of Confederates swarmed upon his troops, and the Pennsylvania Reserves' grip on Prospect Hill began to loosen—and with it, the hopes of Union victory.[43]

Before Meade returned to the front, he already had lost control of his right. James Walker's Confederate brigade had torn into the flank of the 1st Reserves, which sent the regiment reeling down the hill, carrying away the 6th, 4th, and 8th Reserves. The mad throng blasted out of the woods and trampled the novice 142nd Pennsylvania. Breathless veterans scurried past, shouting to the green regiment to "Get out of this, the 'Johnnies' are right behind us!" The rout left the soldiers of the 142nd Pennsylvania in disarray. Walker's Brigade suddenly exploded into their midst, causing the new regiment to flee the railroad. The colonel tried to put the retreat in a better light, stating that the Confederates compelled the 142nd Regiment "to retrace [its] steps precipitously." A more direct private said the Rebels forced him to "run" for his life. He mockingly corrected himself, "retreat, I should say." Frank Holsinger raced to the rear with the rest of Meade's right. His only purpose was to outdistance the Rebels. He ran so hard that he collapsed and vomited in an irrigation ditch. "Why endure this?" the sickened Pennsylvanian wondered. Death seemed almost preferable to the strain. Brushing himself off, the private walked slowly to the rear, concluding, "I determined what is to be will be." He escaped without a scratch. Captain John Eichelberger of the 8th Reserves stumbled during his flight when a bullet passed through his leg. It pushed his kneecap out like a cone. The captain swatted the kneecap flat and resumed his retreat.[44]

Since the collapse of the right, Meade's hold on the left also had begun to deteriorate. Pennsylvanians fought toe to toe with A. P. Hill's and Early's legions, but they had no ammunition, which gave a tremendous advantage to Jubal Early's Confederates. The neat, compact, and organized brigades of Atkinson and Hoke caught the Federals overextended and leaderless. Union resistance crumbled with startling rapidity. The bulk of the disordered Northern mob tumbled down the hill to the RF&P Railroad. Small groups of soldiers covered them with an impromptu rear guard. They delayed the Rebels as long as they could and then fell back. The rear guard sustained enormous casualties. "The loss on that retreat," recalled one of Meade's men, "was fully equal to that on the advance." A 5th Reserves soldier agreed: "coming in was rough but giting out was rougher." The 7th Reserves claimed to be the last regiment to leave Prospect Hill.[45]

Even as Meade's right and left folded, the Confederates closed in on the center. The untried 121st Pennsylvania wandered aimlessly on the wooded heights as it moved in the wake of the 1st and 6th Reserves. The novices encountered Rebel dead and wounded from Gregg's Brigade. "Such a sight," wrote one recruit, "I am in no way anxious to see again." Colonel Chapman Biddle worried that he had outdistanced the Pennsylvania Reserves and strayed beyond support. On his own, Biddle decided to retrace his steps to the railroad. A slight brush with the Stonewall Brigade might have helped make up his mind, though the First Corps historian later insisted that the regiment "was quite loath to retire." During the withdrawal, the 121st Pennsylvania passed the 3rd Reserves advancing up the hill. Apparently the sight of fresh troops did nothing to change Chapman Biddle's disposition; he continued to fall back. Some of his recruits, however, appeared to mix with the veterans and returned to the hill. The loosely reinforced 3rd Pennsylvania Reserves continued to press ahead. An apprehensive Reserves soldier thought they had gotten "too far ahead" of the other regiments through "some mistake or misunderstanding on the part of our Officers."[46]

Colonel Horatio Sickel's 3rd Reserves located the 2nd Reserves on the Military Road, just as Confederates assailed both regiments from opposite directions. The 2nd Reserves, now commanded by Captain Timothy Mealey, fired on the advance of Atkinson's Brigade while the 3rd Reserves tangled with the Stonewall Brigade. The historian of the outnumbered 2nd Reserves wrote that "the foe [was] swarming out on all sides." Another Reserves soldier remembered that the "Rebels were firing on us from the right and left and front and there was no troops to support us. It was terrible to see the men falling all about one." A 121st Pennsylvania man among the Reserves noted, "Our men were dropping very fast and the bullets whistled past our ears like hail." Firing in all directions, the 121st Pennsylvanians posed a special threat to friend and foe alike. Frank Sterling's comrades fired so wildly that they blistered his face with powder burns and almost cost him an eye.[47]

The 2nd Reserves had surprised the 26th Georgia and halted its progress. The 3rd Reserves, on the other hand, checked the 2nd Virginia. But the Reserves saw Confederate reinforcements hurrying through the woods to cut off their line of retreat. The 3rd Reserves called the fight a "rather rough job," with Rebels firing from behind trees and bushes. Three bullets shredded Colonel Horatio Sickel's uniform, and another smashed his binoculars. "We were looking for support," one Pennsylvanian wrote plaintively, but no one came. Caught in a crossfire, the Union soldiers retired before the Stonewall Brigade could surround them. Confederate artillery lashed at the retreating bluecoats. A fleeing Northerner wrote, "the[y] planted several pieces and the[y] did everlastingly rake us coming down that hill." The last of the Pennsylvania Reserves had been driven from Prospect Hill amid a crescendo of fire through which "one could hardly hear the orders of our officers," according to a man in the 3rd Reserves.[48]

Meade refused to concede the battle. The general later told his wife, "The slightest straw almost would have kept the tide in our favor." Meade rode along the railroad, looking "considerably vexed" as he rallied his broken commands. He anchored his left on several stout regiments from C. Feger Jackson's brigade. Most of them never had advanced beyond the railroad grade, so they were still intact. Meade urged Colonel William McCandless—the surprised successor to William Sinclair as brigade commander—to regroup his men to the right of Anderson's (formerly C. Feger Jackson's) brigade. The colonel, known to his soldiers as "Old Buck," enlisted the aid of officers Talley and Sickel to reorder his broken regiments. Few members of the 1st Brigade recognized McCandless, since he had transferred into the brigade only shortly before the battle. Those who did know him had a hard time finding him, as his horse had been killed at the outset of the battle and he was on foot. The colonel missed his mount, as he dashed from group to group, organizing the soldiers behind the railroad embankment. To make themselves more conspicuous, McCandless and Meade seized battle flags to rally the troops. Colonel Chapman Biddle's 121st Pennsylvania redressed on its colors once it reached the tracks. McCandless used its flag as a foundation for reorganizing other units. While Buck McCandless waved the 121st Pennsylvania's standard, Meade took the flag of the 2nd Reserves. As the troops flooded out of the woods and began to gel, Meade summoned his rear guard to fall back. Rebels harried the last pockets of resistance, "capturing many of the men and killing and wounding many more." Meade had recalled the 7th Reserves not a moment too soon.[49]

Federals cobbled together a hurried and feeble line. The troops had no order, no semblance of unity, no coordination, minimal ammunition, and very little hope. Meade watched the Confederates descend the face of Prospect Hill, but refused to withdraw. He kept his toothless command in place, hoping that David Birney's Third Corps division would redeem all that had been lost. But Birney could not possibly recoup the hill if Meade lost his toehold on the railroad.[50]

Confederates on top of Prospect Hill tried to deny Meade the chance. Intermixed Southern commands wasted precious minutes, trying to realign their forces for an advance. Confusion reigned, especially among James Archer's weary Tennesseans. As reinforcements assumed responsibility for the front, the 1st Tennessee slipped to the rear. Lieutenant Colonel Newton J. George, the bloody, ear-pierced successor to Colonel Peter Turney, thought he had been relieved and pulled his regiment out of the shallow trenches. Archer intercepted him and herded the regiment back into line. The Tennesseans had no sooner returned than the whole Confederate line surged ahead in an attack. While Archer coaxed the 1st Tennessee back to the trenches, Edmund Atkinson and Robert Hoke chafed over Meade's stand at the railroad. Some of the Federals along the embankment still had cartridges, which stung the Confederates standing exposed on the hilltop. Hoke mused testily that "it would not do to allow them to remain," and "immediately" ushered his brigade down the slope. Atkinson charged at the same time, goaded by a similar fire and high losses. Confederates bounded down the hillside and through the woods, piercing the air with "the wildest yells and gruff hurrahs." Northerners awaited the onslaught. Rebels spilled into the bottomland. The Yankees met them with one final "terrific and murderous fire." A bullet killed Lieutenant Colonel Thaddeus P. Scott, head of the 12th Georgia—making him the regiment's third commander lost in as many battles. A young protégé of Stonewall Jackson's, Major Edward S. "Ned" Willis, took over the regiment and led it toward the railroad.[51]

Atkinson's 38th Georgia lost its commander before it reached the bottom of the hill. Captain William L. McLeod had led the regiment at Fredericksburg, but a shell concussion knocked him out of the attack; and the regiment rolled ahead without him. Colonel Robert Hoke fell indirectly prey to the sting of a Union minié ball. The brigade commander spurred his mount ahead of the 15th Alabama just as a bullet nipped the horse's ear. The shock dropped the beast to its knees, jolting Hoke loose from the saddle. The horse then sprang up and bolted in a frenzy of pain. Hoke, his foot stuck in the stirrup, could not free himself before the wild animal dragged him, flailing, across the field. Soldiers from the 15th Alabama grabbed the reins and freed the dazed commander. Captain William C. Oates said that Hoke looked "addled for the moment." The colonel staggered uncertainly but insisted on leading the men.[52]

Confederates boiled down the hillside and over the railroad tracks. Some of the Southerners leapt into the ditches and landed literally on the heads of the Federals. The avalanche of Rebels inundated Meade's line, and enemies locked in another bout of close combat. Troops mixed inextricably. Atkinson's Georgia brigade claimed the Northerners offered their most serious resistance at the railroad. Clubbed muskets and bayonets heightened the desperate melee. Hoke charged into better-organized regiments—C. Feger Jackson's, now Anderson's. The large force startled Hoke's Brigade, which lashed out with extraordinary violence to keep from being destroyed. Hoke discovered the Yankees outnumbered his troops after it was too late to disengage, so the degree of viciousness effectively surprised and demoralized the Union defenders.[53]

Archer's minuscule regiments burst over the railroad to Hoke's left. The Tennesseans relied exclusively on bayonets, since they had no ammunition. Fortunately for them, neither did the Federals. Two Virginia regiments from John M. Brockenbrough's Brigade joined Archer's troops. The melee "lasted a few minutes," and pitted the organization of fresh Confederate reinforcements (excluding Archer, of course) against the tired, distended Pennsylvania Reserves. Meade's men flailed impotently and then abandoned the railroad ditch. A Northern soldier called the battle "one of the most disastrous to our Division." Confederates took control of the railroad and restored their original defensive line—all before David Birney's Union division arrived to support Meade. Southerners cheered their success, and even sour Jubal Early, nicknamed the "Wooden Man" for his stoicism, laughed with delight. They had met the crisis and triumphed.[54]

Many of the Pennsylvanians did not escape and ended up as prisoners.

Atkinson and Archer ordered the captured Yankees to the rear. Hoke's Brigade, outnumbered by the Federals, treated their prisoners roughly to ensure compliance. As the Yankees submitted, Hoke's command relaxed its treatment. Atkinson's Brigade claimed that they had captured more prisoners at Fredericksburg than any other unit in Lee's army. Hoke also had a bevy of Federals—in fact, too many for his brigade to handle. Robert Anderson's 9th Pennsylvania Reserves still held the stone wall a short distance away and continued to blister the railroad with fire. Soldiers blue and gray vied for cover in the overcrowded railroad ditches. Hoke ordered a small detail to take the prisoners to the rear, so he could have more cover for his Confederates. Guards herded the Federals out of the ditch while still under fire. Some of the prisoners balked, afraid they would be hit by friendly fire. The detail worried more about their own safety and shoved them ahead. Running a gauntlet, many of the prisoners disappeared before they reached the Confederate rear. Some fell under the fire of their own men. Others took advantage of the commotion to elude their captors. Hoke learned, much to his chagrin, that the Confederates behind him took credit for his prisoners. Jubal Early met a teenage Georgian toting a Yankee lieutenant and three other prisoners to the rear. Jasper Horben of the 38th Georgia presented his captives to Early, and startled the general by revealing that he had captured all four with an empty rifle. Early may have chuckled at Horben's feat, but Atkinson's Brigade had another surprise for the general, as they prepared to follow up their success.[55]

Union general David Birney scrambled to redeem himself before the irascible Meade lost control of Prospect Hill. Birney had scattered his command widely to guard batteries. Now that he had to reinforce the front, he had few troops available. Goaded to action by Meade, the Third Corps general ordered his nearest brigade to send whatever units it had at hand. Brigadier General J. H. Hobart Ward received the orders. He, in turn, told the division leader's older brother, Colonel William Birney, to advance the 38th and 40th New York to the railroad. Even as Colonel Birney aligned his regiments, the Third Corps troops saw Meade's line unraveling. The Confederates spilled down the hillside and captured the railroad just as the New Yorkers started forward. William Birney hurried to reach the Pennsylvania Reserves before their line completely collapsed. The 38th New York marched on the left and the 40th New York took the right. J. H. Hobart Ward rode to the 4th Maine and ordered it to join William Birney's advance. The two New York regiments rolled across the muddy plain, with Ward and the 4th Maine close behind them.[56]

Colonel Birney's two regiments became disorganized when they hit the woods. The 40th New York entered the brush while the 38th New York skirted the field to the south. As soon as the 40th Regiment—known as the Mozart Regiment—breached the woods, the refuse of George Meade's disheartened right came careening through its ranks. James Walker's Confederates had routed the Pennsylvanians, who in turn disrupted the 40th New York. A New Yorker said the Reserves stampeded "like a herd of buffalo." Meade's soldiers warned the Mozart men to "Go back! Go back!" Some of the Pennsylvania Reserves calmed down enough to join the New Yorkers. H. F. Christy of the 11th Reserves survived Meade's attack, only to be captured with Birney's men later. As the Reserves fled to the rear, it became obvious that Birney had arrived too late to save Meade's right.[57]

The 38th New York also met an impasse at that moment. William Birney's men ran into two ditches that stretched across their front. They struck at a particularly deep point. Soldiers tumbled five or six feet into the excavations. The steep sides made the obstacle "almost impassable." Union soldiers clawed their way out as best they could. Some of them halted in the trench to catch their breath. Others found it difficult to climb out of the hole without comrades to pull them out. Some of those who reached the other side pitched back into the cut killed or wounded. Mounted officers pranced along the ditch unable to get across. Colonel William Birney's regiments fragmented in the woods and the ditches. The colonel admitted with misgiving that his command had been "thrown into partial disorder" during the advance.[58]

General Ward caught up with Birney's regiments and helped rally them. He pointed the newly arrived 4th Maine to the right. Ward encouraged all three regiments to advance together. Ward's brigade obliqued to the right. Perhaps Ward was drawn by the stampede of Meade's men, or he was attempting to get around the difficult ditches. Since the three regiments angled into the scrubby marsh, the 38th New York reached the railroad before the others. William Birney's troops crossed the tracks cautiously. The left flank immediately became embroiled in a fight with Atkinson's Georgia brigade. Before the 40th New York and 4th Maine could help, Confederates pinned them down with "a terrific fire." Atkinson's Georgians halted the Federals in moments. Ward estimated that he lost 300 of his 800 effectives during the first five minutes of action. Confederates turned Ward's left flank, catching the 38th New York in a crossfire. Colonel William Birney fell seriously wounded, but remained with his command until he could extricate it from the trap. The regimental color-bearer, John Campbell, fell dead at the outbreak of fighting. Lieutenant Jeffrey Pendergrast saved the standard when the left flank collapsed. When the 38th New York retreated, it uncovered the 40th New York. The Georgians crushed the end of the Mozarters' line and sent them reeling. Colonel Nelson A. Gesner fell wounded but retained command until he extracted his regiment. The 4th Maine, absorbed in a fight in front, did not notice the other units give way. Confederates swarmed around both of the regiment's flanks. Major William L. Pitcher was killed instantly and the Maine men broke. The 4th Maine soldiers, according to an eyewitness, seemed to be "specially unfortunate in the loss of prisoners." Panicked men flooded out of the copse as fast as they could run. General Ward reckoned that he brought back 350 of the 800 soldiers who had entered the forest moments before.[59]

Prior to Ward's advance, the Confederates had crowded the railroad captured from Meade's Pennsylvanians. Georgians of Atkinson's Brigade had barely begun to regroup when they noticed Ward's Yankees penetrate the finger of woods to their left. Shots fired at the 38th New York in front diverted the Northerners into the marsh. Atkinson shifted his brigade up the railroad to intercept the bluecoats. The Rebels struck the flank of Ward's brigade and unraveled the line with remarkable speed. Victorious Southerners pitched across the railroad in pursuit. The brigade rampaged through the forest, with officers coaxing, "Forward boys, forward!" Captain Edward P. Lawton of Atkinson's staff seized the brigade colors and rode the length of the line, exhorting the men to catch the Yankees. Colonel Clement A. Evans of the 31st Georgia admired the captain's recklessness. Stealing an epitaph from Napoleon, he called Lawton "the bravest among the brave." Plucky Confederates chased Ward's broken command, "yelling as they advanced like savages."[60]

Colonel Edmund Atkinson led the charge to the edge of the swamp. He intended to stop and secure the copse against further incursions. Not all of his Confederates pressed ahead with enthusiasm. A skulker from the 60th Georgia cowered behind a stump when Colonel William H. Stiles caught him. The colonel slapped him with the flat of his sword. The recreant, sure that he had been hit by a bullet, whimpered his last mortal prayers. The annoyed officer interrupted the last rites by booting the man. "Get up, sir!" Stiles screamed. "The Lord wouldn't receive the spirit of such an infernal coward." The man jumped up and cried with obvious relief, "Ain't I killed?

Lord be praised!" The reanimated soldier bounded off to catch his regiment before the astonished colonel could kick him again.[61]

Hoke's Brigade, Archer's Brigade, and half of Brockenbrough's Brigade heard Atkinson attack and charged out of the railroad ditches in support. The Confederates on the right had endured a savage fire from Robert Anderson's 9th Pennsylvania Reserves and needed relief. They either had to drive the Northerners away or retreat. Elements of three brigades dashed across the flat ground in a picturesque phalanx. Hoke's troops left the railroad "with one loud cheer." Jackson and D. H. Hill admired the attack and then galloped up the hill. Several days later, D. H. Hill addressed Robert Hoke as "General." The confused colonel asked if Hill was making fun of him. Old Rawhides assured him that Jackson had been impressed by his decisiveness—and a promotion was forthcoming. Another onlooker watched the Confederate attack from atop Prospect Hill. The enthusiastic artillerist, Ben from South Carolina, wrote to his father, "My hat couldn't stay on my head. I would have hollered if I had been killed . . . simply because I couldn't help it."[62]

Archer's and Brockenbrough's men struck the 9th Reserves in front, but the Union musketry held the Confederates at bay. Hoke's Brigade, however, extended beyond the Pennsylvanians' vulnerable left flank. Southern troops crossed the low stone fence and turned the end of Lieutenant Colonel Anderson's line. The Union defenders gave away and scattered. An Alabama soldier said Hoke sent the Yankees "reeling, staggering, [and] breaking" to the rear. They fought for a moment and then "fled precipitously."[63]

The Confederates halted behind the captured wall. Archer and Hoke regrouped their commands. Officers directed prisoners to the rear unescorted. Not too surprisingly, many of them disappeared. The Southern brigadiers prepared to move again, perhaps sparked by Atkinson's advance into the finger of woods. Hoke, however, changed his mind at the last minute when he spied a Federal threat to his right front. Abner Doubleday's torpid division had come to life when Meade's division retreated. Doubleday adjusted his line to guard against a Confederate envelopment. Uncertain of Doubleday's intentions, and probably spotting Birney's division moving up, Archer and Hoke checked their advance at the fence line and waited to see what the Federals would do next. Doubleday's artillery shelled the position, and the Confederates decided that there was no advantage to holding the wall. Jubal Early came to the same conclusion and sent an orderly to withdraw Hoke's Brigade. The Southerners retired to the RF&P Railroad under an annoying shellfire. En route, Hoke received Early's orders.[64]

Archer directed part of his tired command to take cover on the crest of Prospect Hill. While climbing the slope, the 1st Tennessee lost another commander. Lieutenant Colonel Newton J. George caught some shrapnel. Soldiers assisted him to the rear as blood hemorrhaged from his leg, hand, and ear. Captain Matthew Turney reassembled the regiment in the woods, reuniting it with the remnants of Archer's Brigade.[65]

As much as Early and Hoke seemed to be in accord with each other, Jubal Early had no understanding of Atkinson's situation at all. Lost from sight in the densely forested marsh, Edmund Atkinson had strayed well beyond the division commander's wishes. Unlike the prudent withdrawal of Hoke and Archer, Colonel Atkinson allowed his Georgians to press ahead without support. The brigade plunged into the thicket—and beyond recall.

The Georgia brigade nipped at the heels of J. H. Hobart Ward's retreating Yankees. Confederates, in their enthusiasm, reached the edge of the woods and spilled into the plain. Atkinson tried to halt the brigade, but momentum carried the men into the open. A Northerner recalled that the Rebels "poured out of the woods like an avalanche." Union artillery had seen Meade's division give away, and then saw Ward come tumbling back. They soon spotted Atkinson's grayclad soldiers and spattered them with canister. Confederates fell in gory clumps before the shock. The guns belched from two hundred yards away, well within the killing range of those oversized shotguns. The cannon were also close enough to be vulnerable to capture. Artillery crowned a rise just beyond a clear hollow, tempting the Georgians to charge them. Transfixed Southerners stormed out of the woods and across the bottoms. With every yard, the Union guns thundered, "doing a deal of damage to the brigade." Captain Edward Lawton, the fearless staff officer, went down on the edge of the field. A canister load had killed his horse, which fell on the captain and injured his leg. Lawton wriggled free of his mount and hobbled ahead of the attack.[66]

Across the way, Union officers scrambled to blunt the unexpected assault. Captain George F. Randolph, chief of Birney's artillery, blasted the Rebels from several angles. Jastram's and Turnbull's batteries fired into the head of the column while some of Gibbon's and Meade's artillery sleeted canister into the attackers' flanks. The ubiquitous Randolph, on his first official day as division chief of artillery, coordinated his guns with Simpson's and Cooper's guns on the left and Leppien's battery on the right. Colonel Charles S. Wainwright may have offered some help after he had turned Doubleday's guns on

Hoke and Archer. Meanwhile, David Birney concentrated on getting infantry support for Randolph's guns. He ordered General Hiram Berry's brigade to advance.[67]

Just as Birney sent Berry's column forward, he encountered Meade's division falling back. Birney's initial impression, based on Meade's routed right wing, was that the division had run in "utter confusion . . . flying in all directions without order from the field." Birney's division now became the lone obstacle between Stonewall Jackson and the river. Franklin also realized this and hurried John Newton's Sixth Corps division to reinforce Birney, but it would be a while before it arrived. John Reynolds, still fixated with the artillery, perceived that Gibbon's cannon had advanced too far into the field; Atkinson's attack jeopardized Hall's 2nd Maine Battery. The First Corps commander told Birney to leave Berry on the left of Meade's artillery and advance the rest of Ward's brigade, under Colonel Régis De Trobriand, to protect Gibbon's guns. (Charles Wainwright, independent of Reynolds, also concluded that Hall was in danger, but he ordered the battery to retire.) Volcanic George Meade rode up a few minutes later and ordered Birney to throw forward a regiment to help rally his retreating Pennsylvania Reserves. Right behind him, Ward's cut-up command streamed out of the finger of woods.[68]

David Birney detached Colonel Asher S. Leidy's 99th Pennsylvania to rally the disheartened Pennsylvania Reserves. At the same time, he advanced the 57th Pennsylvania to assist Ward. Leidy's 99th Pennsylvania ordered the Reserves to re-form behind it, but the flotsam of soldiers rolled past like an irresistible tide. Reynolds joined Meade, and both officers attempted to stem the retreat. Meade stormed back and forth, trying to halt small knots of men, only to see them vanish moments later. Survivors of the 121st Pennsylvania noted the general was "considerably vexed." The 4th Reserves found out the hard way. When Captain Enos L. Christman failed to rally his men, "Meade cursed him and told him he would have him shot" if he did not do better. A witness wrote grimly that "Meade is a rough customer when under fire." The division shoved through the fastidious ranks of Leidy's 99th Pennsylvania. "The men appeared sullen and disheartened," recalled a Third Corps officer, "as if they had been badly treated and sacrificed." One of Meade's men excoriated the Third Corps troops, "our supports," for being "too late to do us any good." When an immaculate young staff officer ordered the Reserves to rally around him, one dirty veteran threw away his rifle and hissed, "I've had enough of this sort of damned business." Neither Meade, nor Reynolds, nor the 99th Pennsylvania could halt the disconsolate Pennsylvania Reserves. Birhey later claimed: "It was useless; they went right through us." By that time, Meade's division had lost any semblance of order. A nearby New Yorker wrote, "A flag, one or two mounted officers, and a squad of a dozen or twenty men were all that could be recognized as a regimental organization." When a taff officer inquired of one soldier where his command was, the Reserve answered dolefully, "Busted up and gone to hell." The generals gave up and ordered the 99th Pennsylvania to open its ranks. The larger part of Meade's division tramped to the rear. Meade raced back toward the railroad to take charge of his rear guard, and Leidy's 99th Pennsylvania rejoined De Trobriand's command as it closed on Gibbon's batteries.[69]

While the generals wrestled with the Pennsylvania Reserves, Colonel Charles T. Campbell's 57th Pennsylvania dashed into an excruciating predicament. The regiment had advanced to J. H. Hobart Ward's support and reached the area of the drainage ditches when Ward's disorderly troops stampeded past them. A moment later, Atkinson's Georgia brigade roiled into the clearing. The alarmed 57th Pennsylvania, its ranks jostled by the crush of Ward's men, quickly regrouped "under a murderous fire." The regiment dove into the ditches for cover and waited for Ward's men to get out of their way so they could return the fire. Atkinson's Confederates hesitated only a moment at the tree line, and then stormed the isolated 57th Pennsylvania. Rebels overran the ditches and, after a brief struggle, routed the Pennsylvanians. One Northerner called the contest for the ditches "the hottest fight our regiment had ever been in." Colonel Charles Campbell, his arm already in a sling from a previous injury, received several more wounds in his arm and side. The latest wounds appeared to be so serious that many thought Campbell would die, but he eventually recovered. Command devolved upon Captain Ralph Maxwell. He ordered what was left of the regiment to retreat. By then, it was too late for many of the Yankees. Atkinson's Georgians collected more prisoners. Some Federals hid successfully in the ditches, overlooked by the Confederates. Perhaps the attractive Union cannon, glistening on the rise, preoccupied the Georgia brigade. The Southerners closed in on the line of guns with nary a Union regiment in sight.[70]

Birney saw the Confederates chase Ward's troops across the field and worried about his vulnerable artillery. He had pushed Berry's brigade forward on the left, and DeTrobriand to the right, but no one supported Randolph's guns in between—precisely where Atkinson's charge seemed to be heading. Birney needed his third brigade, under Brigadier General John C. Robinson, more than ever. Staff officers galloped across the fields to find the missing

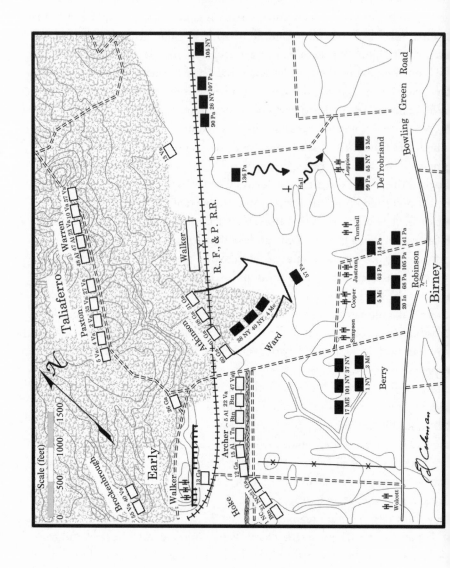

brigade and bring it up. Meanwhile, the widely separated Berry and DeTrobriand braced themselves for the onslaught. The Third Corps soldiers lay
down behind the cannon—the slight rise concealed them from the Confederate attackers. With Robinson's brigade nowhere to be found, Birney fretted
about the gap between Berry and DeTrobriand. Ward's brigade had covered
that sector, but his command had been battered beyond use. The general
desperately ordered Berry to send a regiment to fill the gap previously held
by three regiments. Berry complied half-heartedly, and released the suspect
5th Michigan. Hiram Berry had serious misgivings about the Michigan commander, Lieutenant Colonel John Gilluly, and may have questioned his bravery. He detached the regiment for the dangerous assignment simply because
it stood closest to the hole in the line. Colonel Gilluly jumped at the chance
to clear his name. Mounted conspicuously in front of his regiment, the officer
pointed the 5th Michigan into the breach.[71]

In front of the 5th Michigan, Captain Edward Lawton limped ahead of
Atkinson's Brigade, exhorting the perspiring Georgians to follow him. Jumbled Confederates swarmed to the foot of the rise without a semblance of
order. Climbing the ridge, the Rebels clashed with Lieutenant Colonel Gilluly's 5th Michigan "almost immediately" after the Federals passed in front of
Randolph's guns. The Union colonel rode well ahead of his troops, perhaps
to prove his fearlessness, and fell instantly, killed in a hail of Rebel gunfire.
Major Edward T. Sherlock assumed control of the Michiganders. A Michigan
soldier declared the next few moments to be "decidedly the most severe action
in which the regiment had ever participated." Another recalled that "shells
and bullets struck on all sides of us." The Northern regiment withered and
quickly fell back. John Gilluly's reckless action not only sacrificed his life and
his regiment, but also blocked Randolph's cannon fire, allowing Atkinson to
inch closer to his prize.[72]

Moments after detaching Gilluly, General Berry changed his mind about
sending the 5th Michigan alone. When gunfire erupted, Berry motioned the
3rd Michigan to its aid. Major Moses B. Houghton's 3rd Michigan barely
entered the field before the scattered refuse of Gilluly's 5th Regiment retreated. Some of the 3rd Michigan yearned impetuously to charge into the
smoke-obscured field and confront whatever had routed their fellow states-
men. Calmer heads, however, prevailed. Officers told the soldiers, "Steady
boys, don't fire yet," before turning them around and marching them back
up the rise. The Confederates punished them with a parting shot. Southern
artillery, likely the remnants of R. Lindsay Walker's guns, pounded the Fed-

eral withdrawal with enough force to make it seem like "shells [were] bursting like hail" among the 3rd Michigan. The regiment fell back obediently, even though the Rebels "set up a hideous yelling" that galled the Yankees. Ward's regiments, plus the 57th Pennsylvania, 5th Michigan, and now the 3rd Michigan, had been tossed aside by the relentless Georgians. Broken Union regiments melded into a muddled mob that outnumbered the attackers, but momentum favored Atkinson's Brigade, and the disorganized mass of Union soldiers fled to the protection of Randolph's artillery.[73]

Edmund Atkinson was drawn to the left by Hall's 2nd Maine Battery. He noticed the battery just as it prepared to flee. The endangered cannon had discharged their last rounds when the Confederates screeched out of the timber. Wainwright had ordered the battery to withdraw to safety. Cannon crews hitched the guns hastily and lashed their horses to the rear. Atkinson shouted at his men to stop Hall before he escaped. A cluster of Southern riflemen started shooting the horses from a range of one hundred yards. As horses toppled, veteran cannoneers cut them out of their traces and kept going. Hall managed to save all but one of his guns. Running out of horses, Hall abandoned the last piece. The battery commander spirited his guns to safety and hoped he could return to save the last cannon. When the gunners left, the 38th Georgia raised three loud, raucous cheers and charged up the hill to claim the abandoned piece. Hall's exposed and high-profile battery may have diverted more than the 38th Georgia, as the whole Georgia brigade swerved to the left, across the front of Randolph's battery.[74]

George Randolph ordered his batteries double-shotted with canister. But he looked on impatiently while first Meade's, and then Birney's infantry obstructed his field of fire. The last of Berry's Michiganders cleared his guns just as Atkinson lunged toward Hall's cannon "like a band of wolves." A Union witness said Randolph hesitated, waiting for the best opportunity "to give Mr. Reb a shot." Confederates clambered to within seventy-five yards of the cannon as the 3rd Michigan stumbled out of the way. Jastram's, Turnbull's, Cooper's, and Leppien's batteries all exploded in black powder smoke and whining canister balls. Cooper's battery from Meade's division played upon the Confederates' weak right flank as it wheeled to the left. Union guns blew gaping holes through the amazed Georgians, who fell in windrows. A Third Corps staff officer said the artillery "opened with a vigor I have never seen surpassed." He imagined the cannoneers fired without sponging out their pieces, "as there appeared to be no interval between the roar of the guns." General John F. Reynolds rode prominently between the guns. He stood for while on the rise with Cooper's Battery B, 1st Pennsylvania Light Artillery. Even as the Rebels closed to within fifty yards, and the canister riddled their lines, General Reynolds shouted with delight, "Captain Cooper, you are the bravest man in the army!"[75]

Captain Edward Lawton neared Hall's abandoned gun, encouraging the 38th Georgia to hurry. Randolph's guns unmasked suddenly and scythed across the head of the attacking column. Lawton went down with a mortal wound just below his belt. Startled by the deadly enfilade, Atkinson's disorganized Confederates scattered for cover. A Federal officer testified to the immediate impact of the artillery. He said the field was covered with Rebel dead and dying, heads off, legs off, and arms." "If that was not slaughter," he concluded, "I give up." Union artillery robbed Atkinson of most of his sting in a matter of a moment. Charles Wainwright stated proudly that his cannon effectively had stopped the attack. When General Birney reported that his infantry had saved the guns—and the army—Wainwright called Birney's claim "a most absurd piece of bombast."[76]

While the artillery decimated the Rebels, Birney's men entered the fray. Colonel Régis De Trobriand leveled an oblique fire with his three regiments adjacent to Leppien's battery. The two sides traded shots and casualties, but the Georgians received the worst of it. Atkinson's Brigade appeared to be "melting away like ice under an August sun." Colonel John Hill Lamar of the 61st Georgia received a painful wound and turned over command to Major Charles W. McArthur. A Union bullet had cut off one of Lamar's fingers. Colonel William H. Stiles saw his son and namesake fall. The colonel ran to his son's side despite protests that he would be killed in such an exposed locale. "I will not be killed," the colonel soothed his captain son, "but if I should be, there is no better spot to fall than by the side of my gallant son." Stretcher-bearers evacuated Captain Stiles, and the colonel resumed his duties with the 60th Georgia.[77]

De Trobriand's command suffered significant losses too. Colonel Asher Leidy received a serious wound and relinquished command of the 99th Pennsylvania to Lieutenant Colonel Edwin R. Biles. Major Samuel P. Lee of the 3rd Maine fell with a mutilating thigh wound. The major refused help as long as the battle hung in the balance. The close, noisy combat raged fiercely, since most of Atkinson's energy had been directed in De Trobriand's direction. One veteran of the fight said the action was "enough to make one shudder." Atkinson's Brigade had been checked by DeTrobriand, and soon felt the Federals tear into its right.[78]

General Hiram Berry watched the Confederate right drift across his fron[t] when it started for Hall's battery. Atkinson's Georgians had no idea that [a] Federal brigade lay behind the rise. The Rebels had fixated on what the[y] could see, and they worried about Hall's escape. As a result, the soldier[s] veered to the left, and their right flank drifted in front of Berry. The Unio[n] general divided his time between gauging the moment to strike and keepin[g] his men from ruining the surprise. His biggest problem was getting his bri gade to lie down. The troops loathed to lie in the watery mud, where the[y] sank at least three inches. Raw recruits of the 17th Maine protested that th[e] mud would soil their brand-new uniforms. Eventually, the general prevaile[d] and the soldiers squirmed uncomfortably in the sopping grime. Berry plante[d] the 37th New York on the right, closest to Cooper's battery. The 101st Ne[w] York and the disgruntled 17th Maine formed to the left. Berry placed the 1s[t] New York in a second line as a reserve. The brigadier walked along the battl[e] line, surveying the Georgians and chastising curious Northerners who peake[d] over the rise. He spent most of his time keeping the 17th Maine in line. Th[e] newly minted soldiers yearned to see something of the battle. "Boys, don'[t] expose yourselves any more than you can help," the general admonished[,] "you'll have a chance to see all you want to." After several incidents, Berr[y] lectured the regiment: "Lay down, men! I am here to take care of you, an[d] I'll do it if you will let me and will obey my orders!" The culprits ducked ou[t] of sight.[79]

Convinced that the moment had come, General Berry's voice rang out[,] "Keep cool, boys, and give it to them." Dirty blue ranks stood up, advance[d] to the crest, and delivered a blistering volley. Shocked Rebels reeled as th[e] Yankees rose out of nowhere and fired down the length of their jumbled com mand. Berry stayed with the 17th Maine, telling the new soldiers, "The Stat[e] of Maine is looking at you and expects every man to do his duty today!" T[o] others he entreated, "Remember that the folks at home are thinking of yo[u] now!" Bewildered Confederates stopped in their tracks and fired up the ridg[e] at the Yankees. The exchange generated more violence and damage than th[e] confrontation with De Trobriand's Federals. Berry's front line hit with th[e] power of an "earthquake, tornado, or lightning," according to a participant[.] The Confederate response proved just as thorny. Bullets zipped so close an[d] frequently that they literally tussled men's hair.[80]

Struck by Randolph's artillery and lashed by Birney's infantry, Atkinson'[s] attack quickly gave away. Bloodied Georgians scampered into the neares[t] ditches for cover and found them crowded with refugees from Meade's an[d]

Ward's commands. The Confederate brigade commander, Colonel Edmund Atkinson, also darted for a ditch, but a Union canister ball mauled his left shoulder just as he tumbled into the cover. Plunging in behind him came Captain James D. Van Valkenburg of the 61st Georgia and Lieutenant James M. Goldsmith of the 60th Georgia. Finding himself surrounded by Northerners, Van Valkenburg told the group imperiously that they were his prisoners.[81]

The Confederate attack had come to a sudden end, and the impact fractured the brigade. A renewed assault across the open field was impractical, and retreat seemed unlikely. Colonel Atkinson had disappeared into an irrigation ditch, so the Georgians turned to the next senior officer for direction. Colonel Clement A. Evans of the 31st Georgia cobbled together a patchwork defense at the edge of the hollow. He hoped his line would discourage the Yankees from crossing the rise and would avert disaster for the Confederates. His Georgians concentrated their fire on Berry's brigade and Randolph's artillery.[82]

On the Federal firing line, Birney congratulated the defenders for preserving the thin Union line. Randolph's and Wainwright's artillery, combined with De Trobriand and Berry, had blunted a serious threat to the integrity of Burnside's position. The perpetual concern of keeping the line of retreat open had most of the First and Third Corps officers acting exclusively on the defensive. In that light, Birney still had a dilemma. He had stopped Atkinson, but he had not forced the Confederates to yield their ground. Birney needed to push the Georgians back, but he had expended all of his troops and no one else was available. At that critical moment, the much-anticipated General John C. Robinson arrived on the Bowling Green Road.

John Robinson had chafed by the river for hours, convinced that he should have accompanied Birney's division onto the battlefield. The general waited in vain for Birney to correct the oversight. After several hours, Robinson elected to cross on his own. The general led his column across the lower pontoon bridge and hurried ahead to find the division.[83]

Colorful, gaudy zouaves led the procession over the lower pontoon bridge. The new 114th Pennsylvania, known as Collis' Zouaves, wore distinctive white turbans, brilliantly trimmed jackets, and baggy red pants. Colonel Charles H. T. Collis patterned his regiment assiduously after the French-Algerian units—even recruiting Frenchmen and a vivandière. The regiment entered its first battle lumped with several other Pennsylvania units and one from Indiana, all of which wore standard dark blue tunics and sky blue trou-

sers—and paled in comparison. Many of the other regiments derided the or-
nate zouaves—and their flashy brass band—as mere decorations rather than
soldiers. The envious bluecoats snickered at Collis' "bounty slingers," calling
them "Robinson's Pets" and "Feather bed soldiers." The zouave band set up
at the end of the bridge and regaled the passing brigade with strains of "Hail
Columbia" as the men marched off to battle.[84]

John Robinson conferred with two of Birney's couriers, both of whom
urged him to hurry. The brigade commander passed the word back to the
column and pressed ahead to find Birney. Robinson and his troops waded
through a confused mass of Pennsylvania Reserves and Ward's brigade. Robinson found his commander in the gap behind Randolph's guns, and Birney
told him to fill the space between Berry's and DeTrobriand's brigades. Robinson shook his troops into line, pets and all. The 114th Pennsylvania took
position first while the rest of the brigade came up. Major John A. Danks'
63rd Pennsylvania formed behind Collis, and then shifted to the left of the
zouaves. The rest of the brigade formed a second line, with the 141st Pennsylvania on the right fifty yards behind Collis, followed by the 105th Pennsylvania, the 68th Pennsylvania, and the 20th Indiana. The brigade lay down in
the mud for a moment while the brigade commander figured out what to do
next.[85]

While Robinson reconnoitered, the head of Birney's artillery, George Randolph, appealed to the waiting infantry for help. The artillerists had lost so
many men that they needed assistance in operating the cannon. "Some of you
fellows come up and help us," the artillerymen implored the zouaves. Part of
the 114th Pennsylvania, along with others, jumped at the call. The volunteers
filled out the cannon crews and kept the artillery pressure on Edmund Atkinson's Georgians. The historian for the zouaves claimed the reinforcements
arrived "just in time," which Lieutenant Edward E. Williams confirmed. The
zouave officer wrote that Randolph's guns would have been lost in another
three minutes if the infantry had not come up. Randolph later thanked Collis' Zouaves and asserted that "they belong to us now."[86]

Heavy losses among the artillery men made Birney realize that he had to
clear away the Confederates to save his guns. Birney ordered John Robinson
to attack at once. The bearded officer notified his second line of the pending
assault and directed it to move up a short distance to support the cannon.
Robinson queried the commander of the 141st Pennsylvania, Henry J. Madill, "Colonel, can you hold your men here?" Madill affirmed that he could

"Hold 'em in hell!" Well pleased, Robinson hurried off to ready the front line to attack.[87]

Birney and Robinson rode behind the prostrate 63rd and 114th Pennsylvania. The generals reined their horses near the center of the line and watched the artillery fire. A witness remembered that Birney and Robinson sat their horses "while the cannon balls played around them[,] as calmly as if sitting at home." Birney paused only a moment before he ordered Robinson into the fray. One of Robinson's staff officers raced down the line, reminding the 114th Pennsylvania that this could be the moment to erase all of their comrades' gibes. "Go in Zoo-Zoos," Lieutenant George W. Bratton called; "now is your chance!" Robinson bellowed the order, "Up and at them."[88]

The movement of Robinson's brigade drew a crescendo of Confederate artillery fire. Smoke obliterated the view of the battlefield, and men fumbled forward over the dead and dying soldiers and horses. Robinson rode in front of the 114th Pennsylvania to guide it into its first battle. Almost instantly, a Southern shell exploded, toppling the general's horse and killing his bugler. Two staff officers fell seriously wounded beside them. Private Samuel Hamilton "had his head shot off." The zouaves recoiled in horror. A member of the regiment, William Grew, later testified, "The unhorsing of these riders, who all appeared for the moment to have been killed, flaggered the men in their advance." One of Collis' Zouaves wrote that "there was an alarming pause in the forward movement." Confederate infantry and artillery lashed at the stalled brigade with a tremendous fury. Lieutenant Edward Williams recalled "the fire getting hotter and hotter," and the shells "fairly rained amongst us." In the confusion, no one noticed General Robinson squirming to free himself from his disemboweled horse.[89]

Colonel Charles Collis raced in front and took control. He seized the zouaves' regimental colors and spurred to the center of the line. He reminded his men that some of them had withstood Stonewall Jackson's legions in the memorable Shenandoah Valley Campaign of 1862. He shouted to his troops, "Remember the stone wall at Middletown!" The colonel restored confidence in the ranks. The Pennsylvanians rallied and cheered; and, joined by the 63rd Pennsylvania—and possibly part of the 5th Michigan—charged ahead. The Federals swept past Randolph's guns and down the slope toward the waiting Confederates. "Nothing was to be seen but smoke and dirt flying from cannon balls," mused a nearly blinded zouave. The soldier concluded: "I have heard of hot places; I now know what they are."[90]

The Pennsylvanians and Michiganders halted fifty yards in front of the artillery and pelted the Rebels with a volley. The Georgians responded "with unabated fury." The exchange brought down many soldiers on both sides and led the Federals to call the area "the Slaughter Pen." Some of the Georgians climbed out of their ditches to return the fire. The two ragged lines, blazing thirty yards apart, struck one observer as "a fair stand-up fight." Confederate Colonel Clement Evans, however, did not see it that way. His tattered Georgia regiments could not defeat the fresh and enthusiastic Yankees. Evans had taken command of the Georgians when Atkinson disappeared. Winded Southerners had expended their last cartridges and pleaded for more. Evans had none to give, so he ordered a retreat. Georgians abandoned the ditches and raced for the woods. An uncharitable Northerner gloated, "the Rebs turned and broke like a pack of sheep." A Michigan soldier wrote: "we poured in the bullets as fast as we could—as long as there was a Reb to be seen." Some of the Southerners, like Colonel Atkinson, did not run the gauntlet of fire and remained trapped in the crowded ditches between the lines.[91]

The Federals sprang forward when they saw the Confederates retreat. George Gordon Meade's dogged rear guard joined the right of Robinson's command. Collis stated that Meade was as "brave as a lion . . . under the most terrific artillery fire." Members of the 99th Pennsylvania followed their color-bearer as he strode forward to reinforce Meade's smattering of Reserves. The standard-bearer had his clothes laced with bullets but survived without a scratch. Some of the Union officers struggled to curtail their troops' ardor. General John Robinson freed himself from his dead mount just in time to check his brigade's advance. The excited zouaves wanted to chase the Confederates, and one of them admitted that "our generals had hard work to stop us from following." [92]

Robinson had saved Randolph's artillery and restored the Union line, but he suffered quite a few casualties. Collis' Zouaves lost the most men in the brigade, including Major Joseph S. Chandler and the vivandière, "French Mary" Teppe, to slight wounds. Robinson's second line also suffered serious losses when it advanced to Randolph's immediate support. The historian for Henry Madill's 141st Pennsylvania wrote that "the shot and shell fell around us like hail, and men fell as grain falls before the sickle." Major Thomas Hawkesworth of the 68th Pennsylvania suffered a mortal wound when a shell had crushed his hip.[93]

Charles Collis and his 114th Pennsylvania zouaves received numerous compliments after their first trial by fire. Robinson thanked the regiment personally and claimed that its decisive charge "entitle[s] it to be ranked equal to any of the veteran regiments." Birney commended the regiment "with great enthusiasm and spirit" for saving the Third Corps batteries. Congress later awarded Charles Collis the Medal of Honor "for distinguished bravery at the battle of Fredericksburg."[94]

Birney re-formed a solid defensive line along the Bowling Green Road. Rather than pursue Atkinson's Georgia brigade, the Union general strengthened his position. Birney drew Berry's brigade back to the road to protect his left. Robinson held the center, and Ward reconstituted part of his brigade on the right. Birney improved his position with shallow earthworks along the road. Atkinson's sudden lunge almost had broken through the weakest part of the Federal line. Concerned Union officers concentrated on the Left Grand Division's defenses. Birney seemed justified fifteen minutes later when the Confederates drove Gibbon's division back from the railroad.

Atkinson's attack was harsh and sobering. The aftermath of the charge revealed its dire consequences to both sides. A lieutenant on Jeb Stuart's staff wrote that the dead lay "in heaps" across the Slaughter Pen. Robert E. Lee scanned the carnage from his command post on Telegraph Hill. Lee touched James Longstreet's arm and whispered with emotion, "It is well that war is so terrible, or we would grow too fond of it." The pageantry of the morning had given way to death and mayhem in the afternoon.[95]

The survivors of Atkinson's Brigade struggled through the woods under an annoying artillery barrage. Onlooking Confederates from A. P. Hill's and Early's divisions scrambled for cover because of the bombardment. A cringing Confederate said the "shell and shot tore the air . . . like the hasty ripping of a stout canvas, only intensely magnified." Stonewall Jackson reached Prospect Hill at that time. He "galloped madly" to the crest and paused. Southerners noted that Jackson seemed unconcerned about the cannonade and "coolly . . . sat upon his horse in the midst of the infernal roar of the cannon." To hero-worshipful Louisianans, Stonewall Jackson was the very "incarnation of war." Jackson saw that the crisis had abated and left the artillery to engage in a long-range duel—"in which luxury," one Confederate recalled, "the artillery of both armies indulged to their hearts' content."[96]

Jubal Early reordered the Confederate defenses on Prospect Hill. The general placed half of Hoke's Brigade along the RF&P Railroad, and the other half on the hill in Archer's trenches. The 21st North Carolina, 21st Georgia, and 1st North Carolina Battalion held the tracks, while the 15th Alabama and 12th Georgia moved into the trenches. The extra regiments of Atkinson's Brigade joined Hoke. The hapless 13th Georgia advanced to the railroad, and the 26th Georgia shared Hoke's trenches. Harry Hays' Louisiana brigade marched up the hill, but Hoke's and Atkinson's men already had occupied the earthworks. The artillery storm caught Hays' Brigade in the open, and cannon "swept the exposed crest like a tornado." Jackson withdrew the brigade to better cover. Early, in the meantime, met the bedraggled Georgia brigade streaming back from Atkinson's assault. The general complimented the Georgians for their élan, but taking the officers aside, he lambasted them for recklessly endangering the brigade. After his tirade, Early directed Clement Evans to Hoke's left. Even the comparative shelter of the woods did not protect Jackson's regrouping soldiers. The 1st Tennessee of Archer's Brigade lost another commander, Captain Matthew Turney. Command devolved to Captain Henry J. Hawkins, making him the Hogdrivers' fourth commander in three hours. One of Hawkins' men opined, "I never heard such a crash of timber as the shells and grape made in passing through the woods and falling all around us."[97]

The carnage and wreckage on Prospect Hill shocked the Confederates. A Tennessee officer wrote of the Federals: "their dead covered the ground for nearly a mile in our front." Another Confederate remarked: "The scene which presented itself . . . in our front was sickening in the extreme." Wounded soldiers crawled along the hillside in search of help. Cripples cried aloud for water. The artillery bombardment interrupted "thousands of heart-rending incidents" and left the fallen beyond immediate succor. Sergeant Jacob Heffelfinger endured the fire with a sublime presence of mind. The sergeant of the 7th Reserves had been wounded through both legs and left behind during the retreat. Exposed on the hillside and unable to drag himself to safety, Heffelfinger faced the irony of being blown to bits by his own artillery. The lame soldier swallowed his pain and regrets and updated his diary. "I am still lying where I fell," he wrote in a good hand. "The Rebels have advanced a line over me, so that I am a prisoner." Heffelfinger noted that he was "now exposed to the fire of our artillery which is fearfully destructive." He closed his entry: "All that we gained at so fearful a cost is lost. . . . Death has been doing fearful work today."[98]

About the time Atkinson's Georgians charged into the mouth of Randolph's artillery, General John Gibbon's line began to unravel. Several Union attacks by Gibbon's division had penetrated the marshy woods but could not break the Confederate defenses. Colonel Adrian Root, one of Gibbon's brigade commanders, reported that the Rebels' resistance had stifled his advance. The herty division commander assured Root that reinforcements would arrive soon and encouraged Root to push ahead. Root reorganized his line for another attempt while Gibbon headed to the right. Riding near the railroad, Gibbon received a painful wound: a shell fragment gashed his wrist and shards of metal buried deep in his hand. Gibbon sent word to General Nelson Taylor to take command of the division and then repaired to the hospital. Riding to the rear, the general passed through legions of idle troops. Only then did Gibbon realize that virtually no one was going to reinforce his division.[99]

The only units rushing to Gibbon's assistance were the 26th New York and 90th Pennsylvania of Colonel Peter Lyle's fractured brigade. The regiments returned to the front shortly after Gibbon's belligerent staff officer, Captain Edward Lee, admonished them. Unfortunately, they had no ammunition and had to rely on their bayonets. The two regiments reached the railroad and joined the 107th Pennsylvania. The trek took its toll on the returning soldiers. The 26th New York lost several color-bearers, including a German named Martin Schubert. Schubert had thrown away a medical furlough to stay with his command through the battle. Joseph Keene, an Englishman, was the last to carry the flag. Congress bestowed the Medal of Honor on both men.[100]

Lyle's troops had no sooner arrived than they saw the 136th Pennsylvania retreat from the woods to their left. The Confederates had assailed the isolated regiment while it wandered aimlessly through the marsh. Colonel William Terrill's 13th Virginia, from Walker's Brigade, pitched into the Pennsylvanians' left flank just as Thomas' Georgia brigade struck in front. The new soldiers lasted only a moment under a "perfect storm of lead and iron" before falling back. The Virginians threatened to cut off the Northerners' retreat. The 136th panicked and fled through the wetland. Phillip Petty, the unlikely Medal of Honor winner, smashed his rifle so that the Confederates could not use it and spirited the regimental colors to safety. The brigade commander, Peter Lyle, rallied the 136th Pennsylvania as it came out of the trees. General Nelson Taylor rode up and ordered the regiment to hold its ground at all costs. Officers protested that they had no ammunition. Taylor answered imperiously to use the bayonet. The regiment stood alone somewhere in the field east of the railroad.[101]

Taylor returned to the right before ascertaining the reason for the 136th Pennsylvania's flight. Taylor and Root seemed preoccupied by the deadly effect of Greenlee Davidson's and Joseph Latimer's artillery. Canister sparked off the railroad embankment and rippled through the bluecoats. Greenlee Davidson wrote with pride, "The grove of pines in my front is no longer entitled to the name of a grove." Confederate infantry had re-established their lines and inched forward to crowd the Federals back. The Northerners laid down a severe fire to keep them at a distance. A New York man remembered, "Our regiment . . . loaded and fired as cooly [*sic*] as though we were shooting squirrels." The mounting pressure on the right caused Union commanders to neglect their left. Colonel Adrian Root, unaware of an attack against his left, ordered the 107th Pennsylvania to close on the right. Peter Lyle saw the 107th Pennsylvania shift and did the same with the 26th New York and 90th Pennsylvania.[102]

Edward Thomas' hard-bitten Georgia brigade had saved A. P. Hill's left with "stubborn resistance." When the Yankees retired to the railroad, Thomas' Brigade advanced to recapture the RF&P. Lane's Brigade and Pender's Brigade, under Colonel Alfred Scales, conformed to Thomas' movements; and the three brigades started through the forest en echelon. Thomas just happened to barrel into the lone 136th Pennsylvania at the same time Terrill's 13th Virginia slashed into its left flank and rear. The right of Thomas' Brigade locked the Pennsylvanians in place while the 35th and 45th Georgia curled around their right flank. The Federals faced a double envelopment and backed out of the fight quickly. The Confederates gave chase "completely routing them."[103]

The other Confederate brigades kept pace as well as they could. James Lane advanced only a portion of his brigade. The 7th and 18th North Carolina marched on Thomas' left. The 33rd North Carolina remained behind to rally the rest of the brigade. General William D. Pender had his hand bandaged and returned to see his brigade in motion. He refused to resume command under the circumstances, but stuck close to Colonel Alfred Scales, to offer assistance.[104]

Firing along Nelson Taylor's line subsided just as the crisis mounted. The Federals had depleted their ammunition, and the Confederates closed in for the kill. Losses spiraled upward as the bluecoats could no longer keep the Rebels back. "A fatal fire was still kept up by an unseen foe," reported Colonel James Bates of the 12th Massachusetts, "and our men were falling constantly." Cannon fire added to their misery. Captain Isaac S. Tichenor of the 105th New York cursed the artillery, but regretted it as soon as the cannonade stopped. The captain wondered at the sudden cessation of fire, but then he glimpsed a Confederate battle line hurtling toward his left flank.[105]

The Confederates charged over the railroad tracks before Lyle's troops could close the gap in the front line. The Southerners burst into Tichenor's left flank and drove a wedge into the middle of Taylor's division. Captain Tichenor had spotted the attackers, but had had no time to react. Union and Confederate soldiers grappled hand-to-hand. The outnumbered New Yorkers began to lose ground. Tichenor sent the colors to the rear, but much of the regiment wound up captured. Among the prisoners was the regimental commander, Isaac Tichenor. The Southerners cursed the captain "in language which one gentleman never uses," according to Tichenor, and stripped him of his trappings. While removing his sword belt, the officer "concluded to skip." He threw the sword at his captors and fled to the railroad. Angry Rebels fired at the fugitive. "It hailed bullets almost unparalleled," Tichenor recalled: "every volley seemed to lift me off my feet." The captain managed to escape somehow, but the regiment was not so lucky. "Our gallant old 105th New York," Tichenor ruminated, "was annihilated." While Tichenor's fate still hung in the balance, Captain Abraham Moore tried to rally the surviving members of the regiment. He failed. One soldier explained, "The 105th New York Volunteers was literally killed in action."[106]

Colonel Peter Lyle's command and the 107th Pennsylvania saw the Confederates smash through the 105th New York. At the same time, Southern troops captured the railroad behind them. The Rebels charged them front and rear. Lyle ordered his regiments to abandon the railroad. The 90th and 107th Pennsylvania, and the 26th New York, retreated to where the 136th Pennsylvania had reassembled. Confederates harried their withdrawal, "yelling like perfect devils at their heels." One of the last Federals to leave the railroad ditch fell mortally wounded. William Bacon, adjutant of the 26th New York, collapsed while directing the rear guard. A bullet had splintered his thigh. Soldiers flocked to the popular officer and carried him away. Major Ezra Wetmore knew Burnside's orders forbade the men from leaving their posts to care for the injured, so he turned his back as a cue for the soldiers to evacuate Bacon. The adjutant had predicted his death and told his bearers that he "had fought his last battle." He died that evening. John Shiel, of the 90th Pennsylvania, earned the Medal of Honor when he disregarded Burnside's orders and risked his life to rescue some of the wounded. Lyle's men emulated him and took most of their wounded with them.[107]

The Confederates charged down the railroad ditch and shredded the left wing of Nelson Taylor's Union division. The 104th and 94th New York yielded to the onslaught. The 16th Maine fought until the Rebels lapped into their rear. One Down East soldier recalled, "We almost had to charge to get out of the Confederate lines." Taylor tried to stay the disaster. Dashing to the 12th Massachusetts, he shouted to the commander, James Bates: "Colonel, I am now in command of the division. General Gibbon has been wounded. Keep your position." Bates lamented that he had no ammunition to hold the point. General Taylor promised that he would not have to hold for long, as reinforcements were coming. Observing a column emerge from the finger of woods, he pointed in exultation: "There is your support." Colonel Bates grimaced. He explained that he had seen them before and they were Confederates. Taylor was taken aback. Scrutinizing the line more closely, Taylor realized his error. His position was no longer tenable, as the Rebels swept toward his rear. The general relented and ordered the rest of the division to retreat.[108]

The Confederates recaptured the RF&P Railroad in short order. Commanders had led their men forward with zealous determination. Line officers, such as Captain John T. Jordan of the 49th Georgia, helped set the tone for the attack. A shell fragment wounded the captain, but he refused to be treated. "Forward!" he scolded, "You take care of the Yankees—the ambulance corps will remove me." Edward Thomas blasted the Union line into bits and "swept them off like chaff before the wind." The right of the brigade struck first and turned the flank before the left engaged. The Georgia brigade's fire "piled up" the Yankee dead and left them strewn "a little thicker than you ever saw pumpkins in a new ground," according to one Southron. A Union soldier verified that "the rebs give it to us good and my comrades fell on all sides." When lame Captain Jordan perceived a hesitation in the 49th Georgia, he spurned his medical attendants and re-joined his command. Seizing the colors and brandishing his sword, the bloody officer shouted "Forward Georgians. Follow me 49th!" The excited Confederates roared ahead and struck "like an avalanche." The Federals gave way, and Captain Jordan stumbled to the top of the railroad grade and planted his colors in triumph.[109]

The left regiments of Thomas' Brigade arrived moments later but refused to halt. The 35th and 45th Georgia, along with Lane's two North Carolina regiments, surged across the railroad tracks. They pursued the Yankees for one hundred yards before they clashed with Peter Lyle's rear guard—the large, disorganized 136th Pennsylvania. Leppien's and Thompson's Union artillery also opened with effect. The Confederates traded fire with the

Northerners before General Thomas received a report that his ammunition was "well nigh exhausted." Exhibiting more prudence than had Edmund Atkinson, Thomas retraced his steps to the railroad. The brigadier placed his troops safely behind the railroad grade and asked Pendleton's Louisiana brigade to support him. Colonel Edmund Pendleton, of Taliaferro's division, formed his line close to the railroad, since Thomas alerted him that the Georgians had no cartridges. Another Union attack failed to develop, and the brigades never had to trade places. James Lane returned his brigade to the railroad next to Thomas. Pender and Scales withdrew their brigade to the earthworks behind Greenlee Davidson's artillery. Pender left Alfred Scales in charge of the right two regiments while he took command of the left two. The 16th North Carolina went back to the skirmish line. The Confederate line had been restored at last, and quiet settled over the battlefield south of Fredericksburg. Large-scale fighting ended on Stonewall Jackson's front at 2:30 P.M.[110]

As the resonance of battle diminished, a new sound filled the fields and woods around Prospect Hill. The cries and screams of broken men and beasts swelled with writhing agony. Soldiers pleaded for water to quench their powder-parched lips. Crippled horses whinnied with "hideous unhuman sounds." A Union soldier wrote, "I have not the heart to attempt to describe" the horrible scenes that he saw. Another torment tortured the wounded. Despite the muddy, waterlogged conditions, dry sage grass caught fire from the black powder sparks. Smoldering embers burst into flames and crackled across the battlefront. Injured soldiers, unable to flee, battled the blaze until they succumbed. Alabama men rescued some of the wounded near their lines, but not before "their hair, whiskers, eyebrows, and lashes, had been burned and their faces and hands had been partially roasted." Most soldiers watched the conflagration in appalled silence, powerless to save the wounded trapped between the lines. Flames consumed the disfigured men, "burning many of them to death amid agonizing screams." The heat cooked off their cartridges and marked their passing with sonorous popping sounds. A Tennessee witness reflected that "it was a horrible sight to see them burning to death. . . . I never want to see such a sight again." Another lamented, "Many of the dead were charred and the wounded severely burned by the sage." Fortunately for the myriad of wounded sprawled across the battlefield, the fire was short-lived and consumed only a couple of acres.[111]

Soldiers, North and South, packed the agricultural ditches between the lines, each side claiming the other as its prisoners, but neither able to enforce the point. The men understood their predicament and agreed to let the armies decide their fate. Until one side or the other forwarded skirmishers to occupy the ditches, the clusters of soldiers sat back in near perfect détente. David A. Curriden of the 7th Pennsylvania Reserves took pity on the wounded Confederate colonel Edmund N. Atkinson. After refusing his canteen to the abrasive Captain James D. Van Valkenburg, Curriden offered it to Atkinson. Atkinson declined, as he was in too much pain. Both parties knew that Atkinson would need medical help soon.[112]

Shortly after he completed his new line, General David Birney asked John C. Robinson to advance his pickets. The generals selected the 114th Pennsylvania. Colonel Charles Collis dispatched a line of skirmishers to clear the ditches in front. Captain Frank A. Eliot led the zouave party across the Slaughter Pen. Amid shouts of joy and sighs of resignation, Collis' Zouaves collected the trapped and wounded soldiers, blue and gray. The Confederates ended up as prisoners, including Colonel Edmund Atkinson—the only brigade commander on either side to be captured at Fredericksburg. Zouaves gently removed him from the ditch on a stretcher. David Curriden accompanied Atkinson and Van Valkenburg to the rear. They parted amiably, exchanging addresses. Van Valkenburg would have his revenge, though. A year and a half later at the Battle of the Wilderness, the Confederate officer bluffed an entire Yankee regiment to surrender. The unit he captured was David Curriden's 7th Pennsylvania Reserves. Fortunately for Curriden, he had left the regiment by then.[113]

As Birney patched the front lines and Collis' Zouaves cleared the ditches, a bevy of officers collected around William Franklin's headquarters at the Bernard house. Cavalry general George D. Bayard reposed beneath a tree engaged in pleasantries when Confederate shells began tearing up the garden around the house. "Although entirely exposed," an officer noted, "Bayard seemed to take no notice of the deadly missiles." Other officers took cover behind the tree. Before Bayard could get up, a shell ricocheted off the ground and crushed his hip at the joint. Soldiers spirited the stricken general into the house, where surgeons proclaimed the wound mortal. Bayard accepted their prognosis stoically and dictated his last few words home. Near his death, "shock rendered him delirious," and he shouted commands to the end. General George Bayard was laid to rest six days later, on the date slated to have been his wedding day.[114]

The battle lapsed into fitful silence as both armies listened to the crescendo emanating from Fredericksburg and Marye's Heights. The battle had shifted northward, and grown in fury. Neither side conceded the struggle south of the city had all but ended. Union and Confederate officers prepared for renewed hostilities, while at the same time wondering which side would provoke the clash first.

CHAPTER NINE

"CHEER UP, MY HEARTIES!"

French's Attack

When cannon resonated upriver from Franklin's front marking the beginning of Pelham's duel, Union troops began to stir in the streets of Fredericksburg. Fog clung to the city, obscuring the fields and heights to the west. Federal pickets peered into the mist until they were relieved at 8:00 A.M. Some of the soldiers resumed their excesses where they had left off the night before. Several dissipated Ohioans of Kimball's brigade renewed their drinking spree at first light. Thomas F. Galwey of the 8th Ohio noted that on the morning of December 13, "Many of the men are already drunk again." Others rooted through violated houses, scavenging for overlooked trinkets or food.[1]

Even before Franklin had received Burnside's quixotic orders, General Edwin V. Sumner had his orders to attack. Sumner studied the directive and broke down the assignments for his corps commanders. He sent preliminary orders to the Second and Ninth Corps by 8:15 A.M. Sumner instructed Orlando Willcox to extend the Ninth Corps' left to connect with Franklin's Left Grand Division. Part of Darius Couch's Second Corps would prolong the right and protect the "upper part of the town." The rest of the Second Corps would form "a column of a division" and attack out of Fredericksburg on Hanover and Frederick Streets (mislabeled in the order as "Plank and Telegraph roads") for the purpose of "seizing the heights in rear of the town." Sumner wanted the lead division to "advance in three lines . . . to be covered by a heavy line of skirmishers in front and on both flanks." A second division would be ready "in the same manner" to support the column. Sumner cautioned his men to be careful advancing through the fog lest they collide with their own troops. The Right Grand Division commander concluded the dispatch: "The movement will not commence until you receive orders."[2]

Darius Couch read his instructions and came to the same conclusion that Franklin had earlier, namely, that "seizing the heights" entailed a diversion in favor of the other wing of the army. Sumner intended to force a lodgment in the Confederate defenses, which would keep Longstreet's men busy on the right and allow Franklin's men to carry Prospect Hill without fear of Rebel reinforcements descending on their flank. Unlike Franklin, Sumner and Couch understood their duties as Burnside had conceived them. Curiously, Burnside envisioned Franklin as the main attack, and Sumner as a secondary assault, yet he described both of their operations with the same words—each to "seize" their respective heights. Such inconsistencies bred deadly confusion among Burnside's lieutenants.[3]

Couch summoned his division commanders and gave them their instructions. The corps commander excused O. O. Howard's division from the attack because it had "led into town" on December 11. Couch detailed Howard to guard the upper part of the city. General William H. French would lead the attack against Marye's Heights, and General Winfield S. Hancock prepared to support him. Couch counseled each division to channel its advance in "column of a division," stacking one brigade behind another. The brigades would be spaced two hundred yards apart.[4]

General French was a restless bundle of energy. Another general wrote that he "was often imperious and impatient, but no one ever saw his troops . . . go into action without a thrill of admiration for him." The brigadier drew up his division in the streets north of the railroad. Troops shifted into place, settling into line by 10:00 A.M. Brigadier General Nathan Kimball's "Gibraltar Brigade" formed on Caroline Street, resting its left near the railroad tracks. The general normally commanded six regiments, but on December 13, French added a seventh regiment from Colonel John W. Andrews' brigade. Kimball kept four regiments on Caroline Street, with the 7th (West) Virginia on the left, followed by the 24th New Jersey, the 28th New Jersey, and the 14th Indiana. The other three regiments advanced a block west to Princess Anne Street. The 4th Ohio took the left and rested its flank on the railroad. On the right, the 8th Ohio concentrated near Hanover Street. The 1st Delaware, recently acquired from Andrews' brigade, formed between them.[5]

The rest of French's division appeared dwarfed in comparison to Kimball's brigade. Colonel John W. Andrews' brigade had only three regiments— after French detached the 1st Delaware—the 4th New York, 10th New York, and 132nd Pennsylvania. Colonel Oliver H. Palmer commanded the Third Brigade—also composed of three regiments—the 14th Connecticut, 108th New York, and 130th Pennsylvania. French moved Andrews' brigade from Caroline Street into Princess Anne Street. The soldiers marched up Hanover Street and formed with the 4th New York on the left of the street, while the 10th New York—called the "National Zouaves"—and 132nd Pennsylvania extended to the right of Hanover Street. The 132nd Pennsylvania rested in front of the Fredericksburg courthouse. Palmer's brigade had spent the previous night bivouacked near the upper pontoon crossing. French shifted it to Princess Anne Street where it connected with Andrews' brigade north of Hanover Street. The 14th Connecticut formed on the left near the courthouse. The 130th Pennsylvania held the center, with its right resting on George Street. The 108th New York formed just north of George Street.

While French readied his command, Winfield S. Hancock arrayed his division along the river at the southern end of Fredericksburg. Brigadier General Thomas Francis Meagher's Irish Brigade came to attention in front of the gutted warehouses at the city docks. Colonel Samuel K. Zook's brigade stretched northward along Sophia Street. Brigadier General John C. Caldwell's brigade formed on Zook's right. Later, Hancock shifted Zook to Princess Anne Street in front of Meagher's brigade. Caldwell's troops then closed on the Irish Brigade's right by the railroad.

At 10:00 A.M. French selected Nathan Kimball to lead the attack. French promised to support him with the rest of the division, and Hancock's 1st Division would back up the assault if necessary. Private Marion A. Wixson of the 23rd New York reported to Kimball as a guide. Wixson had been in the Fredericksburg area during the spring of 1862 and knew the ground. Kimball prepared the three regiments on Princess Anne Street to go forward as skirmishers and massed the rest of his brigade as an attacking column. Colonel John S. Mason of the 4th Ohio took command of Kimball's skirmishers and devised an unusual plan of attack. Mason wanted to "throw out a cloud of skirmishers" and attack the Confederate pickets hovering near the western fringe of the city. When the Southerners fell back Mason would pursue them closely, hoping he could drive "the enemy's skirmishers before us, and enter their breastworks simultaneously with them." Mason and Kimball hoped the fleeing Rebels would shield the Federals against Confederate fire from Marye's Heights.[6]

Colonel Mason and his officers identified several exit routes from the city and examined the millrace that girded the backside of Fredericksburg. The race served as a spillway for the canal north of the city, and it ran around Fredericksburg. The millrace split near the railroad on the south end of the city, with one course going underground to the river by Marye's mill, the other flowing southward into Hazel Run. The sluiceway had walls lined with stone and wooden boards, and a bottom five feet deep and fifteen feet wide. Marsena Patrick had tried to drain the millrace the day before, but the stream still had three feet of standing water. Only three bridges crossed the sluiceway, at Prussia Street, Hanover Street, and William Street. Confederate pickets guarded both sides of the stream at two of those bridges. Colonel Mason and his skirmishers needed to capture the bridges swiftly and intact.[7]

The Confederates had prepared a defensive scheme more elaborate than the Federals imagined, and stronger than even the Southerners had guessed. Newly promoted brigadier general Thomas R. R. Cobb, a gangly Georgian, did not have a uniform commensurate to his rank, or even an appropriate overcoat. The new general did, however, improve his defenses with a practiced eye. "We have a magnificent position," the brigadier wrote, "the best perhaps on the line." Cobb placed three regiments—the 18th Georgia, 24th Georgia, and the Phillips Legion—behind a "rock wall . . . which . . . was about 3½ feet high and built against a bank making a very good protection from the enemy." The general left another unit—Cobb's Legion—back in camp behind Howison Hill. Cobb's Legion spent the day supporting Pendleton's artillery. Phillips' Legion anchored Cobb's left behind the stone wall. The 24th Georgia held the center, and the 18th Georgia formed on the right. General Cobb placed the 16th Georgia in reserve behind Marye's Heights, near Howison's Mill on Hazel Run.[8]

Atop Marye's Heights, artillery bristled through the embrasures of freshly dug gun pits. The Washington Artillery stockpiled canister near its guns. Cannoneers removed ammunition chests from the limbers and placed them beside the pits to keep them handy. Drivers sheltered horses and carriages in a ravine behind the Willis cemetery, and the cannoneers bivouacked next to their guns. Bystanders laughed and cringed at the Washington Artillery's efforts. Skeptics condemned the gun pits silhouetted on the virtual crest of the heights. They predicted the summit would become "a slaughter-pen." Colonel J. B. Walton, on the other hand, believed the position had strength. He relaxed, unconcerned, with his staff in the large empty parlor of the Marye mansion. The adjutant of the Washington Artillery wrote, "We are confident of holding our position." James Longstreet worried about the vulnerability of the salient as late as noon on December 13. Major General Richard H. Anderson exacerbated his concerns. The subordinate general wrestled with some inequalities in the ground north of Marye's Heights. His division anchored Lee's left from the Plank Road to the Rappahannock. Stretching his line thin, Anderson feared the Federals might slice through his defenses without difficulty. He warned Longstreet that he might have to pull back.[9]

Longstreet steadied his division commander, but at the same time alerted Cobb and others on Marye's Heights that Anderson's line was weak. Longstreet's courier found Colonel Walton and his staff smoking in the Marye garden. Walton read Longstreet's warning: "If Anderson, on your left, is badly pressed, he will fall back to the second line of heights. Conform to his movements." The artillery commander grimaced, and his adjutant admitted, "The contents of the note looked ominous." Walton forwarded Longstreet's note, via his adjutant, to General Cobb in the Sunken Road. The Georgia officer read the note "carefully," and puffed, "If they wait for me to fall back, they will wait a long time." The brigadier sent his assurances to Lee and Longstreet that he would hold his position "to the last." Lieutenant William Owen returned to the Washington Artillery, convinced that all was right again.[10]

Union colonel John Mason, after consulting his officers, issued attack orders by 10:30 A.M. Colonel Franklin Sawyer's 8th Ohio would move out Hanover Street and rush the Confederates holding the millrace. Meanwhile, Mason would take the 4th Ohio and 1st Delaware out of town on Prussia Street. Once the two wings crossed the millrace, they would unite and head for Marye's Heights. Captain Peter Grubb, 4th Ohio, would guide Colonel Sawyer's column out Hanover Street. Captain John S. Jones of the same regiment assisted Major Thomas A. Smyth's Delawarians in case the regiments got separated during the advance. Mason's force numbered approximately 700 men.[11]

Action started to unfold at 11:00 A.M., when French notified Couch that his division was ready. The Second Corps commander signaled the news across the river and immediately received permission to attack. Kimball relayed the orders to Mason. "Move out now, Colonel," Kimball shouted. "God bless you—good bye!" Sawyer's 8th Ohio rushed into Hanover Street and headed out of Fredericksburg. As soon as the blue column debouched from the city, it met with a quick fire from the Southern pickets posted at the foot of the hill. "Just as we reach the edge of the city and before we have time to deploy," remembered an Ohioan, "we are met by a fire from the enemy's skirmishers." Colonel Sawyer reported, "we had hardly moved a square when the enemy's sharpshooters in considerable force opened a murderous fire upon our front." The 8th Ohio charged and the Confederates fled from the bottoms. The bridge—or what was left of it—had been captured. The Southerners had removed the floorboards, leaving the naked stringers intact. Colonel Sawyer halted at the millrace and stretched his left to find Mason's column.[12]

When Sawyer ran into rifle fire, John Mason's group encountered trouble of a different sort. Mason's column, led by the 4th Ohio, swept into Prussia Street, past the railroad depot, and across the millrace. Confederate skirmishers yielded without a contest, but that made Mason's advance more difficult. Southern artillery—the venerable Washington Artillery—fired on the column as soon as it left the cover of the city. Men began to fall rapidly. "The enemy opened a very heavy cross-fire of artillery," Mason wrote, "doing very great execution." Federals dipped behind the west bank of the millrace, and the shells caromed after them. Lieutenant Colonel James H. Godman, commanding the 4th Ohio (since Mason assumed overall command of the three regiments), fell pierced by shrapnel in the thigh. Captain Gordon A. Stewart took over the regiment and delegated part of the command to Captain Leonard W. Carpenter. Stewart commanded the regiment's left wing while Carpenter led the right. Major Smyth's 1st Delaware moved behind the 4th Ohio's line and extended its flank northward. The "Crazy Delawares"—so called for their propensity for fighting, even amongst themselves—moved along the millrace until they located Sawyer's 8th Ohio. Mason's line was whole again.[13]

The Washington Artillery focused their fire at the southern end to the city. Adjutant William Owen returned from seeing Cobb just as the Federals started their attack. The artillerists spotted the movement while the Yankees were still in Fredericksburg. Walton quickly mounted his black horse, Rebel, and rode to Lieutenant Galbraith's gun pit north of the Plank Road. There, the colonel studied the Federals through his binoculars. Nearby, artillerist Henry H. Baker also watched the blue column enter the field. He wrote that it was "the most impressive and vivid spectacle of grandeur ever witnessed by a soldier." The Louisiana cannoneers stood mesmerized. "We had never

witnessed such a battle-array before," a cannoneer reminisced. "How beautifully they came on!" recalled Adjutant Owen. "Their bright bayonets glistening in the sunlight made the line look like a huge serpent of blue and steel."
As the head of the Federal column left the city, Walton ordered Galbraith to
open fire. The commander watched the first shot strike the column and then
rode to Captain Squires' guns in the center of the line. Walton and Owen
dismounted and sent their horses to safety. Colonel Walton strode between
the guns and roared, "'tention! Commence fir-I-ng!!" Squires', Miller's, and
Eshleman's guns exploded in unison. As Owen put it, "the edge of Marye's
Hill is fringed in flame." The Washington Artillery admired the effect of their
fire. "We could see our shells, bursting in their ranks, making great gaps,"
reported the battalion adjutant. The Louisiana gunners also fired solid shot
with calculated precision. Billowing smoke covered the hill after every discharge, obliterating most of the view. Occasionally, a small break in the cloud
revealed the plain "dotted with patches of blue," which the artilleryman recognized as dead and wounded Yankees.[14]

Union skirmishers braved the cannon fire and surged after the retreating
Confederate pickets. They left the millrace and dashed nine hundred yards
across an open field that tilted upward to the base of Marye's Heights. A
couple of houses and fences dotted the landscape, but otherwise, it was de-
void of cover. The Federals sprinted forward, but mud caked on their boots
and pants and weighed them down. The fleet Rebel pickets reached the
Sunken Road long before the Union soldiers could catch them. General
Thomas R. R. Cobb's Georgia brigade watched the winded bluecoats struggling across the sticky plain and bided its time.[15]

The Northerners pressed on with panting urgency. Shells tore their ranks,
sending "arms, hands, legs and clothing into the air." A Union soldier wrote,
"the hill and slope behind us and among us . . . is horrible and heart-rending." Oncoming Federals trampled the fallen underfoot. The color-bearer of
the 8th Ohio rushed ahead, beckoning his regiment to moved faster. A shell
decapitated the standard-bearer for the 4th Ohio, George B. Torrence, "leaving his blood and brains upon comrades and the flag." In contrast to the
artillery, all remained still along the Sunken Road. When Mason's men
passed a small ripple in the ground, a swale of negligible proportions—all
Hell erupted. Cobb's Georgians stood up from behind their stone wall and
unleashed a devastating volley that paralyzed the Yankees. Colonel Mason
screamed at his men to take cover. Federals dove into the swale and instinctively fired back. Some of the men sought protection behind a thick board

fence enclosing the ten-acre lot of the Fredericksburg fairgrounds, Mercer Square.[16]

Cobb's Brigade had waited for the Federal advance to come closer before they opened fire. Southerners had huddled behind the stone wall, unable to see the results of the Washington Artillery's cannonade. Only the infantry officers stood behind the crouching ranks. Some of the more eager men jumped up occasionally and fired at the oncoming Northerners. "Hold. Don't fire yet," Colonel Robert McMillan stormed at the 24th Georgia. "Wait till I give the order." The men returned to kneeling, passing the agonizing minutes by searching the officers' faces for some indication of what was happening in front. The 24th North Carolina stood to the left of Cobb's Brigade. The Tar Heels gawked unabashedly at the Unionists. "They came in grand style, three or four columns deep," remarked a Carolinian. The enemy closed to two hundred yards. Cobb's men remained silent. Federals approached to one hundred yards. Nervous Confederates in the 24th Georgia implored their commander, "Colonel, we must fire, they are coming too close." Yet Cobb waited, drawing the Yankees closer. Suddenly, the general waved his hat to get everyone's attention, shouting, "Get ready Boys—here they come!" With that, the general gave the order to fire. Officers echoed his command down the line. Colonel McMillan instructed the restive 24th Georgia, "Men, if you do shoot, shoot low." Long lines of gray and butternut scrambled to their feet, rifles appeared atop the stone wall, and a volley exploded across the attackers' path—followed by a second and a third.[17]

Cobb's men blazed away, while officers attempted to gauge the effect through an almost impenetrable cloud of gun smoke. William R. Montgomery of the Phillips Legion noted that the Confederates "poured volley after volley into their ranks which told [with] a most deadening effect." Some of the Georgians, however, needed a little assistance with their weapons. Captain Walter Scott Brewster of the Phillips Legion occasionally took a rifle from an inexperienced soldier and fired it, gently instructing, "There . . . that's the way to fire." Thomas R. R. Cobb, attended by his chaplain, Rufus K. Porter, moved along the line to help direct the fire. "By his powerful presence, counsel and order," Porter wrote admiringly, "he was felt at every point of the line." The Confederate fire stopped the attackers cold. "Here the Legion did more execution than at any engagement of the war," wrote a Confederate. Samuel M. H. Byrd of the Phillips Legion reminisced, "I have been over many spots where the dead were strewn on the battlefields of Virginia, but on no spot did I see so many dead as there was in front of our position."

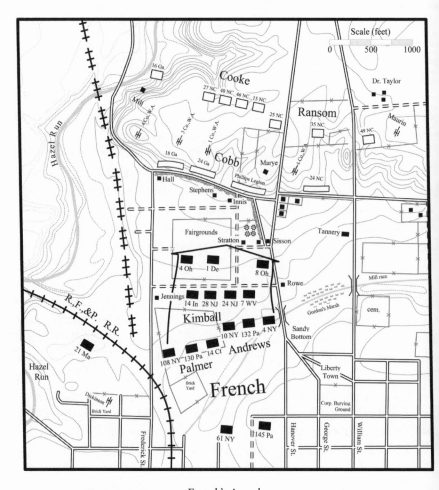

French's Assault

Federal losses littered the field. Confederate casualties, on the other hand, were slight. Several officers fell as they exposed themselves above the wall. Few of Cobb's men had been hit, except for one company of the Phillips Legion, which straddled the intersection of Mercer Street and the Sunken Road.[18]

On the Union side, the 8th Ohio suffered from the stone wall's fire, but also from sharpshooters hidden in the houses along Hanover Street at the base of Marye's Heights. A member of the 4th Ohio mused that "human nature cannot endure such a storm of bullets and not reply." Colonel Sawyer ordered his soldiers to take the buildings. "Then with a lusty cheer we ounded forward," recalled one. Some of the men burst into Allen Stratton's brick house and the adjoining wheelwright shop. Another group forced its way into "the house at the fork in the road"—a small brick grocery belonging o the Sissons family. A woman—perhaps Mrs. Sarah Sissons—had barricaded the door and hidden in the basement. Northerners broke down the door and swarmed inside. Soldiers dragged their wounded comrades into the store and laid them "first on the counters and then as their numbers increased, on the floor." The Ohioans were surprised to discover a lady hiding n the cellar. She seemed absurdly out of place, thought an Ohio man, as she stood "right in the vortex of the whirlpool of destruction." Blueclad soldiers fired through the windows and drew the wrath of gray soldiers behind the wall and along the hilltop. The fire wrecked Sissons' store, as "bullets whistled through it in every direction." "Shells exploded," an 8th Ohio soldier recalled, "shattering, with their terrible detonations[,] every glass in the windows." Sarah Sissons retreated to her cellar again. Meanwhile, Mason's men looked back to Fredericksburg for reinforcements.[19]

When Mason's men had crossed the millrace, Nathan Kimball ordered the rest of his brigade to dress ranks on Caroline Street. The general rode down the line, occasionally stopping to address the men. Reining up in front of the 24th New Jersey, Kimball harangued his troops: "Boys, we are the attacking brigade. I shall expect you to go ahead and open the fight. Keep steady, aim low, and let every man do his duty." Pausing a moment, the general concluded, "Remember you are Jerseymen!" Kimball told another group, "Cheer up, my hearties! This is something we must all get used to." The brigadier sent a guide to Colonel Joseph Snider of the 7th (West) Virginia with orders to move out Prussia Street. A little past 11:30 A.M., the column lurched into motion "with an ominous silence akin to a funeral procession."[20]

The Louisiana artillerists of the Washington Artillery pinpointed the range of the railroad depot by the time Kimball's brigade started past it. The Federals stumbled into "a most murderous fire from the enemy's artillery." A 14th Indiana man wrote that "it seemed we were moving in the crater of a volcano." Kimball reported that shells burst in the ranks, "destroying a company at a time." That undoubtedly was an exaggeration, but it reflects the initial shock of the cannon fire.[21]

The 7th (West) Virginia scrambled across the bridge and dodged north into the protective millrace ravine. The 24th and 28th New Jersey regiments followed the western Virginians into the ravine. The 14th Indiana came last.

Before the brigade reformed, Colonel Snider of the 7th (West) Virginia had fallen wounded by a shell fragment and had to be carried to the rear. Lieutenant Colonel Jonathan H. Lockwood took over his regiment. In a matter of a few minutes, Kimball stretched his right flank to Hanover Street. The left rested on Frederick Street, a road that ran from the city out to the southern end of Marye's Heights. Kimball's new line inverted the order of regiments with the 7th (West) Virginia going from the left flank to the right.[22]

Kimball ordered his brigade to leave their blankets and tents in the millrace ravine. Men piled their effects and left a guard to watch them. The general sputtered a few more ineffectual speeches, telling the troops, "Look out boys. They can't kill all of you but they may hurt some of you." One listener concluded, "Well[,] thought I, that was pretty poor satisfaction or comfort to us." Another wrote that Kimball was a "shallow brained and heartless officer." The brigade commander ordered his troops to fix bayonets, and then called for a charge. The men sprang to their feet and clawed their way out of the ravine.[23]

Dashing into a spongy cornfield, the Federals bogged down in "rough and muddy ground." They were hindered further by "fences and all other obstacles." Southern artillery unleashed a torrent of shells at the oncomers. Kimball's brigade endured "a furious storm of shot, shell and shrapnel." An Indiana soldier wrote, "it was a desperate undertaking . . . but each man resolved to go as far as any other." Lieutenant Colonel Edward A. L. Roberts of the 28th New Jersey reported that his men suffered "a most galling and deadly fire of shot and shell." Men labored across the field as fast as they could suck their feet free from the mud. Many of Kimball's soldiers stopped along the way to return the Confederate fire. Halting to load and shoot slowed Kimball's advance to a crawl and left the men exposed for a prolonged period of time. The general estimated that he lost one-fourth of his command while crossing the plain. Those still in line reached Mason's skirmishers and collapsed in sheer exhaustion. Sprinting four hundred yards over fences and through mire left the men heaving for air and too limp to press farther. Kimball had run his men too far. Now, when Kimball needed them to move swiftly, they were too winded to move at all.[24]

Cobb's Brigade, ensconced behind the stone wall, leveled a punishing fire on the prostrate Federals. An Ohio soldier remembered how "The air [was] alive with fireworks." An Indiana man recalled, "our men were never subjected to a more devouring fire." The Union brigade started to wither "like dry grass before the fire." Kimball clung to the swale, the fairgrounds fence,

nd the Stratton-Sissons buildings. Isolated pockets of Northerners charged
orward, but the Confederates enjoyed every advantage. The heights and the
unken Road appeared "teeming with Gray Backs," a term Northern soldiers
sed to describe the Confederates. A New Jersey man wrote that "in a contest
o unequal, success was impossible."[25]

General Kimball rode conspicuously amid "the sea of bristling bayonets."
His every move drew fire. Galloping to the right, the general suddenly tum-
led from the saddle with a severe wound in his right thigh. Staff officers
ently lifted Kimball and carried him to the rear. The brigadier sent word
o Colonel John Mason to take command. Kimball's party met the division
ommander, William French, near the edge of the city. General French of-
ered his sympathy, and Kimball told him that Mason was in command.[26]

By the time Kimball's aide found Colonel Mason, the Ohio officer already
new of the general's wounding and had assumed command. Mason had
tarted for the right of the brigade when word of Kimball's wound tele-
raphed down the line. He immediately ordered Colonel Sawyer of the 8th
Ohio to take charge of the skirmishers while he took stock of the rest of the
rigade. As Mason surveyed the situation, Lieutenant Joseph R. Swigart of
Kimball's staff dashed up to give him the command officially.[27]

The 14th Indiana, meanwhile, had pressed its attack through "heaps of
lead and wounded" to get closer to the stone wall. Adjutant Thomas C. Bai-
ey dropped out early with a wound. Sergeant John H. Wingert died carrying
he colors. Corporal Thomas Gibson seized the flag, but sustained a flesh
wound in the neck. Others tried to take the standard, but Gibson refused to
give them up. When the attack collapsed, the 14th Indiana lay down. Gibson,
however, continued to stand with his flag. An officer snapped at him "to lay
down the colors." The corporal shouted back, "That is what we are fighting
for." Major Elijah H. C. Cavins, commander of the regiment, commended
he wounded soldier for his bravery, but ordered him to give the flag to someone else and go to the hospital. A survivor of the assault wrote that he had
"never yet seen so many fall in so short a time."[28]

The inchoate 24th and 28th New Jersey regiments quailed before the fire.
Veteran Ohio soldiers took cover behind the blacksmith shop and the brick
grocery, but the Jerseymen lay exposed along a fold in the ground. Bullets
flew among their prostrate ranks, and their effectiveness diminished. One of
the Jerseymen wondered "whether in any of the great battles of the war the
soldiers became more mixed in action." Colonel Moses N. Wisewell fell mortally wounded in the jaw, and Lieutenant Colonel Edward A. L. Roberts took

command of the 28th New Jersey. The 24th New Jersey lost its adjutant, John O. Crowell, killed while rallying the regiment. Thomas Galwey, of the 8th Ohio, noted that the Jersey soldiers "did not exactly run, yet they were very nervous all the time." When the 24th and 28th New Jersey seemed to grow accustomed to the panoply of destruction, two shells blasted their ranks in quick succession. The novices shrank in terror. Seasoned Captain Francis W. Butterfield of the 8th Ohio reassured the New Jersey soldiers that the Confederates could never land three shots in the same spot. "When his words were beginning to reestablish their confidence," a bystander observed, "another shell exploded with a tremendous crash right among them." The horror-stricken recruits bolted for safety. "The poor Jersey boys took to their heels," recorded one old soldier. Lieutenant Colonel Roberts, already under a cloud for making a drunken spectacle of himself in November, failed to redeem his reputation at Fredericksburg. General Sumner cashiered him within a month.[29]

Cobb's men flayed the Federals with a steady, killing fire. A Carolina soldier wrote, "The small arms made one continual noise without a moment's cessation." "So continuous was the roar of musketry on the firing line," recalled a Federal, "that I do not remember hearing the reports of the cannon." General Cobb quickly learned that he would need more ammunition to sustain that level of intensive fire. He sent several requests to the rear for help. Cobb was not certain who actually commanded the salient formed by Marye's Heights and the Sunken Road, so he asked for assistance from several possible sources. Aides searched for Brigadier General Robert Ransom on Marye's Heights, while others skirted the southern end of Willis' Hill to locate Lafayette McLaws. Ransom was the closest superior officer, and his division lined the back of Marye's Heights. Robert Ransom believed he commanded all of the troops in the salient—including Cobb's Brigade—and sent help immediately. Cobb accepted it: though he came from McLaws' division, and mainly looked to McLaws for support, he did not stand on protocol and would welcome assistance from whoever offered it.[30]

Ransom answered first and Confederate reinforcements flocked to the crest of Marye's Heights. The division commander had used Cobb's request to forward Brigadier General John R. Cooke's Brigade to the top of the hill. Cooke, a brother-in-law of J. E. B. Stuart and cousin to the author John Esten Cooke, aligned his four regiments in the hollow behind the Willis cemetery. The 15th North Carolina formed on the left, joined by the 46th North Carolina, 48th North Carolina, and 27th North Carolina. Cooke acted swiftly, but his line moved erratically. The general sent his regiments forward with the wishful injunction: "Now, men, I want you to do this prettily; go on." The 15th North Carolina dropped its knapsacks, and the others probably did the same; then they advanced. Lieutenant Colonel Samuel H. Walkup's 48th North Carolina, however, was not ready. For some reason, Walkup ordered his men to cap their weapons before advancing. As a result, the brigade lurched forward disjointedly, each regiment heading to the crest at its own speed and inclination. Reaching the summit under a "merciless fire and storm of minnie balls and shell," Cooke tried to regroup his command. He planted Lieutenant Colonel William MacRae's 15th North Carolina in front of the Marye house. The rest of the brigade extended to the right. Lieutenant Colonel Walkup's 48th North Carolina huddled behind the brick wall of the cemetery. The other regiments lay down on the crest. Soldiers of the Old North State gaped at "a most magnificent view of the movements" of both the Union and Confederate forces. Occasionally, Cooke's Brigade fired a volley, but it largely refrained from shooting over the heads of Cobb's men. This all but negated its usefulness.[31]

Cooke's Brigade halted on line with the Washington Artillery, but the 27th North Carolina hesitated only a moment, "in the midst of a terrific fire," before it surged down the hillside to the Sunken Road. Gunners "began to throw up their hats and cheer" the charging regiment. The Carolinians responded with a yell and set off for the bottom of the hill. Cobb's Georgia units met the incoming Confederates with more shouts and cheers. The 27th North Carolina lost a dozen soldiers while descending Willis Hill, among them their commander. Colonel John A. Gilmer hobbled into the road with a painful wound to his knee. Major Joseph C. Webb sustained a glancing shot to his wrist, which, he wryly noted, "hurt my coat worse than it did my hide." The reinforcements mingled with Cobb's troops, making the men roughly four files deep. One impetuous Carolinian jumped on top of the wall and taunted the Unionists, "Here is your mistake!" He fired his rifle and hopped down in the road.[32]

Ransom, meanwhile, shifted two regiments from his own brigade to the hilltop. Ransom told them that Cobb needed ammunition and "must be reinforced." He also warned them that "the undertaking was a dangerous one." The 25th and 35th North Carolina hustled into line near the Marye home. Lieutenant Colonel Samuel C. Bryson's 25th North Carolina formed behind the picturesque mansion. Lieutenant Colonel John G. Jones' 35th Regiment moved to its left. Shortly afterward, Ransom ordered Bryson's 25th North

Carolina to support the 15th North Carolina in front of the Marye's house. Bryson's regiment advanced around either side of the house. Closing ranks in the front yard, the 25th North Carolina took position on the immediate left of the 15th North Carolina.[33]

General William French spotted the Confederates shifting on Marye's Heights and assumed the Southerners were massing for a counterattack against his right. French sent a warning to Colonel Mason to "look out for the right." In turn, Mason cautioned Colonel Sawyer, of the 8th Ohio, to be on his guard. Mason also shifted the 7th (West) Virginia to support the 8th Ohio. Lieutenant Colonel Lockwood's Virginians took a beating as they extended the line north of the Telegraph Road. Heavy fire forced the bluecoats to fall back to the Sissons grocery. "My men suffered severely," Lockwood reported. Sawyer's 8th Ohio also crossed Telegraph Road, but came back with the same results. "We were subjected to a most murderous fire of both artillery and small-arms," the commander wrote, "which swept our position." Among the fallen lay the adjutant of the Ohio regiment, Lieutenant David Lewis. A small group of Federals made a lodgment north of Telegraph Road, but they lacked the strength to advance farther. Their role became strictly defensive.[34]

Part of the 8th Ohio reinforced the blacksmith shop between the Stratton house and Sissons' store. The Ohioans filled in where part of the 24th and 28th New Jersey had fallen back in disorder. A dirt lane separated the blacksmith shop from the grocery store. Corporal Samuel Brown swung open a large wooden door from the blacksmith's shop that blocked the lane. Perched in the corner of the shop, Brown fired at the Confederates using the door hinges as a rest. Southern artillery countered by smashing the door with solid shot, though it missed the sharpshooter. The corporal shouted, "Bully for you, by God!" and fired from the new hole.[35]

Federal casualties continued to mount. Wounded men crawled to the grocery store for shelter. Bloody and maimed soldiers filled the building. A burning thirst gnawed at them; wounded begged for water. When canteens ran dry, soldiers searched for a pump. In desperation, they routed the lady out of the basement and demanded water. The Northerners, a veteran wrote, "dragged the poor woman out of her cellar." She told them that the well was behind the store—and between the lines. The bluecoats "forced her out into the pelting shower of missiles to show them the well." Though he never saw her again, the 8th Ohio soldier Thomas Galwey thought the woman "must have gone mad with fear." Later in the day, soldiers reported seeing a disheveled woman sitting among the Yankee corpses, staring blankly into space.[36]

Men fought for what seemed like hours. The Federals could not move, either forward or back, without provoking a fusillade from the stone wall—"that terrible stone wall," as Thomas Galwey called it. Kimball's attack had stalled. Ammunition began to run low, and some of the men relied on the dead and wounded to replenish their supply. Trapped in this predicament, the Union troops became frustrated. One soldier wished aloud: "Great gods, if only one of those shells would take Burnside on the head!" The division commander, William French, hurried reinforcements from the city.[37]

Andrews' and Palmer's brigades had waited for orders near the city courthouse. The clock chimed noon as French sent his last two brigades into the battle. Andrews' brigade led the way, and Palmer followed it.

John Andrews had two veteran regiments—the 4th and 10th New York—but their ranks were thin. Together, they mustered about 500 men. Though the units were small in number, one New Yorker reported that the regiments appeared to be "in good spirits and marching in excellent order." French had taken Smyth's 1st Delaware away from the brigade earlier, but he replaced it with the new 132nd Pennsylvania from Palmer's brigade. "I was glad," wrote Lieutenant Colonel Charles Albright, commander of the Pennsylvanians, "for my boys preferred fighting with and alongside of veterans." O. O. Howard probably was happy to get rid of the 132nd Pennsylvania. The Keystone soldiers had camped near the general's headquarters, and two of Albright's men had stolen his breakfast that morning.[38]

Andrews rearranged his brigade before marching, placing the 132nd Pennsylvania in the middle of the line, with the 4th New York on the left and the 10th New York on the right. The newcomers added 340 men to the brigade, bringing it up to 850—barely a respectable size for a regiment at the beginning of 1862. The 132nd Pennsylvania lacked a majority of its officers, including its colonel and major. Some companies mustered only a single officer, while others were led by noncommissioned officers. The ranking officer, Lieutenant Colonel Albright, though present, wrestled with an obstinate case of laryngitis. Mercifully, the adjutant, Frederick L. Hitchcock, returned from sick leave just as the command joined Andrews' brigade. Hitchcock's healthy vocal cords gave voice to Albright's whispered commands.[39]

Colonel Oliver Palmer commanded a triad of regiments—14th Connecticut, 130th Pennsylvania, and 108th New York. The 14th Connecticut joined

Andrews' right, near the bullet-pocked Saint George's Episcopal Church. Many of the men welled with nervous excitement. "Waiting in suspense . . . with such apprehensions as came to them, seemed worse to endure than a dash upon the field," lamented a Connecticut soldier.[40]

French briefed Andrews and Palmer before he sent them forward. He told Andrews to support Kimball's brigade and that Palmer would back him up. Andrews instructed his subordinates to exit the city the same way Kimball had and take position 150 yards behind Mason's soldiers. The brigade commander informed his subordinates that the brigade would join Mason's line only "as it became weakened." Andrews never intended to take over the attack. Rather, he expected to boost Mason's force so it could renew its attack. Both Andrews and Palmer directed their officers to dismount to avoid being conspicuous targets. Soldiers scuttled into line while mounted leaders surrendered their horses, blankets, and effects to their servants. Colonel Andrews watched the last-minute preparation, and somehow convinced himself that "the men seemed full of enthusiasm, and eager to meet the enemy."[41]

As soon as John Andrews' brigade started down Princess Anne Street, it drew fire immediately from Confederate artillery on Marye's Heights. Southern gunners swept the streets that crossed the Union march. Their shells bowled through the column with terrifying effect. Andrews' brigade had barely moved before the leader of the 10th New York received a disfiguring wound to his head and neck. A shell exploded in Colonel John E. Bendix's face and dropped him in a bloody heap. Captain Salmon Winchester stepped forward and kept the regiment moving. A Northern soldier noted another danger downtown. Confederate shells often exploded against the buildings, hurling shrapnel and bricks with equal velocity. Wounded men literally clogged the street. A shell burst left a member of the 132nd Pennsylvania lying in the thoroughfare with his leg dangling by a bloody tendon. Several men dragged him off the street, but they handled him so roughly that the wounded soldier pleaded to be left alone to die. Even under fire, some soldiers kept their sense of humor. They laughed at lanky George Monroe of the 4th New York, who absently faltered at each intersection to hike his collar and skip across the intersection with his head down as if in a rain shower. Despite the merriment, Monroe appeared "perfectly unconscious of the absurdity of his action."[42]

Andrews' column came under a more destructive "hurricane of iron" when it entered Prussia Street. The Confederates had perfected their aim against Kimball's brigade, and now knew exactly where to direct their fire. Federals darted across the millrace by a brickyard owned by the Mullens or Alers families. A shell cleaved a 4th New York soldier in two and then exploded, killing and wounding another eleven men. Andrews' troops picked their way through the dead and wounded, which slowed their progress and left them vulnerable. Eugene Cory of the 4th New York called this the "most terrific artillery fire we had ever faced." "I can truthfully say that in that moment I gave my life up," reminisced the adjutant of the 132nd Pennsylvania. "I do not expect ever to face death more certainly. . . . It did not seem possible that I could go through that fire . . . and return alive." Nearby, Pennsylvanian John Kistler took a direct hit that tore his arm off at the elbow. Dropping out of ranks, he headed for the hospital, intending to get it dressed so he could return to the fight.[43]

Most of Andrews' brigade hurried across the millrace and dipped behind the rise along the watercourse. The ranks retained reasonable order with the exception of the 132nd Pennsylvania. Colonel Andrews redressed his battle line, which now appeared in inverse order. The 4th New York now held the right, with the 132nd Pennsylvania in the middle and the 10th New York zouaves on the left. The soldiers hugged the ground a few hundred yards behind Mason's (Kimball's) brigade. Andrews made no immediate effort to join Mason, but contented himself with holding the ravine. Even when Palmer's brigade extended his left, Andrews refused to advance. He hoped Mason would somehow succeed on his own, and he feared mixing his command with Mason's ranks. Either way, Mason's brigade fought alone while Andrews' soldiers lay under a punishing artillery barrage.[44]

Oliver Palmer's brigade traversed the same route out of the city. When Andrews' men started down Princess Anne Street, Palmer's officers ordered their men to fix bayonets. After a brief pause, the column lurched into motion. "It came *our* turn now," wrote Major Francis E. Pierce of the 108th New York (emphasis in original). The brigade marched to Prussia Street, hurrying across the exposed intersections. The 14th Connecticut led the way, with the 130th Pennsylvania and 108th New York in trace. Bursting shells and crashing walls engulfed the brigade in smoke, dust, and noise. Edward W. Spangler of the 130th Pennsylvania noted how "screaming shells shattered the roofs of many of the houses[,] scattering the debris over our heads."[45]

The brigade turned into Prussia Street. Houses on the right protected the column until it reached the railroad depot, and "then the storm burst upon them." Confederate artillery wreaked havoc with the Federals channeling through the choke point at the millrace. Colonel Palmer reported: "Their guns appeared to have the exact range of this passage." The bottleneck slowed the advance and created an inviting target. A Connecticut soldier later recalled that "the missiles did murderous work." Sergeant William B. Hincks of the 14th Connecticut wrote, "Canister shot went hopping round the depot yard and on the causeway like enormous marbles, and shells burst, with a hideous crash, on every side."[46]

Palmer's brigade hesitated at the sluiceway. A Pennsylvanian wrote that the bridge was "a most serious and embarrassing obstacle, and very disconcerting under a raking storm of projectiles." "Our men fell like leaves," recalled a New Yorker. One shell tore off both of David Lincoln's legs as he crossed the span. Soldiers in the 14th Connecticut shied away in revulsion. Others stood transfixed by the spectacle. Lincoln smiled weakly, offering his comrades words of encouragement as they filed past. Following the Connecticut soldiers came the Pennsylvanians and New Yorkers. "When crossing a sluice, I noticed several men standing still looking at something," remembered a member of the 108th New York. To the latecomers, Lincoln evenly intoned: "Pass on boys. Don't stop to look at me." At the same time, Captain William McLaughlin herded a portion of the 130th Pennsylvania onto the bridge. Shells carved huge gaps in his ranks. One of the shells decapitated Captain McLaughlin, splattering his brains over the company.[47]

Converging artillery fire and nightmarish scenes like those of Lincoln and McLaughlin unnerved some of the men. The 14th Connecticut's advance degenerated into a chaotic shambles. Some of the 130th Pennsylvania cowered behind the railroad depot. When routed from their shelter, Union soldiers darted across the millrace and hid behind a brickyard, or "Old Ashery." The 108th New York behaved the same way when artillery "swept the brave men away like chaff." A New Yorker wrote, "the shells burst among them with awful havoc."[48]

More men might have fallen had not Lieutenant Colonel Sanford H. Perkins taken the initiative. Perkins, of the 14th Connecticut, told the head of the paralyzed column to follow him. The broken ranks picked through the human debris and sidled to the right, under cover of the millrace depression. Filing up the ravine, the 14th Connecticut overlapped the left of Andrews' brigade, and arrived behind the 10th New York. Unable to find a spot in the line, the New Englanders turned to retrace their march. As Perkins' men about-faced, the surrounding troops jeered them for leaving. The regiment, however, quickly pivoted back into line on the left of the 10th New York and lay down. The rest of Palmer's soldiers re-formed along the ravine. Some of them took cover behind a short stone wall overlooking the waterway.[49]

Several Union soldiers saw a balloon rise above Stafford Heights. Confederate artillery also descried the balloon and hurled several rounds at it, even though it floated well beyond their range. Connecticut lieutenant James L. Townsend blurted out impulsively, "They are firing at the balloon!" "Good God," scoffed Captain Samuel H. Davis, "Townsend is afraid they were firing at the balloon. I should think *somebody* was firing at *us*" (emphasis in original). Laughter rippled down the line.[50]

Thaddeus S. C. Lowe, head of the Federal army's young aeronautic corps, made several balloon ascents on December 13. The intelligence he gathered appeared to be superficial and often wrong, but the novelty of his experiment captivated Union and Confederate soldiers and enticed brash young staff officers to go aloft and see the action. Southerners attempted to shoot down the balloon several times without success, though their best opportunity came when the balloon prepared to leave the ground. Band members of the 1st Rhode Island Cavalry cringed every time Lowe's inflated orb started to rise because enemy shells inevitably rained on their bivouac.[51]

Confederate artillery pummeled Andrews' and Palmer's brigades as they lay behind the millrace embankment. Some of the Southern guns enfiladed Andrews' right flank. "Perhaps the most trying position in which a soldier can be placed is standing still under an artillery fire which he cannot return," reminisced a New Yorker. Another wrote, "Minutes passed which seemed hours to our harassed and comparatively helpless regiment." The 10th New York's new commander, Captain Salmon Winchester, steeled his men by parading in front of his line. Several officers asked the captain to lie down, but he loudly refused, asserting that "he would stand until he was knocked down." Almost immediately, a solid shot snapped his sword in two and smashed his thigh with a fatal wound. Several zouaves carted the dying officer to the rear, and Captain George F. Hopper became the third commander of the National Zouaves within ten minutes. The men became callous of death. The 132nd Pennsylvania watched with indifference as a shell decapitated an officer. "So intense was the situation that even this tragic death received only a passing thought," noted a Keystone soldier. Consensus agreed that "no troops could stand that fire" for long. John Andrews needed to act before his command fell apart. The colonel decided to attack.[52]

Andrews later claimed that he reinforced Colonel Mason's brigade when he thought it no longer could advance on its own. Others thought that Mason's brigade "had been struggling" just to hold its ground. Andrews' brigade climbed out of the muddy ravine and dressed ranks. As soon as the line rose from the depression, the Confederates redoubled their fire. "The very air [was] lurid, and alive with the flashes of guns, and rent with the long shriek of solid shot and shell, and the wicked whistle of grape," attested a 4th New York soldier. Men bit their lips and gulped short breaths as the line started on "one of the most desperate charges of the whole four years of war." They closed ranks every time a shell ruptured their alignment. Shoulder to shoulder, they pressed up the incline toward Marye's Heights.[53]

The attackers marched with measured cadence despite the hellish barrage. Sublime courage became commonplace. "One may ask how such dangers can be faced," reflected Frederick Hitchcock, the adjutant of the 132nd Pennsylvania. "The answer is, there are many things more to be feared than death." Hitchcock dreaded cowardice and failure to fulfill his duty more than Rebel cannonballs. The adjutant wrote: "This is duty. I'll trust in God and do it. If I fall, I cannot die better." Hitchcock probably whispered the sentiment of many of the men on the battlefield, North and South.[54]

Such beliefs carried Andrews' brigade closer to the enemy heights. The Northerners leaned into the fire and reached the prostrate forms of Mason's brigade. Momentum propelled the attackers to the forefront of the battle. The 4th New York passed between the Stratton house and the blacksmith shop. The 132nd Pennsylvania and the 10th New York slipped through a fence and into the spacious Fredericksburg fairgrounds. As the Federals passed the high water mark of Mason's advance, Southern infantry suddenly stood up from behind the stone wall. Several well-directed Confederate volleys blunted the attack in a matter of minutes. The Federals felt "almost blown off our feet, staggering as though against a mighty wind." The Yankees suffered a crippling loss in short order. Nearly one-half of the command had fallen within fifteen minutes of leaving the millrace. Captain Hopper saw many of his 10th New York zouaves "mangled in a most horrible condition." The survivors stumbled back to the swale and sprawled in the mud alongside Mason's brigade. The newcomers joined Mason's dirty ranks in returning the fire. Northerners "went to work with a will," noted New York Captain Hopper, "but it was no use." Pretty soon Federal fire diminished. Rifles became fouled and ammunition grew scarce along the whole line.[55]

Shortly after Andrews' assault, Palmer's brigade took up the attack. The men had endured twenty minutes of shelling along the millrace. From its position,

volley!" Before the 130th Pennsylvania could respond, Southerners rattled off a volley and Colonel Zinn fell dead with a bullet in his brain. Captain William A. Porter, the next senior officer, withdrew the 130th Pennsylvania to the edge of the fairgrounds and ordered it to lie down beside the 14th Connecticut. At the worst possible moment, Captain Porter noticed Union artillery coming into action behind him. Their first shots fell among his men. The Pennsylvanians started to break. Ohio colonel John Mason, in charge of Kimball's brigade, swore "like a trooper" at them and steadied the troops.[61]

The 108th New York drove forward through a storm of shot and shell. The left half of the regiment, south of the fairgrounds' wall, passed only a couple paces beyond the swale before grinding to a halt. The right of the regiment, inside the fairgrounds, lost half of its men before reaching the center of Mercer Square. Several Northerners wrote that the danger of this attack exceeded that of Antietam. "It was a much harder battle than Antietam," John Pellett declared in a letter home. Another remembered, "Antietam was a hard fought field, but this is the most terrible yet in the annals of warfare." The line foundered and then drifted back. Men fell at every step. Soldiers looked for cover, but found little. The barren fairgrounds left them stark and easy targets for the Confederates. "I don't see how a worse place could by any means have been made," concluded a Northerner. Another soldier noted, "when I saw the murderous fire as it swept through the columns of our devoted men, my feelings were indescribable." Private Edward Cotter wrote angrily, "I was so mad that I could have went and helped the rebels—to think of our men marching right into the Jaws of death without any Site to defend themselves." The 108th New York fell back to the east wall of the fairgrounds. Major Francis Pierce confessed, "How any man went up & back again alive is more than I can imagine."[62]

Across the way, the Confederates expanded their fire to rake the entire Union front. From the Sunken Road and the crest of Marye's Heights, Ransom's and Cooke's North Carolinians combined with Cobb's Georgians to blast the Federals. A 10th New York's officer described the field as "a perfect slaughter house." Captain George Hopper, commander of the 10th New York, recalled the swale filling with so many wounded that it was difficult to move along the front line without stepping on them. "The shot, shell and Rifle balls flew like hail," as they skimmed the top of the swale. Hopper walked erect with a stoic fatalism, defying the bullets. He later explained: "There was no use to dodge the little ones, for you was just as likely to run your head in front of one as to get away." Somehow he beat the odds and survived. Other New Yorkers escaped with equally good luck. Some of the men had stuffed their blouses with hard-pressed cakes of tobacco, and when bullets struck them, they deflected or imbedded in the plug tobacco, causing little more than a stunning jolt and a telltale bruise.[63]

The 132nd Pennsylvania did not share Captain Hopper's sang froid. "The nervous strain was simply awful," recalled one soldier. "It can be appreciated only by those who have experienced it." Adjutant Hitchcock remembered, "The atmosphere seemed surcharged with the most startling and frightful things." The dead and wounded outnumbered the living in places. Lying in the middle of the fairgrounds seemed like madness to the Pennsylvanians. One officer argued that it would be better to fix bayonets and make another charge than to sit there "and invite certain destruction." The 132nd Pennsylvania lost its entire color company within minutes of entering Mercer Square. Five men fell bearing the regiment's standards. Lieutenant Henry H. Hoagland saw the fifth man collapse and took the flag. When he raised it, he too slumped mortally wounded. Lieutenant Charles McDougal—already carrying one flag—picked up Hoagland's colors and asked Adjutant Hitchcock to take it. As McDougal handed a flag to Hitchcock a bullet smashed the lieutenant's arm and wrist, spattering blood on the adjutant's face. Hitchcock caught the colors as it flew from McDougal's shattered arm. Another Confederate bullet cut the flagstaff and a shell fragment gouged the adjutant's head. Frederick Hitchcock sank to the ground, calmly thinking, "This is the end." He blacked out still holding the flag. Sergeant Major Austin F. Clapp rolled the adjutant over, gave him up for dead, and retrieved the colors.[64]

Colonel Andrews moved between the knots of men around the Stratton house and the fairgrounds. The brigade commander drew a great deal of fire. Andrews' aide, Lieutenant Theodore H. Rogers, was wounded and stumbled into the brigadier. Soon after, Andrews himself fell disabled. The colonel refused to relinquish command and stayed on the field. Andrews penned a curiously ambiguous report, stating that he had been disabled but turned over command only after the brigade left the field. At that time, he yielded command to Lieutenant Colonel John W. Marshall of the 10th New York. Marshall, however, stated that he took command from Lieutenant Colonel William Jameson of the 4th New York, to whom Andrews was "obliged to surrender the command." Andrews made no mention of Jameson in his account of the battle, and Jameson made no reference to commanding the brigade. Jameson could only have taken command as the brigade left the field, because he was junior in rank to Colonel John D. MacGregor of the 4th New

York, who fell during the withdrawal. Since MacGregor never commanded the brigade, we can presume that Andrews retained control until the withdrawal.[65]

Nearby, Colonel Oliver Palmer watched his brigade wither before him. The ranks had become so torn and mixed that the brigade commander could no longer locate his three regiments. The colonel hovered near the north end of Mercer's Square, where he spotted the flag of the 14th Connecticut. Palmer squatted behind a nearby mound of dirt, and made no further effort to find his brigade. Unknown to him, the 14th Connecticut's banner did not indicate the regiment's position. Color Sergeant Charles E. Dart had planted the flag behind a broken fence post on the perimeter of the fairgrounds, and lay down between Lieutenant Charles Lyman and Corporal John Symonds. A Confederate shell burst in front of them. Gravel from the blast blinded Corporal Symonds, and his eyes swelled to the size of eggs. Shrapnel tore off most of Charles Dart's face. Shell fragments then sawed through the fence post and struck the lieutenant. Sergeant Augustus Foote spotted the faceless color-bearer in his death throes. He crawled over and took his place. Confederates shot Foote in the head and hip when he tried to evacuate the flag. The sergeant lay beneath the upright flag. In his delirium, he begged nearby Union soldiers to kill him. Brigade commander Palmer assumed the standard rammed in the mud marked his brigade's whereabouts. Soon afterward two Connecticut soldiers, Frederick B. Doten and William B. Hincks, asked Colonel Palmer where to find their regiment. Palmer pointed to the flag. The two dashed forward, only to discover the state flag unattended. Apparently Foote had either fainted or crawled away, because neither man noticed him. They furled the banner and spirited it to safety.[66]

Palmer's brigade lingered on the field, but the hope of victory had vanished. "We all felt that success was a forlorn hope," wrote a Pennsylvania soldier. Death and destruction ravaged the prostrate line. Shells screeched overhead and exploded in their ranks, appearing to "lift the earth from its foundation." Bullets rained down on the men like "drops in a summer shower." New Yorkers noted that the dead literally "piled upon each other in scores." A Connecticut soldier asked: "Who can depict the horrors of that scene? What language can adequately portray the awful carnage of that hour?" The 108th New York hurled musketry at the Confederate stone wall to prevent the Rebels from concentrating their fire with total impunity. Federal ammunition disappeared rapidly without any tangible sign of success. The Federal line grew quiet again, and the men looked to the rear for reinforcements and fresh ammunition. John Pellett of the 108th New York wrote angrily: "We could not do anything to them. They had all the advantage of us."[67]

The whirlwind of destruction bred confusion in the prostrate clumps of bluecoats. The excessive loss of leaders stranded troops without a guiding hand, and the lack of ammunition and the fouled pieces left them powerless to fight. When fresh troops under General Winfield Scott Hancock arrived, the beaten remnants of Andrews' brigade drifted back to Fredericksburg. The men ran a gauntlet of fire to get to the city. Colonel John D. MacGregor of the 4th New York received a wound in his arm and needed to be helped off the field. At the same time, Colonel Andrews' wound may have rendered him unfit to command, or he may have become separated from his brigade. His troops rallied beside the millrace under the next senior officer, the 4th New York's Lieutenant Colonel William Jameson. Private John Kistler of the 132nd Pennsylvania re-joined the brigade at the millrace. A shell had severed his arm during the attack. He had the stump bandaged, grabbed a cracker and buoyantly headed for the battlefield. Kistler found Lieutenant Colonel Charles Albright and piped cheerfully between bites of his cracker, "Colonel I hope we shall whip them yet." He was probably the only optimist left in the entire brigade.[68]

Palmer's brigade also left the field in small, disorganized groups. Most of the troops made their way toward the city and carried their wounded with them. Soldiers sometimes tussled for the right to help an injured comrade because it was a means to escape the battle. Parts of French's division lingered along Mercer Square and waited for night in order to retire. The left half of the 108th New York stayed, unaware that the rest of the brigade had fallen back. Lieutenant Colonel Powers retained his position south of the fair grounds, cut off from the rest of the line by the board fence. Many of the Federals along the swale shimmied to the right to get behind the Stratton house. The crowd congregating near the dwelling reminded one man of "a huge cluster of swarming bees extending far back." A chunk of Palmer's brigade gathered at the millrace, even though Confederate shells bedeviled them "with a hellish noise." Some of the wounded could not reach Fredericksburg. They hid in the ruins of an icehouse etched in the bank of the millrace. More than a hundred men crammed into a pit measuring thirty or forty feet square.[69]

Colonel John Mason's brigade—formerly Kimball's—remained on the battlefield. The men held their ground even when the other brigades with drew. Mason clung to the swale with the expectation that fresh reinforcements were coming soon. The Ohio colonel consolidated his line, incorporating men left over from the rest of French's division. He anchored his line on the Stratton house and the Sissons store, with his left drifting halfway down the badly splintered wall of Mercer Square. Mason never knew of the contingent of the 108th New York south of the fairgrounds.[70]

Moments after French's division left the field, Adjutant Frederick Hitchcock regained consciousness. The adjutant of the 132nd Pennsylvania felt blood pulsing from his head wound. The shell fragment had torn his scalp, but fortunately no more. When the next attack, by Hancock's division, swayed closer to the stone wall, the Pennsylvanian saw that "the field about me was literally covered with the blue uniforms of our dead and wounded men." Hitchcock stumbled to his feet and teetered in one direction and then another as he tried to avoid Confederate sharpshooters. A minié ball clipped his leg just above the ankle. It felt "like the stinging cut of a whip." Clambering into the millrace ravine, the adjutant ran into Lieutenant Colonel Charles Albright. The colonel embraced him and hoarsely whispered, "We thought you were killed." The commander tenderly bound Hitchcock's wounds, and Sergeant Major Clapp apologized sheepishly for having pronounced him dead.[71]

Darius Couch, commander of the Second Corps, rode along the edge of the city, trying to get a feel for the fight. Smoke and fog obscured his view, so he returned to Fredericksburg. He dispatched orders to two of his division commanders. He ordered Hancock to take his 1st Division and sustain French's division. Couch also ordered French to renew his attack as soon as Hancock joined him. Telling his subordinates to "carry" the heights, Couch deliberately intensified the action from a demonstration to a full-blown assault. He wanted Longstreet swept off Marye's Heights.[72]

The Second Corps chief stopped at the courthouse on Princess Anne Street and headed inside. Accompanied by General Oliver O. Howard, Couch climbed into the cupola for a better view of the field. Together, they scanned the horizon, and the crusty corps commander watched the final moments of French's attempted breakthrough. "Oh, great God!" he gasped. "See how our men, our poor fellows are falling!" The field was wrapped in chaos. Commands became mixed and scattered by artillery. Dead littered the plateau, and wounded streamed back to the city. Howard wrote, "French's brave division had almost disappeared." The Second Corps commander watched in stupefied horror: "I had never before seen fighting like that, nothing approached it in terrible uproar and destruction." Each charging brigade in succession "would do its duty and melt like snow coming down on warm ground."[73]

Hancock's division took the field as soon as it could, and the bloodied remains of French's command flowed past it heading in the opposite direction. French had given up hope for renewing the attack. Hancock's fresh division could not strengthen his force enough to sustain another assault. French preferred to let Hancock simply replace his division. As a result, the general ordered his survivors back to Fredericksburg. "This was to our division the real end," Connecticut volunteer Henry Stevens remembered, "and it practically dropped out of the fight for the day." French greeted the men as they came back. He told them that it was a "——— hot day for the 13th of December."[74]

General Hancock did not know that French had lost hope, or that he had ordered his men off the field. When Hancock met French's men, he screamed at them to rally and join his command. Hancock's cursing made "the air sulphurous with imprecations." Edward Spangler of the 130th Pennsylvania later wrote with grudging admiration, "Until then I did not know the English language was so rich in eruptive possibilities." French's soldiers ignored the vituperative general and left Hancock's men "to go through the motions."[75]

French's division had never stood a chance of success. Nathan Kimball's plan of using Confederate skirmishers as a shield bogged down in the thick mud of the plateau. It almost certainly had been visionary in any case. His men waded forward as fast as they could, but they closed on the stone wall too slowly and too winded to drive home the attack. Southerners blew back the brigade when it was already disorganized and exhausted. The rapid succession of brigade lines, conceptually spaced two hundred yards apart, never materialized. French held his last two brigades back while Kimball engaged the Confederates alone. Reinforcements, rushed forward after the fact, took a considerable time to issue from the city, dress ranks, and advance. John W. Andrews complicated matters further by deliberately withholding his brigade. The colonel believed that he should support Mason's attack as needed, rather than lead the attack. He somehow convinced himself that Kimball's troops, under Mason, had retained their momentum. Colonel Oliver Palmer had to wait until Andrews advanced before he could move. Impatiently, he shortened the interval between their brigades to 150 yards. French's second and third waves really constituted one attack. Neither brigade had enough man power to cover half of Mason's (Kimball's) front. Andrews moved to the right and opened an avenue for Palmer's attack to the left without overlapping. Ultimately, Confederate artillery doomed all of the Federal attacks to failure. Waves of Union attackers theoretically should have focused the Confederate fire on the forefront brigade, while the following brigades advanced relatively unscathed. The Confederates, however, divided their fire, allotting their infantry to the closest Yankees, and their artillery to the reinforcements channeling out of Fredericksburg. By the time the Federals closed on the stone wall, cannon fire already had disorganized them.

Union losses attest to the effectiveness of the Southerners' fire. Kimball's brigade suffered 520 casualties out of perhaps 2,000 troops. The new men of the 28th New Jersey bore the heaviest casualties of the brigade, losing 193 men out of 665. Andrews' brigade incurred still heavier losses, counting 342 casualties out of 850 men engaged, a loss exceeding 40 percent. The 10th New York lost 9 of its 11 officers. The 132nd Pennsylvania counted 150 casualties out of 340 men—44 percent of the nine-month regiment. The Pennsylvanians also lost their colors. After several men had fallen while holding the standard, the last one carried it off the field despite a serious wound. The delirious soldier stumbled into a church used as a hospital. Still clutching his flag, he fainted and died. Surgeons propped the flag in a corner and subsequently forgot about it. Palmer's brigade recorded the lightest losses, amassing 293 casualties. The 14th Connecticut lost 122 out of 270 men, suffering a 45 percent reduction. Edmund Wade noted later that the wounded commander, Lieutenant Colonel Sanford Perkins, "is most crazy about it and has given notice to the authorities that the Regiment is not fit for duty." French's division had lost nearly one-third of its officers, and a little more than 30 percent of its men.[76]

French's division—minus Mason's brigade, which was still fighting—regrouped on the river. Regimental officers rallied their troops on Sophia Street and called roll. Palmer's brigade re-formed below the railroad bridge, and Lieutenant Colonel Jameson regrouped Andrews' brigade to its right. Lieutenant Colonel John W. Marshall of the 10th New York left a detail at Chatham and hurried across the river to take command of the brigade. Marshall dispatched patrols to scour the city for lost men. French and his staff also helped. They directed numerous soldiers to Sophia Street. Captain Joseph W. Plume, an aide to the general, happened upon the 1st Delaware and on his own initiative returned it to Andrews' brigade.[77]

Major General Ambrose E. Burnside (*center*),
commander of the Army of the Potomac

MOLLUS Collection, USAMHI

General Robert E. Lee,
commander of the Army of Northern Virginia

MOLLUS Collection, USAMHI

50th New York Engineers laying a pontoon bridge under fire, December 11, 1862. Sketch by Alfred R. Waud.

The Federal bombardment of Fredericksburg, as seen from the middle pontoon crossing. The burned railroad trestle appears on the right.

From *Battles and Leaders of the Civil War*

The back of Marye's Heights overlooking Fredericksburg on December 11, 1862. Frank Vizetelly sketched this view from Lee's command post on Telegraph Hill.

Courtesy Fredericksburg & Spotsylvania N.M.P.

The Federal sacking Fredericksburg on December 12, 1862, as witnessed by the artist Arthur Lumley.

Library of Congress

An 1884 view from Stonewall Jackson's position of Prospect Hill. The RF&P Railroad runs along the base of the hill. The copse of woods appears on the left.

The 1884 reunion of Union First Corps veterans on Prospect Hill. The group is standing in front of Archer's earthworks.

Courtesy Fredericksburg & Spotsylvania N.M.P.

The millrace valley. The race had been drained by the time of this postwar photograph. Union troops re-formed under the lip to the left. Marye's Heights appears in the background.

Fields in front of Marye's Heights. Photograph taken from Federal Hill in May 1864. The Stratton house is on the right.

Library of Congress

Kimball's attack against the stone wall, showing the millrace in the foreground along with attackers swarming around the Stratton house, the wheelwright shop, and Sissons' store.

Confederate Washington Artillery on Marye's Heights, December 13, 1862, sketched by Confederate soldier William L. Sheppard.

From James Longstreet, *Manassas to Appomattox* (Philadelphia: Lippincott, 1896)

The stone wall and the Sunken Road

Confederates defending the stone wall on December 13, 1862. The Hall house appears in the background. Drawn by Confederate artist Allen C. Redwood.

From *Battles and Leaders of the Civil War*

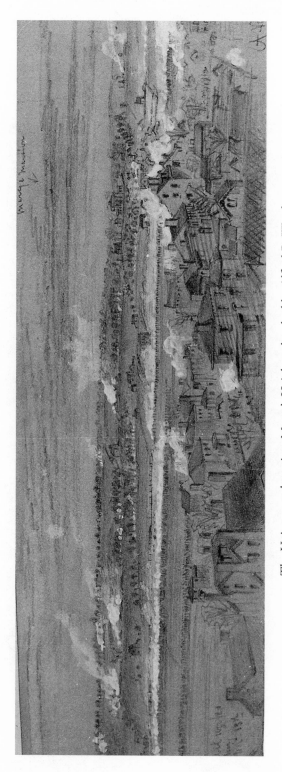

The Union assault against Marye's Heights, sketched by Alfred R. Waud.

A. A. Humphreys' attack against the stone wall. The general appears in the middle of this Alfred R. Waud sketch, doffing his hat.

Library of Congress

Alfred R. Waud's depiction of Burnside's Mud March. The sketch is dated January 21, 1863.

CHAPTER TEN

"THE VALLEY OF DEATH"

Hancock's Attack

Edwin V. Sumner worried about the troops pinned in front of Marye's Heights. The Right Grand Division commander sent an aide aloft in Professor Lowe's balloon at 12:10 P.M., but impatiently hurried forward before the observer could report what he saw. Sumner went to the Lacy house and surveyed the situation. The general yearned to take control of the battle, but Burnside had forbidden him to cross the river. A witness recalled how Sumner "chafed sadly under the restriction." At the collapse of French's attack, the general ordered Lowe's balloon to ascend again. Thaddeus Lowe cut the flight short when gusty winds made the balloon unmanageable. Sumner had to judge the action from his own vantage point. A correspondent close to the general wrote that Sumner habitually removed his false teeth when barking orders and carefully rested his spectacles on his forehead as he studied the movements beyond the Rappahannock. "He paced to and fro in front of the Lacy House, with one arm thrown around the neck of his son," observed a nearby spectator, "his face haggard with sorrow and anxiety."[1]

Across the river the Second Corps commander, Darius Couch, hurried reinforcements to French's division. William French had asked for artillery, and Couch sent forward several batteries. The Second Corps chief of artillery, Captain Charles Morgan, remonstrated that his "artillery could not be advantageously used *until* certain points were cleared" (emphasis in original). French and Couch argued that these points "could not be carried without a saturating artillery concentration." This sparked a row between French and Morgan. French wanted a section of Arnold's Battery A, 1st Rhode Island Artillery, to move across the millrace "to encourage the infantry in their charge." Morgan refused to sacrifice his rifled battery. Morgan's reluctance may have sprung from a mishap in the Ninth Corps at that same time.[2]

General Orlando B. Willcox's Ninth Corps had introduced artillery into the battle already, with poor results. Brigadier General Samuel D. Sturgis ordered a battery to the front when French attacked. Lieutenant George Dickenson's Battery E, 4th U.S. Artillery, rumbled into the spacious lot of Knight's brickyard, an elevated rise immediately south of the railroad. Dickenson's four 10-pounder Parrotts set up under a deluge of Confederate shells. The Federal cannoneers buckled immediately, having borne a flurry of casualties. The cannon crews abandoned their pieces and fled to the nearby buildings. Lieutenant Dickenson rousted them back to work only to be suffocated with more artillery fire. Confederate skirmishers prowled in front, blazing at the battery silhouetted on the hill. Dickenson went down, shot through the forehead, and his men stampeded again. The dying commander lingered only long enough to whisper, "Bury me where I fell."[3]

Lieutenant John Egan took over Dickenson's battery. He rallied enough men to withdraw the guns from the brickyard. Egan reported that "remaining longer all my men would be destroyed." The battery lost 13 men and 5 horses in twenty minutes. The Confederates had ravaged the battery with virtual impunity. Sturgis concurred with Egan's decision. He refused to put any more guns in Knight's brickyard.[4]

Egan's (Dickenson's) battery withdrew to the river, just as other guns lumbered to the front. General French lost the argument about taking artillery beyond the millrace, but he prevailed in getting long-range support for his right flank. He convinced Morgan to place guns on George Street to guard against an enemy counterattack. Couch went farther. He directed several batteries to the outskirts of Fredericksburg. Captain John D. Frank's Battery G, 1st New York Light Artillery, and Captain William A. Arnold's Battery A, 1st Rhode Island Artillery, moved to the last covered block of Hanover Street, a principal street that fed into Telegraph Road. The guns went into battery on a ridge overlooking the canal ditch. They set up next to Mr. Howison H. Wallace's house, Federal Hill, the onetime home of Confederate general Thomas Cobb's maternal grandmother. Arnold had assumed command of his battery that morning when Major John A. Tompkins was promoted. Arnold told his new command that he understood that they had a reputation for fighting and that "he was something of a fighter himself." He expected that they would "stand by him under all circumstances," especially when they rolled into position under heavy fire.[5]

Lieutenant Edmund Kirby's Battery I, 1st U.S. Artillery, moved up the street to their right—George Street. French personally led Kirby's battery to the walled confines of Fredericksburg's Corporation Burying Ground. Kirby found enough room in the cemetery for one section of his guns. Lieutenant George A. Woodruff planted two smoothbore cannon among the neglected tombstones. He had a clear view over a neighboring wagon yard and the ramshackle dwellings of a suburb known loosely as "Liberty Town." This haven for free blacks at the terminus of George Street masked Woodruff's guns and, at the same time, provided some protection for French's right flank.[6]

Fifteen minutes after French's last brigade failed, Union guns opened fire. Federal artillery chief Henry Hunt added several long-range batteries on Stafford Heights to the mix. The cannoneers concentrated on the Confederate Washington Artillery. Nearly every one of their rounds kicked sand and gravel into the faces of the Southern artillerists. One shell struck a lunette right in front of Colonel J. B. Walton and dumped dirt down his shirt. The whitewashed buildings on Willis Hill received numerous hits. One round carried away "a cart-load of bricks." Shot after shot pocked the paint and exposed the orange-red brick underneath. Before the day ended, shells transformed the buildings from white to red. Some of the inexperienced Rebel cannoneers quaked under "the mad screech of their projectiles . . . but it did not curb the enthusiasm," recalled a veteran.[7]

For all their effort, the Union artillery achieved very little. Frank's and Kirby's smoothbores made no impact. Even positioned on a high ridge at the head of Charlotte Street, the members of Battery G, 1st New York, complained that their elevation was much lower than Marye's Heights. This left them at the mercy of the Confederate rifled guns. Poor fuses and low trajectory caused several rounds to land among the Union infantry. General French stopped Frank's guns at once. Morgan compensated by ordering another battery into action by the railroad depot. An orderly seeking Major John A. Tompkins stumbled on Lieutenant Evan Thomas and his Battery C, 4th U.S. Artillery. Thomas assumed the messenger had bungled his name, and moved his 12-pounder Napoleons out Prussia Street. His battery straddled the railroad in front of the station. Thomas proved to be just as ineffective as Frank,

so Morgan pulled him behind a board fence by the depot. Gunner Tully Mc-
Crea called the artillery duel "the hardest fought, bloodiest, and most hotly
contested of the war." Most of the smoothbores suffered without doing any
harm to the Rebels.[8]

Arnold's Rhode Island rifles were the only Union guns effective in the
fight. Unfortunately, as other batteries dropped out, the Confederates focused more attention on Arnold's command. Morgan reported that the battery "suffered an unusual loss of material." At 1:30 P.M., Arnold lost one of
his pieces when a shell knocked a spoke out of a wheel. The crew replaced
the wheel under fire, and eventually re-joined the fray. The contrast between
Arnold's 3-inch rifles and the smoothbore batteries was remarkable. Morgan
pleaded for more rifled cannon. Couch agreed and forwarded a note to the
chief of artillery Henry Hunt: "I am losing, send two rifle batteries." Hunt
sent the guns, but they would not arrive until after 2:00 P.M.[9]

The Confederates had on the whole suffered very little during the bombardment, but Union action managed to inflict two serious losses at this time.
While Thomas Cobb's Georgia brigade crouched behind the stone wall and
weathered the storm, braided officers gathered by the Martha Stephens house.
Cobb conferred with his aide, Captain Walter Brewster, and his ordnance
officer, Captain John McPherson Berrien, and learned from them that he
needed more ammunition. He dispatched several couriers to find help. One
of these messengers found Brigadier General John Rogers Cooke, who went
to see the Sunken Road for himself.[10]

Cooke found Cobb near the Stephens house and proposed bringing his
North Carolina brigade into the Sunken Road. The Carolinians could replenish the Georgians with their own ammunition. The generals agreed, and
Cooke went to fetch his brigade. No sooner had General Cooke turned than
a Yankee bullet struck him in the head, fracturing his skull. Cooke's adjutant,
Captain Henry A. Butler, caught the general and laid him in the road.
Stretcher-bearers carted him down the Sunken Road to Howison's Mill behind Marye's Heights. An ambulance conveyed him to the rear. Butler took
the general to the home of a close friend, Mrs. Elizabeth M. T. B. French.
The Widow French, along with two daughters and a young houseguest,
nursed the general back to health, and John R. Cooke's recovery blossomed
into romance. The general later married the young guest, Miss Nannie
Patton.[11]

Moments after Cooke fell, Cobb was injured. A Union shell crashed
through the Stephens house and burst, wounding Captain John M. Berrien

in the hip and Cobb in the right thigh. A piece of shrapnel had struck Cobb just above the knee, snapping the bone and lacerating the femoral artery.[12]

Staff and line officers rushed to Cobb's aid and, in the process, drew fire from Federal sharpshooters. Captain Brewster fell mortally wounded in the thigh. Lieutenant Colonel Robert T. "Tom" Cook, commander of the Phillips Legion, took a bullet in the head. Captain James M. Johnson took over the Phillips Legion and immediately fell, wounded in the foot. Lieutenant Jules A. Peck, the acting major, replaced Johnson.[13]

Cobb kept his composure. Raising himself on one elbow, he examined his wound and asked "tranquilly" for a tourniquet. Staff officers fashioned one out of a silk handkerchief. Drs. E. D. Newton and Ervin T. Eldridge removed Cobb from the Sunken Road on a stretcher. Jubilant troops sobered at the sight of their commander leaving the field. "The rejoicing ceased for a time," reported a soldier-correspondent for a Charleston newspaper, "and the mourning sat on every countenance as four grief-stricken litter bearers passed down the lines bearing the heroic Cobb." The general tried to cheer them up. He told the Phillips Legion: "I am only wounded Boys, hold your ground like brave men." The brigade commander slipped into shock as they carried him away.[14]

An ambulance conveyed Cobb to the division hospital behind Lee's Hill. Accompanied by Dr. Eldridge, the Reverend R. K. Porter, and Captain Rutherford, the general rallied somewhat. He asked them to tighten the handkerchief on his leg. Attendants carried Cobb into Mrs. Wiet's house on Telegraph Road, where the chief surgeon, Dr. John T. Gilmore, tried to stanch the blood.[15]

Winfield Scott Hancock briefed his brigade and regimental commanders before the 1st Division attacked Marye's Heights. The general stated dryly: "Gentlemen, I have called you together for the purpose of communicating to you the orders of the commanding general. They are imperative and must be carried out at all hazards and at all costs." Hancock selected Samuel K. Zook's brigade to support French. If Zook faltered, Thomas F. Meagher's Irish Brigade would take the lead; and if Meagher faltered, John C. Caldwell's brigade would advance. Hancock explained, "if one or either line should fail the other should pass on and over and so on until the works of the enemy were carried." At the end of the meeting the officers bid each other adieu, as if forever. Samuel Zook later wrote, "I went into the action with no hope of success but with the conviction I was leading my brave battalion to inevitable and useless slaughter." Only the Irish Brigade officers dared to make light of their situation. Colonel Robert Nugent of the 69th New York kidded Colonel Edward Cross of Caldwell's brigade: "Cross, we are going to have hot work to day, but if you get into Richmond before I do, order dinner at the Spottswood House and I will dine with you." The ailing New Englander growled, "So ———— and so ———— Nugent, we are!"[16]

After breakfast, Zook formed his brigade on Sophia Street. By Hancock's orders, he marched up the rocky lane to Caroline Street. Zook filed to the right, resting his right flank, the 53rd Pennsylvania, on the tracks of the RF&P Railroad. The 27th Connecticut came next, followed by the 66th New York and 57th New York. Around 11:00 A.M., the 2nd Delaware and 52nd New York returned from picket duty to extend Zook's line, with the New Yorkers on the far left. Zook had the troops stack arms and dismissed them with the injunction to stay close. Men scattered into the nearby houses and continued their looting from the previous day. "They immediately made a dash for the houses," wrote staff officer Josiah Favill, "and ransacked them from cellar to garret."[17]

The commander of the Irish Brigade, Thomas Meagher, disappeared with several orderlies while the men dressed ranks. The chaplain of the 69th New York, Father James Ouellet (pronounced "Willet") asked if he could "say a word to the men." Colonel Nugent accompanied the prelate as he moved along the line "blessing each man, Catholic and Protestant alike." The care-worn men seemed relieved to see the chaplain. Nugent wrote that they "went into the fight as cheerfully as they would into a ballroom." When the French-Canadian priest finished his absolution, Nugent announced that he would "make an Irishman out of the Father that day."[18]

Meagher returned with two orderlies toting hefty bundles of green boxwood. The men formed in line and Meagher issued a sprig of green to each soldier to adorn his cap. The general explained that it was a badge of their Irish heritage and set an example by placing three large clusters in the brim of his hat. The soldiers embraced the idea enthusiastically and crammed evergreen into their hatbands. Some of the troops hung boxwood wreaths on their colors. "As I looked along the line," reminisced a member of the 116th Pennsylvania, "the men presented a unique appearance, as each hat, from the general's down, was ornamented with a sprig of boxwood." Soldiers in the 63rd, 69th, and 88th New York readily accepted the verdant badges as a surrogate for their missing green flags, which they had shipped home before replacements arrived. A man in the 88th New York wrote, "We all looked gay and felt in high spirits."[19]

The rattle of musketry already sounded French's assault when Meagher, accompanied by Hancock, addressed the individual regiments of what he termed "his little Brigade." Halting before each unit he offered a brief speech "in his eloquent style, and in words of real inspiration." Standing before the colors of the 88th New York, Meagher announced: "Officers and soldiers of the 88th Regiment—In a few moments you will engage the enemy in a most terrible battle, which will probably decide the fate of this glorious, great and grand country—the home of your adoption!" Meagher paused for a moment, and in a stifled voice, continued: "Soldiers—This is my wife's own regiment, 'her own dear 88th,' she calls it, and I know, and have confidence, that with dear woman's smile upon you, and for woman's sake, this day you will strike a deadly blow . . . and bring back to this distracted country its former prestige and glory." The general raised his voice as he ended, "This may be my last speech to you, but I will be with you when the battle is the fiercest; and, if I fall, I can say I did my duty, and fell fighting in the most glorious of causes." Shells burst overhead, heightening the drama. The general climaxed his exhortation with a promise to the 116th Pennsylvania: "And boys I will lead you." Civilian bystanders conceded Meagher's talent for delivering "a florid high falutin speech."[20]

General John C. Caldwell drew his brigade into line beside Meagher's Irishmen. Regimental commanders inspected the ranks. Colonel Edward Cross examined the 5th New Hampshire with an air of impending doom. Troubled by the stomach flu and a nagging premonition, the officer confessed, "Somehow I had an impression that I was to be killed or badly wounded." He attested his will and gave his belongings to the regiment's chaplain. "As God is my witness," Cross wrote of the forthcoming attack; "it seemed to my heart that it was to be a failure." In contrast to his gloom, the colonel discovered his men "cheerful and full of hope." That somewhat offset the New Englander's foreboding.[21]

John Caldwell had divided his brigade earlier that morning. He sent two regiments—the 61st and 64th New York—to relieve French's pickets on Princess Anne Street. Later, Caldwell reinforced them with the untested 145th Pennsylvania. Colonel Nelson A. Miles, an ambitious officer, spread the three regiments along the edge of the city. "It seemed to us," wrote a Pennsylvanian, "that we had never been in better spirits." This 145th Pennsylvania soldier revealed a lack of foresight. Miles placed the 64th New York

on the left and the 61st New York in the middle. Colonel Hiram L. Brown's
euphoric Pennsylvanians held the right.[22]

The rest of Caldwell's brigade formed on Sophia Street, with the 5th New
Hampshire on the right. Beside it lined up Colonel H. Boyd McKeen's 81st
Pennsylvania and Colonel George W. von Schack's 7th New York. Several of
the commanders made speeches and gave their men last-minute instructions.
Cross had listened to Meagher's oratory and sniffed at what he called "one of
those speeches peculiar to the man." In contrast, he spoke plainly to his men.
The colonel "told them it was a bloody strife; to stand firm and fire low; to
close on their colors and be steady." "To the officers," Cross ended, "I only
said that they were expected to do their duty." Caldwell reported his men
ready.[23]

Hancock intended to expand the attack front because the Rebel troops
made the current area of attack too dangerous. While Zook waited below the
railroad, the division commander transferred Meagher and Caldwell to the
center of Fredericksburg. Meagher's troops passed around Caldwell's brigade
at 12:30 P.M. and led the column up Sophia Street. Caldwell's command
closed behind the Irish Brigade. The Yankees and the Irish moved upriver,
weathering heavy shellfire at cross streets. The brigades galloped across the
intersections and regrouped under cover of the next block. Private William
McCarter of the 116th Pennsylvania called the intersections "fatal localities
to many of our men, and although they invariably crossed them on a run and
in single file, many were killed in doing so."[24]

Nelson Miles withdrew the other half of Caldwell's brigade from picket
duty shortly after French attacked. He re-formed the 61st and 64th New York
and the 145th Pennsylvania on Princess Anne Street and shifted them to the
right. Miles marched the column to George Street. He took cover behind the
Presbyterian church and waited for the rest of Hancock's division to come
up.[25]

Hancock's division, meanwhile, was delayed by a number of obstacles that
jerked the column into an awkward stop-start sequence. The wounded from
French's attack broke the column once on Sophia Street. Injured men swelled
the field hospitals along the riverfront, and Hancock's soldiers encountered
numerous "fearful specimens of mangled humanity." Lieutenant Colonel St.
Clair A. Mulholland recalled that "the appearance of dripping blood was not
calculated to enthuse the men or cheer them." Some of French's men carried
an injured officer on a window shutter, his leg dangling by a single tendon.
Hancock's soldiers pleaded with the stretcher-bearers to put him down, but

they ignored the entreaties. Finally, a man stepped out of ranks and cut the tendon with a pocketknife. The leg dropped to the ground with a thud, and the wounded man weakly smiled his gratitude. An uninitiated soldier in the 116th Pennsylvania fainted; his comrades left him on the curb when they resumed the march. An Irish soldier remembered, "It was a time well calculated to try the stoutest hearts."[26]

The column halted again near the foot of George Street. Federal artillery on the outskirts of the city had drawn Confederate fire on the spot that interdicted Hancock's advance. Shells directed at Kirby's battery in the cemetery overshot the mark and caromed into the head of Hancock's division. A shell exploded in the Irish Brigade, wounding Colonel Dennis Heenan, commander of the 116th Pennsylvania, in the hand. Shrapnel decapitated Sergeant John C. Marley, whose body sank to its knees, still clutching his musket. Moments later, Woodruff's section of Battery I, 1st U.S., stopped firing, and the Confederates diverted their cannonade to another area of the city. Hancock's column promptly swung into George Street and started west.[27]

French's attack had failed by this time. As a result, Hancock's troops marched up George Street during a lull in the artillery action, with only an occasional Rebel shell howling overhead. Lieutenant Colonel Mulholland of the Irish Brigade remembered listening to a cat meow above the tread of feet. The column passed the Episcopal and Presbyterian churches (where Barksdale's Mississippians had fought two days earlier) and Kirby's section of Battery I, 1st U.S., in the cemetery. Hancock halted at the edge of Fredericksburg. Meagher's Irish Brigade formed in Liberty Town, at a point where George Street angled downhill toward Hanover Street. Caldwell's brigade took position behind the Irish.[28]

Nelson Miles re-joined Caldwell's command as it passed the Presbyterian church. Caldwell directed him to the end of the column. Artillery fire suddenly rekindled over Caldwell's brigade. A soldier in the 64th New York wrote, "shells and bullets came flying through the street and they killed many of our men before we got to the edge of the city." When the 7th New York passed the Presbyterian church, the 145th Pennsylvania swung into line behind it. The once ebullient newcomers suddenly realized their danger. Many of them jumped out of ranks to shake the Reverend John H.W. Stuckenberg's hand, exclaiming "good bye Chaplain!" The salutations were "the last 'good-bye' that some of them uttered," the minister remembered.[29]

Meagher's and Caldwell's brigades gazed at a battlefield wrapped in flames.

"In full view of the enemy's works, we saw what fearful havoc had been made among the troops of the first assaulting division," recalled a man in the 116th Pennsylvania. "The dead and large numbers of the wounded lay thick in front of the heights." The soldiers looked across four open fields, divided by fences, to Marye's Heights. Battle smoke virtually obscured the sun. "Noonday is turned to dusk by the storm," wrote an officer.[30]

Anticipation and fear welled in Hancock's division. The chaplain of the 145th Pennsylvania admitted that his first battle "almost completely unmannered me." Charles A. Fuller of the 61st New York observed a soldier "who was literally unnerved by fear." Fuller noted that the man's "countenance was distorted by terror, and he was shaking in every limb." Even a veteran warrior like Fuller confessed, "I never exerted more will power to make my legs move in the right direction than just here." One of Hancock's men muttered, "We will fail to carry those heights."[31]

Zook's brigade waited on Princess Anne Street until Couch ordered Hancock to attack. A Connecticut soldier reported that the "most difficult thing to stand up under is the suspense while waiting as we waited in Fredericksburg . . . watching the columns file past us and disappear in the cloud of smoke." The division commander offered Zook's brigade a few words of encouragement before starting. "Hancock . . . rode slowly and proudly up and down the line, surveying the ranks," wrote a Connecticut man, "his countenance wearing an aspect of quiet and cool determination." The general stopped in front of the skittish 27th Connecticut and leaned forward in the saddle. "You are the only Connecticut regiment in my division," he snapped. "Bring no dishonor upon the State you represent." Hancock turned and ordered Zook to move out. The dejected brigade commander "went in like a man going to his execution and without a thought of returning." Zook mounted his horse and started the troops for the field.[32]

The brigade commander divided his six regiments into three groups, instructing each pair of regiments to exit the city by a different street. The right group, composed of the 53rd Pennsylvania and raw 27th Connecticut, used Prussia Street, following the path of French's division. Colonel John R. Brooke assumed command of them. He put his own Pennsylvania regiment in the lead. The second group, the 66th and 57th New York, followed Zook's aide, Lieutenant Charles H. H. Broome. He led them out the first avenue south of the tracks, called Frederick Street. The final group, the 2nd Delaware and 52nd New York, left the city by the next street to the left, named Princess Elizabeth Street. Zook personally directed them.[33]

Confederate fire registered on Zook's brigade as soon as it left Princess Anne Street. A Connecticut Yankee remarked glibly, "As we turned west the fun began." Shells exploded over the three blue columns. A lieutenant on the right reminisced, "as soon as the head of the column appeared in the open, the rebel batteries opened fire and pandemonium at once broke loose." A Pennsylvania soldier wrote that Brooke's column passed through a "hurricane of deadly missiles." A shell knocked over several men in the 27th Connecticut. One of them jumped up and shouted, "I'll have you pay for that!" Zook's aide, Lieutenant Josiah Favill, accompanied Brooke's two regiments. He later described the ordeal: "The whizzing, bursting shells made one's hair stand on end; our guns added to the confusion as they fired over our heads, and the two flights of shot and shell in opposite directions, made a noise above the roar of Niagara."[34]

John R. Brooke hurried his soldiers over the millrace and deflected them to the right. The 53rd Pennsylvania and the 27th Connecticut regrouped along the millrace ravine. Colonel Brooke stopped by Warren Missimer, the first man hit in the 53rd Pennsylvania, and personally dressed his mauled foot. This personal touch impressed Samuel H. Rutter, who reported home, "I never feel [as] safe in going into a fight as when he [Col. Brooke] has command." The 27th Connecticut had lost some of its men when it passed the railroad depot. Rebel guns had "trained upon the spot with fatal accuracy," but the regiment did not panic as it had the day before.[35]

Lieutenant Charles Broome brought forward Captain Julius Wehle's 66th New York and Major N. Garrow Throop's 57th New York. Both regiments had new commanders because their respective heads had fallen on December 11. The two regiments veered to the right, crossed the railroad tracks beyond the millrace, and joined Brooke's line. A New York soldier recalled with gothic detail how "one shell struck a man in the back, cut him in two and sent his entrails flying in all directions." At the same time, another round "filled the air with pieces of flesh, clothing and accoutrements." Both the 66th and 57th New York regiments had suffered significant losses. An officer in the 57th New York reported that "by this time the field was strewn with the dead and dying and the air filled with the wails and groans of the wounded." Among the stricken lay the commander of the 66th New York, Captain Wehle. Captain John S. Hammell took command of the regiment and sent Wehle to the hospital.[36]

Zook's third column started with Colonel William P. Baily's 2nd Delaware, and Colonel Paul Frank followed with the 52nd New York. The column entered the field and crossed the railroad, extending the brigade's left flank. Adjusting his line, Samuel Zook rested his right flank on Hanover Street and his left on the railroad.[37]

Zook's brigade quickly started forward. Soldiers climbed out of the mill-race ravine and over a high board fence. The brigade dashed across the shell-swept field. Confederate artillery chewed up the advancing Federals but failed to deter them. A shell struck Albert Taylor of the 57th New York and "scattered his body so that a piece of his skull struck Corporal Lawrence Floyd." Taylor's head knocked Floyd unconscious. Zook's left contended with artillery rounds and bricks when it slipped through Mr. Aler's, or Mullen's, brick-yard under fire. A novice soldier feared that "every moment would be our last." Later, he reflected, "I am willing to say for one that I was pretty badly scared." Zook, concerned for the 27th Connecticut—or leery of its panic the day before—shifted to the right and accompanied the regiment.[38]

Men thronged up the hill and tripped over French's soldiers holding the swale. Zook's troops flopped on the ground behind the mud-caked bluecoats. Zook waited for all of his men to catch up before he gave the order to "Charge!" Hancock's men stood up and picked their way through French's troops. Rebel artillery continued to hammer Zook's alignment. A New Englander noted that the "shot and shell plow the ground in front, burst over our heads, or make fearful gaps in the line." A staff officer remembered the shells "plowing great furrows in our ranks at every step." A Pennsylvanian, Levi J. Fritz, felt his heart sink as he entered what he called "the open door to the house of death."[39]

Across the field, Confederate infantry waited for the Federals to come closer. Georgians and Carolinians huddled along the Sunken Road. Some peeped over the stone wall to gape at the attackers. An unexpectedly sympathetic North Carolina man recalled that "They were brave men and it looked like a pity to kill them." Confederate colonel Robert McMillan drifted along the line, gauging the Federal approach. At his command, his brigade rose suddenly and fired a volley into Zook's Yankees. Smoke billowed across everything as the Confederate line erupted in flame. The graycoats howled with a contemptuous Rebel yell "which passed along the whole line until the hill fairly rang."[40]

Zook's Federal brigade pressed closer. One Southerner likened it to "a bravery born of desperation." Federals closed to within one hundred yards of the stone wall, but the exposed field made it look "a terrible long distance" farther. Crackling Confederate rifles melded with the deep resonance of the

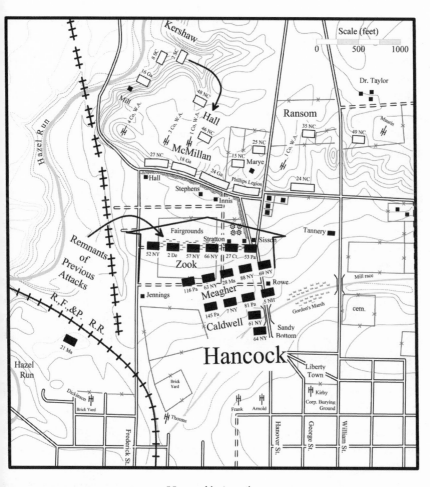

Hancock's Assault

Washington Artillery. Federal wounded littered the ground. One Union soldier looked ahead with dismay and saw that "the upward path was strewn with the dead and wounded; by the dozens." Attackers bowed their heads as if breasting a storm. Some of them involuntarily tugged their hats low over their ears. Union artillery added to the nightmarish swirl. Their cannon continued to fire, and many of their shells landed in Zook's ranks. Second Corps commander Darius Couch was horrified. He shut down the Northern artillery support. "Not a word is spoken" among the attackers, recalled a Connecticut man, and "not a gun fired." The Confederates mauled the silently approaching mass of bluecoats.[41]

Erskine Church of the 27th Connecticut thought the whistling, pelting canister balls sounded like hailstones. The new soldier became surprisingly introspective. "There can be nothing more puzzling than to describe the feelings of a man in battle," he wrote. "You cannot describe it satisfactorily to yourself or others. To march steadily up to the mouths of a hundred cannon while they pour out fire and smoke, shot and shell, in a storm that mows the men like grass is horrible beyond description." Church had read stories of combat heroics, but he concluded that it was "absurd to say that a man can do it without fear." The impressionable private later contradicted himself. "Once fairly in for it your sensibilities are strangely blunted," he told his mother in a letter. "You care comparatively nothing about the sights that shocked you at first." He closed unaffectedly, "Men torn to pieces by cannon shot becomes a matter of course."[42]

Zook's right pressed ahead of his left. The 53rd Pennsylvania and 27th Connecticut wavered a moment, but Colonel Brooke led them to the Stratton house. Staff officer Favill reported that "Brooke was as usual up in front . . . looking after his men, one of the most unconcerned men in the crowd." Brooke took "the crowd" around the brick dwelling. The bulk of the 53rd Pennsylvania passed to the right of the house, and the Connecticut regiment went around both sides of the structure. Brooke re-formed them in an orchard behind the house. The regiments poked their rifles through the orchard fence, "all full of bullet holes and torn with shot." They peppered the stone wall at a distance of eighty-five yards. A small sortie by the 53rd Pennsylvania pushed closer to the wall, but the thrust quickly collapsed, "driven back with terrible slaughter."[43]

The rest of Zook's brigade ran into the same difficulties that had disrupted French's advance. The center of Zook's line slowed to get around the east fence of the fairgrounds. Adjutant James G. Derrickson of the 66th New York complained that the board fence "was very difficult to remove or scale." French's failure to take down the fence only added to the problems of subsequent attacks. Three regiments—the 66th New York, 57th New York, and 2nd Delaware—hacked at the fence while Brooke attacked on the right. At the same time, Colonel Frank's 52nd New York skirted the southern end of Mercer Square and pressed to within one hundred yards of the stone wall. Confederate infantry hid behind the wall, and sharpshooters took position in Joseph Hall's white clapboard cottage. They beat back the foray with ease. When the adjutant of the 52nd New York, Charles Laty, was killed, the regiment gave way. Sergeant Franz X. Reinhardt fell wounded while carrying the colors. Lieutenants Hermann Ehrichs and Emil H. Frank saved the flag. Just as the left fell back, the center of the line broke into Mercer Square. The fairgrounds wall ensured that Zook's attack broke into three ineffective, piecemeal assaults.[44]

A frustrated commander implored his men "Forward!" and Zook's center regiments scrambled over the fence. Dropping into the fairgrounds, the line raced toward the stone wall. Officers cried repeatedly, "Advance. Forward," and the men cheered as they lunged ahead. Crossing the open square, the bluecoats stumbled into the fence-line on the far side of the fairgrounds. Cobb's men had torn down the planking and meshed the timber into an obstruction that resembled an abatis. The tangled boards slowed the attackers as they stepped through the impediment. This allowed the Confederates more time to shoot them down.[45]

Confederate infantry waited for the Yankees to flounder in the tangled boards and then devoured them in fire. The entire front disappeared in "a continuous sheet of flame from base to summit" of Marye's Heights. The attack crumbled. "The losses were so tremendous," reported Josiah Favill, "that before we knew it our momentum was gone." An officer in the 57th New York wrote that his men fell "as fast as I could count." The 66th and 57th New York withered in the storm, losing most of their officers in minutes. By the time the commander Captain John S. Hammell fell, the 66th New York had no more captains. The command devolved to the adjutant, Lieutenant James G. Derrickson. The 57th New York beside it lost its commander and its adjutant. Major N. Garrow Throop fell badly wounded and had to be helped from the field. Before leaving, he turned over the regiment to Captain James W. Britt. The new commander estimated that his regiment had been reduced to approximately 84 men.[46]

Zook's regiments fell to the ground and returned the fire. The units in the fairgrounds clung to a small knoll, roughly on line with the 53rd Pennsylvania and 27th Connecticut. The New York and Delaware soldiers were still exposed and sustained heavy losses. A small boy crawled to the rear, dragging a broken leg by a thread of muscle. The lad asked for the best way to get off the field. A comrade piped up, "Cheer up, my brave boy," and directed him to "follow along that fence and you will get off all right." The youth crawled away, "leaving a trail of blood behind him." No one knew if he ever made it, nor did they have time to care. A member of the 57th New York wrote that similar events happened "too frequent to stir the emotions, yet their impress on one's memory never fades away."[47]

Colonel John R. Brooke attempted another attack against the stone wall. He discovered a stone fence near Sissons' store "that runs at an angle with that which the enemy was using." He shifted a portion of the 53rd Pennsylvania behind the wall. Confederates countered with a "deadly shower of canister and musket balls." Rebel sharpshooters from the 24th North Carolina enfiladed Brooke's stone wall from several houses on Hanover Street. "In a little while," reported a Pennsylvanian, "nearly every man was down." Somewhere in the mix, the 53rd's acting adjutant, Lieutenant George C. Anderson, went down. Brooke sent Lieutenant John H. Root to get more men from Zook, but the messenger was hit before he could deliver the message. The Federals came within fifty yards of the wall, but the Confederates drove them back with fearful losses.[48]

The 24th North Carolina blistered Brooke's men at close range. "Some few of them got within 50 yards of our line," General Ransom reported, "but the whole line were forced to retire in wild confusion." In a rapid exchange of fire, the 24th North Carolina lost its adjutant, Oliver D. Cooke. Lieutenant Colonel John L. Harris also suffered a leg wound, but he refused treatment. "Officers are noticed closely in battle," Harris wrote, "and if the men see their officer shunning the bullets, they will get frightened."[49]

Robert McMillan's brigade, in contrast, slew the Yankees with near impunity. A flabbergasted Southerner noted that "the dead were thick enough to walk on" around the Stratton house and adjoining peach orchard. McMillan moved along the line, "waving his sword and encouraging his men." The troops "seemed to catch the spirit of their leader," reported a Georgian. The 24th Georgia hailed its commander by turning around "in the thickest of the fight" and giving him "three hearty cheers." McMillan thanked the men, but between assaults, he cautioned them to hold their fire "until the enemy should come within musket range." The colonel lured wave after wave of attackers close to his defenses, and the results were cataclysmic. An impressionable Southron remembered: "Blood and brains were scattered everywhere. It was gruesome and sickening."[50]

John R. Brooke rallied his Federals behind the Sissons store. Brooke held the Second Corps' right flank, and he worried that the Confederates might counterattack. The 24th North Carolina edged forward and threatened the Federal's flank, but failed to dislodge it from the houses and yards on Hanover Street. Brooke gave up the notion of attacking and assumed a defensive posture.[51]

Zook reported that his brigade had been "dashed to pieces by shot and torn into shreds by shells." His troops cowered "under the most infernal fire of musketry and artillery—at short, very short range." The brigade commander later confided, "I never realized before what war was. I never before felt so horribly since I was born." A Confederate bullet killed Zook's horse, leaving the colonel "badly stunned." Rumors circulated that he had been killed. Samuel Zook slowly regained his senses and took one of his orderlies' horses. He found the mount unmanageable, so he gave it back and continued on foot.[52]

Zook's regiments quickly ran out of ammunition. Frank's 52nd New York took cover in the unfinished railroad cut to the left of the fairgrounds. The colonel ordered his men to withdraw in small squads, fearing that a large exodus would draw more fire. The 52nd New York rallied in the rail cut, and relied on its bayonets for protection. Fresh troops soon passed to the front, and Frank sent to town for ammunition. One of Sumner's staff officers allegedly told Frank's emissary to replenish his regiment at the river. By the time the 52nd New York retreated, the rest of Zook's brigade had also fallen back.[53]

The last commander of the 66th New York, Adjutant Derrickson, reported that his ammunition gave out and the regiment "gradually retired." Derrickson passively condoned their action. The 66th New York's departure opened a gap in the front line. The 2nd Delaware lost its commander, Colonel William P. Baily, in the middle of the fairgrounds. His successor fell wounded, and Captain Peter McCullough took charge. He pulled the 2nd Delaware back to the swale.[54]

The erstwhile regiments on the right kept their fragile hold on the buildings and backyards along Hanover Street. The 53rd Pennsylvania had pressed so close to the stone wall that the Confederate cannoneers could not depress their guns to hit it. Southern infantry, however, redoubled their fire. A young Pennsylvanian remembered, "The enemy were firing no matter what the provocation." Colonel Brooke reported the wounded gave their ammunition to their comrades before leaving the field. Levi Fritz, however, attested that the "Men who were wounded stayed on the field, shooting until exhausted." Some injured soldiers, unable to shoot, bit cartridges and loaded weapons for others to use. The 27th Connecticut, in contrast, misused its cache of ammunition. Colonel Richard Bostwick complained that his regiment was ineffective because it was "lamentably deficient in arms." Most of the men carried rusted and antiquated smoothbore muskets that Bostwick reported were "unfit for active service." When they exhausted their cartridges, Colonel

John Brooke ordered his men to fix bayonets and sit tight. Another brigade assault had stalled.[55]

In the flagging moments of Zook's attack, Hancock summoned the Irish Brigade to advance in support. General Thomas Meagher's troops marched down George Street to Hanover Street. The area beyond Liberty Town was called Sandy Bottom. The men advanced into Sandy Bottom under an intense artillery barrage. A veteran recalled: "There was a terrible battle fought here . . . compared with which Antietam was nothing." Shells dashed the hard-surfaced road and caromed through the brigade. An Irish soldier wrote, "the cannonballs striking the rock like earth ricocheted, with to all appearances, increased vigor." Some of the men took cover behind dwellings, but General Hancock rode down the sidewalk and rousted them into line.[56]

The Irish Brigade ran headlong into the millrace. The 69th New York broke ranks and funneled across the bridge stringers under precise Confederate artillery fire. The Federals wondered how the Southern cannon had found the "perfect range of the bridge." The Washington Artillery's immediate accuracy is rather surprising considering that Meagher's brigade was the first large group to use the Hanover Street bridge. Once across the sluiceway, Colonel Robert Nugent's 69th New York took cover behind a sharp rise in the millrace ravine. Colonel Patrick Kelly's 88th New York crossed next. Both commands sidled to the right of Hanover Street. The 28th Massachusetts crept across the bridge runners and took position straddling the street. Meagher's first three regiments wasted twenty minutes tiptoeing across the bridge. The rest of the brigade crowded the east bank of the millrace trying to avoid the artillery fire.[57]

Meagher ordered his last two regiments to wade through the water. The 63rd New York became "somewhat demoralized" when it forded the frigid sluiceway. The 116th Pennsylvania, on the other hand, became completely disorganized. Part of the regiment splashed through the water, while the rest scoured the bank for material to build another bridge. Some tried crossing on tree limbs and fell in the water anyway. Thomas Meagher dismounted and crossed the bridge stringers with the aid of two wounded soldiers. The general limped noticeably. The brigade wasted thirty minutes getting across the millrace, all the time under fire.[58]

Meagher had suffered serious losses while crossing the millrace, but lighter than those taken by French and Zook. Sergeant John Strechaback saw a man whose head had been neatly sliced in two by a shell and shouted, "Look at the watermelon." An Irish Brigade soldier remembered the millrace depression forever afterward as "The Valley of Death."[59]

The Irish Brigade had crossed one field, but three more loomed ahead. A sergeant in the 116th Pennsylvania wrote, "we could see the desperate character of the work before us." Meagher re-formed his brigade and issued last-minute instructions. Officers told their men to take off their knapsacks and blankets, and anything else that might encumber them. Hancock reiterated that officers should lead on foot. Confederate fire was so heavy that "a pigeon could scarcely live through it," and he feared horsemen courted almost certain death. The men fixed bayonets and "the clink, clink, clink of the cold steel sounding along the line made one's blood run cold," recollected Private William McCarter of the 116th Pennsylvania. Ready to charge, the nervous soldiers exploded with a cheer.[60]

Hancock had escorted the Irish Brigade to the millrace before returning to get Caldwell's brigade. One of Caldwell's soldiers remembered that "as the road leaves the city, it makes a slight curve, and as we came to that spot the whole view was opened up to us." The brigade suddenly saw and felt the full fury of Marye's Heights. The Northerners boiled down the hillside and into Hanover Street. The 5th New Hampshire took the lead, followed by the 81st Pennsylvania, the 7th New York, the 145th Pennsylvania, the 61st New York, and finally, the 64th New York. The column strung out as it sallied through the debris of Meagher's advance. "The road was littered with some dead, and cast off blankets and knapsacks," recalled one of Caldwell's men. The 145th Pennsylvania found the streets "covered with blankets and overcoats and haversacks and other articles, which had been thrown away in the hurry and excitement." The impediments slowed the advance and left the column ragged by the time it reached the millrace.[61]

The obstacle further deranged Caldwell's line. The watercourse "scattered the men some," according to Colonel Edward Cross, who marched at the head of the column. Shellfire aggravated the situation. A member of the 64th New York described the area as "a bad low place filled with water and mud, and there are maney [sic] dead and wounded men of ours in this mud hole." Some of the men scooted around the wounded and over the stringers; others plunged through the cold water and mud. Caldwell's lead regiments crossed the stream without serious loss, but the last two regiments took a beating. Confederate fire concentrated on the spot just as the 61st New York started to cross. The regiment scampered ahead, but the 64th New York took several hits that left a bloody mess on both sides of the sluiceway. Charles A. Fuller of the 61st New York recalled how "one of the ghastly sights of the war was almost under my feet." A shell had eviscerated a Union soldier, "and in its passage had set fire to his clothing, and there his corpse lay slowly cooking." The 64th New York stepped over the sizzling body while it still convulsed. "I thought he was dead," a Union soldier wrote, "but there was nothing certain about that."[62]

Safely across the millrace, Caldwell's brigade formed in the declivity behind the Irish Brigade. Caldwell's troops struggled to get a foothold in such a crowded, restricted space and on a slippery, muddy slope. Men tripped and slid through the waterlogged slime, but eventually all fell into place.[63]

Hancock worried that the Confederates overlapped his right and might turn his flank. Perhaps Colonel Brooke's run-in with the 24th North Carolina sparked his concern. The division commander ordered Meagher to detach two companies to guard the right flank. A couple of companies from the 69th New York, under Captain James Saunders and Lieutenants Luke Brennan and Robert H. Milliken, dashed to the right and took possession of a small knoll. Within an hour, these three officers would be the only commissioned officers left in the regiment.[64]

Zook's brigade had begun to break by this time. A captain in the 69th New York noted in horror, "God! mark how they fall, see how its ranks are thinned." The lieutenant colonel of the 116th Pennsylvania wrote that Zook's "line waves like corn in a hurricane." The attack collapsed, and the survivors recoiled amid a chorus of Confederate shouts and jeers. Meagher moved promptly to take Zook's place. The general strode in front of his command and yelled, "Irish Brigade, advance." The line sprang forward with a cheer.[65]

The Irish Brigade had barely cleared the millrace ravine when Rebels opened fire on them. Samuel Hunter of the 116th Pennsylvania noted quaintly, "then there was music." The Irish Brigade also suffered enfilading fire from the right. St. Clair Mulholland thought the brigade had ventured "into an arc of fire." The Federals advanced unevenly, with the right racing ahead of the left. The 69th New York pitched across the second fence before the rest of the brigade. The Irish met French's and Zook's men "hugging the earth," and lay down to catch their breath.[66]

Meagher's brigade regrouped and nudged through the human wreckage. Men lying in the swale proved to be a greater obstacle than the millrace. "The Brigade had to walk over them," reported a soldier in the 88th New York, "and stood to be slaughtered like sheep." Staff officers tried to coax the men out of the way. One nettled officer complained, "The devil could not get them to budge an inch farther." The Confederates sprang up and poured several volleys into the attackers. A member of the 63rd New York marveled at how the stone wall disappeared behind "sheets of flame from thousands of muskets." Meagher's troops fell in droves, and the line fragmented before it cleared the swale. Fractured portions of individual regiments pressed closer to the enemy, but the cohesion of the Irish Brigade had been lost while picking its way through the hodgepodge of Federal soldiers.[67]

Part of the 69th New York swept past the Stratton house under a searing fire. "No pen can describe the horrors of this battle," Colonel Nugent wrote. The men stuck close together until they reached the final barrier between them and the Confederates: the orchard fence behind the Stratton house. Some recklessly braved the fire and entered the last field. Confederates tumbled dozens of Nugent's men at a time. The colonel later remembered, "It was a living hell from which escape seemed scarcely possible." One-eyed Captain John Donovan agreed. He wrote that "it was impossible for human nature to withstand this."[68]

Nugent fell severely wounded in his right side. Diminutive James Cavanagh, nicknamed "the Little Major," assumed command. Soon he was wounded in the thigh. Cavanagh yielded the regiment to the third in command, Captain Thomas Leddy. Before leaving, Cavanagh told the 69th New York to "Blaze away and stand to it, boys!" Captain Leddy had re-joined the regiment only the day before, after convalescing six months from a wound in the Seven Days battles around Richmond. He took another bullet at Fredericksburg. It passed through his left arm and returned him to the hospital. Captain John Donovan took command. Balls caught him in the chest and left shoulder. He slumped to the ground, abandoned for dead by his men. By that time, the 69th New York had no one left to command. All of its officers had been cut down.[69]

Donovan lay in a mud puddle barely cognizant of his surroundings. "The battle appeared to me like a dream," he recalled. A nearby explosion covered him with mud. He rose stiffly and searched for the 69th New York. Much of it lay dead and wounded along the Stratton fence; those still unhit had retreated to the swale. Donovan joined them in the depression. In all of the commotion, no one noticed that the colors had vanished. A dying color-bearer attempted to save the flag by hiding it in his tunic. Later, the men discovered his corpse with the standard tucked inside his jacket.[70]

Colonel Patrick Kelly's 88th New York reached the orchard fence a moment after the 69th New York. Kelly's command raced to the fence, looking for protection from the cannon. The 88th New York escaped the canister, but ran into a hail of gunfire from the stone wall. A New Yorker noted that the Rebels hit them with a "dreadful shower of bullets." Another soldier wrote that the musketry rose to a crescendo, "often drowning the notes of the cannon." The Confederates stopped the 88th New York cold. "Our men were mowed down like grass before the scythe of the reaper," reported a Northerner. Kelly's troops tried to return the fire but were slaughtered. An 88th New York soldier wrote, "The men lay piled up in all directions." An Irish Brigade captain declared, "Oh! It was a terrible day. The destruction of life has been fearful, and nothing gained."[71]

A part of the 88th New York sallied beyond the board fence, but melted away instantly. Major William Horgan and Adjutant John R. Young led the forlorn assault. Neither officer came back. Captain William B. Nagle wrote ruefully: "Irish blood and Irish bones covered that terrible field to-day." Colonel Kelly nearly lost his life rallying the refugees of Horgan's assault. While fashioning a crude battle line, a Rebel bullet snipped his suspenders and grazed his spine. Just as Kelly gathered his command, the 28th Massachusetts came up on the left.[72]

Colonel Richard Byrnes had difficulty muscling his command through the prostrate figures of the previous attacks. By the time he redressed his regiment and advanced, most of the 69th and 88th New York had fallen back. The 28th Massachusetts encountered the same one-sided musketry—with the same results. His men erupted momentarily into the confines of the fairgrounds, but the Southern riflemen halted them. A soldier, who apparently kept statistics on such things, claimed the Confederates opened "the longest, and at the same time, the heaviest fire of musketry on record." Major Andrew P. Caracher dropped out of line with a head wound. The rest of Byrnes' regiment backtracked to the swale. A number of soldiers gathered boards from the fairgrounds' fence and stacked them in makeshift barricades. Others drifted to the right to get behind the Stratton house for cover.[73]

The 63rd New York floundered through the jumble of other commands and lost its connection to the rest of the brigade. Major Joseph O'Neill's command divided in two by the fairgrounds fence. Federals forced their way through holes in the fence. Waiting Confederates crushed them with a "steady withering sheet of flame" when they emerged on the other side. A New York captain wrote "many a poor soul [bit] the dust." On the right,

Major O'Neill received a severe wound in his right arm. Command devolved on Captain Patrick J. Condon, but he was with the left wing and did not know that he was in command until later. The 63rd New York also lost its adjutant, Lieutenant Miles McDonald. As the regiment became disorganized, General Meagher waved his sword and reunited the broken wings.[74]

The New Yorkers returned the fire, but their "musketry made no impression" on the stone wall. The Irish watched the Rebels load "at leisure" behind their protective wall and became disillusioned. Many of Meagher's men concluded that Burnside had sent them forward as "a bloody sacrifice." Confederate bullets shredded the 63rd New York's standard, and a piece of shot snapped its staff in two. Dozens of balls honeycombed Color Sergeant Patrick Chambers' jacket, surprisingly without touching him. Someone shouted, "Lie down and fire!" and the 63rd New York hit the ground. Recalling the order, an Irish soldier reminisced, "Fortunately it came, or not a man or officer would have lived." Men blazed away at the Rebels and then rolled over on their backs to reload. This regiment kept the Irish Brigade on the firing line, but it conceded the attack had failed.[75]

The 116th Pennsylvania followed General Meagher into a blinding cloud of battle. Lieutenant Colonel Mulholland wrote that there were "Shells everywhere; a torrent of shells; a blizzard of shot, shell and fire." A Pennsylvania private recounted that shells "burst among us in front, in rear, above and behind us." Gaps appeared in the 116th Pennsylvania's neat alignment, and the troops became confused. Yet the Irish general kept them advancing. Holes developed in the units' alignments so frequently that the troops found it impossible to fill the spaces. The Pennsylvanians met a heavier fire when they approached the fairgrounds. "Soon we forgot the presence of the shells," an officer admitted, "in the shower of smaller missiles that assail[ed] us." Men bowed their heads and pressed on.[76]

Fire engulfed the new regiment at the same moment the brigade commander disappeared. Meagher left the 116th Pennsylvania so he could help re-form the 63rd New York. The new Irish Brigade soldiers found it "impossible amid such a blinding storm of bullets to proceed farther." A ball struck Captain John O. O'Neill in the ribs before it passed through his lungs and lodged next to his spine. When someone asked him where he was hurt, the captain answered breathlessly, "I'm wounded all over." Colonel Heenan received his second wound of the day, which took him out of the battle. Major George H. Bardwell also left seriously injured. Lieutenant Colonel St. Clair Mulholland took command and ordered his men to, "Load and fire at will!"

The 116th Pennsylvania had lost most of its officers by this time, and the colors had fallen several times. The latest commander saw his "men dropping in twos, in threes, in groups" inside the exposed fairgrounds. Mulholland took a bullet in the leg and passed the command to Captain John Teed. A shell fractured Color Sergeant William H. Tyrrell's leg. He rested on one knee and flaunted his colors. Twelve balls ripped his standard and another broke the flagstaff. Tyrrell fell dead with five bullet wounds. "It was simply madness to advance as far as we did," wrote one man, "and an utter impossibility to go farther." The murderous fire forced the men to see "the full absurdity of the attempt to accomplish an utter impossibility." Bodies piled up and the men's cheering trailed off. "They were not there to fight," recounted one officer, "only to die."[77]

The 116th Pennsylvania tumbled back to the swale. There, men competed for shelter behind the tiny shelf of land. Some of the soldiers heaved dead bodies out of the ditch to make room for the living. Others stacked the corpses to make human breastworks. A sergeant remembered: "The only possible shelter we could have from the murderous fire were the dead bodies of our comrades that we would pile up the best we could and get behind." Hundreds of wounded dragged themselves to the Stratton house. They huddled behind the edifice to escape the fire.[78]

Meagher vanished at that moment. The general had concealed a knee suppuration, which surgeons had drained, but the knee became stiff and painful. Barely able to ride, Meagher had reluctantly obeyed Hancock's orders to advance on foot. Leading the 63rd New York, he pulled up lame when he bruised the ulcerated kneecap. The brigade commander disregarded Hancock's orders and hobbled back to get his horse.[79]

The Irish Brigade assault collapsed thirty minutes after it started. The brigade lost its cohesion while passing French's and Zook's troops. The concentrated fire of the Southerners further disrupted it and added confusion. The brigade failed to function as an organization after it passed the swale, and the individual regiments never had a chance after that. The Federals attacked the stone wall piecemeal, which allowed the Confederates to concentrate on each regiment as it came up. The loss of three of the five regimental commanders, coupled with the disappearance of the brigade commander, left the broken Irish Brigade without a unifying head to rally it. Many of the men fled back to the city. Meagher—now on horseback—collected several hundred of them under the banner of the 63rd New York. He marched them back to the river.

The rest of the brigade clung to some of the most advanced positions taken during the day.

Caldwell's brigade started across the killing ground shortly after Meagher's attack. Winfield S. Hancock had tried to hasten the tail of Caldwell's brigade over the millraces before it started. The general found Colonel Nelson Miles trying to form on Caldwell's left flank. The division commander redirected his 61st and 64th New York behind the center of Caldwell's brigade. Hancock returned to the edge of the millrace basin, looking "cool and collected" as he cantered along the crest. To Colonel Cross, the general appeared to be as "brave as a lion." A New York officer recollected, "We expected every minute that he would be shot off from his horse." Mounted orderlies and staff officers fell wounded around him. Confederates unhorsed four of Hancock's five staff officers and sent three of them to the hospital. A Rebel bullet creased Hancock's vest and grazed his stomach. The general mused to one of his aides, "It was lucky I hadn't a full dinner." Caldwell and his retinue joined Hancock in front of the brigade. "General Caldwell," Hancock ordered, "you will forward your brigade at once; the Irish Brigade is suffering severely."[80]

Caldwell's commanders overheard Hancock and gave their men last-minute instructions. Edward Cross told the 5th New Hampshire, "Attention! Every man is expected to do his duty to-day." Still troubled by his premonition, he added, "If I fall never mind me." He ordered the men to fix bayonets. The regimental leaders told their troops that "No man [is] to fire a shot until he is inside the rebel lines." Legions of muddy bluecoats clambered out of the ravine. Caldwell's brigade started forward before Nelson Miles had had time to form his two New York regiments. The right of the brigade surged ahead of the left. The angle of the millrace placed Caldwell's right closer to the Confederates and further exacerbated the distortion in the line. The suddenness of Hancock's orders and Caldwell's compliance left the attacking Federals in some disarray.[81]

The men fumbled across the mud-churned plateau. A newspaper correspondent wrote that Caldwell's brigade disappeared amid "red flashes in the white gloom of a pearly powder cloud." The battle smoke was "laced with streams of jagged flame, and writhing and vibrating as if charged with electricity." The reporter concluded, "It was not war, it was madness." Northern soldiers braved the fire and proceeded toward the stone wall. Moments after starting, a shell exploded in Edward Cross' face. Shrapnel struck him in the chest, mouth, and forehead. The 5th New Hampshire ignored the colonel's fall and rushed ahead. Another shell fragment smacked him in the leg. Cross spit out blood and sand—and several teeth—and began to crawl off the field. He used his sword scabbard as a brace. A bullet punched the scabbard out of his hands and knocked Cross to the ground. "After that warning I concluded to lie still," the colonel wrote, "so placing myself on my back, feet to the foe, I awaited death."[82]

"Leaden hail causes the line to disappear like dew before the morning sun," a corporal in the 5th New Hampshire recalled. Major Edward E. Sturtevant assumed command of the regiment when Cross fell, and led the men closer to Marye's Heights. A New England officer noted, "On all sides men fell like grass before the scythe." Another wrote, "No line could stand their fire." The brigade shrank at every step as men dropped from its thinning ranks. Officers cajoled the survivors to close on the colors.[83]

The 81st Pennsylvania charged across the field, somewhat behind the 5th New Hampshire. To its left came the 7th New York and 145th Pennsylvania. Nelson Miles' two New York regiments strung out in column behind them, with the 61st New York leading and the 64th New York bringing up the rear. Caldwell advanced near the center of his line with Colonel von Schack's 7th New York. An officer under Miles wrote that the next few minutes became a matter of "life or death to us, and the quicker we got near the foot of the Heights where we could lay down, and do some fireing ourselfs, the better it was for us." Clumps of Caldwell's men flocked to the prone lines of French, Zook, and Meagher. Some of them tried to keep going, but most slumped to the ground and took cover with the troops already in the swale.[84]

The 5th New Hampshire shouldered its way through the mass of bodies. The New Englanders reported that they found the previous attackers mixed "in very disorderly condition." Caldwell's men had to be extra careful near those troops because they "were firing wildly at the enemy." Musketry from the swale imperiled more Federals than Rebels. Caldwell's right swarmed past the Stratton house. The left wing of the 5th New Hampshire ran against the brick house and piled to the right to get around the dwelling. "This threw us into a bunch," recalled Sergeant George S. Gove, "and it was here so many of our men were killed and wounded." A hog pen further disrupted the attackers. "After passing the brick house," reported an officer, "all formation of the regimental line of battle was lost." Somewhere past the Stratton house, Major Sturtevant was killed. Lieutenant Charles Dodd, the regimental adjutant, also fell wounded. Soldiers later recovered Dodd, but the major's body was never found.[85]

The Northern mob flocked through Stratton's orchard and reached the board fence. The fence ran parallel to the stone wall fifty yards away. Bullets riddled the fence and dropped a number of Federals in their tracks. "Splinters from the fence, torn off by the enemy's bullets," remembered one soldier, "were flying in every direction." The effect left the dead and dying piled against the wall. Color-bearers pushed to the front, and some of the men rallied on the standards. Individuals pounded holes in the fence to charge the stone wall.[86]

Most of the 5th New Hampshire's color guard never made it past the Stratton orchard. Captain John Murray was shot dead while carrying the national colors. Corporal Smith P. Davis advanced the colors toward the brick house before he fell mortally wounded. Captain James B. Perry brought the flag to the Stratton house. Bullets caught him in the chest and shoulder. Perry fell on Lieutenant Janvrin W. Graves. The lieutenant raised the colors, but could not advance them because he had broken his leg. Graves became the fourth color-bearer in as many minutes.[87]

Lieutenant Graves propped the flag against the wall and revived Captain Perry. The dying captain asked feebly, "How goes the battle?" Graves murmured, "I think it is going against us. The regiment is cut to pieces." James Perry dimmed. "This is my last day; I cannot live," he whispered, "but I would liked to have lived long enough to have seen the battle go in our favor." A little later, Captain Perry inquired, "Where is that dear old flag?" The lieutenant assured him, "I have it here." "Let me see it once more before I die," the captain pleaded. Burying his face in the folds, Perry gently kissed the flag and expired.[88]

The New Hampshire state flag made it to the Stratton's orchard. "Our color bearers were shot down," wrote a New Hampshire soldier, "trying to get over this fence." Some of the soldiers squeezed through holes in the planking, and someone tossed the flag over the fence to them. Private Frank Swift took the colors and started forward alone. A scattering of soldiers caught up with him. Swift collapsed wounded, and Sergeant George S. Gove took the banner. He carried it still closer to the Confederates. Corporal John R. McCrillis joined the party and suggested everyone should lie down. George C. Foss declined. He told McCrillis: "I will stand here until I am hit." A converging fire sleeted through the small group and, predictably, Foss screamed, "I am shot." At the same moment, Sergeant Gove called for help. A piece of shrapnel had struck the color-bearer on the back of the head and paralyzed him. Gove pleaded with McCrillis to save the flag. George Gove had fallen on top of it, so the corporal rolled him over. McCrillis secured the flag and looked around for help. "There was no one in sight to my right or left, except the dead or wounded," he wrote. Fixing his eye on a crack in the fence, he made a break for it. Confederate fire had slackened at that point and McCrillis made his escape. Dodging around the corner of the Stratton house, the corporal took cover with hundreds of other Union soldiers. Very few of the Federals had ventured beyond the Stratton orchard.[89]

The rest of Caldwell's brigade did not advance as far as the 5th New Hampshire. Caldwell reported that "Some of my men, especially on the left, were halted and commenced firing." Part of the 81st Pennsylvania managed to reach the Stratton house with the 5th New Hampshire, but they had been whittled away to nothing. Men foundered in what some of the soldiers called "the Slaughter Pen." A Pennsylvanian recollected, "The fire here was terrific—the hottest I have ever seen." Colonel H. Boyd McKeen dropped out wounded. Major Thomas C. Harkness also fell. Eventually, Captain William Wilson became the 81st Pennsylvania's fourth commander. At the same time, the 7th New York's Colonel von Schack received a slight wound, but he refused to relinquish command. The historian of the Second Corps claimed that the New York regiment had lost eighteen commissioned officers, including the lieutenant colonel and major.[90]

The 145th Pennsylvania fell behind the rest of Caldwell's brigade. The regiment wrestled through the supine lines in the swale and then dealt with the southeast corner of the fairgrounds fence. The Pennsylvanians wasted a good deal of time trying to breach the fence. Colonel Hiram L. Brown sustained serious wounds to his chest and thigh. He surrendered command to Lieutenant Colonel David B. McCreary. Soldiers later counted eighteen bullet holes in the state flag and another thirteen in the national colors. A piece of cannonball sheared the U.S. standard from its staff. By the time the 145th Pennsylvania penetrated the fairgrounds, Lieutenant Colonel McCreary could not find the rest of Caldwell's brigade. Though he had no way of knowing it, McCreary was the only field officer in the entire brigade at that moment who had not been hit. The lieutenant colonel left his regiment in the fairgrounds to look for General Caldwell. After he left, a sizable chunk of the 145th Pennsylvania panicked and fled the field. Caldwell stemmed the rout and returned the 145th Pennsylvania to the front. The general tried to fashion a semblance of order along the swale. Two of Caldwell's staff officers fell wounded as they shadowed their brigade commander. The general constantly urged his brigade forward. At the same time, he discouraged men in the rear from firing into his command. One of Meagher's lieutenants noted that General Caldwell "ineffectively" rallied his brigade.[91]

Colonel Nelson Miles, meanwhile, had brought up his two New York regiments and ordered them to lie down behind Caldwell's line. Hancock, however, had other ideas. He directed his aide, Lieutenant Mitchell, to put Miles on the right flank to ward off a potential counterattack. The 61st and 64th New York moved north running a gauntlet of fire as they passed the brick house, the wheelwright shop, and Sissons' store. New Yorkers piled across Hanover Street and into the backyards of the George Rowe and Thomas F. Proctor houses. A garden with a "tight board fence" neatly delineated Mr. Proctor's property. Colonel Miles ordered his men to lie down behind the wall. "The fence hid the enemy from our sight," recalled a soldier in the 61st New York, "but the distance to their nearest line of rifle pits was short." Miles estimated that the stone wall stood about forty yards beyond the wooden fence. Miles directed the 61st and 64th New York to shoot at the Washington Artillery. The troops could see the guns above the fence, and they harassed the Southern cannoneers as best they could. Under the circumstances, Louisianans may have congratulated themselves for making the gun pits deeper.[92]

Confederates answered with canister, and Miles' men hid behind their wooden fence while splinters and wood chips rained down on them. Only Miles and a sergeant of the 61st New York dared to stand behind the recumbent line. Nelson Miles moved back and forth to get a better look at the Confederate defenses. On the other hand, Sergeant George Joyce simply refused to lie down. He cautioned his men: "Lie low boys. I'll let you know if anything happens," but without heeding his own advice—he received a wound in the foot. The 61st New York's Major William H. Spencer lost a leg to a wound at the same time.[93]

Miles convinced himself that he could capture the stone wall at the foot of Marye's Heights. "We were then within 40 yards of the enemy," he reported, "and it only needed a spirited charge with the bayonet to close in." The colonel sent word to Caldwell that he had an opportunity to storm the works up Hanover Street. All that he needed was the rest of Caldwell's and Zook's brigades to support him. Caldwell met Miles at Sissons' store and Colonel Samuel Zook joined them. The brigade commanders listened to Miles, but argued that supports could not be relied upon for help. Caldwell's brigade was in disarray, and Zook stated that he had no brigade to offer. Miles volunteered to go ahead without the support, but Caldwell and Zook still balked. "I was advised by all my superior officers there not to attempt it alone," Colonel Miles wrote. "I only regret I did not make the attempt alone to carry the hill." Caldwell retorted in his report, "Had there been any support, I should not have hesitated to give him the order," but without reinforcements, "it seemed to me a wanton loss of brave men." Instead of seizing the initiative, Caldwell relegated Miles to guarding the flank beyond Hanover Street.[94]

The matter quickly became moot. As soon as Miles returned to his command a rifle ball struck him in the throat. Many of the New Yorkers did not share Miles' penchant for the attack and looked at his wound as a godsend. Charles Fuller labeled the Confederate missile that hit the colonel "accommodating," because Miles "had to leave the field, somewhat to the longevity account" of the soldiers in the 61st and 64th New York. Spewing blood, Miles gurgled final instructions to Lieutenant Colonel Enos C. Brooks, of the 64th New York, to hold his ground "at all odds." Colonel Brooks soon followed Miles to the rear with a bullet in his arm, which necessitated amputation. Lieutenant Colonel K. Oscar Broady of the 61st New York, assumed responsibility for the two regiments, while Captain William Glenny became the nominal head of the 64th New York.[95]

General John Caldwell started for the right when he heard that Miles had been hit. He proceeded only a short distance before a Confederate bullet pierced his side. Caldwell refused to leave his brigade, but a second bullet lodged in his shoulder, which compelled him to retire. Caldwell was the second Union general and third brigade commander hit in front of the stone wall. Hancock turned over command of the brigade to the already wounded Colonel George W. von Schack of the 7th New York. Later, when Hancock learned that von Schack had concealed his wound out of modesty, the division commander wrote, "Colonel von Shack's [*sic*] conduct at Fredericksburg was heroic."[96]

Hancock had wrecked his entire division. The Confederates had shredded Hancock's brigade-front assaults. Caldwell's brigade lost in excess of 950 men and suffered four of the heaviest regimental losses in the division. Caldwell's charnel statistics came close to doubling either the 527 losses sustained by Zook's brigade or the 545 casualties sustained by Meagher's. Zook and Meagher fielded much smaller brigades, so the losses balanced proportionately. The assiduous Hancock had seen his command brutalized with much deadlier effect than French had suffered. The division lost in excess of 2,000 of the 5,500 men sent into the attack. One of Hancock's soldiers wrote, "The loss of our Division at Fredericksburg was greater than any other Division engaged in that battle." The statistics bore him out; but instead of falling to pieces, a glimmer of hope for the Federal attack still lingered. As General Caldwell headed for the hospital, he saw another division emerge from the city. Chancing upon Colonel Joshua Owen, commander of the Philadelphia Brigade, Caldwell learned that O. O. Howard's division had been ordered to make another attack against the stone wall. Help seemed to be on the way.[97]

At the same time General Caldwell sought the surgeons in blue, surgeons in gray tried to revive General Thomas R. R. Cobb. The Confederate general had sunk deeper into shock. The chaplain, R. K. Porter, cradled Cobb's head in his lap and soothed the general. Cobb cried, "Porter, it is very painful!" He spoke sparingly, unaware that the end was near. At times, the chaplain thought Cobb had drifted into unconsciousness, but the dying man occasionally squeezed the hand of a staff officer to let him know he was still alert. For a while, he stared steadfastly at one of his aides. Around 1:00 P.M., word arrived that Hancock had been repulsed. The pale, dying commander whispered his last words, "Thank God," and passed away.[98]

CHAPTER ELEVEN

"A DEVIL OF A TIME"

Howard and Sturgis Attack

General Oliver Otis Howard hovered close to headquarters, waiting for Darius Couch to commit his division to prolong Hancock's right. When the initial attacks failed, Couch feared the Confederates might retaliate with a counterattack. Howard's division was the only Second Corps unit not engaged, and Couch had no one else to turn to. The corps commander told Howard to forget about protecting the flank and march directly to Hancock's support. The Right Grand Division commander, Edwin Sumner, concurred and ordered the Union Ninth Corps to keep abreast of Howard's advance. Sumner hoped that the Ninth Corps—coupled with the remains of the Second Corps—might provide the force and expanded frontage to carry Marye's Heights. If nothing else, it would discourage the Rebels from counterattacking. A Confederate counterpunch worried the Union high command because it threatened to rout the entire disorganized right wing of Burnside's army. Howard thought Sumner's orders for the Second and Ninth corps to cooperate were "clear and well understood."[1]

Howard summoned his division from the upper pontoon crossing, where his brigades spanned the first three streets parallel to the river. Brigadier General Alfred Sully's brigade guarded Princess Anne Street; Colonel Joshua T. Owen's Philadelphia Brigade used Caroline Street; and Colonel Norman J. Hall's brigade stood on Sophia Street by the bridges. Together, they numbered roughly 3,500 men. Sully's brigade had detached the 1st Massachusetts Sharpshooters from the 15th Massachusetts for picket duty. The sharpshooters fanned across the bottoms north of the Plank Road and bedeviled Confederate artillerymen, thus diverting attention away from the exposed right flank. Owen's Philadelphians sent the 71st Pennsylvania to picket around the unfinished Mary Washington monument. Howard directed Owen to take the nine-month regiment, the 127th Pennsylvania, from Hall's brigade as compensation. The raw regiment boasted three times as many men as any other regiment in the division. Owen told the novices, "the 13th day of December would be a memorable day in American history; and that it would be the 'baptismal day in blood of the 127th Regiment.'"[2]

Shortly after Hancock's attack grounded to a halt, Howard ordered his troops to stow their knapsacks in the neighboring houses, and his officers to proceed on foot. The 127th good-naturedly piled their shiny new gear in a house, never to see it again. Wily veterans quickly replaced all of their worn-out equipment at the greenhorns' expense.[3]

Howard's division left the northern end of the city in the hands of Brigadier General A. Sanders Piatt's tiny Third Corps brigade and marched south. Joshua Owen's Philadelphia Brigade followed Caroline Street to George Street, where it turned west on the trail of Hancock's division. Owen's men halted on the edge of Liberty Town, amid grizzly scenes of "dead men . . . lying promiscuously over the ground; while wounded men were brought in on the sidewalks from the field." The impressionable 127th Pennsylvania noted several "frightful scenes, which stamped themselves indelibly upon the memories of each and every one in that column." The rest of Owen's column—the 69th Pennsylvania, followed by the 106th and 72nd Pennsylvania—did not seem so impressed. The 69th Pennsylvania cheered Kirby's battery as it passed the Corporation Burying Ground. The "Battery Boys," in turn, saluted the "Fighting Brigade."[4]

Hall's and Sully's brigades joined Owen by the cemetery. Colonel Norman Hall's troops marched in silence, "for all know that they must traverse those heaps of dead; that they too, must face that storm of death." The celebrated captain, and doomsayer, Henry L. Abbott recollected that the army went forward "with the conviction, almost the determination, of getting licked." Sully's brigade lagged behind the other brigades, gathering in detachments such as the 34th New York, which had been picketing the city cemetery on Plank Road. General Howard rode down the marching column and encouraged the troops.[5]

Howard joined some of the other Second Corps officers for a last-minute briefing at the knoll on George Street. Wounded Colonel Nelson Miles insisted on seeing Howard and ordered his stretcher-bearers to carry him to the knoll. Miles clasped his neck to stem the bleeding while he advocated an attack north of Hanover Street. Howard also talked to Generals Couch and Hancock. Couch silently scanned the field while Hancock advised Howard to move part of his command directly behind his division. Hancock thought that once his front was stabilized, Howard could extend his right with an attack in column up Hanover Street.[6]

Howard waved Owen's brigade forward. Colonel Owen mounted a large gray horse against orders and headed the column down the hill to Hanover Street. Confederates savaged the column just as it entered Sandy Bottom. "Men were struck down lacerated by the bursting shells," noted a member of the brigade, "while the posts and fences along the road were torn to pieces and the fragments sent flying in the air." The men did not know whether the shrapnel or the splinters from the houses were more dangerous.[7]

The Philadelphia Brigade hit the millrace and found the bridge still unplanked. Owen turned in frustration and thundered, "Men, cross the best way you can, and form on the other side of the canal, under that hill." Soldiers broke ranks and crossed "in twos, in threes and every other way," according to a 106th Pennsylvania man. Before the tail of the column passed, they encountered a man "running with his head off." The decapitated body somersaulted and splashed into the sluiceway. The Philadelphia Brigade reformed in the muddy ravine beneath the plateau. The 69th Pennsylvania took the right, resting its flank on Hanover Street. The 106th Pennsylvania formed next, followed by the 72nd Pennsylvania and 127th Pennsylvania.[8]

Joshua Owen waved good-bye to Couch, Hancock, and Howard, and ordered his brigade to advance. Owen gave the order at 1:10 P.M. The brigade commander's horse fell wounded as soon as the troops left the ravine. Owen jumped free of the mount and led the 69th Pennsylvania on foot. The brigade dashed ahead, "a-yelling at the top of their voices."[9]

Confederates greeted the outburst with "one continued shower of shells and balls." Most of the Federals scampered across the field, but the 127th Pennsylvania maintained a deliberate pace. General Howard admired the nine-monthers' discipline, marching "as straight as on dress parade," but the men suffered terribly because of the injudicious exercise. Owen guided his advance along the axis of Hanover Street. All of the previous attacks had moved perpendicular to the millrace. As a result, the prior assaults had marched diagonally across the plain and engaged the Confederates piecemeal. Owen's orders ensured that the Philadelphians would bring their entire weight to bear on the stone wall simultaneously.[10]

Owen reached the Stratton house and looked for Hancock's line. "To my amazement," he reported, "the two lines which I was told to support I found to have been almost entirely annihilated." The Philadelphia Brigade recognized "some scattered companies and parts of regiments." Most soldiers, however, recalled "one long line of battle, lying down two deep, but it is a line of dead men."[11]

The Philadelphians battled forward into "the very jaws of death." A watching Federal officer marveled: "they faced death like heroes." The soldiers knew they were being "ruthlessly mowed down without the shadow of a chance to capture the foes." Owen agreed: "To advance further would only entail useless slaughter." He ordered his brigade to lie down. Joshua Owen moved along his line shouting, "lie down, close, close, close." Most of the soldiers sprawled on the ground without cover. The 69th Pennsylvania, on the right, hid behind a "slight pale fence" and a few dwellings along Hanover Street. General Howard described the area as "a little hamlet whose straggling buildings gave some protection." The seventh attack against the stone wall had collapsed within ten minutes of leaving the millrace.[12]

Joshua Owen dispatched two companies of Lieutenant Colonel Dennis O'Kane's 69th Pennsylvania to infiltrate the houses on Hanover Street. Federals filled the second story windows to fire on the Confederate cannon crews atop Marye's Heights. The Washington Artillery quickly reduced the sharpshooters' nest "to an utter wreck" and drove the Northerners away. Colonel Owen sent an aide to General Howard telling him it was impossible to carry the heights without more artillery and infantry.[13]

Confederates reinforced the Sunken Road at about the same time the 69th Pennsylvania entered the houses on Hanover Street. Anticipating the Federal move, General Robert Ransom sent three regiments—the 25th, 35th, and 49th North Carolina—to the crest of Marye's Heights. The 49th North Carolina remained on the summit just north of the Plank Road. The 35th North Carolina marched in rear of the Washington Artillery between Plank Road and Hanover Street. Ransom led the 25th North Carolina to the Marye house. They arrived "just in time" for Owen's sortie. The regiment passed around both sides of the mansion and regrouped on the open hilltop to the left of the 15th North Carolina. The Carolinians suffered serious losses in the exposed position. "Men could be seen falling like sheaves before the sickle," recalled one of Ransom's soldiers. He estimated that the regiment lost 120 men in the first two minutes. The Rebels lashed back, firing over the heads of the defenders in the Sunken Road. The 25th North Carolina, however, could not stay there or it would be destroyed. The regiment piled down Hanover Street to the stone wall. The newcomers shouldered into line between the Phillips Legion and the 24th North Carolina. Ransom's reinforcements made sure the bluecoats fell in droves before their fire: "Nothing could live before that sheet of lead that was hurled at them."[14]

Howard saw the 25th North Carolina advance and feared they would attack his right. Owen's men also believed the 25th North Carolina intended to strike their weak flank. When the Rebels raced down Hanover Street, Owen ordered his men to stand and fire a volley. They assumed that their musketry, which "would stagger any line," had blunted the counterattack. Howard encouraged Owen to "hold the position at all hazards." The colonel replied, "Never fear, I will hold the position."[15]

Joshua Owen's Philadelphia Brigade jealously hoarded its ammunition. The commander refused to let his men fire at the stone wall. His decision kept the brigade from wasting its bullets, although it disillusioned many of his soldiers. Howard, on the other hand, marveled at the staying power of Owen's brigade. Later, he plagiarized what every soldier North and South recognized as a hallmark of excellence, and dubbed Owen's command his "Stonewall Brigade."[16]

Howard ordered Norman Hall's brigade to help the Philadelphia Brigade. Hall had waited until Owen's command cleared the millrace before moving. The colonel massed his 800 men in column, as suggested by General Hancock, and waited for Howard's signal to attack. Sometime around 2:00 P.M., Hall's men dashed down George Street to the millrace. The brigade stopped when it discovered the sluiceway blocked by wounded soldiers, fugitives, and stretcher-bearers.[17]

Corps commander Darius Couch altered Hall's course and directed him to the right of the bridge. Hall's brigade splashed through the spillway and re-formed on the far side. The 19th Massachusetts had led the brigade to the bridge, but the 20th Massachusetts ended up on the far right during the confused crossing. The 19th formed on its left. The 59th New York assumed the next spot in line, followed by the 42nd New York and the 7th Michigan. The Michiganders anchored Hall's left on Hanover Street. Couch's sudden change of direction—and switching Hall's brigade from column to line—

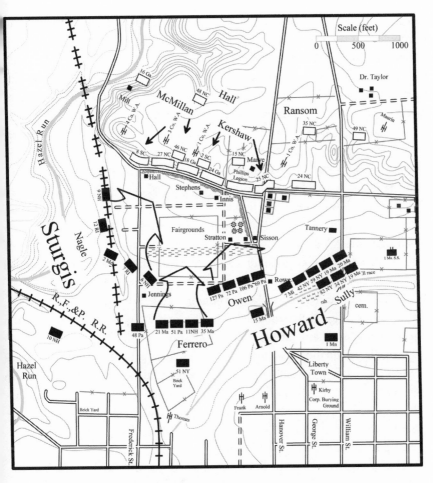

Howard and Sturgis' Advance

may have been planned from the beginning. Hancock's column of attack may have reflected Nelson Miles' recommendation for a bayonet charge, or the general may have thought it was an easier way to cross the millrace. After crossing, Couch probably would have formed Hall's brigade on the right of Hanover Street anyway. When the human logjam on the bridge broke up the movement, Couch channeled his men into line first and then crossed. Either way, Nelson Miles had made his point, and Hall's brigade became the first large force sent north of Hanover Street to attack.[18]

Hall's brigade crawled out of the basin to attack the Confederates beyond the right of Owen's brigade. Northerners stared across four hundred yards of clear, open fields. A member of the Harvard regiment thought the ground unfolded "as smooth as the glacis of a fort" to the base of the heights. Nerves grew taut, and men felt like they would burst. "O dear me I was afraid when I was first under fire," wrote George A. Patch of the 19th Massachusetts, "but if I had run away I should not have conquered my fear any, but on the contrary, should have made myself more" frightened.[19]

As soon as Hall's right stepped out of the bottoms, the 19th Massachusetts stumbled. The regiment had not covered fifty yards before it turned back. Captain Macy's 20th Massachusetts continued to advance alone. Captain Abbott later complained that the brigade functioned "without the slightest notion of what was intended to be accomplished." Part of the confusion stemmed from the fact that Hall had not ordered an advance. The 20th Massachusetts struggled up the slope, unaware of the mixup. "The enthusiasm of the soldiers has been all gone for a long time," declared one officer. He attributed any effort shown by the regiment to "discipline and old associations." Captain Ferdinand Dreher, Macy's senior—and rival for command of the regiment—fell mortally wounded. The rest of the regiment lay down in the field, unable to go any farther.[20]

Brigade commander Norman Hall ordered the renegade 20th Massachusetts to fall back to the millrace. Macy's men withdrew deliberately, much to the admiration of their leader. "I am more proud of this retreat than anything," Macy reported. "It was done coolly." Hall, on the other hand, criticized Macy for charging "without my knowledge, and, in forming line, created some confusion at that point."[21]

Hall straightened out the line and launched a coordinated attack. The brigade surged forward, and the waiting Confederates threw a storm of shot at it. A Michigan soldier wrote, "We received such a withering, deadly fire . . . that it was impossible to get more than half way across that open ground." The left started to waver, but Hall's right slogged up the soggy slope with conviction. Confederate volleys staggered the attackers at 150 to 200 yards from the base of Marye's Heights. A 19th Massachusetts man recalled, "The whole line was enveloped in a cloud of sulphurous smoke, almost hiding the regiments from each other." Groups of men dropped mangled and torn. A New Englander thought, "the slaughter had been beyond description." A sergeant recollected, "No one who has not witnessed such a scene can form any idea of the awfulness of that hour." The 7th Michigan troops lost contact with the rest of the brigade in the black powder haze. One of them wrote, "It seemed as if the earth had opened up and swallowed whole regiments at a ime." The New York regiments retreated to the millrace. The 7th Michigan headed in the same direction. Only the 19th and 20th Massachusetts ventured closer to the Sunken Road.[22]

"What carnage!" a member of the 19th Massachusetts recalled. Soldiers plodded uphill over their own dead. Men lost their footing because "the grass was slippery with their blood." A captain wrote, "We have had a devil of a time here." The line stopped, fired a few spasmodic volleys, and started to unravel. The Southerners focused much of their fire on the sparkling new flags of the 19th Massachusetts. When the men began to lie down—and maintaining the attack seemed hopeless—Sergeant Ronello B. Creasey challenged them, "I will stand by as long as I live . . . come on boys!" Before he moved, a bullet smashed the staff and struck him fatally in the groin. Corporal Winfield Rappell, the other standard-bearer, fell mortally wounded beside him. The death of the flag bearers sent the regiment reeling backward. The 19th Massachusetts halted its recoil when it reached the millrace. The 20th Massachusetts fared better, taking cover behind John Hurkamp's tannery, a large edifice that fronted on Plank Road. Colonel Hall ordered the 20th Massachusetts to hold its ground while he re-formed the rest of the brigade.[23]

Hall rallied his troops and started another attack. One of his soldiers noted acidly: "the tragedy is reenacted." Confederate artillery enfiladed the right. Confederate captain Victor Maurin's Donaldsonville Artillery, from Louisiana, fired down the length of the line from the heights north of the Plank Road. His shot plowed through the blue ranks, rupturing the line. The Federals reached the 20th Massachusetts, but failed to move beyond that point.[24]

Hall reported that human nature doomed his assault. Union soldiers instinctively stopped and fired. The colonel tried to discourage that and prodded them forward, but it proved impossible. Immobilized in an open field, the left of Hall's line gave away again. The 42nd and 59th New York broke first, leaving the 7th Michigan alone on the left. The Michigan soldiers quickly backtracked to the millrace. This left Hall with two Massachusetts units to fight alone.[25]

The 20th Massachusetts sallied from the cover of the tannery only to get jolted by heavy musket fire. Captain Abbott estimated that the regiment lost 63 men in a few minutes, leaving about a hundred soldiers still in the ranks. A Confederate bullet knocked Captain Herbert Mason's sword out of his hand, and he dropped to the ground for cover. The rest of the 20th Regiment did the same.[26]

Captain Harrison G. O. Weymouth led his 19th Massachusetts up the incline until he took a severe wound in the left leg. Surgeons later amputated the limb. Captain Andrew Mahoney assumed command, but fell moments later with wounds in his arm and side. Besides Weymouth and Mahoney eleven other officers of the 19th Massachusetts suffered wounds on December 13. Command ultimately devolved upon Captain Jonathan F. Plympton.[27]

Confederate sharpshooters focused on color-bearers as well as officers. The 19th Massachusetts already had lost two flag holders in the previous assault. Two more bearers fell in quick succession. Martin Bradbure briefly took one of the standards, but died when hit by a bullet that had cut through the staff. Sergeant Charles B. Brown became the seventh man to take the flag. A bullet wound in the head left him stunned. A lieutenant thought the wound was mortal and ordered him to give up the colors. Brown refused, shouting, "I will not give them to any man." He rushed ahead, stumbled, and fell dead, driving the flagstaff into the ground. Lieutenant Edgar M. Newcomb rescued the national colors from the mud while Sergeant Charles L. Merrill picked up the state flag. Both fell instantly. A bullet broke both of Lieutenant Newcomb's legs just below the knees. As he writhed in pain, Newcomb gave the colors to Lieutenant John G. B. Adams. He yelled, "Don't let them go down!" Two more men died caring for the white Massachusetts state flag. Lieutenant Adams soon possessed both flags, making him the eleventh color-bearer within an hour. Adams took the regimental standards and ran for cover behind some nearby buildings. The survivors of the 19th Massachusetts followed him to the tannery. Lieutenant John G. B. Adams' quick thinking rescued the flags and the regiment, and earned him the Congressional Medal of Honor.[28]

One of Hall's men recalled despondently, "We did all that troops could do." Norman Hall "stoutly condemned" the attack "as simply ridiculous." Captain Herbert C. Mason of the Harvard Regiment reminisced, "We did our best, but failed." General Couch agreed. He concluded, "the men were asked to conquer an impossibility." The acerbic Captain Abbott declared that this was "nothing but murder."[29]

Hall's third attack had collapsed, and his men huddled around the tannery or along the millrace. The brigade commander believed that his troops could not make another attack. He reported to General Howard that "Further attempts to advance were hopeless." His men were exhausted, but he thought they could hold their position.[30]

Following Hall's repulse, more Confederates moved to Marye's Heights. Robert Ransom advanced the 46th and 48th North Carolina of Confederate

Edward Hall's brigade to the crest, even though the Washington Artillery partially blocked their movement. Stuck behind the guns, the Carolinians fell victim to Union fire. A shell exploded in the 46th North Carolina, which "knocked down a good many, myself included," mused the regimental commander, Major William L. Saunders. The major, incredibly, was the only one not injured. Moments later, a bullet grazed Saunder's temple, "enough to let the blood ooze." The major "bled most disgustingly and very expensively for I ruined my uniform."[31]

The 48th North Carolina lost its major as soon as it reached the summit. A Yankee ball hit Major Albert A. Hill in the shoulder. The regimental adjutant, John R. Winchester, fell wounded soon after him. Lieutenant Colonel Samuel H. Walkup, leader of the 48th North Carolina, received a sharp wound to the hip. Walkup discounted the injury and continued to command. Lieutenant William F. Beasley ran up to the colonel, clutching his leg. He begged Walkup to "tell his mother he died like a true Southern Soldier." The commander scoffed at Beasley's flesh wound and histrionics.[32]

The Carolinians needed to change their position. The 48th North Carolina withdrew slightly for cover, while the 46th North Carolina advanced to the safety of the Sunken Road. The Tar Heels filed past the Washington Artillery, who hailed the men with three cheers. The Carolinians cheered in kind, and sailed down the slope of Marye's Heights. Major Saunders watched in delight. "It was the proudest day of my life," he insisted: "I could not keep from hollering hurrah for old North Carolina." Laughing as he went down the hill, William Saunders was hit in the mouth by a bullet. It passed through his open mouth and punctured his cheek. A soldier noted wryly, "It was . . . the most abruptly ended laugh heard during the war." Saunders managed to reach the Sunken Road without further mishap, along with most of his command. Colonel Edward Hall, the brigade commander, reported that his troops "suffered but little after arriving" at the stone wall. An astute private concurred, recalling that "behind the stone wall I felt pretty much at home." He thought that anyone who was hurt "after we got behind the fence did it by their own carelessness."[33]

Just as General Robert Ransom committed "every man at my disposal," he met the head of Kershaw's Brigade coming up the back of Willis Hill. Brigadier General Joseph B. Kershaw had sent two regiments to help Cobb's Brigade, as per Lafayette McLaws' orders. Colonel John D. Kennedy's 2nd South Carolina led the march, followed by the 8th South Carolina. The column crossed Telegraph Road and climbed the steep hill. They reached the summit under a terrible shellfire. An explosion in the lead regiment obliterated one young soldier. Robert W. Shand wrote, "His head was in one spot, his brains in another, his body in a third—truly a gruesome sight." Kennedy halted and threw his regiments into line, with the 8th South Carolina on the right.[34]

Kershaw followed them up the slope and made a beeline for the crest of Marye's Heights. Word of Cobb's wounding had compelled McLaws to send Kershaw to take charge of the Sunken Road. The South Carolina general scouted the Marye's Heights salient under a heavy fire. Kershaw ignored the Union marksmen, who, incredibly, stopped shooting at him. The Federals, according to staff officer Shand, admired Kershaw's bravery. The brigadier finished his reconnaissance, doffed his cap, and "bowed thanks" to the Yankees before returning to Kennedy's regiments.[35]

The sight of more Confederate reinforcements dismayed General Howard. He instantly ordered Alfred Sully to reinforce Owen's and Hall's brigades. The division commander sent one regiment to aid Owen's Philadelphia command. Another regiment supported the Federal artillery. The rest went to Hall's brigade. Major Chase Philbrick's 15th Massachusetts filed over the millrace on the bridge struts. The Massachusetts men saw Owen's brigade was engaged in "some hot work." The shellfire threw Sully's column out of sync. A shell tore off a sergeant's left arm and wounded a color corporal and a surgeon's orderly before it killed the regimental surgeon, Dr. S. Foster Haven, Jr.[36]

Major Chase Philbrick concealed his regiment in the millrace ravine and scouted ahead for his intended position. The mass of Federals on Hanover Street made a tempting target for plunging artillery. Several rounds plowed the lip of the ravine and sprayed the men with dirt. A 15th Massachusetts' man reckoned that he "came near getting killed a thousand times." The troops lay down for protection while Major Philbrick looked for Joshua Owen. A sharpshooter's bullet hit Philbrick while in front. Captain John Murkland assumed command.[37]

Murkland shifted the 15th Massachusetts to the left of Hanover Street, and spread his men along the millrace depression. An aide from Colonel Joshua Owen's brigade located the 15th Massachusetts there and ordered them to stay put. "Taking it all round," recalled a Bay State soldier, "it was a rough day."[38]

General Howard sent his brother, Lieutenant Charles E. Howard, to check on Hall's brigade. "I had a feeling akin to terror," Howard later wrote, "when I sent an aid or mounted man to carry an order." They alone rode where no other officers were allowed to go on horseback. Charles Howard returned and exclaimed, "Oh, general, they fired a volley at me, but it passed over my head!" The aide concealed the fact that a piece of shrapnel had gashed his calf and ruined his boots.[39]

O. O. Howard's sibling reported that Hall's brigade needed reinforcements badly. "The destruction of life has been fearful in the extreme," he explained. Howard, in turn, told Sully to take the rest of his brigade to Hall's support. Sully left the 1st Minnesota to guard Kirby's battery while the remaining regiments went to bolster Norman Hall's Yankees. The brand-new 19th Maine led the way, trailed by the 34th and 82nd New York. Sully took his brigade down George Street through a heavy cannonade. "My courage was better at Fredericksburg than it ever was afterwards," reminisced a soldier in the 19th Maine. "I do not think I dodged a single shell or musket ball here, for I was a soldier and I thought it would be cowardly to dodge." Even this reckless soul admitted that "for all that, I could not help thinking of home, and wishing that I was there."[40]

The brigade crossed the millrace at 1:30 P.M. and wheeled right under cover of the embankment. Sully formed his men directly behind Hall's brigade. The 19th Maine took the right, resting its flank on the Plank Road close to Hurkamp's tannery. The 34th New York filled the center, and the 82nd New York guarded the left near Hanover Street. The 19th Massachusetts laughed at the green 19th Maine. "It was amusing to see the effect of the cannon shot on them," one soldier noted. "As each shot passed over the regiment from right to left, the men would duck their heads successively." This reminded him of "the waving of grain in the wind." Hall's soldiers called the newcomers the "Softbread Regiment." Sully, on the other hand, commended the 19th Maine for getting their first whiff of gunpowder and "apparently did not dislike the smell of it." The brigadier ordered his men to lie down behind Hall's brigade for cover.[41]

Sully never considered attacking Marye's Heights. With only three regiments, he intended to support Hall's brigade. "Here we lay expecting each moment to be attacked by the rebel infantry," wrote a member of the 34th New York. "But we were not thus fortunate. A more terrible fate awaited us." Later in the day, Confederate artillery enfiladed their position and made the Union soldiers suffer.[42]

Even as Sully bolstered Hall, the belligerents continued to pepper each other with bullets and shrapnel. A boy in the 24th Georgia jumped on top of the rock wall, waving his hat and cheering until his comrades "could pull him down." Colonel Robert McMillan passed "up and down the line," cautioning his brigade to "keep down behind the wall." While encouraging his old regiment, the colonel clasped his neck and staggered. His son, Garnett, shouted, "Pa, are you hurt?" McMillan smiled. "Hit, but not hurt," he replied cheerfully as he picked up a spent bullet and put it in his vest pocket as a souvenir.[43]

Despite their seeming protection, McMillan's soldiers needed to keep their wits about them, not so much to avoid Yankee fire, but for the misaimed fire of the Confederates behind them. The 15th North Carolina, onetime members of Cobb's Brigade, hovered just above their former mates. The Georgians disliked the Carolinians and had just cause. The 15th North Carolina had taken position south of the Marye house and fired wildly into the Georgians. An irate Rebel recollected, "We did not need or want them." Carolinians rattled the clapboard siding on the Innis house and hit some of their unsuspecting comrades in the back. A soldier in the Phillips Legion concluded "our greatest loss was caused by the guns of our own men stationed on the hill in our rear." Gus Tomlinson risked his life twice to run up the hill and correct the errant fire. Lucius Stone made a third trip, screaming at them that "they were killing our own men." Eventually, the North Carolinians adjusted their aim, much to the relief of everyone in front.[44]

O. O. Howard had wasted the strength of his division in a series of piecemeal attacks astride Hanover Street. Howard had hoped the Ninth Corps would join his left, but much to his chagrin, their attack had not materialized. He complained that "the instructions were clear and well understood," and he had expected help to be there. His three brigades had been thrashed without any cooperation from the Ninth Corps. Darius Couch had engaged Howard when the front line teetered on the brink of collapse and emboldened Confederates threatened to counterattack. He did not have the luxury to coordinate his assault with Orlando B. Willcox's Ninth Corps. Willcox required considerable time to prepare his troops, and by the time he was ready, Howard's division had already ground to a halt. "The word 'support' is an uncertain one," a nettled Howard ruminated, "and often a very unsatisfactory one in battle." The Second Corps had engaged its full force against Marye's Heights, but it failed to even dent the Confederate defenses. By the time General Willcox marshaled the Ninth Corps to support Couch, he discovered there was very little left to support.[45]

*   *   *

Willcox ordered Brigadier General Samuel D. Sturgis to advance his division to Hancock's left just as Howard's attack waned on the right. Sturgis massed his two brigades at the lower end of Sophia Street and Caroline Street. Brigadier General James Nagle's 1st Brigade formed near the middle pontoon crossing. Brigadier General Edward Ferrero's 2nd Brigade stood in the street ahead, near General Willcox's headquarters.[46]

Sturgis earlier had sent the 51st New York from Ferrero's brigade to Knight's brickyard to support Dickenson's Battery E, 4th U.S. Artillery. Prolonged skirmishing along the RF&P Railroad compelled Ferrero to reinforce General George W. Getty's picket line with the 21st Massachusetts. Officers made the Massachusetts regiment take off their aging greatcoats, or overcoats, because their light blue material had faded and they looked as gray as the Rebels' coats. The Bay State soldiers went into action, shivering without their 'miserable gray overcoats." The rest of Ferrero's brigade listened to the picket fire and wryly noted, "That sounds like popping corn."[47]

As the Second Corps assault started, Willcox ordered Ferrero's brigade to the edge of the city. The soldiers became nervous. One man reminisced, "To say that my heart got right up into my mouth don't half express it." An 11th New Hampshire soldier wrote sardonically, "It was the last 'Fall in' to a great many." The brigade filed up Prussia Street and turned right into Princess Anne Street. Ferrero aligned his brigade with the 35th Massachusetts on the right, next to the untested 11th New Hampshire. The 51st Pennsylvania held the left until the 21st Massachusetts returned from Getty's picket line. Ferrero rested his left near the railroad depot. The men lay down on the sidewalk for a moment. The sparkling new uniforms of the 11th New Hampshire contrasted greatly with the faded apparel of the other regiments. From a distance, their jackets appeared to be almost black.[48]

Ferrero harangued his troops before they moved. He told one regiment: "Keep cool: it is good fun when you once get in!" Some of the men doubted his veracity. Ferrero ended his prattle, "I will not ask you to go anywhere that I will not lead you." Many questioned his truthfulness. One captain stated that the general disappeared from that moment on.[49]

Some time after 2:00 P.M., Sturgis gave the order for Ferrero's brigade to attack. The brigade moved out Prussia Street and across the millrace bridge. It came under Confederate cannon firing "with all the fury of the demons." A member of the 21st Massachusetts wrote that the Rebels laid down "the best directed artillery fire that we had ever suffered or seen." The first shell struck a stack of railroad ties, and "in the twinkling of an eye that entire pile was converted to kindling-wood." Ferrero's column dipped into the millrace ravine. Some of the men took cover in Mullens' or Aler's brickyard.[50]

Confederate cannon blasted the brickyard and riddled its strong plank fence. Rebel shot demolished hundreds of bricks, covering the 51st Pennsylvania with reddish brick dust. Shells splintered the wall. "Shells made havoc of that fence," recalled one frightened soldier, "and to me it was the most trying time of the day." Casualties accumulated at an appalling rate. The ravine filled with "men, reduced to mere bundles of rags and mutilated flesh, or with mangled bodies writhing in agony upon the ground." A shell hit Warren Webster of the 21st Massachusetts in the face and his head "flew from his shoulders." Webster's corpse "rolled over, the blood spurted from the neck as water comes from a pump, until the heart pumped the body dry."[51]

Some of the men started crying. One frightened soldier exclaimed: "Oh, dear! they'll kill every one of us; not a d——d one of us will be left to tell the story!" A listening comrade wrote glumly, "he was about right." A man in the 11th New Hampshire "seemed in a terrible mental agony, groaning and taking on." One witness "felt as badly as he [did] but I kept it to myself." A Second Corps unit, the 145th Pennsylvania, panicked and stampeded through Ferrero's brigade. They warned the Ninth Corps men, "Don't go up there; the day is lost!" One of Ferrero's soldiers reported, "They ran so fast, it looked to me as if their feet didn't touch the ground!" Officers chased them, screaming, "Halt! halt you ———, halt!" but it was no use.[52]

On Marye's Heights, Joseph Kershaw ordered Colonel John Kennedy to reinforce the Sunken Road. The general wanted the South Carolinians to march to the crest, fire, and charge down the slope to the Sunken Road. The 2nd and 8th South Carolina advanced smartly, but they soon became separated by the intense barrage that rattled through their ranks. At the summit Kennedy ignored the order to fire. He hurried his men down the hillside at the double-quick. The line cascaded down the slope screeching "like so many wild Indians." A South Carolinian wrote that they "rolled, slid, jumped and stumbled" into the Sunken Road. Federals fired into the Rebels as long as they exposed themselves. Major Franklin Gaillard fell wounded in the face as he tumbled down the hill. Lafayette McLaws' aide, Captain Henry L. P. King, died on the slope in front of the Marye house. A shell fragment glanced off Kershaw's right arm and killed his horse before he reached the road. The general also lost a staff officer to a contusion on the head.[53]

Kershaw shook off his wound and took command of the Sunken Road

He divided the 2nd South Carolina and sent part of it to the right. The rest he dispersed between the 24th Georgia and the Phillips Legion. His troops swelled the ranks behind the wall to four deep.[54]

The 8th South Carolina arrived somewhat later. It had been delayed first by the prone 48th North Carolina lying in its path, and then by the volley at the crest. The regiment lost 28 of its total 31 casualties while coming down the hillside. Kershaw met the 8th South Carolina as it entered the road and directed it to the far right of the salient, near "a creek, which debouched into the valley." The general saw some movement near Hazel Run and feared the Federals might use the stream to threaten his right flank and rear. The Union Ninth Corps probably brought this to his attention when it entered the field south of the unfinished railroad. Prior to that, Kershaw had only encountered Federals coming from Hanover Street. "Now Stackhouse," Kershaw clasped the leader of the 8th South Carolina by the shoulder, "occupy that position and hold [it] against any force that the enemy may send against it." Colonel Eli T. Stackhouse put his regiment on Kershaw's flank just as the Yankees began to test that part of the line.[55]

Soon after Kershaw moved, Ferrero received the order to attack. The brigade commander shouted, "Go in and give it to them." Ferrero's four regiments, comprising 1,850 soldiers, stepped onto the plateau. Colonel Walter Harriman told the 11th New Hampshire, "Be firm and brave boys." Some of Hancock's and French's soldiers saw the newcomers and started cheering and clapping their hands. The dark-uniformed New Englanders drew repeated shouts of encouragement. "Go in, Eleventh New Hampshire, go in!" they cheered. "You are good for it! Go in, bully boys!" The new soldiers did not respond, but trudged tight-lipped through the brickyard. "We didn't cheer much in return," recollected a New Hampshireman, "we had something else of importance on our minds just then."[56]

Ferrero's brigade clambered over a fence and then another. Federals wriggled past those obstacles and reached the fairgrounds under "a most desperate fire." Marye's Heights appeared to them to be a "seething Hell." The 51st Pennsylvania reported that it lost more men during the advance than at any other part of the fight. "They went up boldly," one of Ferrero's men reported, "but many of them got his before they had a chance to fire a gun."[57]

The acting major of the 35th Massachusetts, Captain John Lathrop, wrote of Fredericksburg: *Antietam was nothing to it.* Major Sidney Willard, the acting colonel, relied on personal bravery to lead the regiment. The major strode ahead of the line—against his officers' objections—and ordered the

35th Massachusetts to follow him. He exhorted, "Come on, boys! Remember South Mountain and Antietam!" The men cheered and charged after him. Midway across the field, a bullet slapped the major in the chest. It clanged off of his bulletproof vest and glanced downward into his groin. The commander pitched onto his face. Sidney Willard slowly turned over and gasped, "My God, I am shot!" One of his soldiers tried to carry him to the rear, but the major was too heavy. Captain Lathrop helped drag Willard to the millrace. The wounded officer panted, "You must let me lie down; I can't go any farther." Lathrop sent a private to fetch a stretcher while he stanched the blood. "God's will be done," Willard sighed. "Tell them I tried to do my duty to my country and to the regiment." He died the next day.[58]

Men began to fall as soon as they passed the brickyard. Confederates paid particular attention to the colors nodding ahead of the battle line. Color Sergeant Joseph H. Collins of the 21st Massachusetts was among the first to fall mortally wounded. Color Corporal Elbridge C. Barr died next to him, carrying the white state flag. Sergeant Thomas Plunkett took the national colors from Collins and Corporal Richard Wheeler grabbed the state flag from Barr's death grip. A bullet struck Plunkett's left hand, but he shook it off. A shell burst directly in front of him and shrapnel carried away his right arm and mangled his left. Plunkett fell, wrapped in his flag. Color Corporal Bradley R. Olney untangled Plunkett and found that the color-bearer had lost both of his arms. Olney took the bloody flag and carried it up the hill, making him the fifth color-bearer for the regiment within a couple hundred yards. Plunkett recovered and later became the doorkeeper for the Massachusetts State Assembly.[59]

"It is a mystery . . . how under the sun even one man reached alive the position," marveled a member of the 51st Pennsylvania. The brigade tried to knock down the fairgrounds fence, but the boards were "nailed on perpendicularly, with stout nails and plenty of them." The 51st Pennsylvania forced its way through a hole in the fence. The spot filled quickly with "heaps of dead, dying and wounded." A Unionist remembered dolefully, "The groans of the dying and wounded soldiers when trodden on were heartrending in the extreme." Men ignored the wounded, "who lay weltering in their gore," and forged ahead.[60]

Entering the fairgrounds, Ferrero's loose formations drifted apart. A devastating fusillade from the stone wall scattered the attackers. "The line wavers suddenly, stops and shivers," recalled a member of the 11th New Hampshire "like some great ship that is beaten by a storm and recedes." Several men described Marye's Heights as "one sheet of flame!" The new recruits returned a volley as nearby soldiers cheered, "Give it to 'em, boys; give it to 'em!" The 11th New Hampshire stood in the middle of Mercer Square while "the hissing bullets flew among us in one incessant stream." The dead and dying accumulated underfoot. One of the soldiers remembered, "This was a time to try what men were made of." Some of the men panicked. A frightened soldier bawled, "they will kill every son-of-a-gun of us, not a d——d one will be left to tell the tale." Officers ordered him shut up. "How to get out of that place alive was a puzzle to me," admitted a lieutenant. Even after the fact, he wrote, "I do not think it possible." But for some, fear dissipated as the new soldiers became inured to the exposure of battle. Charles Paige, of the 11th New Hampshire reported, "I felt the dread but that soon left me."[61]

The 11th New Hampshire withdrew to the swale and took its turn lying in the churned-up depression. Men fired from their knees at the invisible foe behind the stone wall. "I was some tired and my knees were wet and covered with mud," recalled one soldier. A young man with calculated nonchalance laid his blouse on the ground and dumped his cartridges on it. He stood up repeatedly and shot at the wall. Late in the afternoon, Rebels killed the determined Northerner.[62]

The 35th Massachusetts entered the fairgrounds near the Stratton house. Captain Stephen W. Andrews had assumed command of the regiment when Major Willard had fallen mortally wounded. He led the regiment to "within a stone's throw of the rebel rifle pits" before the voluminous fire stopped him. Andrews' men fell down behind another regiment, possibly the 127th Pennsylvania of Joshua Owen's Philadelphia Brigade, and returned the musketry.[63]

The left of Ferrero's brigade strayed from the dirt trail of Frederick Street and angled to the right to connect with the 51st Pennsylvania. The 21st Massachusetts regrouped by the southeast corner of the fairgrounds. The historian of the 21st Massachusetts recollected, "I wonder, even now, how we could have escaped with the loss of only *one third* of the number that we took into the fight." Officers did not believe they could reach the Confederate works and stopped trying. Instead, the 21st Massachusetts lay down in the swale. The decision seemed justified when Confederates reinforced the pickets below Hazel Run and opened fire on their flank.[64]

Northern troops loaded their dirty rifles while lying flat on their backs, then rolled over or stood up to shoot. Men on the right fired as fast as they could while those on the left hoarded their ammunition, firing only when the

Rebels exposed themselves. Ferrero ventured near the front, long enough to demand that his brigade fire in regular volleys. "It was horrid to put men in [that] position," a Massachusetts soldier contended. He later wrote his family, "The shells came so near me that the mud filled my ears." Without hope of carrying the heights, Ferrero's troops prayed that they were strong enough to hold the swale. "This was the fiercest battle ever fought on this continent," in the judgment of one Massachusetts soldier.[65]

Edward Ferrero knew his brigade needed help. He asked Sturgis to return his 51st New York. Colonel Robert B. Potter had idled on the edge of the city after Dickenson's battery retired. Accordingly, Sturgis dispatched the regiment to find Ferrero. The 51st New York swung north across the unfinished western rail spur, and into the millrace depression. Colonel Potter immediately turned his command into the field and started for the fairgrounds. Confederate artillery focused their full attention on the tiny command of 300 officers and men. Recently promoted Captain George Washington Whitman—brother to the famous literary figure Walt Whitman—ruminated that "we received the most terrific fire of grape, cannister, percussion Shell, musketry, *and everything else, that I ever saw.*" A shell burst at Whitman's feet and a piece of shrapnel creased his jaw and cheek. The 51st New York reached the swale in a hurry and found Ferrero's brigade.[66]

Potter's 51st New York relieved the 11th New Hampshire and 51st Pennsylvania. Both of those regiments had run out of ammunition. Colonel Potter's men lay down and picked up the fire. Despite the cold muddy ground, a Union soldier reported that "loading and firing of the muskets caused the men to perspire as freely as if they were cradling in the harvest field." Sweaty men took comfort in seeing the 51st New York's mascot—a "large and beautiful black dog," crouching in the swale with them. Unfortunately, the dog received a painful wound, sank quietly in the mud, and died.[67]

The inextricable mix of Second Corps commands—along with the subsequent arrival of Howard's division and Ferrero's brigade—led to a general lack of concert or cooperation. "There was no general officer in actual tangible command of the front line," noted a Ninth Corps soldier, "and no such feeling of unity among the different organizations." Ferrero had left the front to see General Sturgis without telling the next in command. The brigadier allegedly went back to get more reinforcements. Rather than send a messenger to headquarters, Ferrero thought it better—and safer—to talk to Sturgis in person.[68]

The cautious brigadier should have stayed with his command; help was already on its way. Sturgis had ordered General James Nagle's brigade to support Ferrero. Nagle's men had spent the afternoon "penned up between the houses, unable to see anywhere." The brigade moved out, its men glad to escape the narrow streets. The soldiers hated the restricted space, where cannon fire could "cut down" a man "like a dog."[69]

Twenty minutes after Ferrero's brigade left the city, Nagle's brigade formed on Caroline Street, with the 6th New Hampshire on the right, next to the 7th Rhode Island, 2nd Maryland, 12th Rhode Island, and 9th New Hampshire. The 48th Pennsylvania received orders to stay behind in reserve. The Pennsylvanians massed in column on Frederick Street, giving Nagle's brigade the odd appearance of running both parallel and perpendicular to the river, like a large letter L. During a brief lull in the battle, the brigade watched the wounded going to the rear and wondered about their "chances of making a similar exit from the field."[70]

Bullets pattered against the houses and shells showered the street, making a lively racket. One shell bounded into a neighboring battery, crippling three horses and smashing a limber "into kindling." A bullet stung a Pennsylvania officer, who was sitting next to Major James Wren. The wounded man cried out, "O, I am shot! O, I am shot!" Wren admitted that he had "never heard a man hollow [holler] so in my life." The major also recounted that, "It made me feel a little Quear [queer] to find I had escaped so narrowly."[71]

Nagle received the order to advance between 2:20 and 2:30 P.M. At that very moment, George Gordon Meade's breakthrough collapsed and the Pennsylvania Reserves were streaming back toward the Bowling Green Road. Minutes later, Gibbon's division, under Taylor, also lost its hold on the RF&P Railroad. Unaware of these setbacks, Nagle's brigade—some 2,000 strong—filed through the narrow streets and alleyways to the western outskirts of Fredericksburg. Part of the 12th Rhode Island even marched through backyards to keep their place in the line of battle. The advancing Northerners carried an array of fears and expectations. A soldier in the 6th New Hampshire noted that "you could see by the boys' faces who were cowards and who were not." Major Jacob Babbitt, 7th Rhode Island, had written to his wife, "Whould it be my lot to fall, know that it was in defence of our beloved Constitution." On a more personal note, Babbitt vowed: "I will try not to disgrace my native town but do all to enoble it." His last thoughts before going into battle, were of home: "Kiss all the children for me and take in immagination [sic] one long embrace from me for yourself."[72]

The brigade cleared the city and passed through Knight's brickyard and past the Fredericksburg poor house. A 6th New Hampshire man's "heart went pit a pat" under the caustic cannonade. Nagle's brigade guided its attack by Frederick Street, which soon split the command. The 6th New Hampshire and 7th Rhode Island crossed the RF&P Railroad with the street, but the rest of the brigade remained to the left of the tracks. As the line proceeded, the right of the brigade strayed farther from the left by passing north of the unfinished railroad. The left of Nagle's brigade continued south of Frederick Street. The separated lines passed the depot and skirted Thomas' Battery C, 4th U.S. Artillery. A board fence might have protected Nagle's brigade, but Thomas' battery drew heavy fire on the area.[73]

The unfinished rail spur divided Nagle's brigade beyond the general's ability to control it. The 6th New Hampshire and 7th Rhode Island on their own initiative continued moving, while the 2nd Maryland, 12th Rhode Island, and 9th New Hampshire halted briefly along the RF&P Railroad south of the cut. Nagle ran into another problem south of the incomplete railroad. The unfinished rail line angled across his front to Hazel Run and crossed the stream at the base of Marye's Heights. This natural feature, combined with the railroad cut, created a triangle-shaped field immediately south of the unfinished railroad, which shunted attackers to the right and directly into Confederate fire from the stone wall and Willis Hill. Nagle wanted to avoid Hazel Run, so he ordered the bulk of his brigade into the unfinished railroad cut.[74]

The 2nd Maryland started for the railroad at once, and a portion of the 12th Rhode Island followed. The left half of the Rhode Island regiment and the 9th New Hampshire, however, lingered on the RF&P, unaware of the move. The 12th Rhode Island had wrapped around a bend in the railroad bed, and never saw the right wing leave.[75]

A 12th Rhode Island officer happened to go around the corner and discovered the other half of the brigade was missing. He dashed back to his command and started it "in the direction supposed to have been taken by the rest of the regiment." Soldiers followed a trail of wounded men and debris to the unfinished railroad. Along the way, they passed Major Cyrus G. Dyer of the 12th Rhode Island, who had been seriously wounded by a shell fragment.[76]

The 2nd Maryland and the right half of the 12th Rhode Island reached the railroad cut and slid down a twenty-foot bank to the bottom. The left wing of the 12th Rhode Island and the 9th New Hampshire arrived a few minutes later. Pandemonium replaced order as the various regiments became mixed in the railroad cut. Confederate ordnance at Telegraph Hill opened fire down the axis of the incomplete railway. Three Georgia guns from Cap-

tain John P. W. Read's Pulaski Artillery joined a behemoth 30-pounder Parrott from Captain H. N. Ells' Macon, Georgia, Light Artillery, under the
temporary command of Captain George W. Nelson. The guns wreaked
havoc on the Federals who packed the railroad cut.[77]

Nagle needed to extract his brigade from the cut, but he tried to do it one
regiment at a time. He ordered the 2nd Maryland to go first and find the
right wing of the brigade. The rest of the brigade would follow in order.
Nagle hoped to reunite his brigade and wheel into line at the point of attack.
This was a complicated maneuver under the best of circumstances, but Nagle
saw no alternative. The plan disintegrated when the 2nd Maryland balked
under the powerful barrage. Men clung to the embankment, frozen with fear.
Officers tried to coax them out of the cut, but they refused to budge. Nagle
begged the Marylanders to move "with all the eloquence he could command," but without luck. In desperation, the general ordered Colonel
Browne's 12th Rhode Island to go around the 2nd Maryland. The Rhode
Islanders scrambled up the embankment on either side of the Marylanders.
The 9th New Hampshire also climbed out of the cut rather than face the
artillery fire. "Forward, men, forward!" Lieutenant Colonel John W. Babbitt
shouted, "They'll shell hell out of you here!" The disordered brigade met a
fresh burst of artillery fire as it entered the plain, which caused even more
confusion.[78]

While Nagle's left fumbled through myriad difficulties, the right wing
sailed into the fight. The 7th Rhode Island had never been in battle before
and nervously followed the 6th New Hampshire's lead. Crossing the open
plain, the regiments drew a tremendous amount of fire. A bullet hit Michael
Kerr of the 7th Rhode Island in the head and cut "a horribly ragged hole
in his right temple." Friends gasped as his face turned purple. Somehow he
recovered. A shell caught Lieutenant Colonel Welcome B. Sayles in the chest
and completely eviscerated him. Sayles' viscera soaked Colonel Zenas R. Bliss
twenty feet away. The commander of the 7th Rhode Island was "sprinkled
from head to foot with blood and pieces of his lung."[79]

The troops became increasingly angry as they advanced. One diarist alleged that the men neither asked nor offered quarter, provided they could
take the stone wall. The 6th New Hampshire and 7th Rhode Island reached
the swale and took cover. Most of the soldiers hid in the entrance lane to
Mercer Square. Five minutes later, blood-spattered Colonel Bliss gave the
order, "Let them have it."[80]

The 7th Rhode Island troops loaded its weapons and went to the front of the swale to fire. The inexperienced color guard accompanied them and was shot to pieces. The small regimental flag soon displayed sixteen bullet holes and a tear from a shell. Bliss ordered the color company to lie down. The colonel took a spare musket and joined the firing line, where a Confederate bullet grazed Bliss and killed the man standing behind him.[81]

The 7th Rhode Island suddenly surged forward and attacked the stone wall. Colonel Joshua Owen ordered his Philadelphia Brigade to join the assault, but before it could move, the Rebels destroyed Nagle's sortie with "a perfect volcano of flame." A 7th Rhode Island man remembered it as "one of the most merciless slaughters of the entire War." Nagle's men reeled back to the fairgrounds. As the Federals tarried by the entrance gate, bullets shivered it to splinters. "None would believe men could bleed so much," one Federal wrote: "Barrels of blood had apparently been poured on the ground along those places." A bullet creased Adjutant Charles F. Page's forehead and mangled his left eye. Joshua Owen realized the futility of a limited assault and ordered the Philadelphia Brigade to lie down again. Most of Nagle's men joined Owen's brigade in the swale and burrowed into the mud bank for cover.[82]

A portion of the 12th Rhode Island regiment broke through the left of Owen's brigade and fled to the rear. The frightened soldiers yelled, "Retreat! Retreat!" which caused the 127th Pennsylvania to panic. The colonel of the 127th Pennsylvania, William W. Jennings, fell wounded twice at that moment. The new regiment broke at the blood-curdling din of the Rebel yell. One Northerner called the Southern taunt an "unearthly, fiendish yell, such as no other troops or civilized being ever uttered . . . as dissonant as the 'Indian war-whoop,' and more terrible."[83]

The flight of two regiments left "a large gap" between Sturgis' Ninth Corps division and Couch's Second Corps. Without field officers to help him, Colonel Bliss was powerless to stop the 7th Rhode Island's retreat. Wounded Colonel Jennings of the 127th Pennsylvania got lost in the confusion, as did his regimental colors. The color-bearer had been killed and left behind. Sergeant William E. Schaeffer rescued both the colors and the colonel and brought them off the field. Meanwhile, the mob of Northerners splashed back across the millrace. Confederate artillery hurried them on their way. A shell burst behind John F. Kerper of the 127th Pennsylvania and blew him "over the bridge." Landing in the water, the terrified youth clambered underneath the bridge struts for protection. A dozen more soon joined him, all of them standing in water waist deep. Lieutenant Colonel Henry C. Alleman and Major Jeremiah Rohrer checked most of the 127th Pennsylvania at the millrace. They reorganized the men in the ravine, and remained there for the rest of the battle.[84]

The 7th Rhode Island bypassed the roadblock at the millrace and flocked into the city on Hanover Street. The throng obstructed Arnold's Battery A, 1st Rhode Island, at Federal Hill, and drew Confederate fire on its position. The battery men tried to curtail the rout, but General Darius Couch thought it was futile. "Let them go," he hollered at the cannoneers, "when they are out of the way, the good men can do something." A Rhode Island artillerist wrote, "The new troops are not worth a D———!"[85]

Just as the Rhode Islanders left the field, Nagle's left wing entered it. Debouching from the unfinished railroad, Nagle tried to wheel into line with the 6th New Hampshire and the remaining portion of the 7th Rhode Island. But confusion marred his advance. The disorganized 12th Rhode Island and 9th New Hampshire maneuvered around the obdurate 2nd Maryland and reached the edge of the plateau only to be plastered with artillery and rifle salvoes. A lieutenant in the 12th Rhode Island wrote, "it seemed to me there was a perfect hurricane of lead howling, screeching and hissing through the air" above his head. He later testified, "I would not answer for my conduct as a soldier at that particular juncture." The 9th New Hampshire scaled the railroad cut and dressed on the left of the Rhode Islanders.[86]

Nagle could not locate his right wing. The 6th New Hampshire and 7th Rhode Island had stopped well short of where Nagle's left wing entered the field. Instead of wheeling to the left, the 12th Rhode Island and the 9th New Hampshire lunged diagonally toward the wall. Under the circumstances, Nagle's left angled toward the Confederate defenses, rather than meeting it head on.

Colonel Browne's 12th Rhode Island moved to the left of a dirt path that connected Frederick Street to the Sunken Road. Confederate fire killed the color-bearer. Lieutenant John P. Abbott took the standard and forged ahead. Color Sergeant Warren N. DeVolve ambled beside him, darkly forecasting, "You will probably fall in a few moments, and I will be ready to take them." Abbott survived DeVolve's prediction and kept the colors for the remainder of the day. A soldier in the 12th Rhode Island recalled, "If ever I prayed in good earnest it was while I was running the gauntlet of those rebel rifle pits." The men slowed down as they tiptoed through the dead, dying, and wounded. Reaching a point one hundred yards from the southern end of Willis Hill, the regiment lay down and opened fire on the Rebels.[87]

The 9th New Hampshire advanced closer to the Confederate heights than anyone else on that part of the field. Unfortunately, the angle of approached exposed it to enfilade fire. A single volley killed and wounded several members of the color guard, including the standard-bearer, Sergeant Edgar Dinsmore. Lieutenant Charles D. Copp grabbed the U.S. flag from the mortally wounded sergeant. Ned Parsons took the state flag. Lieutenant Copp later received the Medal of Honor for his quick retrieval of the downed standard.[88]

The attackers sprinted over "frightful looking corpses." One body had both of its legs shot off and the stumps stuck straight up in the air. A soldier wrote in his diary that evening: "All was hideous, frightful, hellish." Bullets and other "unseen missiles of death" kicked mud and gravel into the men's faces. One soldier reported that so much "mud spattered in my face . . . that I could hardly see." By the time he reached the foot of the heights, he was "smeared with mud and begrimed with powder." Some of the 9th New Hampshire men paused at a fence. Others ventured a short distance beyond it. The advanced group grounded to a halt under a violent sheet of rifle volleys. Federals took cover behind rocks, hummocks, and swales.[89]

While repulsing Ferrero's assault, Joseph Kershaw's ammunition began to run low. "The muskets became so foul," recalled a Carolinian, "that they frequently had to be wiped." Men used their shirts to swab the weapons clean. The acting adjutant of the 24th North Carolina wrote that the Rebels presented an extraordinary appearance. Gunpowder smeared their faces, and he thought "the boys were as black as cork minstrels." Confederates set up relays to pool their ammunition. Soldiers at the wall kept firing while the men behind them loaded rifles and passed them forward. The constant shooting left some of the riflemen "sore for many days." One of them reported, "our shoulders were kicked blue by the muskets." To maintain that kind of fire required a tremendous amount of ammunition, and that concerned Kershaw.[90]

Fortunately, help was on its way. A half hour after Kershaw left for the Sunken Road, the rest of his brigade received orders to follow. The 3rd South Carolina led the march, followed by the 7th and 15th South Carolina. The 3rd South Carolina Battalion stayed behind to picket the Hazel Run valley near Howison's Mill. The column dashed down the Telegraph Road under a heavy artillery fire. One Confederate recollected that the exploding shells "looked like bursting stars on a frolic."[91]

Kershaw's Brigade charged up the back side of Marye's Heights and regrouped behind the Willis family cemetery. Men barely caught their breath before one of Kershaw's aides directed the 3rd South Carolina to "occupy the crest." Immediately afterward, wounded Major Frank Gaillard rode up, "speaking for . . . Kershaw," and giving "substantially the same order." Colonel James D. Nance started the 3rd South Carolina forward at once. Lieutenant Alfred E. Doby hurried them along, exclaiming that the Marye house "was in danger of being possessed by the enemy." The 3rd South Carolina raced across the heights to the mansion. It formed to the left of the house. The 7th South Carolina shifted behind the Marye home. The 15th South Carolina took position to its right and lay down near the Washington Artillery.[92]

Colonel James Nance advanced the 3rd South Carolina next to the 15th North Carolina. Passing in front of the house, the South Carolinians met "a murderous fire from the enemy." A member of the 3rd South Carolina recalled the storm as "the heaviest fire of Artillery and muskets I ever heard." The line charged over a wire or chain fence, and lay down to fire. Nance fell wounded in the thigh. Soldiers dragged him to the Marye mansion. The colonel turned over command to Lieutenant Colonel William D. Rutherford, but refused to go to the hospital. Rutherford fell pierced in the side, and command devolved upon Major Robert C. Maffett. When the major was wounded in the arm, Captain Rutherford P. Todd took over until he too was hit. Captain William W. Hance then assumed the command. The wounded Colonel Nance advised him to retire the 3rd South Carolina a few paces to the chain fence for cover. Hance fell while trying to execute the withdrawal. His successor, Captain John C. Summer, died instantly when a canister round passed through his head. Captain John K. G. Nance became the seventh and final commander of the 3rd South Carolina, and he was already wounded! No wonder Colonel Nance declined to leave his regiment until it was safe. The unit had been badly shot up in a matter of minutes. The brigade historian wrote sadly: "the dead of the Third Regiment lay in heaps, like hogs in a slaughter pen."[93]

The 7th South Carolina advanced to the Marye house and relieved part of the 3rd South Carolina and 15th North Carolina. The reinforcements took cover behind the fence running in front of the house and refused to venture beyond it. Soldiers stood up to fire and then lay down to reload. The 7th South Carolina, correspondingly, had far fewer casualties than the 3rd South Carolina or the 15th North Carolina.[94]

Nagle's brigade sprawled in front of Willis Hill. The right wing stopped on line with Ferrero's and Owen's brigades, and the left wing pivoted forward at an angle. The 2nd Maryland, holding fast to the unfinished railroad cut, served loosely as a hinge between the wings. The brigade absorbed a tremendous fire in front, but the left suddenly came under a new and unwelcomed fire from behind. [95]

Confederate brigadier general Micah Jenkins exacerbated the Ninth Corps' troubles when he shuttled his South Carolina brigade into Kershaw's old position at the foot of Telegraph Hill. Jenkins had seen Kershaw's 3rd South Carolina Battalion annoy the left flank of the Federal attackers, and decided to reinforce the Southrons along Hazel Run. The Palmetto Sharpshooters of South Carolina combined their fire with that of the 3rd South Carolina Battalion and made such an impression that the Federals thought the Southerners had turned their flank and rear. Northerners fidgeted nervously under the Rebel crossfire.[96]

At that same time, General Edward Ferrero found his division commander behind a brick barn on the outskirts of Fredericksburg. General Samuel Sturgis sat propped against the wall, drinking whiskey from a canteen. Ferrero "came in from the front, much excited." The brigade commander reported that his command "was all cut up," and he wanted to know "why in the ———— he did not send them re-inforcements." Sturgis quietly answered, "Oh, I guess not, General; keep cool." He took a gulp from his canteen and offered it to Ferrero. "Take a little of this," he drawled. A Confederate shot just then plunged through the barn, exiting above Sturgis' head. A watching Pennsylvanian recalled, "A solid shot struck the building . . . throwing brickbats amongst them, and covering the party with dust and dirt." Ferrero and the division staff scattered, but Sturgis finished his drink. The division commander then tossed the canteen to Ferrero, and went around the barn to look at the battle. Coming back, he told the commander of the 48th Pennsylvania, "Now is your time, Colonel, go in." Sturgis released a lone regiment into the field for the second time in an hour.[97]

Colonel Joshua K. Sigfried's 48th Pennsylvania marched over the railroad tracks to Prussia Street before leaving the city. His regiment of 311 officers and men halted near the brickyard under fire. Sigfried went ahead to see where to take his regiment. The men lay down behind the brickyard fence to await his return. Solid shot and shell fragments "played a tattoo" on the wall.[98]

Sigfried spotted Jenkins' South Carolinians maneuvering near the Union left flank and thought they were precursors to a Confederate counterstrike. He rushed the 48th Pennsylvania up Frederick Street to combat the supposed attackers. The Pennsylvanians advanced, as one Northerner recollected, "with death staring us in the face as grim as ever any troops met it." Major Wren saw a private "Cut right in 2 pieces with a shell and his insides lay on the ground alongside of him." They met part of Ferrero's brigade near the swale. The 48th Pennsylvania replaced the 21st Massachusetts, which had expended all of its ammunition. The newcomers dispersed along the fold in the ground. Their right rested on the small frame James Jennings' house. The arrival of the 48th Pennsylvania caused Confederate Micah Jenkins to withdraw his skirmishers behind Hazel Run.[99]

Another attempt at the stone wall had failed, at the cost of another thousand casualties added to the Federal tally. Confederate artilleryman E. Porter Alexander estimated that the Union Second Corps lost 4,114 men in four hours—a sobering 1,000 casualties per hour. Incomplete records from Howard's division lack strength or casualty lists. With some approximations, one gets a sense of the division's loss. Howard estimated his division contained 3,500 men. He also counted 914 casualties for the entire campaign. Excluding the almost 300 men lost in the street fighting on December 11, Howard suffered approximately 610 casualties in the assault on Marye's Heights. That equals an 18 percent reduction of his force. The two Harvard regiments—the 19th and 20th Massachusetts—suffered a total of 167 losses, or 34 percent of their combined strengths. Owen's brigade reported only 258 losses. The Philadelphia Brigade historian later wrote, "The total loss in the brigade . . . [was] astonishingly small," even though the 127th Pennsylvania showed the highest regimental loss in the division, with 146 killed, wounded, and missing. Sully's role as a support is clearly reflected in his low mortality rate. He reported only 122 casualties.[100]

Sturgis' division kept somewhat better records of its strengths and losses. Sturgis tallied 1,011 losses among his 4,475 men. The total loss of the division amounted to 23 percent. Ferrero took 2,150 men (assuming the 51st Pennsylvania had approximately 300 effectives) into action, and he lost between 489 and 509 men. The uncertainty arises from disagreements about the number of men considered missing. Nagle claimed that he had 2,700 men in his command, but the individual regimental rosters—assuming a strength of 600 for the 12th Rhode Island—amounted to only 2,325. Part of the difference may result from the men lost to campaign attrition, sickness, or detachments to other duties. Nagle reported the loss of 522 men, but the individual regiments tallied 696 casualties. Differences arise again over the counting of the missing. The two brigades split the division casualties almost evenly, reflecting equal involvement in the battle.[101]

Howard's and Sturgis' divisions had failed to press their attacks with the urgency, or the ferocity, of the previous assaults. Instead, they husbanded their resources and used them to stabilize the existing line of battle. Part of this caution stemmed from the fact that almost all the troops in Fredericksburg now had been committed to the battle. Only Piatt's small Third Corps brigade—coupled with the 71st Pennsylvania and 8th Illinois Cavalry—covered the northern half of the city. Getty's two-brigade division of the Ninth Corps, and Colonel Samuel Sprigg Carroll's small Third Corps brigade, protected the extreme southern end of Fredericksburg. Just two regiments—the 1st Minnesota, and the 12th New Hampshire of Carroll's brigade—held the center of the city, the equivalent of six city blocks. Burnside needed to reinforce the city's defense and maintain pressure on Marye's Heights. He ordered General Joseph Hooker's Center Grand Division to cross the river and attack.

The Second Corps commander, Darius Couch, had sent an urgent appeal to the artillerist Henry Hunt for rifled artillery. Couch's smoothbore Napoleons were no match for the Rebel guns on Marye's Heights. Hunt received Couch's request between 1:30 and 2:00 P.M. He sent two batteries across the river under Major Alexander Doull of his staff. Doull took Captain Charles Kusserow's Battery D, 1st Battalion, New York Light Artillery, and Captain Richard Waterman's Battery C, 1st Rhode Island Light Artillery. They crossed at the upper pontoon crossing. Brigadier General Amiel W. Whipple's Third Corps division independently contributed a battery of its own.[102]

General Whipple had split his division, sending brigades to either end of Fredericksburg. One reported to the Ninth Corps, and the other guarded the northern end of the city. Two batteries, under Captains Albert A. von Puttkammer and John T. Bruen, idled near the river. Whipple sensed that the tide had turned against the Federal artillery. He hurried von Puttkammer's 11th New York Artillery to the western edge of the city. Von Puttkammer placed two 3-inch rifles on the corner of Amelia Street and Charles Street, and another two a block south on William Street. Bruen's 10th New York Light Artillery remained in reserve because it contained only smoothbores.[103]

Major Doull reported with his rifled pieces right after von Puttkammer became engaged. Couch directed Doull to the Mary Washington monument.

Waterman's artillery went into battery in front of the Gordon house, known as Kenmore. Kusserow's gunners unlimbered to Waterman's right. Richard Waterman's Battery C, 1st Rhode Island, fired rapidly for an hour before tapering off to a more deliberate pace. Kusserow's New York artillery maintained a disciplined, steady fire from the start. As a result, Waterman ran out of ammunition and had to beg for more. Von Puttkammer's battery shared some of their caissons with Rhode Islanders.[104]

Waterman estimated that he fired more than 400 rounds. Kusserow expended 600 rounds. Counterbattery fire cost Waterman one man and four horses; and Kusserow, seven men and one horse. Waterman also reported the loss of one of his 3-inch rifles, which he sent to the rear with a broken axle. The artillerist noted "the very frequent fractures of gun axles of the 3-inch guns." He thought the gun was largely inferior to the 10-pounder Parrott. Second Corps artillery chief Captain Morgan, on the other hand, believed the rifled batteries had rendered invaluable service by offsetting part of the Confederates' great advantage. The three rifled batteries did not turn the tide of battle to the Federals' favor, but they did stabilize the right flank so Couch no longer feared a Confederate counterattack. The addition of artillery on the northern limits of Fredericksburg also gave the Federals a chance to reinforce and expand their picket lines.[105]

Brigadier General A. Sanders Piatt advanced his brigade to the upper reaches of the millrace and the Fredericksburg canal. The 122nd Pennsylvania marched north along the Fall Hill road. Heavy artillery fire forced it to take shelter behind a paper mill and a small cluster of houses. The 124th New York stretched the picket line south from the mouth of the millrace. The 86th New York and 12th New Hampshire extended the line to the left. The operation was unexceptional, but fraught with danger. Confederate sharpshooters became more aggressive, and Piatt feared that he might provoke a counterattack after all. He brought up Captain John T. Bruen's 10th New York Light Battery to drive the Confederates away from the canal. Bruen set up guns at the ends of Charles Street and Prince Edward Street, facing north. While Piatt rode along his picket line, he attempted to jump a gully. His horse stumbled, the saddle shifted, and the general fell flat on his back. The fall dislocated Piatt's back so that he could not move without extreme pain. Stretcher-bearers carted him to the rear, and Colonel Emlen Franklin took over his brigade. The fire dwindled in front and the crisis passed. "We lay down awaiting the order to charge," wrote an officer in the brand-new 124th New York, "but, fortunately . . . it never came."[106]

The addition of rifled artillery to the Federal right may have bolstered the Northern soldiers' morale against a retaliatory Confederate attack, but four batteries could not stop the overall Union right wing from collapsing. Fortunately, Major General Joseph Hooker's Center Grand Division already had started for Fredericksburg. Hooker's reinforcements offered the Right Grand Division a chance to fall back and regroup. Hooker intended to shield Sumner's tired legions, but Burnside had other plans.

CHAPTER TWELVE

"THE DIE IS CAST"

Deep Run and Griffin's Attack

Ambrose Burnside paced in front of the Phillips House, "his saber clattering on the gravel." Concern deepened as the army commander watched wave after wave of Union attackers pour out of Fredericksburg and melt away before the Confederate fire. The crisis absorbed Burnside's full attention, leaving him no time to concentrate on his primary assault. He had listened to the telegraphic messages from Franklin's front, but sent nothing in return. Burnside later told an investigative committee: "I confess I did not think of that part of the field as much as I should have done." The instability of the Fredericksburg front required almost all of his time. News of Meade's and Gibbon's repulse stunned Burnside. He suddenly faced the possibility of defeat. The general sent an aide, Captain James M. Cutts, to Franklin to encourage another assault at once. Anticipating Franklin's compliance, Burnside reinforced the Fredericksburg front. Joseph Hooker would strengthen his fragile front and hopefully re-ignite his diversionary assaults.[1]

William Franklin's front simmered after the repulse of John F. Reynolds' First Corps. Meade and Taylor rallied their divisions behind the Smithfield ravine. Men collected their knapsacks—and noticed how many went unclaimed. George Meade seethed at the loss. Reynolds tried to soothe him, but the implacable division commander snarled, "My God General Reynolds, did they think my division could whip Lee's entire army?" Meade retired to

Franklin's headquarters, where inquirers foolishly asked how he had fared. He showed them his bullet-ruined hat and rejoined acidly, "I found it quite hot for me."[2]

Burnside's aide arrived soon afterward. He found Franklin busily splicing a defensive line together, rather than preparing for another attack. Franklin complained that he needed the entire Left Grand Division—and Birney's division of the Third Corps—just to hold his position. Two brigades of William W. Burns' Ninth Corps' division—Orlando M. Poe's and Daniel Leasure's—had taken position in front of the Bernard house to protect the lower pontoon crossing. General John Newton's Sixth Corps division shifted to the left to cover the Bowling Green Road by Smithfield. Newton stacked his brigades in a gap that had developed between Berry's brigade and Robinson's brigade of Birney's division. At the same time, a large interval remained open between Birney's left and Doubleday's right. Only Wolcott's Battery A, 1st Maryland, covered the gap. A similar opening yawned between Birney's right and the left of Howe's Sixth Corps division. The only reserves Franklin had against a Confederate attack were two brigades of Burns' division. Under the circumstances, Franklin thought it would be foolish to attack. Captain Cutts started back to headquarters to give Burnside the disappointing news. Franklin's decision, however, was not entirely in his hands.[3]

Union and Confederate pickets skirmished most of the day for control of Deep Run. Early in the morning, the 15th New Jersey, a large, untested regiment, had infiltrated the brushy ravine of Deep Run. Following Gibbon's repulse, General William Dorsey Pender sent the 16th North Carolina to reoccupy the area. The 16th North Carolina came abreast of the hidden Federals and received a surprise volley in the flank. Pender's Confederates quickly backed away to the railroad. The minor fracas lasted only a few moments, and both sides settled back into quiet.[4]

General William "Baldy" Smith had witnessed the incident and asked one of his division commanders, General William "Bully" Brooks, to reinforce the skirmish line south of the creek. Smith hoped that this would discourage the Confederates from threatening the 15th New Jersey's flank. Brooks told Brigadier General Alfred T. A. Torbert to strengthen his hold on Deep Run.[5]

Brooks thought a regiment, with another in support, could secure the picket line south of Deep Run. If it required assistance, the division commander gave Torbert permission to use the rest of his brigade. Brooks also lent Torbert two regiments from General David A. Russell's brigade. Brooks and Torbert selected Colonel William B. Hatch's 4th New Jersey to execute the order. The 15th New Jersey would act in support.[6]

Colonel Hatch strode in front of the 4th New Jersey and waved them forward. "Come on boys," he shouted, "follow me." The 4th Regiment—300 strong—sprang after the colonel. Northern troops scrambled across Deep Run and surged toward the railroad. The 16th North Carolina, ensconced behind the embankment, blazed away at the attackers. Captain Joseph W. Latimer's Confederate artillery swung around to join the fight. Torbert reported that Hatch's 4th New Jersey "advanced in a handsome manner under a severe fire." Several companies of the 15th New Jersey, under Major James M. Brown, left the cover of Deep Run to support Hatch's right. Northerners overran the railroad embankment at the moment when the 16th North Carolina expended its last cartridge. Confederates broke and fled before the onslaught. Many of them stampeded right through Latimer's cannon. Others thronged around Greenlee Davidson's guns. Some of the Rebels believed that retreat meant almost certain death. Quite a few of them lay down and played dead to avoid being shot or captured. Colonel Hatch mounted the railroad and loudly announced, "Boys! three cheers for our side!" The bluecoats erupted with huzzahs. The time approached 3:00 P.M.[7]

The instant success of Hatch's sortie surprised both sides. Federals suddenly discovered Latimer's cannon glaring at them from the reverse slope of a knoll, two hundred yards away. The New Jersey soldiers concentrated their fire on the artillery. The abrupt flight of the 16th North Carolina dismayed several Confederate units posted in the woods behind Latimer's knoll. Brigadier General Evander McIver Law, commanding a brigade in John B. Hood's division, had been advised to assist Pender's Brigade whenever he was needed. Law imagined that the entire picket line had collapsed when the fugitives of the 16th North Carolina inundated his lines. His concern grew when Federal sharpshooters "annoyed the artillerymen so much they could not handle their guns." Law promptly advanced his brigade to the support of Latimer's artillery.[8]

Joseph Latimer watched in disgust as the 16th North Carolina abandoned him. He could not hold his position without supports. The Yankees laid down such a heavy fire that he could not remove his pieces either. Gun crews abandoned the cannon and ran for cover. Latimer spotted Law's Brigade in the treeline behind him. He bounded across the field furiously waving his cap. The artilleryman appeared "very excited," as he reined in front of the infantry. "Don't come up here," Latimer shouted, "unless you will promise to support me." Latimer complained that the 16th North Carolina had deserted him. "Go back, Captain, to your battery," the foot soldiers assured him, "this is the old 4th Alabama." "Thank God, I am safe," Latimer allegedly answered as he hurried back to rally his command.[9]

Law marshaled his brigade along the timberline immediately behind Latimer's guns. He hoped his presence there would force the New Jersey troops to back away from the artillery. If that failed, the general intended to attack. Law's Brigade had two Alabama regiments—the 4th and 44th—along with the veteran 6th North Carolina. Two unblooded regiments recently had joined the brigade to boost its strength. The colonels of the 54th and 57th North Carolina petitioned Law for the honor to lead the attack if it became necessary. For the moment, Law moved the whole brigade closer to Latimer's knoll, trusting that the bluecoats would back down.[10]

Law's Brigade lay down on the slope behind the Confederate artillery. Several regiments sent companies ahead to skirmish. They immediately became "hotly engaged." The Southern skirmishers quickly retreated behind the hill. The Yankees had no intention of retreating. In fact, everyone in Law's Brigade watched the rise, anticipating a Union counterattack. "We were in great suspense," recalled a member of the 4th Alabama. But the Union troops never advanced beyond the tracks.[11]

Law ordered the 54th and 57th North Carolina to sweep the Yankees from the railroad. The general accompanied the new regiments past the abandoned cannon and over the knoll. Colonel Archibald C. Godwin's 57th North Carolina assumed the right of the line, and Colonel James C. S. McDowell's 54th North Carolina kept pace on the left. The force possessed approximately 900 men and outnumbered the Federals almost two to one. As they topped Latimer's knoll, the Carolinians received a severe musketry. Nervous recruits slowed down and returned a spattering fire. A portion of the 16th North Carolina, trapped between the lines, was caught in the crossfire. Pender's officers dashed into Law's lines, and diverted their fire away from the 16th North Carolina, caustically telling the 57th North Carolina to "distribute their favors" elsewhere. Independent of Law's movement, the right of Brigadier General George T. "Tige" Anderson's brigade also joined the imbroglio. The 8th Georgia left its position along a Virginia ditch fence and fired across the Deep Run ravine at Torbert's right.[12]

When Law's Confederates closed to within 125 yards of the railroad, the brigadier ordered them to charge. Colonel Godwin seized the colors of the 57th North Carolina and plunged ahead. The regiment responded immediately. Colonel McDowell's 54th North Carolina kept close, but lagged behind. A Texan in Robertson's Brigade called the attack "the prettiest sight I ever saw."[13]

Archibald Godwin planted his standard on the railroad and the 57th North Carolina swarmed into the ditches around him. Southerners fired steadily at the Federals across the railroad embankment, with less than thirty yards between them. The Yankees grudgingly began to yield with heavy casualties. A North Carolinian reported that "the blood flowed as from a butchered hog." A New Jersey soldier agreed that "it was an awful place for me to go."[14]

The fury of the Confederate response startled Alfred Torbert. He immediately asked his division commander for reinforcements. Bully Brooks sent Colonel Henry O. Ryerson's 23rd New Jersey. Several companies of Colonel Henry W. Brown's 3rd New Jersey may have attached themselves inadvertently to Ryerson's column. Latimer's Confederate guns jumped into the action and hit the reinforcements with a scathing fire. Men started dropping as the column filed across Deep Run. In their haste to support Torbert, the 23rd New Jersey soldiers failed to unload their knapsacks and other impedimenta. The column waded through the creek, toting heavy loads, which greatly handicapped their mobility and speed. The sluggish Northerners made an excellent target for Latimer's cannon. A New Jersey soldier complained that the officers "took us in bad."[15]

Even as the 23rd New Jersey trudged forward, Sixth Corps commander William F. Smith reconsidered escalating the battle. He warned William Brooks "that a general engagement might be brought on" if they added more troops. Baldy Smith had not bargained on that. He ordered Torbert's reinforcements to withdraw. The 23rd New Jersey had advanced to within sight of the 4th and 15th New Jersey regiments before Smith's orders stopped it. The 4th New Jersey, and a couple of companies of the 15th New Jersey, were left unaided to handle a mismatched struggle with two Confederate regiments.[16]

Colonel William Hatch's troops relinquished the railroad, and the 4th New Jersey backpedaled to safety. The Confederates surged across the tracks in pursuit. Hatch saw them and ordered his regiment to halt and about-face. The Federals fired a volley into the Rebels. The Carolinians replied, and William Hatch collapsed, mortally wounded, his right leg destroyed. Lieutenant Colonel James N. Duffy assumed command, but the 4th New Jersey broke before he could take over. The 15th New Jersey contingent, under Major

James Brown, scampered back to the ravine along Deep Run. The men carried Major Brown with them. A Confederate ball had passed through his thigh, and the bluecoats evacuated him down Deep Run.[17]

General Torbert watched the fiasco. He appealed to the 23rd New Jersey for help. Colonel Ryerson's command had started to withdraw, on Baldy Smith's orders, but Torbert begged Ryerson to cover the routed 4th New Jersey. The tired soldiers, laden with packs, turned to face Law's assault. Ryerson's Jerseymen fired several volleys into the Carolinians, and then fell back a short distance, only to turn and fire again. The bluecoats, unable to stay the onslaught, continued to give ground. One of Torbert's soldiers recalled that the retreat "was a more difficult movement to execute than the advance."[18]

Seeing the Yankees flushed "like wild turkeys," the excited Confederates pursued them on the run. Colonel Godwin's 57th North Carolina chased after the broken 4th New Jersey, while McDowell's 54th North Carolina followed farther to the left. When the 23rd New Jersey tried to blunt the attack, the 57th North Carolina tore the Yankees to pieces. The 23rd New Jersey reeled in disorder. A Northerner rejoiced in his salvation: "I don't know how we ever got out with our lives." Many of the Northerners discarded their knapsacks to lighten their load and hasten their escape. Even the tempting prize of new packs failed to deter the Confederate charge.[19]

Evander Law's Confederates advanced to within three hundred yards of the Bowling Green Road. Unknowingly, they had charged the weakest seam in Franklin's defenses. The Confederates were headed for the large gap between David B. Birney's Third Corps division and Albion P. Howe's division of the Sixth Corps. Birney later testified that the area had been left "without a soldier, without a man." General Albion Howe's division stood three brigades deep next to Deep Run. Francis Vinton's brigade, now commanded by Brigadier General Thomas H. Neill, formed the front line. Brigadier General Calvin E. Pratt's brigade held the second line, and Colonel Henry Whiting's Vermont brigade made the third.

Ahead of them, five batteries stood on the crest of a ridge. A thin veil of skirmishers from Lieutenant Colonel Charles H. Joyce's 2nd Vermont roamed in front. Artillery could have decimated the 54th and 57th North Carolina, but the stampeding New Jerseymen blocked their fire. The Confederates thus rushed ahead while sustaining very little damage. No one occupied the ground to Law's right front, so the Federals could not offer even an oblique fire.[20]

Just as quickly as the gap opened, it snapped shut. Franklin had summoned Sickles' division from the pontoon bridges for a completely unrelated purpose. Serendipity sent the reinforcements to the gap just as Law's Rebels closed in. Brigadier General Daniel Edgar Sickles, a rakish politico, lothario, and gloryseeker, drove his column across the fields toward the front with an expertise that belied his recent appointment to division command. He led three brigades, but one of them—Brigadier General Joseph B. Carr's—had been stripped of almost all of its strength. Carr had detached four regiments to guard the lower pontoon crossing. He advanced only two regiments—a meager one-third of his command. Colonel George B. Hall's "Excelsior Brigade" came next, followed by Brigadier General Joseph W. Revere's brigade. George Hall had lost a third of his command to various support assignments. He commanded four regiments. Lieutenant Francis W. Seeley's Battery K, 4th U.S. Artillery, and Lieutenant Justin E. Dimick's Battery H, 1st U.S. Artillery, accompanied the division.[21]

The Third Corps commander, George Stoneman, sent several aides to hurry Sickles. Stoneman's assistant adjutant general met Carr's brigade coming over the bridge and ordered it to Howe's support at once. Sickles himself set out to find Howe. He wandered too far to the right and mired down near the mouth of Deep Run. The general finally found Howe's position and shifted his division across the spacious lawn of the Bernard house. Sickles then consulted with Stoneman while his command filled the slot between Howe and Birney. Sickles wheeled his men into line with a surprising amount of dexterity. Carr's truncated brigade took the right. With only two regiments, Carr placed Lieutenant Colonel Benjamin C. Tilghman's 26th Pennsylvania on the left and Lieutenant Colonel Clark B. Baldwin's 1st Massachusetts on the right. George Hall's Excelsior Brigade extended Carr's left to connect with Ward's brigade of Birney's division. His regimental alignment cannot be determined from the evidence available at this time. Sickles held Joseph Revere—a descendant of the Revolutionary War figure—in reserve behind Carr. Lieutenant Seeley's U.S. battery unlimbered in a one-hundred-yard space between Carr's and Hall's brigades. Lieutenant Justin E. Dimick's Battery H, 1st U.S. Artillery, waited in reserve behind Revere's brigade.[22]

Sickles' troops swung into line just as the remnants of Torbert's New Jersey regiments stampeded to the rear. Northern artillerists sprang to their guns as soon as the bluecoats cleared their muzzles. Two Vermont regiments advanced to reinforce the 2nd Vermont skirmish line after the mob had passed Whiting's brigade. The 4th Vermont curled around the end of the long line of batteries and took position on the right of the 2nd Vermont. Whiting also forwarded the 5th and 3rd Vermont to the right of Pratt's brigade. The front line lay down behind the rise to wait for the Rebels to come closer. When the Southerners appeared, the men jumped up and poured a volley into them. Rifle fire meshed with artillery to stun the oncoming North Carolinians. The arrival of Sickles' division added an oblique fire that tore into the Confederate flank. The gap in the Federal line, and the fleeing New Jerseymen, had drawn Law's Southerners close to the Bowling Green Road; but the suddenly unmasked cannon, combined with Howe's skirmishers and Sickles' division, ensured a painful rebuff. Two regiments of Confederates had ventured too far before they realized they had blundered into two divisions.[23]

Evander Law tried in vain to check his explosive Carolinians. Chasing after them, Law's horse tumbled wounded and pinned the general to the ground. Law's aide, Lieutenant Virginius Smith, dashed ahead to restore order, but he fell dead. The attackers rushed on without their leader. Only the unexpected deluge of Yankee fire tempered their ardor. Confederates took instant and staggering losses. One company of the 57th North Carolina lost 40 of its 60 men. Law's men returned the fire, but the Federals had superb cover. Smith's Sixth Corps and Sickles' division hid behind the heavy banks of the Bowling Green Road, and the 15th New Jersey blended into the thickets of Deep Run.[24]

Law freed himself from his mount and re-joined the North Carolinians on the ridge overlooking the Bowling Green Road. He ordered his men back, and they reluctantly obliged. The 57th North Carolina covered the retreat, and the Federals did not pursue. Meanwhile, the rest of Law's Brigade took position along the railroad in front of Latimer's guns. One Alabamian recalled, "The men moved in a bad line." Shellfire discouraged them from joining the 54th and 57th North Carolina. Little did the Federals realize, but Hood had sent the brigade forward with orders to cover Law's retreat. The entire action had lasted fifteen minutes.[25]

General George E. Pickett flew to John B. Hood as soon as Law's Brigade charged past Latimer's guns. He suggested excitedly that they should join the assault, but Hood preferred to withdraw Law's North Carolinians. Longstreet, unaware of the situation, privately censured Hood for his seeming torpidity. The corps commander barely mentioned the event in his official report. He explained later, "the truth is our success was so handsome that I did not care to mar the enjoyment of it by making official trouble."[26]

Hood's veterans greeted the returning Carolinians with "a yell from our

side that made the very earth tremble." Dejected Tar Heels ignored the accla-
mation, assuming that they had failed in their very first attack. They cried
in disgrace. One frustrated Carolinian wrote, "Durn ole Hood." Despite the
division commander's lofty commendations, rumors persisted that Hood had
"no confidence" in the North Carolinians. One bloodied former novice
grumbled, "If we had been some of his Texans he would have let us go on."
The two regiments never reflected on the impossible odds or the intimidating
loss of 270 men. They focused only on the possibility of what might have
been.[27]

Across the battlefield, William Franklin and Baldy Smith also pondered
that scenario. The unexpected Confederate attack made them acutely sensitive to the slightest conflict. Torbert's insignificant effort to restore a picket
line had provoked a powerful counterstroke. The fortuitous arrival of Sickles'
division had prevented a more grievous situation. The encounter had shaken
the Federal commanders, and when Burnside's orders arrived demanding action, Franklin dismissed them out of hand. For the remainder of the day, the
terminally cautious Franklin maintained a strict tactical defensive. The Federals put all of their effort into building a defensive perimeter along the Bowling
Green Road. Quiet again reigned on the fields south of Fredericksburg.

As yet, unaware of Franklin's refusal, Burnside assumed that his Left Grand
Division would renew the offensive below Fredericksburg. To ensure Franklin's success, he mobilized the remainder of Joseph Hooker's Center Grand
Division—Brigadier General Daniel Butterfield's Fifth Corps—and ordered
it against Marye's Heights.

Butterfield's corps consisted of three divisions. The 1st Division, under
Brigadier General Charles Griffin, bivouacked near the middle pontoon
crossing at the boyhood home of George Washington. The 2nd Division,
commanded by Brigadier General George Sykes, held a position above Falmouth, watching the Union far right. The 3rd Division, the untested Pennsylvania command of Brigadier General Andrew A. Humphreys, rested in the
fields next to Burnside's headquarters. Burnside ordered Hooker to put the
Fifth Corps in motion at once. The response unfolded unevenly, as Hooker
forwarded the order to Butterfield, and the Fifth Corps commander sent staff
officers pounding across Stafford Heights. As a result, some divisions received
the directive faster than others. Griffin's division responded first.[28]

Griffin's division had watched the Right Grand Division's attacks against
Marye's Heights. Each assault, according to the well-publicized Lieutenant

Colonel Joshua L. Chamberlain of the 20th Maine, was "swallowed up in the earth, the bright flags quenched in gloom, and only the writhing mass marking the high tide halt." Griffin's division chafed to move. Chamberlain recollected: "We waited in tremulous expectation. . . . If the worst is coming, let us meet it." An officer in the 44th New York muttered aloud, "I would consent to give my right arm to be assured that I could escape this day's peril with my life." Most of the soldiers studied the battle in sullen quiet. Captain Ellis Spear of the 20th Maine wrote, "I think few had any hope of success. For my part, I went in simply to do my duty without enthusiasm or even hope." The more astute soldiers listened for the battle on the left and asked, "For God's sake, where is Franklin?!" Perhaps Burnside should have wondered as well, or perhaps he anticipated an explosion of activity at any moment.[29]

General Butterfield ordered Griffin to cross the middle pontoon bridge shortly after 2:30 P.M. Charles Griffin, a salty old Regular whom the men nicknamed the "King of the War Dogs," gave the men "a searching, wistful look," before leading them over the bridge. Men thumped across the wooden span and received a rude welcome to the city. A wounded man, clutching his neck, jostled the column and sprayed blood on the Fifth Corps soldiers. He gurgled for help, but the frightened newcomers shied away. "No one dared to lend him the assistance which he needed and beseechingly implored," recalled a member of the 22nd Massachusetts.[30]

Butterfield met the head of Griffin's division at the bridge and sent it to Caroline Street. Colonel James Barnes' brigade hurried up the Rocky Lane to the next block. A passing soldier described the rough-hewn road as "a rocky street leading up through two stone-faced walls." The brigade filed right onto Caroline Street and rested under cover of the houses. Lieutenant Eugene Carter, a U.S. Regular officer on Butterfield's staff, searched the column for his two brothers, knowing they would soon be engaged. Tears smeared his cheek as he admitted, "I pray God to save them . . . I shall never live a happy moment if they are killed."[31]

Barnes' brigade muscled through a confused sea of soldiery. "I could see nothing but soldiers," a Pennsylvanian wrote. Others saw long rows of dead men "with their coat tails over their faces." Wounded soldiers streamed past, some wearing the unmistakable boxwood sprigs of the Irish Brigade. The ever-present Rebel artillery rounds crashed into buildings all along the block, dumping bricks, window shutters, and shingles on the men. "It is seldom . . . that the metal [*sic*] of men is tested in column in crowded streets, where there can be no resistance," recollected a Pennsylvania man. Lieutenant Colonel James Gwyn commanded the 118th Pennsylvania—nicknamed the "Corn Exchange" regiment after its bank-sponsor in Philadelphia. Gwyn kept his men busy by drilling them in the manual of arms. Once he had acclimated the troops to their situation, the colonel ordered them to load their weapons. When one youth fumbled several times trying to cap his piece, an older soldier suggested to a lieutenant: "It was a darn shame to take this boy into the fight as he could not load his gun." The embarrassed soldier protested, "Oh yes I can!"[32]

Lieutenant Colonel Gwyn's exercise may have pacified the 118th Pennsylvania, but a Confederate shell ironically made the men forget their fears altogether. The round upset a wooden stoop on a nearby house and revealed crates of tobacco hidden underneath. The men rushed the house and plundered the weed. Gwyn sharply rebuked the men for breaking ranks but may have smiled inwardly at their enthusiasm—he would need that soon enough.[33]

Daniel Butterfield ordered Griffin's division to advance and support Sturgis' Ninth Corps troops at 3:30 P.M. Butterfield, however, modified the order before Griffin could move. The Fifth Corps commander wanted the 1st Division to relieve Sturgis rather than support him. Colonel James Barnes, commander of Griffin's 1st Brigade, prepared to go first. He formed his troops with the 18th Massachusetts on the right, followed by the 25th New York, 13th New York, 118th Pennsylvania, 1st Michigan, 22nd Massachusetts, and 2nd Maine.[34]

Colonel Barnes' brigade marched out Princess Elizabeth Street and Frederick Street south of the railroad. Griffin and Barnes sat on horseback and watched the column file past. One Pennsylvanian stared back, noting that Barnes "was intently observing the temper and bearing of his soldiers."[35]

Barnes' brigade emerged from the city under shellfire. "The roar was deafening," wrote one soldier; "shot and shell screeched in maddening sounds . . . dropping with wonderful accuracy." The first shot hit three members of the 22nd Massachusetts. The shell plunged through the chest of Private William H. Mudgett and passed out his back, splattering his lungs on his comrades. Incredibly, Mudgett survived! Part of Barnes' difficulty came from the proximity of Thomas' Battery A, 4th U.S. Artillery, which drew fire on the locale. The Northern guns "were pounding away," according to one of Barnes' soldiers, "in spite of the severe punishment they were receiving."[36]

Wary new enlistees of the 118th Pennsylvania noticed a number of skulk-

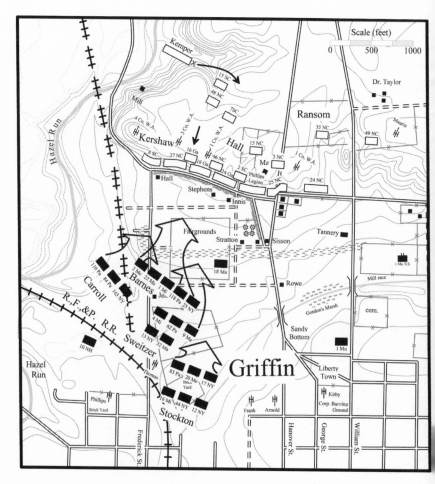

Griffin's Assault

ers hiding in the city. "Their conduct was no incentive and their presence no encouragement," recollected one of Barnes' men. As the regiment passed under a sign advertising "Van Haugen's Variety Shop," a solid shot ripped the sign from its hinges and flung it over their heads. The debris landed in the ranks of the 1st Michigan. Another shell maimed 16 soldiers in the Michigan unit. Their shrieks echoed in the street and undermined morale. "We are no fools!" protested a Pennsylvania soldier. "We can see when we have a chance; here we had none." Yet Barnes' column continued to file out of Fredericksburg and into the millrace depression.[37]

The brigade waded through the millrace. Men struggled to keep their feet against the swift current. Some fell down because of the uneven bottom. Others tripped over unexploded Confederate ordnance. Once across, Union troops scaled a high retaining wall. Others shivered in the millrace until they were hoisted free.[38]

Barnes' right rested on the RF&P Railroad. The rest of the brigade formed on the level ground to the left. The center of Barnes' command stretched across the muddy confines of Knight's brickyard. Large stacks of brick and a shot-torn kiln left little room for the Federals to maneuver. The brigade's attempt to realign caused a delay that paralyzed the Fifth Corps' movements.[39]

Charles Griffin charged into the brickyard to get Barnes' brigade moving. An admiring Massachusetts soldier wrote of Griffin: "He was omnipresent, cool, quick, magnetic, and inspiring." The division commander snapped at Barnes to extend his right across the railroad, and spread the brigade front. At the same time, Griffin silenced Thomas' battery to relieve some of the fire on the spot. Sometime during this interval, the general received a slight wound, making him the second-highest-ranking Union officer hit at Fredericksburg. Griffin refused to leave his command and nursed his wound surreptitiously. As Barnes' brigade crossed the tracks, the division commander announced, "There goes one of my brigades to hell and the other two will soon follow."[40]

Lieutenant Colonel Joseph Hayes led his 18th Massachusetts over the railroad tracks and along the west bank of the millrace as far as he could go. He moved several hundred yards and halted on the spot where he thought Barnes wanted him. The rest of Barnes' brigade uncoiled after Hayes. But a large gap developed between the 18th Massachusetts and the next regiment in line, the 25th New York. The New Yorkers had crossed the railroad, but inexplicably stopped just beyond the tracks. The commander of the 18th Massachusetts reported seeing the rest of the brigade draw up short of his position, but he felt compelled to stay where he was because Barnes and Griffin had designated his location. Barnes later complained that Hayes had exceeded his directions and advanced too far from the rest of the brigade. It appears that the Massachusetts colonel's definition of "as far as possible to the right" differed from the brigade commander's. The intense artillery barrage probably further exacerbated the miscommunication, as Barnes executed the move in a hurried fashion.[41]

Once it had assumed its position, the 18th Massachusetts lay down along the sluiceway. Shells occasionally landed in the ravine. Corporal Richard H.

Holmes stepped out of ranks sheepishly and saluted his commander with his left hand. He asked Colonel Hayes for permission to go to the rear as he apologetically held up a bloody stump where his right arm used to be. The rest of the regiment sat tight, fixed bayonets, and waited for orders to attack.[42]

Griffin found it increasingly difficult to coordinate Barnes' widely separated wings. He sent one of Barnes' aides, Lieutenant Walter S. Davis, to order the 18th Massachusetts to advance. The staff officer told Lieutenant Colonel Hayes, "The General says you may charge if you want to." Hayes did not recognize this as a mandate and answered, "When I have orders." Griffin immediately accosted Hayes, "Colonel, I want some one to charge." Hayes stood his ground and repeated, "I will charge when I have orders." Having run out of patience, Griffin moved to the center of the regiment and personally ordered it to charge.[43]

The 18th Massachusetts scrambled out of the millrace depression. "Now it was neck or nothing," wrote one of Hayes' soldiers. Northerners crammed into line, touched elbows, and billowed across the muddy plateau. Unfortunately, Griffin had sent the 18th Massachusetts into action before the rest of Barnes' brigade was ready. For the third time on December 13, a single regiment entered the field alone. Hayes' command would not see Barnes' brigade again for the rest of the battle.[44]

Lieutenant Colonel Hayes' 18th Massachusetts made a beeline for the Stratton house. Southern shot riddled the regiment. Hayes lamented that his regiment "melted away as we advanced." To a Massachusetts soldier "It seemed that none could live in such a storm of Bulletts." The 18th Massachusetts received the full attention of the Confederate line. The colonel reported, "their whole fire seemed now to be directed upon us." The 18th Massachusetts passed to the left of the brick house and stopped dead against the northeast corner of the fairgrounds.[45]

The 18th hid behind the wall even though "bullets were coming through this fence as thick as hailstones." When Hayes was ready to move, the men pounded the wall with their musket butts. Confederates hit a number of Yankees as they emerged from the openings. The second-in-command of the regiment, Captain George C. Ruby, fell mortally wounded near the fence; in the confusion, his body was never recovered. The 18th Massachusetts forced its way into Mercer Square and tried to re-form on the run. The national and state colors went down several times as both color-bearers fell dead and the entire color guard was hit almost simultaneously. Federals in the swale shouted at the newcomers: "Lie down! You are fools to go any further!" The

18th Massachusetts rattled off three or four volleys before its line collapsed. One Union soldier insisted, "It was utterly impossible" to go beyond this point.[46]

The 18th Massachusetts fled back through the fence and down the slope to the millrace before Colonel Hayes could rally them. The colonel fashioned a semblance of order out of his bloodied regiment. Hayes estimated that he had lost more than half of his command by that time. Joseph Hayes calmed his men with a short address, and then led them back to the front. The troops responded with surprisingly boisterous cheers as they left the millrace. By now, the rest of Barnes' brigade had launched an attack of its own.[47]

James Barnes never saw the 18th Massachusetts disappear. He focused instead on getting his brigade clear of the millrace defile. Many of his troops affixed their bayonets on the run. Some of the wiser soldiers cast off their knapsacks and bedrolls to lighten their load. Barnes' brigade obliqued to the right, perhaps in an effort to shorten the distance between itself and the 18th Massachusetts. As the line rolled forward, regiment after regiment spilled across the railroad tracks, and then the unfinished railroad, until they entered the field below Mercer's Square. Southern guns on Telegraph Hill and Howison's Hill vexed Barnes when he crossed the unfinished railroad. His brigade emerged from the cut, coughing and gagging for air, "half blinded by dust and gravel thrown directly in our faces by the tempest of iron," according to one man. The 13th New York and 118th Pennsylvania joined the 25th New York north of the unfinished railroad. The rest of the brigade—the 1st Michigan, 22nd Massachusetts, and 2nd Maine—remained south of the railroad cut, outdistancing the others.[48]

The 13th and 25th New York on the right headed for the Ninth Corps soldiers lying on the ground ahead of them. Colonel Elisha G. Marshall, nicknamed "Old Bricktop" for his auburn hair, encouraged his 13th New York, "Men, you know your duty. Forward!" The right of Barnes' brigade removed several fences that crossed its path, all the time dodging Confederate artillery fire. A soldier in the 13th New York wrote that the brigade lost much of its cohesion when the men "scrambled for dear life."[49]

Bricktop Marshall shepherded the 13th New York through the storm, riding along the line and offering encouragement. A bullet pierced his breast and deflected upward through his neck. Blood pulsed out of his chest and throat as he relinquished command to Lieutenant Colonel Francis A. Schoeffel. Surgeons somehow saved Marshall's life. The adjutant of the 13th New

York, Job C. Hedges, also dropped out of the advance with a wound in his arm. An observer noted that "the loss in officers was particularly severe."[50]

Barnes' right drifted away from the unfinished railroad. The left regiments obliqued across the railbed to maintain their connection with the brigade. The 1st Michigan trundled across the unfinished railroad first, followed by the 22nd Massachusetts. They reunited with Barnes' command near the whitewashed Jennings house. Barnes' left regiment, the 2nd Maine, caught a tremendous blast of cannon fire while in the unfinished railroad cut and stalled. James Barnes' brigade drove ahead without realizing that the far left regiment had dropped out of the attack. Flashes of fire stabbed through the greasy black smoke, marking the Confederate cannon on Marye's Heights. Barnes' brigade lost momentum and halted near the Jennings house. "As if by a common impulse," recalled one Massachusetts soldier, "every man on the left sank to the ground exhausted."[51]

The Fifth Corps' soldiers had faltered before they could relieve Sturgis' Ninth Corps division. Men hugged a shallow depression behind the Jennings' house while shells played around them. A man in the 22nd Massachusetts shouted: "This is awful; we better go forward!" As he sprang to his feet, a bullet tore through his head, spattering his brains on his comrades. Friends watched in horror as his body slid to the bottom of the depression. "He was gasping in that peculiar, almost indescribable way that a mortally wounded man has," recalled one of his mates. One soldier remembered the image of his "pleading expression, speechless yet imploring." The 22nd Massachusetts surged ahead with defiant huzzahs. Confederates responded with a brutal fire. "It was nothing but one roar," wrote Walter Carter of the 22nd Massachusetts; "even the cheering we gave seemed to be drowned in the terrible noise."[52]

Bluecoats shambled forward in a half-crouching manner, "as though breasting a 'blizzard.'" Barnes' men reached the fairgrounds and tiptoed through the Union soldiers glued to the landscape. A Fifth Corps soldier remembered, "This slope was black with lines of battle lying flat on the ground." Barnes' brigade relieved Nagle's brigade, and part of Ferrero's. Barnes' fresh troops edged ahead of the prostrate lines, and the Ninth Corps division crawled to the rear. Sturgis' command claimed that it left to "make room for the fresh regiments." The field was so densely packed with broken commands that later assaults lost their momentum before passing the swale. Barnes' brigade took over Sturgis' position passively. The brigade did not attempt to attack the stone wall.[53]

Colonel Barnes tried to launch an attack, but without luck. He rode down the line, exhorting his men. He collected his command—with the exception of the 18th Massachusetts (which had fallen back to the millrace) and the 2nd Maine (stuck in the railroad cut)—and prepared to assail the Confederate stronghold. The leader of the 13th New York allegedly rebuffed Barnes' plan, telling him, "I will see you in ——— before I will put my men over that field!" Barnes argued that the Confederate guns would kill them all if they stayed where they were. Lieutenant Colonel Schoeffel retorted, "If you want those guns silenced, say so, and we will silence them." Barnes replied, "Very well, Colonel; take your own course—only stop those guns." The New York officer decided to join the assault.[54]

Barnes' brigade hacked away the remaining portions of the stout fairgrounds fence surrounding Mercer Square. Portions of the fence stood five feet high, and were reinforced by three horizontal boards. Men hastily knocked them down. Some impatient troops leapt over the wall and moved into the middle of the fairgrounds. The youthful John Smith of the Corn Exchange regiment suffered a concussion when a shell blew him over the fence and into a pool of mud.[55]

Mud clung to the attackers' heavy uniforms and weighed them down. Confederate fire paralyzed Barnes' attack from the start. A Pennsylvanian reminisced: "Bullets spoke to me. zip! whiz! bang!! And the shells screeched! Horrible! It was so new to me and wild."[56]

The 118th Pennsylvania lost its major as soon as it entered the fairgrounds. Major Charles P. Herring had nudged his horse along the line, counseling his men to stay cool. A ball caught him in the right arm. A nearby soldier cried out, "This is awful!" "This is what we came here for," the major rejoined as he dismounted. A second ball ripped through Herring's other arm and projectiles shredded his jacket. The wounds forced him to leave the field. Rebels laced hundreds of balls through the Union ranks and particularly their flags. The 118th Pennsylvania counted fourteen holes in its national colors and another ten in the state colors. "Such punishment was unbearable," the regimental historian reported. "What a bloody, one-sided battle this was," John L. Smith wrote. "To say this is awful is tame; it cannot be described. . . . I cannot write the horrors I saw." The rapid increase in casualties, combined with the frustration of being victimized by the Rebels, demoralized the 118th Pennsylvania. The Corn Exchange regiment broke and ran for the unfinished railroad cut. Barnes cut off their rout and rallied the regiment in the field south of Mercer Square. The brigade commander seized the 118th Pennsylvania's tattered colors and rode ahead of the regiment with the injunction "Follow me." The regiment obeyed.[57]

The rest of Barnes' brigade fractured, pushing ahead in small sections. The commander of the 13th New York angled his men into the fairgrounds. He directed his men to fire at the Confederate artillery on Marye's Heights. Southerners, protected by lunettes, continued to operate without much danger. The 1st Michigan halted when its leader, Lieutenant Colonel Ira C. Abbott, suffered a wound in the face from which he "very narrowly escaped" death. The 22nd Massachusetts faltered, rallied, and tried again with no better results. Smoke choked and blinded the troops. Sweat poured off the straining soldiers. Powder and smoke clung to their moist skin, smudging their complexions. Angry Yankees fired and cursed. Some yelling: "Here's for B!" Others shouted: "Give it to them!" or "Put the ———— into them!" In the choking haze of battle, they blazed wildly.[58]

The 2nd Maine had been stranded in the unfinished railroad cut. Cannon fire had disorganized the regiment, and by the time it re-formed, Barnes' brigade had disappeared into the fairgrounds. Lieutenant Colonel George W. Varney led the 2nd Maine up the railroad cut, using the depression to get closer to the stone wall. Confederates on Telegraph Hill kept the column under an intense barrage. A shell fragment struck Colonel Varney on the head and dropped him senseless. Major Daniel F. Sargent assumed command and ordered the regiment out of the cut. More Rebel fire greeted the 2nd Maine as it emerged from a washout in the railroad bank. Both the national and state color-bearers fell wounded. Kennedy Stewart dropped the national flag when a bullet burst his lungs. Edward McKenney instinctively grabbed the standard. When the state colors hit the ground, Sergeant Michael Gallagher picked them up. The 2nd Maine disintegrated almost immediately and drifted back to the railroad. Major Sargent rallied the command and tried again, only to meet with the same results. A third advance after dark reunited the 2nd Maine with Barnes' brigade. Until then, the regiment lay low and fired from the lip of the railroad cut.[59]

By the time the 2nd Maine settled into the cut, the rest of Barnes' brigade had grounded to a halt. Colonel Barnes recognized the difficulty of reaching the stone wall and gave up the attack. He ordered the men to take cover. Division commander Charles Griffin told Barnes to "hold the position at all hazards." The brigade commander dashed along the line, overseeing its defense. Confederate riflemen killed Barnes' horse. The colonel remounted, only to have a second and then a third horse shot from under him. An aide to Barnes, Lieutenant Walter S. Davis, also lost two mounts. Another staff officer wrote that "Col. Barnes acted very bravely." General Griffin reported that Barnes had earned "special notice for his coolness, energy, and marked ability." His ability probably did not exceed that of many of the other Federal commanders, but his poise certainly elevated him above most.[60]

Barnes' brigade dropped to the ground on the edge of the fairgrounds. Men made themselves as small as possible, "hugging the ground as tight as a human body could be made to hold on to the earth." Fighting for room along the swale, as well as protection, soldiers tossed dead bodies out of the swale and stacked them in front as human breastworks. Some of the men found the cover repulsive and horrifying. As time passed, most of them became resigned to its necessity, and viewed the dead with a detached callousness. One Northerner wrote that his brother and he spent the entire afternoon huddled behind a body whose "whole back up to his neck [was] scooped out with a solid shot."[61]

Any movement on the Union line provoked an angry burst of fire from the Confederates. "A raise of the head, or a single turn not unfrequently proved fatal," recalled a Corn Exchange soldier. A New Yorker wrote, "It was almost sure death for a man to even get upon his knees." Some of the Confederates used a house near the stone wall, to get a better shot at Barnes' line. Stationed in the second story of the Joseph Hall house, Rebel sharpshooters fired down on the prone blue figures. Even the fearless James Barnes found it difficult to communicate with his commanders under such fire. He resorted to sending messages forward by one of his aides. Captain John B. Winslow had to crawl to the front on his hands and knees, carrying dispatches in his teeth.[62]

The 22nd Massachusetts tried to silence the fire from the house. Robert G. Carter fired so often that his rifle fouled. Soon his ramrod jammed in the muzzle of the weapon. While trying to coax it free, Carter spotted a Rebel in a window and reflexively fired—ramrod and all. He laughed nervously as he thought of impaling his astonished enemy with a rammer. The Federal fire lasted only a short while before ammunition began to give out. Men all along the line cried for cartridges. Officers turned to the dead and wounded for anything to give them. Just when the fire petered out noticeably, the veterans of Barnes' brigade caught sight of reinforcements in the distance.[63]

Colonel Jacob B. Sweitzer's brigade hurried to join Barnes' command. The brigade had undergone a confusing day of shuffling back and forth. Earlier in the day, Sweitzer's command had tramped across the middle pontoon bridge, only to be halted and countermarched. A short time later, the command recrossed the river, following Barnes' brigade. Sweitzer marched through the city, "moving leisurely." Along the way, the men beheld "chaos let loose." Streets teemed with wounded soldiers, stragglers, ammunition wagons, and batteries. An Irishman in the 9th Massachusetts wrote that "it looked as if 'Pandora's box' had been opened in Fredericksburg." Sweitzer's Bay State Irish stumbled upon the used-up 28th Massachusetts of Meagher's Irish Brigade. Many of the grimy soldiers "shook their heads in a rueful and not reassuring manner." A captain in the Irish Brigade remarked to the reinforcements, "it was the toughest place he had ever been into and that he was sorry to see us going in."[64]

Union artillery on Stafford Heights hurt Sweitzer's progress when its shells exploded prematurely and showered the column with shrapnel. An infantry soldier recollected that "much strong indignation was expressed at the recklessness of such a premature explosion." Another soldier made the 9th Massachusetts laugh when he complained, "This going to the *front* to be shot in the *rear* by one of our own . . . is d—— poor generalship, I say." The brigade quickly left the docks and sidled up Frederick Street to the vicinity of the brickyard.[65]

Sweitzer's brigade stopped, and the men deposited their knapsacks on the sidewalk. Boys from the drum corps stayed behind to mind the gear and take care of the officers' horses. Slipping through a ravine, Sweitzer's men splashed across the lower reaches of the millrace spillway—"a small gully in which lay several bodies"—and took cover behind a fence. Sweitzer organized his troops in two lines. The 9th Massachusetts held the right of the front line. The 62nd Pennsylvania came next, and the 4th Michigan formed on the left. In the second line, the 32nd Massachusetts took the right and the 14th New York formed on the left. The men loaded their rifles and waited for the order to attack.[66]

When Barnes' brigade moved to the attack, Sweitzer shifted his troops to the right. The brigade crossed the railroad tracks and trekked through "marshy ground" along the millrace. A Union soldier wrote that he waded in "very cold slush." Sweitzer had the men trail their arms so they would be inconspicuous as they marched up the ravine. The brigade commander halted his troops and formed a brigade front. Soldiers saw the hideous effects of the battlefield and knew they would soon be part of it.[67]

While Sweitzer maneuvered into position, Colonel Samuel Sprigg Carroll prepared to take his brigade into battle. Carroll's brigade, part of Whipple's division of the Third Corps, had entered the city three hours earlier. Carroll had sent one of his new regiments, the 12th New Hampshire, to the upper end of town to support the artillery at the Gordon house. The rest of the brigade—the 84th Pennsylvania, 110th Pennsylvania, and the untried 163rd New York—crossed the middle pontoon bridge with orders to cooperate with the Ninth Corps. Carroll's men littered the bridge with playing cards as they entered Fredericksburg. Men whispered in grim undertones about the foolishness of continuing the struggle. "It looks to me as if we were going over there to be murdered," noted a Pennsylvania soldier. A man in another regiment used the same terms, declaring, "I will stand to my duty right through if I die for it, but I think it is nothing less than murder to try such a mad scheme." Another proclaimed, "I am sure we cannot take those hills . . . and I think those in high authority if they run us up there against such works will be guilty of the blood of every man slain." Carroll's brigade formed in line of battle along the lower end of Sophia Street. "We are in for it now," a member of the 84th Pennsylvania spoke. "There is no getting out of this. The die is cast."[68]

An irrepressible spirit in the 84th Pennsylvania tried to brush off the solemnity of the moment. "Who would not be a soldier?" the young man asked. "Terms, 'thirteen dollars a month,' and found '—dead on the field!'" Shellfire punctuated the announcement, and the joker rejoined, "Do you hear the music? . . . Now this is melody indeed!" No one shared his levity.[69]

Men hunched along the street and prayed to be spared. Looking around, they found Fredericksburg "bleak, deserted, and comfortless." A soldier in the 110th Pennsylvania wrote, "as for Fredericksburg, part of it is burnt, and the rest destroyed." The rare houses not gutted or ransacked had been taken over as headquarters and hospitals. The troops stacked their arms and idled for two hours before Orlando B. Willcox summoned them at 3:30 P.M. The Ninth Corps commander wanted Carroll to support Sturgis' division. Carroll's brigade marched up Frederick Street to the brickyard, shouldering its way past a tide of mixed military commands. According to a soldier in the 84th Pennsylvania, "The streets by this time were confused and crowded with batteries, ammunition wagons, regiments moving to the front, wounded men hurrying to the rear." En route, Carroll stopped to see General Sturgis.[70]

Carroll's brigade formed behind the RF&P Railroad embankment, past the brickyard. The 163rd New York likely took the right, with the 110th Pennsylvania on the left and the 84th Pennsylvania in the middle. A lieutenant in the 84th asked Colonel Samuel M. Bowman for "a special favor." He wished to be excused so he could pay his respects to George Washington's mother, adding with a smile, "Besides, I think a change of location just now would be good for my health." The colonel replied, "I am very glad to find you so patriotic and sentimental. . . . You will have a chance of meditating on her example and influence right in the thick of the fight." The facetious lieutenant returned to his company.[71]

No one told Sturgis that Griffin's division had started to replace his troops. As a result, the Ninth Corps general ordered Carroll's brigade to the left of his command so he could draw Confederate fire away from his division. Expanding the Federal left, Sturgis hoped would relieve—or at least, diffuse—the pressure on the right. Sprigg Carroll responded instantly, pointing his troops into the field south of the unfinished railroad.[72]

A watching Rebel marveled how "They came up by acres and our boys fired in to the dense masses without the fear of missing." "Their very numbers made this courage more awful," the Southerner remembered. In the middle of Griffin's assaults, Robert Ransom added more troops to the salient. He called his last two regiments from north of Hanover Street. The 49th North Carolina crossed the Plank Road and massed behind the Marye house. The 35th North Carolina advanced to its right and assumed a position on the cleft between Marye's and Willis' hills, but not without loss. Major John M. Kelly was killed in the transfer. Ransom also came close to losing his life, when a ball tore through his lapel. Ransom looked at his collar and remarked in disgust, "Do you see that?" A witness thought Ransom's nonchalance was "one of the coolest things I ever saw in regular action."[73]

The other division commander concerned with the salient also hurried reinforcements to the Sunken Road. Lafayette McLaws informed Kershaw and Ransom that Brigadier General James L. Kemper's Brigade, of Pickett's division, was on its way. At the same time, he reminded Colonel Robert McMillan that General Cobb had left the 16th Georgia in reserve at Howison's Mill behind Marye's Heights. McMillan sent for the regiment immediately. The Georgia regiment suffered some casualties as it entered the Sunken Road. McMillan put the 16th Georgia behind the 24th Georgia. "I was in many hard fought battles," reminisced a newcomer, "but never saw men more cool and more deliberate [than McMillan's Brigade] . . . and I never saw another battlefield so thickly strewn with dead men." One of Kershaw's veterans wrote that "this was one of the fiercest battles of the war."[74]

Samuel Sprigg Carroll ordered his troops to fix bayonets and charge. Angling to the right, the brigade scampered across the triangular plateau and dipped into the unfinished railroad cut. A Pennsylvania soldier called it "a little dash across the open space from one cut to the other." Carroll's brigade plunged down the steep embankment and stumbled unexpectedly into another charging brigade. Carroll had blundered into Sweitzer's command of Griffin's division. Neither brigade was aware of the other until they collided. Both commands moved side by side for a short distance, but the brigades crowded each other and soon became entwined as they vied for space.[75]

Carroll realized that his brigade could not exit the railroad cut until Sweitzer cleared out. The Third Corps officer reported, "I could move no farther without breaking the column." Grudgingly, Carroll yielded the right-of-way to the Fifth Corps troops. The momentary confusion, and lack of cooperation, left Barnes' brigade alone at the front with only the shattered legions of all of the previous assaults.[76]

Completely unaware of Carroll's brigade, Jacob Sweitzer's brigade had chafed along the millrace above Prussia Street. Soldiers soured at the prospect of leading another futile attack. "It was a useless, ill-judged endeavor," a Massachusetts veteran recalled. Confederate shot struck the crest of the ravine frequently and deflected overhead. At 3:30 P.M.—the same time Carroll's brigade started forward—Griffin ordered Sweitzer to support Barnes' brigade. The Federals left the millrace ravine twenty minutes after crossing the sluiceway.[77]

Sweitzer's brigade stormed across the open ground as fast as the men could move. Slick mud made the going sluggish. Self-conscious Northerners thought the Rebels directed all of their fire at them. The roar of musketry sounded "as if a million [fire] crackers were going off under ones nose." Artillery tore great gaps in their ranks. A Pennsylvanian recalled that "grape shot came, whirrrrr, buzzz on every side." A Massachusetts soldier recollected that the Confederates "dropped their shells over and about us with a precision and rapidity that we did not admire in the least." The Federals picked up speed but without relief. One frightened Yankee wrote, "The faster we 'double-quicked,' the faster [the shells] seemed to explode."[78]

Sweitzer's brigade had proceeded only a short distance before the left became entangled with Carroll's brigade in the unfinished railroad. At the same time, Sweitzer's right ran into a herd of Union soldiers stampeding to the rear. A Pennsylvanian wrote, "the crowd of stragglers rushing to the rear . . . threw the brigade into temporary confusion." The 9th Massachusetts and 62nd Pennsylvania tried to stem the rout, but to no avail. The Keystone regiment only added to the problem. Ordered to "Left face," it somehow imagined the command was to "About face." A member of the 62nd recalled, "Our regiment thinking the line was broken wavered a moment and then partly broke." Colonel Jacob Sweitzer and the commander of the 62nd Pennsylvania, Major William G. Lowry, dashed into the confused mass "swinging their hats above their heads on the point of their swords" and rallied the 62nd Pennsylvania on its colors. Once he had settled the brigade, Sweitzer brushed past Carroll and moved to the swale.[79]

Sweitzer's brigade relieved some of the units on the front line. The 4th Michigan replaced the 9th and 11th New Hampshire regiments of Sturgis' division, while the 9th Massachusetts took the place of the 118th Pennsylvania Corn Exchange regiment of Barnes' brigade. Sweitzer's soldiers lay down and opened fire. Meanwhile, the brigade commander met with some of the leaders in the swale. An Irish Brigade officer told the Fifth Corps colonel to stay put, but Sweitzer retorted: "General Griffin says he can take the hill in fifteen minutes. That hill must be taken before sundown." Unable to sway Sweitzer, the Irish officer volunteered, "Come here and I will show you the exact place for your left wing to go in." The two officers reconnoitered the ground together. Sweitzer returned at 3:45 P.M. and ordered his entire brigade shifted to the left. The constant sidling right and left angered some of the regimental leaders. A 9th Massachusetts soldier wrote, "All this waste of time chafed Colonel Guiney and his officers exceedingly."[80]

The brigade shuffled to the left and re-formed opposite the southern end of the stone wall. Sweitzer spurred his horse ahead of the line and, swinging his hat on the tip of his sword, shouted, "Come on, boys, there is nothing here that will hurt us." The men cheered and charged the wall. Confederates lit up the winter twilight and poured musketry into the attackers as they fumbled across a cabbage patch. Sweitzer's horse went down. The colonel mounted another. One of his aides received three wounds; a second fell dead, and a third had his horse shot out from under him. Finally, a bullet struck Sweitzer's leg, and he had to be carried back to the Jennings house.[81]

The Union attackers took a savage beating. A bluecoat noted, "grape and canister and bullets rained down on us." Another recalled how "bullets went singing by our ears like so many bees." A Massachusetts soldier calculated that "in ten minutes, every tenth man was killed or wounded." Marshall Davis, color-bearer of the 32nd Massachusetts, flew across the field, somehow avoiding injury. A comrade called Davis: "the fastest traveller in the line." Men hiked across two board fences and through rows of cabbage plants before the Rebel fire grounded them to a halt. A Pennsylvanian wrote with undisguised amazement, "I don't see how we ever got up there at all." The adjutant of the 62nd Pennsylvania was one of those who did not make it. A cannonball struck James E. Cunningham, and he died without a sound.[82]

General Sturgis later told the Pennsylvania historian Samuel P. Bates that Burnside watched Sweitzer's attack through his field glasses. The army commander inquired, "What troops are those?" When informed they were Sweitzer's command, Burnside said, "No troops ever behaved better in the world." Sweitzer's brigade, however, had become nothing more than a disorganized mob, its regiments "jumbled together in some confusion." Confederate volleys disrupted them thoroughly, and Colonel Francis J. Parker discovered another incredible source of disorder. Hungry soldiers, disdaining the shot and shell, stopped to pick cabbage leaves along the way. By the time the officers herded the men into anything remotely akin to a line, the attack had foundered. Color sergeants planted their flags along the swale, and the men lay down beside them. The attack had fallen apart in ten minutes, despite Burnside's reported delight at its success.[83]

Sweitzer's regiments fired on the Rebels according to their own inclinations. The 62nd Pennsylvania blazed fast and furious. According to one soldier, "We fired as fast as we could load." The 9th Massachusetts took a more deliberate approach. Because they could not distinguish the Confederates behind the stone wall, "the regiment did not as a whole indulge in a useless expenditure of buck and ball." The 32nd Massachusetts caught everyone's eye when it stood erect and fired by files over the heads of the 62nd Pennsylvania and 9th Massachusetts. "They evidently were not satisfied with firing 'at will'," wrote a soldier in the 9th Massachusetts, "for we could continually hear the orders from them: 'Company!' 'Ready!' 'At the stone wall!' 'Aim!' 'Fire!' 'Load!'" Some of the troops, snug behind the rise, shouted, "Bully for the 32d! Give it to 'em!" No matter how the troops discharged their weapons, the Confederates remained elusive. A member of the 9th Massachusetts guessed that "for every 'Johnny' hit, a ton of lead was expended."[84]

Colonel Sprigg Carroll waited in the unfinished railroad for updated orders from Charles Griffin. Carroll initially had taken the field under orders from the Ninth Corps, but when Sweitzer cut him off, the Third Corps officer put himself under Griffin's command as the general in charge of the field. Griffin, however, never knew this and never acted on it. Perplexed by Carroll's inactivity, Ninth Corps commander Orlando Willcox grew impatient. He ordered Carroll to "move straight forward to the crest" of Marye's Heights. Carroll's brigade climbed out of the deep cut shortly after 4:00 P.M., and headed for the center of the fight. The 110th Pennsylvania, on the left, had some difficulty scaling the slippery mud banks amid the congestion of other commands. A large portion of the regiment opted to advance along the unfinished railroad. A Keystone soldier recalled that "numbers of our poor boys sent down the cut" were slaughtered by Rebel artillery. A survivor of this barrage, James C. Hamilton, reported with horror: "It's hard to conceive a more fearful charnel house than that terrible cut." Southern cannon on Telegraph Hill churned the cut into a nightmarish "valley of dead and dying men." A watching Confederate testified, "I saw the bloodiest shot I ever saw in my life. . . . I think it could not have failed to kill or wound as many as 20 men." The artillerist, E. Porter Alexander, noted, "The sight of that shot excited me."[85]

Carroll's brigade fell in behind Barnes' and Sweitzer's commands. The brigade crossed the open mud flat and bogged down in the smoke and noise of battle. Through a break in the black powder haze, a soldier in the 84th Pennsylvania saw "the heights . . . wreathed and fringed with fire and smoke." The sound of battle rattled intolerably in the soldiers' ears, rendering some temporarily deaf. "If you set 1,000 Locomotives to whistling in a smoke shop and make all the noise you can," recalled one veteran, "you will not compete with the noise of this Battle." Carroll's brigade took its place in the swale.[86]

Sprigg Carroll's men may have ventured beyond the recumbent lines of the more recent assaults, but not for long. A proud member of the 84th Pennsylvania declared that Carroll executed "the best Baynet [*sic*] charge on the rebels of the fight," yet the attack collapsed in a matter of a few yards. Carroll's brigade felt the full impact of the Confederate fire. "The hills occupied by the enemy burst forth into flame," recalled one veteran, "as though their very crests had become one vast volcanic crater." The carnage was instant and devastating. A shell struck one man in the 84th Pennsylvania and tore "him all to pecis" before it wounded another "5 or 6 in the Bargan." One of Carroll's men reported, "It was a hard sight to see men fall in the ranks along side of you." Another wrote, "What murder it was," and confessed to feeling "helpless and numb." Carroll retreated quickly to the cover of the swale. The tiny fold in the ground offered only a few scant inches of protection, but it had become a haven for thousands.[87]

The battle degenerated into a struggle without purpose. To many of the Federal soldiers, it appeared they were there to shoot and be shot. A writer from the 32nd Massachusetts recounted that he risked his life for hours in "a battle of which there seems to have been no plan." Sweitzer's brigade, to the left of the fairgrounds, engaged in a deadly contest with Confederates in and around the Hall house. "At intervals the enemy's sharpshooters would climb up the roof of a story and a half house to our left front," recorded a 9th Massachusetts soldier. Bullets rattled through the skimpy board fence protecting the Union solders. "Many spent bullets dropped among us . . . cutting through the clothes and leaving black-and-blue marks," a lieutenant wrote. Quite a few soldiers sustained lumps and bruises, rather than serious injuries, because "the force of the bullets was partially spent as they passed through the boards, slats and rails of the fences." A shellburst directly over a pack of 9th Massachusetts officers nearly killed the regimental commander. When the smoke cleared, Colonel Patrick R. Guiney discovered that his sword scabbard had been cleaved "smoothly" in two.[88]

Seeing his first two brigade shredded, Charles Griffin reluctantly called on his division reserves to replace some of the bloodied units in front. Griffin's 3rd Brigade, commanded by Colonel Thomas B. W. Stockton, had been the last to cross the middle pontoon bridge. Confederate shot plunked into the Rappahannock River on either side of the marching column. "The air was thick with the flying, bursting shells," a Maine soldier recalled, and "there was an unconquerable instinct to shrink beneath it, although knowing it was then too late." When they heard a screaming shell, veteran soldiers knew it had already passed. William Rankin of the 20th Maine jumped when a solid shot slammed into the riverbank beside him. His comrades laughed at him, but by the time they reached the other side of the river, one of them admitted, "there was not much hilarity." Troops bustled across the bridge so quickly that the pontoons began to sway dangerously. Horses reeled and the men scarcely kept their balance. The column scrambled off the bridge and up the bank. Stockton's brigade crossed the Rappahannock at 4:00 P.M.[89]

Griffin's final brigade hurried along Sophia Street, wading through hordes of pillagers, some of them waving wads of Confederate banknotes. One looter handed a roll of bills to a captain, laughing that he might as well get paid before going into battle. Stockton's brigade paraded through the bustle with dramatic fanfare. "Banners wave, bands play, the soldiers cheer, and the rebels shell our advancing columns," recollected a soldier, "but in the thrilling excitement of that hour the shells have lost their terror." Others noted more daunting scenes. Joshua Chamberlain described how "crushed bodies, severed limbs, were everywhere around, in streets, dooryards, and gardens."[90]

Stockton's brigade marched up Frederick Street before turning right and crossing the railroad tracks at the depot. The line halted on Prince Edward Street, overlooking the millrace. Griffin held Stockton in reserve, in case of disaster. The 17th New York rested its right on Charlotte Street. To the left stood the 12th New York, 20th Maine, 44th New York, 83rd Pennsylvania, and 16th Michigan. The midwestern regiment straddled the RF&P Railroad. Federal soldiers took advantage of the meager cover and lay down behind a light wooden fence. The 83rd Pennsylvania hid behind some buildings adjacent to the depot, and the 16th Michigan took cover behind a hardware store.[91]

Cover soon became essential. Union artillery tried to break the deadlocked battle. Confederate artillery responded with a severe barrage that not only blanketed the Union cannon, but raked the edge of the city. Chamberlain recalled, "just then the battle burst forth with new fury." The 20th Maine soldiers spent the next hour "flat in the mud upon our faces," according to Theodore Gerrish. A member of Stockton's brigade reported, "the shells from the enemy [were] flying over and around us at rather a lively rate." A Pennsylvanian remembered, "For an hour the fragments of their shells fell thickly around us and wounded several of our men." Colonel Strong Vincent, commander of the 83rd Pennsylvania, stood conspicuously in front of his regiment to hearten the nervous troops. "Here it was that Colonel Vincent first began to give indications of that bravery for which he afterwards became distinguished," boasted an admiring soldier. "With sword in hand he stood erect in full view of the enemy's artillery, and though the shot fell fast on all sides, he never wavered nor once changed his position." In one case, bugler Oliver W. Norton wrote that when he overcame his fear, he found the shellfire almost poetic. Studying the ruined city, Norton concluded: "after we had done all the damage we could, the rebs played on it with their 'brass horns' from the other side. Between them both there was not much of it left untouched."[92]

Captain Ellis Spear sat on a rock in front of the 20th Maine, petting a small dog "of the rat terrier breed," which whimpered and shook during the cannonade. The commander of the 20th Maine, Colonel Adelbert Ames, conversed quietly with Lieutenant Colonel Chamberlain behind the lines. One of the captains overheard Ames mutter, "This is earnest work." The eavesdropper wrote: "the remark struck me as a very reasonable one and appropriate to the occasion." Unlike Strong Vincent's bravado, the 20th Maine officers appeared to go out of their way to ignore their men during the barrage.[93]

Stockton's brigade watched an endless trail of wounded file past. Men on stretchers, or carried in blankets, were wounded to every degree imaginable— "some mortally, some severely, and some slightly." Stockton's troops again grew quiet and edgy. A Maine soldier testified that the wounded "caused some of us to feel rather scary. I, for one, acknowledge the corn."[94]

Stockton reported that the shellfire caused "quite a number wounded" in his brigade. Some of the wounds, however, were accidental or self-inflicted. Royal F. Dodge of the 20th Maine knelt absently on his musket, discharging a ball through his hand. The frightened soldier assumed the Rebels had shot him. Captain Ellis Spear found it impossible to calm the young man. Dodge ignored the officer, dropped his gun, and sprinted to the hospital.[95]

Twilight descended upon Fredericksburg and started to hide "the lurid field of carnage." Stockton's bluecoats hoped that nightfall might spare them from the battle. As the sun began to set behind the Confederate heights, Charles Griffin summoned his reserves to the Jennings house. The bugles blared and the brigade scrambled into line. Captain Ellis Spear abandoned his stray terrier somewhat apologetically. He wrote later that "I could not charge with a little dog under my arm." An excited captain in the 20th Maine instructed his company to "Remember their Sires," which drew a chorus of laughter.[96]

Stockton's brigade hurried across the millrace just to the right of Prussia Street. Colonel Stockton avoided the Prussia Street bridge because Confederate artillery had pinpointed the span. As a result, troops splashed through four feet of turbid water. The brigade historian noted that the sluiceway created "a serious hindrance, breaking the conformation of the ranks." Soldiers, soaked to the skin, scampered up the bank and into the brickyard. Stockton's brigade re-formed behind a "stout board fence."[97]

Stockton re-formed his brigade in two lines. Every other regiment dropped back to form the second line. The 17th New York took the right of the first line, with the 20th Maine and 83rd Pennsylvania on the left. The 12th New York formed behind the 17th New York. The 44th New York held the middle of the second line, and the 16th Michigan backed up the 83rd Pennsylvania. Stockton's left rested on the unfinished railroad. Griffin explained to Stockton where he needed to go. His brigade would charge to the Jennings house "with only the blazing light of musketry and artillery to guide it." Lieutenant

Colonel Norval E. Welch took advantage of the pause to deliver a "short and spirited address" to the 16th Michigan. The men cheered just as Stockton's bugles announced the attack.[98]

Confusion reigned in Stockton's brigade from the start because some heard the bugles and others did not. Stockton's left heard them plainly and started down the unfinished rail cut. The center of the line also heard the order, but fell behind, trying to breach the brickyard wall. Stockton's right never heard the bugles and remained in position, oblivious to the movement. Confederate artillery focused on the Union advance and added to the pandemonium. The left of the brigade—the 83rd Pennsylvania and 16th Michigan—weathered a terrible storm of ordnance as it moved up the railroad cut. The regiments abandoned the cut, but their ordeal intensified. A Pennsylvanian recalled, "This threw us in some confusion." In the meantime, the 20th Maine and 44th New York became mixed as they tried to pull down the obstinate brickyard fence. Lieutenant Colonel Freeman Conner, commander of the New Yorkers, fell wounded, and Major Edward B. Knox became the new head of the regiment. Eventually the troops broke through the wall and plunged across the miry plateau. The uncertain advance of the center, confused by the darkness and the chance wounding of the 17th New York's adjutant, Lieutenant George S. Wilson, may have severed the link to the right. Stockton thus left behind two New York regiments from the start.[99]

Stockton's brigade flailed across the plain in two groups while the third contingent sat idle. The 83rd Pennsylvania, on the left, piled out of the railroad cut in a mass of confusion. Several companies debouched to the left; the rest went to the right. Colonel Strong Vincent halted his command and retrieved the wayward companies. While traversing the fifteen-foot-deep cut, Vincent's Pennsylvanians tangled with some tough Ninth Corps pickets who created "great confusion" in the attackers' ranks when they refused to get out of the way. Vincent eventually re-formed the 83rd Pennsylvania and started forward again. Moments later, fresh salvos of Confederate fire buffeted the column and drowned out the officers' orders. A Federal soldier recalled that "the ranks became again thrown into some disorder." The 16th Michigan suffered the same travails. Strong Vincent ordered the two regiments to press obliquely to the right.[100]

Stockton's center tried to catch up with the Pennsylvanians and Michiganders. The 20th Maine and 44th New York "advanced over fences and obstructions of all kinds, over bodies both of the dead and the living," Chamberlain reported. A captain remembered seeing blankets unfurled over the corpses. Theodore Gerrish recalled, "The field was thickly covered with the fallen . . . mangled and bleeding, trodden under the feet of the charging column." The men ran into a variety of fences and obstacles. They darted around garden posts, over wire fences, and across deep ditches.[101]

The new troops seemed strangely unaffected by the fire or the carnage. "I do not remember thinking of danger," wrote Ellis Spear, even though he did recollect that "the uproar was immense, & the air was full of the shriek of shells." Colonel Adelbert Ames strode twenty paces ahead of the advancing 20th Maine with his sword unsheathed. A soldier recalled, "with the inspiration derived from such a man as Colonel Ames, it was a very easy thing to face danger and death." Charging across the open field, even Ames had his courage challenged. Confederate artillery north of the Plank Road unexpectedly advanced to the edge of Marye's Heights and enfiladed the Union assault. Captain Victor Maurin's Donaldsonville Artillery fired down the length of Stockton's lines. Ames and Chamberlain looked at each other, and Ames whispered, "God help us now!"[102]

The artillery had an immediate and dreadful impact. As one soldier later recalled, "We picked our way amid bodies thickly strewn." A Maine soldier thought the heights billowed like a volcano. Another believed the hill looked much worse, "which *Hell* only can compare with." Several cannon rounds landed in the 44th New York, "throwing up great bodies of earth." Proceeding farther, the men encountered rifle fire. A New Yorker recollected that it was "doubtful if a single person in the Brigade indulged the hope that any real success could be obtained." Yet the headstrong Yankees persevered. An onlooker in Sweitzer's brigade admired their style: "I saw the Twentieth Maine . . . coming across the field in line of battle as upon parade, easily recognized by their new state colors."[103]

Thomas Stockton reunited his left and center at the Jennings house. The men lay down in the mud for cover, and the officers seemed lost. No one in Stockton's brigade knew where to go once they reached the Jennings house. Vincent sent his adjutant to Stockton for directions, but the staff officer could not find the brigade commander "amid so many troops." Stockton, for his part, could not locate Charles Griffin to get new orders. Even the brigade bugler went searching for Griffin. His efforts ended in "a rap on the head with a board thrown by an exploding shell, [and] a mouthful of gravel raised by a ploughing grape shot."[104]

In five or ten minutes the division commander appeared and ordered Stockton to replace some of the regiments in the front line. Barnes' brigade had exhausted its ammunition and needed help. Stockton asked Adelbert Ames if he could relieve the units directly in front. The colonel replied, "Certainly, sir," and quickly advanced up to the swale to have a look. Happening upon the 22nd Massachusetts, Ames asked, "Who commands this regiment?" Lieutenant Colonel Sherwin came forward, and the two coordinated an exchange of positions. "I will move over your line and relieve your men," Ames explained. "Colonel, my regiment will relieve yours firing, if you will move them [pointing to the 22nd Massachusetts] to the rear." Sherwin readily agreed, and Ames hurried back to get the 20th Maine.[105]

Stockton led the center of his brigade up the slippery slope to the swale, then again lost contact with his left. Some of the previous attackers feared the new troops were making another forlorn assault and tried to halt them. "It's no use, boys; we've tried that," they shouted. "Nothing living can stand there; it's only for the dead!" Stockton's brigade did not venture farther. It relieved the troops in the swale, but "not . . . without a severe trial of the men's courage." The fairgrounds divided the 20th Maine in half. The right shied away from the wall when they saw that "a perfect storm of bullets pierced and shattered the fence every instant." Lieutenant Colonel Chamberlain snapped, "Down with that fence," but the men hesitated to go near it. One of them, George W. Carleton, confessed, "it seemed death to any man to touch it." Chamberlain asked aloud, "You want *me* to do it do you?" and seized the top board. As he pried it loose, the others joined him and tore down the fence in short order.[106]

As soon as Stockton's brigade passed the swale, it felt the full sting of Confederate fire. "The storm of shot and shell and musketry," reported Strong Vincent, "that now poured into us was exceedingly destructive." Another soldier thought that, "When we first went to the front, the battle was raging more terribly than at any other time during the day." The fire certainly had been heavier earlier, but not since Stockton's brigade had arrived on the battlefield. Colonel Stockton never intended his brigade to attack, and he quickly ordered his men to lie down. The brigade engaged in "long range musketry." A 20th Maine soldier wrote that "The utter impossibility of taking the rebel position was manifest to every man in the regiment, but we blazed away at the enemy, and they at us." The brigade fired into the darkness, "guided by the flashes of the fine musketry of the enemy." The lurid explosions mesmerized the soldiers. "The muzzle-flame deepened the sunset red," recalled Chamberlain, "and all was dark."[107]

The left of Stockton's brigade inched instinctively closer to the front.

When he failed to get orders from Stockton, Strong Vincent advanced the 83rd Pennsylvania and 16th Michigan to the swale on his own initiative. He angled his regiments to the left of Sturgis' division and Carroll's brigade. Vincent's command shifted around a little hillock. The colonel ended up placing his two regiments at right angles to the rest of the Federal line. Confederates caught the Yankees in the open and hit them with a destructive fire. The 16th Michigan reported its heaviest losses occurred at this point. A member of the 83rd Pennsylvania recalled, "there is always something more terrible in the crashing of musketry on the battle field than in the roar of the heaviest artillery." Vincent withheld his fire, and darkness saved him from excessive casualties. The colonel also checked his fire because he was uncertain of what lay ahead of him. Vincent could not determine if any friendly forces lay in front. When he asked some retreating Federals, he received nothing but evasive shrugs. Colonel Vincent stopped his firing altogether when he observed some muzzle flashes in front, streaking toward the Confederate stone wall. Several hundred rattled Yankees fell back through his lines. New Jersey soldiers lambasted the 83rd Pennsylvania for shooting them in the back. "Up to that time," a Keystone soldier recounted, "we had supposed there was nothing but rebels in our front."[108]

Four brigades from Hooker's Center Grand Division had taken the field with no results except to lengthen the casualty lists. Griffin's and Carroll's advance had plenty of talented leadership, but lacked coordination. Fifth Corps commander Daniel Butterfield appeared in the thick of action "calm, methodical and determined," even though he lost three orderlies to wounds. Yet Butterfield forfeited any good he might have done by shunning his responsibilities and recklessly riding into battle. His disappearance eliminated any coordination between Griffin's division, Carroll's brigade, and Sturgis' division. All three commands acted on their own accord, with the result that Griffin missed a chance to attack on a multiple brigade-front, and ended up squeezing Carroll out of the advance.[109]

A soldier in Griffin's division wrote, "Some of the grandest charges the world ever saw were made by our troops." Griffin, however, committed his division piecemeal, intent on relieving Sturgis' Ninth Corps troops, rather than taking Marye's Heights. Only later did Griffin try to carry the Confederate defenses, and by then his strength had been spent. Charles Griffin was "omnipresent," or so Robert G. Carter claimed, but he was also wounded and unable to keep his command together. One senses his frustration when he barked at the 18th Massachusetts: "I want *some one* to charge!" In the end, his division lost 926 men in three confused attacks.[110]

Colonel James Barnes suffered the division's heaviest casualties, losing 500 men. The 18th Massachusetts incurred the worst regimental losses—125 out of 290 troops—a 43 percent reduction. Barnes lost three horses in the attack. Colonel Jacob B. Sweitzer's brigade suffered 222 killed and wounded. Sweitzer himself had been hit in the leg and his horse killed. Though carried to the Jennings house, he never relinquished command. His brigade had collided with Carroll's and had fallen into some disarray. The 62nd Pennsylvania came close to breaking and, in the final count, sustained almost twice as many casualties as its sister regiments. Colonel Thomas B. W. Stockton stayed behind as the division reserve, and advanced alone at sunset. The Confederates concentrated all of their might against the brigade, causing 201 casualties, most of them felled by artillery fire. Carroll's tiny brigade marshaled approximately 650 soldiers. Southern defenders sapped it of 111 men in a matter of minutes. Its palsied advance came at the hands of two different division commanders who could not, or would not, communicate with each other. Carroll, as a result, found himself at cross-purposes and without direction.

By this time, the Confederates had nearly perfected their range and accuracy, but two things conspired against them, raising concerns in the Southern ranks. The efficient Washington Artillery had about exhausted its ammunition, and the Union Fifth and Ninth Corps marshaled two more divisions to try the stone wall again.

CHAPTER THIRTEEN

"THE GATES OF HELL"

Final Assaults at Twilight

Ambrose Burnside's aide returned to headquarters shortly after Griffin's division became engaged. The army commander learned too late that William Franklin had declined to attack south of Fredericksburg as he was directed. Griffin's advance, outside of steeling the Ninth Corps' lines, had been pointless. Franklin's cavalier behavior defies logic. He pretended that Burnside's order had been merely a request rather than a demand. Burnside fired off a second peremptory order for Franklin to attack at once. Expecting his subordinate would obey this time, Burnside planned another assault in front of Marye's Heights. This time, a spark of hope blessed his timing.

The Washington Artillery had dominated the battlefield for five hours. They had shelled the Federals with unsurpassed precision, but they had expended hundreds of rounds. Captain Benjamin F. Eshleman notified his commander, Colonel James B. Walton, that his battery was "almost out of ammunition." In truth, all of the batteries had used up their allotment. Battery officers reported that they had fired everything—case shot, shell, and canister. All of the guns had been reduced to a few rounds of solid shot. Gunner Henry H. Baker wrote, "Our ammunition chests are empty, every shot has been hurled at the enemy." The Louisiana commander had forgotten to bring up his ammunition train, so he had no way to replenish his battalion.[1]

General James Longstreet noticed the fire diminished on Marye's Heights. He dispatched his ordnance chief, Captain Osmun Latrobe, to find out why. Latrobe went to Walton and asked how he was doing. The colonel replied, "All right, except we are running short of ammunition and . . . we have not been able yet to get any sent to us." The staff officer told Walton to get help from Lieutenant Colonel Edward Porter Alexander. At the same time, Latrobe ordered the neighboring batteries to cover for the Washington Artillery's declining fire. As he galloped away, Captain Latrobe kidded the Louisianans that it was "too hot for him" to stay.[2]

Burnside talked anxiously with the generals around the Phillips house. His earlier confidence had given way to what one writer described as something "akin to desperation." "His mind," noted an observer, "for the moment, seemed to be unbalanced." Burnside had ordered Franklin in emphatic terms to "advance his whole line." He also directed Joseph Hooker to "put in everything," and carry the heights. Hooker questioned the 2:30 P.M. order. Burnside curtly rejoined, "those heights must be taken. . . . Why should General Hooker ask such a question at this time?" Hooker remonstrated, "I thought that, in view of the terrible losses . . ." but Burnside cut him off, repeating the order. The Center Grand Division commander gave the order to General Andrew A. Humphreys of the Fifth Corps.[3] Burnside told Bull Sumner that Hooker was on his way. Sumner, in turn, notified Darius Couch at 2:40 P.M.: "Hooker had been ordered to put in everything. You must hold on until he comes in." Couch rejoiced. Griffin had replaced the Ninth Corps troops, but no one had rescued the Second Corps. The rest of the Fifth Corps would stabilize the front. As Couch put it, "Hooker's coming was like the breaking out of the sun in a storm."[4]

Andrew A. Humphreys was as delighted as Couch. The often austere general seemed "disposed to be tyrannical" to many, but at the Phillips house he brimmed with excitement. Humphreys bounded out of Burnside's headquarters with enthusiasm. According to his aide, Captain Carswell McClellan, "it was evident to any one acquainted with his manner that gratifying instructions had been received." Humphreys commanded a new division of Pennsylvanians, largely untrained and never in battle before. Six of his eight regiments had enlisted for only nine months. Humphreys, too, had little combat experience. He showed obvious disappointment when he missed the battle of Antietam. Fredericksburg would erase that imagined stigma. He pointed to Marye's Heights and proudly announced, "We *must* gain the crest."[5]

Colonel Peter H. Allabach informed Humphreys' 1st Brigade: "It now remains for us to cross the river, make the final charge, and carry the position." The brigade commander ended, "I wish every man to do his duty." The soldiers cheered accordingly. Humphreys also gave speeches with a much different effect. The general, alleged a soldier in the 155th Pennsylvania, "communicated in a vigorous address" that they would be a "forlorn hope," which was a common term for a sacrificial attack. Even the stoutest warriors thought that Humphreys' speech "made it indeed a very trying occasion, and a test of the soldierly qualities of the command."[6]

Some of Humphreys' soldiers despaired. A nervous trooper in Humphreys' escort told his commander, "I can't go, Captain." "Why not?" the officer asked; "Are you sick?" "No," stammered the soldier. "But I can't go." Tears glistened his cheeks as he bawled, "If I go over there I will be killed." The captain refused to dismiss him, but another soldier interceded. A teamster—and the frightened man's brother-in-law—stepped forward, volunteering, "If you are going to be killed, I will go in your place, and you can take my team till I come back." As the column started forward at 3:00 p.m., the teamster scoffed, "I guess you are a coward, but I will show you I am not one." Whether the teamster-turned-cavalryman survived his gallant gesture is not of record.[7]

Brigadier General Erastus B. Tyler's brigade led the division over the upper crossing. Allabach's brigade followed. The men double-quicked past General Burnside. The army commander attempted to cut through the column, but the soldiers jostled his horse. Burnside chided them, "You need not crowd, boys." Looking over the new division, the army commander told the men, "there is plenty to do over there." An innocent recruit reassured Burnside, "We are ready for the work, General." The leader peeled away, and the column hiked down to the river.[8]

Confederate artillery had made the bridges treacherous areas. A member of Allabach's brigade wrote, "The enemy were doing their best to stop us." Another reported, "Some of the shells did fall uncomfortably close." The column split and took advantage of both of the upper bridges. Tyler's brigade crossed without difficulty. One of Tyler's men noted that he crossed a solid pontoon span with "scarcely the slightest motion being perceptible upon the firm double pontoon bridge." Allabach's brigade, on the other hand, staggered across a loose and swaying bridge, which "kept rocking and swinging to the tread of the soldiers." As the tail of Allabach's brigade stepped onto the bridge, the color guard of the 155th Pennsylvania paused for a moment. John Mackin, known to the regiment as "Uncle," had been visiting his son when the orders came to move. The father instinctively asked for a rifle and was turned down. Officers spotted Mackin marching with the regiment and refused to let him cross the river. They stopped him at the end of the bridge. The old man embraced his son, Corporal John Mackin, Jr., and sorrowfully watched his son march into Fredericksburg. The corporal survived the battle, but died in 1864 in the Wilderness.[9]

Humphreys' division wended past rough-hewn coffins "piled up by the hundreds" near the riverbank. It saw "newly-made graves" in the city. A hush fell over the column. Humphreys tried to keep them from any more demoralizing scenes. The general rode ahead and diverted the wounded down side streets lest his division "should be depressed by the sight." But injured soldiers choked the city. According to a man in Tyler's brigade, he passed "hundreds of wounded men of different regiments, on stretchers and on foot, some with ghastly wounds."[10]

Humphreys halted on Caroline Street and ordered his men to stow their knapsacks inside the houses and stores (presumably the ones not used as hospitals). Soldiers broke ranks and dumped their gear. Humphreys grew impatient and started ahead before everyone had deposited their baggage; some units went into battle still carrying their effects.[11]

Andrew Humphreys doubled up his column and marched up George Street two regiments abreast. The general and his staff led the way. Humphreys' men endured a steady cannon fire but suffered few casualties. A severed tree limb decked Adjutant James C. Noon of the 133rd Pennsylvania. He assured his friends that "he was not struck, but he was all unnerved." He died a few minutes later in the upcoming attack. The wounded men from the battlefield cheered the sharp new division, and were loudly cheered in return. Humphreys formed his division on the rise above Liberty Town. Tyler's brigade moved to the right and took cover in "another street on the outer edge of the place and parallel with the river." The 91st Pennsylvania formed "in line behind a graveyard, the stone wall of which offered some protection." This was the Corporation Burying Ground, and put them close to modern-day Barton Street. Allabach's brigade filed to the left, into an alleyway between George and Hanover Streets. The men surveyed the corpse-littered field ahead of them. The destruction attested to "the hopelessness of the contest." A Union colonel later noted, "there was no chance for success in storming these works." As generals gathered on the crest, one of the lieutenants muttered to his men, "Boys, we're in for it."[12]

Humphreys found Winfield S. Hancock standing alone, "apparently waiting there for some one." A few minutes later, Darius Couch, commander of the Second Corps, joined them. Couch had come from the battlefield after a distressing reconnaissance. "It was evident," according to one of Humphreys' aides, "that General Couch's sympathetic nature was thoroughly aroused by what his troops had been through." Couch had rejoiced when Hooker promised support, but when no one came, he grew discouraged. The shattered Second Corps had exhausted its ammunition. The general feared that his corps would be forced back if supports did not arrive soon. When Couch saw Humphreys he pressured him to help. The Fifth Corps general said it was "an urgent request," and his staff remembered that Couch "was exceedingly solicitous," yet Humphreys refused to budge. The new general responded stolidly, "I am ordered into position here." Couch was dumbfounded; but Humphreys wanted to go forward. He softened. "You are the ranking officer," Humphreys conceded, "and if you will give me an order to do so I will support you at once." Couch gave the order immediately, even though Humphreys came from another grand division. Humphreys ran into Joseph Hooker moments later. The Center Grand Division commander confirmed Couch's orders with the explanation, "General Burnside desired that the heights should be taken before sundown." Hooker advised his subordinate to rely on the bayonet, provided he could survive to get that close.[13]

Humphreys delightedly directed Allabach's brigade to advance between 4:00 and 4:30 P.M. The brigade dashed down the avenue to Hanover Street. Sprinting to the millrace, the men were hit by a renewed artillery barrage. Union guns answered and added to the fearfulness of the moment. "One could not see for the great volumes of smoke," recounted a soldier in Humphreys' party, "and the discharges of the guns on both sides made the earth shake and tremble." Troops spilled across the waterway as the bridge runners remained unaccountably uncovered, even at that late hour. Clambering up the other side, Allabach's men filed to the left of Hanover Street and took cover beneath the oft-used embankment of the ravine. Parties broke off to replank the bridge.[14]

A. A. Humphreys knew nothing of the ground. He had rushed forward without reconnoitering first. He asked Hancock for assistance. The general gave Humphreys his brother, Captain John Hancock. Humphreys, with Captain Hancock and the rest of his staff, splashed across the millrace to get a better look at the battlefield. The large cavalcade was "greeted with a shower of bullets." Humphreys put his staff under cover while he, Captain Hancock, and one or two others rode ahead. Some of Griffin's soldiers saw the general "finely mounted on a light-stepping bay horse." Someone foolishly proposed "Three cheers for General Humphreys," which drew attention to the officer. The division commander wheeled smartly "as though on review," doffed his kepi, and offered "a smile and bow of acknowledgement." The brigade leader, Colonel James Barnes, explained the layout of the troops to Humphreys. He seemed satisfied and turned to get his attack started. Later, the general reported that he "did not know . . . of the ground being encumbered" by the Second Corps troops, or of the swale—"the existence of which I knew nothing of until I got there." His conversation while riding with Hancock's brother casts doubt on the first statement, and his proximity to Barnes and the battle line disparages the second. Humphreys either failed to make the rudimentary observations during his reconnaissance or he conveniently forgot aspects of it after the fact. Either way, Humphreys had seen enough to tell his aide, Captain Carswell McClellan: "M——, the bayonet is the only thing that will do any good here, —tell Colonel Allabach so, and direct him to see that all muskets are unloaded." Loaded weapons might tempt the men to stop and fire. The last thing Humphreys wanted his men to do was stop.[15]

Meanwhile, Erastus Tyler had advanced his brigade behind Allabach's. The brigade kept the doubled columns of regiments as it poured down George Street "until we neared the main road leading westward from town." Confederate shells destroyed the buildings surrounding the intersection of George Street and Hanover Street. The division suffered its first fatality there when a shell severed a man in two. The soldier threw up his hands, gasping, "Oh, my God! take me," and died instantly. A witness described how "the sight of this made some of the boys feel a little queer—a little qualmish." Tyler strung out his column to lessen the chance of another hit.[16]

Tyler's brigade waded through the sluiceway and tried to huddle behind Allabach's troops, but there was no room for the brigade to re-form. Tyler shifted his command to the right of Hanover Street. The men struggled across a swampy meadowland, called Gordon's marsh. The brigade halted its right near Hurkamp's tannery. The men found the spongy morass tough to march through. An officer reported, "The occupation of this meadow appeared to be criminally purposeless." Regimental commanders encouraged their men to close up. The troops responded with loud cheers, much to the anger of the surrounding Federals. Howard's division had occupied the tan-

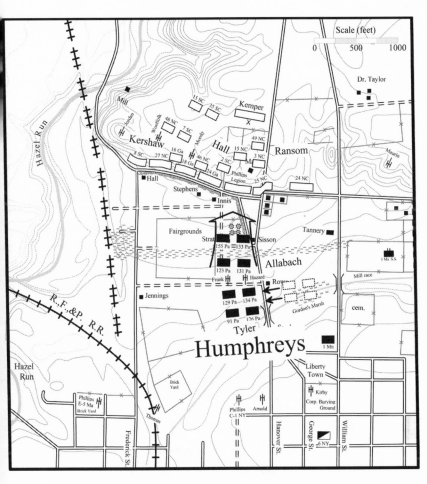

Humphreys' Assault

nery for several hours "without attracting the attention of the enemy's artillery," and they wanted to keep it that way. They roundly condemned the reinforcements for entering the field "with loud cheers," and "attracting the attention of the enemy." A field commander in Sully's brigade wrote that Tyler's troops moved "in a rather noisy manner, and making a good deal of display." As the veterans tried to shush Tyler's brigade, a Confederate officer rode to the crest of Marye's Heights to investigate the commotion.[17]

The Confederate was Captain Osmun Latrobe of Longstreet's staff. The ordnance chief had dashed across the Plank Road to see Captain Victor Maurin's Donaldsonville Artillery. Maurin had posted his Louisiana battery in pits that sat back from the crest of Marye's Heights. This allowed him limited play during the battle. He had harried the Federal infantry with an occasional shot at Hurkamp's tannery. Latrobe begged the battery commander to intensify his efforts because the waning Washington Artillery needed additional firepower. The staff officer was particularly worried about the Federals massed in the swale, a virtual blind spot for artillery. Maurin balked. His guns would have to leave their gun pits and advance to the bald crest, "and to do this, were to meet almost certain death from the guns in front." Maurin's lieutenant, R. Prosper Landry, volunteered to try. The brash young officer ordered up a 10-pounder Parrott. Landry's crew, and Latrobe, manhandled the gun across the bare summit of Marye's Heights.[18]

Several Union cannon opened fire on Landry's piece immediately. Shrapnel pierced one of the gunners through the heart before his cannon had even cleared the gun pit. "The fate of their comrade seemed to inspire my men with renewed determination," Landry reported. They quickly set up, sited the piece, and opened fire. They pumped eight rounds into the Union infantry as fast as they could load. Landry fired with impressive accuracy. As Maurin later reported, "not one shot was lost, but every one telling with frightful effect."[19]

Landry's gun had plenty to shoot at. Burnside had ordered the Fifth Corps into the field, but only Humphreys had amassed his division of 4,500 Pennsylvanians right in front of Landry's gun. Brigadier General George Sykes, appropriately nicknamed "Tardy George," lagged behind with his division of U.S. Regulars, and missed most of the artillery fire.

A Northern soldier in Howard's division remembered, "Here we lay expecting each moment to be attacked by the rebel infantry. But we were not thus fortunate. A more terrible fate awaited us." Landry's new position enfiladed the Federal right. One of the Louisianan shells killed three men and wounded several others in the packed ranks of the 126th Pennsylvania. Another tossed a man ten feet in the air. A third crushed one man, severed the limbs from another, and sprayed the brains of a third "far and wide," before it burst, killing and maiming several more. A nearby bluecoat recalled: "It is said the judgment-day comes but once, and we all felt that it had come for us right then and there." An unseasoned comrade wrote, "it required more cool courage to witness this without flinching, than afterward to go into the charge." A soldier in Humphreys' command recounted, "I have heard of the horrors of the battle field but the reality is terrible." Soldiers bowed their heads fatalistically and waited for the next shell. "It was fearful, it was horrible," a Northerner candidly reminisced. "Brave men turned pale and strong men held their breath." One of Tyler's colonels felt "a dread certainty at every discharge." Several officers took cover behind the tannery. The absence of the officers alarmed some of the troops, who fled back to the millrace. For all their perceived damage, many of the Rebel shells actually plowed into nothing more than the soft earth, spewing clods of mud over the shrinking ranks. Landry's fire had more of a psychological impact than a physical bite.[20]

Several Union batteries challenged the Confederate cannon, and Maurin feared that they had "obtained a perfect range" on Landry, but the lieutenant stood his ground. The Southerners fired deliberately despite the shells and sharpshooters' bullets "flying thick and fast around them." Three Confederates fell wounded. Five horses were also hit. Finally, a Union shell struck Landry's Parrott, breaking a wheel and wounding three more men. Prosper Landry reluctantly abandoned his lopsided piece and withdrew the rest of his crew to safety. For a brief moment, they had terrorized the Union infantry in front of the stone wall, and alleviated some of the pressure on the Washington Artillery.[21]

General Hooker rode along the edge of the city, observing the Confederate fire. He stopped at Federal Hill, overlooking the millrace, and scanned the scene with his field glasses. Nearby, Arnold's Rhode Island battery drew some close fire, but Hooker seemed not to notice. O. O. Howard later wrote of Hooker, "I wondered that he was not shot." Hooker discerned that the Rebel fire had slackened and decided to take a chance. He ordered several batteries into the field to get a better shot at the stone wall. Hooker wanted them to breach the Rebel defenses before Humphreys attacked.[22]

Hooker sent orders to Couch, Howard, and several Second Corps battery commanders. Couch confirmed all of Hooker's edicts, since the Left Grand Division commander was the highest-ranking officer in Fredericksburg. Between 3:45 and 4:00 P.M., Kirby's Battery I, 1st U.S. Artillery, left the Corporation Burying Ground and advanced to the hillside north of Liberty Town. The 1st Minnesota stuck with the guns as support. At the same time, Howard brought forward Captain John G. Hazard's Battery B, 1st Rhode Island Light Artillery. The general had found Hazard and the Second Corps chief of artillery, Captain Charles Morgan, on Caroline Street. Howard explained the situation, saying that guns were needed in the field "to encourage the infantry." Morgan objected, "General, a battery could not live out there." Howard snapped, "Then it must die out there." Hazard calmed Morgan and said he could go anywhere he was needed. The general warned Hazard not to act recklessly and lose his guns, but a nearby observer remembered that Howard "did not care if we lost [the battery]. He expected that we would." Hazard's Rhode Island battery mounted up and rumbled out Hanover Street.[23]

Hazard's guns passed Arnold's Battery A, 1st Rhode Island, at Federal Hill. Arnold's men cheered, "There goes Battery B to h———ll!" General Couch rode alongside, apologizing to Hazard "that he feared we would lose our guns, but that he would rather do that than give up without another desperate effort." None of the generals thought Hazard's battery would come back alive. Clattering across the newly planked millrace bridge, the battery jostled past Sully's brigade, which greeted it with cheers. "The sight of our battery," recalled a New Englander, "appeared to inspire them with a new life." The infantry saw Hazard's guns as the antidote to Landry's Confederate Parrott.[24]

The battery jangled into the field to the left of the Telegraph Road. Musketry sliced through the artillerymen as they emerged from the millrace ravine. "Wee had hardley got on," wrote one gunner, "before our men and horses began to fall." Hazard took position on the brow above the ravine, opposite the Rowe house. His battery stood three hundred yards from the stone wall. The right section of the battery formed on the Telegraph Road, about thirty yards in advance of the other sections. Before the gunners could unlimber their pieces, two more horses and another soldier had fallen. One of the lieutenants took charge of the caissons and parked them in the ravine across the millrace.[25]

Hazard directed his first shots at a house full of sharpshooters menacing Barnes' brigade. Several hits sent the Confederates reeling out the door. "Wee brought them out in a hury," an artillerist boasted. The guns then focused on the stone wall, pounding it with solid shot and shell. Federal fire raged for close to forty-five minutes. When Hazard emptied his limber chests, caisson limbers came forward to replace them.[26]

More Federal guns ran the gauntlet to set up next to Hazard's battery. Hooker dispatched Captain John D. Frank's Battery G, 1st New York Light Artillery, to help. Frank hesitated when he received orders from the head of another grand division. Unable to find his own general, Frank hedged. He left one section behind in case Couch needed it, and led the other four guns to join Hazard. The New York battery took position on Hazard's left. Frank's battery fired solid shot and spherical case shot "with marked effect," according to the captain. Confederate infantry fire appeared to drop off, and Captain Frank reported that the ten Union guns "greatly disconcerted the fire of the enemy's line of infantry." Hazard's men did not share his assessment.[27]

Confederate fire sleeted through the Rhode Island battery. "Our position was a perfect hornet's nest, with the hornets all stirred up," recalled the battery historian. "Minie balls were flying and singing about us." Horses fell one after another. Captain Hazard's mount was killed, and the officer directed his battery on foot. Two of his three section leaders, Lieutenants Horace S. Bloodgood and Joseph S. Milne, also lost their horses, shot from under them. Four sets of wheel horses died and had to be cut from their traces. All told, Hazard's battery lost fifteen horses. A battery man remembered the bullets "flew thick and fast," but "we were too busy to dodge them." Another participant reported: "They were in a most terrible trying position, but did not lose their self-possession for a moment." The Confederates, however, had a decided advantage in position, and worsted the exposed batteries. A Rhode Island artillerist wrote candidly, "Wee got a good licking." Yet the batteries remained largely intact. Neither Hazard nor Frank had lost a single gun. A number of horses had fallen, but very few men. Hazard counted 16 wounded but no fatalities. Frank's battery lost 1 man killed and 5 wounded, along with 5 horses. "It was very remarkable," wrote a gunner in Hazard's battery, "considering our close action with the enemy."[28]

The Confederates admired the courage of the Federal batteries, but the Union supports had mixed emotions about their execution. Hazard met the Rebels during a truce soon after the battle, and a Confederate artillerist told Captain Morgan about seeing "one of the most gallant deeds, performed by a battery." Morgan introduced him to Hazard. The Southerner thrust out a hand, drawling, "Captain, I congratulate you and your men on their deed of gallantry." Few of the bluecoats gave the guns as much credit. The guns only drew fire and added more casualties. A 1st Minnesota soldier recalled sardonically that the men "took the Enemy's intentions to kill us all (in the way of shelling) as good naturedly as we could." General Alfred Sully was not so amenable. He withdrew the 1st Minnesota on his own accord. Sully, already nursing a slight wound in his leg, scoffed, "They might court martial me and be d——d, I was not going to murder my men." A grateful soldier in the 1st Minnesota later expressed, "Our thanks to Gen Sully who dared to disobey orders & get us out of a job that is one of impossibilities." In front of Hazard's and Frank's guns, Owen's Philadelphia Brigade not only braved Rebel fire, but found itself being hit from behind. Low-trajectory shells or premature explosions rattled through the prone ranks, as the Federal gunners attempted to fire just over their heads. "Occasionally a shell would burst short, or the fragments of a sabot would strike among us, and for a moment recall our attention from the front," testified the brigade historian. "Certainly nothing tested the courage of the men more than to be placed in such a position," another soldier recalled, "with shot and shell from both directions, in front and in rear." Colonel Owen, unlike Sully, took it in stride, later applauding the guns for "good service in enabling me to hold my position." Owen appreciated that although the Federal artillery failed to breach the wall, it helped discourage an always possible Confederate counterattack.[29]

At the height of the Federal barrage, Confederate colonel James Walton begged E. Porter Alexander, in Longstreet's name, to replace his battalion. A courier found Colonel Alexander near the Plank Road. Alexander responded immediately, but after the fact thought better of it. "Had I not been new to my command," he reflected, "I would have proposed to send in ammunition, & men too, if necessary, but to object to the exposure necessary of both his teams & mine." Nonetheless, Alexander had promised nine guns. Walton would have to hang on until they arrived. By this time, the Washington Artillery had suffered three fatalities and twenty-three wounded. "We were now so short-handed that every one was in the work," recalled Adjutant William Owen, "officers and men putting their shoulders to the wheels and running up the guns after each recoil." Captain Charles W. Squires reeled when a ball bounced off his chest. Falling into Owen's arms, he whispered, "Send for Galbraith to take command, I'm wounded." The lieutenant assumed command of the 1st Company, and Squires went to the hospital, where he soon recovered. The situation in front grew increasingly urgent.[30]

E. P. Alexander collected four guns from Captain Pichegru Woolfolk's battery; another three from Captain George V. Moody's Madison Light (Louisiana) Artillery; and a two-gun section from Captain Tyler C. Jordan's Bedford (Virginia) Artillery, under Lieutenant Donnell Smith. The batteries "hastened" down the Plank Road, crossing under the fire of Captain A. Burnet Rhett's South Carolina battery. Alexander dispatched Lieutenant Joseph Haskell to quiet its fire until he passed. The Confederates obliged, but the Federals did not. Shells not only harried the oncoming batteries, but also came perilously close to killing Alexander. The colonel glanced up to see a shot bearing down on him. With no time to react, he wondered where it would hit. Incredibly, the shell passed beneath his horse and struck the ground fifteen feet behind him. Not everyone was so fortunate. The battalion commander estimated that he suffered three-quarters of his losses while dashing onto Marye's Heights. Alexander tried to minimize his losses by ordering his crews to move through low spots and covered areas. The lead driver, probably from Jordan's battery, found his path blocked with dead bodies. When he attempted to bypass them, his team and gun overturned in a ditch. This further delayed Alexander.[31]

Walton had anticipated Alexander's arrival. Unable to continue the battle, Walton pulled his Louisiana batteries out of their pits, so that Alexander's guns could occupy them without delay. The Washington Artillerymen ran up their teams, limbered, and bolted off the crest of Marye's Heights. But Alexander was nowhere in sight.[32]

The Union soldiers could not believe their eyes. The Washington Artillery was leaving! One of the Federal brigadiers sent the happy news to his division commander, Winfield S. Hancock, who in turn notified Couch. The Second Corps commander whirled on A. A. Humphreys and trumpeted, "General Hancock says the enemy is retreating; now is your time to go in." The Fifth Corps general sprang across the millrace shouting for his men to attack. Officers stepped in front of their commands, yelling, "They are retreating; forward, men!" Colonel Peter Allabach's brigade stood two regiments deep, the 123rd Pennsylvania and 131st Pennsylvania in front, and the 155th Pennsylvania and 133rd Pennsylvania behind them. Humphreys ordered his troops to rely on the bayonet and demanded that their weapons be emptied. He had the muskets "rung" (by dropping ramrods noisily into the barrel) to prove they were unloaded. Some of the regiments still carried their gear. The 155th Pennsylvania dropped its knapsacks beside the millrace and Colonel Edward J. Allen detailed his youngest boys to stand guard. Humphreys happened upon the youths and directed them "indignantly and profanely" back to ranks. Mounted officers moved to the front. Men touched elbows and roared out of the ravine with a resounding yell.[33]

Humphreys doffed his cap and gave his staff a courtly bow. "Gentlemen," he remarked pleasantly, "I shall lead this charge; I presume of course, you will wish to ride with me." Touching spurs, the general and his entourage moved ahead of the advancing legions. Humphreys later recounted, "the setting sun shining full upon my face gave me the aspect of an inspired being." Humphreys removed his hat and raised his right arm to heaven. The general's son, Lieutenant Henry H. Humphreys, noted that his father "thoroughly impersonated the God of War." Tumult exhilarated the general, and he galloped farther ahead. "I felt gloriously, and as the storm of bullets whistled around me . . . the excitement grew more glorious still," he wrote. "Oh, it was sublime!"[34]

Soldiers saw nothing of the pageantry or glory that excited A. A. Humphreys. Many in the division experienced nothing short of hopelessness. A member of the 131st Pennsylvania thought they had been "sent to the harvest of death in an aimless and hopeless battle." Allabach's brigade came up behind Hazard's and Frank's batteries, and the men hesitated to pass in front of the still-blazing cannon. Infantry commanders quieted the guns with some difficulty. The blue line set off again, marching deliberately across the muddy plateau, which constituted a "sea of mortar" by late afternoon. Confederate small arms fire rattled through the neatly packed ranks. A diarist in the 123rd Pennsylvania wrote, "It was then the balls came thick and fast." Another remembered that the guns created "such a din as I never wish to hear again." Soldiers trampled wounded men and horses, and crossed shattered fences. The surroundings, according to one Keystone State volunteer, "were certainly enough to gratify any studious or morbid desire" to see a battlefield.[35]

Humphreys' attackers ran unexpectedly into a glut of bluecoats in the swale. Mixing with Owen's Philadelphia Brigade, Allabach's troops lost their alignment and impetus. A number of filthy men, who had been there for hours, cried, "Halt!" and tried to restrain Allabach's recruits from going any farther by grabbing at their trousers, coats, and canteens. Some appealed to the newcomers, "Don't go forward, it is useless, you will be killed." Most of Humphreys' Pennsylvanians took their advice and lay down. At least one commander reported that he "deemed it prudent to order the regiment down upon the ground." A soldier in another regiment recalled, "Instantly, every man was flat upon the ground." The shiny rifles meshed with the clatter of the muddy ones, all shooting at the impervious stone wall. Colonel Peter Allabach suddenly discovered that his brigade had disappeared amid the mass of prone soldiery. "My troops," he half-apologized, "not having before been under fire, seemed to think that they were not to go beyond."[36]

Humphreys and Allabach rousted their troops for a renewed assault. Colonel Allabach ordered his officers, where he found them, to quiet the fire. At the same time, Allabach asked Second Corps officers to remove their troops. He implored a major in Couch's corps "to get his men up and charge with me, or go to the rear." The major ignored him. General Humphreys was also busy cursing the Philadelphia Brigade in a high-handed fashion. One of the brigade's historians alleged that Humphreys "accused us of cowardice in no very flattering terms, and ordered us to join his command." Colonel Joshua Owen told Humphreys that he had no order beyond "hold that position." The nonplused general went back to Allabach's brigade.[37]

Humphreys and Allabach extricated their brigade from the mass of blue coats. But the reluctant ranks became easy marks for Confederate infantry. An aide noted in his diary: "Men falling in groups." Mounted conspicuously, Allabach and his staff proved a superb target. The colonel's adjutant general fell, shot through the lungs; an orderly received a dangerous wound in the side; and one of Allabach's aides lost his horse to an exploding shell. Peter Allabach had no one to help him rally his troops until A. A. Humphreys arrived. "I should have found some difficulty in forming line for a second charge," the colonel told Humphreys, "had it not been for your presence in person, cheering the men on." Together, they managed to re-form the brigade and push ahead.[38]

Officers again trotted in front of the line, by Humphreys' orders. Shoving through the prone mix of soldiers, Allabach's brigade cleared the swale and surged toward the stone wall. The division commander rode triumphantly ten yards ahead of his troops, trailed by a line of winded staff officers. They passed the Stratton house, with the 123rd Pennsylvania moving to the left of the house, and the 131st Pennsylvania to the right. The second line closely shadowed the first. The 155th Pennsylvania angled away from Stratton's, sticking to the 123rd's left rear. The 133rd Pennsylvania smacked against the house and boiled around both sides. The brigade caught up with Humphreys fifty yards from the stone wall. A participant wrote that the charge was "one of the grandest events of the war." Then everything collapsed with the arrival of fresh artillery on Marye's Heights.[39]

The sudden departure of the Washington Artillery perplexed Robert E. Lee and James Longstreet. Lee tugged on his subordinate's sleeve and asked, "Look there, what does that mean?" Longstreet had no idea. He turned to Major John W. Fairfax of his staff and snorted, "Go & order Walton to go back there and stay there." Before Fairfax had fairly started, E. Porter Alexander arrived on Marye's Heights. His guns dashed across the crest "at a gallop." Federal artillery and infantry opened a furious storm of fire on the figures silhouetted on the crest. In Alexander's word, "The sharpshooters & the enemy's guns all went for us." The nine gun crews deftly made a beeline for the open pits. "We were emulating greased lightning just then," recalled Colonel Alexander. The batteries quickly dismounted their ammunition chests and sent the limbers and horses to the rear. Twelve horses had fallen before reaching cover.[40]

Alexander's fresh guns pumped a devastating barrage into Humphreys' attackers. Smith's section of Jordan's battery probably held the far right on Willis Hill. Captain Pichegru Woolfolk's four guns took the center, and George

W. Moody's three pieces held the left. Alexander brought forward only smoothbore Napoleons and a 24-pounder howitzer (from Moody's battery). Federal attackers had bunched in front of the artillery battalion. "That," Alexander reported, "was just what we wanted." The Confederate artillery pounded the dense mass, firing canister as fast as the cannon crews could load. Porter Alexander encouraged his batteries to use as much ammunition as necessary before dark. Yankee artillery tried to intervene, but Alexander's men ignored them and concentrated on Humphreys' stunned division.[41]

The Federals had driven close to the stone wall when Alexander suddenly emerged above them. "And then," recalled a Union soldier, "we met the full power of the enemy." Artillery salvos, intertwined with musket fire, created "a sheet of flames that enveloped the head and flank of the column." The Federal lead regiments stood dumbfounded by "the merciless fury of the hidden enemy behind the stone walls . . . and the shot and shell rained upon us." The 131st Pennsylvania took cover behind the houses on Hanover Street. The rear regiments bowled right through the human wreckage. The right of the 155th Pennsylvania collided in confusion with the 123rd Pennsylvania. Once again, the Confederates had transformed the landscape behind the Stratton house into "the great death trap."[42]

Peter Allabach's recruits tried to defy the Rebel fire. "The thought of momentary death rushed upon me," a Union soldier wrote, "and it required every exertion to hush the unbidden fear of my mind." Sulfurous smoke and flame stabbed at the dwindling attackers, leaving the field "covered with dead and wounded." Bullets shredded the colors of the 123rd Pennsylvania and 155th Pennsylvania. The 123rd counted twelve holes in its flag and another through the staff. The 155th Pennsylvania's flag had fourteen holes and a staff fractured by a canister round. Color Sergeant Thomas Wiseman of the 155th fell mortally wounded. Corporal Charles Bardeen dropped dead across him. Corporal George W. Bratten died taking the flag from Bardeen; then Corporal Thomas C. Lawson grabbed the standard before it hit the ground. Lawson ended the day as the only member of the color guard not killed in the fight. The 133rd Pennsylvania had three wounded in its color guard, and several others that ran away. A ball snipped the visor from the cap of a 133rd Pennsylvania soldier, raising a throbbing lump on his temple. "I guess I ripped out two or three 'confounds,'" the man admitted. As Allabach's troops accustomed themselves to the circumstances, a new fire erupted from the rear which completely disrupted them. The soldiers in the swale, overcome with "an excess of enthusiasm," blazed into the backs of the Humphreys' column

Allabach reported that most of the "friendly fire" came from Hazard's battery. "We could go no further," wrote one of Allabach's men, "the carnage was too fearful."[43]

Pennsylvanians dropped to the ground and commenced popping at the stone wall. Some of the regiments sprayed the Confederates with buck and ball, but with disheartening effect. The soldiers heard their bullets spatter harmlessly against the stones. The intense black powder smoke, coupled with the lateness of the day, made it nearly impossible to see the Rebels. The officers were equally frustrated. "There was very little for any officer to do," a soldier in the 131st Pennsylvania noted. Allabach tried to prod the charge along, but the Confederates brought down the colonel's horse, leaving Allabach to search for another mount. For the moment, the brigade had no leader.[44]

General Humphreys roared into the midst of Allabach's brigade and took command. Forcing the line forward again, the general and his staff fell prey to the nightmarish fire. A witness in Humphreys' bodyguard testified, "I never expected to come out alive." Humphreys lost almost his entire staff in a matter of minutes. Five of the seven officers who started the charge lost their horses. Four of the seven men went to the rear wounded. "The greater part of my staff were now on foot," the general reported. Only one horseman remained unscathed with Humphreys—his son, Henry. Together, they exhorted the troops to take the wall. An onlooker wrote that Humphreys "rode along our lines sitting as straight on his saddle . . . as if nothing was the matter, giving advice to the officers & cheering the men." The division commander groused at the soldiers firing blindly, "D——n it, do not waste so much ball." He told them, "Give them the cold steel. That's what the rascals want."[45]

Suddenly, Humphreys' horse, Charley, fell on top of the general. Two bullets had broken the animal's leg. Humphreys sprang up and "let off sulphurous anathemas at the rebels." The commander's passion subsided, and he politely asked for another mount. The brigade and division commanders were both unhorsed, and their attack had folded within ten minutes of starting. Humphreys did not dwell on the results harshly. Turning to his son, Henry, the father beamed, "H——, I am proud of you my boy! You're a chip from the old block!" Another staff officer noted a "peculiar sound" emanating from the general. Humphreys was whistling an odd cheery tune known as "Gay and Happy." The mystified aide later wrote, "I had not known before that he possessed the accomplishment of whistling, and his selection fixed itself permanently on my memory." Humphreys dispatched his son to update Hooker, and when he remounted, he turned to get Tyler's brigade.[46]

Erastus Tyler's brigade needed time to regroup during Allabach's charge. Maurin's Donaldsonville Artillery had wreaked havoc with Tyler's Pennsylvanians. The brigade at one time broke and fled into Gordon's marsh. Alfred Sully tried to stem the rout, but gave up when one of the recruits shrieked, "Don't stop me—I'm demoralized as hell!" Sully had had enough. He told Tyler to get away from his command. Humphreys had come to the same conclusion, and ordered Tyler's brigade back across Hanover Street to "prepare . . . to support or take the place of Allabach's brigade." Allabach's troops were under way before Tyler could move.[47]

Tyler's brigade ran a gauntlet of fire while crossing Hanover Street, and it suffered several casualties making the transition. Tyler guided his column south until the entire brigade stood behind Hazard's and Frank's batteries. Tyler tried to straighten out his disordered and undisciplined ranks. Colonel Matthew S. Quay, former commander of the 134th Pennsylvania, proved to be an indispensable help. Physically feeble, Quay had recently resigned his commission. When he learned of Burnside's offensive, he begged Tyler to let him volunteer for his staff. The brigade surgeon had warned, "If Colonel Quay goes into action, he will die like a fool." The sickly Pennsylvanian retorted: "It may seem foolish; but, I would rather die, and be called a fool, than live, and be called a coward." Now, he shouldered his mount through the throng, getting the brigade ready to attack.[48]

Humphreys joined the brigade to expedite Tyler's advance. The division commander towered above the brigade, trying to restore the soldiers' confidence. Shells continued to threaten and cut overhead "with their unearthly scream." Many of the men ducked and dodged. "Don't juke, boys!" hollered Humphreys. When the general shied from another shot, the boys laughed. "Juke the big ones, boys," the general said, smiling, "but don't mind the little ones!"[49]

Tyler had not re-formed his brigade by the time Humphreys arrived. The close proximity of Hazard's and Frank's artillery hampered his realignment. Limbers passed in and out of his lines as they resupplied the cannon. Confederate artillery rounds overshot the Union guns and landed in Tyler's command. Major George W. Todd of the 91st Pennsylvania fell mortally wounded when a shot tore off his right leg. The constant hammering of the Federal guns made Tyler wonder how he was going to get past them. Hazard showed no inclination to stop, as the battle with E. P. Alexander's battalion had become a matter of self-preservation. Humphreys noted the impediment, and personally went to each gun, ordering it to stop until Tyler's brigade had passed. Time slipped away and the field had grown almost completely dark. The Fifth Corps commander, Daniel Butterfield, sent three plaintive orders, urging Humphreys to take Marye's Heights at once. Humphreys responded, "I had tried the bayonet with one brigade, and was now going to try it with the other." Mollified, Butterfield replied, "Give my compliments to General Humphreys and tell him he is doing nobly—nobly." Butterfield's aide fell wounded while relaying the corps commander's compliments.[50]

A. A. Humphreys ordered Erastus Tyler to attack. Mounted officers again stepped in front of the line. Cantering in front of the troops, Tyler told them: "There is a stone wall up there which I want you to take. You must take it at the point of the bayonet; not a shot must be fired." One of Tyler's regiment recalled the general shouting, "Boys, you are ordered to take that stone wall, and must do it with the bayonet." The ranks cheered loudly, and for the first time, closed ranks "with as much coolness and precision as when on field drill." The brigade formed two lines of regiments just like Allabach's had done. The 134th Pennsylvania took the right front, with the 129th Pennsylvania to its left. The 126th Pennsylvania held the right rear, next to the 91st Pennsylvania.[51]

Tyler took his place by General Humphreys' side. Together, they moved forward in the last glint of the disappearing sun. Humphreys instructed Tyler to aim for the right of Allabach's brigade. The general hoped Allabach's group might be able to join Tyler's men. The division commander then lifted his hat as the signal to attack. Officers shouted for their men to move out. Company commanders, like Captain John Stonebach of the 129th Pennsylvania's Company K, waved their swords. Stonebach bellowed, "Come on K's, follow me." The troops again cheered, and swarmed out of the millrace ravine.[52]

Tyler's brigade nudged through Hazard's and Frank's batteries, and advanced across the churned fields. Men sank up to their ankles in pulpy mud, which caked their uniforms and slowed their progress. Humphreys' second assault suffered not only small arms fire, but fire from Alexander's Confederate artillery, which struck "like a blast from a furnace." Even the indefatigable Humphreys judged that Tyler had charged "under the heaviest fire yet opened." But smoke, mingled with the dying light, made the attackers less distinct and harder to hit. Tyler suffered only slight losses. Shells shrieked and howled, and the charging line of battle tripped and stumbled over the dead from previous assaults. Only the flags seemed to be visible to the Rebels. The standard-bearer for the 129th Pennsylvania was one of the few who fell crossing the plateau. Colonel Jacob G. Frick caught the flag and carried it forward on horseback. A Confederate bullet snapped the flagstaff "in uncomfortable proximity" to the colonel's head. Congress later awarded Frick the Medal of Honor.[53]

Charging Federals found their path blocked by the troops lying in the swale. The Second Corps mass, combined with the survivors of Allabach's brigade, bullied and coerced Tyler's brigade to stop. "The officers commanded halt, flourishing their swords as they lay," Tyler complained. Soldiers shouted and gestured at Humphreys' men to lie down or they would be slaughtered. Tyler's brigade refused. Tyler tried to shoo the broken ranks out of his way. Colonel Matthew S. Quay, the sickly officer serving on Tyler's staff, snapped, "March over them, tramp them down." Breathing life back into the assault earned Colonel Quay the Medal of Honor. Jacob Frick leapt his horse over anyone who got in his way. Tyler's brigade bulled ahead, but the ranks became mixed. "The men got considerably confused," wrote one of Tyler's soldiers, "and by the time we reached our point were entirely so." The snarled mob funneled into "a massive column too large to be managed properly."[54]

Humphreys had hoped Tyler would come up beside Allabach. The whole division could then attack in one extended line. Instead, Tyler's brigade blundered right into Allabach's rear. Momentum carried the throng to the Stratton house. The right regiments of Tyler's command split, going around both sides of the dwelling. Scampering across the backyards and the fairgrounds, the Yankees met "a sudden flash of waving fire," that "for the instant lit up the summit of the stone wall for its entire length." Volleys of lead rippled through the riot of troops. Federals reached the last fence between them and the Rebels, but they could go no farther. A Union observer noted that the Southerners had acquired the "exact range and terrible execution" from "a day's full practice."[55]

Gaps rent the column. Officers and men went down in droves. When Colonel James G. Elder of the 126th Pennsylvania dismounted to help remove a fence, a ball fractured his thigh. One of his color-bearers, Corporal Thomas Daily, helped carry him back to Fredericksburg. Lieutenant Colonel David W. Rowe assumed command of the regiment. The 91st Pennsylvania's Colonel Edgar M. Gregory also dismounted when five bullets brought down his horse. As he stood in front of his men, a bullet smacked his right hand. Lieutenant Colonel William H. Armstrong, commander of the 129th Pennsylvania, also lost a horse shot out from under him. The leader of the 134th Pennsylvania, Lieutenant Colonel Edward O'Brien, was the only regimental officer still mounted, and even he had a "miraculous escape." A ball had passed through his saddle from front to rear directly underneath him. O'Brien's regiment lost its major, John M. Thompson, with a wound in the left hand; and its adjutant, Alfred G. Reed, suffered a mortal thigh break. Soldiers also carted away Captain Herbert Thomas of Humphreys' staff. The officer had lost his horse during Allabach's attack, and being of no further service to the general, returned to the 129th Pennsylvania. When the standard-bearer for the 134th Pennsylvania fell dead, Corporal George E. Jones of the 126th Regiment rescued his colors. No one knew the flag was missing until after the battle. The loss of numerous leaders and color-bearers left the men with little direction.[56]

Several officers were still mounted, and they beckoned the troops to follow them. Humphreys moved ahead of everyone, often turning to shout encouragement to his men. Lieutenant Henry H. Humphreys stuck close to his father, quietly placing himself between the general and the enemy. Three bullets hobbled the youth's horse, and another wounded him in the foot. Erastus Tyler rode nearby, bristling at anyone who tried to stop his troops. Near the Stratton house, a shell fragment caught the general in the chest. When the brigade commander went down, Colonel Quay of Tyler's staff appealed to the men to follow him. "Damn it boys, what are you dodging for?" he swore. "If I can sit on my horse, and the bullets go over my head, they certainly can't hit you." Quay dashed ahead and the men were obliged to stick close. They needed to protect the colonel because he carried all of their pay in his pockets. "My hope is that every man will know that I have this money," Quay wrote, "then my bones won't be left on the field." Humphreys strained to keep Tyler's brigade going. "One more minute," he believed, "and we should have been over the wall."[57]

Blood and gore saturated the ground in front of the stone wall. The division commander described the stone wall as "a sheet of flame," and his troops could not stand up to it. A barrage of bullets rattled against Stratton's orchard fence, reducing it to splinters. One soldier observed "a small tree nearby, which was shaken by bullets as if by a wind." Another remembered dead bodies "hanging on the . . . fence." The first soldier wondered "how any of us could escape." The second marveled "that any returned alive." Tyler's brigade had come within a minute of reaching the stone wall, but no one was left to keep going. Many of the men had fallen dead or wounded, and the survivors dispersed. "It was worse than useless" to continue, wrote a recruit to the hometown newspaper, "as nothing but death stared them in the face." Andrew Humphreys lost his second horse, and another attack collapsed. The second assault had lasted fifteen to twenty minutes.[58]

The survivors clustered along the Stratton fence, returning an ineffective fire, even though Humphreys had forbidden any musketry until the stone wall was taken. The largest contingent huddled in the narrow backyard of Sissons' store. Confusion turned to panic when Union troops behind them opened fire. Bullets sprinkled through Tyler's brigade, which, the general recalled, "unfortunately took effect upon us." Several key officers fell in the mistaken fire. The brigade commander reported that a second volley from the rear brought his command to a halt. The Pennsylvanians complained vigorously, but the fire failed to dissipate.[59]

Tyler's brigade quickly gave way, "retiring under a fire that would have been madness to have continued to resist." The troops endured "but a moment," according to one of the regimental officers, before they flew from the field. Humphreys, Tyler, and sundry others tried to stem the rout, but without success. "My efforts were the less effective since I was again dismounted," reflected Andrew Humphreys. Even after mounting the wounded Colonel Elder's horse, he could not stop the panic. Frail and sickly, Captain Wharton "was run over and badly tramped" when he tried to halt the 126th Pennsylvania.[60]

Confederates spotted the Federal retreat and redoubled their fire. Humphreys tried to halt his broken command by the swale, but the men stampeded past him. Large portions of the 131st and 133rd Pennsylvania from Allabach's brigade joined the rout. The mob became jumbled with the Federal artillery. A gunner remembered: "in thay went and back thay came as quick as thay went in." A more agitated artilleryman wrote, "The effect of infantry running through a battery is, of course, most demoralizing." But no one in the batteries flinched. Humphreys sent his escort to help Tyler stop the rout at the millrace. "They are cutting my men to pieces," Humphreys mused. "Get them here as quick as you can." The escort sounded recall. A. A. Humphreys rode back to the swale and directed what was left of Allabach's brigade to cover the retreat. General Joseph Hooker bitterly testified later, "Finding I had lost as many men as my orders required me to lose, I suspended the attack." He ordered Humphreys to withdraw the remainder of his command.[61]

Allabach's brigade split into two sections. The 123rd and 155th Pennsylvania held the left, and elements of the 131st and 133rd Pennsylvania clung to the right. Humphreys sent Allabach, still on foot, to retire the right to the millrace ravine. The division commander covered Allabach's retreat personally with the 123rd and 155th Pennsylvania. Humphreys again exuded bravado. The general rode behind the rear guard, crooning the song "I Will Be Fat and Greasy Still." Disbelieving Federals wondered at Humphreys and then joined in. The two regiments sang with their division leader "in thundering tones" as they retired. Critical Confederates reported that they sent the Yankees "actually howling back to their beaten comrades."[62]

Humphreys' division rallied on either side of Hanover Street by the millrace. Allabach's brigade concentrated north of the road. His men appeared "defeated but not dismayed." They quickly reorganized. "We lay down on the cold damp ground," a diarist noted, "to pass the night." Tyler's brigade re-formed with more difficulty, and darkness exacerbated the confusion. Officers rallied their commands around the regimental colors. Several commanders yearned against reason to attack again. Captain John H. Walker of the 126th Pennsylvania roused his company even though he was wounded in the right shoulder. He declared that "One arm was enough to lead his men to another charge." He only left the field when Lieutenant Colonel David W. Rowe gave him peremptory orders. Humphreys' attack was over.[63]

Captains Hazard and Frank withdrew their artillery with Humphreys' blessing. The batteries left at a walk. Hazard had lost so many horses that he abandoned one of his limbers, and his left section had to haul their guns off by hand. General Howard met the returning batteries and "complimented each officer personally." One of the gun crew recollected "the generalls [*sic*] sayed thay never expected to see us come out again with our Battery." Humphreys and the guns yielded the front to the newly arrived division of Brigadier General George Sykes and his highly touted U.S. Regulars. The Regulars spread out one brigade, under Major George L. Andrews, covering Hanover Street; and another, commanded by Lieutenant Colonel Robert C. Buchanan, guarding William Street on the right. Brigadier General Gouverneur K. Warren held his small brigade of New Yorkers in reserve in Liberty Town. Meanwhile, the battle continued to flare southwest of Fredericksburg, where the Ninth Corps made one final attempt to seize Marye's Heights.[64]

Humphreys' division, some 4,500 strong, lost more than 1,000 men in the course of forty-five minutes. Allabach's brigade had started with approximately 2,300 troops. It suffered 562 losses, a reduction exceeding 24 percent of the command. By far the heaviest casualties happened in the two right regiments that split north of the Stratton house. The 131st Pennsylvania lost 175 troops. The 133rd Pennsylvania sustained 184 casualties out of an estimated 500 men. Their losses also reflect the confusion caused by Tyler's rout. Attrition dropped off among the two left regiments, with the 155th Pennsylvania counting only 68 killed, wounded, or missing.[65]

Erastus Tyler's brigade counted 2,100 effectives after detaching 100 men for various details. The two lead regiments sustained the heaviest losses. The 129th Pennsylvania took 139 casualties, and the 134th Pennsylvania suffered 148. The second line had casualties significantly lighter. The total loss of 454, or 23 percent of the brigade, suggests the quickness of the attack, where the frontrunners sustained the largest losses and little difference appeared between those on the right or left of the Stratton house. Humphreys lost almost a quarter of his command, but boasted that his division had come closer to capturing the stone wall than any other attack. Allabach perpetuated the notion. "The old boys," the colonel reminisced, "got nearer the gates of Hell (the stone wall) than any other regiment engaged in that battle." This led to years of controversy between the Fifth Corps and Second Corps veterans over who got the closest to the stone wall, and even to disputes between Allabach and Tyler's soldiers. None of the disputes ended to anyone's satisfaction.[66]

General Andrew Atkinson Humphreys reveled in his first experience of battle. Steeped in an outdated infatuation for glory, the general pranced around the battlefield, recklessly exposing himself. He later told a friend, "I felt like a young girl of sixteen at her first ball." Then he thought better of it, and corrected himself: "I felt more like a god than a man." Whether a girl or a god, Humphreys never gave any clear leadership to his command. He merely set it loose and joined in the panoply. Humphreys would mature later and gain a wide recognition for his talents, but at Fredericksburg he showcased only his enthusiasm. His division may have gotten among the closest to the stone wall, but it also ended in the most disorganized rout. Its sacrifice was futile, and its commander ineffectual.[67]

The Confederates celebrated in the aftermath of Humphreys' debacle, little realizing that the Federals were preparing for one final desperate attempt to capture Marye's Heights. Ninth Corps commander Orlando Willcox had learned about Humphreys' assault perhaps after it had begun. Trying to offer support, he ordered Brigadier General George Washington Getty to advance his division. Getty's command, composed of two brigades, had a predominant number of new regiments that had no campaign or battle experience. Some of the units had joined their brigades literally the day before Burnside attacked Fredericksburg. One brigade commander reported that "two-thirds of the men had never been under fire." A member of the 13th New Hampshire concurred: "We were not hardened warriors. We were simply N.H. farmer boys, who had never committed any more bloody deed than killing a cat."[68]

Colonel Rush C. Hawkins commanded Getty's 1st Brigade. He had earned some notoriety by training the 9th New York (Hawkins') Zouaves, and struck many as a strong leader, though rumors persisted about his secret dissipation. The 2nd Brigade followed Colonel Edward Harland, a virtually unknown quantity from the 8th Connecticut. Getty, as a result of the inexperience of his soldiers and their commanders, had hoped to avoid using them at Fredericksburg.[69]

The troops had spent the day nestled in relative safety near the Fredericksburg gas works. The smell offended the men, but it seemed more congenial than that of the battlefield. Soldiers amused themselves by arranging contests to re-create George Washington's fabled coin toss across the river. Contestants hurled stones from the city wharves. Allegedly, a "huge fellow from Michigan" was the only one to reach the other side.[70]

Confederate shells often landed uncomfortably near the docks. Federal artillery on Stafford Heights responded, and frequently their rounds detonated prematurely, mauling the Ninth Corps soldiers. Members of Getty's division particularly blamed a New York "German" battery and a Connecticut battery. Diederichs' Battery A, 1st New York Light Artillery, fired from a position just above the docks, and immediately to its left frowned Batteries B and M, 1st Connecticut Heavy Artillery. Between them, they managed to keep the Union men ducking, and the Rappahannock River "in a constant state of disturbance." Shells knocked over stacks of rifles, wounded men, and crushed the skull of one of Hawkins' Zouaves. Peter Smithwick, a six-foot seven-inch giant, took a hit in the shoulder. He casually pocketed the shrapnel—"about the size of a hen's egg"—as a souvenir and returned to ranks. A diarist noted darkly, "As yet no one to day has been hit by rebel shells while our own guns are killing us by the wholesale!" Officers dispersed their men to minimize the chances of any one getting hurt.[71]

The sun had turned a hazy red and begun to sink over the horizon. The Ninth Corps soldiers, according to one of them, "began to flatter ourselves that we should not be called upon." Then a winded orderly dashed up to

Getty, and speculation ran through the ranks "like wildfire." The idea of another assault seemed preposterous. "We can scarcely give the rumor any credence," recalled a New Englander, "and the movement is roundly condemned on all hands as sheer folly." The imperious order to "Fall in!" silenced all doubters. George Getty instructed Colonel Hawkins at 5:00 P.M. to attack the southern end of Willis Hill. Harland's brigade would move in support—to reinforce a breakthrough; or, more likely, to cover a retreat. The two brigades would issue from the southern end of the city, re-form on the RF&P Railroad, and then advance.[72]

Hawkins' brigade tramped up the Rocky Lane, the 9th New York Zouaves leading the way. The column formed line of battle between Knight's brickyard and the Slaughter house, Hazel Hill. Harland's command pushed through the city in two columns. The right column, led by the 21st Connecticut followed by the 4th Rhode Island, took one street. The other column, composed of the 8th, 16th, and 15th Connecticut regiments, moved up a parallel road. Reuniting on Princess Anne Street, Harland's brigade formed to the left of Hawkins' command. The 4th Rhode Island crossed paths with Buckley's Rhode Island battery. One of the artillery officers recognized the regiment and cried, "Boys, remember that old Rhode Island is looking at you to-day." A worried foot soldier muttered back, "By jabers, we'd rather be looking at Rhode Island about these times."[73]

Reaching the edge of Fredericksburg, Getty's division caught its first glimpse of the battlefield. "Not until then did we know whether the day had been lost or won," recounted a Connecticut soldier. But upon peering through the fences, "the truth flashed on us in an instant." Even as the men loaded their weapons and fixed bayonets, some shook their heads. "It was going wrong, wrong, and we all knew it," a Ninth Corps soldier remembered. Another wrote, "The prevailing idea and feeling in Gen. Getty's Division is that our assault will be fruitless; but it must be done." Onlookers prayed for the red sun to go down, but it had another half hour of light left. Lieutenant Charles B. Gafney of the 13th New Hampshire grumped, "I wish I could get up there and kick that thing down!"[74]

Getty's division formed in an instant and charged. They tore down fences and scampered around buildings, dressing their lines on the fly. The troops broke into a run, dashed down a steep bank, and hurtled the millrace. Muddy, soaking soldiers sprinted to the RF&P Railroad "as fast as legs would carry us," recollected one of Hawkins' soldiers. Troops sloughed off knapsacks, haversacks, blankets, and even greatcoats, in an effort to lighten their loads and move faster. They passed through rough fields and smooth; over fences, ditches, mud bogs, "and about every thing else" that could impede their progress. Confederate artillery made the going lively. Some of E. P. Alexander's missiles overshot the attackers and landed in Hazel Run. They churned the stream, creating the illusion of boiling water.[75]

Hawkins' brigade regrouped at the railroad embankment. Harland's brigade lagged behind, further disrupted by obstacles and artillery. Hawkins understood, incorrectly, that he needed to send a regiment to support Captain Charles A. Phillips' 5th Massachusetts Battery, which had set up behind the brickyard. He assigned the 9th New York to the artillery. Hawkins compensated by pulling the 10th New Hampshire—one of his own regiments—off the picket line. The colonel formed his troops into a narrow, deep battle line, reminiscent of what Emory Upton would orchestrate at Spotsylvania Court House in May 1864. He placed the 103rd New York and 25th New Jersey in his front line. Behind them, he positioned the 10th and 13th New Hampshire regiments. The 89th New York formed a third line behind the 13th New Hampshire. But Hawkins commenced his attack before his line had completely jelled. The 10th New Hampshire hesitated. The commander was reluctant to move because he thought the 9th New York would relieve it. When the New Yorkers failed to show up, the New Englanders grew restless and joined the attack. Hawkins' rush to get started may have stemmed from a frustrated attempt to aid the dying moments of Humphreys' attack, to beat the setting sun, or to escape the crowding of Harland's brigade and Phillips' battery along the railroad embankment.[76]

Generals Hooker and Getty reconnoitered the field in Hawkins' front. Hooker, conspicuously mounted on a white horse, ranged up and down the unfinished railroad under intense sharpshooter fire. Getty reproached Hooker for recklessly exposing himself, but the Center Grand Division commander could not be bothered. "Gen. Hooker seemed to care little for the danger or for the remonstrance," Getty noted after the battle.[77]

George W. Getty wanted to coordinate Hawkins' assault with some of the Fifth Corps units lying on the other side of the unfinished railroad. He sent his aide, Captain Hazard Stevens, "to communicate with the commander of a large body of men on the right front." Stevens darted across the rail cut, searching for someone in charge. Blundering into Sweitzer's brigade, of Griffin's division, the aide talked to Colonel Patrick R. Guiney of the 9th Massachusetts: "Colonel, General [Getty] wants you to take your regiment and charge on the enemy's works." Officers gathered around the aide and ques-

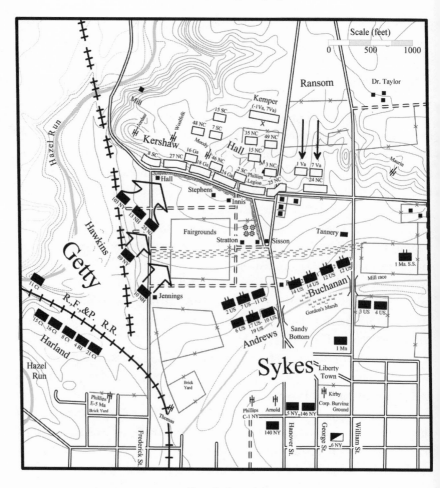

Getty's Assault

tioned his veracity. Guiney quietly reproached him, "You go and tell your general that I take my orders from my immediate superiors." The aide quickly departed. An indignant officer in the 9th Massachusetts exploded: "The man, or general, who sent such a message as that, must be either drunk, crazy, or a confounded ass—or all three put together!" Upon returning to Getty, Stevens diplomatically reported that he could not find anyone in command. Getty's division would attack alone.[78]

Harland's brigade moved into the meadow behind Hawkins' command. Rebel artillery punished the exposed brigade. "It would be impossible to convey the awfulness of the situation," wrote a Connecticut soldier. Another soldier recalled the fire, shouts, and hanging smoke created as realistic a scene of "Dante's *Inferno* as it is possible to illustrate it anywhere this side of the infernal regions." The winded colonel of the 15th Connecticut panted to his men, "A perfect storm of bullets, boys; a perfect storm!" Meanwhile, Lieutenant Colonel Joseph B. Curtis rode between the diverging wings of his 4th Rhode Island, shepherding them back together. While he was haranguing his regiment, a Confederate shell burst overhead, killing him. Major Martin P. Buffum should have taken command, and may have done so, but at least one source alleged that he had remained in town, and Captain James T. P. Bucklin took over.[79]

Getty halted Harland's troops in low ground, which darkness made difficult to see. The soldiers in the 16th Connecticut plunged blindly into a pond when their commander, Captain Charles L. Upham, ordered them to "Lay down and rest." Since they were standing in three feet of water, a soaked Federal recalled, "the order . . . struck us as rather comical." The men exploded in laughter. The imperious regimental commander demanded, "What's that laughing for?" A puckish private bandied back, "Come and see." Upham stormed toward the impudent voice—and fell into the water. Hastily retreating, he ordered the regiment out of the pond. "Men can Lie down here," he seethed as the regiment laughed at his foible.[80]

Phillips' battery fell silent, paralyzed by the heavy attrition of artillerymen. Desperate for help, Captain Charles Phillips appealed to the 4th Rhode Island for volunteers. Phillips asked, "Where is your colonel?" The men replied, "Dead." "Who is the next in command?" Phillips inquired. When told that it was Major Buffum, he wanted to know, "Where is he?" "Back in the city," came the reply. "Who is the next in command?" "Captain Bucklin." "Where is he?" sputtered the tired cannoneer. Before he heard another excuse, Phillips gave up and dashed to the next command. He found the 21st Connecticut more accommodating. Even with the extra hands, Phillips soon quit the uneven contest and fell back to town. Between Harland and Phillips, no wonder Hawkins was so anxious to start his attack.[81]

Thirty minutes had elapsed since the division left the city docks. Darkness covered much of the battlefield. Marye's Heights loomed ahead like "a great black hill." Rush Hawkins ordered his brigade forward between 5:30 and 5:45 P.M. Sliding over the RF&P Railroad, Hawkins' brigade crossed the triangular plateau. The line strayed into a mud bog that momentarily halted the attack. The left regiment in the front line—the 103rd New York—had been stopped cold. The 25th New Jersey also struggled when its left mired in the mess. The right wing, moving on higher ground, kept going. The second line, composed only of the 13th New Hampshire (because the 10th New Hampshire was still waiting to be relieved), also had its line riven by the marsh. As a result, the 13th New Hampshire halted until the left wing could be extricated from the mud slough. The left wing passed in front of the right. In an effort to keep going, the 13th New Hampshire wedged between the two halves of the 25th New Jersey. The 89th New York trailed aimlessly behind. Hawkins' line completely lost its order. It emerged from the bog more like a riot than a brigade. A veteran reminisced, "This mud accident damaged, if it did not destroy, the effective power" of Hawkins' brigade.[82]

The colonel of the 13th New Hampshire, Aaron F. Stevens, was too sick to keep up with his regiment much less keep order. He had lost twenty pounds because of his illness, and according to his subordinates, he looked ten years older. Stevens complained that it was impossible for him to "eat, drink, or *smoke*" (emphasis in original). He had ridden his horse into battle, but the high-banked RF&P forced him to dismount and limp ahead on foot. Plunging into the bog, Stevens floundered in mud "above my knees from which I never could have got out." A hefty private yanked Stevens out of the muck and carried him to safety. Exhausted, the officer lay down and summoned his horse again.[83]

The marshy low ground drained into the unfinished railroad at a bubbling spring, known locally as Cold Spring. Hawkins' troops straggled into the unfinished railroad cut by the spring and tried to straighten out their line. The 103rd New York had drifted to the left and probably halted along Hazel Run, though conceivably it entered the unfinished railroad and never ventured beyond it. Elements of the 25th New Jersey filled the railroad cut or fumbled through Cold Spring. The 10th New Hampshire was hastening to catch up, but had yet to re-join the brigade. This left the 13th New Hampshire and 89th New York intact, with a tiny portion of the 25th New Jersey in tow. The men lay down until Hawkins could reorganize "and a new start taken."[84]

Hawkins' Federals had suffered little real damage, and the Confederate fire had all but stopped. The Rebels thought Humphreys' attack had ended the Union assaults for the day; and Southerners failed to see the new threat maneuvering through the darkness. "Suddenly the cannonading and musketry of the enemy ceased; the shouts of our men also were hushed, and nothing was heard along the line," recalled the commander of the 13th New Hampshire. "For a few minutes," a private remembered, "there is an ominous silence in our front." Another soldier called it a "mysterious silence." Federals took advantage of the reprieve to re-form quietly along the unfinished railroad cut.[85]

Officers struggled unsuccessfully to reorder the brigade. The 25th New Jersey was beyond help and the 13th New Hampshire teetered on the brink of confusion. George Getty asked Major Edward Jardine, of the 9th New York Hawkins' Zouaves, to straighten out Colonel Stevens' regiment. The diminutive major spurred his horse to the crest of the railroad and harangued the troops. Seeing no improvement, he changed tactics and shouted, "Thirteenth New Hampshire, you love your country, you are brave men, and you came out here to fight for her—now, go in!" The Hampshiremen scrambled out of the ditch and trampled any Jerseymen who got in their way. A jumbled mass of bluecoats bolted into the field, only a hundred yards from the stone wall. This began what one Union soldier believed to be "one of the most dangerous infantry charges ever made on this continent."[86]

Men picked up speed and exploded with a pent-up cheer. The shout alerted the Confederates to the unforeseen danger. Colonel E. Porter Alexander stood talking to the gunners of Jordan's battery when the Yankees roared out of the darkness. Alexander sheepishly admitted, "If they had not started with a cheer I don't think that I, at least, would have known they were coming; for I could not see them." Instinctively, the Confederate artillerists depressed their guns and spewed canister into the blackness. When the Northerners fired back, Alexander ordered his crews to concentrate "canister at the gun flashes." Corporal James A. Logwood of Jordan's battery aimed his piece and stepped back to fire. Alexander instructed him to lower the elevation some more. The gunner fell mortally wounded before he could obey. Alexander stepped over the dying man and aimed the weapon himself.[87]

The motley vestige of Hawkins' brigade fumbled toward the stone wall. Men tripped over a myriad of unseen dead and wounded. Crossing a low stone fence, the Federals approached to within fifty yards of the Confederate line when they plainly heard the chilling Rebel order: "Ready, Aim—Fire!" A New Hampshire soldier wrote that the next moment was "terrible beyond words to describe." Another noted, "It was a sight magnificently terrible." A blinding sheet of flame exploded in the attackers' faces. The discharge lit up "much of the scene, revealing long, dense rows of rebel heads and leveled muskets." Others saw "the heads of the rebels now and then in the flashes of light, and distinctly hear their officers' words of command." Another recalled, "the flash revealed the mass of slouched hats, and glistening gun barrels." The assault stopped dead in its tracks.[88]

Both sides found their proximity to each other alarming. To one Federal soldier, it seemed "the powder from their musketry burned in our very faces, and the breath of their artillery was hot upon our cheeks." Others remembered seeing "gun wads, or cartridge bags, fly over us, and some of them fall burning, smoking and stinking among us." A New Hampshire man had difficulty judging the distance to the Rebels, but when a bullet blistered his nose, he declared them to be "pesky near." The 25th New Jersey collapsed under the strain. Men fled through the uncertain ranks of the 13th New Hampshire, creating "considerable confusion." Both regiments retreated through the 89th New York. Most of the brigade tumbled back into the cut and landed on top of the troops already there. Some did not reach the cut in time. Two panicked soldiers knocked over a private in the 13th New Hampshire, and all three tumbled into the railroad cut together. When the New Englander regained his senses, he asked the others to get off of him. When they did not respond, he discovered that both of them were dead. A member of Hawkins' brigade reported, "almost every regiment that went into the fight that night got all broke up."[89]

Rush Hawkins and his officers rallied the brigade in the rail cut. A Union soldier remembered that there was "a babel of orders and commands," as they furiously re-formed. A part of the 13th New Hampshire had not panicked, and held its ground close to the stone wall. Captain George N. Julian reported that "it was impossible to rally the men alone while at the extreme front." Julian paced in front of his small command trying to fashion a line. Fortunately for the captain, the Southerners failed to spot him.[90]

The battle took on a strange allure in the darkness. Musket flashes and cannon provided a dazzling array of fireworks—from "the bright spark of a rebel explosive bullet, to the instant glare of a locomotive headlight, as the cannon discharge and the shell burst." One participant imagined that he saw "twenty thousand flashes a minute." A New Yorker wrote, "At this time, the grandest scene of the battle was to be witnessed . . . the air was brightly illuminated with a grand pyrotechnic display." A New Englander thought, "The whole scene is royally magnificent; and well worth going five thousand miles to see." Some claimed that a thousand licks of flames lit up the night simultaneously. The unseen missiles spattered around the hapless Federals like "a lot of small buzz-saws." Striking the ground, bullets kicked stones and dirt over the attackers and, according to one, "tickled us in the face."[91]

The Confederate fire looked worse than it actually was. The majority of Hawkins' brigade hunkered down safely in the railroad cut, hidden from the barrage. The portion of the brigade clinging to the plain lay down and let the bullets pass overhead. Darkness made it difficult to see, so the Confederates blazed away at a target they imagined to be much farther away. "If it had been in the day time so that they could have seen our position," surmised a New England soldier, "they would have killed about every one of us." The sense of danger frightened some Yankees. Robert W. Varrell, the hefty, three-hundred-pound color-bearer of the 13th New Hampshire, suddenly realized that his immense girth worked to his disadvantage. Dropping the national colors, he headed for the rear, insisting that he was hurt. "He rapidly fell away to a mere shadow of his former self," reported Captain Matthew T. Betton, "and did no duty after the battle." In contrast, Sergeant William R. Duncklee took charge of the New Hampshire state colors, even after sustaining a nasty wound in the side of his head. Duncklee also retrieved the national flag abandoned by Varrell.[92]

The commander of the 10th New Hampshire, Colonel Michael T. Donohoe, hustled forward and proposed that the brigade take another stab at the stone wall. Before they started far into the field however, they received a blistering fusillade from the flank and rear that robbed them of their momentum. The left of Griffin's division had not recognized Hawkins' brigade in the darkness. The 83rd Pennsylvania and 20th Maine fired on the Ninth Corps troops when they cut across their front. Hawkins' men screamed for the Federals to stop shooting. "Everybody, from the smallest drummer boy up, seemed to be shouting to the full extent of his capacity," reported Hawkins. The brigade commander braved the fire to quiet the Fifth Corps troops. The incident lasted approximately seven minutes, according to Hawkins, but a member of the 13th New Hampshire argued that "minutes are hours in a place like this." The attack fell apart, and the survivors took flight.[93]

The 10th New Hampshire pulled back immediately. The tiny portion of the 25th New Jersey ceased firing, and to their relief, discovered that both the Federal and Confederate lines stopping shooting at them. The 13th New Hampshire probably aided—and benefited from—this experiment. Commanders tried to rally their troops again, but the men were too confused and edgy. A member of the 25th New Jersey worried about their proximity to the foe, and cried plaintively, "We will all be captured if we remain here." The head of the regiment later admitted that this wailing caused considerable consternation in the regiment. As a result, the final portion of Hawkins' brigade abandoned the plain without orders. Escaping from the extreme front proved tricky, as the Rebels discovered the move and lit up the night with renewed fury. Other Federals responded to the fire, catching Hawkins in another crossfire. One of the last to fall back, S. Millet Thompson wrote that the Confederates opened a "perfect storm" on his regiment, but "the Union bullets are as dangerous for us to face in retreating." Men crawled off the field on their hands and knees. Major Jacob J. Storer of the 13th New Hampshire had gained the railroad cut, but lost his sword when it fell out of its scabbard because of this unmartial posture. He returned to the plain at once and retrieved his sword.[94]

Hawkins' aggregation of regiments filled the rail cut. The brigade commander led them quietly back to the RF&P Railroad. Members of the 13th New Hampshire stumbled upon a commander of another regiment sitting alone near Cold Spring, looking somewhat disoriented. The men inquired if he was hurt. "No," he replied, "but I am all bedaubed." They left him to fend for himself.[95]

Hawkins' troops regrouped behind Harland's brigade. The 10th and 13th New Hampshire regiments formed the nucleus upon which the other units dressed. The time approached 6:30 or 7:00 P.M. before Hawkins' had the majority of his command in hand. In the darkness, many of the men wandered aimlessly, unable to find their units. "You can imagine better than I can describe," wrote a private, "the anxiety with which we inquired after friends." Colonel Michael Donohoe stood on the railroad grade bellowing for his command, not only to rally, but to make another attack. His gesture did not amount to anything. Rush Hawkins reported his repulse to Getty, and the division commander ordered his brigade to fall back to the area of the Poor House.[96]

Edward Harland's brigade stood post along the railroad, aware that it was the last organized body in that sector of the battlefield. Officers cautioned their men to stay quiet and keep watch. The fervent adjutant of the 15th Connecticut took the opportunity to preach melodramatically: "For God's sake, for the sake of your wives & children, as you value your own safety, & the safety of the army, do keep perfectly still." He warned others: "The safety of the army depends on you tonight."[97]

Darkness closed the action on the Confederate right at about the same time. Stonewall Jackson had spent the late afternoon trying to goad the Federals into another attack. He replaced or replenished some of the batteries along the Second Corps line. Colonel Reuben L. Walker yielded the gun pits on Prospect Hill to Colonel J. Thompson Brown's artillery reserve. Willie

Pegram, still smarting from the fact that his men had abandoned their guns earlier, requested to stay behind.[98] Captain William P. Carter's King William Artillery of Virginia cantered up to take Pegram's place, but the young captain refused to leave. Carter came forward and stood awestruck by the scene on the hill: "Dead men between the guns and under their very mouths; broken wheels of which there were a multiplicity; over-turned caissons, one of which had blown up; horses shot in every conceivable way, some dead, some plunging in the last agonies of that grim monster. One poor animal, I well remember, was walking about with all of that portion of his face below his eyes entirely carried away by a solid shot or shell."[99]

Carter found Pegram sitting on the trail of a broken gun, whittling a stick. Carter asked, "Halloo, Captain, what's all this rumpus?" Pegram looked up sadly and replied, "We've been having a big row up here." Carter tried to ease his friend to the rear, suggesting, "The boss sent me to unlimber in your rear, and keep you from crawling." Pegram snorted, "Is that so? Well, you have come too late; I am past crawling." The bespectacled artillerist nodded to the dead, "We have not had the time or chance to move them." Glancing at young William Carter, he asked, "Do you want to come in?" The newcomer stammered a weak "yes," but ventured that there was no room for his guns. Pegram cut him short, "Plenty of room!" The King William Artillery unlimbered in the pits next to Pegram's battery.[100]

Captain William J. Poague's Rockbridge (Virginia) Artillery came forward at the same time. Poague's gunners set up in pits right behind their famous Lexington neighbor, Stonewall Jackson. The general scanned the field, trying to figure out a way to compel the Union army to attack again. Wheeling on Poague, the general ordered him to engage the Federal artillery in front. Jackson hoped Poague would provoke an assault, or at least develop the Yankees' strength. Poague grimaced at the dangerous order, but barked the necessary commands under Jackson's watchful eye. Confederate shells arced into the Federal lines, answered by a deluge of Yankee shells in return. "Such a tempest of shot and shell I never have witnessed anywhere during the war," confessed the captain. Somewhat surprised by the unanticipated flare-up, other Confederate batteries quickly joined the fray. Carter's King William Artillery and Pegram's Letcher Artillery combined their fire with the Rockbridge guns. Captain Greenlee Davidson, still holding his position by Bernard's Cabins, also jumped into the fight.[101]

Federal fire blanketed the Confederate artillery placements. Every time the Southerners committed more guns, the Federals seemed to invest twice as many. A Virginian wrote, "Pandemonium broke loose again on 'Dead Horse Hill.'" Northern shrapnel knocked down the King William Artillery's flag twice from atop the gun pit. A shell hit a Confederate cannon, killing and wounding nine members of the crew. Carter became tangled with two horses that had been gutted by a shell. "They dropped like logs and never kicked," the captain recalled. Among the more regrettable losses to the King William Artillery was that of Bull-face Mike, a circus horse whose fearlessness made him a battery pet. A shell struck him squarely on the nose. A shell caught a Virginia gunner between the shoulder blades and flung his lifeless body three feet into the air. A solid shot sizzled between Carter and Pegram, causing Pegram to tumble backward with his feet in the air. Carter thought his friend had been hit. Pegram assured him that he was okay, but mused, "the windage from that solid shot made it a close shave, I can tell you."[102]

A gaudily attired officer, replete with the latest traps, stood quietly near Carter's battery. The captain admired the silent officer's finery, but thought, "there was something about that man that did not look so new after all." Carter ventured aloud "that those big guns over the river had been knocking us about pretty considerably during the day." The horseman shot him a glance, and Carter realized that he had been talking to General Jackson. "I knew in an instant who it was before me," the artillerist recollected. "The clear-cut chiseled features, the thin, compressed and determined lips, the neatly-trimmed chestnut beard, the calm, steadfast eye, the countenance to command respect." Stonewall studied the young man for a second, and then rode away without leaving any further instructions.[103]

Greenlee Davidson's artillery suffered a deluge of Yankee fire. The captain maintained the fight until an incoming shell blew up one of his limbers, scorching the ground and severing a gunner in two. The explosion cast the dead man's clothes into the treetops. Davidson's batteries abandoned the contest. J. Thompson Brown's artillery gave up the fight at about the same time. Lieutenant Colonel Lewis Minor Coleman, surprised by the unexpected duel, found it difficult to bring up two howitzers from Captain Willis J. Dance's Powhatan (Virginia) Artillery. The deputy commander of Brown's battalion stormed up to Captain Poague and demanded, "Who ordered you to open fire?" Poague answered that Jackson had, but Coleman raged, "Well, I take the responsibility of ordering you to stop." Colonel Brown arrived and also wanted an explanation. Poague obliged them, but the Federals continued to pound the hill. Moments later, Lieutenant Colonel Coleman felt the annoying sting of shrapnel burn his leg. He dismissed it as a flesh wound.

But his boot welled with blood, the wound became infected, and much later it proved fatal.[104]

Stonewall Jackson left Prospect Hill when he realized the Northerners would not attack. Instead, he turned his efforts to making an assault of his own. As daylight waned, the general reconnoitered the Union positions quickly, looking for an opportune spot to strike. Federal artillery had shown that the Union Third Corps positions would be difficult to assail, so Jackson focused on the Federal left flank. The laconic Stonewall impatiently thrust a fist toward the Yankees, murmuring, "I want to move forward, to attack them." Jackson had an hour of daylight left in which to strike.[105]

Jackson, accompanied by an aide, went out through Jeb Stuart's lines and prowled in front of Abner Doubleday's position. The Confederate noted that Doubleday had contracted his left flank—drawing Meredith's and Rogers' brigades closer to the intersection Pelham had made famous—and thought this might betray some hidden weakness. The adorned general and his braided lieutenant, James Power Smith, also had captured the attention of the Northern picket line. When the duo strayed too close, a bullet sizzled between Jackson and Smith. The youthful aide winced. "Mr. Smith," Jackson said dryly, "had you not better go to the rear? They may shoot you!" The staff officer refused to leave his commander, but he appreciated Jackson's brevity on reconnaissance. Returning to his lines, Jackson consulted with Stuart and hatched a plan to attack the Union left.[106]

Jackson probably dispatched his idea to Lee immediately, and then prepared to attack. The general wanted the entire Second Corps to advance, with Stuart on his right and John B. Hood on his left. Jackson planned to launch the assault at sunset, so the long shadows would mask his movement and the last glint of light would spotlight his target. Artillery would precede the attackers, breaching the Federal defenses and causing confusion in their ranks. Unfortunately, the architect for the most ambitious attack of the day— ideally, encompassing 35,000 plus men—had only minutes to prepare and execute it before it would be too dark. Staff officers dispersed through the woods, summoning various commands to their jump-off positions. The normally efficient staff fell short in the sudden scramble to attack. Some of Jackson's division commanders never received their notice for the grand assault. Major Alexander S. "Sandie" Pendleton fell wounded by a spent bullet before he could notify General William B. Taliaferro's division. Lieutenant Joseph G. Morrison, aide and brother-in-law to Jackson, could not find Jubal Early until it was practically too late. A. P. Hill, D. H. Hill, and Hood all received their orders, but Jackson had only two-thirds of his force aware of the attack, much less ready.[107]

Jubal Early first learned of the attack when D. H. Hill's division came forward from its reserve position. The men pressed ahead urgently, "double-quick thro' the woods," according to a soldier in Rodes' Brigade. Early demanded an explanation. One of Hill's lieutenants, Brigadier General Alfred H. Colquitt, told him about the pending twilight assault. D. H. Hill joined them, and confirmed the attack order. After the fact, the weary Lieutenant Morrison gave Early his notice. Early stormed to the front, unable to collect his widely scattered division in time for the attack. The captious subordinate happened upon Jackson and explained that his command was spread across the entire front. Jackson encouraged Early to advance with whatever he could manage. Jubal Early even alleged that Jackson gave him command of the right wing of the attack. More likely, Jackson asked Early to coordinate with Stuart.[108]

Confederates marshaled for the attack behind the railroad and along the crest of Prospect Hill. Early deployed two brigades—Hoke's and Hays'—along the RF&P tracks. D. H. Hill formed on the hill behind him. Ramseur's Brigade, under Colonel Bryan Grimes, stood closest to Poague's Rockbridge Artillery on the right of the division. Brigadier General Robert E. Rodes took up the line to Grimes' left, followed by Brigadier General George Doles' Georgia brigade. Colquitt's Brigade likely completed the line. D. H. Hill was missing one of his brigades, the North Carolina command of Colonel Alfred Iverson. It remained in the rear, without orders and oblivious to the circumstances. A. P. Hill continued the line north of the marsh, taking control of one of Early's brigades. Colonel James A. Walker's Virginia command formed on his right, with Thomas' Georgia brigade next, followed by Lane's and Pender's brigades. Colonel Daniel Hamilton's (Gregg's) Brigade formed in reserve behind Walker. Stuart's cavalry and Hood's First Corps division completed the alignment on either end of Jackson's line.[109]

Worried about the declining daylight, Jackson ignored the fact that half his troops were not ready to go. He ordered his artillery to the front, and ten batteries rumbled across the railroad tracks. Dropping trails, the cannon quickly opened on Doubleday's and Birney's Federal divisions. The first salvo came at twilight, and by 5:00 P.M., all of Jackson's guns had come into play. Jackson watched carefully from a spot near Lieutenant William K. Donald's section of Captain John M. Lusk's battery. Northern artillery responded immediately. According to Sandie Pendleton, the Federals unleashed a barrage, "the heaviest I ever saw, surpassing that at Malvern Hill." William Carter wrote that the Yankees raked Prospect Hill "in a most merciless manner." Jackson's attempt to smother the Union guns had failed completely. The general rescinded his attack orders and withdrew his forces back to the woods, personally accompanying Donald's guns to the rear. "It is seldom, in this country at least," chronicled a Northern historian, "that the artillery played such an important battle as it did at Fredericksburg." For the North at least, it had thwarted the most aggressive Confederate commander and his designs to launch the largest attack of the battle.[110]

Word of the canceled attack sped rapidly along the line. "There was not a man in the force," alleged Jubal Early, "who did not breathe freer when he heard the orders countermanding the movement." A North Carolinian concurred that the orders arrived "in the nick of time." The news, however, failed to reach one division before it was too late. D. H. Hill assumed the end of the bombardment signaled the beginning of the attack. Blinded by darkness and dense vegetation, Hill missed the withdrawal of the artillery. He rode conspicuously in front and led Doles' Brigade across the railroad. Rodes' and Grimes' brigades followed, but Colquitt clung to his position on Prospect Hill. Either Jackson's cancellation arrived in time to stop him, or the thick woods hid the advance. The woods proved difficult and divisive. Doles cleared the edge of the woods with little trouble. So did Grimes; but Rodes' Brigade split in two when it splashed through the marsh between them. William S. Campbell of the 5th Alabama reported, "It being nearly dark, we could scarcely see, consequently, the brigade became badly mixed up." The left of Rodes' Brigade, consisting of the 5th, 6th, and 26th Alabama, cleared the swamp and scampered after Doles' Brigade. The right of the brigade—the 3rd and 12th Alabama—reached the edge of the woods sometime later and stopped under a punishing barrage. Rodes' left also felt the fire, forcing the Alabamians to lie down in the field. "We dodged down to the ground," recalled one of Rodes' soldiers, "and lay as still as mice." The Federals turned their fire on Grimes' Brigade and drove it back. The division commander rode around the field with an air of disdain for the shellfire. "If there ever was an officer whose conduct under fire was calculated to inspire confidence and courage in his followers, that officer was Gen. D. H. Hill," wrote one of his men. Hill wished the Federals would attack him. He joked with General Doles, that "he would rather see the Yankees advance upon us in that position than to see the face of a pretty woman."[111]

Hoke's Brigade advanced hesitantly when it saw D. H. Hill move. It crossed the railroad tracks, but stopped well short of Rodes' and Doles' brigades. Hoke's men had removed all of their equipment prior to the assault, but when the call came, they clung to the railroad embankment. Officers prodded the troops forward even though they secretly sympathized with them. Captain William C. Oates, of the 15th Alabama, reminisced later that he too wanted to stay behind "if I could honorably have done so."[112]

Jackson's belated reprieve caught up with D. H. Hill and Jubal Early in the open flatland between the lines. The division commanders spirited their commands back to Prospect Hill under "a horrible red glare . . . of a spherical case shot," that in the darkness, seemed to light up "the whole heavens." Some of Rodes' advanced troops waited until pitch dark before falling back. Soldiers settled along the railroad and conjectured on what might have been. William McClendon of the 15th Alabama forever after harbored "a peculiar horror of night fighting." Jubal Early believed Jackson had courted disaster. "Nothing could have lived," the crotchety general believed, "while passing over that plain under such circumstances." Fortunately, Stonewall Jackson had abandoned the scheme before it really got started. Three and a half brigades had charged across the railroad and were easily recalled. The rest of the corps never left the staging area, so casualties remained light. Jackson, normally morose about setbacks, seemed strangely unperturbed, and was uncommonly pleasant and talkative for the rest of the evening. Jackson even consented to sit for a portrait artist later that night. He modeled for the highly respected Alexander Galt, but then he slipped into a "profound sleep" within a couple of minutes.[113]

Jeb Stuart had gone forward at the same time Jackson's artillery opened fire. When Jackson gave up the attack and recalled his troops, he notified Stuart, but the cavalry leader continued to press the Yankee left flank. Confederate cavalry brushed through staunch, unforgiving hedgerows, and crowded Doubleday's division. Many of the hedges probably had openings cut by Fitz Lee's troopers or Pelham's gunners during the day, making maneuvering easier for the cavalrymen. Complete darkness masked Stuart's tiny command, even with Pelham blazing in the van. Stuart drove ahead of his lines, disdaining the closeness of the Union fire. A Yankee bullet glanced off his saddle, close to his leg, and another pierced his collar. Stuart tested Doubleday's retracted line until he was satisfied that no weak point existed on the Union flank. He stopped his troopers, and they faded back into the hedgerows and the darkness. The cannon fire ebbed, and silence seeped across the battlefield. The Battle of Fredericksburg had come to an end. Unruffled, Stuart returned to Hamilton's Crossing, where he impressed a number of soldiers with his trademark "gentlemanly deportment and kindness of heart." An infantry private encountered the cavalry chief that evening and thought him "very polite indeed." Stuart took pride in his role at Fredericksburg. He had started the battle on his own, and he had ended it as well.[114]

CHAPTER FOURTEEN

"DECIDING THE FATE OF OUR COUNTRY"

The Aftermath of Battle

Night steeped the battlefield in darkness and cast an eerie pall over the combatants. Only an occasional shot, the shrieks of the wounded, and the creaking of ambulances carting the maimed to hospitals broke the stillness. A member of the Philadelphia Brigade recalled that "the wounded lay everywhere about us, and to assist the stretcher-bearers in finding them quickly, these poor fellows were told by their comrades to groan continually until they were found." A Federal officer remembered listening to the haunting peal of the bell in Saint George's Episcopal Church. Surgeons, North and South, plied their scalpels by candlelight in churches and houses, where windows were cloaked to prevent the light from drawing fire. Even with their best precautions, a Union doctor died in the George Rowe house when a glint of light betrayed his presence. Small groups of soldiers wandered the field or straggled into Fredericksburg, searching for their comrades. A Northern surgeon remembered "witnessing scenes that angels weep over if they ever weep."[1]

James Longstreet reinforced the Sunken Road at the foot of Marye's Heights during the night. Brigadier General James L. Kemper replaced the 24th North Carolina with the 1st and 7th Virginia Infantry. Joseph Kershaw also brought the 3rd South Carolina and 15th South Carolina into the road. Kershaw ordered the Confederates to fire volleys into the darkness to discourage a night attack. Rush Hawkins' assault had raised some concerns for the safety of the Sunken Road.[2]

Union soldiers shifted along the swale to get comfortable for the night. Some foraged for food and blankets among the dead. Sometimes they got more than they bargained for. A Union party stumbled into an icehouse near the millrace and found it "literally torn to pieces with shell, and bodies, blood, hair, brains, and the flesh strewed the floors and walls." A Massachusetts soldier in Barnes' brigade discovered a full haversack protruding from under a dead officer. He thrust his hand into the bag and to his horror, "encountered not hard bread, but a paste of hard, clotted blood mingled with flour." The impressionable scavenger wrote, "I fled from the spot; I foraged no more, for I *was not hungry again that night*" [emphasis in original].[3]

Others searched the field for wounded and missing comrades. Captain George N. Stone of the 7th Rhode Island was fairly sure where his lieutenant colonel had fallen. He took a squad to recover the body. The group "stumbled over the bodies of the dead," unable to see anything in the pitch dark. "The only means of identification," according to a New Englander, "was the sense of touch." Men scattered and "fumbled over each corpse they encountered." Eventually one of them found a body with shoulder straps. As he moved his hands down the corpse, he discovered that "the chest was completely shattered, one hand passing entirely within the cavity made by the exploding shell." After confirming this was Lieutenant Colonel Welcome B. Sayles, the squad scooped his remains onto a blanket and carried them back to the city.[4]

It was a dark and cheerless night. Joshua Chamberlain remembered that he spent the night curled up with cadavers, pulling their capes over his head for warmth. One of his captains, however, alleged that Chamberlain slept under a blanket between the leader of the 20th Maine and the brigade commander. "There was a singular conflict in our breasts," recalled a Union private. "We were wishing the hours away, and yet dreaded to have the darkness disappear."[5]

Meanwhile, across the river, Burnside convened a council of war to decide what to do next. The grand division commanders gathered at the Phillips house. Their gloomy reports depressed Burnside, who struggled to stay awake. A witness thought the army commander appeared "dead with sleep" and showed "evidences of great nervous exhaustion." Burnside ended the discussion after an hour when he announced that he personally would lead the

Ninth Corps in an assault on Marye's Heights in the morning. The Fifth Corps would act in support. In a sense, Burnside had superseded his subordinates, both Sumner and Hooker. The Center Grand Division commander protested vehemently. One officer reported that Hooker's "whole appearance and manner of talking indicated disapproval and almost insubordination." The other generals also objected, but Burnside refused to change his mind. The meeting disbanded, and the grand division chiefs reconvened a council of their own. William Franklin approached Burnside later that night and proposed another attack on Stonewall Jackson, like they had discussed before. The army commander refused. After Franklin's poor performance, Burnside evidently would rather rely on the Ninth Corps.[6]

Troubled by his generals' reports, Burnside crossed the river to assess the situation for himself. The general talked to several officers in the city. "I went all over the field on our right," he later attested. Union soldiers everywhere frowned on the idea of another attack. By morning, Burnside left Fredericksburg, admitting, "I found the feeling to be rather against an attack . . . in fact it was decidedly against it." Burnside ignored the consensus and determined to try again anyway. The army commander returned to his headquarters and notified Sumner to prepare the Ninth Corps for action. He specifically ordered that the troops be arranged in "a column of attack by regiments." Perhaps Hawkins' near-success the previous evening encouraged Burnside, who concluded that a compact unit with a small front might reach the stone wall whereas Hawkins' disheveled units had failed. Burnside did not appear to consider the darkness as a reason for Hawkins' nearness to the stone wall.[7]

Robert E. Lee had relished the outcome of the battle so far. He sat up late into the night hosting a plethora of gilded generals at his headquarters. The officers found the general "in the highest spirits." Lee listened to the result of Jackson's hard-fought battle on the right and noted Jackson's assurance that he could maintain his front. Underscoring Stonewall's satisfaction, Longstreet exuded confidence that nothing could penetrate the Confederate left. He had punished seven Union assaults and not one Northerner had reached his lines. The Confederates had triumphed so handily that it was hard for them to believe that Burnside had thrown his best punch. Only John Bell Hood dissented from their opinion. When Hood entered Lee's tent at 10:00 P.M., the commander immediately asked him what he thought of the Union attacks. Hood replied, "Burnside was whipped." Lee disagreed, certain that Burnside had yet to make his "principal attempt," which he reckoned would come at dawn. Lee hoped the Federals would crush themselves on the morrow, and then the Army of Northern Virginia might even consider assuming a counteroffensive.[8]

With that in mind, Robert E. Lee readied his army for the prospective battle. He ordered Jackson to "obtain as many wagons as possible," emptying them if necessary, and send them to Guiney Station for ammunition. Lee wanted the men and artillery rearmed that night "and every thing ready by daylight tomorrow." He closed his message to the religious corps commander, "I am truly grateful to the Giver of all victory for having blessed us thus far in our terrible struggle. I pray he may continue it." Jackson dispatched Major George H. Bier to Guiney in haste. The Second Corps commander, meanwhile, rearranged his lines. A. P. Hill's division yielded the front to fresh troops who carried a full complement of cartridges. William Taliaferro's and Jube Early's troops spread out and improved some of the low ditches Hill's men had defended. A. P. Hill and D. H. Hill moved their men back to the Hamilton farm and caught up on some much-needed rest.[9]

Longstreet made only minor adjustments to his defenses. Lafayette McLaws offered to relieve Kershaw's South Carolina brigade from duty on the Sunken Road. Kershaw replied that his position "was the post of danger, and therefore was the post of honor." He begged to stay, feeling that he had earned the right. McLaws next asked Colonel Robert McMillan if Cobb's Brigade would like relief, but the Georgian declined as well. Brigadier General Paul Semmes protested about being left out. "I knew that Gen. Semmes was fretting to share the dangers and honors," sympathized McLaws, but Kershaw and McMillan deserved the front. They had fought hard, proved their reliability, and exhibited high morale—none of which Semmes' men had had a chance to show. Kershaw and McMillan consolidated their brigade lines rather than leaving them amalgamated. The South Carolinians took the left, and McMillan's men shifted to the right. James Kemper's men supported Kershaw. E. P. Alexander brought up the rest of Jordan's battery and replaced Victor Maurin's battered Louisiana guns. The artillerists dug all night, repairing and improving the gun pits on Marye's Heights. Alexander occasionally launched a rocket over the Federal lines to discourage a night attack. Artillery chief William N. Pendleton ordered the gunner to fire "incendiary shell" at the houses on the edge of the city "so that we can see what the enemy is doing." Without the proper shells, Alexander improvised, with mixed results. All of the troops in the Sunken Road labored through the night, improving the stone wall and entrenching gaps in the wall where avenues like Mercer Street entered. Many of the men used bayonets to pry loose the frozen ground. Skirmishers from the 3rd South Carolina and 27th North Carolina crept softly in front of the wall after 9:00 P.M., setting up a picket line. Stationed thirty yards from the enemy, the Confederates netted a number of disoriented prisoners, who strayed into their hands. "Many of their recruits came into our lines," a North Carolina soldier boasted. In the middle of the night, Southern pickets captured a Federal orderly bearing dispatches for Griffin's division to support an attack in the morning. They whisked the courier off to headquarters.[10]

Lee briefed the Richmond authorities on the events of December 13. He wrote to the War Department at 9:00 P.M.: "About 9 A.M. the enemy attacked our right, and as the fog lifted the battle ran from right to left; raged until 6 P.M.; but, thanks to Almighty God, the day closed [with assaults] repulsed along our whole front. Our troops behaved admirably, but as usual, we have to mourn the loss of many brave men. I expect the battle to be renewed at daylight. Please send this to the President."[11]

Before midnight, the captured orderly arrived at Lee's headquarters with his valuable information. The mounted Federal apparently carried orders preparing for a morning assault. It is impossible to determine whether the missing orders emanated from the Ninth Corps—which would spearhead Burnside's December 14 assault—or from Griffin's division of the Fifth Corps, which would support it. Wherever the order originated, it confirmed everything that Lee had suspected. He reiterated his orders to the generals to dig in and be ready by dawn.[12]

December 14 dawned frigid. The weather observer in Georgetown noted the temperature was forty degrees at 7:00 A.M., but gusty winds made it feel much colder. Mists again shrouded the battlefield. Kemper's Virginia brigade stared vigilantly into the fog, looking for the anticipated attack. Whispers electrified the line, warning that the Yankees were advancing. Tall forms appeared faintly in the distance, and "the whole brigade discharged their pieces almost simultaneously." The volley drew no reprisal, and the stoic forms held their ground. This confused the anxious Southerners, who continued to study their adversary. "As they didn't seem to advance very fast, we cooled down a little," wrote one of the eagle-eyed sharpshooters. Moments later the mist thinned to reveal that they had fired at a fence. The young zealots sheepishly waited for the real attackers to come.[13]

Soldiers North and South felt certain that Burnside must attack. "Every one expected to see the battle renewed again," recalled a Rebel in Pickett's division. A Union soldier agreed unhappily: "the present is dark and the future—shall I say—darker?" From a Northern perspective, no one could sally out of Fredericksburg without heavy losses because "the town . . . was at the mercy of the enemy." Federal commanders offered no reassurances, and morale sagged. James Longstreet, in contrast, inspired his men that morning. He told his First Corps: "Let every man of us summon all his spirit and all his strength to this encounter." He anticipated that "if we beat our foe in this engagement, the war may terminate with it." Longstreet warned his troops that "every soldier should feel that upon his own individual efforts may hang the success or failure" of the battle. That sentiment echoed in Jackson's camps. "We broke the backbone of Burnside's army," reported topographer Jed Hotchkiss. "Today will go far towards deciding the fate of our country."[14]

Newspaperman Murat Halstead returned to Washington on December 14 and promptly informed Secretary of the Treasury Salmon Chase what was happening in Fredericksburg. Halstead frightened Chase with gory details of defeat, and later reiterated his observations to the president. Railroader Herman Haupt arrived in the capital later that day and was immediately buttonholed by Pennsylvania congressman John Covode. Haupt related some of the news from the front, which depressed the politician. Covode dragged Haupt to see the president at 9:00 P.M. Hearing bad news for the second time that day, Lincoln asked Haupt and Covode to come with him to see General Halleck. The president interrupted a dinner party at Halleck's residence on I Street, between Fifteenth and Sixteenth Streets. Lincoln ushered the general-in-chief into a side room with Haupt and Covode. The railroad superintendent repeated his observations to Halleck. When Haupt finished, the president commanded Halleck to "telegraph orders to General Burnside to withdraw his army." Halleck paced the room for a moment before responding, "I will do no such thing." He did not know enough about the situation to foist orders on Burnside from afar. "If we were personally present and knew the exact situation, we might assume such responsibility," he reasoned. "If such orders are issued, you must issue them yourself. I hold that a General in command of an army in the field is the best judge of existing conditions." Haupt interjected that Burnside could retreat without loss at any time he wanted, which instantly soothed the president. There was no need to rush. Lincoln sighed, "What you say gives me a great many grains of comfort." Washington would let Burnside continue his campaign.[15]

Union generals drifted into Edwin Sumner's headquarters throughout the early morning of December 14. Generals Willcox, Hunt, and Pleasonton sat in the Phillips house while others milled around the outbuildings. "Our Hdqrs & grounds," noted Sumner's son-in-law, "were literally jammed with Generals." Officers spoke openly against the new attack. A staff officer wrote "Nearly all disapproved of the attack which Genl. Burnside had ordered." In the Ninth Corps, both George Getty and Rush Hawkins seriously condemned the plan. They, and others, appealed to Sumner to intercede with the army commander. As the time neared 10:00 A.M., the only one noticeably missing was Burnside.[16]

The general arrived at the Phillips house fifteen minutes late for his own attack. He appeared uncertain of his plans. Heading upstairs, he gazed out the window and then requested Professor Lowe to take his balloon aloft for a better view. The aeronaut declined because high winds made it too dangerous for the balloon. Sumner took the opportunity to quietly suggest to Burnside that he needed to talk to his subordinates. "General, I hope you will desist from this attack," the elder whispered. "I do not know of any general officer who approves of it, and I think it will prove disastrous to the army." Burnside heeded his confidant's suggestion. "Advice of that kind," he later wrote "caused me to hesitate." He had expected discord from almost all of his officers, but not Sumner. Sumner had supported him faithfully in all things. He postponed the attack and summoned a council of war.[17]

Across the battlefield, Robert E. Lee resumed his place on Telegraph Hill. Longstreet reconnoitered for much of the morning before he reported to Lee at his command post. Jackson arose to "an amusing war of words." He asked his body servant, Jim Lewis, to saddle his favorite mount, Little Sorrel. Lewis protested against riding the same horse two days in a row. The general demanded his horse. But Jim triumphed when he brought out a different horse which the general took without comment. The Confederate high command gathered to await the attack, but it never materialized. Around noon, Lee and Jackson left Telegraph Hill to take a look at the southern end of the line. Riding through Hood's positions, the generals invited the division commander to accompany them. The men cheered Lee, but some of them still wondered at Jackson's unaccustomed attire. One group of Hood's soldiers speculated on Jackson's identity: "Stonewall h——ll! Who ever saw old Stonewall dressed up?" Overhearing the debate, the corps commander smiled self-consciously, causing the men to laugh and cheer. Lee surveyed the indolent Federals in front of Prospect Hill and returned to his headquarters, convinced that Burnside had changed his mind about attacking. "General," he confronted Longstreet on his return, "I am losing faith in your friend General Burnside."[18]

Lee tried to provoke an attack late in the afternoon. He ordered Hood to withdraw the center of his line from the Lansdowne Valley. Robertson's Texas Brigade and Tige Anderson's brigade abandoned their entrenchments along the valley floor and fell back to the ridge by Dr. Rennolds' house. They left with great fanfare. A watching newspaperman noted, "the keen flash of their arms was seen, and their bands playing Dixie plainly heard." Pickets remained behind to offer a show of resistance in case Burnside snapped at the bait. After testing his right and left, Lee hoped the Federals might take the Southern withdrawal as a sign of weakness in the center. If he could lure the enemy closer, the Confederates on either side of the valley—Pickett's and Taliaferro's divisions—could trap the Yankees in a well-planned crossfire. Unknown to Lee, Burnside and his subordinates remained cloistered in the Phillips' house, and the ruse went largely unnoticed.[19]

Unable to lure Burnside into his trap, Lee spent the rest of the day improving his fortifications. The strength of Longstreet's front had exceeded Jackson's, with obvious terrain features neatly incorporated into the defensive scheme. Stonewall's men labored arduously on December 14 to make their positions just as strong. Jackson commanded Taliaferro to "send all your picks & spades" to Prospect Hill. A detail of two men for each tool reported to Jackson personally, who set them to working on the crest of the hill. Jackson hastened the digging, confiding to his friend, Alexander R. Boteler, "Burnside has doubtless discovered by this time that it's useless for him to make any further attempts on the left and left center of our line." That only left Jackson's right, and the general wanted to be ready. Work progressed well into the evening. A listening Pennsylvanian remembered, "at night we could hear the rebels chopping trees and strengthening their fortifications." Some of the grayclad troops pried up the remaining tracks of the RF&P, and incorporated the wooden ties into their breastworks. Lee approved of all of the work. "My army," he allegedly told a staff officer, "is as much stronger for these new entrenchments as if I had received reinforcements of 20,000 men."[20]

Longstreet's Confederates spent the day engaged in a one-sided duel with the Federals pinned down in front of Marye's Heights. Sharpshooters along the stone wall and atop Marye's Heights peppered the field, shooting at anything that moved. "We commenced firing at any and every thing moving in our front," recalled Nathan C. Bartley of the 7th Virginia. Most of the Northerners flattened themselves on the ground, unable to twitch without provoking a volley. The Confederates "were wasting so much ammunition and doing so little damage," that officers permitted only three men from each company to shoot at a given time. The fire became regular, but every so often a daring Yankee would dart across the front, sparking a volley. "Sometimes we would see a man run from one house to another," a Virginian wrote, "and we would fire hundreds of shots at him." Even under sporadic explosions of fire, the Rebels largely refrained from shooting at the Rowe house and the buildings adjacent to the fairgrounds. Yellow flags fluttered over the houses, denoting them as hospitals. Confederates concentrated on the bluecoats lying in the swale.[21]

E. Porter Alexander wished to join the duel but held back. Longstreet had forbidden him from using any ammunition unless in a crisis. The heavy guns frowned menacingly, but quietly. Alexander remembered "the day as a very disagreeable one" for him. Moving along the line, the artillery commander drew fire from Union sharpshooters posted in Hurkamp's tannery on Plank Road. The Northerners had loopholed the building, giving them firing ports to harass any Confederate who showed himself on the street. Alexander crossed Plank Road several times, gambling with one particular sniper. "He had several shots at me during the day," the colonel recalled, "& though he missed me every time, I acquired a special animosity to him." By the end of the day, the artillerist complained to Longstreet about his ordeal with the "particularly bad nest of sharpshooters in a brick tanyard." Longstreet told his young lieutenant that fresh ammunition had just arrived from Richmond and he could spare a "few score shell" for Alexander "to get even with them."[22]

Confederate infantry along the Sunken Road continued a droning standoff between snipers, which consumed much of the day. The sergeant major of one of the South Carolina regiments fell dead on the picket line. Henry Gooden of the 2nd South Carolina risked his life to fetch water from a nearby well. He returned safely, only to be killed by a bullet passing through both of his lungs. A Georgia soldier on a similar errand retreated from the well "amid a hail of bullets." Rebels retaliated and blanketed the ground in front with dead and wounded Unionists. "The fields," wrote a South Carolinian, "were blue with Yankee dead." Another imagined that "the ground between the lines was nearly bridged with the wounded, dead and dying Federals."[23]

Wounded Yankees between the lines begged for help. They pleaded desperately for water. Soldiers on both sides heard the heart-wrenching cries, "Water, water, for God's sake, water!" The appeals affected many, but no one could render assistance. Any attempt from either side to aid the injured immediately sparked a angry fusillade of fire. "No one dared to go to the relief of the wounded," a 16th New York soldier recalled, "because the appearance of a head above the breastworks was the signal for a volley." Twenty-year-old Sergeant Richard Rowland Kirkland, of the 2nd South Carolina, felt particularly moved by the pathos. He asked General Kershaw if he could take water to the injured Northerners. "General," he beseeched, "I can't stand this." "Kirkland," the general answered, "don't you know that you would get a bullet through your head the moment you stepped over the wall?" The youth was willing to take that risk. "If you will let me," the sergeant stated, "I am willing to try it." Kershaw acquiesced. He told the sergeant, "I will not refuse your request, trusting that God may protect you." Kirkland asked if he could have a white flag to stop the shooting, but Kershaw could not allow it; military protocol forbade such a usage. "All right, Sir," he replied, "I'll take the chances." Kershaw watched the sergeant leave the Stephens house with "feelings of profound admiration."[24]

Kirkland filled several canteens at Martha Stephens' well, and then entered the field between the lines. Federals immediately opened fire. A watching Georgian thought the bullets were so concentrated that it seemed "a bird could not escape them." Kirkland reached the first wounded Federal and knelt to give him a drink. The Carolinian placed a knapsack under the Northerner's head, covered him with a blanket, and then moved on to the next man. The Federals stopped shooting and watched. Troops on both sides cheered as the brave sergeant moved from soldier to solder. The ceasefire may have prompted others to come forward with more water. The historian for Kershaw's Brigade remembered the event with a Georgian running between the lines with water. "A squad," according to a staff officer, "went out after dark on the same charitable mission." At least one Federal procured water for the discomfited, which an admiring Rebel called "the coolest performance I witnessed . . . during the war." Whether Kirkland acted alone, or pioneered a host of encounters and somehow became a composite for all of the works of mercy, is hard to determine. Seventeen years after the battle a newspaper correspondent begged for the name of the man who gave water to his enemies; General Joseph Kershaw responded instantly, naming Richard Kirkland as the "Angel of Marye's Heights." Regardless of who should get the credit, the act of humanity far transcended the individuals who performed it. "Such deeds as this," wrote a Northern soldier, "are the redeeming features of war."[25]

* * *

On the other side of the Rappahannock River, Burnside and his generals argued behind closed doors. All of the grand division and corps commanders attended the council of war except Franklin's generals, who dared not leave their front for even a brief time. No one at the meeting supported Burnside's preference for another assault. Officers voted unanimously to remain on the defensive, and Burnside yielded "with expressions of greatest reluctance." The council, however, failed to offer any alternative solutions. None of the generals wanted to abandon Fredericksburg and retreat. Leaving the field to the Rebels would be a clear-cut admission of defeat, and no one wanted to face that responsibility. Without a convenient change of base, McClellan's old cronies appeared at a loss about what to do, and Burnside refused to press them. Instead, he dismissed the council at 4:00 P.M., hoping that an unforeseen opportunity might arise to change their minds. Expectant staff officers waited outside anticipating orders. "Such constant scenes of excitement" strained the staff "to the highest point" of anxiety. When the generals announced the attack had been canceled, everyone relaxed. "After the Council broke up," one staff officer told his wife, "our horses were unsaddled & the staff breathed freer again."[26]

Deeply chagrined, Burnside sat down to dinner with Sumner. Hooker and Butterfield, along with several others, joined them. After eating, Burnside left the party to see the commanders in Fredericksburg. The army commander sought out several junior officers to get their opinions on another attack in light of the council of war. "I . . . found that the same impression prevailed among them," he reported. The general returned to the Phillips house and ordered William Franklin and Edwin Sumner to report to him at once. Burnside explained the situation and asked Franklin's opinion for the record. Franklin "was of exactly the same opinion" as all of the others. The commander dismissed the generals at 10:00 P.M., still no closer to resolving the deadlock at Fredericksburg. Burnside sent his aide, Major William Goddard, to Washington that night to consult with Halleck. Perhaps he hoped a word from the War Department would strengthen his subordinates' resolve. Goddard did not see the general-in-chief until 6:00 P.M. on December 15, and by then Burnside had made up his mind.[27]

The Southern army whiled away the day waiting for Burnside to attack. One Carolina doctor worried that "The result of the fight is not yet decisive." He believed that when victory did come, "there will be bloody work." The ever-aggressive Porter Alexander believed that "no one conceived that the battle was over, for less than half our army had been engaged." The Army of

Northern Virginia had spent an emotionally draining day. "Just imagine our feelings," wrote a Virginian under Stonewall, "as we lay there all day . . . expecting every moment to be rushed together in deadly conflict." The day ended without resolution. Intense Confederates prepared to spend another freezing night on the battlefield. As far as they were concerned, victory had been postponed until December 15. Lee informed Richmond that, "with the exception of some desultory cannonading and firing between skirmishers, he [Burnside] had not attempted to renew the attack." Lee requested that additional supplies and ammunition be forwarded at once. The Confederate generals remained confident that Burnside would surely attack the next day.[28]

The night sky heightened the anticipation of Lee's army when it appeared to forecast Confederate success. A brilliant illumination lit up the horizon. The Aurora borealis—or Northern Lights—radiated over the battlefield for over an hour starting at 6:15 P.M. "The heavens were filled with long streaks of pale yellow light then blended together and turned to a blood red," recounted a wide-eyed witness. It first appeared as a dim reflection from below the horizon and grew until it covered the sky. One of Jackson's veterans described it "Shooting up its steady and well defined columns, each tinted in separate and distinct hues and thus continued for many minutes then all gradually faded away." The majestic display unfurled its rays across the sky like a fan. An awestruck Confederate remembered, "The awe and beauty of this natural apparition as it appeared on that night . . . will ever hold a place in memory." Because the Northern Lights were rarely seen in those parts, soldiers assumed it had profound symbolism. "An omen," cried a member of the Richmond Howitzers, "an omen of the fight." Artillerists suggested that "the heavens were hanging out banners and streamers and setting off fireworks in honor of our victory." With such breathtaking displays to lull the Southerners to sleep, no wonder they believed Burnside would meet further disaster the next day.[29]

Some Confederates took advantage of the bright skies to plunder the dead for warmer clothing. Men had spent days coveting the overcoats and shoes of the Union corpses strewn in front. Longstreet's veterans ogled tons of enticing material, but refrained because of the proximity of the Federals in the swale. Anyone crossing the stone wall did so at his own peril. Jackson's men, on the other hand, roamed freely along the railroad and through the coppice, helping themselves to loot from hundreds of Yankee bodies. Captain William C. Oates of the 15th Alabama ordered his entire regiment to collect shoes. The hunters thoroughly scoured the bodies. A nearby Carolinian wrote that many of the soldiers stripped the corpses "of every stitch of clothing." Several ludicrous encounters resulted from the hasty search for clothes. A Confederate attempting to wrench loose a pair of shoes jumped when the "corpse" laconically asked to keep them a bit longer. "Beg pardon, sir," the startled Rebel stammered, "I thought you had gone above." A sleeping Alabamian awoke to discover someone stealing the boots off his feet, shortly after he had taken them from a dead Yankee. The ensuing scuffle forced Captain Oates to rectify the situation by confiscating the boots for himself. By morning, marauders pretty well had gleaned the field in front of Prospect Hill. Someone even had lifted the uniform coat from General Conrad Feger Jackson's body.[30]

Stonewall Jackson had had little chance to sleep over the past three days and was beginning to show it. Jackson encouraged his friend Alexander Boteler to "return to camp, get your supper and go to bed," because he felt sure they would "likely . . . have a very busy day tomorrow." The congressman gratefully accepted quarters in Jackson's tent, later acknowledging, "The advice was timely and too good to be neglected." The general spent part of the evening at Lee's headquarters comparing notes on the day. Later he visited with Virginia governor John Letcher. Perched on a stool between his guests, Jackson nodded into a "profound sleep" while the party continued to banter and read.[31]

Later in the evening, a brigade orderly from Maxcy Gregg roused the general from his slumber. "General," he announced, "Gen. Gregg has sent me to say to you that he will be glad to see you before he leaves us. We fear that he will not live until morning." Jackson listened while the staff officer explained that Gregg wished to apologize for some past criticisms of Jackson. "Poor fellow," murmured the general, "I feared that his wound was mortal, but did not think the end so near." He dismissed the orderly with the uncharacteristic message: "Give my love to him and say that I will see him as soon as I can get there." Dr. Hunter H. McGuire, medical director of Jackson's corps, reported to Jackson at 4:00 A.M., confirming that Gregg "was beyond hope." Jackson ordered the tired physician back to the dying general; then he dressed quietly so as not to awaken Congressman Boteler.[32]

Maxcy Gregg struggled in silent agony at Thomas Yerby's home, Belvoir. Numerous officers visited the dying general, offering prayers and final words of hope. David Gregg McIntosh, the South Carolina artillerist, sat in the corner, keeping vigil over his distant kinsman. No one saw him hunched in the shadows. A. P. Hill crept into the room alone when Gregg was asleep, and tenderly kissed him on the forehead before slipping out as quietly as he came.

Brigade chaplain J. Monroe Anderson knelt beside the general when Gregg awoke. The general motioned him closer, whispering in his ear, "Mr. Anderson, I would kneel if I could." Dr. McGuire arrived shortly afterward; and Jackson hard on his heels.[33]

Maxcy Gregg tried to stammer an apology, but Jackson assured the dying man that he had not been offended. "The doctors tell me that you have not long to live," Jackson said kindly as he took his subordinate's hand. "Let me ask you to dismiss this matter from your mind and turn your thoughts to God and to the world to which you go." Gregg's eyes welled with tears. "I thank you," he choked, "I thank you very much." The general passed away quietly before daybreak. A houseguest recalled, "He looked very handsome as he lay in his last sleep." Stonewall Jackson rode silently back to camp with Dr. McGuire. The medical director broke the silence by asking his chief how they were going to cope with the expected Union attack that morning. Jackson, still deeply affected, snapped, "Kill them, sir! kill every man!"[34]

The first light of December 15 sparked renewed activity along the battle lines. The day dawned warm; temperatures reached sixty-eight degrees in the afternoon. Skirmishers heated up too, reflexively popping away at one another. Federal troops studied the growing Confederate earthworks, and began excavating trenches of their own. Artillery punctuated the morning with sporadic blasts. But the Confederates generally maintained a disdainful silence, challenging the Union army to come closer. "Today we opened on them both right & left with artillery," a Northern signalman wrote, "but met with very little response." A Pennsylvania diarist wondered whether "we are going to retreat or expect a severe contest." The stillness made him observe, "Both parties act very (strange) cautious." A rumor circulated through the Army of the Potomac that Sigel's Reserve Grand Division had arrived upriver to flank the Confederates while Burnside diverted Lee's attention. (Sigel's forces were en route to the army, but would not arrive at Stafford Court House for several more days.) Stonewall Jackson rotated his divisions again, giving the front to D. H. Hill's troops. A. P. Hill formed the second line; and Taliaferro and Early went into reserve. Jackson ordered Taliaferro to turn over all of his entrenching tools to the troops in front, and the digging continued.[35]

Burnside rose early on the balmy morning of December 15 and went directly to Sumner's headquarters. Climbing the stairs to the second floor, he scanned the Confederate lines with a telescope. A few minutes later, the general slumped down the steps crestfallen. "Genl. Burnside came down," remembered Sumner's son-in-law, William Teall, "much depressed in feelings." The Confederates had improved their defenses dramatically during the night. Under the circumstances, Burnside saw no way he could convince his subordinates to attack the Rebels now. He had run out of options. The commanding general "announced his determination to resign." Sumner quickly took the general aside, and scolded him that "he must not think such a thing." The second-in-command thought Burnside was overreacting; he should take a closer look at the battlefield. Mulling over Sumner's advice, the general mounted and went into Fredericksburg to talk to some of his subordinates. Perhaps their morale might exceed his expectations.[36]

Burnside spent most of the day discoursing with his officers downtown. Any hopes that they would reconsider an assault quickly vanished. The notion of attacking was overshadowed by the prevailing concern that the army would be attacked. This fear was confirmed when renewed picket fire caused several regiments to break. A flood of demoralized soldiers fled into the lower city, raising the alarm that the Confederates were counterattacking. The attack never materialized, and the Federals re-established their picket line without further mishap. Dejected, Burnside rode back to headquarters late in the afternoon. He sent invitations his grand division chiefs to dine with him that evening.[37]

Meanwhile, Lieutenant Colonel E. Porter Alexander had a personal score to settle with the Federal sharpshooters ensconced in Hurkamp's tannery. The Northerners had vexed him on December 14. When they opened on the Rebels again at dawn, Alexander happened to be nearby. He determined to "rout them." The tannery squatted in a hollow, making it difficult for the Confederates to hit it with artillery. Alexander thought Moody's battery had the best angle of fire. A 24-pounder howitzer just south of Plank Road stood four hundred yards from the sharpshooters. The Southern artillery commander studied a low intervening ridge as he calculated the trajectory. He figured that he might be able to skim a shell off the top of the ridge and its downward curve could strike the building. Alexander aimed the howitzer himself, spending several minutes "to get all exact." Stepping back, he ordered the weapon discharged. The artillery round barely cleared the hill before it arced downward. The cannon crew heard the shell crash into the building and explode, and "at once there came a cheer from our picket line." An excited infantryman scurried up Marye's Heights, shouting gleefully, "That got 'em! You can hear them just a hollering & a groaning in there." Alexander's meticulous shot wounded a number of U.S. Regulars and forced the rest to seek safer climes. The Confederates had nullified the only advantage the Federals had claimed on the Marye's Heights front, and they did it with one shot.[38]

Wounded still covered much of the field, begging and crying for help. Most of them lay trapped between the lines. Their pitiful cries grew weaker and less numerous with each passing hour, as many succumbed to their wounds and the elements. "The poor wounded," recollected Jeb Stuart's Prussian staff officer, Heros von Borcke, "were in a miserable state after their long exposure to cold and hunger."[39]

Union general Franklin took advantage of the lull to seek help for the few injured men still alive. A Federal officer approached Stonewall Jackson's line waving a white handkerchief. Confederate pickets stood up along a ditch-fence and motioned the lieutenant closer. Brigadier General Robert Rodes met the Unionist at the fence. The Northern emissary proposed an informal truce to collect the wounded. Rodes declined such an unofficial arrangement, asking instead for a formal written request that he could pass along to his superiors. Union litter-bearers who already had entered the field were summarily shooed away. The unsuccessful Federal returned to his lines, promising to get the proper authority. Two hours later, another white flag heralded one of Franklin's staff officers with a small escort. A watching Southerner called the chastened Yankees "the prettiest sight . . . I ever saw in my life." The horsemen stopped one hundred yards in front of the pickets and Rodes went out to parley with them. He returned with a verbal request from Franklin for a truce. He forwarded the petition to Jackson. The Second Corps commander rejected it, and demanded the application be properly submitted in writing. Franklin's representative acquiesced; Stonewall Jackson, well satisfied, granted a truce for the remaining hour of daylight.[40]

Captain Edwin V. Sumner, Jr., son of the Right Grand Division commander, represented the Federals during the truce. Jackson sent Lieutenant James Power Smith, of his staff, to handle the Confederate arrangements. Jackson cautioned his newest aide, "If you are asked who is in command on our right do not tell that I am, and be guarded in your conversation." Some of the Confederate officers mirrored Jackson's caution, forbidding their men to fraternize with the enemy. General Rodes warned his pickets, "Now, boys these Yankees are going to ask you questions and you must not tell them anything. Be very careful about this." "General," a private interrupted, "may we not tell them that we whipped them yesterday?" Rodes chuckled and said, "Yes, you can tell them that." Another interjected, "General may we not tell that we can whip them tomorrow again?" Amid approving laughter, Rodes relented, "Yes, yes, go on, go on. Tell them what you please."[41]

Federal ambulances trundled into the field. Details fanned across the battlefield, collecting the dead and wounded. Southern detachments met them at the picket line, to gather the dead Georgians from the Slaughter Pen. Together, Northerners and Southerners broke the spongy ground, digging graves for the slain. They excavated long trenches and buried the bodies en masse. A Confederate picket thought it "was a grand sight" to see the parties working together, "and at the same time a very simple affair." Burial parties barely collected the bodies before time ran out on the truce. Many of the corpses lay abandoned in heaps at collection points. In a hurry to finish, some Confederates crammed bodies into the railroad ditches, and kicked down the embankments on top of them. While these groups raced through their macabre chore, the 4th North Carolina disposed of the rotting horseflesh on Dead Horse Hill. Soldiers threw the carcasses on huge bonfires. The number of dead horses made at least one soldier wonder how "anyone could have passed through this place without being killed." Federals rescued their wounded and whisked them off to Falmouth. Waiting trains carried them to Aquia Landing, where ships conveyed them to hospitals in Washington and Alexandria. Rufus Ingalls made arrangements with Quartermaster General Meigs to transport 3,500 wounded men.[42]

While soldiers toiled in the dirt, officers turned the field into "quite a reunion." Old army friends embraced and inquired about acquaintances. Both sides, according to a bystander, "gladly clasped hands and seemed greatly delighted to see each other." Jeb Stuart and Rooney Lee sought out a number of their former associates. Only Lieutenant Smith seemed uncomfortable with the familiarity. A Federal officer named John Junkin, a brother to Jackson's first wife, recognized Stonewall's aide and asked him to relay a message from Jackson's father-in-law. Somewhat baffled, Smith responded, "I will do so when I see Gen. Jackson." Junkin smiled pleasantly and replied, "It is not worth while for you to try to deceive us. We know that Gen. Jackson is in front of us." The young Confederate said nothing more.[43]

Many of the work parties emulated the officers and put aside their gravedigging to trade goods. "Let the dead bury their dead," a Union lieutenant told a Southern artillerist with a biblical flare, "and we will have a talk." Hundreds of soldiers mingled "in the most friendly manner," swapping pipes, tobacco, coffee, and knives. One Confederate walked away with a new canteen, a nice cup, several haversacks with crackers, and a sack of coffee. Some incidents of friction occurred, but they only accentuated the prevailing good feelings indulged in by both sides for the moment. A Federal martinet, for example, objected to a lanky Alabama soldier carrying away a new Enfield rifle. He told the Rebel to drop it, but the Confederate ignored him. Unsheathing his sword, the Federal ordered the man to desist "with a fierce oath." The unimpressed Southerner pointed to the officer's boots, drawling, "I will shoot you tomorrow and get them boots," and then strode away. Federal captain Edwin Sumner said with amusement to James P. Smith, "That fellow has gotten just what he deserved. He won't sleep a wink tonight." The hour slipped away and the truce ended. Both sides retreated to their respective positions and resumed their war-like postures. The peaceful, almost festive, interlude seemed ludicrously out of place. A Carolina soldier reflected, "What a strange thing is war."[44]

Burnside sat down to dinner with his grand division commanders and one or two other generals. Burnside brooded through the meal. One of Sumner's staff officers noted, "He looks careworn & I really feel a sympathy for him." The commander notified the assemblage that he "had decided to withdraw to this side of the river." After dark, the Army of the Potomac would recross the Rappahannock River. He charged Hooker with evacuating the city and Franklin would handle the left. Burnside intended to keep a small force in Fredericksburg and below, just enough "to hold the town and the bridgeheads." Franklin telegraphed the news to William F. Smith to get started on preparations. Dinner ended at 5:00 P.M., and Franklin and Hooker left to begin the retreat. Sometime later, Burnside's aide, Major Goddard, wired from Washington that Halleck "decidedly disapproved of recrossing the river." Halleck encouraged Burnside to resume the attack or, at least, entrench the bridgehead. Halleck himself telegraphed shortly afterward, cryptically assuring Burnside that "you will be fully sustained in any measures you may adopt in regard to unreliable officers." He refused to officially counsel an attack, hedging, "we cannot judge here; you are the best judge." By then, it was too late. Burnside's army had already started to retreat.[45]

Baldy Smith alerted the commands on Burnside's left to get ready to move at dark. Hooker returned to Fredericksburg to do the same. Engineers carpeted the bridges with hay and sod "to deaden the sound" of the retreat. Some of the bridge teams even removed their shoes to avoid unnecessary noise. Soldiers muffled the batteries, ambulances, and wagons by wrapping their wheels in straw. Darkness hid all of their activity by 7:00 P.M., when Franklin arrived at the lower pontoon crossing. Federal officers ordered their men to pack their knapsacks carefully and light fires in the bivouacs. The bluecoats burned mammoth piles of trash, including "used cracker boxes and everything of a combustible nature." A timely wind from the northwest fanned the flames into roaring conflagrations. A watching New Yorker later recalled, "the wind howled among the trees."[46]

Hidden behind the luminous pyres and howling wind, Franklin's Federals slipped down to the river. Ambulances had evacuated most of the field hospitals during the afternoon. Artillery now followed their ruts to the lower pontoon crossing. After the guns came the infantry. Tramping in two or three columns, the foot soldiers abandoned the front and converged on the bridgehead. The soldiers fell back rapidly and silently. "Not a word was spoke," recounted a Northern diarist. "The canteens, cups & accouterments did not rattle & jingle as usually," a signal officer attested; "all seemed to be conscious that on the silence depended their lives." Any noise from Franklin's command might alert the Confederates to what was happening. "It was a sad retreat," recalled a member of the 1st U.S. Cavalry. "The remains of many comrades," he noted regretfully, "remained on the battlefield," which added to the somberness of the withdrawal.[47]

Pickets maintained their posts while the infantry disappeared. Franklin carefully withdrew his forces from left to right, starting with the troops farthest from the bridges and ending with those closest to them. The Sixth Corps, by this arrangement, covered the retreat in case the Confederates suddenly intervened. Doubleday's and Taylor's (Gibbon's) divisions arrived at the river first. Meade's Pennsylvania Reserves trailed them. Stoneman's two Third Corps divisions took up the march next. Bottlenecks choked the bridgehead, but the engineers and generals smoothed out any confusion and kept the columns flowing. Smith's Sixth Corps slowly fell in behind them, completing the crossing by 2:00 A.M. Union cavalry roamed through the darkness, silently switching places with the infantry pickets. The last of the foot soldiers retreated in the same order as their divisions—starting with the troops at Smithfield, and then those at Mannsfield and The Bend. Torbert's brigade claimed to be the last infantry to leave the field. The cavalry screen fell back shortly afterward. Before departing, they herded the stragglers and skulkers ahead of them. The last troops crossed the bridges at 3:00 A.M. In all the excitement, no one noticed the 114th Pennsylvania zouave band. They had conducted a concert at Birney's headquarters that afternoon and then lay down in the Smithfield ravine to get some rest. Somehow, they slept through the exodus of 60,000 soldiers.[48]

In Fredericksburg, Hooker ordered George Sykes' U.S. Regulars to replace the pickets around the city. Sentinels relieved by Sykes found Fredericksburg astir with troops exiting the city. Like Franklin's troops, Sumner and Hooker's men had evacuated most of their wounded during the afternoon. Confederate observers had noted their ambulances creaking over Stafford Heights and the new Federal entrenchments laid out by General Gouverneur K. Warren on the edge of the city. They assumed it prefaced another attack. Fredericksburg remained remarkably quiet throughout the retreat. Naive citizens occasionally thrust their heads out of windows, and candles illumined "the streets packed with multitudes." Nervous Yankees hissed, "Put out that light! put out that light!" and civilians disappeared behind closed shutters. Hooker and his subordinates hurried the troops through a maze of city streets. Officers feared that their men might panic when they learned that most of the army was retreating. "Should a panic occur," wrote a staff officer, "none can tell the extent of the disaster which would unavoidably ensue." Hooker's men remained calm despite the evacuation of Sumner's Right Grand Division.[49]

The Center Grand Division commander studied the situation and seriously doubted that he could hold a bridgehead at Fredericksburg. Sometime before 10:00 P.M., Hooker sent a note to Burnside recommending the complete evacuation of the west bank. "Hooker felt it his duty," recalled the army chief, "to represent . . . the condition in which I was leaving the town and the troops in it." Daniel Butterfield went to see Burnside in person. At Hooker's behest, the Fifth Corps commander elaborated that he needed more men to hold the bridgehead. After a lengthy discussion, Burnside admitted, "I felt that the troops I proposed to leave behind would not be able to hold the town." The commander notified Hooker that he "partially decided to withdraw the whole command." The ambiguous orders made Fighting Joe Hooker's predicament even more confusing. Burnside finally relented at 1:00 A.M., ordering Hooker to pull out his entire force and abandon the bridgehead. The subordinate eagerly complied.[50]

Members of Woodbury's volunteer engineer brigade awoke "quite unexpectedly" to the blare of bugles after midnight. Grabbing their arms and a day's rations, the bridgebuilders started for the river. "What occasioned the movement we could not imagine," remembered a sleepy soldier in the 50th New York Engineers. Passing Burnside's headquarters, the engineers suddenly encountered a "multitude of troops . . . coming back across the river." The engineers understood at once why they had been summoned. "We knew what our duty was very well," wrote one of them. Woodbury's volunteers hastened to the river and started dismantling the bridges they had risked everything to build five days before.[51]

Winds grew stronger at 9:30 P.M., gusting and howling through the sullen ranks of the retreating bluecoats. Only the staff officers on Stafford Heights reveled in the weather. One of them recognized that: "the sound of the movement . . . must necessarily be borne from the city in this direction." William Teall wrote that "so good a night" for retreat probably "could not again be had" in a year. The wind blew all of the incidental noise of retreat away from the prowling Confederate pickets. Stars shown brightly until 1:00 A.M. on December 16. The night air felt agreeably warm and balmy at sixty degrees. Two hours later, thunderheads rolled in and buffeted the marchers with sheets of rain. A Pennsylvania soldier noted in his diary: "found myself disagreeably wet & cold & the wind howling . . . rain coming down in torrents." The cloudburst lasted for three hours.[52]

Engineers cut their anchors at dawn, just as soon as the last troops had tramped across the pontoon bridges. Severing their tie to the bank, workers swung the entire span adeptly to the Stafford riverbank. Once they grounded it, work teams swiftly dismantled the pontoons. They unlashed all of their equipment: balks, chesses, and rails, and loaded them into wagons. Engineers wrestled with their bulky tools, making the ground "very muddy and disagreeable." Woodbury's men stowed the last of their gear by 12:00 noon and headed back to camp by 2:00 P.M. Individual bluecoats and small groups of stragglers collected on the far shore and on the city riverfront. Engineer details ferried them to safety throughout the early morning. Everything went smoothly and as planned. "As a retreat, or whatever you call it," critiqued a New Yorker, "it was the most admirably accomplished and its secrecy was characteristic of Burnside."[53]

Lee's Confederates rested through the storm, oblivious to the withdrawal, though some of Stonewall Jackson's men had their suspicions. Southern pickets studied the curious bonfires glowing along William Franklin's front. They stood in marked contrast to the pitch darkness that engulfed the city of Fredericksburg (where even civilians with candles were driven indoors). Staring at the flames, a transfixed North Carolina captain suddenly realized a "scarcely perceptible, though incessant flickering of the lights." Colonel Bryan Grimes, commanding Ramseur's Brigade of D. H. Hill's division, also noted the dancing glimmer of the fires. He believed the Yankees were marching past the flames in silhouette, which created the shimmering illusion. Such a large-scale movement betrayed a major shift of the Federal army. But was it an attack or a retreat? The lateness of the hour, combined with the rain, strongly suggested a withdrawal. Grimes reported the retrograde to D. H. Hill, who promptly discounted the North Carolinian's alarm. The Federals "were not going to retreat," Old Rawhides Hill assured the colonel, "until after another effort." Hill returned to his sleep, and the Tar Heel colonel sat in the rain watching the beguiling flicker of lights, hoping the general was right.[54]

Dawn brought an eerie silence to the battlefield. Curious Confederates strained their eyes to catch a glimpse of their silent foe. Generals prepared for the decisive moment of battle. Lafayette McLaws reinforced the Sunken Road with Micah Jenkins' South Carolina brigade. Anxious Paul Semmes gratefully replaced McMillan's fatigued brigade. A member of the 6th South Carolina wrote that all of the Southrons labored "under the impression that the big fight was to come off today." Morale remained high on Marye's Heights. A new arrival studied the defenses and reported, "The whole Yankee nation could not have driven us . . . from that position by storm." Yet nothing stirred in front. Longstreet began to worry. At 2:00 A.M., the First Corps commander ordered Jenkins to send two companies to "scout the town." Colonel Asbury Coward called for volunteers from the 5th South Carolina to go "see if Burnsides was still there." Thomas Collins led the first foray. Entering the city, he wandered the streets briefly before returning with nine prisoners. He single-handedly had convinced them that the town was in Confederate hands. Two companies entered the city next, rounding up an additional 150 Federals lost or left behind.[55]

South of town, Stonewall Jackson's skirmishers also began to stir. Parties of Walker's, Rodes', and Grimes' brigades moved cautiously across the Slaughter Pen. Jeb Stuart dispatched Captain W. W. Blackford at the same time "to see what the enemy was about." The lone horseman dashed across the open fields in a precautionary zigzag pattern. Running into the 5th Alabama, Stuart's aide met his brother, Major Eugene Blackford, and together they scouted to the river. John B. Hood summoned Captain A. C. Jones to investigate his front with a detachment from the 3rd Arkansas. All of these troops crossed the Bowling Green Road without trouble, and some went all the way to the river without spotting a Yankee. One detachment stumbled on the slumbering musicians of the Collis' Zouaves nestled in the muddy Smithfield ravine. Confederates roused the bleary-eyed bandleader, Frank Rauscher, and asked him what he was doing there. Assuming they were Union provost guards, Rauscher grumbled that he had his orders, adding that they should mind their own business and he would mind his. He paused when he saw the armed soldiers "grimly smile at my response." The Southerners confiscated the band's silver German-crafted instruments and sent the troupe to Libby Prison in Richmond.[56]

Confederates re-established their picket lines on the river. Some zealous Southerners dashed to the river opposite the lower pontoon crossing within an hour of the bridges' being taken up. Seeing engineers on the opposite bank, excitable pickets opened fire. Union artillery answered and dispersed them with a few well-aimed rounds. Trying to avoid a similar encounter, Confederate captain A. C. Jones hailed the Union picket at Deep Run, "Hello there, Mr. Yank." The Northerner responded, "Hello, yourself." Jones inquired, "I want to know if it is peace or war." The reply came back, "If you won't shoot, I won't." "I wish to make a bargain with you," the Rebel proposed. "I intend to place a line of pickets on this side of the river. If you will not fire upon them, we will agree to keep the peace." Blue and gray pickets resumed their peaceful vigils for the first time in a week.[57]

Bryan Grimes notified D. H. Hill that the Union army had escaped. Harvey Hill passed the information on to Jackson. Minutes later, Lee and Jackson charged up Prospect Hill and accosted D. H. Hill. "Who says the enemy have gone?" Jackson demanded. "Colonel Grimes," Hill replied. Whirling on the North Carolina colonel, Stonewall snapped, "How do you know?" The field officer reported that he had been to the river and back without trouble and that the bridges had been removed. Robert E. Lee and his subordinates suddenly realized that Burnside had given them the slip before they could complete their victory. Grimes noticed that "there was a look of deep chagrin and mortification, very apparent to the observer, on the countenance of each, though nothing of the sort was expressed in words." Lee returned to Telegraph Hill, crestfallen. Reflecting on his army, Lee wrote, "I believe they share with me my disappointment that the enemy did not renew the combat of the 13th." A week later, on Christmas, General Lee still mulled over his disappointment, telling his family, "I was holding back . . . and husbanding our strength and ammunition for the great struggle." "Had I divined that it was to have been his only effort," Lee recounted, "he would have had more of it." Burnside's withdrawal galled the Confederate commander, because he had received reports of the possible retreat but discounted them. "I had my suspicions," he admitted, "but could not believe they would relinquish their hopes after all their boasting and preparation." Lee considered the battle only half won.[58]

Contrary to Lee's disappointment, word of the Federal retreat electrified the Confederate line. The ranks erupted in spontaneous cheers and celebration. A Carolina doctor who had feared the battle had not been decisive enough on December 13 wrote enthusiastically, "Recent developments have demonstrated otherwise." Soldiers along the route of Lee's ride back to Telegraph Hill greeted him with tumultuous hurrahs. Jackson and Longstreet also received their share of affectionate shouting. Even Virginia governor John Letcher galloped the length of the Confederate line, basking in cheers. John Bell Hood rode through his division, telling each regiment "there is not a live Yankee on this side of the river." "The boys begin to yell," remarked a Texan: "it comes nearer and nearer to us as each succeeding brigade takes up the chorus." At one point, Hood laughed, "Boys, you all did such great works here last night that you scared the Yankees." Amid the gratified celebrants, only the dour Stonewall Jackson mirrored Lee's chagrin. "I did not think that a little red earth would have frightened them," he snarled. "I am sorry that they are gone. I am sorry I fortified."[59]

A myriad of Union wounded thronged the railhead at Falmouth Station. Open cars, padded with hay and pine boughs, conveyed the injured to Aquia Landing. Delays ensued as ships jockeyed for dock space. Eventually these steamboats, laden with wounded, carried the wounded to Washington on the morning of December 17, sixteen to eighteen hours after evacuating Fredericksburg. In contrast, Herman Haupt's efficient transportation teams could make the same journey in just six hours.[60]

Ambrose Burnside, looking "careworn & miserable," wandered into Edwin Sumner's headquarters after the last troops had marched off of Stafford Heights. He picked disconsolately at his breakfast. "Poor man," William Teall thought, "How I did pity him." Sumner tried to cheer up his commander. He told Burnside that "under the circumstances," the retreat was "very creditable." "There was not a gun or anything else lost," he reported. "The entire army returned without accident." Burnside took little consolation in the best march he had ever orchestrated. The retreat had been executed with masterly precision, but a waiting message from Halleck dampened any satisfaction: "The President desires that you report the reason of your withdrawal as soon as possible." "No man," Burnside said sadly, "can know what this has cost me!"[61]

Confederates reoccupied Fredericksburg by mid-morning. First impressions of the devastation stunned the Southerners. Shelling from both sides had destroyed whole blocks of houses and businesses. One soldier concluded that "There are but few houses worth repairing." Division commander William Taliaferro wrote, "I have never yet before in all the horrible scenes of destruction & havoc it has been my sad fortune to witness during this war seen anything equal to it. Every house is pierced by cannon balls or splintered by bullets." Doors had been wrenched off their frames, and many of the dwellings had been reduced to "burning ruins." "Still smouldering fires meet you at every turn," the Virginian mused. "Churches, orphan asylums [are] all torn to pieces." Fresh graves marred "almost every yard & enclosure." Residents of Fredericksburg dribbled home cautiously to take stock of their losses. A Carolina soldier recounted, "The beautiful City of Fredericksburg is now in ruins." Some of the scars still survive in the city as it enters the twenty-first century.[62]

Southern troops roamed the battlefield, confiscating clothing and equipment from the dead. The ground in front of Marye's Heights "was thronged with men who thought nothing of stripping a Yankee," recalled a South Carolina man. "I can't imagine how to illustrate the scene." A bystander likened the exercise to "drawing the hide off a squirrel." One fellow held the corpse by the head while another drew off the overcoat around its feet. Threadbare Confederates marveled at the quality of the spoils: "The Yankees are very well clad," and their overcoats were "of the very best material." Within hours, the blue-covered field turned dazzling white, as most of the bodies had been stripped naked. Confederate troops enjoyed the warm uniforms, but their officers worried about distinguishing friends from foes. Jackson and Longstreet ordered the men to dump the uniforms.[63]

The promise of more action in a new locale interrupted the Confederate revels. Just as the Army of the Potomac disappeared behind Stafford Heights, Federals reappeared at Port Royal. Lieutenant Commander Samuel Magaw's light-draft fleet had patrolled the Rappahannock off Oaken Brow on December 15, where it made contact with Colonel Benjamin Franklin "Grimes" Davis of the 8th New York Cavalry. Together, Magaw and Davis hatched a diversion to take some of the pressure off Burnside's front at Fredericksburg. Davis paraded his regiment on the riverbank opposite Port Royal on the 15th while Commander Magaw gave the Confederate garrison an ultimatum to evacuate. Magaw informed the local commander that the Federals needed Port Royal and would bombard the town if it did not surrender. He also planted a gullible contraband on shore with "a big story" confirming that the Yankees were massing on the opposite bank. Magaw advised the Confederates that they had until dawn to evacuate all of the noncombatants from Port Royal. Lieutenant Colonel Zachariah S. McGruder of the 10th Virginia Cavalry acknowledged Magaw's warning and notified the citizens of Port Royal

:o leave at once. The Union navy and cavalry returned the next morning, out before Grimes Davis' videttes started demonstrating, word arrived that Burnside had withdrawn. Davis and Magaw stopped to assess the situation. Hearing nothing of Burnside's guns upriver and seeing little stirring in Port Royal, the pair decided to scrap the mission. The navy hove to, dropping back to a position in the river below the town. Davis' 8th New York Cavalry faded back into its former positions near King George Court House.[64]

Robert E. Lee reacted swiftly to the news of action brewing at Port Royal. Assuming that the unexpected disappearance of Burnside corresponded with the sudden emergence of an unknown force at Port Royal, Lee supposed the Federal offensive had shifted farther downriver. Hoping to get another crack at the Northerners, Lee dispatched Stuart's cavalry and Jackson's corps to meet the incursion at Port Royal. Stuart dashed ahead in the van. Stonewall Jackson promptly filled the roads behind him. Jubal Early's division started at 10:00 A.M., followed by the two Hills. Taliaferro's division sidled off the battlefield, taking A. P. Hill's former camps at the Yerby house. Longstreet's corps retained its positions, keeping watch over Fredericksburg.[65]

Stuart's cavalry galloped into Port Royal to find that the Federals had vanished. Locating the naval vessels anchored at rest in the river below, Stuart reported that the Federals had abandoned the feint. He hurried word back to Jackson and Lee that the crisis had passed. Jackson's troops crammed the road to Port Royal, cheering Jackson every step of the way. Early's division pressed on into the evening, reaching Port Royal after dark. D. H. Hill's troops halted nine miles south of Prospect Hill and camped by the side of the road. A. P. Hill's frazzled division collapsed at the Moss Neck plantation of Richard Corbin. Jackson bivouacked in the woods close to the manor house. The night grew cold and miserable. "The Gen. Froze out," Jed Hotchkiss noted, "and we hunted up a house." Drawn to the mansion—"one of the most beautiful buildings I have seen in this country," Jackson thought—the staff begged the lady of the plantation for supper. Mrs. Roberta C. Corbin lavished a bountiful meal upon the general and his staff, and begged Jackson to stay the night. Jackson told his wife that the invitation "was thankfully accepted, and I had a delightful night's rest." Indeed, all of Jackson's soldiers and staff relished the sleep. Hotchkiss "slept soundly . . . the first time for several days." The exhausted staff, groomed to rise before dawn, snored until 10:00 A.M. on December 17; and Jackson with them. Burnside's third offensive had come to an end, and Lee's weary soldiers took advantage of the break.[66]

The armies slipped into an informal quiescence by the evening of Decem-

ber 16. Peace returned to the Rappahannock Valley, and men on both side.
rested in camp. "This is the first quiet evening in many days," wrote a Union
staff officer. "We stand now precisely where we did before we crossed the
river minus the killed & wounded."[67]

Marching into Stafford Court House and Dumfries that day, Franz Sige
arrived with the Federal Eleventh Corps. Henry Slocum's Twelfth Corp
shifted to Fairfax Court House. Their arrival negated Burnside's losses at
Fredericksburg and would prove that Burnside was nothing if not resilient
The army head not only balked at the idea of going into winter quarters, but
now he furiously devised a plan for another offensive. Perhaps feeling pressured by Washington to erase the worst military disaster yet associated with
the Lincoln administration, Burnside concocted another strategy on December 17. He may have hurried his plans when Henry Halleck demanded a
meeting at Aquia Landing that night. At 2:00 P.M., December 17, the army
commander convened another of his customary councils of war. The grand
division commanders critiqued the last operation, and Burnside fished for
suggestions. The army chief took their information and consulted with Halleck at 10:00 P.M. The two met again the next night at 5:30 P.M. Nothing is
known of the two exchanges. Halleck may have visited simply to determine
the extent of the defeat, or he may have advocated another forward move.
Burnside's renewed activity strongly suggests that Halleck encouraged another offensive, and the army commander readily obliged him.[68]

CHAPTER FIFTEEN

"PLAYED OUT!"

Dumfries Raid and the Mud March

Even as Ambrose Burnside plotted his next move, the armies cleared away the debris of the last battle. Wounded filled the hospitals or awaited transportation to Washington. Dead bodies littered the battlefield, and prisoners needed to be exchanged. And the Federal government launched an investigation to pinpoint the cause of Burnside's defeat.

Union hospitals sprang up everywhere, filled with "wounded men almost without number." Overflowing hospitals presented "quite a melancholy appearance." Surgeons toiled for days performing mass amputations. In many cases, they did not bother to remove the victim's boots or shoes. Orderlies carried away severed arms and legs in bushel baskets. A member of the 76th New York saw "20 bushels of lims [limbs] in one pile." Cemeteries popped up in the fields adjacent to the hospitals. "Hundreds bit the dust," recalled a hospital steward, "but one gets used to such seens [scenes] quicker than you would think possible."[1]

The Christian Commission helped alleviate some of the suffering. The Reverend Alexander Reed, general agent for the commission, wangled his way to the front without a pass. Unable to attain one in Washington, he turned to Herman Haupt for help. The railroader appointed Reed a "brakeman in the service of the Military Railroad Department." Reed confessed that he knew nothing about engineering. "When you get to Falmouth," Haupt said slyly, "if you do not like the service you can resign." The Christian Commission's agent brought vital supplies and tents to ease the burden on the medical corps. The cumulative effect of those efforts yielded a noticeable drop in mortality. One in four wounded died at Antietam; one in three during the battles of Kennesaw Mountain and Atlanta. But Burnside's army suffered only one fatality in seven. Dr. J. T. Heard attributed this to improved care: "In no previous battle witnessed by me were the wounded so promptly and well cared for throughout the army as at Fredericksburg."[2]

Across the river, slain soldiers still covered the field in front of Marye's Heights. "I have never seen men lay so thick," reported a correspondent for the Charleston *Daily Courier*. "You can't imagine what a horrible spectacle I witnessed," a Georgia private told his family. A South Carolina officer had "never seen or conceived of such havoc." Brigadier General Cadmus M. Wilcox confessed, "I have seen several battle fields in this war where *I thought* the enemy lay in heaps but on this there were more to the acre than I ever [had] seen before." A Confederate soldier counted 484 dead bodies in one acre. Another estimated that in one spot, six hundred yards square, "a man could not walk along without stepping on dead bodies." W. W. Blackford of Stuart's staff described the field looking as "blue as if it had been covered with blue cloth." A veteran remembered, "I saw hundreds of men lying dead, shot in all parts and some with their heads, legs, arms, etc. shot off, and mangled in all manner and shapes." Osmun Latrobe of Longstreet's staff examined the destruction closely. "I rode over the battle field, and enjoyed the sight of hundreds of dead Yankees," the staff officer gloated. "Saw much of the work I had done in the way of severed limbs, decapitated bodies, and mutilated remains of all kinds. Doing my soul good."[3]

Robert E. Lee was appalled that the Union army had left behind its dead. In an unprecedented gesture, Lee asked Burnside to bury their bodies. Longstreet's chief of staff, Major G. Moxley Sorrel, conveyed Lee's request to Generals Wadsworth and Parke on December 16. James Wadsworth asked how many dead remained on the field. "I ask Major," he explained, "so as to make my burying parties strong enough." Longstreet's chief of staff replied, "I cannot possibly guess with any approach to accuracy. I have only ridden through the slain in front of Marye's Hill." There, he imagined he had seen eight hundred bodies. Wadsworth exclaimed, "My God, my God!" The Federals agreed to send a detail of one hundred men across the river, commanded by one field officer and two lieutenants. Edwin Sumner decided to postpone action until the next morning, since it was so late. Sorrel assured Lee that the Yankees would forward burial parties on December 17.[4]

Sumner put Colonel John R. Brooke, head of the 53rd Pennsylvania, in charge of the burial party. Brooke's command, drawn from various regiments, crossed the river shortly after sunrise on December 17. A Union soldier claimed that "The weather being cool, the task was not so repulsive as at Antietam." But some of the participants found it plenty dreadful: "enough to sicken one of war."[5]

A Confederate escort greeted the Northerners when they landed. Enemies shook hands, and the group set off for the battlefield. Brooke assigned his work crews to designated lots to look for bodies. Soldiers "commenced the solemn task" of digging trenches and filling them with corpses. Some workers used wooden planks to cart the bodies to the grave.[6]

A Confederate recalled that some of the teams struggled because "the bodies of the slain had frozen to the ground." A disgusted member of the 27th Connecticut wrote that the bodies "were frozen and most of them had turned black." Some bluecoats used pick-axes to pry them from the ice.[7]

Confederates—many still clad in the uniforms of the dead Yankees—watched the macabre work. Generals Lafayette McLaws and William Barksdale rode close enough for Brooke's men to see they were "dressed in old clothes and looked shabbily enough." Some of the Unionists eluded the guards and dumped dozens of bodies in Wallace's icehouse. The remains were not discovered until after the war.[8]

Brooke's detail recrossed the river at the end of the day. A Southern woman sent them back with "the most wrathful imprecations." She damned them for demolishing her house and wished that "all of the Yankees were dead." In contrast, the armed Rebels parted with the bluecoats "in the most friendly manner." They shook hands and exchanged goods. "What a pity that we must fight," wrote a returning Union soldier.[9]

Brooke had buried 620 men in front of Marye's Heights, but another 400 had yet to be interred. With Burnside's permission, Federals buried them on December 18. Hard-packed ground made graves little more than shallow trenches crammed with bodies. "Their burying parties were making hideous work with the dead soldiers," Confederate Major Sorrel declared critically. Lee protested to the Union commander, but there was little that Burnside could do about it. By nightfall, all of the Union dead had been interred in one fashion or another. A Union laborer wrote in his diary: "I shall not soon forget the appearance of those dead bodies. Death is a solemn thing any-where, but in such a manner it is dreadful."[10]

While Brooke buried the dead, Provost Marshal Marsena Patrick negoti-ated a prisoner exchange. The Confederates had proposed the exchange at 8:30 A.M. on December 17. Grizzled General Patrick marched 459 Southern captives (almost all of them taken from A. P. Hill's division) to the Rappa-hannock at noon and traded them for an unknown number of Federals. Wil-liam Franklin took formal charge of the exchange and concluded it to everyone's satisfaction.[11]

Burnside finished all of these macabre chores just in time to deal with the U.S. Congress's Committee on the Conduct of the War. Radical elements of the Republican Party empowered the committee to investigate—and deter-mine the blame for—the fiasco at Fredericksburg. Henry Halleck dashed down to Aquia Landing on December 18 to prepare Burnside for the con-gressmen's arrival. The committee's six members landed the next day, led by Benjamin F. Wade of Ohio and Zachariah Chandler of Michigan. The politicians took over Burnside's headquarters, where they interrogated Burn-side, Sumner, and Franklin. The next day, they questioned Hooker, the dar-ling of the Radicals. The inquiry ended at 4:00 P.M. on December 19, and the committee returned to Washington. Back in the capital, they grilled Henry Halleck and Montgomery Meigs. Ultimately, they vilified Franklin for being a willful dullard (and conveniently, a practicing Democrat and con-firmed McClellan disciple), who had destroyed Burnside's strategy.[12]

The commander acted with a renewed sense of urgency, since turmoil racked Washington in the aftermath of Fredericksburg. The gold standard fluctuated dramatically in New York. Governor Horatio Seymour openly de-nounced the administration and its unconstitutional acts. Secretary of State William Seward, pressured by Radical Republicans in Congress, proffered his resignation. Marsena Patrick wrote of Seward, "the news is too good to be true and wants confirmation—May it be confirmed!" Lincoln secured Secre-tary of the Treasury Salmon Chase's resignation as well. As a leader for the Radicals, his removal would negate Seward's. The president, however, re-jected both of their resignations—thus retaining the balance of rival (and hos-tile) factions inside his cabinet and the party.[13]

Bad news continued to pour in. The highly acclaimed naval wonder, the *Monitor*, sank off of Cape Hatteras on January 4. "The reverses . . . have had a very chilling effect upon all of us," reported an old army hand, "and the loss of the 'Monitor' . . . seems to add to our calamities about as much as we can bear." All of these setbacks combined to depress the Army of the Potomac. The army reached a low point just as Burnside prepared another "On to Richmond" drive.[14]

In contrast, Confederates across the river toured the Fredericksburg battlefield with self-satisfaction. Sightseers clearly distinguished the actions in front of Prospect Hill and the stone wall as two separate and distinct battles—drawing a historical parallel to Napoleon's twin victories of Jena and Auerstädt. "I availed myself of the opportunity . . . to ride over the *two* battle fields," wrote a soldier in the 57th Virginia. He noted, "On the right the fighting was less concentrated, but the slaughter was more terrible." Southerners heartily agreed with the Yankee observation, "Lee never gained a cheaper victory."[15]

Burnside, in the midst of so many distractions, prepared his army for another move. He ordered more pontoons to replace the shot-riddled boats lost at Fredericksburg. Replacements arrived after January 3. Until then, engineers made do with the existing boats. They spent weeks patching and corking holes. Ambrose W. Thompson, a New York engineer, counted thirty-eight holes in one pontoon.[16]

The Northern commander reorganized his army during the interlude. George Meade reminded Burnside that he was a major general in charge of a division while three brigadiers led corps. Burnside therefore gave Meade the Fifth Corps on Christmas Day (much to the shock and consternation of the deposed commander, Dan Butterfield). James Wadsworth, who arrived after the battle, took over Doubleday's division of the First Corps; and Abner Doubleday transferred to the 3rd Division. John C. Robinson transferred from the Third Corps to take command of the 2nd Division after the wounding of John Gibbon. He supplanted the uninspiring Nelson Taylor.[17]

Robert E. Lee used the time after Fredericksburg to spread his forces up and down the river, again covering all of the likely points of attack from Banks Ford to Port Royal. Within a couple of weeks, the Richmond government weakened Lee's army when it ordered Ransom's division to North Carolina on January 3.[18]

Lee's army empathized with the natives of Fredericksburg. Their homes and businesses had been vandalized and destroyed, and the impoverished citizenry faced a dire winter ahead. Members of the 3rd Arkansas shared their rations with them—"and they were slim enough, God knows," noted a well-intentioned captain. Their kindness reaped an unprecedented amount of goodwill. Other commands raised money for the inhabitants. Several units vied to outdo each other's generosity. Stonewall Jackson and James Longstreet each donated several hundred dollars of their own pay. Robert Ransom, before leaving for North Carolina, personally solicited his officers' charity. He set the tone by donating $100—one-third of his month's salary. The philanthropy of the ragtag army saved many civilians from utter ruin.[19]

Lee's cavalry, meanwhile, spent the weeks after Fredericksburg harassing Federal supply lines. Wade Hampton crossed upriver at Rappahannock Station on December 17 with a small foray. Dividing his forces, Hampton swooped down on a Federal camp along Occoquan Creek. The Confederate raiders captured a wagon train crossing the stream. Lieutenant Colonel William T. Martin of the Jeff Davis Legion forced the wagon guard—who were on the other side of the creek—to surrender and come over on a ferry boat. Hampton gobbled up half the train before the 17th Pennsylvania Cavalry and a couple of companies of the 6th Pennsylvania Cavalry appeared on the opposite bank. Colonel Richard H. Rush of the 6th stumbled into Hampton while en route to the Army of the Potomac. The Pennsylvanian attempted to hold the Confederates in place while a detachment turned their flank via Selectman's Ford. Hampton anticipated the move and blocked the ford. Confederate cavalry withdrew without menace, and returned to camp on December 19 laden with 150 prisoners, 20 wagons, and 30 stands of arms. Burnside wired Brigadier General Julius Stahel, Franz Sigel's cavalry chief, to "please see that a strong guard is thrown out at once . . . even to the whole of your command if necessary." Skirmishing continued for the next few days at Kelly's Ford, Catlett's Station, and Brentsville.[20]

Christmas passed uneventfully and served as a time of reflection for the troops on both sides. Homesickness and frustration marked the occasion for many, making the second Yuletide of the war particularly melancholy. Union soldiers in Hancock's division used a Christmas Eve review to show their displeasure for Burnside. The army commander joined Sumner for the 5:00 P.M. parade. The Irish Brigade hailed Sumner with enthusiastic cheers "but not so with Genl. Burnside," according to a staff officer. They met him with stone silence. Embarrassed, Sumner quietly appealed to the brigade to cheer—for his sake.[21]

Desertion rose to epidemic proportions. A New Jersey artillerist reported that desertion escalated because "the result of the battle of Fredericksburg was demoralizing to the army." Commissary and quartermaster departments

added to the army's misery, barely able to meet its daily minimal requirements. One soldier recalled that these departments "were in the worst condition we ever knew." Union soldiers answered roll call in tattered rags. Officers
and men grew surly and insubordinate; discipline slackened, and no one had
been paid in months. "There is gloom and despondency throughout the entire command," admitted Burnside. Desertions revealed the intensity of the
army's dissatisfaction. The Army of the Potomac and the Washington defenses aggregated a force of 326,750 troops. Of that force, the authorities
counted 86,330 absent by the end of January 1863—a reduction of 27 percent. Gabriel Colby of the 124th New York deserted on Christmas Day.
When recaptured, he offered the excuse that "so many were sick of the service
after Fredericksburg."[22]

Officers in the Army of the Potomac spent the holidays getting drunk.
"Christmas was a dull day at our Camp," wrote a sanctimonious signal officer, "but the Army all through as a general thing enjoyed itself *hugely.*" The
inefficient commissary somehow acquired enough whiskey to issue a gill "to
all who applied for it" on Christmas Eve. "The result," recalled Louis Fortescue, "was the Army of the Potomac on the 25th was as drunk as an *owl.*"
Visitors to General Dan Sickles' camp noted that "Whiskey punches flowed
like rain." Sickles and his staff became so furiously drunk that they had to
buck and gag one of the staff officers, who in his cups attacked several of the
aides with his saber. Pilgrims who continued on to Hooker's headquarters
found things "in the same elegant condition with the exception of the buck-
ing and gaging [*sic*]." New Year's Day brought more of the same behavior.
"We had a gay time," the ever-drinking Fortescue reported, "and then 'I am
sorry to say' the party got beautifully inebriated." Few officers made it to roll
call the next day. The besotted drum major of a Pennsylvania regiment ended
up in the guardhouse when he blared the wrong bugle call in camp, much to
the annoyance of the bleary-eyed sufferers.[23]

Across the Rappahannock, the Army of Northern Virginia showed more
restraint during the holidays. "I spent a most quiet and uninteresting Xmas,"
William Taliaferro told his wife. "Nothing to eat or drink but a lrg piece of
beef & cold water." William Cocke of Pickett's division complained about
the tedium of his Christmas fare: "Isn't it too hard to have to dine on the
same old thing today that I've had for seven or eight months past? You cannot
imagine how it made my mouth water to read about . . . 'fine mackerel.'"
Some Confederates supplemented their diet creatively for the holidays. Diminutive General Billy Mahone, "not unmindful of creature comforts," kept

a pen of turkeys beside his tent. On Christmas morning, he discovered the pen empty and his dinner gone. Some South Carolinians hatched a scheme to get as drunk as the Yankees. Earle Lewis of the 5th South Carolina commandeered an officer's frock and a sword, organized a "so-called provost guard," and visited several neighboring Virginia brigades which he understood "had whiskey to sell." Claiming to be from Longstreet's headquarters, Lewis confiscated the alcohol and carried it back to camp. "We had a terrible spree in camp," reported the officer defrauded of his coat, "the boys nearly all getting drunk and kicking up a terrible hurrah!" Awakened by the commotion, General Micah Jenkins seethed at the unseemly display. He waited until morning before he harangued the hungover Carolinians "very severely for our drunken and disorderly conduct."[24]

Stonewall Jackson spent Christmas hosting a dinner party for Lee, Stuart, and Pendleton, among others, set amid the splendor of Moss Neck. Guests were surrounded by lavish pictures of racehorses and fighting gamecocks. Jeb Stuart feigned disappointment announcing that Jackson's tastes indicated "a great decline in his moral character, which would be a grief and disappointment to the pious old ladies of the South." The indomitable host blushed coyly. At the dinner table, Stuart speared a pat of butter stamped with a fowl, telling the party to behold the Jackson coat-of-arms. The meek general blushed again in delight. Even Lee joined in the fun, kidding Jackson for having a waiter in a white apron. He accused the Second Corps commander and his staff of "playing soldiers," and of living too well. He invited them to his headquarters to see how real soldiers fared.[25]

New Year's came and went with little difference in the daily regimen of the Confederate army. Robert E. Lee took time away from his demanding schedule to transact a little personal business before the end of the year. Preempting the forthcoming Emancipation Proclamation, Lee manumitted the Custis family slaves on December 29.[26]

Jeb Stuart had left Jackson's Christmas party to embark on another raid behind enemy lines. Stuart hoped to institute a "system of irritation," by disrupting Burnside's supply lines. News had leaked that Burnside had issued three days' cooked rations and filled his wagons with another ten days' worth of supplies on December 26. Stuart wanted to develop the Union army's intentions. The cavalry leader amassed three brigades—Hampton's, Fitz Lee's, and Rooney Lee's—at Kelly's Ford on the afternoon of December 26. The raiders, some 1,800 strong with four guns, forded the river and separated. Fitz Lee set out for the Telegraph Road north of Chopawamsic Creek and then would proceed toward Dumfries. Rooney Lee moved directly against Dumfries; and Hampton headed for the Occoquan again.[27]

Rooney Lee reached Dumfries about mid-morning and found it heavily guarded. Demonstrations forced the Federals to withdraw north of Quantico Creek. Fitz Lee gained the Telegraph Road without incident and pushed on to Dumfries. Stuart considered attacking Dumfries with both brigades, but prisoners revealed that the Yankees had a substantial force. The Confederate general opted to skirmish for the rest of the day. After dark, he withdrew to strike another target.[28]

Stuart bivouacked near Coles' Store for the night. Hampton joined him there after a brief foray to Occoquan. Hampton's cavalry had routed the 17th Pennsylvania Cavalry at sunset, before falling back. His Confederates had captured a number of wagons and prisoners. Stuart sent them south along with two of his guns that had run out of ammunition.[29]

The Confederates broke camp early on December 28 and descended on Occoquan in force. Stuart's Rebels surprised a Federal scouting column at Greenwood Church and sent it reeling. Once again, the unlucky 17th Pennsylvania stampeded to escape the Southern host. A telegrapher reported the "desperate charges" of the Pennsylvanians were "going full speed *to the rear*" (emphasis in original). The 5th Virginia Cavalry chased the Yankees across Selectman's Ford. The 3rd Virginia Cavalry then took the lead, galloping right into the camp of the 3rd Pennsylvania Cavalry. Federals fled in every direction, leaving the Rebels to ransack their camp. Stuart detached Hampton to capture the village of Occoquan, while the rest of his column turned north toward Burke's Station. Hampton ultimately drew up short of the town because of darkness. He broke off the action and set out to join Stuart again.[30]

Stuart by then had captured the Union post at Burke's Station. Fitz Lee had flanked the hamlet and destroyed the railroad bridge over Accotink Creek, while Stuart led a sortie straight into the village. The Rebels overran the station before the military telegraph operator could raise the alarm or disarm his equipment. Stuart's cavalry pillaged the telegraph office while the general read through official dispatches from Major General Samuel P. Heintzelman's headquarters in Washington. Stuart analyzed the Federal dispositions as revealed in the messages, and prepared to move on, but not before he had a little fun. He ordered a telegrapher in his command named Shepard to send a message to the Union quartermaster general in Washington. Stuart's communiqué complained that the quality of mules recently furnished to the army were "so inferior" that they greatly embarrassed him "in moving his captured wagons." Having revealed his position, Stuart ended his transmission, cut the telegraph wires, and headed west.[31]

Traveling by night, Stuart's van pushed toward Fairfax. The head of the column stumbled into an ambush about a mile from the county seat. The Federal garrison had been warned of Stuart's approach by some of the refugees from Burke's Station. Stuart withdrew and went into camp. He ordered large bonfires lit to deceive the Yankees while the Confederate column veered north across the turnpike between Fairfax Court House and Annandale. Safely on the way to Vienna, Stuart called in his rear guard from the camp. Stuart traveled from Vienna to Frying Pan on December 29. The next day, the Confederates reached Warrenton. Union prisoners arrived in town "sore, exhausted, and faint." Stuart's raiders returned to Culpeper on the last day of 1862. They had bagged 25 wagons and 200 prisoners during the week-long sojourn behind Union lines.[32]

Federal troops in northern Virginia failed miserably trying to catch Jeb Stuart's raiders. Stuart had intercepted Heintzelman's orders at Burke's Station and knew more about the Federals' whereabouts than they knew themselves. Burnside largely ignored the raid initially, leaving the Washington department to handle the affair. The army commander, by coincidence, had sent a mounted expedition to the upper fords of the Rappahannock on December 30. Alfred Pleasonton's column of 4,000 cavalry started for Warrenton in preparation for the army's next offensive. An infantry column left Potomac Creek in support, bound for the confluence of the Rappahannock and Rapidan Rivers. Burnside's plans changed abruptly at 10:00 P.M., when the War Department ordered the army commander to intercept Stuart as he returned through Warrenton. "The telegram of course produced an entire change of programme," recalled a Union staff officer, "and they were immediately ordered back to pursue J. E. B. Stuart." Pleasonton approached Warrenton cautiously on December 31. Winter weather numbed his soldiers, who fidgeted in the saddle for warmth. "It was bitter cold," complained a member of the 1st U.S. Cavalry. The Federals discovered Stuart's rear guard still in town. Pleasonton's horsemen formed in squadrons on the outskirts of Warrenton and charged in; but the Southerners were gone. "As we rode in on one side," wrote a bemused Union trooper, "Stuart's Cavalry rode out on the other side." Unable to block Stuart's escape, Pleasonton let the Rebels go and withdrew to Kelly's Ford.[33]

Confederate lieutenant R. Channing Price wrote that the Dumfries Raid was the "longest, most dangerous and most brilliant Expedition that the Cavalry has yet given to an admiring public." Stuart staff officer and cavalry aficionado Henry B. McClellan reported that Stuart's raid was "unproductive of any great material results," but it demonstrated that a "bold leader" like Stuart could operate behind Union lines with near impunity for a week. The Confederate chief had some fun with Montgomery Meigs and may have uncovered Burnside's intention to turn Fredericksburg, if for no other reason than the brush with Pleasonton's 4,000-man force at Warrenton, which refused to fall back any farther than Kelly's Ford.[34]

Before Stuart launched the Dumfries Raid, Burnside finalized plans for another move to Richmond. He had reconnoitered the Rappahannock below Fredericksburg and encouraged some of his subordinates to do the same. He personally requested Brigadier General John Newton, an engineer noted for his large breakfasts and creature comforts, to scout the river with a critical eye. In the meantime, he ordered General James Wadsworth to construct corduroy roads to improve the flow of traffic to the river. Gray-haired James Wadsworth personally superintended the construction, and occasionally waded into the mud to lend a hand. "To see a major-general condescend to assist in road-building, was rather gratifying to the democratic ideas of the privates," noted a soldier in the 76th New York. The general told his men "that honest labor is not degrading." The laborers nicknamed him "Old Corduroy." Activity animated much of the riverbank southeast of Fredericksburg. "There were two or three points," recalled Burnside's chief of staff, John Parke, where "preparations were going on." The Union army commander used some of these sites as a subterfuge to mask his real intentions. Parke admitted, "The real point of crossing the general only knew."[35]

Burnside decided his army was "in a fighting condition" by December 26, even though he knew that that was not a consensus. "There was a diversity of opinion upon that point among the general officers," General Parke later told the Committee on the Conduct of the War. The Union commander thought enough time had elapsed since the Battle of Fredericksburg for the army to resupply, re-equip, and recover from its fatigue. He secretly had molded a plan to cross the Rappahannock simultaneously above and below Fredericksburg. He selected a crossing point seven miles below the old town, near the mouth of Muddy Creek and opposite James Seddon's house. At the same time, Union cavalry under General William W. Averell would strike across the Rappahannock upriver at Kelly's Ford. "It was my intention to make a feint above the town," Burnside explained, "which could have been turned into a positive assault if I found we were discovered below." On December 26, the army commander ordered his lieutenants to prepare three days' cooked rations, fill the wagons with enough supplies for ten days, and collect a twelve-day supply of beef cattle. He wanted the army to be ready to move within twelve hours.[36]

William Averell took 2,500 "of the best cavalry in the army," including 1,000 "picked men," and started upriver. Joseph Hooker detached Barnes' infantry brigade to accompany the cavalry. Burnside instructed Averell to cross at Kelly's Ford and take the 1,000 picked men to Raccoon Ford on the Rapidan River. The 1,500 remaining cavalry would demonstrate in front of Warrenton and Culpeper to keep the Confederates away from Averell's strike force. The infantry intended to hold the Confederates' attention at Richards and Ellis' fords. Averell's fleet force of 1,000 troopers would then be free to strike the Virginia Central Railroad at Goochland or Carter's Station. The cavalry would tear up the tracks. When they reached the James River Canal they would blow up locks and dismantle bridges on the Richmond and Lynchburg Railroad. Averell also hoped to destroy a trestle bridge where the Richmond, Petersburg and Weldon Railroad crossed the Nottaway River. At the end of the expedition, Averell planned to head east and join Major General John J. Peck at Suffolk. Steamers would carry the raiders back to Aquia Landing. While Averell's column headed to its jump-off at Kelly's Ford, Burnside started his move to Muddy Creek.[37]

The Federal commander forged ahead regardless of Stuart's raid and poor morale, expecting to start his fourth offensive on December 31. Stuart's raid delayed Burnside's start, but two Union generals completely halted the operation. Brigadier Generals John Newton and John Cochrane went to Washington on December 30 to inform "someone in Washington" about the poor state of morale in the army before it undertook another winter offensive. Cochrane ostensibly took leave "by reason of sickness," but in reality, he had political connections to the Radical Republicans.[38]

Morale troubled the fleshy John Newton. "I became painfully aware," he later testified, "that the troops in my division and the whole army had become exceedingly dispirited." Talking to his superiors, Newton understood the problem "arose from a want of confidence in General Burnside's military capacity." The Sixth Corps division commander said that this conviction was "almost universal." Baldy Smith later tried to exculpate himself by blaming most of the dissatisfaction—"which was openly expressed"—on Joe Hooker'.

men. When Burnside asked Newton to critique his crossing site at Muddy Creek, the engineer soured. "I saw the place where he intended to cross," Newton recalled, "and it appeared to me to be as bad, if not a little worse, than the place we had crossed at the first time." Burnside listened to Newton, but he intended to cross there anyway.[39]

Encouraged by Franklin and Smith, Newton decided the powers in Washington needed to know the danger of taking dispirited troops into battle again so soon after Fredericksburg. Smith and Franklin gave Newton and Cochrane leave, knowing full well their intentions. Newton even asked his superiors for advice. He volunteered to see the president if they wanted him to, or he might seek "some of the prominent members" of Congress. The senior generals remained noncommittal, leaving Newton to later tell the Committee on the Conduct of the War: "I received no advice or consent from either of them," even though they cleared his departure on the very eve of a new campaign.[40]

Newton and Cochrane left early on December 30. Cochrane thought that they should go see either Senator Henry Wilson of Massachusetts or Moses F. Odell, the New York representative on the Joint Committee on the Conduct of the War. They arrived in the capital at 3:00 P.M. and checked into a hotel. Cochrane left Newton to find the congressmen. The brigadier was unable to locate either one of them. Congress had recessed for the holidays, and many of the politicians, including Wilson and Odell, had left town. Ironically, if the Sixth Corps generals had stayed with the army, they might have talked to Vice President Hannibal Hamlin and six other congressmen, who visited the army on New Year's Eve. Running out of options, Cochrane decided to see the president. Cochrane's friend Secretary of State William H. Seward saw the general at the White House. Cochrane explained his visit and begged Seward for help. The secretary of state did not want to interfere in War Department business and suggested that Cochrane go see Edwin Stanton or Henry Halleck. Cochrane answered that he wanted to avoid official channels. Seward understood and made an appointment for the generals to see Lincoln that afternoon.[41]

The generals arrived at the White House at the appointed time and were ushered into the president's office. Newton launched into a discourse on military positions and the fragile morale of the soldiers. Cochrane thought Newton had strayed from the point. Later he attested, "General Newton spoke upon subjects of which I had declined to speak." Newton, himself, admitted that he found himself "in a very delicate position." He did not want to tell the president explicitly that the army had no confidence in Burnside. "I could not tell him that, although . . . that was my firm belief." The division commander instead described the demoralizing state of the army without broaching the subject of the cause. He hoped that Lincoln would discover the reason on his own. Lincoln became agitated. He presumed the two generals represented a cabal of officers that wanted "to replace the commander." The dangerous tone of the conversation alarmed Cochrane. "The impression that such was the President's understanding," he recounted, "startled me." Cochrane interjected that they did not want Burnside removed. Newton, also taken aback, said that he only wanted to notify someone in authority about the condition of the army. They thought the army stood on the brink of disaster, and another defeat on the Rappahannock might mean the end of the Army of the Potomac. "If it should be unsuccessful for any reason," Cochrane warned, "the influence of the disaster upon the cause of the whole country would be ruinous." Newton encouraged Lincoln to ascertain the facts for himself. Lincoln calmed down and told the generals that he was glad they had confided in him. As he showed them out, the president promised that "good would come of the interview."[42]

Back in Virginia, the Army of the Potomac, far from being demoralized, prepared for action. "We are having splendid weather for military operations," wrote a Connecticut artillerist: "Something must be done." The army's chief of staff agreed: "The roads are good and the weather fine." E. S. Allen, one of Thaddeus Lowe's "aeronauts," reported on December 30 that the "heaviest body of [Rebel] troops I judge, are North and West of the City." Robert E. Lee appeared to be shifting troops away from Fredericksburg to counter Averell's cavalry movement to Kelly's Ford. Barnes' brigade forded the Rappahannock at Richards' Ford on December 31 after a brief skirmish. Burnside had everything ready to spring his forces below Fredericksburg. But then a telegram from President Lincoln stopped everything.[43]

Lincoln's cable to Burnside arrived, much to the general's surprise, during the night of December 30: "I have good reason for saying that you must not make a general movement without letting me know of it." General Parke wrote, "The order came upon him like a thunderbolt." Burnside wondered how to interpret the dispatch, uncertain what had prompted it and what it meant. In a single sentence, Burnside had lost control of his army. He retained nominal command of the Army of the Potomac, but he could no longer exercise authority without first checking with Lincoln. The general complied dejectedly, and canceled his offensive. Lincoln's interference angered Burnside, but the general was more troubled that his plans had been leaked. He had made a conscious effort to hide his plans from everyone, confiding in only two staff officers and Henry Halleck. Presumably, Halleck would have briefed the president long ago. No one knew when the offensive would begin except Burnside, yet Lincoln's dispatch arrived just at the moment of starting. Newton and Cochrane went to Washington when they saw that a movement was imminent, but neither one of them had known the time it would commence. Parke, on the other hand, suggested that Lee's Confederates did know Burnside's plans. "The enemy were prepared," he recalled philosophically, "by having a force ready to oppose us." (The early signs of Lee's army marching west had been greatly exaggerated.) If that indeed was the case, Lincoln's message did not come a moment too soon. Still, an air of indecision marked the army's on-again-off-again preparations. "I am greatly disgusted," wrote Provost Marsena Patrick, "but there is no help I suppose." Burnside was more distressed by the conspiratorial lack of trust among his generals.[44]

The Northern commander asked to see the president at once. He took a steamer to Washington, arriving on New Year's Day. On that momentous day—Lincoln signed the Emancipation Proclamation into effect—Burnside went to see the president early in the morning. The general demanded to know why his plans had been canceled. Lincoln answered that he understood none of the prominent officers under Burnside had any faith in the movement and that the army was "dispirited and demoralized." Burnside was shocked. He countered that none of his subordinates could have known his plans because he deliberately kept the details from them. "General Halleck knew it," Burnside said, but "none of them knew my plans." The army commander demanded to know who told the president that the army was demoralized. Lincoln declined to name names. Burnside dropped the matter and begged permission to start his offensive at once. Lincoln again refused. He doubted the "feasibility of making the entire movement," especially after Lee had taken measures to thwart it. On the other hand, the president voiced some regret that Burnside had stopped Averell's raid.[45]

Burnside felt powerless. Unable to commence operations or learn who had snitched, Burnside observed, "I ought to give up the command of the Army of the Potomac." He thought the lack of faith in him, voiced by the army and the country, and now by the president, thoroughly undermined his ability to command. "It is the duty of every public man," Burnside declared, "who found himself an impediment to the accomplishment of the greatest amount of public good, to give way to some other person who possessed the public confidence." While on the subject, Burnside thought that the public outcry against Secretary of War Stanton and General-in-Chief Halleck warranted their resignations as well. Lincoln refused to comment and asked Burnside to come back later in the day.[46]

The president asked Stanton and Halleck to attend the second meeting, at which Burnside again pressed Lincoln to accept his resignation. Unintimidated by Stanton and Halleck, he reiterated that they should resign as well. The army commander later wrote that he never demanded their resignations, he merely stated that it would be the expedient thing to do. Halleck seemed somewhat confused. He claimed that he knew Burnside's plans but only now had learned that Lincoln had canceled them. Talk of his resignation did nothing to smooth his ruffled disposition. Stanton sat unmoved, detached. Having drawn a line in the sand, Burnside demanded that Lincoln dismiss the officers who had visited him. He had his suspicions about Newton and Cochrane, since their leave coincided with everything crashing to a halt. Halleck backed Burnside, and with typical ambiguity, approved of *their* dismissal. The president refused. Burnside left the second meeting rebuffed again. He returned the next morning to appeal one last time for the president to approve his plans and cashier his enemies. He was spurned on both accounts.[47]

Marsena Patrick noted that Burnside returned to the army greatly deflated. The general left his last interview and sailed back to Aquia Landing, arriving mid-morning of January 2. Patrick saw him soon afterward, "feeling badly." Burnside confided to his provost marshal that Lincoln would not let him move the army. "Every thing hangs by the eyelids," the junior officer recounted in his diary. "Our onward to Richmond has stopped very suddenly," wrote a signal officer in the Sixth Corps. "What the next move will be it is very hard to say." Burnside would have agreed, now that he had very little say about the movement of the army.[48]

The weather continued to mock Burnside. A staff officer reported that January 2 had been "warm, almost like spring"—perfect conditions for an advance. Life in the sunny camps continued with its daily regimen, spiced occasionally with the fanfare and panoply of war. Lieutenant Colonel William W. Teall, of Sumner's staff, interrupted his duties on January 8 to escort a Georgia widow, and the remains of her husband, Captain Edward Lawton, to the Confederate side of the river. Captain Lawton, of Atkinson's Brigade, had died from a mortal wound received on December 13. When Mrs. Lawton requested the body be taken home, Teall resolved "that the thing should be done handsomely." He led a procession of sparkling zouaves from the 10th New York to the river with arms reversed and drums muffled. Mrs. Lawton sobbed and clung to the Yankee officer's arm. "Col[onel] I needn't tell you how grateful I feel," she whispered. Taken aback, Teall also cried.[49]

General Joseph Kershaw, of South Carolina, donning a short cloak, met the party on the riverbank. Teall, with knightly flourish, placed Mrs. Lawton's arm in his. Kershaw spoke with emotion, "Col[onel] we feel grateful for y[ou]r kind attention. I thank you for it." Shaking the young widow's hand, the Union officer spoke softly, "Goodbye Madam—God bless you." Retreating to his boat, "oppressed with sadness," Teall hastened back across the river. The scene stood in vivid contrast to the mundane activities of the camps along the Rappahannock Valley.[50]

Burnside, meanwhile, drafted another plan of attack. He conceded that his previous offensive had been ruined by time. The swaggering cavalryman Alfred Pleasonton had learned that the army's maneuvers were common knowledge in Washington, and he identified certain Southern sympathizers who knew all about Averell's cavalry mission. Edwin Sumner confirmed that Lee's army acted like it knew Burnside's intentions. He reported the Rebels were "hard at work" erecting fresh earthworks on the river near Seddon's.[51]

Burnside, Halleck, and Lincoln undertook a vigorous correspondence as they hashed out a new offensive for the Army of the Potomac. The president unexpectedly asked Burnside to try another forward movement, in light of other campaigns and happenings. Major General John G. Foster, commander of the Department of North Carolina, had led a Federal force of 10,000 into the Carolina interior on December 11. He had taken Kinston on December 14 and pushed on to Goldsboro. Foster had burned four miles of the Weldon and Wilmington Railroad before withdrawing to New Berne. Robert E. Lee detached Ransom's division southward on January 3, adding the hard-bitten D. H. Hill, ostensibly to rally the people of North Carolina to his banner. Lee later noted that the Northern press had reported that 75,000 troops had left the Army of Northern Virginia to reinforce the Carolina coast—and part of them then went west to Braxton Bragg. "These were made use of as arguments," Lee told the War Department with a great deal of truth, "that impelled General Burnside to make his last attempt."[52]

Encouraged to strike Lee while he was weakened, Burnside searched the river for another crossing point. He personally reconnoitered the ground above Falmouth, mistrusting his backbiting subordinates. While taking a "very thorough" look at the river west of Fredericksburg, Burnside continued preparations opposite Muddy Creek, perhaps as an alternative site; or, more likely, a ruse. As late as January 15, Burnside still wandered the riverbank, looking for places to cross. Members of Berdan's Sharpshooters saw him riding unattended near Banks Ford. One of them "wondered what his thoughts were." Marsena Patrick often found his commander preoccupied. "Burnside is rather obtuse in his conceptions and very forgetful," he jotted in his diary. The Federal commander pored over maps, studied spy reports, and quizzed the provost marshal to exhaustion. Patrick procured guides for Burnside from his old brigade, many of whom had served at Fredericksburg the previous spring. Burnside wanted to know details about the terrain between the river and the Plank and Telegraph Roads.[53]

The Union commander ultimately decided to launch his fifth offensive upriver from Fredericksburg at Banks and U.S. Fords. He would not divide the army this time, instead taking his whole force across the two upper fords. Activity, meanwhile, continued at Muddy Creek to deceive the Southerners. Burnside spirited his pontoon trains out of camp, keeping them under cover near Berea Church on the road to the fords. He intended Franklin and Hooker to spearhead the move simultaneously, and Sumner would follow twenty-four hours later. Burnside, personally, did not like this plan nearly as much as the old one. "It was not so good," he testified. "But I could not make the other for the enemy knew all about it." John Parke, in contrast, thought the new plan was better and had a "stronger probability of success." Because it was intended as a surprise, Burnside hoped the army could secure the south bank before Lee could react, thus turning the Confederates out of their fortified defenses.[54]

Critics in the army quickly discredited Burnside's proposal. Charged with leading the advance to U.S. Ford, Baldy Smith reconnoitered the route. He denounced the enterprise with "forceful remarks" to the chief engineer, Colonel Cyrus Comstock. The colonel answered that Burnside had selected the position himself and would not reconsider. Others disliked using Banks Ford. A member of the 1st Pennsylvania Reserves wrote: "the river here above the tide runs swift over a rocky bed, and even if the pontoons had got to the bank I doubt if they could have been layed down." Of course, later campaigns would prove that bridges readily could be placed at Banks Ford, despite the rocky, rippling water.[55]

When he had everything ready, Burnside requested the authority from the president or Halleck to move. The army chief admitted that "nearly all of the general officers" opposed his plan, but he was willing to bear full responsibility for its outcome. All he wanted was some general directions. Burnside later explained, "I did feel that General Halleck ought at least to sanction the move." Lincoln had counseled Burnside not to put the Army of the Potomac at risk. Still smarting from the president's patronizing admonition, the normally affable general stated bluntly that he had "no other plan of campaign for this winter." If Lincoln rejected it, the army commander again offered his resignation. Burnside's patience had worn thin. He refused to consider the third alternative—to sit tight and wait for Lee to make a mistake. "I am not disposed to go into winter quarters," he informed Halleck. The general-in-chief responded that he always favored a forward movement, but he would not assume responsibility for how and when it should be made—a curious statement, since Lincoln expressly controlled both of those variables. The Washington government appeared to be distancing itself from Burnside against probable defeat, rather than giving its support to ensure victory. The commander of the Army of the Potomac ultimately assumed full responsibility for the final decision—he would go ahead.[56]

Burnside ordered his grand division commanders to move on January 17. Sumner would demonstrate in front of Fredericksburg, while Franklin marched to U.S. Ford, and Hooker to Banks Ford. Sigel's Reserve Grand Division would shift south from Stafford Court House to fill the gap between Sumner and the columns heading upriver. Burnside, however, postponed the operation at the last minute when Confederates started spreading upriver, creating conflicting intelligence regarding their position. The Northern commander kept his lieutenants on alert. He told Sigel and Slocum to move on Monday, January 19. Unknowing Federal soldiers hoped the delay portended something more permanent. "The respite was most welcome both to me and I doubt not the whole Army," wrote a hopeful Connecticut Yankee, "for I tell you they are not anxious for a fight."[57]

Burnside needed to know what the Rebels were up to. He asked Marsena Patrick to send a spy across the river to ascertain the Confederate positions. Patrick sent Ebenezer McGee, a Fredericksburg-area native and reputed employee for the RF&P Railroad, to scout the other side of the Rappahannock. McGee crossed the river and came back two nights in a row. He reported that the Southerners had dispatched an undetermined force to U.S. Ford, but nothing to Banks Ford. Delighted with the prospect of catching the Confederates divided, Burnside rewarded the spy with $1,500 and modified his plans. He ordered his army to move on January 20, with both Franklin and Hooker converging on Banks Ford.[58]

Union troops gathered to hear Burnside's latest general order. "The movements of our troops in N.C. and the Southwest had drawn off and divided the Rebel forces on the Rappahannock," Burnside proclaimed, "therefore the Gen. Commanding, regards this as the auspicious moment, in the providence of God, to strike a blow." Last-minute preparations sent men scrambling for rations and ammunition. Army surgeons evacuated the sick from the camps to Aquia Landing. (Unfortunately, no one alerted the Aquia officials, who promptly shipped them back to the then-empty camps to fend for themselves.) William F. Smith, commander of the Sixth Corps and leader of Burnside's advance, convened a council of war. Despite his own doubts, Smith allegedly told his generals to put aside their misgivings and give the army commander their full cooperation. "I should expect the 6th Corps to preserve its high reputation," he concluded, regardless of the outcome of the campaign.[59]

Blue-clad troops formed on the morning of January 20, ready to start at a "minute's notice." Sumner's Second Corps commenced demonstrating on the river below Fredericksburg. At noon, Franklin's Left Grand Division started marching to the right. Smith's Sixth Corps led the way over dirt lanes heading toward Berea Church. Hooker's Center Grand Division kept pace with Franklin's column on the Warrenton Road. Stoneman's Third Corps took the lead. Hooker's column veered southwest at Payne's farm on a path leading past R. England's farmstead. Franz Sigel's Eleventh Corps slipped into place above Falmouth and covered Burnside's line of communications. Brigadier General Julius Stahel's cavalry guarded the RF&P Railroad from Aquia to Brooke's Station. Brigadier General Adolph von Steinwehr's division held the railroad from there to Falmouth. Brigadier General Carl Schurz, German radical from the failed 1848 revolution, covered the Warrenton Road from Falmouth to Burnside's main force, near Berea Church. Sigel held his third division, Brigadier General Nathaniel C. McLean's, in reserve to guard the Potomac Creek railroad bridge and Belle Plain. Henry W. Slocum's Twelfth Corps shifted from Fairfax Court House and Dumfries to Wolf Run Shoals and the Occoquan. Later, Slocum moved his two divisions to Stafford Court House. Union cavalry under William Averell demonstrated at Kelly's Ford, to draw attention away from the main body.[60]

Excellent weather, unseasonably warm with fluffy cumulus clouds floating overhead, combined with the activity and excitement of a new campaign, re-invigorated the army. "No one [was] sorry to move," recalled a New Hampshire soldier; "almost anything is preferable to this vile camp." Others approached the march with uncertainty. Private Miles Peabody hoped the army would be "more successful this time than we were before." Reflecting on the possibilities, he recounted: "It will be a terrible battle and many more lives will be sacrificed on the altar of their Country." Lingering doubts still haunted a segment of the army, leading some to question the move. Peabody admitted that his regiment, the stalwart 5th New Hampshire, "feels rather downhearted at the prospect" of another battle. Some of the veterans alleg-edly said "that they will not go into another fight." A New Yorker wrote home, "Now for another Onward to Richmond tomorrow. . . . For my part, I feel very little confidence in our success." Although he was not particularly critical of Burnside, a 16th New York soldier reported: "We have as good a Gen. to command us as we ever had, but this make five times we have started for the Rebel Capital"—and this latest move appeared to be the least likely to succeed of them all.[61]

A day's march eased some of the tension. The late start guaranteed a short, easy hike. Men basked in the "pleasant, but cloudy" day and enjoyed hard-surfaced roads. An artillerist in Clark's battery reported, "The roads were good." A Sixth Corps officer confirmed the report: "the roads were never in better condition," which allowed the head of the columns to reach their desti-nations in plenty of time. Those in the rear still dealt with the inevitable traffic snarls. "It was forward and halt, every five minutes until after dark," recalled one soldier. Altogether, doubts started to vanish and soldiers began to give Burnside the benefit of the doubt. A member of the 82nd Pennsylva-nia thought that the army was "quite well and in good spirits" as it went into bivouac on the evening of January 20.[62]

Burnside transferred his headquarters to G. W. Wroton's farm on the road crossing England Run. His movement had begun flawlessly, with successful demonstrations below Fredericksburg and the march upstream undetected. Lee had not shifted any of his troops, convincing the Northern commander that his secrecy was still intact. Burnside told Baldy Smith: "With good weather we were 48 hours ahead of them." He made a few last-minute prepa-rations for crossing Banks Ford in the morning. He ordered the 2nd U.S. Sharpshooters to protect the bridge builders. At 8:00 P.M., the general sent Clark's Battery B, 1st New Jersey Artillery, to Banks Ford, but the guide got lost, leaving the battery stranded in a maze of unmapped country lanes and cow paths.[63]

Burnside exhausted himself while checking on every detail for the crossing. Baldy Smith thought the commander looked haggard and distracted. Smith, albeit not an impartial witness, wrote that the general seemed "nearly crazy from anxiety and want of sleep." The Sixth Corps commander certainly overstated his case, but Burnside did need rest. It took little effort to convince him to take a nap in Smith's tent. The subordinate general stood guard at the tent flap to make sure no one disturbed him. After "some time" Burnside emerged from the tent "refreshed," just in time to face a new crisis.[64]

Burnside awoke to raindrops pattering on his tent. A staff officer in Humphreys' division noted that the rain commenced at 7:00 P.M. Baldy Smith wiped the first droplets from his forehead and said he was "devoutly thankful, for I knew the campaign was ended." The corps commander embellished his certainty, but the rain added a new variable that could potentially cripple the operation. As Burnside had stipulated, he was forty-eight hours ahead of Lee "with good weather." The army commander returned to his headquarters to wait out the storm. Orders stood for the Army of the Potomac to cross Banks Ford in the morning.[65]

But rain continued to fall all night long. It grew stronger and more violent, and mixed with sleet as temperatures fluctuated. Wind howled through the camps, blowing away shelter tents and keeping soldiers wet and miserable. A Pennsylvanian wrote that it was "one of the hardest storms that I have seen since I joined the army." A New Hampshire soldier reported, "it came down good and the wind blew like 'old nick.'" A 2nd U.S. Sharpshooters man remembered the northwest wind "blew a gale." To a member of Owen's Philadelphia Brigade, "it rained as if the world was coming to an end." Morning offered no respite, and the deluge continued to drench the shivering ranks. "It rained more or less all day and night," recounted a Sixth Corps man. Another soldier noted in his diary on January 21, "Still raining *hard.*" Drizzle continued to mock Burnside's efforts on January 22 before clearing off the next morning; but by then, the Union campaign was in shambles. Unbeknownst to Burnside, he had walked into an immense storm front that dropped several inches of rain in Washington in a two-day period.[66]

The Union army awoke on January 21, after a comfortless night, to discover "every thing [was] one sea of mud." Roads had become slick, then muddy, and in a short time, they were transformed into a pool of "liquid mud." The geological strata of Stafford County, Virginia, consisted of a hard

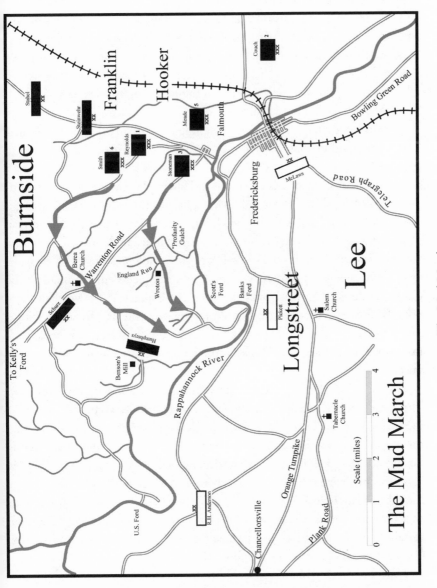

The Mud March

crust of surface clay beneath which one interested party discovered "some kind of earth without any consistency." Water penetrated the clay and saturated the sandy loam underneath, which liquefied, leaving the surface crust unsupported. Wagons, caissons, limbers, and ambulances rutted the softened crust until it collapsed, causing the "very bottom to drop out of the roads." "The mud is not simply on the surface," reported the French officer Régis de Trobriand, "but penetrates the ground to a great depth." Army wagons and vehicles sank up to their hubs; and men foundered up to their knees. A U.S. Sharpshooter who wallowed through the mire, concluded that "there was no bottom to the mud." Similarly, a dismounted cavalryman, floundering in a field, cursed aloud that "the whole bottom had fallen out of the blessed country."[67]

Burnside re-evaluated his situation on January 21. Even though the Rappahannock had risen dramatically overnight and the current raged through the rocky defile of Banks Ford, the Union commander had a sizable portion of his army and engineers within striking distance. He decided to go ahead with the march. Soldiers packed their wet tents and blankets, which made "a load heavy enough to discourage a mule." A rumpled Pennsylvanian in the Corn Exchange Regiment imagined that his blanket alone weighed forty pounds. Soldiers formed in ranks, "dripping wet and half frozen." "Not a man," noted an artillerist from Maine, "had a dry thread on and we all suffered much from the cold." Horses and men shivered as they set off for Banks Ford.[68]

Marchers found the mud relentless and getting worse by the hour. "In some places it was so sticky that it pulled off our shoes every few minutes," recalled a fatigued First Corps man. In shallower spots, soldiers discovered the ground "slippery as ice." A Unionist wrote, "Men were continually falling down and being helped up." Exhaustion sapped the troops of their hilarity. "So saddened were the men," a Northern soldier remembered, that "no one thought of laughing." A disgusted New Jersey man complained in his diary that the mud was so viscous that "you put your foot down and you are not certain you will not have to get some horse to pull you out." Pretty soon, even horses could not rescue the foot soldiers.[69]

Man and beast alike discovered the road surfaces treacherous locales. Wheeled vehicles had churned the roads into a "regular mortar-bed." Rain combined with an unseasonable thaw to draw the hardened frost out of the ground, making "the most awful roads I ever saw," according to a 5th New Jersey participant. Artillery sank deeper into the mire and cannon crews wrestled mightily to keep them moving. Continued precipitation thoroughly wore out the men. They eventually left the guns stuck fast in the road. Foot soldiers plodded slowly behind, in a grungy slime "knee deep in the best places." They helped to free the guns on occasion or rescue the horses and mules. One officer confessed, "I never saw anything equal to it." Bully Brooks' division tried to corduroy the road, placing logs under the wagons "to keep them from going out of sight entirely." The planking submerged and so did the vehicles.[70]

Engineers hitched extra horses and mules to their valuable pontoon train to keep it going. Sometimes a single pontoon required double or even triple teams to drag it forward. Batteries harnessed eight to twenty-eight horses to each gun carriage, and even then, "they could hardly get along." Animals struggled against the elements, churning the mud ever deeper. Exhaustion overcame many of the horses. They stumbled, fell over, and drowned. Animals died by the score. Men tried to extricate the beasts but could do little to help them. Some became so entrapped that soldiers had to shoot them. "Thousands of horses and mules dropped down dead in their harness," wrote a horrified 15th New Jersey private. He counted fifty-two carcasses in a mile, and at one point he saw ten horses in a twenty-yard stretch.[71]

The pontoon train inched its way closer to the river. Hours passed with scant progress. Making matters worse, engineers discovered that someone had tampered with their wagons, stealing the linchpins that fixed the wheels to the axles. Brigadier General Daniel Woodbury ordered guards posted around his wagons with orders to "bayonet the first man found meddling with the wheel." Drivers grew increasingly despondent over the "hopelessness of the affair." When they could go no farther, teamsters unhitched their mules and horses and rode away, leaving the abandoned hulks sinking in the mud. The engineers had no choice but to stop for the day. Posting guards by each boat—"a needless proceeding, as it could not get away," observed one wag— the begrimed engineers straggled into the woods to make camp. As Humphreys' division slogged past the boats, a disconsolate guard shouted, "The Army of the Potomac's on one Hell of a move!"[72]

Whole regiments pitched in to keep part of the train moving. A single wagon often required 150 men tugging on ropes with horses and mules to free it from the bog. Some pontoons would not budge even with ropes manned by entire regiments. The hard work left behind a trail of worn-out soldiers. Men floundered only a few feet before collapsing breathless. The 15th New Jersey called a recuperative halt "every hundred yards." When the

22nd New York ventured farther without a break, only a dozen men remained in ranks with a single captain. "We waded on, with all the enthusiasm gone out of us," wrote an overtaxed Northerner.[73]

The army reached an impasse in a particularly treacherous ravine along England Run. The path to Banks Ford passed through the deep defile near Burnside's headquarters. Men wrestled with pontoons, carriages, wagons, and ambulances, pushing and dragging them uphill and down. Teamsters coaxed and bedeviled their fagged horses to unprecedented extremes, regardless of their proximity to Burnside's sensitive ears. The infantry "unanimously" christened the ravine "Profanity Gulch." A New York private noted that by the end of January 21 "the ravine became impassable and the effort was abandoned." Guns littered the low ground, cemented into place. Exhausted soldiers littered the woods, desperate for rest. Burnside's advance had been reduced to a crawl.[74]

The Union commander spent a nervous day, hoping against logic that his army could slough through the morass. Fifteen pontoons managed to slither into position near the river before the day ended, but Burnside needed a minimum of five more to complete even one bridge. The general learned the rest of the pontoons "could no more be moved than the pyramids." General Woodbury had notified Burnside early on to expect a "great delay." The head of the Army of the Potomac promptly put his timetable on hold. He wired General Sumner, "I have just learned from Gen Woodbury of a great delay in the arrival of pontoons." He thought Sumner's grand division "will probably not be needed until late in the day. I will give you an hour's notice before moving." Night came without further word. After dark, Burnside realized he had been too optimistic. He telegraphed Hooker, "It is not at all likely that we will attempt to cross tomorrow." The Union army would need January 22 to close up.[75]

The evening of January 21 rained as menacingly as the night before. Mud worsened with every hour. "Dead horses and mules lay by hundreds where they had been stalled or smothered by the mud." The army sprawled across the chaotic countryside. Berdan's Sharpshooters huddled near the river. The van of the Sixth Corps rested wearily in drenched woods about a mile from the river. The rest of the army strung out all the way to Falmouth. Soldiers sat through another rain-driven night to "wait for daylight, but not to sleep." They sulked without supper because "it was impossible to make a fire as it was raining so hard we had no fuel."[76]

The next day brought more rain and another titanic struggle against the forces of nature. Rations ran out, and regiments issued a gill of whiskey to each man "in place of food." Animals still sank up to their bellies. Teamsters, "noted the world over for their proficiency in profanity," used "their whole catalogue of oaths, with many new combinations invented for the occasion." But, as a worn-out onlooker noted, "it was no use." Burnside's army simply wallowed in place. A portion of the Sixth Corps detected another problem looming on the other side of the river. "We could . . . easily distinguish at night the enemy's camp fires opposite us." Soldiers in Brooks' division feared that "they expected and wished an attack from us." Lee had found them out.[77]

Burnside's preliminary moves came while Robert E. Lee was away, and Longstreet and Jackson were at odds. Lee had gone to Richmond to consult with the president. News of another Union offensive cut the conference short, and the general hurried back to Fredericksburg. Until he returned, James Longstreet was the acting commander of the army. He had examined the Federal movements and forwarded all of the intelligence to Lee in Richmond. He also ordered the army "under arms, prepared to take the field." Stonewall Jackson, perhaps influenced by Burnside's previous designs or Sumner's demonstrations, believed Burnside would cross below Fredericksburg. Longstreet, on the other hand, thought Burnside would cross the Rappahannock above Fredericksburg. The neck of land between the Rappahannock and the Potomac was too narrow and marshy to the east. It made the route below Fredericksburg impracticable for a major military movement. He obviously did not give much credence to Burnside's initial proposal to strike across the river at Muddy Creek. Jackson offered to take his entire corps downriver to anticipate the Union advance. Longstreet disagreed, suggesting that Jackson should continue to guard his part of the Rappahannock while Longstreet's corps moved upriver to block the upper fords. According to Longstreet, Jackson balked at his command. "He was not satisfied," Longstreet reminisced many years later, "and demurred against authority less than General Lee's." Exerting his seniority, Longstreet demanded compliance, leaving the Second Corps chief with no recourse but to protest. Lee arrived in time to settle the issue before Burnside had committed any serious moves. The general set off on a two-day reconnaissance that convinced him that Burnside's bedraggled army had concentrated near Hartwood Church. He put Longstreet's forces in motion to intercept them.[78]

Lee ordered two divisions to Banks and U.S. Fords. Longstreet selected

Richard H. Anderson's and George E. Pickett's divisions. He cautioned each of them to "move at once with your command . . . [and] endeavor to conceal your movements from the enemy." Officers dragged their men onto muddy parade grounds on January 21, read them Lee's orders, and started for the fords at once. The divisions left so suddenly that the troops had no time to pack or prepare. They left behind their "clothing, blankets, cooking utensils, rations and everything in camp." Longstreet's divisions slogged fifteen miles "over miserable roads" in the time it took Burnside to cover four miles. Roads may have seemed "miserable," but the macadamized Orange Turnpike and several planked roads allowed the Confederates to move with greater efficiency than Burnside. Anderson's division reached the area of Tabernacle Church on the Plank Road while Pickett halted at Salem Church on the Turnpike. They advanced pickets to the river and the next day moved up in force. Anderson covered U.S. Ford and Pickett guarded Banks Ford. Both divisions immediately started entrenching.[79]

Rain and wind lashed Longstreet's Confederates with the same ferocity that crippled Burnside's command. Men shivered in the "drenching cold rain." "The winds howled about us," recalled a frozen member of Pickett's division. Heavy gusts added an unexpected element of danger as the troops marched through miles of pine forests: "Many trees were torn up by the roots, endangering the lives of the men." Reaching their destinations, Anderson's and Pickett's troops established camps in name only as they huddled in the mud "without tents or shelter."[80]

Confederates settled into the mud and slush, even though they suffered "something fearful," according to Jet Holland of the 17th Virginia. He remembered it as "one of the most trying times of this War." To stay warm, shivering Southrons gratefully volunteered to erect earthworks by the fords. Men toiled around the clock to pile mud and logs breast high in crude trenches and gun pits. In short order, members of Brigadier General Richard B. Garnett's Brigade were able to claim: "We are well fortified here . . . and have no fears they can pass us here, even though they may have a much larger force than we have." Robert E. Lee spent his birthday, January 21, examining the defenses with Jeb Stuart. He found the works well constructed but wretchedly manned. The army commander quietly admonished Georgia brigadier general Ambrose Wright for the "deplorable condition" of his command. He had Wright send his wagons back to camp for supplies. "The errand was fruitless," noted a Georgian, as "everything had been stolen by troops of other commands." Pickett's battalions warmed themselves by meager fires on January 21—the campfires spotted by the Sixth Corps. The next morning, Pickett's artillery shelled the woods on the opposite side of the Rappahannock River. The barrage surprised the Yankees. Bluecoats fled from their bivouacs, but not before seven or eight had been killed or wounded. Union guns offered no reprisal, being cemented in mud too far to the rear to help.[81]

After the confusion died down from the Rebel artillery's "warm reception," Union soldiers heard Confederate pickets taunting them. "Say! Yanks!" exclaimed a Southerner. "We'll be over in the morning and haul your guns and pontoons out of the mud for you." Another offered, "We'll build your bridges, and escort you over." The fun continued throughout the day: "Why didn't you let us know you were not going to cross again at Fredericksburg?" "We had a first-class reception fixed up for you, last time—if you had only come where we lived." "Say Yank, when are you all coming over here with your eight days rations? We are awfully hungry over here." Union soldiers seethed quietly, but they bristled when some clever Confederates painted a message on a barn roof: "Burnside stuck in the mud." "It might [have] been fun for them," recalled one Yankee, "but it was death to us." Unfortunately, the Northerners could not deny it; as one New Yorker confessed, "it was literally so," and that was what really stung. Burnside's army had to "grin and bear all these buffets of evil fortune." Southerners enjoyed the reaction to their sign so much that they erected another one with the same message opposite Falmouth.[82]

Morale collapsed in the Union army on January 22. Officers sought solace in drink. A New Jersey soldier in the Sixth Corps estimated that "on that day two-thirds of the prominent officers were drunk." Major Alexander Way of the 1st New Jersey wrote in frustration, "I am tired and sick of being bamboozled around hither and yon according to the caprice of those in authority and gaining nothing." Way was not alone. He alleged that "almost every officer in the army speak [*sic*] in the same way."[83]

Joseph Hooker boasted to Marsena Patrick that he could command the army "when he will say the word." On the march to Banks Ford, the Center Grand Division commander "stoutly protested so reckless a venture," selectively forgetting his own proposal to cross U.S. Ford in November. Patrick excused Hooker's uncivil tongue with the presumption that "He must be drunk." But Hooker's vitriol stirred others to complain. Some of the generals vented their criticisms "in a very public manner." Several officers even denigrated Burnside in front of his staff, who loyally reported it to the army commander. Patrick secretly confided to his diary that even the "Officers at Head Quarters are much disgusted" with Burnside for "a certain want of decision, even in Small Matters." He closed his entry wondering if this "last sad attempt" might be "more disastrous to him" than the defeat at Fredericksburg.[84]

Trouble spread throughout the officer corps. First Corps brigade commander Colonel Peter Lyle appeared to be "despondent and disconsolate." Brigade and regimental officers looked and acted "mad enough to curse and kill all mankind," according to an old veteran. Even Burnside's one true friend, Edwin Sumner, complained. He chastised the other officers for grousing, but in the end, he admitted that Burnside had lost control. "There is a great deal too much croaking," Sumner reported: "there is not sufficient confidence." The gray-maned general later said the want of confidence ultimately cost Burnside his command, not incompetence. "If he made a mistake, I made one too," the loyal subordinate professed, "for I certainly approved the steps, one by one, that he took." Happenstance and mud, however, had the army flailing about for a scapegoat.[85]

Common soldiers, worn out by mud, rain, and sleet, and "frozen like a board," mirrored the mood of their officers. Members of the 118th Pennsylvania asked backtracking regiments if they had seen the "Burnside stuck in the mud" sign. The units responded in unison, "H——l with Burnsides!" Other regiments shouted at every passing officer, "Burnside's supply train stuck in the mud!" Abandoned and ransacked wagons ornamented the gloomy countryside. "Supplies of every kind lay thickly everywhere," wrote a Massachusetts man. He guessed that it would cost the Federal government millions of dollars to replace what had been "so foolishly lost."[86]

Unfortunately for the men, the item most urgently needed at the front was food, and it was stuck far in the rear. "I never knew before what it was to suffer with hunger," recalled the adjutant of the 16th Maine. He and the colonel and the major lived for two days on six crackers. Hungry mules tried to eat the pontoon boats. In desperation engineers fed the mules soft pine rails. "Wherever that occurred," a soldier recollected, "it looked as though a saw-mill had once been there." Horses in Harn's 3rd New York Battery ate each other's manes and tails. Undernourished and overworked horses dropped dead by the hundreds. The Fifth Corps lost between 2,000 and 3,000 horses during the Mud March; and the Pennsylvania Reserves counted 364 dead mules and horses in the five-day maneuver.[87]

Some well-meaning officers issued a dram of whiskey to the soldiers "in small doses" to ward off the chill. Alcohol on empty bellies, combined with exhaustion and discontent, sparked several belligerent confrontations. Thirst and hunger drove members of the 134th Pennsylvania to loot the mud-trapped wagons for more whiskey. By the soldiers' own admission, the whiskey they found left them "much the worst for it." Several Federals had to be carried back to camp on litters because they were too drunk to walk. Another regiment suffered "a regular drunken row" in the middle of the night. Officers reduced several noncommissioned officers to the ranks and sent "a squad of Privates" to the guard house before they restored order. One sergeant became "so wrought up" that he attempted "to whip the Colonel right on the spot." A New York captain in a different corps reprimanded the sergeant of the guard for drinking and threatened to take his stripes. The sergeant grabbed a pistol and "rushed like a madman looking for the Captain." The officer hid behind a tree and waited for the sergeant to pass, when he cut him down with his sword. The sergeant was placed in an ambulance and never seen again. In another regiment a regular gunfight broke out between officers and a teamster. The colonel of a Rhode Island regiment "got mad" when a wagon blocked his path. "He accordingly drew his sword and pitched into the teamster," wrote an onlooker. The teamster retaliated with a club and "got the better of the Colonel." Captains rescued their commander, firing their revolvers at the teamster. The wagoner escaped with only the loss of a horse. The provost marshal arrested all of the officers and held them for court-martial. The head provost, Marsena Patrick, despaired: "Every body was in the dumps."[88]

Men had reached the breaking point. They plodded through mud, carrying "as much as fifty pounds of the sacred soil" on their shoes. A Pennsylvanian noted "they all look pretty near worn down." Men grumbled about being sent on a "tom fools errand" upriver. "Oh, the curses that night breathed on the move" exceeded any that the soldiers had indulged in before. They complained about "the war, the Generals, the Government, and everything." A 16th Maine soldier wrote to his family: "You at home cannot imagine the terrible pickle the Army of the Potomac was in." All of Burnside's plans had collapsed before he could even reach the river. Some soldiers wondered where they would have been if they had left a day earlier. "Thank God we didn't go over," recalled one, "for if we had moved one day sooner and had got over the river the whole army would have 'gone up' for sure." Soldiers felt like they had been mismanaged again by unfeeling politicians and incompetent generals. Soldiers in the 12th Massachusetts voiced their displeasure by shouting down Burnside's orders with: "Played out! Played out!" If he did not do something quickly, Ambrose Burnside faced a more serious problem than losing the campaign—he faced losing his army.[89]

Burnside decided to abandon the campaign. His rations had run out, his artillery and pontoons were frozen in the mud, and his officers openly opposed him. When the general and his staff revisited Banks Ford on the evening of January 21, they learned that the ground could not facilitate a major move across the river. Yet Burnside did not cancel the move until the next morning. The general wrote: "I then determined to order the commands back to their original encampments." Even then, Burnside waited, hoping to deflect some of the responsibility. He asked Halleck to meet him at Aquia Landing, or if Halleck preferred, he could "run up to Washington for an hour." He started for Aquia at 9:00 A.M. When he arrived, he found an icy reply from the general-in-chief. Halleck told Burnside that if he came to Washington, he would be responsible for "voluntarily leaving his command at that time." Burnside "did not care to assume" that responsibility and telegraphed back, "I shall not go up." Instead, he issued verbal orders for Hooker and Franklin to bring their grand divisions back to Falmouth. The general sent some of his staff "by special boat" to let Halleck know the state of the army and the reasons for ending the campaign; and then he retired to his camp to await the return of his army.[90]

Burnside's orders arrived late in the day. Hooker and Franklin opted to start their retreat the next morning. Rain diminished to an annoying drizzle on January 23. The army was awash in a sea of mud. Bully Brooks' division became the rear guard, while the rest of the army struggled to backtrack through the morass. The difficulty of moving became even more complicated in retreat. Federal troops had floundered for the past two days over poor roads, but now they needed to retrace their steps over ground they had thoroughly chewed up during the advance. The mire kept the army from reaching Banks Ford, and it also hindered its return to camp. A New Jersey soldier wrote, "We could not go on & we could not get back." Wagons, ambulances, caissons, and guns littered the roads, fields, and forests of Stafford County. "It was several days before they were dug out and dragged into camp," reported an infantryman. Nearly the whole army labored to corduroy the liquefied roads. They commandeered fences and cut down trees, laying them in the road and covering them with brush.[91]

Dingy ranks broke up and men headed for camp any way they could. "In squads of twos and threes," wrote the historian of the 12th Massachusetts,

"Burnside's unfortunate army splashed, swam, and floundered in the endeavor to regain its old camping-grounds." A participant noted, "the march home was a trying one," with the men generally marching "upon their own hook." Spared the humiliating mud march, Ninth Corps troops watched an endless parade of "straggling soldiers," who came in "muddy, wet, ugly, sour and insubordinate." Some of the men did not reach camp until January 26.[92]

The Army of the Potomac returned to its encampment humiliated. The troops reacted with anger and despondency. A diarist reported, "The soldiers were a good deal dispirited." A Pennsylvania officer wrote home that the army was "disheartened and disgusted." Even years later, men called the Mud March: "Burnside's futile campaign." One veteran mused, "The army did not get far," but then added wryly, "except *down* in the mud." As the last stragglers trudged into camp, a Fifth Corps officer wrote a single line in his diary: "Jan. 24: Weather good. . . . Poor Burnsides!"[93]

Meanwhile, the Union commander drafted a controversial order that would cause a political furor. General Orders No. 8 cashiered wholesale a number of officers in the Army of the Potomac. Burnside leveled charges against Hooker, Franklin, Smith, Brooks, Newton, Sturgis, Ferrero, Cochrane, and Lieutenant Colonel Joseph H. Taylor, the assistant adjutant general of the Right Grand Division. Burnside blamed Hooker for promoting distrust with his disparaging criticisms. Hooker, Burnside wrote, was "a man unfit to hold an important commission." He charged Bully Brooks with "complaining" about government policy and demoralizing his command. John Newton and John Cochrane needed to go because they had breached the army's security by divulging classified information—to the president! Burnside wanted Franklin, Smith, and Colonel Taylor removed for being "strong opponents to a move across the Rappahannock." The army commander reported that they had been "very open and public" in their opinions, and Burnside believed that "they could no longer be useful to that army." Sturgis, in consequence of a "misrepresentation" was relieved because he was inexplicably absent during the Mud March. Burnside later learned that Sturgis had a good reason for being away and expunged his record. The general hoped that this wide-ranging purge of officers would rectify the poor cooperation of the army's hierarchy. Burnside directed his adjutant to publish the order at once.[94]

Only two members of Burnside's staff knew about General Orders No. 8, and one of them tried to talk the general out of releasing it. They agreed that their chief's order "was a just one," but they worried about its legal and political ramifications. Burnside did not wield the power to get rid of so many leaders—that was the president's prerogative. They feared that Burnside would force Lincoln to carry out the order or openly deny the charges. Burnside agreed. He determined to put the order before the president, along with his resignation, and let Lincoln chose one or the other. The army commander wired Washington on the evening of January 23 for a meeting. While waiting for nightfall, Burnside watched the army struggle back to camp. Spotting Generals Franklin and Smith passing, he disingenuously invited them to lunch. Over a boned turkey, Burnside appeared to be "fitful in his moods," according to Baldy Smith. Sometimes he was pleasant and talkative; but at other times he lapsed into taciturn brooding. Smith, in no flattering terms, thought this was a symptom of Burnside's "apparent absent-mindedness." As his guests left the table, Burnside obtusely promised, "You will presently hear of something that will astonish you all!"[95]

Burnside left for Washington at 8:00 P.M. He arrived in Washington eleven hours later. Going straight to the White House, Burnside presented General Orders No. 8 and his resignation to Lincoln. The commander informed the president that he could not lead the army unless drastic changes were made. He reminded the chief executive that he never had sought the command and only wished to retire to civil life if Lincoln deemed him unfit for service. Burnside told the president that he did not want to do anything to weaken the government, suggesting that he would take the responsibility for removing the malcontents. "I think you are right," replied Lincoln, "but I must consult with some of my advisors about this." Burnside soured. "If you consult with anybody," he grumbled, "you will not do it, in my opinion." Lincoln explained uneasily, "I cannot do that; I *must* consult with them." The general deflated. He sighed, "You are the judge and I will not question your right to do as you please." Lincoln asked Burnside to stay in Washington while he sorted this out, but the general insisted that he had to get back to the army. Lincoln asked him to come back the next day.[96]

The Union commander returned to Washington at 6:00 A.M. the following day. He went directly to the White House, but was not allowed to see the president. Burnside went to Willard's Hotel for breakfast, and returned to see Lincoln, Stanton, and Halleck. The president informed the general that he had decided to relieve him and put Joseph Hooker in command. Lincoln said that "the unfortunate state of existing circumstances" compelled him to make the change. Howling radicals pressured him to save the nascent

Republican Party. They advocated strongly the elevation of their idol, Hooker. Lincoln saw no alternative but to bow to their wishes. Burnside quietly professed that he was not surprised and expected as much. "I suppose, Mr. President," Burnside answered stoutly, "you accept my resignation, and all I have to do is to go to my home." Lincoln "warmly" replied, *"General, I cannot accept your resignation; we need you, and I cannot accept your resignation."* Instead, the president gave the lion-hearted soldier a thirty-day leave so they could find him another command.[97]

Before Burnside left Washington, he learned that Lincoln had notified the army of the change in command. Burnside was shocked to hear that he and Sumner had been relieved, each "at his own request," when in fact, neither one had asked to be relieved. In Sumner's case, it was just as well. The ancient soldier retired to Syracuse, New York, where he died peacefully on March 21, 1863. Burnside, on the other hand, took great umbrage at the term "relieved." He protested to the War Department that Lincoln's phrasing was "very unjust." The general tendered his resignation and insisted that Halleck accept it immediately. The general-in-chief squirmed nervously, blaming the Secretary of War for the phrasing of the order. He had no power over Stanton's words. Burnside challenged him: "You can go to the secretary of war and say to him that this order does not express the facts of the case." No longer trusting Halleck to do the right thing, the deposed general went to Stanton's office to restate his case and resign. Stanton empathized with the disgruntled warrior. The secretary pointed out, however, that Burnside's resignation would injure the cause and destroy his already frayed reputation. "I don't care a snap about myself," Burnside huffed, "for I feel that I am right." But then he took a deep breath and acquiesced: "I do not want to injure the cause."[98]

The Army of the Potomac underwent another upheaval. Ambrose E. Burnside was done; Joseph Hooker assumed command; Sumner quit to New York; and Franklin and Smith were relieved by the new army chief. Hooker dissolved the grand divisions, and all of the corps commanders reported directly to him. "Everything," declared an army insider, "looked in a state of confusion." Many doubted Hooker's capacity for higher command. "It is no less than madness," wrote one general, "to put an officer at the head of a great Army in the field because some ordinary uninstructed men call him smart." General Erasmus Keyes, the sycophant admirer of Montgomery Meigs thought that Hooker was "not more capable perhaps" than Burnside. The army had undergone a storm of chaos and innuendo that would be difficult to overcome. Success for the Army of the Potomac in the future appeared to be a dim reckoning at best during the winter of 1862–1863; but for now, the army needed to rest and refit. The Federals called an end to the Fredericksburg campaign.[99]

General Robert E. Lee had never doubted the ultimate outcome of the campaign. He had foiled all of Burnside's designs and confidently prepared to hold the Rappahannock line for an indefinite period. He recognized that part of his victory had been luck—the delayed pontoons, the timely rain of the Mud March—and he took steps to be better prepared for future operations. He ordered the Army of Northern Virginia to fortify the Rappahannock River and guard all of the possible crossing points from Port Royal to the confluence of the Rappahannock and the Rapidan. "I laid out lines for field-works and rifle-pits covering all approaches by the upper fords," Longstreet reported. Confederates entrenched as far west as U.S. Ford. From U.S. Ford, Longstreet re-fused the left flank of the army southward, extending it to cover the roads leading to Chancellorsville. When engineers had done little more than mark the line, Longstreet left the army for a temporary assignment in southeast Virginia. Taking Hood and Pickett's divisions with him, Longstreet left McLaws and R. H. Anderson to continue the work. The project dragged, hampered by the magnitude of the undertaking and the paucity of tools. "The total inefficiency of the supply of tools," Richard Anderson wrote, "keeps back the work." The line re-fused from the river never truly materialized, but Longstreet's defenses on the river showed a surprising sophistication that kept the Yankees at bay for the winter.[100]

Stonewall Jackson also erected earthworks, which rivaled Longstreet's. The chief engineer of the Second Corps, Captain James Keith Boswell, wrote in January, "We are now engaged in fortifying the river from Port Royal to Massaponax." A. P. Hill's division erected a line that the young captain judged to be "a very good one." On the other hand, Boswell argued constantly with D. H. Hill about his deployment. "I am paying particular attention to Genl. D. H. Hill's line," Boswell told a friend. "You know Genl. D. H.'s fancy for acting Engineer." In the course of a few weeks, Confederates had erected an almost continuous line of earthworks and trenches along thirty-five miles of the Rappahannock River. Jackson's de facto chief of staff, Major Sandie Pendleton, boasted, "The world has never seen such a fortified position." Redoubts and sunken batteries crowned every hill above and below Fredericksburg. Lee, in fact, had more redoubts than cannon, but the line's menacing appearance easily deterred the Yankees from any more operations on that stretch of the river. Their work done, or the imperative for work at least diminished, the Fredericksburg campaign was over.[101]

EPILOGUE

"Not the Same Troops We Started With"

Ambrose Burnside packed up his belongings and left the Army of the Potomac on January 27. General Patrick noted, "there seemed to be some feeling." The deposed commander shook a few hands and offered his adieu. "Farewell Gentlemen," he sighed, "there are no pleasant reminiscences for me connected with the Army of the Potomac." He left on the noon train for Aquia Landing.[1]

Joseph Hooker assumed command and reorganized the army. His soldiers had wallowed in a deadly ennui for so long that their confidence had disappeared. A Sixth Corps officer reported, "They are not the same troops we started with." General John Newton testified, "I don't know what is the matter with them, but they have not got the same spirit they started with." Hooker's flair and administrative talent soon righted the army, and morale improved. One soldier wrote in his diary: "Since Hooker . . . I think there never was better discipline. . . . He is liked very much & has proven himself the right man in the right place *so far*." Hooker's shortcomings would soon become evident during the spring Chancellorsville Campaign.[2]

Robert E. Lee's Army of Northern Virginia settled into its winter camps on the other side of the Rappahannock. Even as Lee divided his forces and materially weakened the army, his Confederates continued to harass, pressure, and embarrass the Federals with numerous cavalry raids. Lee relied on a single-track railroad for a steady trickle of supplies. Shortages of food and fodder caused the Confederates to disperse further. Much of the cavalry and reserve artillery moved beyond Lee's immediate recall. The rest of the army supplemented its diet by living off the land. The Army of Northern Virginia had entered a winter of scarcity that made it anxious and even more aggressive in the 1863 campaigns. Yet its strong morale would endure—and even thrive. Victory at Chancellorsville in May allowed Lee to seize the strategic initiative and advance into Pennsylvania for the summer of 1863.[3]

Fredericksburg stands out among the landmark campaigns of the Civil War. It saw the clash of the two largest armies ever engaged in the war. It gave Robert E. Lee his most resounding victory over the Union army and solidified his place among Confederate leaders. Fredericksburg correspondingly proved to be the worst embarrassment the Lincoln administration had suffered so far in the conflict. Lincoln had pushed Burnside to gain the victory he needed to redeem his presidency. Instead, the defeat at Fredericksburg further compromised his position with the hostile Congress that convened at the beginning of December. Lincoln also prodded his other field commanders for victory, and their results were just as disappointing. Confederate Earl Van Dorn single-handedly turned back Ulysses S. Grant's drive to Vicksburg. The Southern raider had burned Grant's supply base at Holly Springs, Mississippi, on December 20, compelling the Federals to abandon the campaign. William T. Sherman's independent bid for Vicksburg met defeat at Chickasaw Bayou on December 29. William S. Rosecrans gained a limited victory over Braxton Bragg after several confused days of fighting at Murfreesboro, Tennessee. The Confederates withdrew on January 2, but Rosecrans' Union army was too disorganized to capitalize on the success. Burnside's failures caused more furor than all of the others' setbacks. His proximity to Washington and the high-profile nature of his operations put Burnside under closer scrutiny than Grant, Sherman, or Rosecrans. His reverses easily outweighed any success Rosecrans might have earned in remote Middle Tennessee. Lincoln refused to dwell publicly on his losses, blaming his reverses obliquely on circumstances, and never acknowledged his culpability in creating those circumstances.[4]

The men of the Army of the Potomac had no difficulty placing the blame for their defeat. Burnside had been the architect of their failure. A Pennsylvania Reserve wrote that "any person of common sense with no military ability would know that it was impossible" to attack Fredericksburg. Burnside had

handled the operation "very badly." A New Jersey observer told his the hometown newspaper, "It is as clear as the sunshine . . . that he has not the capacity
for moving an army of this magnitude." Confederates noted that Union pickets "universally . . . are loud in their denunciations of Burnsides." The general, for his part, admitted his shortcomings. "My Fredericksburg campaign
failed," he recounted in mid-1863, "and I assumed the responsibility of the
failure." The deposed commander swallowed all of the blame, but he easily
could have spread the wealth between those above him, namely, Lincoln,
Stanton, and Halleck, and those below, including Hooker, Franklin, and just
about everyone mentioned in General Orders No. 8. Instead, Burnside shouldered the full censure without excuse.[5]

While Burnside remained silent, others decried the meddling of the president and the politicians. "There is something wrong," a Connecticut heavy
artilleryman warned, "somewhere at Washington I think." Fiery Colonel
Emory Upton wrote: "There is imbecility somewhere but it does not do to
breathe it." He informed his correspondents, "Our defeats emanate from
Washington." One soldier reported that "No army ever entered the field like
this one—brave." He predicted, "one victory would make it enthusiastic; two
formidable; three irresistible." Yet victory eluded it. Even Connecticut legisla-
tor Jonathan Lymann W. Coe thought victory achievable, but "the President
has got to stop acting as Commander-in-Chief."[6]

The Army of the Potomac believed the homefront clamored for a decisive
winter campaign, which led to Burnside's rise and their current predicament.
Uninformed newspapers and hometown demagogues had complained that
McClellan moved too slowly and Burnside actually moved too fast, and was
impulsive and reckless. A 15th Massachusetts correspondent concluded, "We
see the *fruits* of the removal of McClellan every day." Many in the army
hoped that the beloved Little Mac would return; but they knew that success
whether under McClellan or Hooker, could only be achieved if "the people
. . . all keep quiet and let the army alone."[7]

The Union army also blamed the war-hawking abolitionists and peace
loving Democrats for undermining their objectives. It attributed the Freder
icksburg Campaign directly to mounting pressure from the abolitionist
movement. In the acrimonious aftermath of Burnside's campaign, soldier
argued that radical abolitionism was counterproductive to the military's con
servative objectives. "I do not blame 'Sides' for the Fredericksburg disaster,
professed a frustrated Pennsylvanian, "but I do blame you Abolitionists at
home for crying out 'On to Richmond' until at last he succumbed." Connect

icut soldier Edward W. Peck stood in a decided minority when he proclaimed: "Lincoln has not backed down from his proclamation. Thank God
for it. Slavery is doomed." Nonetheless, the Emancipation Proclamation
came at the darkest moment in the war for the Union, and many thought
they saw a corollary.[8]

Northern soldiers believed that they had been sabotaged by the other political extremists who wished to settle the war with peaceable negotiations, recognize the Confederacy's independency, and bring the volunteer soldiers
home. The Copperheads, as Union loyalists derisively labeled them, intensified their efforts in 1862 to subvert the Union war effort. They preached civil
disobedience and helped facilitate desertion. Homefront pressure encouraged
mass defections from the army. "There are lots of copperheads in our
county," recalled a Pennsylvanian, "and it is these desperados that create so
much dissatisfaction in the army." Newspapers published the peace Democrats' "treasonable language," leaving many soldiers feeling isolated, guilty,
and unappreciated. "The infernal newspapers," wrote a Union man, "do
more to demoralize the army than anything else."[9]

Most Confederates celebrated the remarkable victory at Fredericksburg,
but Robert E. Lee and his chief subordinates were disappointed by the outcome. Of all of their campaigns, Lee and Longstreet considered Fredericksburg and Second Manassas as their most "fruitless victories." Lee told
Longstreet that "victories such as these were consuming us, and would eventually destroy us." With limited resources, Lee needed a decisive victory to
justify his losses. "Fruitless victory for us," recalled General Longstreet, "was
about equivalent of a defeat to the Federals, and only left the result to time."
The First Corps commander undoubtedly overdramatized his case with the
benefit of hindsight, but he more than likely captured Lee's concern.[10]

The Army of Northern Virginia, in contrast, thought the campaign on the
Rappahannock had been the most decisive yet in the war—and they looked
for meaningful results. "Burnside's defeat will doubtless tend to bring the war
to a close sooner than otherwise," reported a Virginian in Pickett's division.
Southerners wrote scornfully of Burnside's ability: "No one but an ass would
have attempted to do what he did." They had soundly defeated "Burnside's
best troops," and that enhanced a growing perception of Southern invincibil-
ity. A Georgia officer noted, "This army can never be whipped by all the
power of Yankeedom combined." A member of the 8th Georgia voiced the
widespread belief that "we can whip a million of them." The only room for
doubt came from their counterpart armies in the west. News of Braxton

Bragg's withdrawal from Murfreesboro, Tennessee, restrained their jubilation. "Every defeat . . . in the West makes for us another battle," recounted an observant Rebel. "We beat the enemy in Virginia; he beats our armies in the West." Lee's army believed that Southern independence could only be achieved through its own accomplishments, which further enhanced the Confederates' self-esteem.[11]

Lee's troops exuded confidence. Soldiers began to speculate about what they had dared not utter before—peace. "I think if many more engagements with them are as destructive as the last, it will bring the war to a close," hoped a South Carolinian. General Cadmus M. Wilcox wrote home optimistically: "Heaven is on our side and . . . we have a bright and happy future before us. . . . I honestly believe that the war is near its end." This anticipation left the Confederacy ill prepared for the hardships of a long conflict. The war continued for two more years, and the South suffered crippling shortages for much of that time.[12]

Robert E. Lee had molded a disjointed, green organization into an efficient army in his first seven months of command. A North Carolinian wrote after Fredericksburg, "Genl. Lee . . . has the entire confidence of the Southern army." They idolized him, admired him with reverential awe. Captain Richard Irby of the 18th Virginia, while at Fredericksburg, learned that he had a new son. When asked to name the child, the captain replied, "As he was born just as the great victory of the 13th was being consummated under Gen. Robert E. Lee, I think we must name him after him." Irby prayed that his son would "prove to be as good, if not as great" as Lee. Confederates already esteemed the fascinating Stonewall Jackson. As an officer in the 8th Florida related, "He is a very plain man, but is a host within himself." But the emergence of Lee, *with* Jackson, created a tandem that promised tremendous success. No one suspected that they had fought their last full battle together.[13]

The Battle of Fredericksburg can be broken down into two separate and distinct actions. The fighting along Stonewall Jackson's front unfolded some distance from the struggle on James Longstreet's front. Jackson's ordnance chief William Allan, who would become a prominent writer, noted that Burnside's advance "led to two entirely separate battles fought three miles apart, between which there was no connection or interdependence, either on his [the Union] side or on that of the Confederates." Federal staff officer Abner R. Small came to the same conclusion, acknowledging that "There had been two battles, and we knew that both had been lost." Burnside's army had lost close to 13,000 men and gained nothing for its efforts. The Confederates reported approximately 4,500 casualties, but there appears to have been some exaggeration, allowing barefoot men leave to re-equip themselves and for slightly injured men to enjoy the holidays at home. Northern soldiers noted the disparity in casualties and the unusual placement of those losses. Close to 8,000 men had fallen in front of the stone wall, while Franklin lost 5,000 more at Prospect Hill. Burnside had sustained more casualties in his diversion than in his main attack. Correspondingly, the Confederates lost approximately 1,000 men on the Marye's Heights sector of the battlefield, and Jackson suffered close to 4,000 casualties in repulsing the Union First Corps.

Stonewall Jackson's 4,000 losses compared closely to Franklin's 5,000, attesting to the savage closeness of the fighting south of Fredericksburg. Jackson's engagement proved to be the decisive action on the December 13, and can be rightfully called the true *Battle* of Fredericksburg. Jackson's victory often has been relatively overlooked because of the more dramatic aspects of Longstreet's portion of the fight. The extreme disproportion of losses in front of Marye's Heights—eight Union casualties for every one Confederate—fixed attention on the astonishing defense that had bloodied several Union corps. Yet the Northerners never had a chance of success against Marye's Heights. Not one Union soldier even reached Longstreet's line. Without the hope of affecting the outcome of the fight, the action at Marye's Heights cannot be considered as tactically significant as that of Prospect Hill. In comparison to Jackson's battle it should be called the *Slaughter* of Fredericksburg. The profoundly savage and visceral nature of Longstreet's fight overshadows Jackson's battle of Fredericksburg even today and often mistakenly diverts the emphasis of study for the battle. [14]

The Confederate corps commanders implemented two entirely different modes of defense. Longstreet guarded six miles of the eight-mile front because he had the benefit of highly defensible terrain. With only half of the army defending three-fourths of the front line, Longstreet relied on the natural strength of Marye's Heights and its corresponding hills to repel his assailants. The First Corps commander had erected elaborate defenses and improved upon them in the weeks leading up to the battle. He kept very few reserves. Stonewall Jackson's line did not have the strong topographic features that defined Longstreet's line, but he did have reserves. The Second Corps commander constructed a well-conceived defense based on the depth of his reserves. Earthworks were scanty, and hasty miscalculations led to severe repercussions. Jackson had assumed an organized unit could not penetrate the

swampy finger of woods in his front. He left a six-hundred-yard gap undefended in A. P. Hill's line. The entire Confederate high command knew
about the opening and prescribed artillery to cover it from several angles. No
one, however, made allowances for the disorganized Federals that in fact
stormed through the unguarded interval. A. P. Hill's culpability must be
shared by Jackson and Lee, both of whom approved of his dispositions.

The two methods of defense also revealed two different military ideologies.
Longstreet maintained a static defensive line with minimal reinforcements
required to sustain Marye's Heights and the stone wall. Troops in the Sunken
Road salient were in a potentially dangerous situation should the Union army
turn either flank, but combined firepower eliminated any threat. Longstreet
had designed a brilliant, complex defensive scheme. Jackson, on the other
hand, engaged in a fluid, close-quarters, and costly fight with the Federals
once they had breached his positions. The action became a confused melee,
punctuated with numerous hand-to-hand encounters. Jackson's counterattacks resulted in a disproportionate amount of Confederate losses. Yet his fire
and intensity also provided the most likely avenue of counterattack—and success—and that threat preyed constantly upon William Franklin's concerns,
making the Union wing commander excessively cautious.

The Confederates on Lee's right fought largely without the strong presence
of Jackson or A. P. Hill. During the critical moment of Meade's breakthrough, both commanders apparently were missing. Jackson had accompanied D. H. Hill's division south of Prospect Hill to meet an anticipated
Union thrust against Stuart's cavalry. He returned to the hill shortly after
Early had restored order. A. P. Hill's whereabouts remain a mystery even
today. Fleeting encounters with Lieutenant McKendree of the artillery and
with the 1st Tennessee suggest that Hill was involved in the action, but his
impact on the management of the battle seems to have been minor. As a
result, most of the brigades involved on Jackson's front fought independently,
cooperating only by happenstance. All of the brigade commanders, with the
exception of John R. Jones (who hid behind a tree), and possibly Paxton and
Brockenbrough, performed effectively and acquitted themselves well. Among
Jackson's division commanders, Jubal Early redeemed his past indiscretions
and showed an initiative that Lee and Jackson came to rely on. In future
campaigns, they would entrust him with more independent decisions. Stuart
provided exceptionally good intelligence and showed sound judgment during
his raids. His cavalry moved with virtual freedom behind Union lines because
of his careful planning and preparation.

Operations on Longstreet's static front afforded fewer opportunities for officers to distinguish themselves. McLaws and Ransom both reported that they had commanded the salient around the Sunken Road and Marye's Heights, and in a sense, each did. Both of them fed reinforcements and ammunition into the battle in a timely manner. Barksdale's unorthodox defense of the riverfront showed imagination and pluck. The Mississippian left an indelible mark on the future of the American military experience. Cobb's conviction in the killing potential of the stone wall had come to fruition through his careful management of his brigade. His death marked one of the few high-ranking casualties incurred behind the wall. Kershaw's leadership, despite a slight wound, ensured a solid defense of the Sunken Road, regardless of the chaos that resulted from mixing his commands. E. Porter Alexander proved that he was a premier artillerist with a trustworthy eye for terrain. Even though J. B. Walton was the nominal chief of artillery for the First Corps, Longstreet came to rely almost exclusively on Alexander's ability.

Few Federal commanders showed inspired leadership during the Fredericksburg Campaign. William Franklin divorced himself from Burnside's plans and the battle when orders failed to match his expectations. He hid in his Mannsfield headquarters, isolated from his command. He knew nothing of Meade's troubles getting reinforcements, or of his repulse, until the division commander showed up at his headquarters after the fact. John F. Reynolds had been the coordinating officer for the attack against Jackson, making him the pivotal officer on Burnside's left. But when Meade needed him most, he had vanished. A close search of the records reveals that Reynolds spent most of his time worrying the artillery about ephemeral details rather than monitoring the overall situation. At one time or another, every battery in the First Corps encountered, received advice from, or took orders from Reynolds. His fondness for the guns—being an old artillerist—made him completely ineffective when Meade sought critical reinforcements. David B. Birney's rigid adamancy doomed Meade's attack to failure and showed a disturbing lack of cooperation between subordinates. Birney may have felt constrained by Reynolds to sit tight, but the fluid situation should have made him more accommodating and willing to help. If nothing else, he should have queried his commander for advice. In the end, only Meade and Gibbon showed initiative and assertiveness. A Northern soldier reported after the battle, "General Meade was possibly the best general in the Army . . . that day." A general at Franklin's headquarters said that "Meade went in and by God he went in like a gentleman. There was not a braver or cooler man on the field." Gibbon had recently risen to division command and successfully proved his competence. His star, like Meade's, was rising. The First Corps historian, J. H. Stine, wrote that "General Meade had come within a hair's breath of achieving a great success." Franklin's failure cost 5,000 casualties, or roughly 38 percent of Burnside's total losses. The Left Grand Division's smaller loss can only be attributed to Franklin's reluctance to involve more troops in the combat. Those engaged suffered inordinate losses.[15]

Burnside's attacks against Marye's Heights showcased a sublime courage among the participants who dashed themselves against the Confederate defenses, but it revealed little in the way of generalship. Hooker, Couch, Hancock, and Griffin all showed a reckless personal bravery, defying the odds and charging into the fray. A. A. Humphreys went out of his way to exhibit his mettle. His fearlessness was admirable, but his complete lack of control over his division proved that personal audacity was no substitute for leadership. Willcox and Sturgis not only avoided leading their troops, but were drunk to boot. The only officers to distinguish themselves on the right were Burnside's artillery chief, Henry J. Hunt, and Second Corps division commander, Winfield S. Hancock. Hunt handled his guns with expert zeal and showed innovation when establishing the bridgeheads on December 11. Hancock revealed an aptitude for decisive higher command that ultimately came to fruition at Gettysburg. Regardless of the officers, good or bad, the story of the Slaughter of Fredericksburg revolves largely around the individual acts of heroism performed by the common soldiers. As one Northerner wrote aptly, "It was a horrible business, relieved only by the wonderful gallantry of the men and officers."[16]

Despite the campaign's momentous importance in the winter of 1862–63, Fredericksburg has been little studied or understood. Even though it was one of the few decisive encounters between the two premier armies in North America, scholars, more often than not, have overlooked Fredericksburg because it is wedged between several critical marquee battles. It ended as a Confederate victory barren of any long-term results. The action occurred at the low-ebb point of two major offensives for Lee—the Maryland and Gettysburg campaigns. "Lee's Greatest Victory" at Chancellorsville and the dramatic so-called High Water Mark at Gettysburg completely eclipsed the unadorned victory at Fredericksburg. This made Fredericksburg frustrating for the South. Federals also refused to dwell on the most distracted campaign undertaken by the Army of the Potomac since First Manassas, or Second

Manassas for that matter. Malaise lingered and festered into worse scenarios, like Chancellorsville. Seven months after Fredericksburg, Gettysburg captivated Northern memory as the moment of vindication and redemption. Burnside's campaign signified all that was wrong with the Federal war effort, from unrealistic political machinations to soft, accommodating generals to poor leadership, and finally to an internal discord among officers who refused to cooperate. Fredericksburg was easily forgotten in light of other experiences. The majority of the Confederates at Fredericksburg were not actually engaged and did not talk about it; and the majority of the Federals who *were* actively engaged did not want to talk about it.

The Fredericksburg Campaign wrought a remarkable season of change. The December encounter proved to be the last battle fought by the majestic full might of both armies. The Army of the Potomac and the Army of Northern Virginia never met in battle again with such immense, burgeoning legions. Fredericksburg was the final battle of the celebrated Confederate triumvirate of Lee, Jackson, and Longstreet. In many ways, it was also the last action of the established two-corps incarnation of the Army of Northern Virginia. Longstreet missed the Chancellorsville campaign, and Jackson was dead before he returned. Ransom's division left the army shortly after Fredericksburg and would not return until after Gettysburg. Fredericksburg also ended the tenures of D. H. Hill and William B. Taliaferro with Lee's army. Both had angered Lee and Jackson, and both promptly received transfers to other departments, where they could vex other commanders on the coast and in the West.

James Longstreet may have compared the losses suffered at Fredericksburg and Chancellorsville, and attempted to exert more influence over Lee during the Gettysburg Campaign. Numerous studies state that Longstreet became more defensive minded as a result of Fredericksburg. Hood and Pickett, rested from their sojourn in southeast Virginia in 1863, played paramount roles at Gettysburg. In fact, George Pickett eagerly jumped at the chance that ultimately destroyed his effectiveness as a leader.

Robert E. Lee learned two valuable lessons at Fredericksburg in regard to earthworks and artillery. The army became inculcated in the use of fieldworks as a result of Fredericksburg. When Confederates had no cover like the stone wall to exploit, they created their own—digging hasty field fortifications and trenches. This development, also embraced by the Union army, altered the course of the war. Frontal assaults would continue to be brutal one-sided affairs that disproportionately favored the defender. For his artillery, Lee continued to mass his batteries into a battalion system. Their re-formation had begun before Fredericksburg and was completed in the aftermath of the winter campaign. Southern staff officer and artillerist Armistead L. Long wrote of Fredericksburg, "It was here for the first time that the Confederate artillery was systematically massed for battle." The results impressed Lee. He encouraged the Southern artillery to play more important and effective roles in upcoming battles—Chancellorsville would be called the greatest day in the history of Confederate artillery; and little compared to the magnificent barrage that preceded Pickett's Charge.[17]

The Army of the Potomac also underwent numerous changes as a result of Fredericksburg. The removal of Burnside marked the end of many generals' terms in the field. Sumner, Franklin, Smith, and Cochrane left the army immediately, never to return. The elevation of Hooker, along with Meade, Howard, Sickles, and Butterfield, gave the army a new makeup and philosophy. Reforms in diet, formation of a cavalry corps, and formalized intelligence gathering may be balanced against the reduction of the field artillery. Hooker disbanded the battalion system, probably due to the poor artillery showing in front of Fredericksburg. Hooker personally had positioned Frank's battery during the Fredericksburg battle, and preferred to keep that power with the infantry generals. Engineers continued to play a crucial role as long as the Federal army operated on the Rappahannock River. The army learned to construct bridges away from the cover of cities; and it readily became accepted that infantry needed to establish bridgeheads in advance. Hooker threw bridges across the Rappahannock below Fredericksburg at the opening of his Chancellorsville Campaign, ferrying elements of the First and Sixth Corps across the river beforehand. For the remainder of the war, bridges laid upriver at Banks, Ely's, Germanna, and U.S. Fords required infantry to secure both banks before construction. Surprisingly, the Union army showed a willingness to continue pursuing winter campaigns. The Army of the Potomac crossed the Rapidan River the next winter during the Mine Run Campaign and saw considerable activity around Petersburg during the winter of 1864–65. These campaigns differed fundamentally from Burnside's campaign because George G. Meade never committed the army without logistics already in place and functioning before he moved.

After Fredericksburg, the Union Ninth Corps left the army and spent the next year and a half roving through several departments, participating in the Vicksburg and East Tennessee campaigns. It returned to the Army of the Potomac in the spring of 1864, but never received total recognition from the other corps as an integral part of the old army. The Ninth Corps lacked the fundamental credentials for acceptance into the jealous fraternity of the Army of the Potomac. It had missed the galvanizing solidarity of the Peninsula Campaign and the redemption of Gettysburg. Only grudgingly did the veterans allow the Ninth Corps badge to appear on the postwar Army of the Potomac medal, and that was narrowly justified by their participation in the Overland Campaign of 1864–65. The Ninth Corps would always be considered outsiders. The arrival of the Eleventh and Twelfth Corps offset the departure of the Ninth Corps, not only in numbers, but in future service as scapegoats.

Even though history sometimes has glossed over Fredericksburg with generalizations, certain legends and misperceptions have endured about the December 1862 battle. Traditional interpretation focuses exclusively on the fighting around Marye's Heights and the stone wall. The tremendous futility and slaughter as wave after wave of Union attackers bludgeoned themselves against safely ensconced Confederates has a certain appeal that lures students away from the truly decisive part of the battlefield at Prospect Hill. The Federals who attacked Marye's Heights suffered unspeakable losses without the hope of success or recompense. The decisive aspect of the battle pivoted on the closely contested fighting around Prospect Hill. A Federal soldier explained the difference between the two conflicts after the war: "The dreadful slaughter in front of Marye's Hill at no time approached success, but, however brave, the efforts of the troops at that point were from the first utterly hopeless. Meade's were the only troops that broke through the enemy's lines, and saw victory, for a short time perched upon their banners."[18]

In terms of morale, the difference between the two actions struck George G. Meade particularly hard. He stated that he would have preferred attacking Marye's Heights rather than penetrating Jackson's line, because temporary victory "made me feel worse . . . than if we had been repulsed from the first." Meade mirrored the sentiment of the army during that winter of discontent. He passed along a rumor to his wife that Halleck had promised that the Union army "shall go to Richmond 'if it has to go on crutches,'" which (as over ten thousand cripples were made the other day) seems likely to occur before long." Meade, like many, was uncertain about the future. No one knew if the Union would survive or if the Confederacy would achieve independence. All the general knew was that the army had been embarrassed at Fredericksburg and he wanted to avenge it somehow. "I do not know what to make of the political condition of the country," Meade confided to his wife. "One thing I do know, I have been long enough in the war to want to give them one thorough good licking before any peace is made." "And to accomplish this," he pledged, "I will go through a great deal." True to his word, Meade led the Army of the Potomac by the time of Gettysburg, and retained command to the close of the war. Fredericksburg had left a stigma that could only be removed by the vindication of Gettysburg and the redemption of Appomattox.[19]

NOTES

ABBREVIATIONS

B&L	Buel, Clarence C., and Robert U. Johnson, eds., *Battles and Leaders of the Civil War*, 4 vols. (New York, 1884–1888).
CWLM	Civil War Library and Museum, Philadelphia
CWMC	Civil War Miscellaneous Collection, United States Army Military History Institute
CWT	Civil War Times Illustrated Collection, United States Army Military History Institute
FRSP	Fredericksburg and Spotsylvania National Military Park, Fredericksburg
GAS&SM	*Grand Army Scout and Soldiers' Mail*
GDAH	Georgia Department of Archives and History, Atlanta
HCW	Harrisburg Civil War Round Table Collection, United States Army Military History Institute
HSP	Historical Society of Pennsylvania, Philadelphia
JCM	Jefferson County Museum, Charles Town
LC	Manuscript Department, Library of Congress
LLC	Lewis Leigh Collection, United States Army Military History Institute
MDAH	Mississippi Department of Archives and History, Jackson

MMO	Massachusetts Military Order of the Loyal Legion Collection, United States Army Military History Institute
MOC	Eleanor S. Brockenbrough Library, Museum of the Confederacy, Richmond
MOLLUS	*Military Order of the Loyal Legion of the United States*, 70 vols. (1887–1915).
MOLLUS Collection	Military Order of the Loyal Legion of the United States Collection, United States Army Military History Institute
NA	National Archives, Washington, D.C.
NYSL	New York State Library and Archives, Albany
NCDAH	North Carolina Department of Archives and History, Raleigh
OHS	Ohio Historical Society, Columbus
OR	*The War of the Rebellion: A Compilation of Official Records of the Union and Confederate Armies*, 128 vols. (Washington, D.C., 1890–1901). Unless otherwise stated, all references are to series 1.
ORN	*Official Records of the Union and Confederate Navies in the War of the Rebellion*, 31 vols. (Washington, D.C., 1895–1929).
ORS	*Supplement to the Official Records of the Union and Confederate Armies.* 70 vols. (Wilmington, N.C., 1994–2000).
RJC	U.S. Congress, *Report of the Joint Committee on the Conduct of the War*, 37th Cong., 3rd sess., no. 108, 3 vols. (Washington, D.C., 1863).
PMHSM	*Papers of the Military Historical Society of Massachusetts*, 14 vols. (Boston, 1881–1918).
SHC, UNC	Southern Historical Collection, University of North Carolina
SHSP	*Southern Historical Society Papers*, 49 vols. (Richmond, 1876–1944).
TSL	Tennessee State Library and Archives, Nashville
UDC	United Daughters of the Confederacy
UM	University of Michigan, Ann Arbor
USAMHI	United States Army Military History Institute, Carlisle, Pa.
USC	University of South Carolina, Columbia
USMA	United States Military Academy, West Point
VHS	Virginia Historical Society, Richmond
VSL	Virginia State Library, Richmond

PROLOGUE: "POOR BURN FEELS DREADFULLY"

1. Catharinus P. Buckingham memoir, OHS.

2. Louis-Phillipe-Albert d'Orleans comte de Paris, *History of the Civil War in America* (Philadelphia, 1876), 2:555–56; *OR,* vol. 19, pt. 2, 545; Buckingham memoir.

3. Buckingham Memoir, OHS.

4. Ibid.; William Marvel. "The Making of a Myth: Ambrose E. Burnside and the Union High Command at Fredericksburg," in *The Fredericksburg Campaign: Decision on the Rappahannock,* ed. Gary W. Gallagher (Chapel Hill, 1995), 2–3.

5. Buckingham Memoir, OHS.

6. Ibid.; Stephen W. Sears, *George B. McClellan: The Young Napoleon* (New York, 1988), 340.

7. Sears, *McClellan,* 341.

8. E. B. Long, *The Civil War Day by Day: An Almanac* (Garden City, 1971), 247; Unidentified soldier, "Burnside's Mud March Made Twenty-one Years Ago," unidentified newspaper clipping, MOLLUS Collection, USAMHI.

9. Allan Nevins, *War for the Union* (New York, 1960), 2:322.

10. Ibid., 319–21.

11. Ibid., 263; Donaldson Jordan and Edwin J. Pratt, *Europe and the American Civil War* (Boston, 1931), 117; Lynn M. Case and Warren F. Spencer, *The United States and France: Civil War Diplomacy* (Philadelphia, 1970), 547.

12. Jordan and Pratt, *Europe and the American Civil War,* 140; Nevins, *War for the Union,* 2:89–90.

13. Albert B. Moore, *Conscription and Conflict in the Confederacy* (New York, 1924), 211, 354, 360.

14. Ezra Warner, *Generals in Blue* (Baton Rouge, 1964), 57; Benjamin P. Poore, *The Life and Public Services of Ambrose E. Burnside: Soldier, Citizen* (Providence, 1882), 36, 42.

15. Vorin E. Whan, *Fiasco at Fredericksburg* (State College, 1961), 9–11.

16. Bell I. Wiley, *Life of Johnny Reb* (Baton Rouge, 1943), 290–91.

17. *OR,* 181–86 (unless otherwise noted, all references are from series I, vol. 21); Jennings Cropper Wise, *Long Arm of Lee* (Lynchburg, Va., 1915), 2:411; T. E. Morris, manuscript notebook on Fredericksburg area battlefields, FRSP, 61–68; Warren Ripley, *Artillery and Ammunition of the Civil War* (Charleston, S.C., 1984), 15, 366, 370, 374.

CHAPTER ONE: "TO CRIPPLE THE REBEL CAUSE"

1. James F. J. Caldwell, *History of a Brigade of South Carolinians Known First as "Gregg's" and Subsequently as "McGowan's Brigade"* (Philadelphia, 1866), 86; A. C. Jones, *Confederate Veteran* 20 (1912): 464; Francis W. Dawson, *Reminiscences of Confederate Service* (Charleston, S.C., 1882), 83; John R. Sloan, *Reminiscences of the Guilford Grays* (Washington, D.C., 1883), 48.

2. Walter H. Taylor, *Lee's Adjutant: The Wartime Letters of Colonel Walter Herron Taylor,* ed. R. Lockwood Tower (Columbia, S.C., 1995), 46.

3. Henry A. White, *Robert E. Lee and the Southern Confederacy* (New York, 1898), 233.

4. Douglas Southall Freeman, *R. E. Lee* (New York, 1934–1936), 2:421; Robert E. Lee, Jr., *Recollections and Letters of General Robert E. Lee* (New York, 1904), 79–80; Walter H. Taylor, *Four Years with General Lee* (New York, 1877), 76; Emory Thomas, *Bold Dragoon: The Life of J. E. B. Stuart* (New York, 1986), 188; James I. Robertson, Jr., *General A. P. Hill: The Story of a Confederate Warrior* (New York, 1987), 160.

5. James D. McCabe, *Life and Campaigns of General Robert E. Lee* (New York, 1867), 276; Freeman, *Lee,* 2:419; Henry Lord Page King Diary, SHC, UNC; Richard Lewis, *Camp Life of a Boy of Bratton's Brigade* (Charleston, S.C., 1883), 34.

6. Harold B. Simpson, *Hood's Texas Brigade: Lee's Grenadier Guard* (Waco, 1970), 193; R. Lewis, *Camp Life,* 34; Mary Anna Jackson, *Memoirs of "Stonewall" Jackson* (Louisville, 1895), 351; Taylor, *Lee's Adjutant,* 45.

7. John Bratton, letter, Oct. 1862, SHC, UNC; Henry D. McDaniel, *With Unabated Trust* (Monroe, 1977), 112; John Hampden Chamberlayne, *Ham Chamberlayne: Virginian,* ed. C. G. Chamberlayne (Richmond, 1932), 141; Richard M. McMurry, *John Bell Hood and the War for Southern Independence* (Lexington, Ky., 1982), 63; William S. Campbell, letter, Oct. 5, 1862, Don Cearley Collection, FRSP.

8. Armistead L. Long, Philadelphia *Weekly Times,* Jan. 6, 1886; *A Historical Sketch of the Quitman Guards, Company E, Harris' Brigade* (New Orleans, 1866), 37; William W. Blackford, *War Years with Jeb Stuart* (New York, 1945), 183; McCabe, *Life and Campaigns of Lee,* 298.

9. Sloan, *Guilford Grays,* 50; *Historical Sketch of the Quitman Guards,* 36; Joseph B. Polley, *Hood's Texas Brigade* (New York, 1910), 137; Robert Stiles, *Four Years under Marse Robert* (New York, 1903), 127; King Diary, SCH, UNC; William F. Smith, "The Military Situation in Northern Virginia from the 1st to the 14th of November, 1862," in *PMHSM,* 3:107–108; James Longstreet, *From Manassas to Appomattox* (Philadelphia, 1896), 291; R. Lewis, *Camp Life,* 34.

10. W. F. Smith, "Military Situation," 3:106–107; Longstreet, *From Manassas to Appomattox,* 291.

11. Henry A. Chambers, *Diary of Captain Henry A. Chambers,* ed. T. H. Pearce (Wendell, N.C., 1983), 66, 68; Freeman, *Lee,* 2:427; J. William Jones, *Life and Letters of Robert Edward Lee, Soldier and Man* (New York, 1906), 218.

12. W. F. Smith, "Military Situation," 3:108–109; John C. Ropes, *The Story of the Civil War* (New York, 1894–1898) 1:444.

13. *Historical Sketch of the Quitman Guards,* 36; Ada Christine Lightsey, *The Veteran's Story* (Meridian, 1899), 24; King Diary, SHC, UNC; Thomas, *Bold Dragoon,* 190.

14. *OR,* vol. 19, 2, pp. 550–51; Newton Martin Curtis, *From Bull Run to Chancellorsville: The Story of the Sixteenth New York Infantry* (New York, 1906), 217; William T. H. Brooks, letter, Oct. 2, 1862, William T. H. Brooks Papers, USAMHI.

15. *OR,* vol. 19, pt. 2, pp. 137, 162, 555; *OR,* vol. 51, pt. 1, pp. 940–41; James H. Ogden III, "Prelude to Battle: Burnside and Fredericksburg, November 1862," *Morningside Notes* (1988): 7, 11 n.

16. Ogden, "Prelude to Battle," 3; Jane Howison Beale, *The Journal of Jane Howison Beale of Fredericksburg, Virginia,* ed. Barbara P. Willis (Fredericksburg, 1979), 60; Herndon, letter, Nov. 9, 1862, Montgomery C. Meigs Papers, LC.

17. Ogden, "Prelude to Battle," 7.

18. Horatio C. Haggard, "Cavalry Fight at Fredericksburg," *Confederate Veteran* 21 no. 6 (June 1913): 295; Noel G. Harrison, *Fredericksburg Civil War Sites* (Lynchburg, 1995), 1:127–28.

19. Herndon, letter, Nov. 9, 1862, Meigs Papers, LC; Ogden, "Prelude to Battle," 4, 7.

20. Haggard, "Cavalry Fight at Frederickburg," 295; Ogden, "Prelude to Battle," 7.

21. *OR,* vol. 19, pt. 2, p. 163; Ogden, "Prelude to Battle," 7.

22. Ogden, "Prelude to Battle," 7.

23. *OR,* vol. 19, pt. 2, p. 163; Ogden, "Prelude to Battle," 8; Beale, *Journal,* 64–65.

24. *OR,* vol. 19, pt. 2, p. 163; Franz Sigel, dispatch, Nov. 11, 1862, Ambrose E. Burnside Papers, NA; Franz Sigel, dispatch, Nov. 13, 1862, Burnside Papers.

25. Herndon, letter, Nov. 9, 1862, Meigs Papers, LC.

26. Marsena R. Patrick, *Inside Lincoln's Army,* ed. David S. Sparks (New York, 1964), 173; Samuel Parmalee, letter, Dec. 26, 1862, Special Collections, Duke University; Brooks letter; Clark S. Edwards, letter, Jan. 15, 1862, Wiley Sword Collection, USAMHI; Jacob W. Haas, letter, Jan. 3, 1863, HCW.

27. Patrick, *Inside Lincoln's Army,* 173; John Gibbon, *Personal Recollections of the Civil War* (New York, 1928), 98.

28. Louis Fortescue, letter, Nov. 14, 1862, Louis Fortescue Paper, HSP; Charles B. Fairchild, *History of the 27th Regiment New York Volunteers* (Binghamton, 1888), 111; Patrick, *Inside Lincoln's Army,* 174; John L. Mitchell, letter to the editor, *Wellsboro (Pa.) Agitator,* Dec. 3, 1862; Luther C. Furst Diary, HCW; William R. Plum, *The Military Telegraph during the Civil War in the United States* (Chicago, 1882), 241.

29. Fortescue, letter, Nov. 14, 1862, Fortescue Papers, HSP; Patrick, *Inside Lincoln's Army,* 174; Stephen W. Sears, *Landscape Turned Red: The Battle of Antietam* (New Haven, 1983), 344; Frederic E. Ray, *"Our Special Artist": Alfred R. Waud's Civil War* (Mechanicsburg, 1994), 40–41.

30. Patrick, *Inside Lincoln's Army,* 174–75; Bruce Catton, *Mr. Lincoln's Army* (Garden City, 1951), 330; Charles R. Johnson, letter, Nov. 12, 1862, Gregory R. Coco Collection, USAMHI.

31. Hiram S. Sickles, letter, Nov. 6, 1862, Hiram S. Sickles Papers, NYSL; Paul A. Oliver, letter, Nov. 10, 1862, Princeton; William D. Whyckoff, letter, Nov. 9, 1862, CWMC; Fairchild, *History of 27th New York,* 111.

32. Patrick, *Inside Lincoln's Army,* 175; Charles G. Evens, letter, Nov. 12, 1862, Burnside Papers, NA; David R. Larned, letter, Nov. 9, 1862, Daniel R. Larned Papers, LC.

33. Ambrose E. Burnside, quoted in *RJC,* 649; Herman Haupt, *Reminiscences of General Herman Haupt* (Milwaukee, 1901), 153; *OR,* vol. 19, pt. 2, pp. 549, 550–51; Larned letter.

34. Haupt, *Reminiscences,* 158–59.

35. Burnside, quoted in *RJC,* 643–44.

36. Ibid., 643.

37. Ibid., 643–44.

38. Ibid., 644–45; *OR,* 100.

39. Haupt, *Reminiscences,* 159–60; Henry F. Clarke, dispatch to John G. Parke, Nov. 14, 1862, Burnside Papers, NA.

40. Haupt, *Reminiscences,* 160; *OR,* vol. 19, pt. 1, p. 464.

41. William Marvel, *Burnside* (Chapel Hill, 1991), 167; Haupt, *Reminiscences,* 180; Augustus Woodbury, *General Halleck and General Burnside* (Boston, 1864), 6; William B. Franklin, quoted in *RJC,* 661.

42. Haupt, *Reminiscences,* 160.

43. Ibid., 154–55.

44. Edwin V. Sumner, quoted in *RJC,* 657; *OR,* vol. 19, pt. 2, p. 572; Erasmus D. Keyes, letter, Nov. 25, 1862, Montgomery C. Meigs Papers, LC; Daniel P. Woodbury, quoted in *RJC,* 648; Plum, *Military Telegraph,* 241; Wesley Brainerd, *Bridge Building in War Time,* ed. Ed Malles (Knoxville, 1997), 93.

45. *ORS,* 3:655; Frank A. O'Reilly, *"Stonewall" Jackson at Fredericksburg: The Battle of Prospect Hill* (Lynchburg, 1993), 6; Marvel, "Making of a Myth," 3; Warner, *Generals in Blue,* 447–48.

46. *OR,* vol. 19, pt. 2, p. 579; Henry J. Halleck, quoted in *RJC,* 645.

47. Burnside, to Cullum, Nov. 19, 1862, Burnside Papers, NA.

48. King Diary, SHC, UNC; Henry B. McClellan, *The Life and Campaigns of Maj.-General J. E. B. Stuart* (Boston, 1885), 186; Charles S. McClenthen, *Narrative of the Fall and Winter Campaign* (Syracuse, 1863), 20; O'Reilly, *Jackson at Fredericksburg,* 7.

49. King Diary, SHC, UNC.

50. *OR,* 84; Burnside, to Cullum, Nov. 19, 1862, Burnside Papers, NA; Whyckoff, letter, Nov. 19, 1862, CWMC.

51. Burnside, quoted in *RJC,* 646, 561; James H. Stine, *History of the Army of the Potomac* (Philadelphia, 1892), 253.

52. *OR,* 84–85.

53. Burnside, to Cullum, Nov. 19, 1862, Burnside Papers, NA; Furst Diary, HCW.

54. Ropes, *Story of the Civil War,* 1:451; *OR,* vol. 18, p. 777; *OR,* 1013–14; William Allan, "Fredericksburg," in *PMHSM,* 3:127; Leander E. Woollard Diary, FRSP.

55. Woollard Diary, FRSP.

56. *OR,* 1014.

57. Alfred M. Scales, *The Battle of Fredericksburg: An Address* (Washington, D.C., 1884), 8; James L. Nichols, *General Fitzhugh Lee: A Biography* (Lynchburg, 1989), 44; O'Reilly, *Jackson at Fredericksburg,* 9; Burnside to Cullum, Nov. 19, 1862, Burnside Papers, NA; *OR,* 1017–78, 1019, 1026.

58. Bureau of the Census, *Eighth Census of the United States,* National Archives Microcopy 653, roll 1380: Spotsylvania/Fredericksburg; John T. Goolrick, *Historic Fredericksburg: The Story of an Old Town* (Richmond: Whittet and Shepperson, 1922), 34; Freeman, *Lee,* 2:433; Benjamin C. Rawlings, *Benjamin Cason Rawlings, First Virginia Volunteer for the South,* ed. Byrd Tribble (Baltimore, 1996), 37.

59. John Bigelow, *The Chancellorsville Campaign* (New Haven, 1910), 32; Evan M. Woodward, *Our Campaigns* (Philadelphia, 1865), 70; George A. Bruce, *The Twentieth Regiment of Massachusetts Volunteer Infantry* (Boston, 1906), 192; Frank A. O'Reilly, "One of the Greatest Military Feats of the War," *Journal of Fredericksburg History* 2 (1997): 1.

60. Woollard Diary, FRSP.

61. *ORS,* 3:737; Sumner, quoted in *RJC,* 657.

62. Burnside to Cullum, Nov. 19, 1862, Burnside Papers, NA; *ORS,* 3:737; Sumner, quoted in *RJC,* 657.

63. Sumner, quoted in *RJC,* 657; Woollard Diary; Beale, *Journal,* 65.

64. Woollard Diary, FRSP.

65. Ogden, "Prelude to Battle," 9–10.

66. Sumner, quoted in *RJC,* 657; Burnside to Cullum, Nov. 19, 1862, Burnside Papers, NA.

67. Patrick, *Inside Lincoln's Army,* 177; Burnside, quoted in *RJC,* 652; Woodbury, *Halleck and Burnside,* 9.

68. Burnside to Cullum, Nov. 19, 1862, Burnside Papers, NA; Burnside, quoted in *RJC,* 652, 654; *OR,* 104–105.

69. Burnside to Cullum, Nov. 19, 1862, Burnside Papers, NA; Burnside, quoted in *RJC,* 646.

70. Woollard Diary, FRSP.

71. George F. R. Henderson, *"Stonewall" Jackson and the American Civil War* (New York, 1904), 2:301; Armisted L. Long, "Annals of War," *Philadelphia Weekly Times,* Jan. 6, 1886.

72. *OR,* 1020; *OR,* vol. 51, pt. 2, p. 647–48; Allan, "Fredericksburg," 3:128; Long, "Annals of War," *Philadelphia Weekly Times,* Jan. 6, 1886; Longstreet, *From Manassas to Appomattox,* 293; Clifford Dowdey and Louis Manarin, *The Wartime Papers of R. E. Lee* (New York, 1961), 339.

73. Lafayette McLaws, letter, Nov. 17, 1862, Lafayette McLaws Papers SHC, UNC; McLaws, letter, Nov. 22, 1862, McLaws Papers, SHC, UNC; Lightsey, *Veteran's Story,* 24; R. Lewis, *Camp Life,* 35; James R. Boulware Diary, VSL.

74. Long, "Annals of War," *Philadelphia Weekly Times,* Jan. 6, 1886; R. E. Lee to Jefferson Davis, Nov. 25, 1862, quoted in Dowdey and Manarin, *Wartime Papers of Lee,* 345; Allan, "Fredericksburg," 3:146.

75. White, *Lee and the Southern Confederacy,* 240; William N. Pendleton, letter, Dec. 13, 1862, William N. Pendleton Papers, SHC, UNC; Alan T. Nolan. "Confederate Leadership at Fredericksburg," in *The Fredericksburg Campaign: Decision on the Rappahannock,* ed. Gary W. Gallagher (Chapel Hill, 1995), 30.

76. Simpson, *Hood's Texas Brigade,* 192; Harold B. Simpson, *Gaines' Mill to Appomattox* (Waco, 1963), 113; Josiah W. Mosely Diary, Ralph G. Poriss Collection, USAMHI; Woollard Diary, FRSP.

77. Stine, *Army of the Potomac,* 255; Patrick, *Inside Lincoln's Army,* 179.

78. McLaws, letter, Nov. 22, 1862, SHC, UNC; Patrick, *Inside Lincoln's Army,* 179–80; Woollard Diary, FRSP.

79. McLaws, letter, Nov. 22, 1862, SHC, UNC; McCabe, *Life and Campaigns of Lee,* 305.

80. Patrick, *Inside Lincoln's Army,* 180.

81. Boulware Diary, VSL; McLaws, letter, Nov. 22, 1862, SHC, UNC; Betty H. Maury Diary, LC; Patrick, *Inside Lincoln's Army,* 180; Longstreet, *From Manassas to Appomattox,* 296; Cadmus M. Wilcox, letter, Dec. 17, 1862, Cadmus M. Wilcox Papers, LC.

82. McLaws, letter, Nov. 22, 1862, SHC, UNC; Allan, "Fredericksburg," 3:130; Simpson, *Hood's Texas Brigade,* 195; Burnside, quoted in *RJC,* 646.

CHAPTER TWO: "THE ENEMY WILL BE MORE SURPRISED"

1. Anna Jackson, *Memoirs,* 377–78.

2. Lenoir Chambers, *"Stonewall" Jackson* (New York, 1959), 2:259–60, 261; *SHSP,* 33:21.

3. Anna Jackson, *Memoirs,* 352; James Power Smith, letter, 24 April 1863, Jedediah Hotchkiss Papers, LC; Chambers, *Jackson,* 2:261.

4. Chambers, *Jackson,* 2:252; O'Reilly, *Jackson at Fredericksburg,* 10; Sidney Carter, *Dear Bet: The Carter Letters* (Greenville, 1978), 85.

5. Chambers, *Jackson,* 2:261–62; Jedediah Hotchkiss, letter, 16 April 1897, Hotchkiss Papers, LC.

6. Douglas Southall Freeman, *Lee's Lieutenants* (New York, 1942–1944), 2:319; O'Reilly, *Jackson at Fredericksburg,* 10.

7. O'Reilly, *Jackson at Fredericksburg,* 10; William C. Oates, *The War between the Union and the Confederacy* (New York, 1905), 165; James C. Nisbet, *Four Years on the Firing Line* (Chattanooga, 1915), 118; James I. Robertson, Jr., *Stonewall Jackson: The Man, the Soldier, the Legend* (New York, 1997), 643.

8. Stiles, *Four Years under Marse Robert,* 190; Robertson, *Jackson,* 643.

9. Chambers, *Jackson,* 2:263, 266–67.

10. Ropes, *Story of the Civil War,* 453; *ORS,* 3:656.

11. Ropes, *Story of the Civil War,* 454; *OR,* 1031, 1033.

12. Chambers, *Jackson,* 2:268; James Power Smith, in *SHSP,* 43:25.

13. *London Times,* Jan. 1, 1863; Chambers, *Jackson,* 2:271.

14. McClellan, *Stuart,* 187; O'Reilly, *Jackson at Fredericksburg,* 11; Richard H. Anderson, dispatch, Dec. 5, 1862, Richard H. Anderson Letterbook, MOC.

15. Lafayette McLaws, "The Battle of Fredericksburg," in *Addresses Delivered before the Confederate Veterans of Savannah, Georgia* (Savannah, 1895), 79, 83; R. H. Anderson, dispatch, Dec. 5, 1862, Anderson Letterbook, MOC; Gilbert Moxley Sorrel, *Recollections of a Confederate Staff Officer* (New York, 1905), 133.

16. O'Reilly, *Jackson at Fredericksburg,* 11.

17. Edward Porter Alexander, order, Nov. 22, 1862, Edward Porter Alexander Papers, SHC, UNC; Edward Porter Alexander, *Fighting for the Confederacy: The Personal Recollections of General Edward Porter Alexander,* ed. Gary W. Gallagher (Chapel Hill, 1989), 167; Stine, *Army of the Potomac,* 259.

18. McClellan, *Stuart,* 187–88; Freeman, *Lee,* 2:437; Richard L. T. Beale, *History of the Ninth Virginia Cavalry in the War between the States* (Richmond, 1899), 55–56.

19. Keyes, letter, Nov. 25, 1862, Meigs Papers, LC; Patrick, *Inside Lincoln's Army,* 181.

20. Brainerd, *Bridge Building,* 93; Woodbury, *Halleck and Burnside,* 9; Frank B. Williams, *Reminiscences of the Fiftieth New York Regiment Engineers* (Washington, D.C., n.d.), 4.

21. *OR,* 86; *RJC,* 647; Woodbury, *Halleck and Burnside,* 9.

22. Brainerd, *Bridge Building,* 94; *OR,* 86; Woodbury, *Halleck and Burnside,* 9.

23. Woodbury, *Halleck and Burnside,* 9; Brainerd, *Bridge Building,* 94.

24. F. Williams, *Fiftieth New York Engineers,* 7–8.

25. Woodbury, *Halleck and Burnside,* 9; Brainerd, *Bridge Building,* 94.

26. Brainerd, *Bridge Building,* 94–95.

27. Daniel P. Woodbury, quoted in *RJC,* 649; Brainerd, *Bridge Building,* 97; Woodbury, *Halleck and Burnside,* 9.

28. Burnside, quoted in *RJC,* 651–52; Brainerd, *Bridge Building,* 97.

29. Clark Baum, letter, Dec. 2, 1862, Clark Baum Papers, Tim Garret Collection, FRSP; *OR,* 87.

30. Halleck, quoted in *RJC,* Keyes, letter, Nov. 25, 1862, Meigs Papers, LC.

31. BW, letter to the editor *Rochester Democrat and American,* Dec. 20, 1862; Brainerd, *Bridge Building,* 97; *OR,* 86–87.

32. Burnside, quoted in *RJC, 651, 655;* Woodbury, *Halleck and Burnside,* 11.

33. Burnside, quoted in *RJC,* 651.

34. Haupt, *Reminiscences,* 165; *OR,* vol. 12, pt. 3, p. 815.

35. Bartholomen Dailey, letter, Nov. 22, 1862, Bartholomen Dailey Letters, Mary Washington College; John Smart, letter, Nov. 20, 1862, John Smart Papers, FRSP; Woodbury, *Halleck and Burnside,* 10.

36. Baum, letter, Dec. 2, 1862, Baum Papers, Garret Collection, FRSP; Smart, letter, Nov. 20, 1862, Smart Papers, FRSP; Haupt, *Reminiscences,* 166.

37. Haupt, *Reminiscences,* 165–66, 168; R. E. Coughlin, *Engineer Operations in Past Wars* (Fort Humphreys, Va., 1926), 91; Smart, letter, Nov. 20, 1862, Smart Papers, FRSP; Francis A. Lord, *Lincoln's Railroad Man, Herman Haupt* (Rutherford, N.J., 1969), 175; Frank A. O'Reilly, "The Pennsylvania Reserves at Fredericksburg," *Civil War Regiments* 4 no. 4 (1995): 2–3.

38. Herman Haupt, dispatch, Nov. 21, 1862, Burnside Papers, NA; Lord, *Haupt,* 177; S. Dean Canan, *History of Cambria County, Pennsylvania* (New York, 1907), 248

39. Lord, *Haupt,* 178; Haupt, *Reminiscences,* 165–67.

40. *OR,* 103; Louis Fortescue, letter, Dec. 6, 1862, Fortescue Papers, HSP; Henry S. Hall, *Personal Experience under Burnside and Hooker* (Kansas City, 1889), 5; Burnside, letter, Nov. 19, 1862, Burnside Papers, NA.

41. Burnside, letter, Nov. 19, 1862, Burnside Papers, NA; Woodbury, *Halleck and Burnside,* 7.

42. Sumner, quoted in *RJC,* 659; Edwin V. Sumner, letter, Nov. 23, 1862, Burnside Papers.

43. Samuel T. Cushing, *The Acting Signal Corps* (Kansas City, 1892), 13; Brainerd, *Bridge Building,* 98.

44. Paul M. Angle and Earl Schenck Miers, *The Living Lincoln: The Man, His Mind, His Times, and the War He Fought, Reconstructed from His Own Writings* (New Brunswick, N.J., 1955), 515; Patrick, *Inside Lincoln's Army,* 182–83.

45. Angle and Miers, *Living Lincoln,* 515–16.

46. Patrick, *Inside Lincoln's Army,* 184; Samuel Magaw, dispatch, Nov. 22, 1862, Burnside Papers, NA.

47. *ORS,* 3:656; Longstreet, *From Manassas to Appomattox,* 300; Henderson, *Jackson,* 2:305; Robert J. Driver, Jr., *The 1st and 2nd Rockbridge Artillery* (Lynchburg, Va., 1987), 34; William S. Campbell, letter, Dec. 17, 1862, Cearley Collection, FRSP; *ORN,* 5:191; George P. Wallace, letter, Dec. 5, 1862, West Virginia Collection, University of West Virginia.

48. Hall, *Personal Experience,* 5; Fortescue, letter, Dec. 6, 1862, Fortescue Papers, HSP; Edgar Richards, letter, Dec. 7, 1862, CWMC; Furst Diary, HCW; Vorhees, letter to the editor, *Hunterdon (N.J.) Republican,* Dec. 19, 1862.

49. Curtis, *From Bull Run to Chancellorsville,* 219; Sumner, quoted in *RJC,* 658; O'Reilly, *Jackson at Fredericksburg,* 12; R. Lewis, *Camp Life,* 36.

50. Burnside, quoted in *RJC,* 654

51. *OR,* 64; William W. Teall, letter, Dec. 9, 1862, William W. Teall Papers, Small Collection, TSL; Burnside, letter, June 7, 1863, Burnside Papers, NA; Marvel, "Making of a Myth," 6; James H. Wood, *The War* (Cumberland, Md., 1910), 103.

52. William W. Teall, letter, Dec. 10, 1862, Teall Papers, TSL; Glenn Tucker, *Hancock the Superb* (Indianapolis, 1960), 100; Francis A. Walker, *History of the Second Army Corps* (New York, 1891), 156; Darius N. Couch, "Sumner's 'Right Grand Division,'" in *B&L,* 3:107.

53. Couch, "Sumner's 'Right Grand Division,'" 108; Patrick, *Inside Lincoln's Army,* 186.

54. Patrick, *Inside Lincoln's Army,* 186.

55. Brainerd, *Bridge Building,* 149; *OR,* 170; F. Williams, *Fiftieth New York Engineers,* 107.

56. Gilbert Thompson, *The Engineer Battalion in the Civil War* (Washington, D.C., 1910), 25; Brainerd, *Bridge Building,* 149.

57. A. T. Williams, letter, Dec. 14, 1862, in *Elmira Weekly Advertiser and Chemung County Republican,* Dec. 27, 1862 (also appears in David S. Moore, *I Will Try to Send You All the Particulars of the Fight* [Albany, 1995] 107); McLaws, "Battle of Fredericksburg," 74; Brainerd, *Bridge Building,* 150.

58. Sumner, quoted in *RJC,* 658; O'Reilly, *Jackson at Fredericksburg,* 12–14.

59. *ORN,* 5:191–94.

60. Ibid., 191, 194.

61. Ibid., 191, 192.

62. Ibid., 195.

63. *OR,* vol. 18, 54; Albert Maxfield and Robert Brady, Jr., *Roster and Statistical Record of Company D, of the Eleventh Maine Infantry Volunteers* (New York, 1890), 17.

64. Longstreet, *From Manassas to Appomattox,* 301.

CHAPTER THREE: "A SCENE OF WILDEST CONFUSION"

1. *OR,* 173; G. Thompson, *Engineer Battalion,* 25; Baum, letter, Dec. 11, 1862, Baum Papers, Garret Collection, FRSP; Brainerd, *Bridge Building,* 150.

2. *OR,* 175, 179; F. Williams, *Fiftieth New York Engineers,* 7–8; Brainerd, *Bridge Building,* 150; Baum, letter, Dec. 11, 1862, Baum Papers, Garret Collection, FRSP; A. Williams, *Elmira Weekly Advertiser and Chemung County Republican,* Dec. 27, 1862.

3. Brainerd, *Bridge Building,* 151; Baum, letter, Dec. 11, 1862, Baum Papers. Garret Collection, FRSP.

4. Brainerd, *Bridge Building,* 153–54.

5. Ibid., 152; Thomas J. Owen, "Back in War Times," *Athens (Pa.) Gazette,* March 11, 1897; Williams, letter to the editor, *Elmira Weekly Advertiser and Chemung County Republican,* Dec. 27, 1862; Baum, letter, Dec. 11, 1862, Baum Papers, Garret Collection, FRSP; *OR,* 168.

6. Baum, letter, Dec. 11, 1862, Baum Papers, Garret Collection, FRSP; Brainerd, *Bridge Building,* 152; "Weather Journal Recording Observations at . . . Georgetown, D.C., June 1858–May 1866," microfilm call #CL-1024, National Weather Records Center, Asheville, N.C.

7. Williams, letter to the editor, *Elmira Weekly Advertiser and Chemung Republican,* Dec. 27, 1862; Brainerd, *Bridge Building,* 154.

8. Josiah M. Favill, *The Diary of a Young Officer* (Chicago, 1909), 206; Frederick Pfisterer, *New York in the War of the Rebellion* (Albany, 1912), 3:2650, 2653; *Annual Report of the*

Adjutant-General of the State of New York for the Year 1901 (Albany, 1902), 764, 867; *Berks, Chester, and Montgomery (Pa.) Ledger,* Dec. 30, 1862; Al M. Gambone, *The Life of General Samuel K. Zook* (Baltimore, 1996), 238.

9. *OR,* 69–70, 181; Edward G. Longacre, *The Man behind the Guns: A Biography of General Henry J. Hunt* (South Brunswick, N.J., 1977), 128.

10. *OR,* 181; Longacre, *Man behind the Guns,* 129.

11. *OR,* 181.

12. Charles S. Wainwright, *Diary of Battle: The Personal Journals of Colonel Charles S. Wainwright,* ed. Allan Nevins (New York, 1962), 132, 135; *OR,* 182; Noel G. Harrison, *Gazetteer of Historic Sites related to the Fredericksburg and Spotsylvania National Military Park* (Fredericksburg, 1989—copy in FRSP), 2: 8. Wainwright called White Oak Church "a very small building not bigger or more pretentious than one of our country school houses."

13. *OR,* 212, 1126–27.

14. *OR,* 194, 1126–27; unknown author (a member of Seeley's Battery K, 4th U.S.), letter, Dec. 18, 1862, *Franklin (N.Y.) Visitor,* Jan. 6, 1863.

15. *OR,* 198, 202, 1126–27.

16. Ibid., 1126–27.

17. Ibid., 182, 194, 198, 199, 213, 217; John H. Rhodes, *The History of Battery B, 1st Regiment Rhode Island Light Artillery* (Providence, 1894), 137; Walker, *Second Corps,* 146; Jacob Roemer, *Reminiscences of the War of the Rebellion* (New York, 1897), 96.

18. Brainerd, *Bridge Building,* 154; A. Williams, letter to the editor, *Elmira Weekly Advertiser and Chemung County Republican,* Dec. 27, 1862; Baum, letter, Dec. 11, 1862, Baum Papers, Garret Collection, FRSP.

19. Williams, *Fiftieth New York Engineers,* 8; John D. Billings, *Hard Tack and Coffee* (Boston, 1887), 386.

20. F. Williams, *Fiftieth New York Engineers,* 8; Billings, *Hard Tack and Coffee,* 386; Brainerd, *Bridge Building,* 155.

21. F. Williams, *Fiftieth New York Engineers,* 8; Billings, *Hard Tack and Coffee,* 386.

22. Billings, *Hard Tack and Coffee,* 386–87.

23. Ibid., 387; Baum, letter, Dec. 11, 1862, Baum Papers, Garret Collection, FRSP; A. Williams, letter to the editor, *Elmira Weekly Advertiser and Chemung County Republican,* Dec. 27, 1862.

24. Brainerd, *Bridge Building,* 154; Baum, letter, Dec. 11, 1862, Baum Papers, Garret Collection, FRSP.

25. *OR,* 175, 179, 345; A. Williams, letter to the editor, *Elmira Weekly Advertiser and Chemung County Republican,* Dec. 27, 1862.

26. Harrison, *Fredericksburg Civil War Sites,* 1:97–98. Harrison states that the bridge measured 420 feet in length.

27. Brainerd, *Bridge Building,* 154.

28. Baum, letter, Dec. 11, 1862, Baum Papers, Garret Collection, FRSP.

29. A. Williams, letter to the editor, *Elmira Weekly Advertiser and Chemung County Republican,* Dec. 27, 1862.

30. J. R. Mehen, "An Incident of Fredericksburg," *Confederate Veteran* 23 (Sept. 1915): 407; Josiah F. Murphey, *Nantucket Experience Including the Memoirs of Josiah Fitch Murphey,*

ed. Richard F. Miller and Robert E. Mooney (Nantucket, 1994), 83; James Dinkins, "Barksdale's Mississippi Brigade at Fredericksburg," *SHSP* 36, p. 19; *OR,* 600, 601, 605.

31. Lafayette McLaws, "The Confederate Left at Fredericksburg," *B&L,* 3: 86; John F. H. Claiborne Memoir, p. 20, John F. H. Claiborne Papers, SHC, UNC.

32. Bruce, *Twentieth Massachusetts,* 193, 196; *OR,* 603.

33. McLaws, "Confederate Left at Fredericksburg," 3:86; Wise, *Long Arm of Lee,* 1:375; Freeman, *Lee's Lieutenants,* 2:334; Chambers, *Jackson,* 2:276; Sanford W. Branch, letter, Dec. 17, 1862, typescript, Margaret Branch Sexton Collection, University of Georgia; Harrison, *Fredericksburg Civil War Sites,* 2:65; Bruce, *Twentieth Massachusetts,* 193; *OR,* 600, 601, 605; Claiborne Memoir, p. 20, Claiborne Papers, SHC, UNC.

34. *OR,* 175; Brainerd, *Bridge Building,* 155; Baum, letter, Dec. 11, 1862, Baum Papers, Garret Collection, FRSP.

35. *OR,* 601.

36. Brainerd, *Bridge Building,* 156; J. S. Wheeler, letter to the editor, *Cohoes (N.Y.) Cataract,* Dec. 20, 1862; Baum, letter, Dec. 11, 1862, Baum Papers, Garret Collection, FRSP; Gilbert Frederick, *The Story of a Regiment: Being a Record of the Military Services of the Fifty-seventh New York State Volunteer Infantry* (n.p., 1895), 116; Thomas J. Owen, "Back in War Times," *Athens (Pa.) Gazette,* March 11, 1897; *OR,* 168. Both Brainerd and Wheeler thought the time was 4:00 rather than 5:00 A.M., but that does not agree with the sequence of the signal guns and Barksdale's initial fire.

37. Owen, "Back in War Times," *Athens (Pa.) Gazette,* March 11, 1897; Brainerd, *Bridge Building,* 157. Thomas Owen thought Captain Perkins' brother served on Brigadier General Daniel Butterfield's Fifth Corps staff and had finagled the orders to send the body home with Owen as an escort.

38. Baum, letter, Dec. 11, 1862, Baum Papers, Garret Collection, FRSP; Brainerd, *Bridge Building,* 156; A. Williams, letter to the editor, *Elmira Weekly Advertiser and Chemung County Republican,* Dec. 27, 1862; *OR,* 175. Baum reported that all of the 50th New York captains had been struck, but one did not report to the hospital. Brainerd and McDonald were the only other captains, and both of them were in the hospital before noon.

39. R. P. McCormack, "Crossing at Fredericksburg," *National Tribune,* Dec. 21, 1899; *OR,* 179, 346, 601; Charles Graham, "Crossing under Fire," *National Tribune,* March 29, 1900.

40. Unknown author (in Seeley's battery), letter, Dec. 18, 1862, *Franklin (N.Y.) Visitor,* Jan. 6, 1863; *OR,* 194, 196.

41. *OR,* 182; *ORS,* 3:763–64; Charles H. Morgan, manuscript report, Dec. 18, 1862, Henry Jackson Hunt Papers, LC; J. H. Rhodes, *Battery B, 1st Rhode Island,* 138.

42. *OR,* 182, 197, 1126–27; J. H. Rhodes, *Battery B, 1st Rhode Island,* 138.

43. Unknown author (Seeley's battery), letter, *Franklin (N.Y.) Visitor,* Jan. 6, 1863; *OR,* 182–83; Favill, *Diary,* 209; Wheeler, letter to the editor, *Cohoes (N.Y.) Cataract,* Dec. 20, 1862; Frederick, *Story of a Regiment,* 117; *Berks, Chester, and Montgomery (Pa.) Ledger,* Dec. 30, 1862.

44. Baum, letter, Dec. 11, 1862, Baum Papers, Garret Collection, FRSP; C. R. Lyon, letter, Dec. 18, 1862, Lyon Family Papers, United States Military Academy; Favill, *Diary,* 209; *OR,* 168, 170, 183, 196.

45. Frederick, *Story of a Regiment*, 116.

46. Ibid., 116–17; Walker, *Second Corps*, 148.

47. Frederick, *Story of a Regiment*, 116; Favill, *Diary*, 208–209.

48. *OR*, 600, 605.

49. Ibid., 167; L. VanLoan Naisawald, *Grape and Canister* (New York, 1960), 238; Wainwright, *Diary of Battle*, 137.

50. Brainerd, *Bridge Building*, 289; G. Thompson, *Engineer Battalion*, 25; *OR*, 167, 169; *Beaver (Pa.) Weekly Argus*, Dec. 24, 1862.

51. Harrison, *Fredericksburg Civil War Sites*, 2:101–102; *OR*, 604.

52. G. Thompson, *Engineer Battalion*, 26.

53. *Clearfield (Pa.) Raftsman's Journal*, Jan. 7, 1863; G. Thompson, *Engineer Battalion*, 26; *OR*, 168.

54. *OR*, 214, 216; Wainwright, *Diary of Battle*, 137.

55. *OR*, 168, 604, 621; Evander McIvor Law, letter, Aug. 23, 1866, Evander McIvor Law Letters, SHC, UNC; *Athens (Ga.) Southern Banner*, Jan. 7, 1863; Blackford, *War Years*, 191–92; William A. Fletcher, *Rebel Private Front and Rear* (Beaumont, Tex., 1908), 47–48.

56. *OR*, 168, 169, 604, 621; Evander McIvor Law, letter, Aug. 13, 1866, Law Letters; SHC, UNC; *Athens Southern Banner*, Jan. 7, 1863; Blackford, *War Years*, 192; Fletcher, *Rebel Private Front and Rear*, 48; G. Thompson, *Engineer Battalion*, 26.

57. Anonymous writer, in *New York at Gettysburg*, ed. William F. Fox (Albany, 1900), 3:1088; Charles S. Wainwright Journals, 5 vols. Henry E. Huntington Society, San Marino, Calif. (all citations are to volume 1); *OR*, 168, 604, 621; E. M. Law, letter, Aug. 23, 1866 Law Letters, SHC, UNC; George Hillyer, letter to the editor, *Athens (Ga.) Southern Banner*, Jan. 7, 1863; Blackford, *War Years*, 191–92; Fletcher, *Rebel Private Front and Rear*, 48; G. Thompson, *Engineer Battalion*, 26; John J. Toffey, letter, Dec. 27, 1862, John J. Toffey Papers, FRSP; Naisawald, *Grape and Canister*, 244; Greenlee Davidson, *Captain Greenlee Davidson, C.S.A.: Diary and Letters, 1851–1863*, ed. Charles W. Turner (Verona, Va., 1975), 62; O'Reilly, *Jackson at Fredericksburg*, 16–17.

58. *OR*, 183.

59. Fletcher, *Rebel Private Front and Rear*, 48; Harrison, *Fredericksburg Civil War Sites*, 2:229.

60. Joseph White Woods Reminiscences, United Daughters of the Confederacy Bound Typescripts, vol. 4, no. 144, GDAH; *OR*, 168, 169, 171, 599; Claiborne Memoir, p. 21, Claiborne Papers, SHC, UNC; *Clearfield (Pa.) Raftsman's Journal*, Jan. 7, 1863.

61. Brainerd, *Bridge Building*, 158; *OR*, 170. Brainerd quoted Woodbury repeating Burnside's orders.

62. A. Williams, letter to the editor, *Elmira Weekly Advertiser and Chemung County Republican*, Dec. 27, 1862; Brainerd, *Bridge Building*, 158; Baum, letter, Dec. 11, 1862, Baum Papers, Garret Collection, FRSP.

63. Brainerd, *Bridge Building*, 158.

64. Ibid.; Baum, letter, Dec. 11, 1862, Baum Papers, Garret Collection, FRSP.

65. Baum, letter, Dec. 11, 1862, Baum Papers, Garret Collection, FRSP, Brainerd, *Bridge Building*, 160–61.

66. *OR*, 176, 179.

67. A. Williams, letter to the editor, *Elmira Weekly Advertiser and Chemung County Republican,* Dec. 27, 1862; Baum, letter, Dec. 11, 1862, Baum Papers, Garret Collection, FRSP.

68. John Sullivan Court-Martial, Oct. 15, 1863, NARA RG 153, LL 1332, NA; A. Williams, letter to the editor, *Elmira Weekly Advertiser and Chemung County Republican,* Dec. 27, 1862; *OR,* 179.

69. *OR,* 170, 176; A. Williams, letter to the editor, *Elmira Weekly Advertiser and Chemung County Republican,* Dec. 27, 1862; Brainerd, *Bridge Building,* 158; John T. Davidson, untitled speech, in *New York at Gettysburg,* ed. William F. Fox (Albany, 1900), 3:1093. Woodbury reported the time as 10:00 A.M., while Williams recalled the hour as 11:00 A.M. Perhaps Woodbury took custody of the 8th Connecticut party at 10:00 and arrived on the scene at 11:00.

70. Order, Dec. 11, 1862, 1:20 P.M., William B. Franklin Papers, LC.

71. *OR,* 183; Longacre, *Man behind the Guns,* 131.

72. J. H. Rhodes, *Battery B, 1st Rhode Island,* 138.

73. Wainwright, *Diary of Battle,* 137; J. H. Rhodes, *Battery B, 1st Rhode Island,* 138.

74. *OR,* 182, 197, 198, 202. Kinzie also named the Wood brothers and claimed "that the stocks were made out of one piece of wood, and not in two parts, according to the Ordnance Manual."

75. Bruce, *Twentieth Massachusetts,* 208; Mehen, "Incident at Fredericksburg," 407; William M. McKinney Abernathy, "Our Mess: Southern Army Gallantry and Privations," MDAH.

76. Mehen, "Incident at Fredericksburg," 407; David Lang, "Civil War Letters of Colonel David Lang," ed. Bertram H. Groene, *Florida Historical Quarterly* 54 (Jan. 1976): 348; *OR,* 601; Bruce, *Twentieth Massachusetts,* 208.

77. John F. H. Claiborne, "Gen. Wm. Barksdale and Barksdale's Brigade," p. 23, Claiborne Papers, SHC, UNC; Steven C. Hawley, "Barksdale's Mississippi Brigade at Fredericksburg," *Civil War History* 40, no. 1 (1994): 20.

78. Longacre, *Man behind the Guns,* 132; Oliver Otis Howard, *Autobiography of Oliver Otis Howard* (New York, 1907), 1:323; Whan, *Fiasco at Fredericksburg,* 40–41; *OR,* 170; Brainerd, *Bridge Building,* 163; A. Williams, letter to the editor, *Elmira Weekly Advertiser and Chemung County Republican,* Dec. 27, 1862.

CHAPTER FOUR: "A FIERCE AND DEADLY CONTEST"

1. H. H. Ring, "Under Heavy Fire: Crossing the Rappahannock with the 7th Mich.," *National Tribune,* April 29, 1897; Murphey, *Nantucket Experience,* 85. Ring stated, "I was standing close by them [Burnside and Hall], gave the matter close attention, and heard all that was said at this time."

2. McCormack, "Crossing at Fredericksburg"; *OR,* 315, 346; Graham, "Crossing under Fire."

3. *OR,* 170, 183; Albert B. Weymouth, *A Memorial Sketch of Lieut. Edgar N. Newcomb* (Malden, Mass., 1883), 107.

4. Baum, letter, Dec. 11, 1862, Baum Papers, Garret Collection, FRSP; *OR,* 174, 180; Dailey, letter, Dec. 14, 1862, Dailey Letters, Mary Washington College.

5. *OR,* 170, 176.

6. Ibid., 174, 180.

7. Ibid., 183, 194, 196, 199, 201, 202, 214.

8. McLaws, "The Confederate Left at Fredericksburg," 3:87; *OR,* 603.

9. McLaws, "The Confederate Left at Fredericksburg," 3:87; A. Williams, letter to the editor, *Elmira Weekly Advertiser and Chemung County Republican,* Dec. 27, 1862; *OR,* 603.

10. A. Williams, letter to the editor, *Elmira Weekly Advertiser and Chemung County Republican,* Dec. 27, 1862; *OR,* 170, 177; Baum, letter, Dec. 11, 1862, Baum Papers, Garret Collection, FRSP; Frederick W. Oesterle, "Incidents Connected with the Civil War," CWT.

11. A. Williams, letter to the editor, *Elmira Weekly Advertiser and Chemung County Republican,* Dec. 27, 1862; Oesterle, "Incidents" CWT; A. B. Weymouth, *Newcomb,* 107; Ring, "Under Heavy Fire," April 29, 1897.

12. Baum, letter, Dec. 11, 1862, Baum Papers, Garret Collection, FRSP; *OR,* 262, 283; Oesterle, "Incidents," CWT; Bruce, *Twentieth Massachusetts,* 198. Hall counted 31 prisoners, and division commander O. O. Howard estimated 30 to 40 captured Confederates.

13. *OR,* 601.

14. Ibid., 262; Oesterle, "Incidents," CWT; *History of the Nineteenth Massachusetts Volunteer Infantry* (Salem, Mass., 1906), 168; George N. Macy, letter, Dec. 20, 1862, MMO; Bruce, *Twentieth Massachusetts,* 198; Harrison G. O. Weymouth, "The Crossing of the Rappahannock by the Nineteenth Massachusetts," in *B&L,* 3:121; Warren H. Cudworth, *History of the First Regiment Massachusetts Infantry* (Boston, 1866), 316.

15. Wheeler, letter to the editor, *Cohoes (N.Y.) Cataract,* Dec. 20, 1862; *OR,* 177; Samuel S. Partridge, letter, Dec. 17, 1862, FRSP.

16. Harrison, *Fredericksburg Civil War Sites,* 1:91; *OR,* 174, 177.

17. Macy, letter, Dec. 23, 1862, MMO; *OR,* 283; Bruce, *Twentieth Massachusetts,* 199; Murphey, *Nantucket Experience,* 87.

18. *OR,* 310, 315, 619; McCormack, "Crossing at Fredericksburg"; Graham, "Crossing under Fire."

19. *OR,* 174, 176, 180; John Smart, letter, Dec. 13, 1862, Smart Papers, FRSP; Dailey, letter, Dec. 14, 1862, Dailey Letters, Mary Washington College.

20. *OR,* 310, 314, 315.

21. O. O. Howard, *Autobiography,* 1:324; Bruce, *Twentieth Massachusetts,* 200; *OR,* 274, 276, 277, 283.

22. *History of the Nineteenth Massachusetts,* 169; John G. B. Adams, *Reminiscences of the Nineteenth Massachusetts Regiment* (Boston, 1899), 50; Dinkins, "Barksdale's Mississippi Brigade at Fredericksburg," 22.

23. *History of the Nineteenth Massachusetts,* 169; Adams, *Reminiscences,* 50; H. G. O. Weymouth, "Crossing," 3:121; Moncena Dunn, quoted in *History of the 118th Pennsylvania Volunteers (Corn Exchange)* (Philadelphia, 1888), 117. As mentioned later in the text, Dunn was an officer in the Nineteenth Massachusetts.

24. *OR,* 601; J. C. Lloyd, "The Battles of Fredericksburg," *Confederate Veteran* 23 (1915): 500; *History of the Nineteenth Massachusetts,* 169.

25. Richard F. Fuller, *Chaplain Fuller* (Boston, 1863), 303; Cudworth, *First Massachusetts,* 316; Joseph E. Hodgkins, *The Civil War Diary of Lieut. J. E. Hodgkins,* ed. Kenneth C. Torino (Camden, N.J., 1994), 16; *History of the Nineteenth Massachusetts,* 171; Adams, *Reminiscences,* 50; *OR,* 600; H. G. O. Weymouth, "Crossing," 3:121; Dunn, quoted in History of the *118th Pennsylvania,* 117.

26. *OR,* 183, 212, 214; Roemer, *Reminiscences,* 96.

27. Howard, *Autobiography,* 1:324; Walker, *Second Corps,* 151.

28. Walker, *Second Corps,* 152; Howard, *Autobiography,* 1:324; *History of the 127th Regiment Pennsylvania Volunteers* (Lebanon, Pa., 1902), 120.

29. *OR,* 277, 283, 285; Henry Ropes, letter, Dec. 18, 1862, Henry Ropes Family Papers, Boston Public Library; Macy, letter, Dec. 20, 1862, MMO; Bruce, *Twentieth Massachusetts,* 200–201; Joseph R. C. Ward, *History of the 106th Pennsylvania Volunteers* (Philadelphia, 1906), 131. Ropes confirmed that Hall gave Macy the "no quarter" orders but added, "it was not of course obeyed."

30. Howard, *Autobiography,* 1:324; Macy, letter, Dec. 20, 1862, MMO; Bruce, *Twentieth Massachusetts,* 201; *History of the Nineteenth Massachusetts,* 171.

31. Macy, letter, Dec. 20, 1862, MMO; Bruce, *Twentieth Massachusetts,* 201; *History of the Nineteenth Massachusetts,* 171; Murphey, *Nantucket Experience,* 87; Ropes, letter, Dec. 18, 1862, Ropes Family Papers, Boston Public Library; Oliver Wendell Holmes, Jr., *"Touched by Fire": Civil War Letters and Diary of Oliver Wendell Holmes, Jr.,* ed. Mark De Wolfe (Cambridge, Mass., 1947), 90.

32. Dinkins, "Barksdale's Mississippi Brigade at Fredericksburg," 22; William Davis, letter, Dec. 16, 1862, MDAH; Bruce, *Twentieth Massachusetts,* 201; Macy, letter, Dec. 20, 1862, MMO; Ropes, letter, Dec. 18, 1862, Ropes Family Papers, Boston Public Library.

33. Ropes, letter, Dec. 18, 1862, Ropes Family Papers, Boston Public Library; Macy, letter, Dec. 20, 1862, MMO; W. Davis, letter, Dec. 16, 1862, MDAH.

34. Murphey, *Nantucket Experience,* 88; Ropes, letter, Dec. 18, 1862, Ropes Family Papers, Boston Public Library; Macy, letter, Dec. 20, 1862, MMO; *OR,* 283.

35. Macy, letter, Dec. 20, 1862, MMO.

36. Weymouth, *Newcomb,* 107; *History of the Nineteenth Massachusetts,* 171; Adams, *Reminiscences,* 50; W. Davis, letter, Dec. 16, 1862, MDAH.

37. Hodgkins, *Civil War Diary,* 16; Adams, *Reminiscences,* 51.

38. Adams, *Reminiscences,* 51; A. B. Weymouth, *Newcomb,* 107; Albert Henly, memoir, FRSP.

39. Henry L. Abbott, *Fallen Leaves: The Civil War Letters of Major Henry Livermore Abbott,* ed. Robert Garth Scott (Kent, Ohio, 1991), 149; Macy, letter, Dec. 20, 1862, letter, MMO; Murphey, *Nantucket Experience,* 89; Bruce, *Twentieth Massachusetts,* 206; *History of the Nineteenth Massachusetts,* 172; *OR,* 283, 285.

40. *OR,* 285, 600, 605.

41. Ibid., 271, 274, 276, 605. Humphreys identified George Street as "the street leading from the Episcopal Church," meaning St. George's Church on the corner of George and Princess Anne Streets.

42. Ward, *106th Pennsylvania,* 131; *OR,* 605.

43. *OR,* 601.

44. Charles H. Banes, *History of the Philadelphia Brigade* (Philadelphia, 1876), 135–36; Ward, *106th Pennsylvania,* 131; *OR,* 277.

45. *OR,* 277.

46. Stiles, *Four Years under Marse Robert,* 130; McLaws, "Battle of Fredericksburg," 77.

47. Benjamin G. Humphreys, "The Sunflower Guard," p. 7, Claiborne Papers, SHC,

UNC; Hawley, "Barksdale's Mississippi Brigade at Fredericksburg," 32; *OR,* 277, 605; Stiles, *Four Years under Marse Robert,* 130.

48. Stiles, *Four Years under Marse Robert,* 130; Freeman, *Lee's Lieutenants,* 2:338; Murphey, *Nantucket Experience,* 126; Abbott, *Fallen Leaves,* 159–60.

49. Banes, *Philadelphia Brigade,* 137; John Smart, letter, Dec. 17, 1862, Smart Papers, FRSP; Bruce, *Twentieth Massachusetts,* 208; *History of the Nineteenth Massachusetts,* 171; Oesterle, "Incidents" CWT; Ward, *106th Pennsylvania,* 132–33; Patrick, *Inside Lincoln's Army,* 187.

50. Banes, *Philadelphia Brigade,* 135; Abbott, *Fallen Leaves,* 155–56; Howard, *Autobiography,* 1:325.

51. Elisha H. Rhodes, *All for the Union: The Civil War Diary and Letters of Elisha Hunt Rhodes,* ed. Robert H. Rhodes (New York, 1985), 89–90.

52. *OR,* 216, "Franklin's 'Left Grand Division,'" in 449, 523; William F. Smith, *B&L,* 3:131; Rhodes, *All for the Union,* 90.

53. Howard, *Autobiography,* 1:325; Baum, letter, Dec. 11, 1862, Baum Papers, Garret Collection, FRSP.

54. *OR,* 310, 315; Howard, *Autobiography,* 1:325. Howard detailed how he laid out a defensive line, but he made no mention of establishing contact with the lower portion of town. Owen's brigade had held the far left of Howard's line and seemed to be the likely body to find Hawkins.

55. *OR,* 571; Sorrel, *Recollections,* 129.

56. Murphey, *Nantucket Experience,* 84; Baum, letter, Dec. 11, 1862, Baum Papers, Garret Collection, FRSP; F. Williams, *Fiftieth New York Engineers,* 5; Bruce, *Twentieth Massachusetts,* 201.

CHAPTER FIVE: "THE MOST GOTHIC OF GOTHS"

1. T. M. Mitchell Diary, FRSP; Woods Reminiscences, UDC Bound Typescripts, vol. 4, no. 144, GDAH; John F. Stegeman, *These Men She Gave: Civil War Diary of Athens, Georgia* (Athens, 1964), 73.

2. *OR,* 607, 625; William H. Kirkpatrick, letter, Jan. 23, 1863, UDC Bound Typescripts, vol. 2, no. 133, GDAH.

3. Constantine Hege, letter, Dec. 15, 1862, LLC.

4. Samuel H. Walkup Journal, Duke; J. C. Webb, quoted in Thomas F. Hickerson, *Echoes of Happy Valley* (Chapel Hill, n.d.), 71.

5. Chambers, *Jackson,* 2:279; *ORS,* 3:720; R. Channing Price, letter, Dec. 17, 1862, R. Channing Price Papers, SHC, UNC; Jmaes R. Cole, *Miscellany* (Dallas, Tex., 1897), 205; J. H. Wood, *The War,* 103.

6. Archibald D. Norris Diary, FRSP; Junius Kimble Reminiscences, MOC; Samuel Angus Firebaugh Diary, CWMC; *OR,* 569; William H. Moore, letter, Jan. 4, 1863, FRSP. Norris wrote of the ditch: "took our position in line-of-Battle behind a ditch cut for a fence along the edge of the forest."

7. Kimble Reminiscences, MOC; Andrews, "Tige Anderson's Brigade at Fredericksburg," *Atlanta Journal,* Nov. 16, 1901.

8. James Power Smith, *With Stonewall Jackson in the Army of Northern Virginia* (Gaithersburg, Md., 1982), 28; Vivian Minor Fleming Reminiscences, FRSP; Edward Hall Armstrong, letter, Dec. 15, 1862, Duke; *ORS,* 3:720; W. S. Campbell, letter, Dec. 17, 1862, Cearley Collection, FRSP.

9. William R. M. Slaughter, letter, Jan. 4, 1863, VHS; Jubal A. Early, *Autobiographical Sketch and Narrative of the War between the States* (Philadelphia, 1912), 170; "Milas," *Staunton Spectator,* Jan. 6, 1863; *ORS,* 3:720.

10. William M. Owen, "A Hot Day on Marye's Heights," *B&L,* 3:97; William M. Owen, *In Camp and Battle with the Washington Artillery of New Orleans* (Boston, 1885), 176.

11. W. M. Owen, "Hot Day," 3:97; *OR,* 573.

12. E. H. Sutton, *Civil War Stories* (Demorist, Ga., 1910), 19.

13. Cole, *Miscellany,* 209–10; Charles E. Davis, *Three Years in the Army: The Story of the Thirteenth Massachusetts Volunteers* (Boston, 1894), 162; J. F. Shaffner, letter, Dec. 21, 1862, Shaffner Papers, NCDAH.

14. Sutton, *Civil War Stories,* 19.

15. *OR,* 107–108.

16. Macy, letter, Dec. 20, 1862, MMO; Ward, *106th Pennsylvania,* 135; Charles H. Eager, letter, Dec. 12, 1862, LLC.

17. Howard, *Autobiography,* 1:326; Ward, *106th Pennsylvania,* 135; Andrew E. Ford, *The Story of the Fifteenth Regiment Massachusetts Volunteer Infantry* (Clinton, Mass., 1898), 223; *OR,* 269, 271, 276, 284.

18. George F. Sprenger, *Concise History of the Camp and Field Life of the 122d Regiment, Pennsylvania Volunteers* (Lancaster, Pa., 1885), 140.

19. *OR,* 314, 316, 331.

20. Furst Diary, HCW; S. Millett Thompson, *Thirteenth Regiment of New Hampshire Volunteer Infantry* (Boston, 1888), 37; Teall, letter, Dec. 12, 1862, TSL; T. E. Manchester, "The Twelfth Rhode Island," *Boston Journal,* no. 125, n.d.

21. Sprenger, *122nd Pennsylvania,* 139–40; Manchester, "Twelfth Rhode Island," *Boston Journal,* no. 125; Isaac Morrow, letter, Dec. 21, 1862, HCW; Charles F. Walcott, *History of the Twenty-first Regiment Massachusetts Volunteers* (Boston, 1882), 240; Charles C. Paige Memoir, p. 21, Wendell W. Lang Collection, USAMHI. Sources vary on time of crossing by as much as 12:30 P.M. to 3:00 P.M.

22. Oliver Christian Bosbyshell, *The Forty-eighth in the War* (Philadelphia, 1895), 96; Albert A. Pope Diary, CWMC; Charles H. Weygant, *History of the 124th Regiment N.Y.S.V.* (Newburgh, N.Y., 1877), 64; *OR,* 395; Sprenger, *122nd Pennsylvania,* 140; Richard Moe, *The Last Full Measure: Life and Death of the First Minnesota Volunteers* (New York, 1993), 213.

23. Walcott, *Twenty-first Massachusetts,* 240.

24. Sheldon B. Thorpe, *The History of the Fifteenth Connecticut Volunteers* (New Haven, 1893), 33; William J. Abernathy, reminiscences, CWMC; Charles S. Granger Diary, CWMC; William H. Relyea Memoir, Connecticut Historical Society; Henry C. Marshall, letter, Dec. 14, 1862, UM.

25. *OR,* 351; Abernathy, reminiscences, CWMC; Leland Q. Barlow, letter, Dec. 24, 1862, Connecticut Historical Society; Marshall, letter, Dec. 14, 1862, UM; Granger Diary, CWMC.

26. O'Reilly, *Jackson at Fredericksburg,* 21; S. M. Thompson, *Thirteenth New Hampshire,* 27.

27. O'Reilly, *Jackson at Fredericksburg,* 21.

28. *OR,* 523, 524, 529, 535; William F. Smith, Dec. 12, 1862, dispatch to William B. Franklin, Franklin Papers, LC.

29. McClenthen, *Narrative,* 34; E. M. Stephenson, letter, Dec. 21, 1862, E. M. Stephenson Papers, HSP; Tully McCrea, *Dear Belle* (Middletown, Conn., 1965), 176.

30. McClenthen, *Narrative,* 34; Edward J. Nichols, *Toward Gettysburg: A Biography of General John F. Reynolds* (State College, Pa., 1958), 100, 137.

31. McClenthen, *Narrative,* 15, 34; Samuel P. Bates, *History of Pennsylvania Volunteers 1861–65* (Harrisburg, 1869–1871), 1:254; Warner, *Generals in Blue,* 129–30; Richard M. Bache, *Life of General George Gordon Meade* (Philadelphia, 1897), 571. Meade once explained his temper to a kinsman, observing that "any man would rather be sworn at than prayed for by his enemy."

32. H. Seymour Hall, "Personal Experiences," CWMC; *OR,* 332.

33. Wainwright, *Diary of Battle,* 138; McClenthen, *Narrative,* 35–36; Bates, *Pennsylvania Volunteers* 1;254; Stine, *Army of the Potomac,* 276.

34. David W. Judd, *The Story of the Thirty-third N.Y.S.V.* (Rochester, N.Y., 1864), 252–53; Wainwright, *Diary of Battle,* 138–39; George W. Stevens, *Three Years in the Sixth Corps* (Albany, 1866), 170.

35. Henry R. Pyne, *The History of the First New Jersey Cavalry* (Trenton, 1871), 104; William B. Franklin, quoted in *RJC,* 712; Thompson A. Snyder Recollections, FRSP; Aurelia Austin, *Georgia Boys with Stonewall Jackson* (Athens, 1967), 57.

36. Pyne, *First New Jersey Cavalry,* 104; William P. Lloyd, *History of the First Regiment Pennsylvania Reserve Cavalry* (Philadelphia, 1864), 38; Edward P. Tobie, *History of the First Maine Cavalry, 1861–1865* (Boston, 1887), 105; Bates, *Pennsylvania Volunteers,* 3:386.

37. Haupt, *Reminiscences,* 176.

38. S. T. Cushing, "The Acting Signal Corps," 12–13; *OR,* 152, 153.

39. Jacob L. Greene, *Gen. William B. Franklin and the Operations of the Left Wing at the Battle of Fredericksburg* (New York, 1900), 11; Gibbon, *Personal Recollections,* 103; McClenthen, *Narrative,* 36; J. F. Shaffner, letter, Dec. 15, 1862, Shaffner Papers, NCDAH; James B. Thompson, *The Civil War Letters of Lieutenant James B. Thompson,* ed. Richard Sauers (Baltimore, 1995), 126.

40. Teall, letter, Dec. 12, 1862, Teall papers, TSL; 126; Marvel, *Burnside,* 102; William P. Hopkins, *The Seventh Rhode Island Volunteers* (Providence, 1903), 56.

41. Patrick, *Inside Lincoln's Army,* 188; *OR,* 269, 276; unknown author, in *New York at Gettysburg,* ed. William F. Fox, 2:662.

42. Owen, *In Camp and Battle,* 182; *OR,* 574; Favill, *Diary,* 210.

43. McClenthen, *Narrative,* 36; William B. Franklin, *A Reply of Maj.-Gen. William B. Franklin to the Committee on the Conduct of the War* (New York, 1863), 1; Franklin, quoted in *RJC,* 662, 707; Frank Fowler, letter, Dec. 20, 1862, New London Historical Society; G. T. Stevens, *Three Years,* 170; Teall, letter, Dec. 12, 1862, Teall Papers, TSL.

44. Louis N. Chapin, *A Brief History of the Thirty-fourth Regiment N.Y.S.V.* (New York, 1903), 80; Roland E. Bowen, *From Ball's Bluff to Gettysburg . . . and Beyond: The Civil War*

Letters of Roland E. Bowen, ed. Gregory Coco (Gettysburg, 1994), 142; Richard H. Lee, letter, Dec. 17, 1862, Salmon Brook Historical Society; Abernathy, reminiscences, CWMC; S. M. Thompson, *Thirteenth New Hampshire,* 40; Jacob Babbitt, letter, Dec. 11, 1862, no. 2085, Park Collection, FRSP.

45. J. Granville Leach, "History of the Twenty-fifth New Jersey Volunteer Regiment, Company F," *Cape May County Magazine of History and Genealogy* (Cape May, 1974), 107; Ford, *Fifteenth Massachusetts,* 225; Charles E. Davis, letter, Dec. 16, 1862, Brown; Aaron K. Blake, letter, Dec. 18, 1862, CWMC; Asaph R. Tyler, letter, Dec. 15, 1862, in "Letters of a Soldier," FRSP; Herbert C. Mason, letter, Dec. 20, 1862, MMO; Macy, letter, Dec. 20, 1862, MMO; Leland Q. Barlow, letter, Dec. 16, 1862, Connecticut Historical Society.

46. Ford, *Fifteenth Massachusetts,* 224; Walter N. Eames, letter, Dec. 20, 1862, Murray J. Smith Collection, USAMHI; *History of the First Regiment Minnesota Volunteer Infantry* (Stillwater, Minn., 1916), 266; Pope Diary, CWMC.

47. William Lucas, letter, Dec. 18, 1862, CWMC; Guilford, letter to the editor, *Philadelphia Weekly Times,* June 16, 1886; Barlow, letter, Dec. 16, 1862, Connecticut Historical Society; Blake, letter, Dec. 18, 1862, CWMC; John H. W. Stuckenberg, *I'm Surrounded by Methodists: Diary of John H. W. Stuckenberg,* ed. David T. Hedrick and Gordon Barry Davis, Jr. (Gettysburg, 1995), 40.

48. Ward, *106th Pennsylvania,* 133–35; Banes, *Philadelphia Brigade,* 138; Thomas F. Galwey, *The Valiant Hours* (Harrisburg, 1961), 59.

49. Abbott, *Fallen Leaves,* 156; Macy, letter, Dec. 20, 1862, MMO; Frank Plympton, letter, Dec. 16, 1862, FRSP; Stuckenberg, *I'm Surrounded by Methodists,* 38.

50. Unidentified soldier [69th New York], memoir, Kenneth H. Powers Collection, USAMHI; Howard, *Autobiography,* 1:325; Favill, *Diary,* 210–11.

51. Miles H. Peabody, letter, Dec. 1, 1862, CWMC; Leach, *Twenty-fifth New Jersey,* 107; unidentified soldier [64th New York], reminiscences, p. 36, Indiana University; Fritz, letter to the editor, *Berks, Chester, and Montgomery (Pa.) Ledger,* Dec. 30, 1862; Eames, letter, Dec. 20, 1862, Smith Collection, USAMHI; Bates, *Pennsylvania Volunteers,* 4:1170; S. M. Thompson, *Thirteenth New Hampshire,* 41.

52. John Lehman, letter, Dec. 15, 1862, UM; Ward, *106th Pennsylvania,* 133.

53. Charles A. Fuller, *Personal Recollections of the War of 1861 Sherburne, N.Y., 1906),* 78; Ford, *Fifteenth Massachusetts,* 223; Lucas, letter, Dec. 18, 1862, CWMC; Henry H. Holt, letter, Dec. 17, 1862, LLC.

54. James Wren, *From New Berne to Fredericksburg,* ed. John M. Priest (Shippensburg, Pa., 1990), 97.

55. Ward, *106th Pennsylvania,* 132; Oscar D. Robinson, diary, Oscar D. Robinson Papers, Dartmouth; A. B. Martin, letter, Dec. 19, 1862, CWMC; Pope Diary, CWMC; Lehman, letter, Dec. 15, 1862, UM; Hopkins, *Seventh Rhode Island,* 43; Favill, *Diary,* 210; Abbott, *Fallen Leaves,* 156; Rufus P. Staniels, letter, Dec. 16, 1862, FRSP; *Reunions of the Nineteenth Maine Regiment Association* (Augusta, Me., 1878), 8.

56. Bruce, *Twentieth Massachusetts,* 210; Mason, letter, Dec. 19, 1862, MMO; Davis, letter, Dec. 16, 1862, Brown.

57. *History of the 127th Pennsylvania,* 122; Howard, *Autobiography,* 1:325; S. M. Thompson, *Thirteenth New Hampshire,* 42–43; Stuckenberg, *I'm Surrounded by Methodists,* 38; Favill,

Diary, 211; Matthew J. Graham, *The Ninth Regiment New York Volunteers (Hawkins' Zouaves)* (New York. 1900), 386.

58. Graham, *Ninth New York,* 384; Patrick, *Inside Lincoln's Army,* 189.

59. Fowler, letter, Dec. 20, 1862, New London Historical Society; Edward K. Wightman, *From Antietam to Fort Fisher,* ed. Edward G. Longacre (Rutherford, N.J., 1985), 99; Ward, *106th Pennsylvania,* 134; Banes, *Philadelphia Brigade,* 138.

60. C. R. Lyon, letter, Dec. 18, 1862, Lyon Family Papers, USMA; Fritz, letter to the editor, *Berks, Chester, and Montgomery Ledger,* Dec. 30, 1862; Herbert C. Mason, letter, Dec. 19, 1862, MMO; Harvey Henderson Diary, NYSL; Davis, letter, Dec. 16, 1862, Brown.

61. Unidentified soldier, letter headed "Headquarters 57th Regt. New York Volunteers," Dec. 17, 1862, FRSP; Favill, *Diary,* 210; Frederick, *Story of a Regiment,* 119.

CHAPTER SIX: "THE JAWS OF DEATH"

1. "Weather Journal Recording Observations," National Weather Records Center; O'Reilly, *Jackson at Fredericksburg,* 26.

2. Early, *Autobiographical Sketch,* 170–71; *Yorkville* (S.C.) *Enquirer,* Dec. 24, 1862.

3. William J. Pettit, "The Boys Who Wore the Gray," *Bulletin of the Fluvanna County Historical Society,* no. 42 (Oct. 1986): 52; Hugh Brogan, ed., *The Times Reports the American Civil War* (London, 1975), 92; John Esten Cooke, "The Right at Fredericksburg," *Philadelphia Weekly Times,* April 26, 1879; Freeman, *Lee's Lieutenants,* 2:346–47; J. P. Smith, *With Stonewall Jackson,* 28–29.

4. Freeman, *Lee's Lieutenants,* 2:349; J. P. Smith, *With Stonewall Jackson,* 30; Caroline Morton, memoir, May 28, 1928, Battlefield Commission Papers, FRSP; Shaffner, letter, Dec. 21, 1862, Shaffner Papers, NCDAH.

5. George F. R. Henderson, *The Campaign of Fredericksburg* (London, 1891), 58; John P. Dyer, *The Gallant Hood* (Indianapolis, 1955), 155.

6. Henderson, *Fredericksburg,* 59; Ambrose Powell Hill, letter, Nov. 14, 1862, manuscript no. 1St92C4, Georgia Callis West Papers, VHS; Murray Forbes Taylor, memoir, Murray Forbes Taylor Papers, VHS; Freeman, *Lee's Lieutenants,* 2:353; James J. Archer, "The James J. Archer Letters: A Marylander in the Civil War," pt. 1, *Maryland Historical Magazine* 65, no. 2 (June 1961): 140.

7. *OR,* 654; *Charleston Daily Courier,* Dec. 15, 1862; Robert K. Krick, "Maxcy Gregg: Political Extremist and Civil War General," *Civil War History* 19, no. 4 (1973): 5; John C. Haskell, *The Haskell Memoirs,* ed. Gilbert E. Govan and James W. Livingood (New York, 1960), 122.

8. Archer, "Letters," 140.

9. *OR,* 675–76.

10. Alton J. Murray, *South Georgia Rebels* (St. Mary's, Ga., 1976), 301; Jere Malcolm Harris, letter, Dec. 17, 1862, FRSP; Nisbet, *Firing Line,* 123.

11. Henderson, *Fredericksburg,* 59.

12. *Staunton Spectator,* Dec. 16, 1862; Tivoll, letter to the editor, *Atlanta Southern Confederacy,* Dec. 25, 1862; *Yorkville* (S.C.) *Enquirer,* Dec. 24, 1862; R. C. Price, letter, Dec. 17, 1862, Price Papers, SHC, UNC.

13. A. Long, "Fredericksburg," *Philadelphia Weekly Times,* Jan. 16, 1886.

14. Wise, *Long Arm of Lee,* 1:378.

15. David Gregg McIntosh, "A Ride on Horseback in 1910," p. 22, David Gregg McIntosh Papers, SHC, UNC; William Ellis Jones Diary, UM; John O'Farrell Diary, MOC; *OR,* 649.

16. John B. Brockenbrough, letter, Nov. 3, 1901, FRSP.

17. Wise, *Long Arm of Lee,* 1:378; Davidson, *Greenlee Davidson,* 63; J. B. Brockenbrough, letter, Nov. 3, 1901, FRSP; William W. Goldsborough, *The Maryland Line in the Confederate Army* (Baltimore, 1900), 275.

18. J. B. Brockenbrough, letter, Nov. 3, 1901, FRSP; *OR,* 637; Robert K. Krick, *The Fredericksburg Artillery* (Lynchburg, 1986), 41; Davidson, *Greenlee Davidson,* 63, 69.

19. *OR,* 638; Murat Halstead, unidentified newspaper clipping, FRSP.

20. Cooke, "The Right at Fredericksburg," *Philadelphia Weekly Times,* April 26, 1879; R. C. Price letter, Dec. 17, 1862, Price Papers, SHC, UNC; John Warwick Daniel, "Notes on Fredericksburg," John Warwick Daniel Papers, University of Virginia.

21. William B. Franklin, letter, Jan. 6, 1881, Box 1, St. Clair A. Mulholland Papers, "Franklin's 'Left Grand Division,'" CWLM; W. F. Smith, "Franklin's 'Left Grand Division,'" 3:133; A. Wilson Greene, "Opportunity to the South: Meade versus Jackson at Fredericksburg," *Civil War History* 33, no. 4 (1987): 298.

22. Isaac R. Pennypacker, *General Meade* (New York, 1901), 97; Franklin, quoted in *RJC,* 55; Marvel, "Making of a Myth," 12.

23. James A. Hardie, letter, March 12, 1863, Burnside Papers, NA.

24. *OR,* 71; O'Reilly, *Jackson at Fredericksburg,* 32.

25. Franklin, quoted in *RJC,* 708; Marvel, *Burnside,* 176; John Esten Cooke, *Stonewall Jackson: A Military Biography* (New York, 1866), 371.

26. Hardie, letter, March 12, 1863, Burnside Papers, NA.

27. Burnside, letter, June 7, 1863, Burnside Papers, NA; Burnside, quoted in *RJC,* 55; Marvel, "Making of a Myth," 10.

28. Wainwright, *Diary of Battle,* 143; William Swinton, *Campaigns of the Army of the Potomac* (New York, 1882), 245; Pennypacker, *Meade,* 97.

29. Franklin, letter, Jan. 13, 1881, Mulholland Papers, CWLM; Nichols, *Toward Gettysburg,* 151; Reynolds, quoted in *RJC,* 698, 702.

30. Josiah R. Sypher, *History of the Pennsylvania Reserve Corps* (Lancaster, Pa., 1865), 112–13; George Gordon Meade, *Life and Letters of George Gordon Meade* (New York, 1913), 1:337, 339; Edwin R. Gearhart, "Reminiscences of the Civil War," pt. 2, *The Spur—Life in Virginia Past and Present* 6, no. 12 (April 1956): 17; J. V. Morgan, letter to the editor, *National Tribune,* Jan. 25, 1925.

31. Wainwright, *Diary of Battle,* 139; *OR,* 520.

32. Sypher, *Pennsylvania Reserves,* 121–23, 318, 416–17.

33. Canan, *History of Cambria County* 2:249.

34. Gibbon, *Personal Recollections,* 100–101; Bates, *Pennsylvania Volunteers,* 1:254.

35. *OR,* 461.

36. Franklin, quoted in *RJC,* 661; Henry J. Hunt, quoted in *RJC,* 689. Hunt refuted Franklin's claim, testifying that his reserve artillery was "amply sufficient" to protect the bridges and cover the Federal line of retreat.

37. W. F. Smith, "Franklin's 'Left Grand Division,'" 3:134.

38. L. B. Hutchison, letter, Dec. 18, 1862, FRSP; John J. Toffey, letter, Dec. 15, 1862, John J. Toffey Papers, FRSP; G. T. Stevens, *Three Years,* 171.

39. Burnside, quoted in *RJC,* 653; Sypher, *Pennsylvania Reserves,* 411; J. L. Greene, *Franklin,* 22; *OR,* 510; Wainwright, *Diary of Battle,* 141; George E. Jepson, "A War Anniversary," *Boston Journal,* Dec. 13, 1892.

40. Jepson, "A War Anniversary," *Boston Journal,* Dec. 13, 1892; *OR,* 518.

41. Jepson, "A War Anniversary," *Boston Journal,* Dec. 13, 1892.

42. McClenthen, *Narrative,* 37; *OR,* 485; Jepson, "A War Anniversary," *Boston Journal,* Dec. 13, 1892.

43. Woodward, *Our Campaigns,* 233; William W. Hassler, *Colonel John Pelham: Lee's Boy Artillerist* (Richmond, 1960), 145–46; Price, letter, Dec. 17, 1862, Price Papers, SHC, UNC.

44. Price, letter, Dec. 17, 1862, Price Papers, SHC, UNC; George W. Shreve, "Reminiscences of the Stuart Horse Artillery," R. Preston Chew Papers, JCM.

45. Cooke, *Jackson,* 37; Shreve, "Reminiscences,"; Wise, *Long Arm of Lee,* 1:382.

46. Shreve, "Reminiscences"; O'Reilly, *Jackson at Fredericksburg,* 41.

47. *Clearfield (Pa.) Raftsman's Journal,* Jan. 7, 1863; Naisawald, *Grape and Canister,* 249.

48. Shreve, "Reminiscences."

49. H. H. Matthew, letter, April 10, 1908, MOC; Wise, *Long Arm of Lee,* 1:383; Cooke, "The Right at Fredericksburg," *Philadelphia Weekly Times,* April 26, 1879.

50. Edgar A. Jackson, ed., *Three Rebels Write Home* (Franklin, Va., 1955), 80.

51. Bates Alexander, "Seventh Regiment," *Hummelstown (Pa.) Sun,* Oct. 25, 1895.

52. Ibid.; J. V. Morgan, letter to the editor, *National Tribune,* Jan. 25, 1925.

53. Bates, *Pennsylvania Volunteers,* 1:950; Naisawald, *Grape and Canister,* 249; *Clearfield (Pa.) Raftsman's Journal,* Jan. 7, 1863; Alexander Doull, quoted in *RJC,* 687.

54. Shreve, "Reminiscences"; Naisawald, *Grape and Canister,* 249; *Clearfield (Pa.) Raftsman's Journal,* Jan. 7, 1863.

55. George W. McCracken "Dedication of Monument—39th Regiment Infantry," in *Pennsylvania at Gettysburg* (Harrisburg, Pa., 1904), 1:268; *OR,* 511; Asa Brindle, letter, Dec. 18, 1862, Ward Family Papers, Detroit Public Library.

56. Brindle, letter, Dec. 18, 1862, Ward Family Papers; William Speed, letter, Dec. 15, 1862, UM; Wainwright Journal, Huntington Library; Samuel R. Beardsley, letter, Dec. 17, 1862, Samuel R. Beardsley Collection, USAMHI; Stine, *Army of the Potomac,* 277.

57. Wainwright Journal, Huntington Library; Philip Mercer, *The Life of the Gallant Pelham* (Macon, Ga., 1929), 137; Beardsley, letter, Dec. 17, 1862, Beardsley Collection.

58. J. C. Haskell, letter, May 12, 1906, John Warwick Daniel Papers, Duke; Beardsley, letter, Dec. 17, 1862, Beardsley Collection.

59. Cooke, "The Right at Fredericksburg," *Philadelphia Weekly Times,* April 26, 1879; Naisawald, *Grape and Canister,* 250.

60. Hassler, *Pelham,* 148.

61. Haskell, letter, May 12, 1906, Daniel Papers, Duke.

62. Price, letter, Dec. 17, 1862, Price Papers, SHC, UNC.

63. Nichols, *Toward Gettysburg,* 151; Reynolds, quoted in *RJC,* 699.

64. *OR,* 462; Naisawald, *Grape and Canister,* 250; Wainwright Journal, Huntington Library; Wainwright, *Diary of Battle,* 141.

65. Wainwright, *Diary of Battle,* 139; Abner R. Small, *The Road to Richmond* (Berkeley, 1939), 63; McClenthen, *Narrative,* 37; *OR,* 486, 490; J. B. Thompson, *Civil War Letters,* 127.

66. Wainwright, *Diary of Battle,* 141; Naisawald, *Grape and Canister,* 250; Nichols, *Toward Gettysburg,* 156.

67. Naisawald, *Grape and Canister,* 250–51, 258.

68. *OR,* 458.

69. *Clearfield (Pa.) Raftsman's Journal,* Jan. 7, 1863; Ben, letter to the editor, *Charleston Daily Courier,* Dec. 30, 1862; *Charleston Mercury,* Dec. 25, 1862.

70. McIntosh, "Ride on Horseback," p. 27, McIntosh Papers, SHC, UNC; Walter Clark, ed., *Histories of the Several Regiments and Battalions from North Carolina in the Great War, 1861–1865* (Goldsboro, N.C., 1901), 4:236; John William Ford Hatton Memoir, p. 376, microfilm, accession #9243, LC.

71. Caldwell, *South Carolinians,* 91; *Philadelphia Inquirer,* Dec. 25, 1862; Bates, *Pennsylvania Volunteers,* 1:969; Whan, *Fiasco at Fredericksburg,* 65.

72. *OR,* 480, 510, 518; O'Reilly, *Jackson at Fredericksburg,* 203 n. 19; B. Alexander, "Seventh Regiment," *Hummelstown (Pa.) Sun,* Nov. 4, 1895.

73. Whan, *Fiasco at Fredericksburg,* 65; *OR,* 496.

74. Reynolds, quoted in *RJC,* 699; W. Speed, letter, Dec. 15, 1862, UM; Snyder Recollections, FRSP; Owen Jones, unpublished report, FRSP; Lloyd, *First Pennsylvania Cavalry,* 42.

75. Naisawald, *Grape and Canister,* 258.

76. Ben, letter to the editor, *Charleston Daily Courier,* Dec. 30, 1862; J. A. Braddock Reminiscences, MOC; John H. Moore, "Fredericksburg," *Southern Bivouac,* Aug. 1882, pp. 181–82; W. H. Moore, letter, Jan. 4, 1863, FRSP; Wood, *The War,* 103.

77. McIntosh, "Ride on Horseback," p. 28, McIntosh Papers, SHC, UNC; Henry Flick, "Official Record of Henry Flick," HCW.

78. Wise, *Long Arm of Lee,* 1:384; Alfred Rupert, letter, Dec. 21, 1862, Chester County Historical Society.

79. Wise, *Long Arm of Lee,* 1:384; *Clearfield (Pa.) Raftsman's Journal,* Jan. 7, 1863; Jacob M. Marsh Diary, Chester County Historical Society; Flick, "Official Record," HCW.

80. *History of the 121st Regiment Pennsylvania Volunteers* (Philadelphia, 1893), 27; William Hamilton, letter, Dec. 18, 1862, LC; Whan, *Fiasco at Fredericksburg,* 66; Ben, letter to the editor, *Charleston Daily Courier,* Dec. 30, 1862.

81. Woodward, *Our Campaigns,* 235; B. Alexander, "Seventh Regiment," *Hummelstown (Pa.) Sun,* Nov. 4, 1895.

82. William E. S. Whitman and Charles H. True, *Maine in the War for the Union* (Lewiston, Me., 1865), 394; Davis, *Three Years in the Army,* 165; Jepson, "A War Anniversary," *Boston Journal,* Dec. 13, 1892.

83. Ben, letter to the editor, *Charleston Daily Courier,* Dec. 30, 1862; W. E. Jones Diary, UM; William P. Carter, "My First View of a Famous Confederate Officer," *Southern Bivouac,* April 1885, p. 368.

84. Ben, letter to the editor, *Charleston Daily Courier,* Dec. 30, 1862.

85. Ibid.

86. McIntosh, "Ride on Horseback," p. 31, McIntosh Papers, SHC, UNC; Price, letter, Dec. 17, 1862, Price Papers, SHC, UNC; W. E. Jones Diary, UM; *OR,* 649.

87. Wise, *Long Arm of Lee*, 1:384.

88. Ibid.; *Yorkville Enquirer*, Dec. 24, 1862; Daniel, "Notes on Fredericksburg," Daniel Papers, University of Virginia.

89. John W. Brockenbrough, letter, Oct. 25, 1874, Brockenbrough Papers, University of Virginia; Daniel, "Notes on Fredericksburg," Daniel Papers, University of Virginia.

90. *OR*, 665; Davidson, *Greenlee Davidson*, 65.

91. Asher W. Garber, "Staunton's Brave Artillery Boy," *Richmond Dispatch*, Oct. 24, 1895.

92. Naisawald, *Grape and Canister*, 252; Reynolds, quoted in *RJC*, 701; Henry Taylor Memoir, FRSP.

93. B. Alexander, "Seventh regiment," *Hummelstown (Pa.) Sun*, Oct. 25, 1895.

94. Small, *Road to Richmond*, 65; Whitman and True, *Maine in the War*, 394.

95. Bates, *Pennsylvania Volunteers*, 1:969; Naisawald, *Grape and Canister*, 256–57.

96. *Clearfield (Pa.) Raftsman's Journal*, Jan. 7, 1863; Wainwright Journal, Huntington Library; "Confederate States," *Staunton Spectator*, Feb. 17, 1863; William B. Bailey, letter, Dec. 17, 1862, HCW; Garber, letter to the editor, *Richmond Dispatch*, Oct. 24, 1895.

97. William T. Poague, *Gunner with Stonewall* (Jackson, Tenn., 1957), 57; Wise, *Long Arm of Lee*, 1:385; Wainwright, *Diary of Battle*, 141; *Clearfield (Pa.) Raftsman's Journal*, Jan. 7, 1863.

98. Wainwright, *Diary of Battle*, 142; Wainwright Journal, Huntington Library.

99. Wise, *Long Arm of Lee*, 1:285; Reuben B. Pleasants, *Contributions to a History of the Richmond Howitzers Battalion*, pamphlet no. 3 (Richmond, 1884), 59; Price, letter, Dec. 17, 1862, Price Papers, UNC; H. B. McClellan, *Stuart*, 194.

100. Wills Lee Reminiscences, p. 5, FRSP; Pleasants, *Richmond Howitzers Battalion*, 59; Pleasants, reprinted in *SHSP*, 12:467.

101. Pleasants, *Richmond Howitzers Battalion*, 59; Cooke, "The Right at Fredericksburg," *Philadelphia Weekly Times*, April 26, 1879; Steven Dandridge, letter, Dec. 19, 1862, Bedinger-Dandridge Papers, Duke.

102. W. Lee Reminiscences, p. 5, FRSP; Wainwright, *Diary of Battle*, 142;

103. Price, letter, Dec. 17, 1862, Price Papers, UNC; W. Lee Reminiscences, p. 5, FRSP; Henry B. McClellan, "The Gallant Pelham and His Gun at Fredericksburg," *SHSP*, 12:469.

104. Bates, *Pennsylvania Volunteers*, 1:727.

105. John W. Keely, "Reminiscences," *Atlanta Constitutional Magazine*, March 15, 1931, p. 20; Tally, "Campaigns of the Army of Northern Virginia," *Confederate Veteran*, March 1900, p. 109; Robert K. Krick, *Lee's Colonels: A Biographical Register of the Field Officers of the Army of Northern Virginia* (Dayton, 1991), 64; W. H. Moore, letter, Jan. 4, 1863, FRSP.

106. *OR*, 656; McCall, letter to the editor, *Confederate Veteran*, Jan. 1895, p. 19; Benjamin Haskins, "Gen. James Archer," *Confederate Veteran*, Dec. 1894, p. 355; Furgeson S. Harris, "Jas. J. Archer," *Confederate Veteran*, Jan. 1895, p. 18; J. H. Moore, "Fredericksburg," *Southern Bivouac*, Aug. 1882, p. 183; Archer, "Letters," 138, 141.

107. J. H. Moore, "Fredericksburg," *Southern Bivouac*, Aug. 1882, p. 183; Kimble Reminiscences, MOC; W. H. Moore, letter, Jan. 4, 1863, FRSP.

108. Cyndi Dalton, *The Blanket Brigade* (Union, Me., 1995), 93; John G. Bryant Memoir, FRSP; G. T. Stevens, *Three Years in the Sixth Corps*, 173; Henry G. Milans, "Eyewitness

to Fredericksburg," ed. Doug Land *North-South Trader's Civil War* 19, no. 6 (Christmas 1992): 23.

109. John W. Haley, *The Rebel Yell and Yankee Hurrah: The Civil War Journal of a Maine Volunteer*, ed. Ruth L. Silliker (Camden, Me., 1985), 61; St. Clair A. Mulholland, "Battle of Fredericksburg," *Philadelphia Weekly Times*, April 23, 1881.

110. Bates, *Pennsylvania Volunteers*, 4:465; Haley, *Rebel Yell and Yankee Hurrah*, 58; *OR*, 368; Birney, quoted in *RJC*, 705; George R. Snowden, "Address of Capt. George R. Snowden," in *Two Reunions of the 142d Regiment Pa. Vols.*, ed. Horatio N. Warren (Buffalo, N.Y., 1890), 51.

111. McIntosh "Ride on Horseback," p. 31, McIntosh Papers, SHC, UNC; Ben, letter to the editor, *Charleston Daily Courier*, Dec. 30, 1862; *History of the 121st Pennsylvania*, 28; Evan M. Woodward, *History of the Third Pennsylvania Reserve* (Trenton, N.J., 1883), 208; *Philadelphia Inquirer*, Dec. 25, 1862; Bates, *Pennsylvania Volunteers*, 1:586, 615, 950; B. Alexander, "Seventh Regiment," *Hummelstown (Pa.) Sun*, Jan. 10, 1896.

112. B. Alexander, "Seventh Regiment," *Hummelstown (Pa.) Sun*, Nov. 4, 1895.

CHAPTER SEVEN: "A TERRIBLE SLAUGHTER IN OUR RANKS"

1. *Pennsylvania at Gettysburg*, 1:222; B. Alexander, "Seventh Regiment," *Hummelstown (Pa.) Sun*, Nov. 10, 1895; A. Rupert, letter, Dec. 21, 1862, Chester County Historical Society; H. F. Christy, "The 'Reserves' at Fredericksburg," *National Tribune*, Sept. 19, 1901.

2. O. R. Howard Thomson and William H. Rauch, *History of the "Bucktails": Kane's Rifle Regiment of the Pennsylvania Reserve Corps* (Philadelphia, 1906), 233.

3. Gearhart, "Reminiscences," 16; Bates, *Pennsylvania Volunteers* 1:727, 851; *History of the 121st Pennsylvania*, 28; *OR*, 491, 591; David Craft, *History of the One Hundred Forty-first Regiment Pennsylvania Volunteers* (Towanda, Pa., 1885), 35; J. V. Morgan, letter to the editor, *National Tribune*, Jan. 22, 1925.

4. W. H. Johnson, letter to the editor, *Atlanta Southern Confederacy, Dec. 30, 1862; OR*, 660.

5. Keely, "Reminiscences," 20; *Pittsburgh Post*, Dec. 24, 1862.

6. *OR*, 660.

7. Robert T. Mockbee, "Historical Sketch of the 14th Tennessee," MOC; Keely, "Reminiscences," 21; Robert E. McCulloch, "Fourteenth Tennessee Infantry," in *The Military Annals of Tennessee*, ed. John B. Lindsley (Nashville, 1886), 1:326; *OR*, 661; Wood, *The War* 107; W. H. Moore, letter, Jan. 4, 1863, FRSP. The Mockbee piece was attested to be accurate by General William McComb.

8. Robert Taggert Diary, LLC; Hiram Houghton Diary, Western Michigan University; Joseph O. Kerbey, *On the Warpath* (Chicago, 1890), 134; *OR*, 657; H. F. Christy, "The 'Reserves' at Fredericksburg," *National Tribune*, Sept. 19, 1901.

9. Bates, *Pennsylvania Volunteers*, 1:791; Ada Craig Truxell, ed., *Respects to All: Letter of Two Pennsylvania Boys in the War of the Rebellion* (Pittsburgh, 1962), 35; B. Alexander, "Seventh Regiment," *Hummelstown (Pa.) Sun*, March 11, 1895; *Beaver (Pa.) Weekly Argus*, Dec. 24, 1862; Thomson and Rauch, *Bucktails*, 233–34; *Pennsylvania at Gettysburg*, 1;248; *OR* 518.

10. B. Alexander, "Seventh Regiment," *Hummelstown (Pa.) Sun,* Nov. 4, 1895; Bates, *Pennsylvania Volunteers,* 1:586; *History of the 121st Pennsylvania,* 28; *OR,* 518.

11. *OR,* 520; B. Alexander, "Seventh Regiment," *Hummelstown (Pa.) Sun,* Dec. 6, 1895.

12. Meade, quoted in *RJC,* 692; Sypher, *Pennsylvania Reserves,* 417.

13. Kerbey, *On the Warpath,* 134; T. Brent Swearingen, letter, March 9, 1863, Arthur Dehon Papers, USAMHI; J. W. McFarland, letter to the editor, *Pittsburgh Post,* Dec. 24, 1862; *Philadelphia Inquirer,* Dec. 19, 1862; Norris Diary, FRSP; Samuel Clark, letter, Dec. 17, 1862, FRSP.

14. *OR,* 139; Thomson and Rauch, *Bucktails,* 234; J. V. Morgan, letter to the editor, *National Tribune,* Jan. 22, 1925.

15. B. Alexander, "Seventh Regiment," *Hummelstown (Pa.) Sun,* Dec. 6, 1895; Reuben Schell, letter, Dec. 17, 1862, FRSP; Norris Diary, FRSP.

16. *Pennsylvania at Gettysburg,* 1:248.

17. Woodward, *Our Campaigns,* 235; *Beaver (Pa.) Weekly Argus,* Dec. 24, 1862; B. Alexander, "Seventh Regiment," *Hummelstown (Pa.) Sun,* Dec. 6, 1895; *OR,* 520.

18. Bates, *Pennsylvania Volunteers,* 1:762, 4:465.

19. Bates, *Pennsylvania Volunteers,* 4:465; Franklin Boyts, diary, Franklin Boyts Papers, HSP.

20. Frank Holsinger, "How Does One Feel under Fire?" in *War Talks in Kansas: A Series of Papers Read before the Kansas Commandery* [etc.], ed. Military Order of the Loyal Legion of the United States, Kansas Commandery (Kansas City, 1906), 294.

21. Richard C. Halsey, letter, Dec. 15, 1862, UM; Boyts, diary, Boyts Papers, HSP; F. Boyts, letter, Dec. 21, 1862, Boyts Papers, HSP; Bates, *Pennsylvania Volunteers,* 4:465.

22. Woodward, *Third Pennsylvania Reserves,* 209; *OR,* 520–21; Jacob Heffelfinger Diary, CWT.

23. *OR,* 519; Woodward, *Our Campaigns,* 235; B. Alexander, "Seventh Regiment," *Hummelstown (Pa.) Sun,* Dec. 6, 1895; John Clinton, letter, Dec. 24, 1862, CWLM; Thomson and Rauch, *Bucktails,* 234; *OR,* 517, 519; William Sinclair, Compiled Service Record, NA.

24. Bates, *Pennsylvania Volunteers,* 1:699; *OR,* 519; Caldwell, *South Carolinians,* 92; Joseph J. Norton, address, 1866, Joseph J. Norton Papers, USC.

25. Caldwell, *South Carolinians,* 92; Norton, 1866 address, Norton Papers, USC; Berry Benson, *Berry Benson's Civil War Book: Memoirs of a Confederate Scout and Sharpshooter,* ed. Susan W. Benson (Athens, 1962), 32; W. A. Miles certificate, Norton Papers, USC.

26. Flick, "Official Record," HCW; Bates, *Pennsylvania Volunteers,* 1:699; O'Reilly, "Pennsylvania Reserves," 17.

27. Caldwell, *South Carolinians,* 92; Norton, 1866 address, Norton Papers, USC; Flick, "Official Record," HCW; Rupert, letter, Dec. 21, 1862, Chester County Historical Society.

28. Caldwell, *South Carolinians,* 94; Bates, *Pennsylvania Volunteers,* 1:699; Wood, *The War,* 108.

29. Rupert, letter, Dec. 21, 1862, Chester County Historical Society; Benjamin J. Ashenfelter, letter, Dec. 23, 1862, CWMC; Flick, "Official Record," HCW; Woodward, *Third Pennsylvania Reserves,* 208; *OR,* 513.

30. Bates, *Pennsylvania Volunteers,* 1:699.

31. Bates, *Pennsylvania Volunteers,* 1:851; Evan M. Woodward, Compiled Service Record, NA.

32. Keely, "Reminiscences," 20; John H. Moore, "Seventh Tennessee Infantry," in *Military Annals of Tennessee,* ed. John B. Lindsley (Nashville, 1886), 1:238.

33. Woodward, *Our Campaigns,* 235; Bates, *Pennsylvania Volunteers,* 1:586.

34. *OR,* 657, 659; Archer, "Letters," 139.

35. *OR,* 659; Woodward, *Third Pennsylvania Reserves,* 214; S. B. King, letter to the editor, *Cumberland Valley (Pa.) Journal,* Dec. 18, 1862; W. H. Johnson, letter to the editor, *Atlanta Southern Confederacy,* Dec. 30, 1862; Woodward, *Our Campaigns,* 235.

36. Woodward, *Our Campaigns,* 235–36; Evan M. Woodward Medal of Honor nomination, Evan M. Woodward Papers, HSP; B. Alexander, "Seventh Regiment," *Hummelstown (Pa.) Sun,* Dec. 6, 1895.

37. *Carlisle (Pa.) Herald,* Dec. 26, 1862; *The Medal of Honor of the United States Army* (Washington, D.C., 1948), 119, 121.

38. J. H. Moore, "Fredericksburg," *Southern Bivouac,* Aug. 1882, pp. 182–83; H. F. Christy, "The 'Reserves' at Fredericksburg," *National Tribune,* Sept. 19, 1901.

39. Mockbee, "Historical Sketch," MOC; Kimble Reminiscences, MOC; J. H. Moore, "Fredericksburg," *Southern Bivouac,* Aug. 1882, pp. 182–83.

40. *OR,* 657 Kimble Reminiscences, MOC.

41. *OR,* 661; Kerbey, *On the Warpath,* 134; McCulloch, "Fourteenth Tennessee Infantry," 1:326.

42. J. H. Moore, "Fredericksburg," *Southern Bivouac,* Aug. 1882, p. 182; J. H. Moore, "Seventh Tennesses Infantry," 1:238; *OR,* 660.

43. W. H. Moore, letter, Jan. 4, 1863, FRSP; J. H. Moore, "Seventh Tennessee Infantry," 1:238; *OR,* 659–60.

44. W. H. Moore, letter, Jan. 4, 1863, FRSP; J. H. Moore, "Seventh Tennessee Infantry," 1:238; John Fite, "The Memoirs of John A. Fite, 7th Tennessee," 93, typescript copy in Gettysburg National Military Park.

45. Bates, *Pennsylvania Volunteers,* 1:728, 919; *Carlisle (Pa.) Herald,* Dec. 26, 1862; Thomson and Rauch, *Bucktails,* 234; Sypher, *Pennsylvania Reserves,* 418.

46. Bates, *Pennsylvania Volunteers,* 1:851–52; H. F. Christy, "The 'Reserves' at Fredericksburg," *National Tribune,* Sept. 19, 1901; James H. McIlwaine, letter, Dec. 14, 1862, CWMC; Woodward, *Third Pennsylvania Reserves,* 215.

47. Freeman Cleaves, *Meade of Gettysburg* (Norman, Ok., 1960), 91; Meade, *Life and Letters,* 1:338; Bache, *Meade,* 240.

48. J. V. Morgan, letter to the editor, *National Tribune,* Jan. 22, 1925.

49. W. Clark, *Histories,* 475, 556; Evan Smith, lettr, Dec. 22, 1862, Evan Smith Papers, Duke; *OR,* 654.

50. W. Clark, *Histories,* 1:373, 2:35, 657; *OR,* 654.

51. *OR,* 654; W. Clark, *Histories,* 2:657; William Grove Morris, letter, Dec. 18, 1862, SHC, UNC.

52. Reynolds, quoted in *RJC,* 700; *OR,* 486; Gibbon, quoted in *RJC,* 715; McCoy, "The 107th Penna. Vet. Volunteers at South Mountain, Antietam, and Fredericksburg," *Phildelphia Weekly Times,* Jan. 4, 1888; Wainwright, *Diary of Battle,* 143.

53. *OR,* 503; Bates, *Pennsylvania Volunteers,* 3:70; Jepson, "A War Anniversary," *Boston Journal,* Dec. 13, 1892; *Berks and Schuylkill Journal,* Jan. 3, 1863.

54. *OR,* 504; Jepson, "A War Anniversary," *Boston Journal,* Dec. 13, 1892; St. Clair A. Mulholland, *Military Order Congress Medal of Honor Legion of the United States* (Philadelphia, 1905), 174.

55. McClenthen, *Narrative,* 38; McCoy, "The 107th Penna. Vet. Volunteers," *Philadelphia Weekly Times,* Jan. 4, 1888; Bates, *Pennsylvania Volunteers,* 3:858.

56. George A. Hussey, *History of the Ninth N.Y.S.M.* (New York, 1889), 225; William Henry Locke, *The Story of a Regiment* (Philadelphia, 1868), 165; *OR,* 654.

57. *OR,* 654; Bates, *Pennsylvania Volunteers,* 1:255; McClenthen, *Narrative,* 31; Locke, *Story of a Regiment,* 165; John W. Jaques, *Three Years' Campaign of the Ninth N.Y.S.M.* (New York, 1895), 129, 132; Hussey, *Ninth N.Y.S.M.,* 224–25.

58. *OR,* 503; Kimball, "My Army Life," *Boston Journal,* no. 125, copy in FRSP; Benjamin F. Cook, *History of the Twelfth Massachusetts Volunteers* (Boston, 1882), 80; W. Clark, *Histories,* 1:374, 2:556.

59. W. Clark, *Histories,* 2:475; James H. Lane, reminiscences, James H. Lane Papers, NCDAH; *OR,* 665; E. Smith, letter, Dec. 22, 1862, Smith Papers, Duke.

60. Phillip Petty Memoir, FRSP; Cook, *Twelfth Massachusetts,* 83; Mulholland, *Medal of Honor,* 170.

61. Canan, *History of Cambria County,* 249; Bates, *Pennsylvania Volunteers,* 3:858; McCoy, "The 107th Penna. Vet. Volunteers," *Philadelphia Weekly Times,* Jan. 4, 1888; McClenthen, *Narrative,* 38; Small, *Road to Richmond,* 65; *OR,* 486.

62. McCoy, "The 107th Penna. Vet. Volunteers," *Philadelphia Weekly Times,* Jan. 4, 1888; *OR,* 490; Kimball, "My Army Life," *Boston Journal,* no. 125, copy in FRSP; Dalton, *Blanket Brigade,* 93.

63. *OR,* 486, 487; Kimball, "My Army Life," *Boston Journal,* no. 125, copy in FRSP; McClenthen, *Narrative,* 39; Small, *Road to Richmond,* 66; Stine, *Army of the Potomac,* 272–73.

64. Small, *Road to Richmond,* 66; McClenthen, *Narrative,* 39; *OR,* 486, 494; McCoy, "The 107th Penna. Vet. Volunteers," *Philadelphia Weekly Times,* Jan. 4, 1888; Stine, *Army of the Potomac,* 273–74. McCoy wrote that Gibbon personally led the 107th Pennsylvania in the attack.

65. *OR,* 655.

66. Ibid., McClenthen, *Narrative,* 39; E. Smith, letter, Dec. 22, 1862, Smith Papers, Duke; Noah Collins Diary, Isaac London Collection, NCDAH; W. G. Morris, letter, Dec. 18, 1862, SHC, UNC; W. Clark, *Histories,* 2:475, 556; Evander A. Robeson, letter, Dec. 17, 1862, reprinted in *Bladen (N.C.) Journal,* Dec. 7, 1961; Dalton, *Blanket Brigade,* 91; J. B. Thompson, *Civil War Letters,* 124; Stine, *Army of the Potomac,* 274.

67. H. B. Howard Diary, William Womble Papers, NCDAH; Dalton, *Blanket Brigade,* 91; J. B. Thompson, *Civil War Letters,* 124.

68. *OR,* 654–55; W. Clark, *Histories,* 2:557.

69. *OR,* 487, 491–92, 655; W. Clark, *Histories,* 1:375, 2:557.

70. Bates, *Pennsylvania Volunteers,* 3:858; *OR,* 487, 490–92, 495; Dennis T. McCarty, letter, Dec. 22, 1862, MOLLUS Collection; Whitman and True, *Maine in the War,* 433; Isaac S. Tichenor, letter, Jan. 13, 1893, Isaac S. Tichenor Papers, FRSP; McClenthen, *Narrative,* 39–40.

71. *OR,* 487, 493; Tichenor, letter, Jan. 13, 1893, Tichenor Papers, FRSP; "Ithaca,"

Elmira (N.Y.) Sunday Telegram, n.d., in Tichenor Papers, FRSP; McClenthen, *Narrative,* 34; Halstead, unidentified newspaper, copy in FRSP.

72. McClenthen, *Narrative,* 40; *OR,* 487; Small, *Road to Richmond,* 66.

73. J. V. Morgan, letter to the editor, *National Tribune,* Jan. 22, 1925.

CHAPTER EIGHT: "GETTING HILL OUT O' TROUBLE"

1. Meade, quoted in *RJC,* 692; Birney, quoted in *RJC,* 705; Craft, *141st Pennsylvania,* 30. Birney stated that he received the call fifteen minutes after Meade entered the woods.

2. Craft, *141st Pennsylvania,* 30; *OR,* 374; Philippe Régis de Keredern De Trobriand, *Four Years with the Army of the Potomac* (Boston, 1889), 353; William Watson, *Letters of a Civil War Surgeon* (Lafayette, Ind., 1961), 41.

3. *OR,* 368; Naisawald, *Grape and Canister,* 257–58; George Lewis, *The History of Battery E, First Regiment Rhode Island Light Artillery* (Providence, 1892), 127; Birney, quoted in *RJC,* 705; Haley, *Rebel Yell and Yankee Hurrah,* 58; De Trobriand, *Four Years,* 365–67.

4. Gibbon, quoted in *RJC,* 715; *OR,* 368; Whitman and True, *Maine in the War,* 71; De Trobriand, *Four Years,* 368.

5. Birney, quoted in *RJC,* 705; Pennypacker, *Meade,* 102.

6. Meade, quoted in *RJC,* 693; Birney, quoted in *RJC,* 705; Pennypacker, *Meade,* 102; *Carlisle (Pa.) Herald,* Dec. 26, 1862; *OR,* 454, 462.

7. *OR,* 487; McClenthen, *Narrative,* 37, 40; Whitman and True, *Maine in the War,* 384.

8. *OR,* 501; Gibbon, quoted in *RJC,* 715.

9. O'Reilly, *Jackson at Fredericksburg,* 111.

10. McCall, letter to the editor, *Confederate Veteran,* Jan. 1895, p. 19; *OR,* 660.

11. McCall, letter to the editor, *Confederate Veteran,* Jan. 1895, p. 19; William F. Fulton, *The Family Record and War Reminiscences of William Frierson Fulton* (n.p., 191_), 55; *OR,* 657; W. H. Johnson, letter to the editor, *Atlanta Southern Confederacy,* Dec. 30, 1862.

12. *OR,* 650; Kerbey, *On the Warpath,* 133–34; Wayland Fuller Dunaway, *Reminiscences of a Rebel* (New York, 1913), 57; Robert E. L. Krick, *Fortieth Virginia* (Lynchburg, 1985), 18–19; J. J. Renfroe, letter to the editor, *Southern Bivouac,* Sept. 1886, p. 262.

13. Early, *Autobiographical Sketch,* 172; William A. McClendon, *Recollections of War Times* (Montgomery, Ala., 1909), 159; *Confederate Veteran,* Oct. 1905, p. 459; Nisbet, *Firing Line,* 124; *OR,* 670.

14. *OR,* 663–64; J. W. Daniel, unidentified newspaper clipping, Dec. 13, 1905, Daniel Papers, University of Virginia; W. R. M. Slaughter, letter, Jan. 4, 1863, VHS; Early, *Autobiographical Sketch,* 172.

15. J. W. Daniel, unidentified newspaper clipping, Dec. 13, 1905, Daniel Papers, University of Virginia; *OR,* 664.

16. *OR,* 665, 670; Early, *Autobiographical Sketch,* 172; Charles W. McArthur, letter, Jan. 29, 1863, typescript, copy at Kennesaw Mountain National Military Park; *Augusta (Ga.) Daily Constitutionalist,* Jan. 6, 1863

17. *OR,* 670; Veritas, letter to the editor, *Savannah Republican,* Jan. 6, 1863; McArthur, letter, Jan. 29, 1863, Kennesaw Mountain.

18. *OR,* 664, 670; Guillaume, letter to the editor, *Sandersville (Ga.) Central Georgian,* Jan.

14, 1863; Henderson, *Jackson,* 2:318–19; J. H. Moore, "Fredericksburg," *Southern Bivouac,* Aug. 1882, p. 183; Kerbey, *On the Warpath,* 137.

19. *OR,* 664, 672–73; Russell, "Description of the Battle of Fredericksburg," *Winchester (Va.) Times,* Feb. 11, 1891; Early, *Autobiographical Sketch,* 173–74.

20. *OR,* 664, 670; Oates, *War between the Union and the Confederacy,* 166.

21. Early, *Autobiographical Sketch,* 174; Slaughter, letter, Jan. 4, 1863, VHS; *OR,* 665, 674; Henry E. Handerson, *Yankee in Gray* (Cleveland, 1962), 53.

22. W. Clark, *Histories,* 4:170.

23. Ibid., 2:170; J. R. Cole, *Miscellany,* 208; Scales, *Fredericksburg,* 16; Davidson, *Greenlee Davidson,* 64.

24. Davidson, *Greenlee Davidson,* 64; William D. Pender, *The General to His Lady: The Civil War Letters of William Dorsey Pender,* ed. William W. Hassler (Chapel Hill, 1965), 195–96; Samuel A. Ashe Reminiscences, NCDAH; W. Clark, *Histories,* 2:170; Scales, *Fredericksburg,* 16.

25. Russell, "Description of the Battle of Fredericksburg," *Winchester (Va.) Times,* Feb. 11, 1891; Caldwell, *South Carolinians,* 94; Henry W. Wingfield, "Diary of Capt. Henry W. Wingfield 58th Va. Reg.," *Bulletin of the Virginia State Library* 16, nos. 2–3 (July 1927): 20; Wood, *The War,* 109.

26. *OR,* 664, 673; Miles, letter to the editor, *Staunton Spectator,* Jan. 6, 1863; Samuel D. Buck, *With the Old Confeds* (Baltimore, 1925), 74; G. T. H. Greer, diary, G. T. H. Greer Papers, VSL; Joseph Way, letter, Feb. 1, 1863, Chester County Historical Society.

27. *OR,* 664, 674; Whitman and True, *Maine in the War,* 394; Miles, letter to the editor, *Staunton Spectator,* Jan. 6, 1863; Greer diary, Greer, Papers, VSL.

28. *OR,* 664.

29. Ibid., 653; Jasper, letter to the editor, *Augusta (Ga.) Daily Constitutionalist,* Jan. 14, 1863. Revised orders came at midday.

30. Ibid., 653, 655; W. Clark, *Histories,* 2:35.

31. Davidson, *Greenlee Davidson,* 66; Truthful Spectator, letter to the editor, *Sandersville (Ga.) Central Georgian,* Jan. 7, 1863; letter to the editor, Jasper, *Augusta (Ga.) Daily Constitutionalist,* Jan. 14, 1863; *Atlanta Southern Confederacy,* Jan. 13, 1863.

32. Jasper, letter to the editor, *Augusta (Ga.) Daily Constitutionalist,* Jan. 14, 1863; Dalton, *Blanket Brigade,* 95.

33. Jasper, letter to the editor, *Augusta (Ga.) Daily Constitutionalist,* Jan. 14, 1863; Veritas, letter to the editor, *Augusta (Ga.) Daily Constitutionalist,* Dec. 23, 1862.

34. Veritas, letter to the editor, *Augusta (Ga.) Daily Constitutionalist,* Dec. 23, 1862; Marion H. Fitzpatrick, *Letters to Amanda* (Culloden, Ga., 1976), 30; James T. McElvaney, letter, Dec. 19, 1862, typescript, FRSP; *Atlanta Southern Confederacy,* Dec. 27, 1862.

35. *Atlanta Southern Confederacy,* Jan. 13, 1863; Jasper, letter to the editor *Augusta (Ga.) Daily Constitutionalist,* Jan. 14, 1863; Truthful Spectator, letter to the editor *Sandersville (Ga.) Central Georgian,* Jan. 7, 1863.

36. *OR,* 676–77; Elisha F. Paxton, *The Civil War Letters of Frank "Bull" Paxton* (New York, 1907), 64, 66.

37. *OR,* 684; W. B. Colston Memoir, p. 22, FRSP.

38. *OR,* 678.

39. Paxton, *Civil War Letters,* 68; Colston Memoir, p. 22, FRSP; G. R. Bedinger, letter, Dec. 23, 1862, Bedinger-Dandridge Papers, Duke; Woodward, *Third Pennsylvania Reserves,* 218.

40. Bedinger, letter, Dec. 23, 1862, Bedinger-Dandridge Papers, Duke.

41. *OR,* 678, 681, 686–87; John O. Casler, letter, April 9, 1906, Bidgood Papers, VSL.

42. Nisbet, *Firing Line,* 125.

43. Pennypacker, *Meade,* 103; *OR,* 366–67; Frederick L. Hitchcock, *War from the Inside* (Philadelphia, 1904), 134.

44. Gearhart, "Reminiscences," pt. 1, 17; H. N. Warren, *142nd Pennsylvania,* 18; Holsinger, "How Does One Feel under Fire?" 294–95.

45. B. Alexander, "Seventh Regiment," *Hummelstown (Pa.) Sun,* Dec. 6, 1895; Woodward, *Third Pennsylvania Reserves,* 209; J. V. Morgan, letter to the editor, *National Tribune,* Jan. 22, 1925; S. Clark, letter, Dec. 17, 1862, FRSP.

46. Bates, *Pennsylvania Volunteers,* 4:31; *Philadelphia Inquirer,* Dec. 25, 1862; Woodward, *Our Campaigns,* 237; J. Frank Sterling, letter, Dec. 14, 1862, Rutgers; Stine, *Army of the Potomac,* 268; Milans, "Eyewitness to Fredericksburg," 23.

47. Woodward, *Our Campaigns,* 237, 245; *OR,* 512; Clinton, letter, Dec. 24, 1862, CWLM; Stine, *Army of the Potomac,* 268; Sterling, letter, Dec. 14, 1862, Rutgers; Milans, "Eyewitness to Fredericksburg," 23.

48. Milans, "Eyewitness to Fredericksburg," 23; Clinton, letter, Dec. 24, 1862, CWLM.

49. Meade, *Life and Letters,* 1:340; *History of the 121st Pennsylvania,* 30; Woodward, *Our Campaigns,* 237; *Philadelphia Inquirer,* Dec. 25, 1862.

50. Bates, *Pennsylvania Volunteers,* 1:851.

51. *OR,* 659, 670, 672; Nisbet, *Firing Line,* 124; Oates, *War between the Union and the Confederacy,* 166; Guillaume, letter to the editor *Sandersville (Ga.) Central Georgian,* Jan. 14, 1863; Shepherd G. Pryor, *A Post of Honor: The Pryor Letters* ed. Charles R. Adams, Jr. (Fort Valley, Ga., 1989), 294–96; William H. Hodnatt Diary, GDAH; Early, *Autobiographical Sketch,* 180.

52. Guillaume, letter to the editor, *Sandersville (Ga.) Central Georgian,* Jan. 14, 1863; Randolph, letter to the editor, *Sandersville (Ga.) Central Georgian,* Jan. 7, 1863; Scales, *Fredericksburg,* 14; Oates, *War between the Union and the Confederacy,* 166–67.

53. Nisbet, *Firing Line,* 124; Martin W. Brett, memoir, typescript, FRSP; *OR,* 670; McClendon, *Recollections of War Times,* 160.

54. Early, *Autobiographical Sketch,* 174; Nisbet, *Firing Line,* 124; Mockbee, "Historical Sketch," MOC; *Philadelphia Inquirer,* Dec. 25, 1862; Swearingen, letter, March 9, 1863, Dehon Papers, Wiley Collection, USAMHI; Randolph, letter to the editor, *Sandersville (Ga.) Central Georgian,* Jan. 7, 1863; Ruper, letter, Dec. 21, 1862, Chester County Historical Society.

55. Nisbet, *Firing Line,* 124; McClendon, *Recollections of War Times,* 160; *Savannah Republican,* Dec. 22, 1862; Oates, *War between the Union and the Confederacy,* 166; W. Clark, *Histories,* 2:158; Guillaume, letter to the editor, *Sandersville (Ga.) Central Georgian,* Jan. 14, 1863.

56. *OR,* 368, 373; Birney, quoted in *RJC,* 705.

57. *OR,* 368, 372–73; De Trobriand, *Four Years,* 269–370.

58. De Trobriand, *Four Years,* 270; *OR,* 370–71, 372–73.

59. *OR,* 369, 372, De Trobriand, *Four Years,* 270–71; H. F. Christy, "The 'Reserves' at Fredericksburg," *National Tribune,* Sept. 19, 1901.

60. *OR,* 369, 670–71; Clement A. Evans, *Intrepid Warrior,* ed. Robert Grier Stephens, Jr. (Dayton, 1992), 138; Guillaume, letter to the editor, *Sandersville (Ga.) Central Georgian,* Jan. 14, 1863; *Savannah Republican,* Dec. 22, 1862; Bates, *Pennsylvania Volunteers,* 2:250.

61. Stiles, *Four Years with Marse Robert,* 135.

62. Oates, *War between the Union and the Confederacy,* 166; Early, *Autobiographical Sketch,* 174; Slaughter, letter, Jan. 4, 1863, VHS; Nisbet, *Firing Line,* 125; Wilson T. Jenkins Reminiscences, NCDAH; *Richmond Dispatch,* Aug. 9, 1898; Ben, letter to the editor, *Charleston Daily Courier,* Dec. 30, 1862.

63. *OR,* 522, 672.

64. Ibid., 657, 659, 665, 672; Oates, *War between the Union and the Confederacy,* 167; Early, *Autobiographical Sketch,* 175.

65. W. H. Moore, letter, Jan. 4, 1863, FRSP.

66. *Savannah Republican,* Dec. 22, 1862; *OR,* 671; Whitman and True, *Maine in the War,* 394; *Sandersville (Ga.) Central Georgian,* Jan. 14, 1863.

67. Naisawald, *Grape and Canister,* 257–58; G. Lewis, *First Rhode Island Light Artillery,* 127; *OR,* 374.

68. Franklin, quoted in *RJC,* 709; Bates, *Pennsylvania Volunteers,* 2:249; *Medal of Honor,* 175; Birney, quoted in *RJC,* 705.

69. Nathan Pennypacker, letter, Dec. 19, 1862, Nathan Pennypacker Papers, Chester County Historical Society; Douglas R. Harper, *"If Thee Must Fight": A Civil War History of Chester County, Pennsylvania* (West Chester, Pa., 1990), 182–83; H. F. Christy, "The 'Reserves" at Fredericksburg," *National Tribune,* Sept. 19, 1901; G. T. Stevens, *Three Years,* 171; Thomson and Rauch, *Bucktails,* 236; *History of the 121st Pennsylvania,* 38; Andrew J. Alexander, *The Life and Services of Brevet Brigadier General Andrew Jonathan Alexander* (New York, 1887), 119.

70. Bates, *Pennsylvania Volunteers,* 2:250; Silas Gore, letter, Dec. 18, 1862, FRSP; Eli C. Strouss, letter, Dec. 19, 1862, CWT; *Pennsylvania at Gettysburg,* 1:326. Strouss stated that they were hit principally by the 61st Georgia.

71. *OR,* 374; Whitman and True, *Maine in the War,* 71; Michigan Adjutant-General's Department, *Fifth Michigan Volunteer Infantry,* vol. 5 of *Record of Service of Michigan Volunteers in the Civil War* (Kalamazoo, 1905), 31.

72. Michigan Adjutant-General's Dept., *Fifth Michigan Volunteers,* 31; William Gilson, letter, Dec. 18, 1862, FRSP.

73. Daniel G. Crotty, *Four Years Campaigning in the Army of the Potomac* (Grand Rapids, 1874), 73; *OR,* 376; Bates, *Pennsylvania Volunteers,* 2:250.

74. Guillaume, letter to the editor, *Sandersville (Ga.) Central Georgian,* Jan. 14, 1862; Whitman and True, *Maine in the War,* 394; Wainwright, *Diary of Battle,* 144; McClenthen, *Narrative,* 41.

75. Crotty, *Four Years Campaigning,* 73; De Trobriand, *Four Years,* 369; George S. Rollins, letter, Dec. 20, 1862, CWT; Strouss, letter, Dec. 19, 1862, CWT; Bates, *Pennsylvania Volunteers,* 2:25; *OR,* 671; A. J. Alexander, "Fredericksburg: Recollections of the Battle," *Philadelphia Weekly Times,* Feb. 23, 1887; *Pennsylvania at Gettysburg,* 2:877.

76. *Savannah Republican,* Dec. 22, 1862; *OR,* 671; Early, *Autobiographical Sketch,* 175; H. Taylor Memoir, FRSP; Wainwright Journal, Huntington Library.

77. *Medal of Honor,* 175; Early, *Autobiographical Sketch,* 180; *OR,* 671; William H. Stiles, letter, Dec. 15, 1862, Emory.

78. *OR,* 369–70; De Trobriand, *Four Years,* 371; Rollins, letter, Dec. 20, 1862, CWT.

79. *Medal of Honor,* 175; Edwin B. Houghton, *The Campaigns of the Seventeenth Maine* (Portland, 1866), 31–32; Haley, *Rebel Yell and Yankee Hurrah,* 58–59; D. V. Lovell, letter, Dec. 19, 1862, CWMC; *OR,* 374.

80. Houghton, *Seventeenth Maine,* 32; Haley, *Rebel Yell and Yankee Hurrah,* 59; V.A.S.P., letter to the editor, *Savannah Republican,* Jan. 1, 1863; Whitman and True, *Maine in the War,* 448.

81. Strouss, letter, Dec. 19, 1862, CWT; Veritas, letter to the editor, *Savannah Republican,* Jan. 6, 1863; *OR,* 671.

82. De Trobriand, *Four Years,* 370.

83. *OR,* 365–66; William Grew, *Fredericksburg* (n.p., 1899—copy in CWLM).

84. Grew, *Fredericksburg; Philadelphia Inquirer,* Dec. 19, 1862; *Philadelphia Weekly Times,* April 24, 1886; Frank Rauscher, *Music on the March, 1862–65* (Philadelphia, 1892), 33.

85. *OR,* 365, 367; Craft, *141st Pennsylvania,* 32; Mulholland, *Medal of Honor,* 170; *Philadelphia Inquirer,* Dec. 19, 1862; Kate M. Scott, *History of the One Hundred and Fifth Regiment of Pennsylvania Volunteers* (Philadelphia, 1877), 65; James P. Coburn, letter, Dec. 17, 1862, James P. Coburn Papers, USAMHI; O'Reilly, *Jackson at Fredericksburg,* 213 n. 36.

86. Edward E. Williams, letter, Dec. 19, 1862, Williams Papers, FRSP; Bates, *Pennsylvania Volunteers,* 3:1185; *Philadelphia Weekly Times,* April 24, 1886; *Philadelphia Inquirer,* Dec. 19, 1862; Grew, *Fredericksburg.*

87. *OR,* 365; Coburn, letter, Dec. 17, 1862, Coburn Papers, USAMHI; Craft, *141st Pennsylvania,* 33; John D. Bloodgood, *Personal Reminiscences of the War* (New York, 1893), 52.

88. *Philadelphia Weekly Times,* April 24, 1886; Bates, *Pennsylvania Volunteers,* 2:493; William H. Morrow, *Under the Red Patch: The Story of the Sixty-third Regiment Pennsylvania Volunteers* (Pittsburgh, 1908) 166.

89. *OR,* 366; *Philadelphia Weekly Times,* April 24, 1886; *Philadelphia Inquirer,* Dec. 19, 1862; Grew, *Fredericksburg;* Williams, letter, Dec. 15, 1862, Williams Papers, FRSP.

90. Grew, *Fredericksburg* Williams, letter, Dec. 19, 1862, Williams Papers, FRSP; *Philadelphia Inquirer,* Dec. 19, 1862; Mulholland, *Medal of Honor,* 170; Morrow, *Under the Red Patch,* 166.

91. *OR,* 367; Randolph, letter to the editor, *Sandersville (Ga.) Central Georgian,* Jan. 7, 1863; Guillaume, letter to the editor, *Sandersville (Ga.) Central Georgian,* Jan. 14, 1863; *Philadelphia Inquirer,* Dec. 19, 1862; Gilson, letter, Dec. 18, 1862, FRSP.

92. *Medal of Honor,* 176; Williams, letter, Dec. 18, 1862, Williams Papers, FRSP; Bates, *Pennsylvania Volunteers,* 2:493.

93. *Philadelphia Weekly Times,* April 24, 1886; *OR,* 366; Craft, *141st Pennsylvania,* 33, 38; De Trobriand, *Four Years,* 371.

94. Mulholland, *Medal of Honor,* 170.

95. Wainwright Journal, Huntington Library; Philip H. Power, letter, Dec. 20, 1862, LLC; Edward Porter Alexander, *Military Memoirs of a Confederate* (New York, 1907), 302.

96. Handerson, *Yankee in Gray,* 53; Keely, "Reminiscences," 20.

97. Early, *Autobiographical Sketch,* 175; *OR,* 665, 672; Oates, *War between the Union and the Confederacy,* 167; Joseph C. Stiles, letter, Jan. 7, 1863, Huntington Library; W. H. Moore, letter, Jan. 4, 1863, FRSP.

98. J. H. Moore, "Seventh Tennessee Infantry," 1:238; Keely, "Reminiscences," 20; Heffelfinger Diary, CWT.

99. *OR,* 487; Gibbon, quoted in *RJC,* 715; McCoy, "The 107th Penna. Vet. Volunteers," *Philadelphia Weekly Press,* Jan. 4, 1888; Gibbon, *Personal Recollections,* 105; Wainwright, *Diary of Battle,* 143.

100. *OR,* 496, 499; William J. Bacon, *Memorial to William Kirkland Bacon* (Utica, N.Y., 1863), 37; McCoy, "The 107th Penna. Vet. Volunteers," *Philadelphia Weekly Press,* Jan. 4, 1888; Bates, *Pennsylvania Volunteers,* 3:858–59.

101. *OR,* 497, 502; Canan, *History of Cambria County,* 249; Mulholland, *Medal of Honor,* 170; Veritas, letter to the editor, *Augusta (Ga.) Daily Constitutionalist,* Dec. 23, 1862.

102. *OR,* 487, 491, 495; Abner R. Small, *The Sixteenth Maine Regiment in the War of the Rebellion* (Portland, 1886), 65; Davidson, *Greenlee Davidson,* 64; Charles Barber, letter, Dec. 21, 1862, FRSP; McClenthen, *Narrative,* 40; Bates, *Pennsylvania Volunteers,* 3:858–59.

103. Truthful Spectator, letter to the editor, *Sandersville (Ga.) Central Georgian,* Jan. 7, 1863; *OR,* 653; Jasper, letter to the editor, *Augusta (Ga.) Daily Constitutionalist,* Jan. 14, 1863.

104. W. Clark, *Histories,* 2:36, 687; *OR,* 655.

105. *OR,* 490, 498, 509; I. S. Tichenor letter, March 17, 1893, Tichenor Papers, FRSP.

106. *OR,* 490; Tichenor, letter, March 17, 1893, Tichenor Papers FRSP; Ithaca, letter to the editor, *Elmira (N.Y.) Sunday Telegram,* n.d., Tichenor Papers, FRSP; Stine, *Army of the Potomac,* 275.

107. *OR,* 497, 501; Davidson, *Greenlee Davidson,* 66; Bacon, *Memorial,* 39, 41–2; McClenthen, Narrative, 44; *Medal of Honor,* 120.

108. *OR,* 498; Small, *Sixteenth Maine,* 67; Dalton, *Blanket Brigade,* 91.

109. Veritas, letter to the editor, *Augusta (Ga.) Daily Constitutionalist,* Dec. 23, 1862; Jasper, letter to the editor, *Augusta (Ga.) Daily Constitutionalist,* Jan. 14, 1863; Truthful Spectator, letter to the editor, *Sandersville (Ga.) Central Georgian,* Jan. 7, 1863; J. VanLew McCreery Recollections, p. 11, VHS; Dalton, *Blanket Brigade,* 95.

110. Fitzpatrick, *Letters to Amanda,* 30; Jasper, letter to the editor, *Augusta (Ga.) Daily Constitutionalist,* Jan. 14, 1863; *OR,* 503, 653; W. Clark, *Histories,* 2:557; Scales, *Fredericksburg,* 16.

111. Fleming Reminiscences, 21, FRSP; Brett, memoir, typescript, FRSP; Canan, *History of Cambria County,* 249; McClendon, *Recollections of War Times,* 160; Slaughter, letter, Jan. 4, 1863, VHS; Weston A. Smith, *The Anson Guards* (Charlotte, N.C., 1914), 168; W. H. Moore, letter, Jan. 4, 1863, FRSP; Norris Diary, FRSP.

112. *Carlisle (Pa.) Herald,* Dec. 26, 1862; Bates, *Pennsylvania Volunteers,* 1:728.

113. *Philadelphia Inquirer,* Dec. 19, 1862; Strouss, letter, Dec. 19, 1862, CWT; *OR,* 366; James M. Goldsmith Reminiscences, GDAH; Bates, *Pennsylvania Volunteers,* 1:728; *Carlisle (Pa.) Herald,* Dec. 26, 1862.

114. A. J. Alexander, "Fredericksburg: Recollections of the Battle," *Philadelphia Weekly*

Times, Feb. 23, 1887; Samuel H. Merrill, *The Campaigns of the First Maine and First District of Columbia Cavalry* (Portland, 1866), 83; Samuel J. Bayard, *Life of George Dashiel Bayard* (New York, 1874), 273–74; William W. Teall, letter, Dec. 14, 1862, Teall Papers, Small Collection, TSL.

CHAPTER NINE: "CHEER UP, MY HEARTIES!"

1. Galwey, *Valiant Hours,* 59.
2. Couch, "Sumner's 'Right Grand Division,'" 3:110.
3. Walker, *Second Corps,* 158.
4. Couch, "Sumner's 'Right Grand Division,'" 3:111.
5. Howard, *Autobiography,* 1:339. "West" is in parentheses because the State of West Virginia did not exist at the time of the Fredericksburg campaign, becoming a state in June 1863—at the time of Fredericksburg these troops were recognized as Virginians. The author adds the qualifier "West" to differentiate this Federal regiment from the Confederate Virginia units.
6. *OR,* 290.
7. Harrison, *Fredericksburg Civil War Sites,* 2:160.
8. Thomas Reade Rootes Cobb, letter, Dec. 6, 1862, Thomas Reade Rootes Cobb Papers, University of Georgia; David L. Preston, "The Glorious Light Went Out Forever: The Death of Brig. Gen. Thomas R. R. Cobb," *Civil War Regiments* 4, no. 4 (1995): 28; Mitchell Diary, FRSP; *OR,* 607; Woods Reminiscences, UDC Bound Typescript, Vol. 4, no. 144, GDAH; Dent, letter to the editor, *Atlanta Journal,* Aug. 10, 1901; Charles J. McDonald Conway diary, GDAH; Byrd, letter to the editor, *Cedartown (Ga.) Standard,* May 5–16, 1914.
9. Owen, *In Camp and Battle,* 181.
10. Owen, *In Camp and Battle,* 184; *OR,* 575; Owen, "Hot Days," 3:97.
11. *OR,* 291.
12. Couch, "Sumner's 'Right Grand Division,'" 3:111; Franklin Sawyer, *A Military History of the Eighth Regiment Ohio Volunteer Infantry* (Cleveland, 1881), 94; Galwey, *Valiant Hours,* 59–60; *OR,* 298.
13. *OR,* 292; William Kepler, *History of the Fourth Regiment Ohio Volunteer Infantry in the War for the Union* (Cleveland, 1886), 95.
14. Henry H. Baker, *A Reminiscent Story of the Great Civil War . . . Second Paper* (New Orleans, 1911), 43, 45; *OR,* 574; Owen, *In Camp and Battle,* 186; Owen, "Hot Day," 3:98.
15. *OR,* 608; Mitchell diary, FRSP.
16. Kepler, *Fourth Ohio,* 96–97; Galwey, *Valiant Hours,* 61; Harrison, *Fredericksburg Civil War Sites,* 1:30.
17. *Athens (Ga.) Southern Banner,* Jan. 7, 1863; Sutton, *Civil War Stories,* 20; Charles S. Powell, "War Talks," Duke; William R. Montgomery, letter, Dec. 17, 1862, William R. Montgomery Papers, USC.
18. Montgomery, letter, Dec. 17, 1862, Montgomery Papers, USC; *Athens (Ga.) Southern Banner,* Jan. 7, 1863; Stegeman, *These Men She Gave,* 74; Byrd,"Phillips Legion," *Cedartown (Ga.) Standard,* May 5–16, 1914.
19. Galwey, *Valiant Hours,* 61; Harrison, *Fredericksburg Civil War Sites,* 2:172–73.

20. James J. Reeves, *History of the Twenty-fourth Regiment, New Jersey Volunteers* (Woodbury, N.J., 1889), 19; *OR*, 295, 299; Benjamin Borton, *On the Parallels* (Woodstown, N.J., 1903), 64–65.

21. David Beem, Memoir, p. 25, David Beem Papers, memoir, Indiana Historical Society; *OR*, 290.

22. *OR*, 290, 294, 299. Kimball and Cavins identified the road on the brigade's left as "Telegraph Road" or the "so-called Telegraph Road." Hanover Street ran into the Sunken Road at the base of Marye's Heights, where it became the Telegraph Road—Frederick Street also ran into Telegraph Road just as it rounded the southern terminus of Willis Hill and appears on the map as a direct tie-in to Telegraph Road, which may have been the source of the misidentification.

23. *OR*, 290; Reeves, *Twenty-fourth New Jersey*, 20; George A. Seaman, letter, Dec. 10, 1862, FRSP; Beem, memoir, p. 23, Beem Papers, Indiana Historical Society.

24. *OR*, 290, 296–97; Reeves, *Twenty-fourth New Jersey*, 20; Beem memoir, p. 25, Beem Paper, Indiana Historical Society. Kimball admitted that "those left with me were exhausted by the fatigue of clearing away fences and marching so far at double-quick."

25. Galwey, *Valiant Hours*, 61–62; Beem, memoir, p. 26, Beem Papers, Indiana Historical Society; E. D. Mason, letter, Dec. 15, 1862, Nathan Kimball Papers, Indiana University; Reeves, *Twenty-fourth New Jersey*, 20.

26. Borton, *On the Parallels*, 65; *OR*, 290, 292; E. D. Mason, letter, Dec. 15, 1862, Kimball Papers, Indiana University.

27. *OR*, 292.

28. W. Houghton, "Charge at Marye's Heights," *National Tribune*, Dec. 16, 1897; D. Beem, letter, Dec. 14, 1862, Beem Papers, Indiana Historical Society; Beem, memoir, p. 27, Beem Papers, Indiana Historical Society.

29. Gabriel Grant Memoir, New-York Historical Society; *OR*, 290, 296; Galwey, *Valiant Hours*, 63–64; Edward A. L. Roberts Compiled Service Record, NA.

30. John D. Damron, letter, Dec. 17, 1862, Ann Penn Wray Collection, University of Tennessee; Borton, *On the Parallels*, 69.

31. Hickerson, *Echoes of Happy Valley*, 71; Walkup Journal, Duke; H. A. Butler, "Fredericksburg—Personal Reminiscences," *Confederate Veteran* 14 (April 1906): 181; *OR*, 629; Lunsford R. Cherry, letter, Dec. 20, 1862, Lucy Cherry Crisp Papers, Duke; HHG, newspaper article, clipping in Stephen B. Weeks scrapbook "History and Biography of North Carolina," vol. 5, Stephen B. Weeks Papers, SHC, UNC; Cooke, quoted in in J. A. Graham, letter to the editor, *Philadelphia Weekly Times*, Sept. 22, 1883.

32. Sloan, *Guilford Grays*, 55; Hickerson, *Echoes of Happy Valley*, 72; Cooke, quoted in J. A. Graham, letter to the editor, *Philadelphia Weekly Times*, Sept. 22, 1883.

33. W. Clark, *Histories*, 2:297; *OR*, 625.

34. *OR*, 293, 298, 299.

35. Galwey, *Valiant Hours*, 63.

36. Ibid., 61; J. W. Ames, "In Front of the Stone Wall at Fredericksburg," 3:122.

37. Kepler, *Fourth Ohio*, 98; Galwey, *Valiant Hours*, 62.

38. *OR*, 304, 309; Bates, *Pennsylvania Volunteers*, 4:244; Hitchcock, *War from the Inside*, 113–14.

39. *OR*, 309; Bates, *Pennsylvania Volunteers*, 4:244.

40. Henry S. Stevens, *Souvenir of Excursion to Battlefields by the Society of the Fourteenth Connecticut Regiment* (Washington, D.C., 1893), 79–80; Charles Page, *History of the Fourteenth Regiment Connecticut Volunteer Infantry* (Meridian, Conn., 1906), 81–82.

41. H. S. Stevens, *Souvenir,* 81; *OR,* 300, 303, 308; Hitchcock, *War from the Inside,* 125.

42. George Hopper, letter, Dec. 21, 1862, CWMC; Charles W. Cowtan, *Services of the Tenth New York Volunteers (National Zouaves) in the War of the Rebellion* (New York, 1882), 163; Eugene A. Cory, "A Private's Recollections of Fredericksburg," in *Personal Narratives of Events in the War of the Rebellion: Rhode Island Soldiers and Sailors Historical Society* (Providence, 1884), 22–23; Hitchcock, *War from the Inside,* 118.

43. Cory, "A Private's Recollections," 24; Hitchcock, *War from the Inside,* 117, 119; Bates, *Pennsylvania Volunteers,* 4:244.

44. Hitchcock, *War from the Inside,* 117; *OR,* 303, 305.

45. Page, *Fourteenth Connecticut,* 82–83; Francis E. Pierce, letter, Dec. 17, 1862, FRSP; Morris R. Darrohn Recollections, Antietam National Battlefield Park; H. S. Stevens, *Souvenir,* 82; Edward W. Spangler, *My Little War Experience* (York, Pa., 1904), 64.

46. H. S. Stevens, *Souvenir,* 82; *OR,* 300.

47. Spangler, *My Little War Experience,* 65; Trume, letter to the editor, *Rochester Democrat and American,* Dec. 22, 1862; H. S. Stevens, *Souvenir,* 86; Darrohn Recollections, Antietam National Battlefield Park.

48. Page, *Fourteenth Connecticut,* 83; Spangler, *My Little War Experience,* 64; Trume, letter to the editor, *Rochester Democrat and American,* Dec. 22, 1862.

49. H. S. Stevens, *Souvenir,* 82–83; Page, *Fourteenth Connecticut,* 83–84.

50. Henry P. Goddard, *Regimental Reminiscences of the War of the Rebellion* (Middletown, Conn., 1877), 11.

51. George H. Sargent diary, Dec. 13, 1862, Huntington Library.

52. Hopper, letter, Dec. 21, 1862, CWMC; Cory, "A Private's Recollections," 23; Cowtan, *National Zouaves,* 164–65; *OR,* 308; Hitchcock, *War from the Inside,* 123–24.

53. *OR,* 303; Cowtan, *National Zouaves,* 165; Cory, "A Private's Recollections," 24.

54. Hitchcock, *War from the Inside,* 117.

55. Cowtan, *National Zouaves,* 165; Cory, "A Private's Recollections," 25; Hopper, letter, Dec. 21, 1862, CWMC; Hitchcock, *War from the Inside,* 120.

56. H. S. Stevens, *Souvenir,* 83; *OR,* 300; Goddard, *Regimental Reminiscences,* 11.

57. Longstreet, "The Battle of Fredericksburg," in *B&L,* 3:79; Pierce, letter, Dec. 18, 1862, FRSP; Page, *Fourteenth Connecticut,* 86; Goddard, *Regimental Reminiscences,* 11.

58. John Pellett, letter, Dec. 21, 1862, CWMC; Spangler, *My Little War Experience,* 65;

59. Pierce, letter, Dec. 17, 1862, FRSP; Owen, *In Camp and Battle,* 189; Baker, *Reminiscent Story,* 48; Spangler, *My Little War Experience,* 66; H. S. Stevens, *Souvenir,* 83; Palmer, letter to the editor, *Rochester Democrat and American,* Dec. 23, 1862. Pierce identifies the south wall as "a fence which runs up the hill."

60. Page, *Fourteenth Connecticut,* 90–91; Goddard, *Regimental Reminiscences,* 12; Edmund H. Wade, letter, Dec. 16, 1862, UM; H. S. Stevens, *Souvenir,* 86; *OR,* 51, 300.

61. *OR,* 300, 302; Spangler, *My Little War Experience,* 66.

62. Pellett, letter, Dec. 21, 1862, CWMC; Trume, letter to the editor, *Rochester Democrat and American,* Dec. 22, 1862; Edward Cotter, letter, Jan. 23, 1863, CWMC; Pierce, letter, Dec. 17, 1862, FRSP.

63. Hopper, letter, Dec. 21, 1862, CWMC; Cowtan, *National Zouaves,* 162.

64. Hitchcock, *War from the Inside,* 118, 121–22,123, 126; *OR,* 309; Bates, *Pennsylvania Volunteers,* 4:244.

65. *OR,* 303, 305, 307.

66. Page, *Fourteenth Connecticut,* 86–88; H. S. Stevens, *Souvenir,* 83–85. Lyman recounted that the wounding of Dart and Symonds occurred along the millrace, but the timing of Foote's wounding and Palmer's location of the flag make it more plausible that it occurred at this point.

67. Spangler, *My Little War Experience,* 66; Page, *Fourteenth Connecticut,* 85; Trume, letter to the editor, *Rochester Democrat and American,* Dec. 22, 1862; Darrohn Recollections, Antietam National Battlefield Park; *OR,* 300; Pellett, letter, Dec. 21, 1862, CWMC.

68. *OR,* 303, 305, 307, 309; Bates, *Pennsylvania Volunteers,* 4:244.

69. H. S. Stevens, *Souvenir,* 84; Page, *Fourteenth Connecticut,* 88, 91–92; Spangler, *My Little War Experience,* 66; Pierce, letter, Dec. 18, 1862, FRSP

70. *OR,* 291.

71. Hitchcock, *War from the Inside,* 122–23, 125–26; *OR,* 309.

72. Couch, quoted in Spangler, *My Little War Experience,* 74; Couch, "Sumner's 'Right Grand Division,'" 3:113.

73. Howard, *Autobiography,* 1:341; Couch, "Sumner's 'Right Grand Division,'" 3:113.

74. H. S. Stevens, *Souvenir,* 83; Goddard, *Regimental Reminiscences,* 12.

75. Spangler, *My Little War Experience,* 66–67; H. S. Stevens, *Souvenir,* 83.

76. *OR,* 131; Hopper, letter, Dec. 21, 1862, CWMC; Bates, *Pennsylvania Volunteers,* 4:244; Page, *Fourteenth Connecticut,* 95; Goddard, *Regimental Reminiscences,* 12; Wade, letter, Dec. 16, 1862, UM.

77. H. S. Stevens, *Souvenir,* 85; *OR,* 305, 306.

CHAPTER TEN: "THE VALLEY OF DEATH"

1. Albert D. Richardson, *The Secret Service: The Field, the Dungeon, and the Escape* (Hartford, 1865), 329, 332; Teall, letter, Dec. 13, 1862, Teall Papers, Small Collection, TSL.

2. *ORS,* 3:764; McCrea, *Dear Belle,* 172; Thomas M. Aldrich, *The History of the First Regiment Rhode Island Light Artillery* (Providence, 1904), 161.

3. *OR,* 318; Naisawald, *Grape and Canister,* 262; Roemer, *Reminiscences,* 102; McCrea, *Dear Belle,* 176.

4. *OR,* 318, 319.

5. Ibid., 266, 287; Harrison, *Gazetteer,* 2:33; Aldrich, *First Rhode Island Light Artillery,* 161.

6. *OR,* 287; Aldrich, *First Rhode Island Light Artillery,* 161; Harrison, *Fredericksburg Civil War Sites,* 2:225; McCrea, *Dear Belle,* 176.

7. *OR,* 658; Baker, *Reminiscent Story,* 45; Owen, "Hot Day," 3:99.

8. *OR,* 232, 289; McCrea, *Dear Belle,* 172, 176.

9. *ORS,* 3:764, 766; William C. Barker, letter, Dec. 17, 1862, Rhode Island Historical Society; Naisawald, *Grape and Canister,* 263.

10. *Charleston Daily Courier,* Dec. 30, 1862; Preston, "The Glorious Light," *New York*

Times, Dec. 26, 1862; J. H. Lumpkin Dec. 30, 1862, Lumpkin Papers, University of Georgia. The New York *Times* identified Berrien as Captain Herring. Preston correctly identifies the ordnance officer.

11. Elizabeth M. A. Wynne, *Genealogies and Traditions* (Indiana, Pa., 1931); Butler, "Fredericksburg—Personal Reminiscences," 181; William C. Davis, "John Rogers Cooke," in *The Confederate General* ed. William C. Davis, ([Harrisburg], 1991), 2:25.

12. *New York Times,* Dec. 26, 1862; Lumpkin, letter, Dec. 30, 1862, Lumpkin Papers, University of Georgia; E. J. Elridge, letter, April 2, 1887, Carlton-Newton-Mell Collection, University of Georgia.

13. *Athens (Ga.) Southern Banner,* Jan. 7, 1863; *New York Times,* Dec. 26, 1862; Montgomery, letter, Dec. 17, 1862, USC.

14. *New York Times,* Dec. 26, 1862; Elridge, letter, April 2, 1887, Carlton-Newton-Mell Collection, University of Georgia; Sutton, *Civil War Stories,* 22; Preston, "The Glorious Light," 37; *Charleston Daily Courier,* Dec. 30, 1862; Montgomery, letter, Dec. 17, 1862, USC; Lumpkin, letter, Dec. 30, 1862, Lumpkin Papers, University of Georgia.

15. Preston, "The Glorious Light," 35, 37, 44; Lumpkin letter, Dec. 30, 1862, Lumpkin, Papers, University of Georgia; A. J. McBride, "Banner Battle of the War," *Atlanta Journal,* May 4, 1901; Elridge, letter, April 2, 1887, Carlton-Newton-Mell Collection, University of Georgia; Stegeman, *These Men She Gave,* 75; J. H. Beale, *Journal,* 75.

16. Robert Nugent, "The Sixty-ninth Regiment at Fredericksburg," in *Third Annual Report of the State Historian of the State of New York* (Albany, 1898), 39; Samuel K. Zook, letter, Dec. 16, 1862, CWMC; Robert Nugent, "The Irish Brigade," in *New York at Gettysburg,* ed. William F. Fox (Abany, 1900), 2:489; William Child, *History of the Fifth Regiment New Hampshire Volunteers* (Bristol, N.H., 1893), 151.

17. Winthrop D. Sheldon, *The Twenty-seventh: A Regimental History* (New Haven, Conn., 1866), 25; Favill, *Diary,* 210; Fritz, letter to the editor, *Berks, Chester and Montgomery (Pa.) Ledger,* Dec. 30, 1862; *OR,* 254, 255, 256, 258.

18. William McCarter, "My Life in the Army," HSP; Nugent, "The Sixty-ninth," 40.

19. Samuel D. Hunter, "Charge of the Irish Brigade on Marye's Heights," *GAS&SM,* Oct. 6, 1883; Mulholland, letter to the editor, *Philadelphia Weekly Times,* April 23, 1881; McCarter, "My Life in the Army," HSP; John Donovan, letter to the editor, *New York Irish-American,* Jan. 3, 1863; William McClelland, letter to the editor, *New York Irish-American,* Jan. 10, 1863.

20. McCarter, "My Life in the Army," HSP; Donovan, letter to the editor, *New York Irish-American,* Jan. 3, 1863; McClelland, letter to the editor, *New York Irish-American,* Jan. 10, 1862; Hunter, "Charge of the Irish Brigade," *GAS&SM,* Oct. 6, 1863; *Yorkville Enquirer,* Dec. 24, 1862.

21. Child, *Fifth New Hampshire,* 151–52.

22. Bates, *Pennsylvania Volunteers,* 4:519; *OR,* 233, 236, 238; C. A. Fuller, *War of 1861,* 78; Stuckenberg, *I'm Surrounded by Methodists,* 40–41.

23. *OR,* 49, 233, 238; Bates, *Pennsylvania Volunteers,* 2:1170; Child, *Fifth New Hampshire,* 152.

24. Child, *Fifth New Hampshire,* 150, 152, 155; McCarter, "My Life in the Army," HSP; Bates, *Pennsylvania Volunteers,* 2:1170.

25. Unidentified soldier (64th New York) Reminiscences, p. 36, Indiana University; C. A. Fuller, *War of 1861,* 78; *OR,* 236.

26. McCarter, "My Life in the Army," HSP; St. Clair A. Mulholland, *The Story of the 116th Regiment Pennsylvania Volunteers* (Philadelphia, 1903), 43; William McCarter, "Fredericksburg's Battle," *Philadelphia Weekly Times,* Sept. 8, 1883.

27. McCarter, "My Life in the Army," HSP; Mulholland, "Battle of Fredericksburg," *Philadelphia Weekly Times,* April 23, 1881.

28. Mulholland, *116th Pennsylvania,* 45.

29. *OR,* 233; Unidentified Soldier (64th New York) Reminiscences, p. 36, Indiana University; Stuckenberg, *I'm Surrounded by Methodists,* 41.

30. McCarter, "Fredericksburg's Battle," *Philadelphia Weekly Times,* Sept. 8, 1883; Hunter, "Charge of the Irish Brigade," *GAS&SM,* Oct. 6, 1883; Donovan, letter to the editor, *New York Irish-American,* Jan. 3, 1863.

31. Stuckenberg, *I'm Surrounded by Methodists,* 41; C. A. Fuller, *War of 1861,* 79.

32. Fritz, letter to the editor, *Berks, Chester and Montgomery (Pa.) Ledger,* Dec. 30, 1862; *OR,* 254; Erskine M. Church, letter, March 15, 1863, Park Collection, FRSP; Sheldon, *Twenty-seventh Connecticut,* 25, 26; Zook, letter, Dec. 16, 1862, CWMC.

33. *OR,* 254, 257; Fritz, *Berks, Chester and Montgomery (Pa.) Ledger,* Dec. 30, 1862; Sheldon, *Twenty-seventh Connecticut,* 26; Frederick, *Story of a Regiment,* 119.

34. Favill, *Diary,* 211; Fritz, letter to the editor, *Berks, Chester and Montgomery (Pa.) Ledger,* Dec. 30, 1862; Sheldon, *Twenty-seventh Connecticut,* 27.

35. Samuel H. Rutter, "The Civil War Correspondence of Samuel Hockley Rutter," *Bulletin of the Historical Society of Montgomery County, Pennsylvania* 19 (1975): 348; Sheldon, *Twenty-seventh Connecticut,* 26–27.

36. Frederick, *Story of a Regiment,* 121; Unidentified soldier, letter headed "Headquarters 57th Regt. New York Vols.," Dec. 17, 1862, FRSP; *OR,* 259.

37. *OR,* 254.

38. Jacob H. Cole, *Under Five Commanders: or, A Boy's Experiences with the Army of the Potomac* (Paterson, N.J., 1906), 120, 121; Favill, *Diary,* 211; Church, letter, March 15, 1863, FRSP; *OR,* 261.

39. Favill, *Diary,* 211; Sheldon, *Twenty-seventh Connecticut,* 27; Fritz, letter to the editor, *Berks, Chester and Montgomery (Pa.) Ledger,* Dec. 30, 1862.

40. Owen, *In Camp and Battle,* 189; Powell, "War Talks," Duke; Baker, *Reminiscent Story,* 48; *Charleston Daily Courier,* Dec. 30, 1862.

41. Baker, *Reminiscent Story,* 48; Favill, *Diary,* 211; Fritz, letter to the editor, *Berks, Chester and Montgomery (Pa.) Ledger,* Dec. 30, 1862; Sheldon, *Twenty-seventh Connecticut,* 27; Church, letter, March 15, 1863, FRSP; Frederick, *Story of a Regiment,* 121.

42. Church, letter, March 15, 1863, FRSP.

43. Favill, *Diary,* 212; Sheldon, *Twenty-seventh Connecticut,* 28; C. R. Lyon, letter, Dec. 18, 1862, Lyon Family Papers, USMA.

44. *OR,* 257, 260; Harrison, *Gazetteer,* 1:105.

45. Frederick, *Story of a Regiment,* 121; Unidentified soldier, letter headed "Headquarters 57th[etc.]," Dec. 17, 1862, FRSP; Favill, *Diary,* 211; C. R. Lyon, letter, Dec. 18, 1862, Lyon Family Papers, USMA.

46. Favill, *Diary,* 211; Unidentified soldier, letter headed "Headquarters 57th[etc.]," Dec. 17, 1862, FRSP; *OR,* 258, 260.

47. J. H. Cole, *Under Five Commanders,* 121.

48. Fritz, letter to the editor, *Berks, Chester and Montgomery (Pa.) Ledger,* Dec. 30, 1862; *OR,* 261.

49. *OR,* 625; J. L. Harris, "Transcription of Civil War Papers—John L. Harris," in *Civil War Documents Granville County, North Carolina* (Oxford, N.C., 1997), 56–57; Powell, "War Talks," Duke.

50. Powell, "War Talks," Duke; *OR,* 608; *Charleston Daily Courier,* Dec. 30, 1862.

51. *OR,* 261.

52. Zook, letter, Dec. 16, 1862, CWMC.

53. *OR,* 257.

54. *OR,* 230, 256, 260.

55. C. R. Lyon, letter, Dec. 18, 1862, Lyon Family Papers, USMA; *OR,* 255, 261; Fritz, letter to the editor, *Berks, Chester and Montgomery (Pa.) Ledger,* Dec. 30, 1862; Frederick, *Story of a Regiment,* 121.

56. James Madigan, letter to the editor, *New York Irish-American,* Dec. 27, 1862; Unidentified soldier (69th New York) Memoir, Kenneth H. Powers Collection, USAMHI; *OR,* 249.

57. Nugent, "The Sixty-ninth," 41; Mulholland, *116th Pennsylvania,* 45; McClelland, letter to the editor, *New York Irish-American,* Jan. 10, 1863; *OR,* 241, 246.

58. John Dwyer, *Address of John Dwyer* (New York, 1914), 3; *OR,* 241, 248, 250; McCarter, "My Life in the Army," HSP; Hunter, "Charge of the Irish Brigade," *GAS&SM,* Oct. 6, 1883.

59. McCarter, "My Life in the Army," HSP

60. Hunter, "Charge of the Irish Brigade," *GAS&SM,* Oct. 6, 1883; Unidentified Soldier (69th New York) Memoir, Powers Collection, USAMHI; Donovan, letter to the editor, *New York Irish-American,* Jan. 3, 1863; McCarter, "Fredericksburg's Battle," *Philadelphia Weekly Times,* Sept. 8, 1883; Mulholland, "Battle of Fredericksburg," *Philadelphia Weekly Times,* April 23, 1881; McCarter, "My Life in the Army," HSP

61. C. A. Fuller, *War of 1861,* 79; Stuckenberg, *I'm Surrounded by Methodists,* 41.

62. Child, *Fifth New Hampshire,* 153; Unidentified Soldier (64th New York) Reminiscences, p. 37, Indiana University; C. A. Fuller, *War of 1861,* 79.

63. *OR,* 233, 234.

64. Unidentified Soldier (69th New York) Memoir, Powers Collection USAMHI; *OR,* 241; Nugent, "The Sixty-ninth," 41; Robert Nugent to St. Clair A. Mulholland, Jan. 5, 1881, Mulholland Papers, CWLM.

65. Donovan, letter to the editor, New York *Irish-American,* Jan. 3, 1863; Mulholland, "Battle of Fredericksburg," *Philadelphia Weekly Times,* April 23, 1881; McClelland, letter to the editor, *New York Irish-American,* Jan. 10, 1863; Hunter, "Charge of the Irish Brigade," *GAS&SM,* Oct. 6, 1883.

66. Hunter, "Charge of the Irish Brigade," *GAS&SM,* Oct. 6, 1883; Mulholland, "Battle of Fredericksburg," *Philadelphia Weekly Times,* April 23, 1881; Donovan, letter to the editor, *New York Irish-American,* Jan. 3, 1863; *OR,* 250; John Dwyer, "63d Regiment Infantry," *New York at Gettysburg,* ed. William F. Fox (Albany, 1900), 2:500.

67. Madigan, letter to the editor, *New York Irish-American,* Dec. 27, 1862; Unidentified Irish Brigade officer, letter to the editor, *New York Irish-American,* Dec. 27, 1862; McCarter, "My Life in the Army," HSP; Dwyer, "63d Regiment Infantry," 2:500.

68. Nugent, "The Sixty-ninth," 42, 69; Nugent, "The Irish Brigade," 2:489; Donovan, letter to the editor, *New York Irish-American,* Jan. 3, 1863.

69. Nugent, letter, Jan. 5, 1881, Mulholland Papers, CWLM; Unidentified Soldier (69th New York) Memoir, Powers Collection, USAMHI; Nugent, "The Sixty-ninth," 43.

70. James J. Smith, "69th Regiment Infantry," *New York at Gettysburg,* ed. William F. Fox (Albany, 1900), 2:508–9; David P. Conyngham. *The Irish Brigade and Its Campaigns* (New York, 1867), 352.

71. Donovan, letter to the editor, *New York Irish-American,* Jan. 3, 1863; McClelland, letter to the editor, *New York Irish-American,* Jan. 10, 1863; Madigan, letter to the editor, *New York Irish-American,* Dec. 27, 1862; Nagle, letter to the editor, *New York Irish-American,* Dec. 27, 1862.

72. Nagle, letter to the editor, *New York Irish-American,* Dec. 27, 1862; Unknown officer, Irish Brigade, letter to the editor, *New York Irish-American,* Dec. 27, 1862; Donovan, letter to the editor, *New York Irish-American,* Jan. 3, 1863; Unknown officer, letter to the editor, *New York Irish-American,* Dec. 27, 1862. The unidentified officer noted that Young was still alive and trapped between the lines as late as Monday, Dec. 15, 1862.

73. Unknown officer, Irish Brigade, letter to the editor, *New York Irish-American,* Dec. 27, 1862; *OR,* 245, 246; Nugent, "The Sixty-ninth," 44.

74. *OR,* 248, 250; Dwyer, "63d Regiment Infantry," 2:500; Nugent, "The Sixty-ninth," 44.

75. Dwyer, *Address,* 4; Dwyer, "63d Regiment Infantry," 2:500.

76. Mulholland, "Battle of Fredericksburg," *Philadelphia Weekly Times,* April 23, 1881; Mulholland, *116th Pennsylvania,* 48; McCarter, "Fredericksburg's Battle," Philadelphia *Weekly Times,* Sept. 8, 1883.

77. Mulholland, *116th Pennsylvania,* 48, 60; McCarter, "My Life in the Army," HSP; Colimore, "A Father in the Civil War" (interview with Mulholland's daughter), *Philadelphia Inquirer,* Aug. 30, 1986; *OR,* 253; Hunter, "Charge of the Irish Brigade," *GAS&SM,* Oct. 6, 1883; Bates, *Pennsylvania Volunteers,* 2:1230. McCarter made the point that Mulholland fell after the colonel and major had already been wounded.

78. Hunter, "Charge of the Irish Brigade," *GAS&SM,* Oct. 6, 1883; Mulholland, "Battle of Fredericksburg," *Philadelphia Weekly Times,* April 23, 1881.

79. Unknown officer, letter to the editor, *New York Irish-American,* Dec. 27, 1862; *OR,* 242; Michael Cavanagh, *Memoirs of General Thomas Francis Meagher* (Worcester, Mass., 1892), 467. An unidentified officer in Meagher's confidence related the nature of the suppuration and the operation to alleviate it. Meagher wrote to his wife—curiously addressed to: "Mrs. Br. Gen. Meagher"—that his knee had been bruised.

80. *OR,* 237; C. A. Fuller, *War of 1861,* 79; Child, *Fifth New Hampshire,* 152, 155; Unidentified Soldier (64th New York) Reminiscences, p. 37, Indiana University; John W. Forney, *Life and Military Career of Winfield Scott Hancock* (Philadelphia, 1880), 335; Charles A. Clark, "Campaigning With the Sixth Maine," in *MOLLUS, Iowa Commandery* (Des Moines, 1879), 416.

81. Child, *Fifth New Hampshire,* 153, 155; *OR,* 233.

82. Murat Halstead, unidentified newspaper, FRSP; Child, *Fifth New Hampshire,* 153.

83. Child, *Fifth New Hampshire,* 150, 154, 156.

84. Brodie, "Fredericksburg: The Charge on the Stone Wall," *GAS&SM,* Oct. 6, 1883; Unidentified Soldier (64th New York) Reminiscences, p. 38, Indiana University.

85. *OR,* 235; Child, *Fifth New Hampshire,* 150, 158, 161, 164. Janvrin W. Graves, in Child, specified that the major fell beyond the brick house.

86. Child, *Fifth New Hampshire,* 156, 164.

87. Ibid., 160.

88. Ibid., 160–61.

89. Ibid., 150, 156, 157, 158, 164.

90. *OR,* 230, 233, 234; Bates, *Pennsylvania Volunteers,* 2:1170; Francis A. Walker, "Reams Station," *PMHSM* (1905), 5:288.

91. Stuckenberg, *I'm Surrounded by Methodists,* 44; *OR,* 234, 239, 250; Bates, *Pennsylvania Volunteers,* 5:520.

92. Harrison, *Gazetteer,* 1:139; "Notes on Thomas F. Proctor houses," Noel G. Harrison Papers, FRSP; C. A. Fuller, *War of 1861,* 80; *OR,* 237.

93. C. A. Fuller, *War of 1861,* 80–81; Isaac Plumb Memoir, CWMC.

94. *OR,* 233, 237; C. A. Fuller, *War of 1861,* 81.

95. *OR,* 237; Plumb Memoir, CWMC.

96. *OR,* 233–34, 236; Winfield S. Hancock to New York governor, Aug. 23, 1863, Frederick M. Dearborn Collection, Harvard.

97. *OR,* 129; Plumb Memoir, CWMC.

98. Lumpkin, letter, Dec. 30, 1862, Lumpkin Papers, University of Georgia; Preston, "The Glorious Light," 37; Stegeman, *These Men She Gave,* 75.

CHAPTER ELEVEN: "A DEVIL OF A TIME"

1. Ford, *Fifteenth Massachusetts,* 228; *OR,* 278; Francis W. Palfrey, *The Antietam and Fredericksburg* (New York, 1882), 168; O. O. Howard, *Autobiography,* 1:338.

2. Ward, *106th Pennsylvania,* 143; *OR,* 272, 278, 279; *History of the First Minnesota,* 265; *History of the 127th Pennsylvania,* 123.

3. *History of the 127th Pennsylvania,* 125; Jeremiah Rohrer Diary, Pennsylvania State Archives.

4. Silas Adams Reminiscences, CWMC; *History of the 127th Pennsylvania,* 126; Ward, *106th Pennsylvania,* 143; *Philadelphia Inquirer,* Dec. 31, 1862.

5. *History of the Nineteenth Massachusetts,* 178, 179; Abbott, *Fallen Leaves,* 152; *OR,* 274–75.

6. O. O. Howard, *Autobiography,* 1:342; Joseph R. C. Ward, "The Philadelphia Brigade at Fredericksburg," *GAS&SM,* Nov. 10, 1888; Ward, *106th Pennsylvania,* 137, 143; *Philadelphia Inquirer,* Dec. 31, 1862; Bruce, *Twentieth Massachusetts,* 215; *OR,* 284.

7. *OR,* 278; Ward, *106th Pennsylvania,* 143; Banes, *Philadelphia Brigade,* 141.

8. Ward, *106th Pennsylvania,* 143; *Philadelphia Inquirer,* Dec. 31, 1862; *History of the 127th Pennsylvania,* 126; Banes, *Philadelphia Brigade,* 141; Bates, *Pennsylvania Volunteers,* 2:702; *OR,* 281.

9. Ward, *106th Pennsylvania,* 143, 144; *Philadelphia Inquirer,* Dec. 31, 1862; *OR,* 278; Bates, *Pennsylvania Volunteers,* 2:702; F. M. Alexander, "A Reminiscence of the Late Unpleasantness," *Hummelstown (Pa.) Sun,* Jan. 5, 1914.

10. Ward, *106th Pennsylvania,* 144; Rohrer Diary, Pennsylvania State Archives.

11. Banes, *Philadelphia Brigade,* 141; Ward, *106th Pennsylvania,* 138, 144; *OR,* 278; *Philadelphia Inquirer,* Dec. 31, 1862.

12. *History of the 127th Pennsylvania,* 111, 127; William H. Myers, letter, Jan. 5, 1863, GWMC; Bates, *Pennsylvania Volunteers,* 2:702; Ward, *106th Pennsylvania,* 144; O. O. Howard, *Autobiography,* 1:340.

13. Bates, *Pennsylvania Volunteers,* 2:702; *OR,* 278.

14. *OR,* 625; W. Clark, *Histories,* 2:297; Chambers, *Diary,* 75.

15. *OR,* 278; Ward, *106th Pennsylvania,* 144; *Philadelphia Inquirer,* Dec. 31, 1862.

16. Ward, *106th Pennsylvania,* 146; *Philadelphia Inquirer,* Dec. 31, 1862; Banes, *Philadelphia Brigade,* 141; *OR,* 278.

17. Bruce, *Twentieth Massachusetts,* 215, 216; *OR,* 284; *History of the Nineteenth Massachusetts,* 179; Macy, letter, Dec. 20, 1862, MMO.

18. Abbott, *Fallen Leaves,* 148; Macy, letter, Dec. 20, 1862, MMO; Bruce, *Twentieth Massachusetts,* 216; *OR,* 284, 285; *History of the Nineteenth Massachusetts,* 179; Foster, "Crossing at Fredericksburg," *National Tribune,* Jan. 25, 1900.

19. *History of the Nineteenth Massachusetts,* 179; Bruce, *Twentieth Massachusetts,* 214–15; George H. Patch, letter, Dec. 23, 1862, LLC.

20. Abbott, *Fallen Leaves,* 148, 149; Macy, letter, Dec. 20, 1862, MMO. Governor John A. Andrews of Massachusetts appointed Macy as the commander of the 20th Massachusetts, even though Captain Dreher's commission predated Macy's. The men thought Dreher made a terrible commander and preferred Macy.

21. Macy, letter, Dec. 20, 1862, MMO; *OR,* 284.

22. *History of the Nineteenth Massachusetts,* 182; Oesterle, "Incidents," CWT; *OR,* 284.

23. *History of the Nineteenth Massachusetts,* 180, 182; William B. Hoitt, letter, Dec. 15, 1862, LLC; Patch, letter, Dec. 23, 1862, LLC; Adams, *Reminiscences,* 53; *OR,* 284.

24. *History of the Nineteenth Massachusetts,* 182; Adams, *Reminiscences,* 53.

25. *OR,* 284.

26. Abbott, *Fallen Leaves,* 149; Mason, letter, Dec. 19, 1862, MMO.

27. *OR,* 284; *History of the Nineteenth Massachusetts,* 180; Adams, *Reminiscences,* 53; Plympton, letter, Dec. 16, 1862, FRSP.

28. Patch, letter, Dec. 23, 1862, LLC; Adams, *Reminiscences,* 53; A. B. Weymouth, *Newcomb,* 112; *History of the Nineteenth Massachusetts,* 180–81; Hoitt, letter, Dec. 15, 1862, LLC. Adams said he moved to the left, and the 19th Massachusetts supported his assertion. But other evidence—including a later encounter with the 19th Maine on the field—suggests the regiment moved to the right and joined the 20th Massachusetts behind the tannery. Weymouth's Newcomb eulogy remarks that they moved "nearer the Pike" and halted behind houses "fronting the Pike." This was the Plank Road.

29. Abbott, *Fallen Leaves,* 149, 154; Mason, letter, Dec. 14, 1862, MMO; *History of the Nineteenth Massachusetts,* 183.

30. *OR,* 284.

31. William L. Saunders, letter, Dec. 30, 1862, SHC, UNC.

32. Walkup Journal, Duke.

33. Saunders, letter, Dec. 20, 1862, SHC, UNC; W. Clark, *Histories,* 3:70; Hickerson, *Echoes of Happy Valley,* 72.

34. *OR,* 588, 592, 598, 626; Mac Wyckoff, *History of the Second South Carolina Infantry* (Fredericksburg, Va., 1994), 54; Robert W. Shand Reminiscences, USC.

35. Shand Reminiscences, USC; Wyckoff, *Second South Carolina,* 56.

36. O. O. Howard, *Autobiography,* 1:342–43; *OR,* 269; Eames, letter, Dec. 20, 1862, M. J. Smith Collection, USAMHI; *OR,* 271; Ford, *Fifteenth Massachusetts,* 225.

37. Bowen, *From Ball's Bluff,* 142; *OR,* 271; Eames, letter, Dec. 20, 1862, M. J. Smith Collection, USAMHI; Ford, *Fifteenth Massachusetts,* 225; Eager, letter, Dec. 14, 1862, LLC.

38. Eames, letter, Dec. 20, 1862, M. J. Smith Collection, USAMHI; *OR,* 271; Eager, letter, Dec. 14, 1862, LLC.

39. O. O. Howard, *Autobiography,* 1:344; Charles H. Howard, letter, Dec. 13, 1862, William T. H. Brooks Papers, LC.

40. C. H. Howard, letter, Dec. 13, 1862, Brooks Papers, LC; *OR,* 269; 276; Chapin, *Thirty-fourth New York,* 80; *Reunions of Nineteenth Maine,* 8.

41. *OR,* 269, 270, 275; *Reunions of Nineteenth Maine,* 179; W., *Lewiston (Me.) Daily Evening Journal,* Oct. 16, 1862.

42. WSW, *Herkimer County (N.Y.) Journal,* Dec. 25, 1862; *OR,* 269; Silas Adams Reminiscences, CWMC. Some of the 19th Maine sources said that they assumed a position near a paper mill and the Mary Washington monument. There is a paper mill north of the monument, but the regiment entered the field south of the monument, placing them in much closer proximity to the tannery.

43. Sutton, *Civil War Stories,* 21.

44. Ibid., 28; John L. G. Wood Reminiscences, UDC Bound Typescripts, GDAH; Benjamin L. Mobely, letter, Jan. 30, 1863, Emory. Mobely wrote of the 15th's transfer from Cobb's Brigade: "the 15th N.C. Regt. is gone and I am glad of it."

45. O. O. Howard, *Autobiography,* 1:338, 344.

46. *OR,* 325; Leander W. Cogswell, *A History of the Eleventh New Hampshire Regiment* (Concord, N.H., 1891), 53.

47. *OR,* 287, 325, 330; Walcott, *Twenty-first Massachusetts,* 240; Cogswell, *Eleventh New Hampshire,* 53.

48. *OR,* 325, 328; John C. Currier, *From Concord to Fredericksburg: A Paper Prepared and Read before the California Commandery* [etc.], War Paper (Military Order of the Loyal Legion of the United States, California Commandery) Series, no. 15 ([San Francisco?], 1896), 11; Cogswell, *Eleventh New Hampshire,* 53, 55, 61.

49. Cogswell, *Eleventh New Hampshire,* 53; William Marvel, *Race of the Soil: The Ninth New Hampshire* (Wilmington, N.C., 1988), 99; Pope Diary, CWMC. Ferrero made several appearances on the field that Pope must have missed.

50. *OR,* 329; Cogswell, *Eleventh New Hampshire,* 54; Thomas H. Parker, *History of the Fifty-first Regiment of Pennsylvania Volunteers* (Philadelphia, 1869), 269; Walcott, *Twenty-first Massachusetts,* 241; Paige Memoir, Lang Collection, USAMHI.

51. Parker, *Fifty-first Pennsylvania,* 269; Paige Memoir, p. 22, Lang Collection, USAMHI;

Walcott, *Twenty-first Massachusetts,* 241; James M. Stone, *Personal Recollections of the Civil War* (Boston, 1917), 111, 112.

52. Paige memoir, p. 22, Lang Collection, USAMHI; Cogswell, *Eleventh New Hampshire,* 54–55, 62.

53. *OR,* 592; William M. Crumley reminiscences, Emory; W. R. Montgomery, letter, Dec. 17, 1862, Montgomery Papers, USC; Wyckoff, *Second South Carolina,* 56.

54. *OR,* 589, 592.

55. *OR,* 598–99; Walkup Journal, Duke; William R. Stackhouse and Walter F. Stackhouse, *The Stackhouse Family* (Morehead City, N.C., 1993), 184.

56. Pope Diary, CWMC; Parker, *Fifty-first Pennsylvania,* 270; Paige Memoir, p. 22, Long Collection, USAMHI; Cogswell, *Eleventh New Hampshire,* 54.

57. *OR,* 329; Currier, *From Concord to Fredericksburg,* 12; Cogswell, *Eleventh New Hampshire,* 55; Parker, *Fifty-first Pennsylvania,* 270.

58. C. A. Bartol, *The Nation's Hour: A Tribute to Major Sidney Willard* (Boston, 1862), 20, 50, 52; Pope Diary, CWMC; Jason Smith, letter, Dec. 16, 1862, Alonzo and Jason Smith Collection, USAMHI.

59. Stone, *Personal Recollections,* 110; *OR,* 327; Walcott, *Twenty-first Massachusetts,* 241.

60. Parker, *Fifty-first Pennsylvania,* 270–71.

61. Currier, *From Concord to Fredericksburg,* 12–13; Cogswell, *Eleventh New Hampshire,* 55, 57; Paige Memoir, p. 24, Lang Collection, USAMHI.

62. Paige Memoir, p. 24, Lang Collection, USAMHI; Cogswell, *Eleventh New Hampshire,* 57–58.

63. *OR,* 52; Jason Smith, letter, Dec. 16, 1862, A. and J. Smith Collection, USAMHI; Pope Diary, CWMC.

64. Walcott, *Twenty-first Massachusetts,* 241; Stone, *Personal Recollections,* 110–11.

65. Stone, *Personal Recollections,* 111; Walcott, *Twenty-first Massachusetts,* 242; *OR,* 325; James Pratt, Dec. 16, 1862 letter, James Pratt Papers, CWMC; Pope Diary, CWMC.

66. *OR,* 325, 330; George W. Whitman, *Civil War Letters of George Washington Whitman,* ed. Jerome M. Loving (Durham, N.C., 1975), 75, 152.

67. *OR,* 330; Parker, *Fifty-first Pennsylvania,* 273.

68. Walcott, *Twenty-first Massachusetts,* 244–45; *OR,* 325; George C. Rable, "It Is Well That War Is So Terrible: The Carnage at Fredericksburg," in *The Fredericksburg Campaign: Decision on the Rappahannock,* ed. Gary W. Gallagher (Chapel Hill, 1995), 53.

69. Oscar Lapham, "Recollections of Service in the Twelfth Regiment, R.I. Volunteers," in *Personal Narratives of Events in the War of the Rebellion: Rhode Island Soldiers and Sailors Historical Society* (Providence, 1885), 27–28; Robinson, diary, Robinson Papers, Dartmouth.

70. Lapham, "Recollections of Service," 28; Joseph Gould, *The Story of the Forty-eighth* (Philadelphia, 1908), 97; Bosbyshell, *The Forty-eighth in the War,* 97; Wren, *From New Berne,* 96; Hopkins, *Seventh Rhode Island,* 43.

71. Hopkins, *Seventh Rhode Island,* 42; Lymann Jackman, *History of the Sixth New Hampshire Regiment* (Concord, N.H., 1891), 122; Bosbyshell, *The Forty-eighth in the War,* 97; Wren, *From New Berne,* 96.

72. Robinson, diary, Robinson Papers, Dartmouth; T. A. Manchester, "The Twelfth Rhode Island," *Boston Journal,* n.d.; A. A. Batchelder diary, FRSP; Babbitt, letter, Dec. 10, 1862, Park Collection, FRSP.

73. Batchelder diary, FRSP; Jackman, *Sixth New Hampshire*, 122; Hopkins, *Seventh Rhode Island*, 43–44, 47; *OR*, 319.

74. *OR*, 319; Lapham, *Recollections of Service*, 30; Marvel, *Race of the Soil*, 100.

75. Lapham, *Recollections of Service*, 29, 30; George W. Diman, *Autobiography and Sketches of My Travels by Sea and Land* (Bristol, R.I., 1896), 49; *OR*, 324.

76. *OR*, 320, 324; Lapham, *Recollections of Service*, 30.

77. *OR*, 320, 565, 567, 587; Manchester, "The Twelfth Rhode Island," *Boston Journal*, n.d.; Lapham, *Recollections of Service*, 31; Diman, *Autobiography*, 49; Daniel E. Hurd, "My Experiences in the Civil War," Daniel Emerson Hurd Collection, USAMHI; Wise, *Long Arm of Lee*, 1:370, 380.

78. *OR*, 320–21, 324; Hurd, "My Experiences," Hurd Collection, USAMHI; Marvel, *Race of the Soil*, 100; Lapham, *Recollections of Service*, 31–32.

79. *OR*, 320, 323; Hopkins, *Seventh Rhode Island*, 44–45.

80. Jackman, *Sixth New Hampshire*, 122; Hopkins, *Seventh Rhode Island*, 44–46; Batchelder Diary, FRSP. Hopkins stated that the men were in close proximity to the 51st New York of Ferrero's brigade.

81. Hopkins, *Seventh Rhode Island*, 44–46.

82. Ward, *106th Pennsylvania*, 138, 145; Ward, letter to the Editor, *Philadelphia Inquirer*, Dec. 31, 1862; *OR*, 279, 323; Hopkins, *Seventh Rhode Island*, 45–46.

83. J. Chandler Gregg, *Life in the Army* (Philadelphia, 1868), 79–80; Rohrer Diary, Pennsylvania State Archives; *History of the 127th Pennsylvania*, 132; William P. Conrad, letter, Jan. 20, 1863, Save the Flags Collection, USAMHI.

84. Jackman, *Sixth New Hampshire*, 123; Guilford, "The 127th Penna. Infantry at the Capture of Fredericksburg," *Philadelphia Weekly Times*, June 16, 1886; Bates, *Pennsylvania Volunteers*, 4:161; John F. Kerper Reminiscences, FRSP; *History of the 127th Pennsylvania*, 132.

85. Barker, letter, Dec. 17, 1862, Rhode Island Historical Society.

86. Lapham, *Recollections of Service*, 32.

87. Ibid., 32–33, 35; Diman, *Autobiography*, 50.

88. *OR*, 322; Marvel, *Race of the Soil*, 100–101.

89. Hurd, "My Experiences," Hurd Collection, USAMHI; Robinson, diary, Robinson Papers, Dartmouth.

90. Powell, "War Talks," Duke; D. Augustus Dickert, *History of Kershaw's Brigade* (Newberry, S.C., 1899), 187.

91. *OR*, 595; Robert Franklin Fleming Memoir, FRSP; Dickert, *Kershaw's Brigade*, 183.

92. *OR*, 593–94, 597, 599.

93. Ibid., 589, 594–95, 596; Charles A. Malloy, diary, Charles A. Malloy Papers, USAMHI; Dickert, *Kershaw's Brigade*, 187.

94. *OR*, 597; J. J. McDaniel, "Diary of Battles, Marches and Incidents of the Seventh S.C. Regiment," p. 18, FRSP.

95. Marvel, *Race of the Soil*, 101.

96. *OR*, 322.

97. Gould, *Story of the Forty-eighth*, 97–99; Bosbyshell, *The Forty-eighth in the War*, 97; *OR*, 322.

98. Gould, *Story of the Forty-eighth,* 99.

99. Bosbyshell, *The Forty-eighth in the War,* 97; *OR,* 322; Bates, *Pennsylvania Volunteers,* 1:1195; Gould, *Story of the Forty-eighth,* 100; Harrison, *Fredericksburg Civil War Sites,* 2:182; Wren, *From New Berne,* 95.

100. E. P. Alexander, *Military Memoirs,* 304; *OR,* 130, 269–71, 276, 280; Banes, *Philadelphia Brigade,* 146; Ward, *106th Pennsylvania,* 146; J. C. Gregg, *Life in the Army,* 80; *History of the Nineteenth Massachusetts,* 181; Abbott, *Fallen Leaves,* 149; Mason, letter, Dec. 14, 1862, MMO; Ford, *Fifteenth Massachusetts,* 229.

101. *OR,* 321, 323–24, 327, 329, 330; Bartol, *Nation's Hour,* 49; Currier, *From Concord to Fredericksburg,* 15; G. W. Whitman, *Civil War Letters,* 152; Jackman, *Sixth New Hampshire,* 123; Hurd, "My Experiences," Hurd Collection, USAMHI; Robinson, diary, Robinson Papers, Dartmouth; Wren, *From New Berne,* 95; Lapham, *Recollections of Service,* 36.

102. *OR,* 184; *ORS,* 3:764.

103. *ORS,* 3:744; *OR,* 393.

104. *ORS,* 3:745; *OR,* 193.

105. *OR,* 193; *ORS,* 3:746.

106. *OR,* 393, 395; Morrow, letter, Dec. 21, 1862, HCW; Sprenger, *122nd Pennsylvania,* 141; Weygant, *124th New York,* 67.

CHAPTER TWELVE: "THE DIE IS CAST"

1. Halstead, unidentified newspaper, copy in FRSP; Burnside, quoted in *RJC,* 56; Burnside, letter, June 17, 1863, NA; Franklin, quoted in *RJC,* 56.

2. Meade, quoted in *RJC,* 693; Cleaves, *Meade,* 92; Thomson and Rauch, *Bucktails,* 236; William F. Smith, *Autobiography of Major General William F. Smith,* ed. Herbert M. Schiller (Dayton, 1990), 62; Bache, *Meade,* 240.

3. Franklin, quoted in *RJC,* 56.

4. W. Clark, *Histories,* 4:170; Little Mack, letter to the editor, *Hunterdon (N.J.) Republican,* Jan. 2, 1863; Alanson A. Haines, *History of the Fifteenth Regiment New Jersey Volunteers* (New York, 1883), 31.

5. O'Reilly, *Jackson at Fredericksburg,* 169.

6. Haines, *Fifteenth New Jersey,* 33.

7. Samuel B. Fisher, letter, Dec. 28, 1862, LLC; W. Clark, *Histories,* 4:170; Scales, *Fredericksburg,* 15; Little Mack, letter to the editor, *Hunterdon (N.J.) Republican,* Jan. 2, 1863; Kenneth W. Jones, "The Fourth Alabama: First Blood," *Alabama Historical Quarterly* 38 no. 3 (spring 1974): 200.

8. Davidson, *Greenlee Davidson,* 65–66; O'Reilly, *Jackson at Fredericksburg,* 169; J. R. Cole, *Miscellany,* 212.

9. Robert T. Cole, *From Huntsville to Appomattox,* ed. Jeffrey D. Stocker (Knoxville, 1996), 82.

10. J. R. Cole, *Miscellany,* 212; Scales, *Fredericksburg,* 15; W. Clark, *Histories,* 1:309.

11. R. T. Cole, *From Huntsville to Appomattox,* 82.

12. W. Clark, *Histories,* 4:170–71. S. W. Branch, letter, Dec. 17, 1862, University of Georgia.

13. H. Walter Berryman, letter, Dec. 27, 1862, FRSP.

14. W. Clark, *Histories,* 3:408; H. W. Berryman, letter, Dec. 27, 1862, FRSP; Edward Mount, letter, Dec. 23, 1862, CWMC.

15. Haines, *Fifteenth New Jersey,* 33; Mount, letter, Dec. 23, 1862, CWMC.

16. *OR,* 528; Haines, *Fifteenth New Jersey,* 33.

17. Little Mack, letter to the editor, *Hunterdon (N.J.) Republican,* Jan. 2, 1863; Haines, *Fifteenth New Jersey,* 33; *Hunterdon (N.J.) Republican,* Dec. 19, 1863.

18. A. Ellis, letter, Nov. 14, 1868, E. P. Alexander Papers, SHC, UNC; W. Clark, *Histories,* 4:171; Little Mack, letter to the editor, *Hunterdon (N.J.) Republican,* Jan. 2, 1863; Haines, *Fifteenth New Jersey,* 33.

19. Berryman, letter, Dec. 27, 1862, FRSP; W. Clark, *Histories,* 3:268, 408; L. Voorhees, letter to the editor, *Hunterdon (N.J.) Republican,* Dec. 26, 1862; Mount, letter, Dec. 23, 1862, CWMC.

20. Evander McIvor Law, letter, Oct. 15, 1866, E. P. Alexander Papers, SHC, UNC; Birney, quoted in *RJC,* 706–707; Mount, letter, Dec. 23, 1862, CWMC.

21. *OR, 378, 379.*

22. *OR,* 379.

23. G. T. Stevens, *Three Years,* 171.

24. R. T. Cole, *From Huntsville to Appomattox,* 82; James A. Lowery, letter, Dec. 17, 1862, FRSP; E. A. Patterson Reminiscences, FRSP; W. Clark, *Histories,* 1:309; Law, letter, Oct. 15, 1866, E. P. Alexander Papers, SHC, UNC; *Selma (Ala.) Morning Reporter,* Dec. 29, 1862.

25. Jones, "The Fourth Alabama Infantry," 201.

26. *ORS,* 3:805.

27. Austin, *Georgia Boys with Stonewall Jackson,* 57; W. Clark, *Histories,* 3:269; Polley, *Hood's Texas Brigade,* 189.

28. *OR,* 404; Robert Goldwaite Carter, *Four Brothers in Blue* (Washington, D.C., 1913), 193; *History of the 118th Pennsylvania,* 122; John L. Smith, letter, Dec. 26, 1862, John L. Smith Papers, CWMC.

29. Joshua L. Chamberlain, "My Story of Fredericksburg," *Cosmopolitan Magazine,* Jan. 1913, 152; Ellis Spear, "My Story of Fredericksburg and Comments Thereon," unpublished memoir, 1914. FRSP; Eugene A. Nash, *A History of the Forty-fourth Regiment New York Volunteer Infantry* (Chicago, 1911), 115; Ellis Spear, *The Civil War Recollections of General Ellis Spear,* ed. Abbott Spear (Orono, Me., 1997), 298.

30. Chamberlain, "My Story of Fredericksburg," 152; Everson, "Forward against Marye's," *Philadelphia Weekly Times,* n.d.; Hayes Reminiscences, Joshua L. Chamberlain Papers, LC; R. G. Carter, *Four Brothers,* 207; *OR,* 404; John B. Winslow, letter, Dec. 17, 1862, FRSP; John L. Parker, *History of the Twenty-second Massachusetts Infantry* (Boston, 1887), 225; Cicero, letter to the editor, *Rochester Democrat and American,* Dec. 22, 1862.

31. R. G. Carter, *Four Brothers,* 194, 199; *OR,* 408; John O'Connell Reminiscences, CWMC; *History of the 118th Pennsylvania,* 122.

32. J. L. Smith, letter, Dec. 26, 1862, J. L. Smith Papers, CWMC; Everson, "Forward against Marye's," *Philadelphia Weekly Times,* n.d.; O'Connell Reminiscences, CWMC; *History of the 118th Pennsylvania,* 122, 124.

33. *History of the 118th Pennsylvania,* 125; J. L. Smith, Dec. 26, 1862, letter, J. L. Smith Papers, CWMC.

34. *OR,* 404, 408; Scorer, letter to the editor, *Rochester Daily Union and Advertiser,* Dec. 20, 1862; R. G. Carter, *Four Brothers,* 207; J. L. Parker, *Twenty-second Massachusetts,* 225; *History of the 118th Pennsylvania,* 128.

35. *History of the 118th Pennsylvania,* 125; William P. Alderman, Dec. 17, 1862, letter, FRSP; *OR,* 405.

36. *History of the 118th Pennsylvania,* 125, 126; R. G. Carter, *Four Brothers,* 194; J. L. Parker, *Twenty-second Massachusetts,* 225.

37. *History of the 118th Pennsylvania,* 126; J. L. Smith, letter, Dec. 15, 1862, J. L. Smith Papers, CWMC.

38. Everson, "Forward against Marye's," *Philadelphia Weekly Times,* n.d.; *History of the 118th Pennsylvania,* 127; J. L. Smith, letter, Dec. 15, 1862, J. L. Smith Papers, CWMC; R. G. Carter, *Four Brothers,* 195.

39. J. L. Smith, letter, Dec. 26, 1862, J. L. Smith Papers, CWMC; R. G. Carter, *Four Brothers,* 185; *History of the 118th Pennsylvania,* 128; J. L. Parker, *Twenty-second Massachusetts,* 225.

40. J. L. Parker, *Twenty-second Massachusetts,* 226; R. G. Carter, *Four Brothers,* 195, 199, 213; James H. Mundy, *Second to None: The Story of the Second Maine Volunteer Infantry* (Scarborough, Me., 1992), 216. Lieutenant Eugene Carter, of the U.S. Regulars, noted in a letter, "General Griffin is wounded slightly."

41. Hayes Reminiscences, Chamberlain Papers, LC; *OR,* 409.

42. Hayes Reminiscences, Chamberlain Papers, LC.

43. Ibid.

44. Everson, "Forward against Marye's," *Philadelphia Weekly Times,* n.d.

45. Ibid.; Alderman, letter, Dec. 17, 1862, FRSP; Hayes Reminiscences, Chamberlain Papers, LC.

46. Erastus W. Everson, quoted in *The Fifth Army Corps* by William H. Powell (New York, 1896), 388, 389; Hayes Reminiscences, Chamberlain Papers, LC.

47. Hayes Reminiscences, Chamberlain Papers, LC; Alderman, letter, Dec. 17, 1862, FRSP.

48. R. G. Carter, *Four Brothers,* 195, 307; J. L. Parker, *Twenty-second Massachusetts,* 226; Michigan Adjutant General's Department, *Record of Service,* 1:23.

49. Draper, "Marye's Hights" [*sic*], *National Tribune,* May 5, 1898; Cicero, letter to the editor, *Rochester Democrat and American,* Dec. 22, 1862.

50. *OR,* 405, 409; W. G., letter to the editor, *Rochester Democrat and American,* Dec. 22, 1862; Scorer, letter to the editor, *Rochester Daily Union and Advertiser,* Dec. 20, 1862; A. G. Cooper, letter to the editor, *Rochester Daily Union and Advertiser,* Dec. 20, 1862.

51. R. G. Carter, *Four Brothers,* 195; J. L. Parker, *Twenty-second Massachusetts,* 226.

52. R. G. Carter, *Four Brothers,* 195–96, 207.

53. Ibid., 196; J. L. Parker, *Twenty-second Massachusetts,* 226; Cicero, letter to the editor, *Rochester Democrat and American,* Dec. 22, 1862; *OR,* 322, 328, 408; Pope Diary, CWMC.

54. Michigan Adjutant General's Department, *Record of Services,* 1:23; Draper, "Marye's Hights" [*sic*], *National Tribune,* May 5, 1898. Draper stated that he stood 10 feet from the

participants during the exchange, but he misidentified the parties as Burnside and Marshall. Draper's lapse casts some doubt on his veracity.

55. *History of the 118th Pennsylvania,* 128–29; J. L. Smith, letter, Dec. 26, 1862, J. L. Smith Papers, CWMC.

56. Ibid., 129.

57. Ibid., 129; *OR,* 405; Winslow, letter, Dec. 17, 1862, FRSP.

58. *OR,* 409; R. G. Carter, *Four Brothers,* 196, 208; J. L. Parker, *Twenty-second Massachusetts,* 227.

59. *OR,* 405, 409; Mundy, *Second to None,* 216–17; O'Connell Reminiscences, CWMC; R. G. Carter, *Four Brothers,* 208.

60. *OR,* 405, 409; Winslow, letter, Dec. 17, 1862, FRSP.

61. *History of the 118th Pennsylvania,* 130; J. L. Smith, letter, Dec. 26, 1862, J. L. Smith Papers, CWMC; William M. Hemmenway Reminiscences, CWMC; R. G. Carter, *Four Brothers,* 208.

62. *History of the 118th Pennsylvania,* 130; Cooper, letter to the editor, *Rochester Daily Union and Advertiser,* Dec. 20, 1862; R. G. Carter, *Four Brothers,* 196; Winslow, letter, Dec. 17, 1862, FRSP.

63. R. G. Carter, *Four Brothers,* 196.

64. Bates, *Pennsylvania Volunteers,* 2:455; Coston Rohrer, letter, Dec. 17, 1862, Emory; Michael H. MacNamara, *History of the Ninth Regiment Massachusetts Volunteers* (Boston, 1899), 254. Rohrer listed the order of march as: 14th New York leading, followed by 9th Massachusetts, 62nd Pennsylvania, 4th Michigan, and 32nd Massachusetts.

65. MacNamara, *History of the Ninth Regiment,* 255.

66. Francis J. Parker, *History of the Thirty-second Regiment Massachusetts Volunteers* (Boston, 1880), 130; Bates, *Pennsylvania Volunteers,* 2:455; Rohrer, letter, Dec. 17, 1862, Emory; MacNamara, *History of the Ninth Regiment,* 255; Michael H. MacNamara, *The Irish Ninth* (Boston, 1867), 159.

67. MacNamara, *History of the Ninth Regiment,* 255; F. J. Parker, *Thirty-second Massachusetts,* 130; Rohrer, letter, Dec. 17, 1862, Emory.

68. Jesse B. Young, *What a Boy Saw in the Army* (New York, 1894), 144; James C. Hamilton Memoir, typescript, CWLM.

69. Young, *What a Boy Saw,* 144–45.

70. Joseph H. Leighty, letter, Dec. 26, 1862, CWMC; Young, *What a Boy Saw,* 136; Hamilton Memoir, CWLM; *OR,* 397. Hamilton called Frederick Street "Fredericksburg Street."

71. Young, *What a Boy Saw,* 145.

72. *OR,* 397; Anthony Washie, "Story of Enoch T. Baker," CWMC.

73. Walkup Journal, Duke; *OR,* 628–29; Chambers, *Diary,* 75; H.H.G., "An Incident," in newspaper "History and Biography of North Carolina," by S. B. Weeks, Weeks Papers, SHC, UNC.

74. *OR,* 608; Eye-witness, letter to the editor, *Athens Southern Watchman,* Dec. 24, 1862; J. W. Woods Reminiscences, vol. 4, UDC Bound Typescripts, GDAH; Crumley Reminiscences, Emory.

75. Young, *What a Boy Saw,* 147; Leighty, letter, Dec. 26, 1862, CWMC; Robert C. Lam-

berton Diary, Western Reserve; Hamilton Memoir, CWLM; Thomas E. Merchant, *Eighty-fourth Regiment, Pennsylvania Volunteers Address* (n.p., 1889), 56.

76. *OR,* 397; Washie, "Enoch T. Baker," CWMC.

77. Henry B. James, *Memories of the Civil War* (New Bedford, Mass., 1898), 27; Rohrer, letter, Dec. 17, 1862, Emory.

78. Thomas Josiah, letter, Dec. 11, 1862, FRSP; Rohrer, letter, Dec. 17, 1862, Emory; MacNamara, *History of the Ninth Regiment,* 255. Josiah started his letter dated Dec. 11, but continued his narrative over the course of the battle.

79. Bates, *Pennsylvania Volunteers,* 2:455–56; Rohrer, letter, Dec. 17, 1862, Emory.

80. John M. Bancroft Diary, Bancroft Collection, UM; Rohrer, letter, Dec. 17, 1862, Emory; MacNamara, *The Irish Ninth,* 160.

81. William F. Robinson, letter, Dec. 18, 1862, Michigan Historical Collection, UM; Bates, *Pennsylvania Volunteers,* 2:456; MacNamara, *History of the Ninth Regiment,* 256.

82. Rohrer, letter, Dec. 17, 1862, Emory; MacNamara, *History of the Ninth Regiment,* 255; F. J. Parker, *Thirty-second Massachusetts,* 131; Bates, *Pennsylvania Volunteers,* 2:456.

83. Bates, *Pennsylvania Volunteers,* 2:456; MacNamara, *The Irish Ninth,* 160; F. J. Parker, *Thirty-second Massachusetts,* 132; W. F. Robinson, letter, Dec. 18, 1862, Michigan Historical Collection, UM.

84. Rohrer, letter, Dec. 17, 1862, Emory; MacNamara, *History of the Ninth Regiment,* 257; F. J. Parker, *Thirty-second Massachusetts,* 132.

85. *OR,* 397; Washie, "Enoch T. Baker," CWMC; Hamilton Memoir, CWLM; E. P. Alexander, *Fighting for the Confederacy,* 175–76.

86. Lamberton Diary, Western Reserve; Young, *What a Boy Saw,* 147; Thomas Goldsborough, letter, Dec. 25, 1862, FRSP.

87. Goldsborough, letter, Dec. 25, 1862, FRSP; Young, *What a Boy Saw,* 150; Hamilton Memoir, CWLM.

88. F. J. Parker, *Thirty-second Massachusetts,* 132; MacNamara, *History of the Ninth Regiment,* 257.

89. Spear, *Recollections,* 19, 299; Chamberlain, "My Story of Fredericksburg," 152; Chamberlain, letter to the editor, *Bangor Daily Whig and Courier,* Dec. 27, 1862; *OR,* 411, 413; Amos M. Judson, *History of the Eighty-third Pennsylvania Volunteers* (Erie, Pa., 1865), 58.

90. Spear, *Recollections,* 19; Theodore Gerrish, *Army Life: A Private's Reminiscences of the Civil War* (Portland, Me., 1882), 76; Chamberlain, "My Story of Fredericksburg," 152.

91. Holman S. Melcher, *With a Flash of His Sword: The Writings of Major Holman S. Melcher,* ed. William B. Styple (Kearny, N.J., 1994), 11; *OR,* 411; Edward Hill, "The Last Charge at Fredericksburg," in *Proceedings of the Third Brigade Association, First Division, Fifth Army Corps* (New York, 1892), 34; Judson, *Eighty-third Pennsylvania,* 58; Alfred M. Apted Memoir, CWMC.

92. Spear, "My Story," FRSP, 44; Spear, *Recollections,* 19, 20; Chamberlain, letter to the editor, *Bangor Daily Whig and Courier,* Dec. 27, 1862; Gerrish, *Army Life,* 76; Unsigned letter to the editor, *Brunswick (Maine) Telegraph,* Jan. 2, 1863; Judson, *Eighty-third Pennsylvania,* 58; Oliver Willcox Norton, *Army Letters, 1861–1865* (Chicago, 1903), 130.

93. Spear, "My Story," p. 41, FRSP; Spear, *Recollections,* 20.

94. *Brunswick (Maine) Telegraph,* Jan. 2, 1863.

95. *OR,* 411; Spear, *Recollections,* 19–20, 300.

96. Judson, *Eighty-third Pennsylvania,* 58; *OR,* 411; Hill, "The Last Charge," 34; Spear, *Recollections,* 20; Spear, "My Story," p. 41, FRSP.

97. Hill, "The Last Charge," 35–36.

98. Ibid., 35; Apted Memoir, CWMC; *OR,* 411. Stockton claimed that his objective was predetermined, calling the Jennings house "the position designated."

99. Hill, "The Last Charge," 33, 35; *OR,* 411; Chamberlain, letter to the editor, *Bangor Daily Whig and Courier,* Dec. 27, 1862; Spear, "My Story," p. 42, FRSP; Nash, *Forty-fourth New York,* 115. Spear challenged Chamberlain's allegation that the 12th and 17th New York regiments failed to advance, scoffing that that would make Stockton a "pretty careless brigade commander."

100. Judson, *Eighty-third Pennsylvania,* 58; *OR,* 413.

101. Chamberlain, letter to the editor, *Bangor Daily Whig and Courier,* Dec. 27, 1862; Spear, *Recollections,* 301; Gerrish, *Army Life,* 77.

102. Spear, *Recollections,* 300; Gerrish, *Army Life,* 77; Melcher, *With a Flash of His Sword,* 13; Chamberlain, "My Story of Fredericksburg," 153.

103. George W. Carleton, letter, Jan. 8, 1866, Yale; Melcher, *With a Flash of His Sword,* 13; Nash, *Forty-fourth New York,* 115; R. G. Carter, *Four Brothers,* 196.

104. *OR,* 413; Norton, *Army Letters,* 130; *Brunswick (Maine) Telegraph,* Jan. 2, 1863.

105. Cicero, letter to the editor, *Rochester Democrat and American,* Dec. 22, 1862; R. G. Carter, *Four Brothers,* 196; J. L. Parker, *Twenty-second Massachusetts,* 227; *Brunswick (Maine) Telegraph,* Jan. 2, 1863.

106. Chamberlain, "My Story of Fredericksburg," 153; Carleton, letter, Jan. 8, 1866, Yale.

107. *OR,* 413; *Brunswick (Maine) Telegraph,* Jan. 2, 1863; Gerrish, *Army Life,* 77; Chamberlain, "My Story of Fredericksburg," 153.

108. *OR,* 413; Judson, *Eighty-third Pennsylvania,* 57, 58; Apted Memoir, CWMC.

109. Hill, "The Last Charge," 34.

110. J. L. Smith, letter, Dec. 15, 1862, J. L. Smith Papers, CWMC; R. G. Carter, *Four Brothers,* 195; Hayes Reminiscences, Chamberlain Papers, LC.

CHAPTER THIRTEEN: "THE GATES OF HELL"

1. Owen, *In Camp and Battle,* 191; *OR,* 574; Baker, *Reminiscent Story,* 58.

2. Owen, *In Camp and Battle,* 190–91.

3. J. G. Hutchison, " Fredericksburg," in *War Sketches and Incidents,* ed. Iowa Commandery, Military Order of the Loyal Legion of the United States (Des Moines, 1889), 272; Joseph R. Orwig, *History of the 131st Pennsylvania Volunteers* (Williamsport, Pa., 1902), 113; *Under the Maltese Cross* (Pittsburgh, 1910), 96–97.

4. J. H. Rhodes, *Battery B, 1st Rhode Island Light Artillery,* 142; Orwig, *131st Pennsylvania,* 113.

5. *The Fifth Reunion of the 155th Regiment Penna. Volunteers* (Pittsburgh, 1896), 28; Carswell McClellan, *General Andrew A. Humphreys at Malvern Hill and Fredericksburg* (St. Paul, Minn., 1888), 12. The emphasis is in the original.

6. Nathaniel W. Brown, letter, Dec. 23, 1862, FRSP; *Under the Maltese Cross,* 95.

7. Yard, "Unable to Help," *National Tribune,* March 1, 1894.

8. *OR,* 443; John W. Phillips, letter, Dec. 18, 1862, FRSP; Samuel L. North, letter, Dec. 18, 1862, CWMC; Orwig, *131st Pennsylvania,* 113.

9. James M. Kincaid Reminiscences, Bucknell; James B. Ross Diary, Historical Society of Western Pennsylvania; William J. Armstrong, *Red-tape and Pigeon-hole Generals* (New York, 1864), 232; Orwig, *131st Pennsylvania,* 114; *Under the Maltese Cross,* 95–96.

10. Orwig, *131st Pennsylvania,* 114; *Under the Maltese Cross,* 95; C. McClellan, *Humphreys,* 12; Armstrong, *Red-tape,* 234.

11. J. G. Hutchison, "Fredericksburg," 268; Orwig, *131st Pennsylvania,* 116; *OR,* 438–39; Phillips, letter, Dec. 18, 1862, FRSP.

12. Adolfo Fernandez Cabada Diary, CWMC; Orwig, *131st Pennsylvania,* 114; Kincaid Reminiscences, Bucknell; Erastus B. Tyler Report, Office of the Adjutant General, Department of Military Affairs, Pennsylvania State Archives; Armstrong, *Red-tape,* 233–34.

13. *OR,* 430, 432; Andrew A. Humphreys to Swinton, May 10, 1866, in Henry H. Humphreys, *Major General Andrew Atkinson Humphreys United States Volunteers at Fredericksburg and Farmville* (Chicago, n.d.), 27; Cabada Diary, CWMC; C. McClellan, *Humphreys,* 13–14, 19.

14. Yard, "Unable to Help," *National Tribune,* March 1, 1894; Orwig, *131st Pennsylvania,* 115; William Wertz, "Story of the 133d Regiment: Taken from the Diary of a Veteran," CWMC; *OR,* 446.

15. MacNamara, *History of the Ninth Regiment,* 256; A. McClellan, *Humphreys,* 13, 14; *OR,* 430–31; Humphreys, *Humphreys at Fredericksburg,* 17, 20, 21.

16. Armstrong, *Red-tape,* 234–35; *Miners Journal,* Jan. 3, 1863.

17. *OR,* 275, 276, 439; Phillips, letter, Dec. 18, 1862, FRSP; Armstrong, *Red-tape,* 235; North, letter, Dec. 18, 1862, CWMC.

18. *OR,* 620; R. Prosper Landry Diary, CWMC.

19. *OR,* 620.

20. WSW, letter to the editor, *Herkimer County (N.Y.) Journal,* Dec. 15, 1862; *OR,* 439, 440; Armstrong, *Red-tape,* 236; *Miners Journal,* Jan. 3, 1863; North, letter, Dec. 18, 1862, CWMC; Chapin, *Thirty-fourth New York,* 82.

21. *OR,* 621; Landry Diary, CWMC.

22. *OR,* 225.

23. *History of the First Minnesota,* 268; B, letter to the editor, *Glen Falls (N.Y.) Messenger,* Jan. 20, 1863; Chester F. Hunt, letter, Dec. 19, 1862, Earle M. Hess Collection, USAMHI; Ziba C. Thayer, letter, Dec. 23, 1862, FRSP; *OR,* 225, 267; Orwig, *131st Pennsylvania,* 116; J. R. Rhodes, *Battery B, 1st Rhode Island,* 139.

24. J. R. Rhodes, *Battery B, 1st Rhode Island,* 139; B, letter to the editor, *Glen Falls (N.Y.) Messenger,* Jan. 20, 1863.

25. B, letter to the editor, *Glen Falls (N.Y.) Messenger,* Jan. 20, 1863; Thayer, letter, Dec. 23, 1862, FRSP; *OR,* 267–68; J. R. Rhodes, *Battery B, 1st Rhode Island,* 139.

26. Thayer, letter, Dec. 23, 1862, FRSP; *OR,* 268; J. R. Rhodes, *Battery B, 1st Rhode Island,* 139–40.

27. *OR,* 289.

28. Ibid., 289; J. R. Rhodes, *Battery B, 1st Rhode Island,* 140–41; B, letter to the editor, *Glen Falls (N.Y.) Messenger,* Jan. 20, 1863; Thayer, letter, Dec. 29, 1862, FRSP.

29. J. R. Rhodes, *Battery B, 1st Rhode Island,* 143; Charles H. Howard, letter, Dec. 13, 1862, Brooks Papers, LC; Davis, letter, Dec. 16, 1862, Brown; Moe, *Last Full Measure,* 213; John Q. Imholte, *The First Volunteers: History of the First Minnesota* (Minneapolis, 1963), 110; Ward, *106th Pennsylvania,* 139; Banes, *Philadelphia Brigade,* 142; *OR,* 279.

30. E. P. Alexander, *Fighting for the Confederacy,* 177–78; Owen, *In Camp and Battle,* 190–92.

31. *OR,* 576; E. P. Alexander, *Fighting for the Confederacy,* 178.

32. E. P. Alexander, *Fighting for the Confederacy,* 178.

33. Orwig, *131st Pennsylvania,* 113, 124; Hutchison, "Fredericksburg," 268; C. McClellan, *Humphreys,* 15; Brown, letter, Dec. 23, 1862, FRSP; *Under the Maltese Cross,* 97; Carol Reardon, "The Forlorn Hope: Brig. Gen. Andrew A. Humphrey's Pennsylvania Division at Fredericksburg," in *The Fredericksburg Campaign: Decision on the Rappahannock,* ed. Gary W. Gallagher (Chapel Hill, 1995), 89. Orwig identified General John C. Caldwell as the one who notified Hancock, but Caldwell had left the field wounded before this.

34. C. McClellan, *Humphreys,* 15; Henry H. Humphreys, *Andrew Atkinson Humphreys: A Biography* (Philadelphia, 1924), 179; Humphreys, *Humphreys at Fredericksburg,* 10; Reardon, "The Forlorn Hope," 89.

35. Orwig, *131st Pennsylvania,* 116; Ross Diary, Historical Society of Western Pennsylvania; Brown, letter, Dec. 23, 1862, FRSP.

36. *OR,* 443, 446; Humphreys, *Humphreys at Fredericksburg,* 12, 14; Brown, letter, Dec. 23, 1862, FRSP; Wertz, "Story of the 133d Regiment," CWMC.

37. C. McClellan, *Humphreys,* 27; *OR,* 443; Ward, *106th Pennsylvania,* 138; Banes, *Philadelphia Brigade,* 143.

38. *OR,* 443; Cabada Diary, CWMC.

39. Humphreys, *Humphreys at Fredericksburg,* 12; *OR,* 443, 446; Brown, letter, Dec. 23, 1862, FRSP; *Under the Maltese Cross,* 102; Wertz, "Story of the 133d Regiment," CWMC.

40. *OR,* 576; E. P. Alexander, *Fighting for the Confederacy,* 178.

41. E. P. Alexander, *Fighting for the Confederacy,* 179.

42. Humphreys, *Humphreys at Fredericksburg,* 18; Wertz, "Story of the 133d Regiment," CWMC; *OR,* 444–45; Ross Diary, Historical Society of Western Pennsylvania; Orwig, *131st Pennsylvania,* 112; Hutchison, "Fredericksburg," 265.

43. Brown, letter, Dec. 23, 1862, FRSP; John H. Kerr, *Oration Delivered at the First Reunion of the 155th Regiment Pennsylvania Veteran Volunteers* (Pittsburgh, 1875), 9; *Under the Maltese Cross,* 101; *OR,* 445, 448; C. McClellan, *Humphreys,* 28.

44. *Under the Maltese Cross,* 102; John C. Anderson, letter, Jan. 10, 1863, CWMC; Brown, letter, Dec. 23, 1862, FRSP; Orwig, *131st Pennsylvania,* 119.

45. Anderson, letter, Jan. 10, 1863, CWMC; Yard, "Unable to Help," *National Tribune,* March 1, 1894; *OR,* 432, C. McClellan, *Humphreys,* 15.

46. C. McClellan, *Humphreys,* 16, 34; *OR,* 431; Humphreys, *Humphreys: A Biography,* 178; Kerr, *Oration,* 9; Yard, "Unable to Help," *National Tribune,* March 1, 1894.

47. *Reunions of the Nineteenth Maine,* 72; *OR,* 275, 431; Abbott, *Fallen Leaves,* 154.

48. *OR,* 440; Martin L. Werkeiser, "Recollections of Fredericksburg," CWMC; J. M. Clark, petition for Medal of Honor, June 6, 1888, Matthew S. Quay Papers, University of Pittsburgh.

49. William O. Campbell Diary, FRSP.

50. *OR,* 431, 437; Tyler Report, Pennsylvania State Archives; Humphreys, *Humphreys at Fredericksburg,* 28–29; C. McClellan, *Humphreys,* 17; Reardon, "The Forlorn Hope," 93.

51. Phillips, letter, Dec. 18, 1862, FRSP; Armstrong, *Red-tape,* 239; Tyler Report, Pennsylvania State Archives; *OR,* 431, 437; Reardon, "The Forlorn Hope," 94.

52. *OR,* 431, 439, 440; Yard, "Unable to Help," *National Tribune,* March 1, 1894; Cabada Diary, CWMC; Werkeiser, "Recollections of Fredericksburg," CWMC.

53. Yard, "Unable to Help," *National Tribune,* March 1, 1894; *OR,* 432, 437; Phillips, letter, Dec. 18, 1862, FRSP; Armstrong, *Red-tape,* 237; Werkeiser, "Recollections of Fredericksburg, CWMC; Jacob G. Frick Medal of Honor File, NA.

54. *OR,* 433, 437, 440; J. M. Clark, petition for Medal of Honor, June 6, 1888, Quay Papers, University of Pittsburgh; Frick Medal of Honor File, NA; Phillips, letter, Dec. 18, 1862, FRSP.

55. Ted Alexander, *The 126th Pennsylvania* (Shippensburg, Pa., 1984), 44; Armstrong, *Red-tape,* 240.

56. *Miners Journal,* Jan. 3, 1863; *OR,* 438; 440–41; Tyler Report, Pennsylvania State Archives; Phillips, letter, Dec. 18, 1862, FRSP; W. O. Campbell Diary, FRSP.

57. *OR,* 432; Cabada Diary, CWMC; Humphreys, *Humphreys at Fredericksburg,* 22, 28; C. McClellan, *Humphreys,* 34; J. M. Clark, petition for Medal of Honor, June 6, 1888, Quay Papers, University of Pittsburgh; Ted Alexander, *126th Pennsylvania,* 44.

58. W. O. Campbell Diary, FRSP; *Miners Journal,* Jan. 3, 1863; Yard, "Unable to Help," *National Tribune,* March 1, 1894; Henry Christiancy Diary, CWMC; *OR,* 432.

59. Tyler Report, Pennsylvania State Archives; *OR,* 437; Armstrong, *Red-tape,* 240–41.

60. *OR,* 432, 440, 441; Tyler Report, Pennsylvania State Archives.

61. *OR,* 432; B, letter to the editor, *Glen Falls (N.Y.) Messenger,* Jan. 20, 1863; Thayer, letter, Dec. 29, 1862, FRSP; Yard, "Unable to Help," *National Tribune,* March 1, 1894; Hutchison, "Fredericksburg," 269; Hooker, quoted in *RJC,* 668; Humphreys, *Humphreys: A Biography,* 178.

62. *OR,* 432, 626; Humphreys, *Humphreys at Fredericksburg,* 10; Orwig, *131st Pennsylvania,* 124; *Under the Maltese Cross,* 102; Hutchison, "Fredericksburg," 269.

63. Ross Diary, Historical Society of Western Pennsylvania; *OR,* 268, 441, 446; Brown, letter, Dec. 23, 1862, FRSP; Armstrong, *Red-tape,* 241.

64. B, letter to the editor, *Glen Falls (N.Y.) Messenger,* Jan. 20, 1863; Hunt, letter, Dec. 19, 1862, Hess Collection, USAMHI; Timothy J. Reese, *Sykes' Regular Infantry Division, 1861–1864* (Jefferson, N.C., 1990), 178–79; Alfred Davenport, *Camp and Field Life of the Fifth New York Volunteer Infantry* (New York, 1879), 345.

65. *OR,* 137; Brown, letter, Dec. 23, 1862, FRSP.

66. *OR,* 137, 436–37, 440; Humphreys, *Humphreys at Fredericksburg,* 9; *Fifth Reunion, 155th Pennsylvania,* 5.

67. Humphreys, *Humphreys: A Biography,* 180.

68. *OR,* 336; Charles W. Washburn, "Record of Service," American Antiquarian Society.

69. Leach, *Twenty-fifth New Jersey,* 109.

70. S. M. Thompson, *Thirteenth New Hampshire,* 45, 68.

71. Wightman, *From Antietam,* 89; S. M. Thompson, *Thirteenth New Hampshire,* 49;

Thorpe, *Fifteenth Connecticut,* 35; Abernathy, "Just a Little Late, but Most Welcome," *Waterbury (Conn.) American,* n.d. [1911–1913], clipping in Abernathy Papers, CWMC; Granger Diary, CWMC.

72. *The Story of the Twenty-first Regiment Connecticut Volunteers* (Middletown, Conn., 1900), 72; *OR,* 332, 335; S. M. Thompson, *Thirteenth New Hampshire,* 45, 50; Staniels, letter, Dec. 16, 1862, FRSP. Thompson interviewed Getty after the war and learned that "the southeast corner [was] the point aimed at" as the objective.

73. Wightman, *From Antietam,* 89; S. M. Thompson, *Thirteenth New Hampshire,* 56; Orville S. Kimball, *History and Personal Sketches of Company I, 103rd N.Y.S.V.* (Elmira, 1900), 158-59; *OR,* 348; George H. Allen, *Forty-six Months with the Fourth R.I. Volunteers* (Providence, 1887), 169.

74. *Story of the Twenty-first Connecticut,* 72; Abernathy, "Just a Little Late, but Most Welcome," *Waterbury (Conn.) American,* n.d., [1911–1913], CWMC; Abernathy, letter, undated, Abernathy Papers, CWMC; Lee, letter, Dec. 17, 1862, Brook Historical Society; S.M. Thompson, *Thirteenth New Hampshire,* 50, 53.

75. Graham, *Ninth New York,* 377; Kimball, *103rd New York,* 159; Aaron F. Stevens, to governor, Dec. 22, 1862, New Hampshire Historical Society; Washburn, "Record of Service," p. 29, American Antiquarian Society; *OR,* 340; Blake, letter, Dec. 18, 1862, CWMC; Wightman, *From Antietam,* 90.

76. *OR,* 332, 337, 343, 346; Stevens, letter, Jan. 5, 1863, New Hampshire Historical Society; Kimball, *103rd New York,* 159.

77. S. M. Thompson, *Thirteenth New Hampshire,* 54.

78. *OR,* 332; MacNamara, *History of the Ninth Regiment,* 258–59.

79. Abernathy, "Just a Little Late, but Most Welcome," *Waterbury (Conn.) American* n.d. [1911–1913], CWMC; *OR,* 354; Allen, *Fourth Rhode Island,* 170.

80. Relyea memoir, Connecticut Historical Society.

81. S. M. Thompson, *Thirteenth New Hampshire,* 57, 58; Washburn, "Record of Service," p. 30, American Antiquarian Society; *OR,* 336; Allen, *Fourth Rhode Island,* 169–70; Fowler, letter, Dec. 20, 1862, New London Historical Society.

82. S. M. Thompson, *Thirteenth New Hampshire,* 58.

83. Stevens, letter, Jan. 5, 1863, New Hampshire Historical Society.

84. *OR,* 336, 341; Stevens to governor, Dec. 22, 1862, New Hampshire Historical Society; S. M. Thompson, *Thirteenth New Hampshire,* 58; Holt, letter, Dec. 17, 1862, LLC.

85. Stevens to governor, Dec. 22, 1862, New Hampshire Historical Society; *OR,* 341; S. M. Thompson, *Thirteenth New Hampshire,* 57, 66.

86. Washburn, "Record of Service," pp. 29–30, American Antiquarian Society; S. M. Thompson, *Thirteenth New Hampshire,* 57, 58, 72; Wightman, *From Antietam,* 97.

87. E. P. Alexander, *Fighting for the Confederacy,* 179.

88. S. M. Thompson, *Thirteenth New Hampshire,* 59, 63, 67; *OR,* 340; Stevens to governor, Dec. 22, 1862, New Hampshire Historical Society.

89. Stevens to governor, Dec. 22, 1862, New Hampshire Historical Society; *OR,* 338, 346; S. M. Thompson, *Thirteenth New Hampshire,* 58, 69; Blake, letter, Dec. 18, 1862, CWMC.

90. S. M. Thompson, *Thirteenth New Hampshire,* 59, 65.

91. Leach, *Twenty-fifth New Jersey,* 108; S. M. Thompson, *Thirteenth New Hampshire,* 58, 60, 61; John H. E. Whitney, *The Hawkins Zouaves* (New York, 1866), 168.

92. Blake, letter Dec. 18, 1862, CWMC; S. M. Thompson, *Thirteenth New Hampshire,* 60, 68, 70.

93. *OR,* 336, 337; S. M. Thompson, *Thirteenth New Hampshire,* 60.

94. *OR,* 337, 343; S. M. Thompson, *Thirteenth New Hampshire,* 62, 69; Stevens to governor, Dec. 22, 1862, New Hampshire Historical Society; Staniels, letter, Dec. 16, 1862, FRSP. As it was, three soldiers were captured when they approached too close to the stone wall to escape. Confederate pickets brought them in.

95. S. M. Thompson, *Thirteenth New Hampshire,* 62.

96. Washburn, "Record of Service," p. 31, American Antiquarian Society; S. M. Thompson, *Thirteenth New Hampshire,* 62; Holt, letter Dec. 17, 1862, LLC; *OR,* 336, 347.

97. Abernathy, memoir, Abernathy Papers, CWMC; Thorpe, *Fifteenth Connecticut,* 35; Asaph R. Tyler, letter, Dec. 15, 1862, FRSP.

98. O'Reilly, *Jackson at Fredericksburg,* 174.

99. William Carter, "Dead Horse Hill," *Home-maker* 3, no. 4 (Jan. 1890).

100. W. Carter, "Dead Horse Hill."

101. Ibid.; Poague, *Gunner with Stonewall,* 57; Davidson, *Greenlee Davidson,* 66.

102. W. Carter, "Dead Horse Hill."

103. Ibid.; Poague, *Gunner with Stonewall,* 57.

104. Davidson, *Greenlee Davidson,* 64; Wise, *Long Arm of Lee,* 1:392; V. M. Fleming Reminiscences, p. 25, FRSP.

105. O'Reilly, *Jackson at Fredericksburg,* 176.

106. Robert L. Dabney, *Life and Campaigns of Lieut-Gen. Thomas J. Jackson ("Stonewall" Jackson)* (New York, 1866), 613.

107. O'Reilly, *Jackson at Fredericksburg,* 176–77.

108. W. S. Campbell, letter Dec. 17, 1862, Cearley Collection, FRSP; *OR,* 666; Early, *Autobiographical Sketch,* 176–77.

109. O'Reilly, *Jackson at Fredericksburg,* 177–78; Slaughter, letter, Jan. 4, 1863, VHS; E. H. Armstrong, letter, Dec. 18, 1862, Duke; Early, "Stonewall Jackson at Fredericksburg," *Historical Magazine* 8 (July 1870): 34.

110. W. Carter, "Dead Horse Hill"; Stine, *Army of the Potomac,* 280; O'Reilly, *Jackson at Fredericksburg,* 178; William N. Pendleton, *Memoirs of William Nelson Pendleton,* ed. Susan P. Lee (Philadelphia, 1893), 247.

111. W. S. Campbell, letter, Dec. 17, 1862, Cearley Collection, FRSP; John H. Harris, "Diary," appendix to *Confederate Stamps, Old Letters, and History,* by Raynor Hubbell (n.p., 1959), 8; E. H. Armstrong, letter, Dec. 18, 1862, Duke; Slaughter, letter Jan. 4, 1863, VHS; J. A. Strikeleather Reminiscences, NCDAH; William M. Norman, *A Portion of My Life* (Winston-Salem, 1959), 156.

112. Oates, *War between the Union and the Confederacy,* 167–68.

113. *Staunton Spectator,* Dec. 26, 1862; *Yorkville (S.C.) Enquirer,* Dec. 24, 1862; Slaughter, letter, Jan. 4, 1863, VHS; Norman, *Portion of My Life,* 156; W. S. Campbell, letter Dec. 17, 1862, Cearley Collection, FRSP; McClendon, *Recollections of War Times,* 161; Early, *Autobiographical Sketch,* 178; Roy Bird Cook, *The Family and Early Life of "Stonewall" Jackson* (Charleston, W. Va., 1924), 188.

114. Cooke, "The Right at Fredericksburg," *Philadelphia Weekly Times,* April 26, 1879; V. M. Fleming Reminiscences, p. 22, FRSP; J. H. Harris, "Diary," 8; O'Reilly, *Jackson at Fredericksburg,* 180–81.

CHAPTER FOURTEEN: "DECIDING THE FATE OF OUR COUNTRY"

1. Banes, *Philadelphia Brigade,* 143; A. J. Alexander, "Fredericksburg: Recollections of the Battle," *Philadelphia Weekly Times,* Feb. 23, 1887; Aldrich, *First Rhode Island Light Artillery,* 162–63; A. Stokes Jones, letter, April 19, 1863, HCW.

2. Robert Ransom, "Ransom's Division at Fredericksburg," *B&L,* 3:95; *OR,* 599.

3. R. G. Carter, *Four Brothers,* 197–98; John Day Smith, *History of the Nineteenth Maine Volunteers* (Minneapolis, 1909), 30.

4. Hopkins, *Seventh Rhode Island,* 48; Rable, "It Is Well That War Is So Terrible," 54.

5. Chamberlain, "My Story of Fredericksburg," 154; Spear, "My Story," p. 49, FRSP; Gerrish, *Army Life,* 78.

6. William Teall, "Ringside Seat at Fredericksburg," *Civil War Times Illustrated,* May 1965, pp. 28–29; Greene, *Franklin,* 25–26; Burnside, quoted in *RJC,* 653; Franklin, quoted in *RJC,* 5.

7. Burnside, quoted in *RJC,* 653.

8. John Bell Hood, *Advance and Retreat* (Philadelphia, 1880), 50; Freeman, *Lee,* 2:466.

9. White, *Lee and the Southern Confederacy,* 240–41; O'Reilly, *Jackson at Fredericksburg,* 183.

10. McLaws, "Battle of Fredericksburg," 88; *OR,* 590, 597; Wyckoff, *Second South Carolina,* 58; E. P. Alexander, order, Dec. 13, 1862, E. P. Alexander Papers, SHC, UNC; E. P. Alexander, order, Dec. 13, 1862, 6 P.M., E. P. Alexander Papers, SHC, UNC; E. P. Alexander, *Fighting for the Confederacy,* 180; Sloan, *Guilford Grays,* 56.

11. *OR,* 547.

12. Freeman, *Lee,* 2:467; Longstreet, *From Manassas to Appomattox,* 316.

13. "Weather Journal Recording Observations," National Weather Records Center; John E. Dooley, *John Dooley, Confederate Soldier,* ed. Joseph T. Durkin (Washington, D.C., 1945), 80–81.

14. Boulware Diary, VSL; George L. Andrew, letter, Dec. 14, 1862, Huntington Library; John Hill Brinton, *Personal Memoirs of John H. Brinton Major and Surgeon, U.S.V., 1861–1865* (New York, 1914), 215; R. H. Anderson Letterbook, MOC; Hotchkiss, letter, Dec. 14, 1862, LC.

15. Murat Halstead, "Battle of Fredericksburg," unidentified newspaper, clipping in FRSP; Haupt, *Reminiscences,* 177.

16. Teall, letter, Dec. 14, 1862, Teall Papers, Small Collection, TSL.

17. Ibid.; Burnside, quoted in *RJC,* 653.

18. Hood, *Advance and Retreat,* 50; Anna Jackson, *Memoirs,* 370; John W. Stevens, *Reminiscences of the Civil War* (Hillsboro, Tex., 1902), 89–90; Longstreet, "Battle of Fredericksburg," 3:82.

19. *Athens (Ga.) Southern Banner,* Jan. 7, 1863; Halstead, "Battle of Fredericksburg," unidentified newspaper, clipping in FRSP; Kittrell J. Warren, *History of the Eleventh Georgia Volunteers* (Richmond, Va., 1863).

20. A. S. Pendleton, order, Dec. 14, 1862, William B. Taliaferro Papers, William and Mary; Alexander Boteler, "A Night with Jackson," *Columbus (Ga.) Enquirer,* Aug. 10, 1881; Canan, *History of Cambria County,* 250; Freeman, *Lee,* 2:468; Heros von Borcke, *Memoirs of the Confederate War of Independence* (New York, 1938), 2:132–33.

21. Nathan C. Bartley, "The Battle of Fredericksburg," *Fredericksburg Free-Lance,* Dec. 24, 1910; Nathan C. Bartley, letter, March 5, 1929, Duke.

22. E. P. Alexander, order, Dec. 14, 1862, E. P. Alexander Papers, SHC, UNC; E. P. Alexander, *Fighting for the Confederacy,* 180–81.

23. Henry C. Conner, letter, Dec. 18, 1862, Henry Calvin Conner Papers, USC; Shand Reminiscences, USC; Dickert, *Kershaw's Brigade,* 197; Crumley Reminiscences, Emory; B. M. Ellison and B. F. Emanuel, *The Humane Hero of Fredericksburg: The Story of Richard Kirkland* (Lancaster, S.C., 1962), 11.

24. Ellison and Emanuel, *Kirkland,* 11; Wyckoff, *Second South Carolina,* 59; Kershaw, letter to the editor, *Charleston News and Courier,* Feb. 6, 1880.

25. Ellison and Emanuel, *Kirkland,* 11–12; McBride, "Banner Battle of the War," *Atlanta Journal,* May 4, 1901; Fleming Reminiscences, FRSP; Shand Reminiscences, USC; Kershaw, letter to the editor, *Charleston News and Courier,* Feb. 6, 1880; Wyckoff, *Second South Carolina,* 59–60; Unidentified Union soldier, "Fredericksburg during the Civil War," Schoff Collection, UM.

26. Burnside, quoted in *RJC,* 653; Teall, letter, Dec. 14, 1862, Teall Papers, Small Collection, TSL.

27. Burnside, quoted in *RJC, OR,* 122.

28. Shaffner, letter, Dec. 15, 1862, Shaffner Papers, NCDAH; Alexander, *Memoirs,* 311; *OR,* 547; Russell, "Description of the Battle of Fredericksburg," *Winchester (Va.) Times,* Feb. 11, 1891.

29. "Weather Journal Recording Observations," National Weather Records Center; Oliver S. Coolidge, "Letter 125," Duke; Wood, *The War,* 110; Henry R. Berkeley Diary, MOC; J. VanL. McCreery Recollections, p. 11, VHS; Stiles, *Four Years under Marse Robert,* 137.

30. Oates, *War between the Union and the Confederacy,* 168; H. R. Berkeley Diary, MOC; Lowry Shufford memoir, NCDAH.

31. Boteler, "A Night with Jackson," *Columbus (Ga.) Enquirer,* Aug. 10, 1881; Cook, *Early Life of Jackson,* 188; Darwin Lambert, *Undying Past of Shenandoah National Park* (Niwot, Colo., 1989), 106.

32. Boteler, "A Night with Jackson," *Columbus (Ga.) Enquirer,* Aug. 10, 1881; Anna Jackson, *Memoirs,* 370; R. K. Krick, "Maxcy Gregg," 22.

33. McIntosh, "Ride on Horseback," pp. 32–33, McIntosh Papers, UNC; J. M. Anderson, Jan. 9, 1863, letter, Maxcy Gregg Papers, USC; Charleston *Mercury,* Dec. 30, 1862.

34. Chambers, *Jackson,* 2:302; Dabney, *Jackson,* 623; Rable, "It Is Well That War Is So Terrible," 49; Matilda Hamilton Diary, possession of Robert K. Krick, from the files of George H. S. King, copy in FRSP; Henderson, *Jackson,* 2:326.

35. Furst Diary, HCW; Child, *Fifth New Hampshire,* 162; A. Smead order to Taliaferro, Dec. 15, 1862, Taliaferro Papers, William and Mary.

36. Teall, letter, Dec. 15, 1862, Teall Papers, TSL.

37. Ibid.

38. E. P. Alexander, *Fighting for the Confederacy,* 181–82.

39. Borcke, *Memoirs,* 2:141.

40. *Charleston Mercury,* Dec. 30, 1862; Unidentified soldier, letter, Dec. 19, 1862, Harvey E. Shepperd Collection, FRSP; Thomas Read Evans Winn, letter, Dec. 18, 1862, Winn Papers, Emory.

41. James Power Smith Memoir, Hotchkiss Papers, LC.

42. O'Reilly, *Jackson at Fredericksburg,* 186–87; Louis C. Duncan, *The Medical Department of the United States Army in the Civil War* (Washington, D.C., 191_), 30.

43. J. P. Smith Memoir, Hotchkiss Papers, LC.

44. McClenthen, *Narrative,* 45; H. R. Berkeley Diary, MOC; W. S. Campbell, letter, Dec. 17, 1862, Cearley Collection, FRSP; J. P. Smith Memoir, Hotchkiss Papers, LC; Thomas D. Boone, *Before the Rebel Flag Fell* (n.p., 1968), 50.

45. Teall, letter, Dec. 15, 1862, Teall Papers, TSL; Smith, "Franklin's 'Left Grand Division,'" *B&L,* 3:138; *OR,* 122, 451.

46. James W. Kenney Memorandum of Service, CWMC; Unidentified Union soldier, "Fredericksburg during the Civil War," Schoff Collection, UM; Gearhart, "Reminiscences of the Civil War," pt. 2, p. 17; Franklin B. Hough Reminiscences, p. 16, FRSP.

47. Furst Diary, HCW; Isaac R. Dunkelberger Memoir, Michael Winey Collection, USAMHI.

48. Haines, *Fifteenth New Jersey,* 36; Edward Hagerty, *Collis' Zouaves* (Baton Rouge, 1997), 132.

49. Teall, letter, Dec. 15, 1862, Teall Papers, TSL; Reese, *Sykes' Regular Infantry Division,* 184; Davenport, *Fifth New York,* 353–54; Anna Jackson, *Memoirs,* 371.

50. Burnside, quoted in *RJC,* 653.

51. Ambrose W. Thompson, journal, Ambrose W. Thompson Papers, LC.

52. Teall, letter, Dec. 15, 1862, Teall Papers, TSL; Furst Diary, HCW.

53. A. W. Thompson, journal, A. W. Thompson Papers, LC.

54. W. Clark, *Histories,* 2:226; Bryan Grimes, *Extracts of Letters of Major-General Bryan Grimes* (Raleigh, N.C., 1884), 26.

55. *ORS,* 3:806; Bratton, letter, Dec. 16, 1862, SHC, UNC; John D. McDonnell Memoir, Winthrop College.

56. O'Reilly, *Jackson at Fredericksburg,* 189; Rauscher, *Music on the March,* 35; W. W. Blackford, *War Years,* 194; A. C. Jones, "Inaugurating the Picket Exchange," *Confederate Veteran* 26 (1918): 155.

57. A. W. Thompson, journal, A. W. Thompson Papers, LC; A. C. Jones, "Inaugurating the Picket Exchange," 155.

58. Grimes, *Extracts of Letters,* 26–27; White, *Lee and the Southern Confederacy,* 252–53; Gary W. Gallagher, "The Yanks Have Had a Terrible Whipping: Confederates Evaluate the Battle of Fredericksburg," in *The Fredericksburg Campaign: Decision on the Rappahannock,* ed. Gary W. Gallagher (Chapel Hill, 1995), 115, 130–31.

59. Shaffner, letter, Dec. 21, 1862, Shaffner Papers, NCDAH; Milas, letter to the editor, *Staunton Spectator,* Jan. 6, 1863; J. W. Stevens, *Reminiscences of the Civil War,* 90; Bartlett Yancey Malone, *Whipt 'Em Everytime* (Jackson, Tenn., 1960), 66–67; Robertson, *Jackson,* 664; "The Haversack," *The Land We Love* 1, no. 1 (May 1866): 117.

60. Duncan, *Medical Department,* 30; Rable, "It Is Well That War Is So Terrible," 59.

61. Teall, letter, Dec. 16, 1862, Teall Papers, TSL; Sumner, quoted in *RJC,* 659; Halleck, dispatch, Dec. 16, 1862, Burnside Papers, NA.

62. William E. Cocke, letter, Dec. 25, 1862, William E. Cocke Papers, VHS; Taliaferro, letter, Dec. 29, 1862, Taliaferro Papers, William and Mary; J. Mark Smither, letter, Dec. 28, 1862, Smither Papers, Hill Junior College; Lewis, *Camp Life,* 37; Gallagher, "Yanks Have Had a Terrible Whipping," 127.

63. Lewis, *Camp Life,* 37.

64. *OR,* 856; O'Reilly, *Jackson at Fredericksburg,* 190–91.

65. Freeman, *Lee,* 2:473; Henderson, *Jackson,* 2:336.

66. Early, *Autobiographical Sketch,* 184; E. H. Armstrong, letter, Dec. 18, 1862, Duke; Hotchkiss, letter, Dec. 17, 1862, Hotchkiss Papers, LC; Anna Jackson, *Memoirs,* 372–73.

67. Teall, letter, Dec. 16, 1862, Teall Papers, TSL.

68. Teall, letter, Dec. 17, 1862, Teall Papers, TSL; Daniel R. Larned, dispatch, Dec. 18, 1862, CWMC.

CHAPTER FIFTEEN: "PLAYED OUT!"

1. Teall, letter, Dec. 16, 1862, Teall Papers, Small Collection, TSL; O. S. Coolidge, Letter 125, Duke; James Coye, letter, Dec. 24, 1862, FRSP.

2. Haupt, *Reminiscences,* 174; Duncan, *Medical Department,* 18, 25.

3. *Charleston Daily Courier,* Jan. 17, 1863; Gallagher, "Yanks Have Had a Terrible Whipping," 127; John L. G. Wood, letter, Dec. 18, 1862, UDC Bound Typescripts, vol. 2, GDAH; C. M. Wilcox, letter, Dec. 17, 1862, Wilcox Papers, LC; Blackford, *War Years,* 196; J. G. Montgomery, letter, Jan. 9, 1863, FRSP; Osmun Latrobe Diary, VHS.

4. Teall, letter, Dec. 16, 1862, Small Collection, Teall Papers, TSL; Sorrel, *Recollections,* 146; Franklin dispatch, Burnside Papers, NA; Edwin V. Sumner, dispatch, Dec. 16, 1862, MMO.

5. Duncan, *Medical Department,* 29; Unidentified Soldier [27th Connecticut] Diary, FRSP.

6. Unidentified Soldier [27th Connecticut] Diary, FRSP.

7. Ibid.; Duncan, *Medical Department,* 29–30. Duncan dismisses the tales of frozen bodies and ground as "fiction," but corroborative evidence suggests it occurred to some degree.

8. Duncan, *Medical Department,* 30.

9. Unidentified soldier [27th Connecticut] Diary, FRSP.

10. Sorrel, *Recollections,* 147; Unidentified Soldier [27th Connecticut] Diary, FRSP.

11. Teall, letter, Dec. 17, 1862, Small Collection, Teall Papers, TSL; Patrick, *Inside Lincoln's Army,* 193.

12. Teall, letter, Dec. 19, 1862, Teall Papers, Small Collection, TSL; *RJC,* 103.

13. Longstreet, *From Manassas to Appomattox,* 317; Patrick, *Inside Lincoln's Army,* 194–5, 201.

14. Patrick, *Inside Lincoln's Army,* 199; D. Beem, letter, Jan. 18, 1863, Beem Papers, Indiana Historical Society.

15. William H. Stewart, *A Pair of Blankets* (New York, 1911), 75; Cook, *Twelfth Massachusetts,* 85.

16. G. Thompson, *Engineer Battalion,* 27; A. W. Thompson, letter, Feb. 8, 1863, Thompson Papers, LC.

17. Meade, *Life and Letters,* 1:341; Henry G. Pearson, *James S. Wadsworth of Geneseo* (New York, 1913), 168.

18. *Historical Sketch of Quitman Guards,* 41.

19. Sloan, *Guilford Grays,* 58–59; A. C. Jones, "Arkansas Soldiers in Virginia," *Confederate Veteran* 20 (1912): 464; William A. Blair, "Barbarians at Fredericksburg's Gate: The Impact of the Union Army on Civilians," in *The Fredericksburg Campaign: Decision on the Rappahannock,* ed. Gary W. Gallagher (Chapel Hill and London, 1995), 158.

20. H. B. McClellan, *Stuart,* 189–90; Plum, *Military Telegraph,* 356; *ORS,* 3:657.

21. Teall, letter, Dec. 24, 1862, Teall Papers, TSL.

22. Michael Hanifen, *History of Battery B, First New Jersey Artillery* (Ottowa, Ill., 1905), 41; Burnside, quoted in Curtis, *From Bull Run to Chancellorsville,* 224; *OR,* vol. 25, pt. 2, p. 15; Gabriel Colby Court-Martial Papers, NA.

23. Fortescue, letter, Jan. 9, 1863, HSP; James C. Thickerstum, letter, Dec. 25, 1862, CWMC.

24. Taliaferro, letter, Dec. 29, 1862, Taliaferro Papers, William and Mary; Cocke, letter, Dec. 25, 1862, Cocke Letters, VHS; Westwood A. Todd Reminiscences, SHC, UNC; Charles T. Loehr, *War History of the Old First Virginia Infantry Regiment* (Richmond, 1884), 33; R. Lewis, *Camp Life,* 38.

25. Freeman, *Lee,* 2:476; Anna Jackson, *Memoirs,* 379; James Power Smith, "Personal Memories of Lee," *Richmond Times-Dispatch,* Jan. 20, 1907.

26. Freeman, *Lee,* 2:476.

27. H. B. McClellan, *Stuart,* 196–97; Burnside, quoted in *RJC,* 716.

28. H. B. McClellan, *Stuart,* 197.

29. Ibid., 199; Thomas, *Bold Dragoon,* 195; *OR,* 736, 737.

30. H. B. McClellan, *Stuart,* 200–201; John W. B. Thomason, *J. E. B. Stuart* (New York, 1930), 351.

31. Plum, *Military Telegraph,* 358; Thomas, *Bold Dragoon,* 199.

32. Plum, *Military Telegraph,* 357–58; H. B. McClellan, *Stuart,* 202; William H. Mills, "From Burnside to Hooker: The Transfer of the Army of the Potomac," *Magazine of American History* 15 (1885): 47.

33. *ORS,* 3:657; Teall, letter, Jan. 2, 1863, Teall Papers, Small Collection, TSL; Dunkelberger Memoir, Winey Collection, USAMHI.

34. R. C. Price, letter, Jan. 2, 1863, SHC, UNC; H. B. McClellan, *Stuart,* 196; Mills, "From Burnside to Hooker," 47.

35. Burnside, quoted in *RJC,* 716; Mills, "From Burnside to Hooker," 44; Parke, quoted in *RJC,* 726; Abram P. Smith, *History of the Seventy-sixth Regiment New York Volunteers* (Syracuse, N.Y., 1867), 197.

36. Parke, quoted in *RJC,* 726, 728; Burnside, quoted in *RJC,* 716–17; Mills, "From Burnside to Hooker," 44.

37. Mills, "From Burnside to Hooker," 44; Burnside, quoted in *RJC,* 717; Teall, letter, Dec. 29, 1862, Teall Papers, Small Collection, TSL; A. Wilson Greene, "Morale, Maneuver, and Mud: The Army of the Potomac, December 16, 1862–January 26, 1863," in *The Freder-*

cksburg Campaign: Decision on the Rappahannock, ed. Gary W. Gallagher (Chapel Hill, 1995),
80–81.

38. Newton, quoted in *RJC,* 731; Cochrane, quoted in *RJC,* 742.

39. Newton, quoted in *RJC,* 730–31, 733; William F. Smith, "Burnside Relieved," *Magazine of American History* 15 (1885): 197.

40. Newton, quoted in *RJC,* 735; A. W. Greene, "Morale, Maneuver, and Mud," 183–84,
89.

41. Mills, "From Burnside to Hooker," 45–46; Cochrane, quoted in *RJC,* 743, 746.

42. Mills, "From Burnside to Hooker," 46–47; Cochrane, quoted in *RJC,* 742; Newton,
quoted in *RJC,* 731, 737.

43. Edward W. Peck, letter, Jan. 3, 1863, CWMC; Parke, quoted in *RJC,* 727; Thaddeus
. Lowe Correspondence, American Institute of Aeronautics and Astronautics Papers, LC;
Charles A. Stevens, *Berdan's Sharpshooters in the Army of the Potomac* (St. Paul, 1892), 228–29.

44. Mills, "From Burnside to Hooker," 47; Parke, quoted in *RJC,* 727, 728; Patrick, *Inside
Lincoln's Army,* 197.

45. Burnside, quoted in *RJC,* 718, 722; Mills, "From Burnside to Hooker," 48; Parke,
quoted in *RJC,* 727.

46. Burnside, letter, May 24, 1863, Burnside Papers, NA.

47. Mills, "From Burnside to Hooker," 48; Burnside, letter, May 24, 1863, Burnside Papers, NA.

48. Teall, letter, Jan. 2, 1863, Teall Papers, Small Collection, TSL; Patrick, *Inside Lincoln's
Army,* 199; Fortescue, letter, Jan. 9, 1863, HSP.

49. Teall, letter, Jan. 2, 1863, letter, Jan. 8, 1863, Teall Papers, Small Collection, TSL.

50. Teall, letter, Jan. 8, 1863, Teall Papers, Small Collection, TSL.

51. Mills, "From Burnside to Hooker," 48; Burnside, quoted in *RJC,* 718; Teall, letter,
Dec. 29, 1862, Teall Papers, Small Collection, TSL.

52. Mills, "From Burnside to Hooker," 48; *OR,* vol. 14, p. 762–63; Freeman, *Lee,*
:478–79.

53. Burnside, quoted in *RJC,* 719; Wyman S. White, *The Civil War Diary of Wyman S.
White,* ed. Russell C. White (Baltimore, 1991), 120; Patrick, *Inside Lincoln's Army,* 202–203.

54. Mills, "From Burnside to Hooker," 48; Burnside, quoted in *RJC,* 725; Parke, quoted
n *RJC,* 728; A. W. Greene, "Morale, Maneuver, and Mud," 195.

55. W. F. Smith, "Burnside Relieved," 198; A. Rupert, letter, Jan. 26, 1863, Chester
County Historical Society.

56. Burnside, quoted in *RJC,* 719; Burnside, letter, Jan. 5, 1863, FRSP; Mills, "From
Burnside to Hooker," 48.

57. Burnside, dispatch, Jan. 17, 1863, Reel 120, Secretary of War Records, NA; Mills,
From Burnside to Hooker," 49; Paul E. Owen, letter, Jan. 31, 1863, Trinity College.

58. Patrick, *Inside Lincoln's Army,* 203; Mills, "From Burnside to Hooker," 49; Burnside,
dispatch, Jan. 27, 1863, Reel 120, Secretary of War Records, NA.

59. Thomas W. Stephens Diary, CWMC; Joseph C. Taber Diary, CWT; Robert W.
Elmer Diary, CWMC; W. F. Smith, "Burnside Relieved," 197.

60. Edmund D. Halsey Diary, Edmund Halsey Papers, USAMHI; S. W. Gordon Diary,
CWMC; Mills, "From Burnside to Hooker," 49; A. Rupert, letter, Jan. 26, 1863, Chester

County Historical Society; Thomas Conningher, letter, Jan. 25, 1863, Rudolph L. Hearle Collection, USAMHI; Theodore A. Dodge, letter, Jan. 22, 1863, LC; *OR,* 754; Charles Elihu Slocum, *Life and Services of Major-General Henry Warner Slocum* (Toledo, Ohio, 1913), 64.

61. S. M. Thompson, *Thirteenth New Hampshire,* 100; M. Peabody, letter, Jan. 20, 1863, CWMC; George Hill, Jr., letter, Jan. 16, 1863, CWMC.

62. Halsey, diary, Halsey Papers, USAMHI; Hanifen, *Battery B, First New Jersey Artillery,* 41; Furst Diary, HCW; Taber Diary, CWT.

63. Patrick, *Inside Lincoln's Army,* 205; Burnside, quoted in *RJC,* 723; Hanifen, *Battery B, First New Jersey Artillery,* 44; W. S. White, *Civil War Diary,* 122.

64. W. F. Smith, "Burnside Relieved," 198, 200.

65. Cabada diary, CWMC; W. F. Smith, "Burnside Relieved," 198.

66. Furst Diary, HCW; Taber Diary, CWT; A. K. Blake, letter, Jan. 25, 1863, CWMC; W. S. White, *Civil War Diary,* 121; Gordon Diary, CWMC; "Weather Journal Recording Observations," National Weather Records Center.

67. Cook, *Twelfth Massachusetts,* 86; Taber Diary, CWT; De Trobriand, *Four Years,* 409; George B. Sanford, *Fighting Rebels and Redskins: Experience in Army Life of Colonel George B. Sanford, 1861–1892,* ed. E. R. Hageman (Norman, Okla., 1969), 193; T. Conningher, Jan. 25, 1863, Hearle Collection, USAMHI.

68. Charles H. Veil Reminiscences, CWMC; Haines, *Fifteenth New Jersey,* 38; William B. Westervelt, "Lights and Shadows of Army Life," CWMC; John L. Smith, letter, Jan. 25, 1863, FRSP; T. Conningher, letter, Jan. 25, 1863, Hearle Collection, USAMHI; William H. Peacock, letter, Jan. 28, 1863, CWMC.

69. Charles A. Harrison Diary, Robert L. Brake Collection, USAMHI; G.K., "Burnside's Mud March," unidentified newspaper, clipping in MMO.

70. C. H. Veil Reminiscences, CWMC; W. H. Myers, letter, Jan. 24, 1863, CWMC; Thomas W. Stanley, letter, Jan. 24, 1863, FRSP; Unidentified Union soldier, "Fredericksburg during the Civil War," Schoff Collection, UM; E. Richards, letter, Jan. 27, 1863, CWMC; C. A. Harrison Diary, Brake Collection, USAMHI.

71. Mills, "From Burnside to Hooker," 49; Gordon Diary, CWMC; Kenney Memorandum of Service, CWMC; Westervelt, "Lights and Shadows," CWMC; T. Conningher, letter, Jan. 25, 1863, Hearle Collection, USAMHI; H. H. Jenkins Diary, Huntington Library; Dayton E. Flint, letter, Jan. 27, 1863, CWMC.

72. G. Thompson, *Engineer Battalion,* 28; W. O. Campbell Diary, FRSP.

73. Mills, "From Burnside to Hooker," 49; Fortescue, letter, undated, HSP; Furst Diary, HCW; H. H. Jenkins Diary, Huntington Library; Hall, *Personal Experience,* 8.

74. Hall, *Personal Experience,* 8–9; W. H. Peacock, letter, Jan. 28, 1863, CWMC.

75. Mills, "From Burnside to Hooker," 49; Haines, *Fifteenth New Jersey,* 39; G. B. Sanford, *Fighting Rebels and Redskins,* 193; Daniel R. Larned, letter, Jan. 28, 1863, LC; Burnside telegrams (2), Jan. 21, 1863, Reel 120, Secretary of War Papers, NA.

76. Haines, *Fifteenth New Jersey,* 39; Gordon Diary, CWMC; Mills, "From Burnside to Hooker," 50; Hall, *Personal Experience,* 8; W. S. White, *Civil War Diary,* 121.

77. Westervelt, "Lights and Shadows," CWMC; Haines, *Fifteenth New Jersey,* 39–40.

78. Freeman, *Lee,* 2:479; Longstreet, *From Manassas to Appomattox,* 323; Taylor, *Four Years,* 82–83.

79. R. H. Anderson, order, Anderson Letterbook, MOC; Ambrose R. Wright Order Book, CWT; E. A. Shiver, "Who Ate the Dog?" *Atlanta Journal,* Feb. 15, 1902; Edgar A. Warfield, *A Confederate Soldier's Memoirs* (Richmond, Va., 1936), 139.

80. E. A. Warfield, *Memoirs,* 139; Stewart, *Pair of Blankets,* 77.

81. E. A. Warfield, *Memoirs,* 139; Jet Holland, letter, Jan. 30, 1863, William Meade Dame Papers, FRSP; William A. Young, Jr., and Patricia C. Young, *Fifty-sixth Virginia Infantry* (Lynchburg, Va., 1990), 69; E. A. Shiver, "Who Ate the Dog?" *Atlanta Journal,* Feb. 15, 1902; P. E. Owen, letter, Jan. 31, 1863, Trinity College; T. Conningher, letter, Jan. 25, 1863, Hearle Collection, USAMHI.

82. Mills, "From Burnside to Hooker," 50; W. S. White, *Civil War Diary,* 123; Unidentified Union soldier, "Fredericksburg during the Civil War," Schoff Collection, UM; T. Conningher, letter, Jan. 25, 1863, Hearle Collection, USAMHI; Cook, *Twelfth Massachusetts,* 87.

83. Mills, "From Burnside to Hooker," 50; Fortescue, letter, Jan. 29, 1863, HSP; D. E. Flint, letter, Jan. 27, 1863, CWMC; Alexander Way, letter, Dec. 17, 1862, FRSP.

84. Patrick, *Inside Lincoln's Army,* 204, 206–207; Mills, "From Burnside to Hooker," 50; Burnside, quoted in *RJC,* 719.

85. G.K., "Burnside's Mud March," MMO; Sumner, quoted in *RJC,* 660.

86. Dunkelberger Memoir, Winey Collection, USAMHI; J. L. Smith, letter, Jan. 25, 1863, FRSP; Aldus Jewell, letter, Jan. 25, 1863, CWMC; G.K., "Burnside's Mud March," MMO.

87. Dalton, *Blanket Brigade,* 99; Gilbert Thompson Memoir, LC; William A. Moore recollections, CWMC; A. W. Thompson, letter, Feb. 8, 1863, LC; P. A. Oliver, letter, Feb. 3, 1863, Princeton; B. F. Ashenfelter, letter, Jan. 28, 1863, CWMC; Unidentified soldier [1st Massachusetts Cavalry], letter, Jan. 24, 1863, Emma A. Legg Papers, Duke; Frank W. Dickerson, letter, Jan. 23, 1863, CWMC.

88. W. O. Campbell Diary, FRSP; P. E. Owen, letter, Jan. 31, 1863, Trinity College; W. A. Moore Recollections, CWMC; Dalton, *Blanket Brigade,* 99; Patrick, *Inside Lincoln's Army,* 206. Abner Small identified the gunfight participants as Rhode Island officers.

89. W. S. White, *Civil War Diary,* 123; Taber Diary, CWT; T. Conningher, letter, Jan. 25, 1863, Hearle Collection, USAMHI; G.K., "Burnside's Mud March," MMO; Dalton, *Blanket Brigade,* 98–99; Cook, *Twelfth Massachusetts,* 86.

90. Burnside, quoted in *RJC,* 719; D. Larned, letter, Jan. 28, 1863, Larned Papers, LC; Mills, "From Burnside to Hooker," 50.

91. W. S. White, *Civil War Diary,* 123; Kenney Memorandum of Service, CWMC; P. A. Owen, letter, Jan. 31, 1863, Trinity College; Stanley, letter, Jan. 24, 1863, FRSP.

92. Cook, *Twelfth Massachusetts,* 87; S. M. Thompson, *Thirteenth New Hampshire,* 103.

93. Furst Diary, HCW; Fortescue, undated letter, HSP; George W. Whipple Pension Record, NA; Cabada Diary, CWMC.

94. Mills, "From Burnside to Hooker," 51–52; Burnside, letter, May 24, 1863, Burnside Papers, NA.

95. Mills, "From Burnside to Hooker," 52; Marvel, *Burnside,* 214; W. F. Smith, "Burnside Relieved," 198.

96. D. Larned, letter, Jan. 28, 1863, Larned Papers, LC; Mills, "From Burnside to Hooker," 52–53; Marvel, *Burnside,* 214.

97. Mills, "From Burnside to Hooker," 53.

98. Ibid., 54, 56; Burnside, quoted in *RJC*, 721.

99. Furst Diary, HCW; Keyes, letter, Dec. 19, 1862, Meigs Papers, LC. Though Keyes wrote before Burnside's removal, speculation had already buzzed in Washington about Hooker's imminent ascension to command.

100. *OR*, vol. 14, p. 763; Longstreet, *From Manassas to Appomattox*, 323–24; R. H. Anderson, letter, Jan. 22, 1863, Anderson Letterbook, MOC.

101. James Keith Boswell, letter, Jan. 5, 1863, Alfred Landon Rives Papers, Duke; Freeman, *Lee*, 2:480; Pendleton, *Memoirs*, 256–57.

EPILOGUE

1. Patrick, *Inside Lincoln's Army*, 208; Fortescue, letter, undated, HSP; A. W. Greene, "Morale, Maneuver, and Mud," 215.

2. Newton, quoted in *RJC*, 739; Furst Diary, HCW.

3. Hood, *Advance and Retreat*, 51.

4. Gallagher, "Yanks Have Had a Terrible Whipping," 119–20; O'Reilly, *Jackson at Fredericksburg*, 192.

5. Thomas W. Dick, letter, Jan. 8, 1863, Dickinson College; Coe, letter to the editor, *Hackettstown (N.J.) Gazette*, Jan. 8, 1863; Tivoll, letter to the editor, *Atlanta Southern Confederacy*, Dec. 25, 1862; Burnside, letter, June 7, 1863, Burnside Papers, NA.

6. E. W. Peck, Jan. 3, 1863, letter, CWMC; Emory Upton, letter, Dec. 23, 1862, CWMC; Coe, letter to the editor, *Hackettstown (N.J.) Gazette*, Jan. 8, 1863.

7. C. H. Eagar, letter, Jan. 27, 1863, LLC; Coe, letter to the editor, *Hackettstown (N.J.) Gazette*, Jan. 8, 1863.

8. J. W. Haas, letter, Jan. 3, 1863, HCW; E. W. Peck, letter, Jan. 3, 1863, CWMC.

9. Furst Diary, HCW.

10. Longstreet, letter, July 25, 1873, in Richard Rollins, "'The Ruling Ideas' of the Pennsylvania Campaign," *Gettysburg Magazine*, no. 17 (1997): 15; Gallagher, "Yanks Have Had a Terrible Whipping," 113.

11. *Athens (Ga.) Southern Banner*, Jan. 7, 1863; H. W. Berryman, letter, Dec. 27, 1862, FRSP; S. W. Branch, letter, Dec. 17, 1862, Margaret Branch Sexton Collection, University of Georgia; McDaniel, *With Unabated Trust*, 130.

12. R. Lewis, *Camp Life*, 36; C. M. Wilcox, letter, Dec. 17, 1862, Wilcox Papers, LC.

13. J. D. Damron, letter, Dec. 17, 1862, Ann Penn Wray Collection, University of Tennessee; Richard Irby, letter, Dec. 19, 1862, FRSP; Richard Floyd, letter, July 13, 1862, Governor John Milton Papers, University of South Florida.

14. Allan, "Fredericksburg," 136; Small, *Road to Richmond*, 69; *OR*, 133–34; 137–42.

15. Pennypacker, *Meade*, 103; Cleaves, *Meade*, 95; Stine, *Army of the Potomac*, 267.

16. Sanford, *Fighting Rebels and Redskins*, 192.

17. Long, "Fredericksburg," *Philadelphia Weekly Times*, Jan. 6, 1886.

18. *History of the 121st Pennsylvania*, 28.

19. Meade, *Life and Letters*, 1:340, 354.

BIBLIOGRAPHY

MANUSCRIPTS

American Antiquarian Society, Worcester, Mass.
        Charles W. Washburn, "Record of Service"
Antietam National Battlefield, Sharpsburg, Md.
        Morris R. Darrohn Recollections
Boston Public Library, Boston, Mass.
        Henry Ropes Family Papers
Brown University, Providence, R.I.
        Charles E. Davis Letter
Bucknell University, Lewisburg, Pa.
        James M. Kincaid Reminiscences
Chester County Historical Society, West Chester, Pa.
        Jacob M. Marsh Diary
        Nathan Pennypacker Papers
        Alfred Rupert Letters
        Joseph Way Letter
Civil War Library and Museum, Philadelphia, Pa.
        John Clinton Letter
        James C. Hamilton Memoir
        St. Clair A. Mulholland Papers
Connecticut Historical Society, Hartford, Conn.
        Leland Q. Barlow Letters

       William H. Relyea Memoir

Dartmouth College, Hanover, N.H.

       Oscar D. Robinson Papers

Detroit Public Library, Detroit, Mich.

       Asa Brindle Letter, Ward Family Papers

Dickinson College, Carlisle, Pa.

       Thomas W. Dick Letter

Duke University, Durham, N.C.

       Edward Hall Armstrong Letter

       Nathan C. Bartley Letter

       George R. Bedinger Letter, Bedinger-Dandridge Papers

       James Keith Boswell Letter, Alfred Landon Rives Papers

       Lunsford R. Cherry Letter, Lucy Cherry Crisp Papers

       Oliver S. Coolidge Letter

       Steven Dandridge Letter, Bedinger-Dandridge Papers

       John Warwick Daniel Papers

       Emma A. Legg Papers

       Samuel and Uriah M. Parmalee Letter, Special Collections

       Charles S. Powell, "War Talks"

       Evan Smith Papers

       Samuel H. Walkup Journal

Emory University, Atlanta, Ga.

       William Macon Crumley Reminiscences

       Benjamin L. Mobely Letter

       Coston Rohrer Letter

       William H. Stiles Letter

       Thomas Read Evans Winn Papers

Fredericksburg and Spotsylvania National Military Park, Fredericksburg, Va.

       William P. Alderman Letter

       Jacob Babbitt Letters, Park Collection #2085

       Charles Barber Letter

       A. A. Batchelder Diary

       Clark Baum Papers, Tim Garret Collection

       H. Walter Berryman Letter

       Martin W. Brett Memoir

       John B. Brockenbrough Letter

       Nathaniel W. Brown Letter

       John G. Bryant Memoir

       Ambrose E. Burnside Letter

       William O. Campbell Diary

       William S. Campbell Letters, Don Cearley Collection

       Erskine M. Church Letter, Park Collection #3845

       Samuel Clark Letter

       William B. Colston Memoir

James Coye Letter
Robert Franklin Fleming Memoir
Vivian Minor Fleming Reminiscences
William Gilson Letter
Thomas Goldsborough Letter
Silas Gore Letter
Murat Halstead, Unidentified Newspaper
Matilda Hamilton Diary, from the files of George H. S. King
Jere Malcolm Harris Letter
Noel G. Harrison Papers
Steven Hawley, "Barksdale's Mississippi Brigade at Fredericksburg," Thesis,
Copy on File
Albert Henly Memoir
Jet Holland Letter, William Meade Dame Papers
Franklin B. Hough Reminiscences
L. B. Hutchison Letter
Richard Irby Letter
Owen Jones Unpublished Report
Thomas Josiah Letter
John F. Kerper Reminiscences
Wills Lee Reminiscences
James A. Lowery Letter
J. J. McDaniel, "Diary of Battles, Marches and Incidents of the Seventh S.C. Regi-
ment"
James T. McElvaney Letter
T. M. Mitchell Diary
J. G. Montgomery Letter
William H. Moore Letter
T. E. Morris, Notebook on Fredericksburg Area Battlefields
Caroline Morton Memoir, Battlefield Commission Papers
Archibald D. Norris Diary
Samuel S. Partridge Letter
E. A. Patterson Reminiscences
Phillip Petty Memoir
John W. Phillips Letter
Francis E. Pierce Letter
Frank Plympton Letter
Reuben Schell Letter
George A. Seaman Letter
John Smart Papers
John L. Smith Letter
Thompson A. Snyder Recollections
Ellis Spear, "My Story of Fredericksburg and Comments Thereon," 1914
Rufus P. Staniels Letter

        Thomas W. Stanley Letter

        Henry Taylor Memoir

        Ziba C. Thayer Letter

        Isaac S. Tichenor Papers

        John J. Toffey Papers

        Asaph R. Tyler, "Letters of a Soldier"

        Unidentified Soldier [27th Connecticut] Diary

        Unidentified Soldier, Letter Headed: "Headquarters 57th Regt. New York Vols."

        Unidentified Soldier, Letter, Harvey E. Shepperd Collection

        Alexander Way Letter

        Edward E. Williams Papers

        John B. Winslow Letter

        Leander E. Woollard Diary

Georgia Department of Archives and History, Atlanta, Ga.

        Charles J. McDonald Conway Diary

        James M. Goldsmith Reminiscences

        William H. Hodnatt Diary

        United Daughters of the Confederacy Bound Typescripts

                William H. Kirkpatrick Letter, Vol. 2, no. 133

                John L. G. Wood Reminiscences, Vol. 2

                Joseph White Woods Reminiscences, Volume 4, no. 144

Gettysburg National Military Park, Gettysburg, Pa.

        "The Memoirs of John A. Fite, 7th Tennessee"

Harvard University, Cambridge, Mass.

        Winfield S. Hancock Letter, Frederick M. Dearborn Collection

Hill Junior College, Hillsboro, Texas

        J. Mark Smither Papers

Historical Society of Pennsylvania, Philadelphia, Pa.

        Franklin Boyts Papers

        Louis Fortescue Papers

        William McCarter, "My Life in the Army"

        E. M. Stephenson Papers

        Evan M. Woodward Papers

Historical Society of Western Pennsylvania, Pittsburgh, Pa.

        James B. Ross Diary

Huntington Library, Henry E. Huntington Society, San Marino, Calif.

        George L. Andrew

        H. H. Jenkins Diary

        George H. Sargent Diary

        Joseph C. Stiles Letter

        Charles S. Wainwright Journals, 5 Volumes

Indiana Historical Society, Indianapolis, Ind.

        David Beem Papers

Indiana University, Bloomington, Ind.

Nathan Kimball Papers

Unidentified Soldier [64th New York] Reminiscences

Jefferson County Museum, Charles Town, W.Va.

George W. Shreve, "Reminiscences of the Stuart Horse Artillery," R. Preston Chew
Papers

Kennesaw Mountain National Military Park, Marietta, Ga.

Charles W. McArthur Letter Typescript

Library of Congress, Manuscript Division, Washington, D.C.

American Institute of Aeronautics and Astronautics Papers

William T. H. Brooks Papers

Joshua L. Chamberlain Papers

Theodore A. Dodge Letter

William B. Franklin Papers

William Hamilton Letter

John William Ford Hatton Memoir, Microfilm Acc. #9243

Jedediah Hotchkiss Papers

Henry Jackson Hunt Papers

Daniel R. Larned Papers

Betty H. Maury Diary

Montgomery C. Meigs Papers

Ambrose W. Thompson Papers

Gilbert Thompson Memoir

Cadmus M. Wilcox Papers

Mary Washington College, Fredericksburg, Va.

Bartholomen Dailey Letters

Mississippi Department of Archives and History, Jackson, Miss.

William M. McKinney Abernathy, "Our Mess: Southern Army Gallantry and Privations"

William Davis Letter

Museum of the Confederacy, Richmond, Va.

Richard H. Anderson Letterbook

Henry R. Berkeley Diary

J. A. Braddock Reminiscences

Junius Kimble Reminiscences

H. H. Matthew Letter

Robert T. Mockbee, "Historical Sketch of the 14th Tennessee"

John O'Farrell Diary

National Archives, Washington, D.C.

Ambrose E. Burnside Papers

Gabriel Colby Court Martial Papers

Jacob G. Frick Medal of Honor File

Edward A. L. Roberts Compiled Service Record

Secretary of War Records, 1863 Microfilm, Reel #120

William Sinclair Compiled Service Record

        John Sullivan Court-Martial, RG 153, LL 1332.
        George W. Whipple Pension Record
        Evan M. Woodward Compiled Service Record
National Weather Records Center, Asheville, N.C.
        "Weather Journal Recording Observations at . . . Georgetown, D.C., June 1858
            May 1866," Microfilm call #CL-1024
New Hampshire Historical Society, Concord, N.H.
        Aaron F. Stevens Letter
New London Historical Society, New London, Conn.
        Frank Fowler Letter
New-York Historical Society, New York, N.Y.
        Gabriel Grant Memoir
New York State Library, Special Collections, Albany, N.Y.
        Harvey Henderson Diary
        Hiram S. Sickles Papers
North Carolina Department of Archives and History, Raleigh, N.C.
        Samuel A. Ashe Reminiscences
        Noah Collins Diary, Isaac London Collection
        H. B. Howard Diary, William Womble Papers
        Wilson T. Jenkins Reminiscences
        James H. Lane Papers
        J. F. Shaffner Papers
        Lowry Shufford Memoir
        J. A. Strikeleather Reminiscences
Ohio Historical Society, Columbus, Ohio
        Catharinus P. Buckingham Memoir
Pennsylvania State Archives, Harrisburg, Pa.
        Jeremiah Rohrer Diary
        Erastus B. Tyler Report, Office of the Adjutant General, Department of Military
            Affairs
Princeton University, Princeton, N.J.
        Paul A. Oliver Letter
Rhode Island Historical Society, Providence, R.I.
        William C. Barker Letter
Rutgers University, New Brunswick, N.J.
        J. Frank Sterling Letter
Salmon Brook Historical Society, Granby, Conn.
        Richard H. Lee Letter
Tennessee State Library and Archives, Nashville, Tenn.
        Small Collection
                William W. Teall Papers
Trinity College, Hartford, Conn.
        Paul E. Owen Letter
United States Army Military History Institute, Carlisle, Pa.

Robert L. Brake Collection
      Charles A. Harrison Diary
Samuel R. Beardsley Collection
      Samuel R. Beardsley Letter
William T. H. Brooks Papers
James P. Coburn Papers
Civil War Miscellaneous Collection
      William J. Abernathy Papers
      Silas Adams Reminiscences
      John C. Anderson Letter
      Alfred M. Apted Memoir
      Benjamin J. Ashenfelter Letters
      Aaron K. Blake Letters
      Adolfo Fernandez Cabada Diary
      Henry Christiancy Diary
      Edward Cotter Letter
      Frank W. Dickerson Letter
      Robert W. Elmer Diary
      Samuel Angus Firebaugh Diary
      Dayton E. Flint Letter
      S. W. Gordon Diary
      Charles S. Granger Diary
      H. Seymour Hall, "Personal Experiences"
      William W. Hemmenway Reminiscences
      George Hill, Jr., Letter
      George Hopper Letter
      Aldus Jewell Letter
      James W. Kenney Memorandum of Service
      R. Prosper Landry Diary
      Daniel R. Larned Dispatch
      Joseph H. Leighty Letter
      D. V. Lovell Letter
      William Lucas Letter
      A. B. Martin Letter
      James H. McIlwaine Letter
      William A. Moore Recollections
      Edward Mount Letter
      William H. Myers Letter
      Samuel L. North Letter
      John O'Connell Reminiscences
      Miles H. Peabody Letters
      William H. Peacock Letter
      Edward W. Peck Letter
      John Pellett Letter

Isaac Plumb Memoir
Albert A. Pope Diary
James Pratt Papers
Edgar Richards Letters
John L. Smith Papers
Thomas W. Stephens Diary
James C. Thickerstum Letter
Emory Upton Letter
Charles H. Veil Reminiscences
Anthony Washie, "Story of Enoch T. Baker"
Martin L. Werkeiser, "Recollections of Fredericksburg"
William Wertz, "Story of the 133d Regiment: Taken from the Dairy of a
	Veteran"
William B. Westervelt, "Lights and Shadows of Army Life"
William D. Whyckoff Letter
Samuel K. Zook Letter
Civil War Times Illustrated Collection
Jacob Heffelfinger Diary
Frederick W. Oesterle, "Incidents Connected with the Civil War"
George S. Rollins Letter
Eli C. Strouss Letter
Joseph C. Taber Diary
Ambrose R. Wright Order Book
Gregory A. Coco Collection
Charles R. Johnson Letter
Edmund D. Halsey Papers
Harrisburg Civil War Round Table Collection
William B. Bailey Letter
Henry Flick, "Official Record of Henry Flick"
Luther C. Furst Diary
Jacob W. Haas Letter
A. Stokes Jones Letter
Isaac Morrow Letter
Rudolph L. Hearle Collection
Thomas Conningher Letter
Earle M. Hess Collection
Chester F. Hunt Letter
Daniel Emerson Hurd Collection
Daniel E. Hurd, "My Experiences in the Civil War"
Wendell W. Lang Collection
Charles C. Paige Memoir
Lewis Leigh Collection
Charles H. Eager Letters
Samuel B. Fisher Letter

   Constantine A. Hege Letter
   William B. Hoitt Letter
   Henry H. Holt Letter
   George H. Patch Letter
   Philip H. Power Letter
   Robert Taggert Diary
 Charles A. Malloy Papers
 Massachusetts Military Order of the Loyal Legion Collection
   G.K, "Burnside's Mud March"
   George N. Macy Letter
   Herbert C. Mason Letters
   Edwin V. Sumner Dispatch
 Military Order of the Loyal Legion of the U.S. Collection
   Dennis T. McCarty Letter
   Unidentified soldier, "Burnside's Mud March Made Twenty-one Years
    Ago," unidentified newspaper clipping
 Ralph G. Poriss Collection
   Josiah W. Mosely Diary
 Kenneth H. Powers Collection
   Unidentified soldier [69th New York] Memoir
 Save the Flags Collection
   William P. Conrad Letter
 Alonzo and Jason Smith Collection
   Jason Smith Letters
 Murray J. Smith Collection
   Walter N. Eames Letter
 Wiley Sword Collection
   Clark S. Edwards Letter
 Bell I. Wiley Collection
   T. Brent Swearingen Letter, Arthur Dehon Papers
 Michael Winey Collection
   Isaac R. Dunkelberger Memoir
United States Military Academy, West Point, N.Y.
 C. R. Lyon Family Papers
University of Georgia, Athens, Ga.
 Sanford W. Branch Letters, Margaret Branch Sexton Collection
 Thomas Reade Rootes Cobb Papers
 E. J. Eldridge Letter, Carlton-Newton-Mell Collection
 J. H. Lumpkin Papers
University of Michigan, Ann Arbor, Mich.
 John M. Bancroft Diary, Bancroft Collection
 Richard C. Halsey Letter
 William Ellis Jones Diary
 John Lehman Letter

Henry C. Marshall Letter
William F. Robinson Letter, Michigan Historical Collection
William Speed Letter
Unidentified Union soldier, "Fredericksburg during the Civil War," Schoff Collection
Edmund H. Wade Letter
University of North Carolina, Chapel Hill, N.C.
Southern Historical Collection
Edward Porter Alexander Papers
John Bratton Letter
John F. H. Claiborne Papers
Henry Lord Page King Diary
Evander McIvor Law Letters
David Gregg McIntosh Papers
Lafayette McLaws Papers
William Grove Morris Letter
William N. Pendleton Papers
R. Channing Price Papers
William L. Saunders Letter
Westwood A. Todd Reminiscences
Stephen B. Weeks Papers, "History and Biography of North Carolina"
University of Pittsburgh, Pittsburgh, Pa.
Matthew S. Quay Papers
University of South Carolina, Columbia, S.C.
Henry Calvin Conner Papers
Maxcy Gregg Papers
William R. Montgomery Papers
Joseph J. Norton Papers
Robert W. Shand Reminiscences
University of South Florida, Tampa, Fla.
Richard Floyd Letter, Governor John Milton Papers
University of Tennessee, Knoxville, Tenn.
John D. Damron Letter, Ann Penn Wray Collection
University of Virginia, Charlottesville, Va.
John W. Brockenbrough Papers
John Warwick Daniel Papers
University of West Virginia, Morgantown, W.Va.
George P. Wallace Letters, West Virginia Collection
Virginia Historical Society, Richmond, Va.
William H. Cocke Papers
Ambrose P. Hill Letter, Georgia Callis West Papers
Osmun Latrobe Diary
J. VanLew McCreery Recollections
William R. M. Slaughter Letter

Murray Forbes Taylor Papers
Virginia State Library, Richmond, Va.
James R. Boulware Diary
John O. Casler Letter, Bidgood Papers
G. T. H. Greer Papers
Western Michigan University, Kalamazoo, Mich.
Hiram Houghton Diary
Western Reserve Historical Society, Cleveland, Ohio
Robert C. Lamberton Diary
William and Mary, College of; Williamsburg, Va.
William B. Taliaferro Papers
Winthrop College, Rock Hill, S.C.
John D. McDonnell Memoir
Yale University, New Haven, Conn.
George W. Carleton Letter

NEWSPAPERS AND PERIODICALS

Athens (Ga.) Southern Banner, Jan. 7, 1863.
Athens (Ga.) Southern Watchman, Dec. 24, 1862.
Athens (Pa.) Gazette, March 11, 1897.
Atlanta Constitutional Magazine, March 15, 1931.
Atlanta Journal, 1901–1902.
Atlanta Southern Confederacy, 1862–1863.
Augusta (Ga.) Daily Constitutionalist, 1862–1863.
Bangor (Maine) Daily Whig and Courier, Dec. 27, 1862.
Beaver (Pa.) Weekly Argus, Dec. 24, 1862.
Berks and Schuylkill (Pa.) Journal, Jan. 3, 1863.
Berks, Chester, and Montgomery (Pa.) Ledger, Dec. 30, 1862.
Bladen (N.C.) Journal, Dec. 7, 1961.
Boston Journal, Dec. 13, 1892.
Brunswick (Maine) Telegraph, Jan. 2, 1863.
Carlisle (Pa.) Herald, Dec. 26, 1862.
Cedartown (Ga.) Standard, May 5, 16, 1914.
Charleston Daily Courier, 1862–1863.
Charleston Mercury, Dec. 25, 30, 1862.
Charleston News and Courier, 1862–1880.
Civil War Times Illustrated, May 1965.
Clearfield (Pa.), Raftsman's Journal, Jan. 7, 1863.
Cohoes (N.Y.) Cataract, Dec. 20, 1862.
Columbus (Ga.) Enquirer, Aug. 10, 1881.
Confederate Veteran, 1894–1915.
Cumberland Valley (Pa.) Journal, Dec. 18, 1862.
Elmira (N.Y.) Sunday Telegram, 1862–1863.

Elmira (N.Y.) Weekly Advertiser and Chemung County Republican, Dec. 27, 1862.

Franklin (N.Y.) Visitor, Jan. 6, 1863.

Fredericksburg Free-Lance, Dec. 24, 1910.

Glen Falls (N.Y.) Messenger, Jan. 20, 1863.

Grand Army Scout and Soldiers' Mail, 1883–1888.

Hackettstown (N.J.) Gazette, Jan. 8, 1863.

Herkimer County (N.Y.) Journal, Dec. 15, 25, 1862.

Hummelstown, (Pa.) Sun, 1895–1914.

Hunterdon (N.J.) Republican, 1862–1863.

Land We Love, vol. 1, 1866.

Lewiston (Maine) Daily Evening Journal, Oct. 16, 1862.

London Times, Jan. 1, 1863.

Miner's Journal, Jan. 3, 1863.

National Tribune, 1894–1925.

New York Irish-American, 1862–1863.

New York Times, Dec. 26, 1862.

Philadelphia Inquirer, 1862–1986.

Philadelphia Weekly Press, Jan. 8, 1888.

Philadelphia Weekly Times, 1879–1898.

Pittsburgh Post, Dec. 24, 1862.

Richmond Dispatch, 1895–1898.

Richmond Times-Dispatch, Jan. 20, 1907.

Rochester (N.Y.) Daily Union and Advertiser, Dec. 20, 1862.

Rochester (N.Y.) Democrat and American, Dec. 20, 22, 23, 1862.

Sandersville (Ga.) Central Georgian, Jan. 7, 14, 1863.

Savannah (Ga.) Republican, 1862–1863.

Selma (Ala.) Morning Reporter, Dec. 29, 1862.

Southern Bivouac, 1882–1886.

Southern Historical Society Papers, 1876–1944.

The Spur—Life in Virginia Past and Present, March, April 1956.

Staunton Spectator, 1862–1863.

Waterbury (Conn.) American, 1911–1913.

Wellsboro (Pa.) Agitator, Dec. 3, 1862.

Winchester (Va.) Times, Feb. 11, 1891.

Yorkville (S.C.) Enquirer, Dec. 24, 1862.

OTHER PUBLISHED PRIMARY SOURCES

Abbott, Henry L. *Fallen Leaves: The Civil War Letters of Major Henry Livermore Abbott.* Ed. Robert Garth Scott. Kent, Ohio: Kent State University Press, 1991.

Adams, John G. B. *Reminiscences of the Nineteenth Massachusetts Regiment.* Boston: Wright and Potter Printing Company, 1899.

Aldrich, Thomas M. *The History of the First Regiment Rhode Island Light Artillery.* Providence: Snow and Farnham, Printers, 1904.

Alexander, Andrew Jonathan. *The Life and Services of Brevet Brigadier General Andrew Jonathan Alexander.* New York: n.p., 1887.

Alexander, Edward Porter, *Fighting for the Confederacy: the Personal Recollections of General Edward Porter Alexander.* Ed. Gary W. Gallagher. Chapel Hill: University of North Carolina Press, 1989.

————. *Military Memoirs of a Confederate.* New York: Charles Scribner's Sons, 1907.

Allan, William. "Fredericksburg." In *Papers of the Military Historical Society of Massachusetts,* Vol. III, 1899.

Allen, George H. *Forty-six Months with the Fourth R.I. Volunteers.* Providence: J. A. and R. A. Reid, Printers, 1887.

Ames, J. W. "In Front of the Stone Wall at Fredericksburg." In vol. 3 of *Battles and Leaders of the Civil War,* ed. Clarence C. Buel and Robert U. Johnson. New York: Century Publishing, 1887.

Annual Report of the Adjutant-General of the State of New York for the Year 1901. Series no. 27. Albany: J. B. Lyon, 1902.

Archer, James J. "The James J. Archer Letters: A Marylander in the Civil War." *Maryland Historical Magazine* 65, no. 2 (June 1961).

Armstrong, William H. *Red-tape and Pigeon-hole Generals.* New York: Carlton, Publisher, 1864.

Bacon, William J. *Memorial to William Kirkland Bacon.* Utica, N.Y.: Roberts, Printer, 1863.

Baker, Henry H. *A Reminiscent Story of the Great Civil War . . . Second Paper.* New Orleans: Ruskin Press, 1911.

Banes, Charles H. *History of the Philadelphia Brigade.* Philadelphia: J. B. Lippincott, 1876.

Bartol, C. A. *The Nation's Hour: A Tribute to Major Sidney Willard.* Boston: Walker, Wise, 1862.

Bates, Samuel P. *History of Pennsylvania Volunteers 1861–1865,* 5 vols. Harrisburg: B. Singerly, 1869–1871.

Bayard, Samuel J. *Life of George Dashiel Bayard.* New York: G. B. Putnam's Sons, 1874.

Beale, Jane Howison. *The Journal of Jane Howison Beale of Fredericksburg, Virginia.* Ed. Barbara P. Willis. Fredericksburg: Fredericksburg Foundation, 1979.

Beale, Richard L. T. *History of the Ninth Virginia Cavalry in the War between the States.* Richmond: B. F. Johnson, 1899.

Benson, Berry. *Berry Benson's Civil War Book: Memoirs of a Confederate Scout and Sharpshooter.* Ed. Susan W. Benson. Athens: University of Georgia Press, 1962.

Billings, John D. *Hard Tack and Coffee.* Boston: George M. Smith, 1887.

Blackford, William W. *War Years with Jeb Stuart.* New York: Charles Scribner's Sons, 1945.

Bloodgood, John D. *Personal Reminiscences of the War.* New York: Hunt and Eaton, 1893.

Boone, Thomas D. *Before the Rebel Flag Fell.* N.p., 1968.

Borcke, Heros von. *Memoirs of the Confederate War of Independence.* 2 vols. New York: Peter Smith, 1938.

Borton, Benjamin. *On the Parallels.* Woodstown, N.J.: Monitor-Register Print, 1903.

Bosbyshell, Oliver Christian. *The Forty-eighth in the War.* Philadelphia: Avil Printing, 1895.

Bowen, Roland E. *From Ball's Bluff to Gettysburg . . . and Beyond: The Civil War Letters of Private Roland E. Bowen.* Ed. Gregory Coco. Gettysburg: Thomas Publications, 1994.

Brainerd, Wesley. *Bridge Building in War Time*. Ed. Ed Malles. Knoxville: University of Tennessee Press, 1997.

Brinton, John Hill. *Personal Memoirs of John H. Brinton Major and Surgeon, U.S.V., 1861–1865*. New York: Neale, 1914.

Brown, Thomas Watson. "The Military Career of Thomas R. R. Cobb." *Georgia Historical Society Journal* 45 (1961).

Bruce, George A. *The Twentieth Regiment of Massachusetts Volunteer Infantry*. Boston: Houghton, Mifflin, 1906.

Buck, Samuel D. *With the Old Confeds*. Baltimore: H. E. Houck, 1925.

Buel, Clarence C., and Robert U. Johnson, eds. *Battles and Leaders of the Civil War*. 4 vols. New York: Century, 1887–1888.

Bureau of the Census. *Eighth Census of the United States*. National Archives Microcopy 653, roll 1380: Spotsylvania/Fredericksburg.

Butler, H. A. "Fredericksburg—Personal Reminiscences." *Confederate Veteran* 14 (April 1906).

Caldwell, James F. J. *History of a Brigade of South Carolinians Known First as "Gregg's" and Subsequently as "McGowan's Brigade."* Philadelphia: King and Baird, Printers, 1866.

Canan, S. Dean. *History of Cambria County, Pennsylvania*. New York: Lewis, 1907.

Carter, Sidney. *Dear Bet: The Carter Letters*. Greenville, S.C.: Keys Printing, 1978.

Carter, Robert Goldwaite. *Four Brothers in Blue*. Washington, D.C.: Press of Gibson Brothers, Inc., 1913.

Carter, William. "Dead Horse Hill." *Home-maker* 3 no. 4 (January 1890).

Chamberlayne, John Hampden. *Ham Chamberlayne: Virginian*. Ed. C. G. Chamberlayne. Richmond: Press of Dietz Printing Co., 1932.

Chamberlain, Joshua L. "My Story of Fredericksburg." *Cosmopolitan Magazine*, January 1913.

Chambers, Henry A. *Diary of Captain Henry A. Chambers*. Ed. T. H. Pearce. Wendell, N.C.: Broadfoot Bookmark, 1983.

Chapin, Louis N. *A Brief History of the Thirty-fourth Regiment N.Y.S.V.* New York: published by the author, 1903.

Child, William. *History of the Fifth Regiment New Hampshire Volunteers*. Bristol: R. W. Musgrove, Printer, 1893.

Civil War Documents Granville County, North Carolina. Oxford: Granville County Historical Society, 1997.

Clark, Charles A. "Campaigning with the Sixth Maine." In *Military Order of the Loyal Legion of the United States, Iowa Commandery*. Des Moines: Kenyon Press, 1879.

Clark, Walter, ed. *Histories of the Several Regiments and Battalions from North Carolina in the Great War, 1861–65*. 5 vols. Goldsboro: State of North Carolina, 1901.

Cogswell, Leander W. *A History of the Eleventh New Hampshire Regiment*. Concord: Republican Press Association, 1891.

Cole, James R. *Miscellany*. Dallas: Press of Ewing B. Bedford, 1897.

Cole, Jacob H. *Under Five Commanders; or, A Boy's Experiences with the Army of the Potomac*. Paterson, N.J.: News Printing Co., 1906.

Cole, Robert T. *From Huntsville to Appomattox*. Ed. Jeffrey D. Stocker. Knoxville: University of Tennessee Press, 1996.

Cook, Benjamin F. *History of the Twelfth Massachusetts Volunteers*. Boston: Twelfth Regimental Association, 1882.

Cooke, John Esten. *Stonewall Jackson: A Military Biography*. New York: D. Appleton, 1866.

Cory, Eugene A. "A Private's Recollections of Fredericksburg." In *Personal Narratives of Events in the War of the Rebellion: Rhode Island Soldiers and Sailors Historical Society*. Providence: Rhode Island Sailors and Soldiers Historical Society, 1884.

Couch, Darius N. "Sumner's 'Right Grand Division.'" In vol. 3 of *Battles and Leaders of the Civil War*, ed. Clarence C. Buel and Robert U. Johnson. New York: Century, 1887.

Cowtan, Charles W. *Services of the Tenth New York Volunteers (National Zouaves) in the War of the Rebellion*. New York: Charles H. Ludwig, 1882.

Craft, David. *History of the 141st Regiment Pennsylvania Volunteers*. Towanda: published by the author, 1885.

Crotty, Daniel G. *Four Years Campaigning in the Army of the Potomac*. Grand Rapids: Dygert Brothers, 1874.

Cudworth, Warren H. *History of the First Regiment Massachusetts Infantry*. Boston: Walker, Fuller, 1866.

Currier, John C. *From Concord to Fredericksburg: A Paper Prepared and Read before the California Commandery* [etc.]. War Paper (Military Order of the Loyal Legion of the United States, California Commandery) Series, no. 15 [San Francisco?]: California Commandery, 1896.

Curtis, Newton Martin. *From Bull Run to Chancellorsville: The Story of the Sixteenth New York Infantry*. New York: G. P. Putnam's Sons, 1906.

Cushing, Samuel T. *The Acting Signal Corps*. Kansas City: Franklin Hudson, 1892.

Davenport, Alfred. *Camp and Field Life of the Fifth New York Volunteer Infantry*. New York: Dick and Fitzgerald, 1879.

Davidson, Greenlee. *Captain Greenlee Davidson, C.S.A.: Diary and Letters, 1851–1863*. Ed. Charles W. Turner. Verona, Virginia: McClure Press, 1975.

Davis, Charles E. *Three Years in the Army: The Story of the Thirteenth Massachusetts Volunteers*. Boston: Estes and Lauriet, 1894.

Dawson, Francis W. *Reminiscences of Confederate Service*. Charleston, South Carolina: News and Courier Book Presses, 1882.

De Trobriand, Philippe Régis de Keredern. *Four Years with the Army of the Potomac*. Boston: Ticknor, 1889.

Dickert, D. Augustus. *History of Kershaw's Brigade*. Newberry, S.C.: Elbert H. Aull Company, 1899.

Diman, George W. *Autobiography and Sketches of My Travels by Sea and Land*. Bristol [R.I.]: Press of the Semi-Weekly Bristol Phoenix, 1896.

Dinkins, James. "Barksdale's Mississippi Brigade at Fredericksburg." *Southern Historical Society Papers* 36.

Dooley, John E., ed. by Joseph T. Durkin. *John Dooley, Confederate Soldier*. Washington, D.C.: Georgetown University Press, 1945.

Dowdey, Clifford, and Louis Manarin, eds. *The Wartime Papers of R. E. Lee*. New York: Bramhall House, 1961.

Dunaway, Wayland Fuller. *Reminiscences of a Rebel*. New York: Neale, 1913.

Duncan, Louis C. *The Medical Department of the United States Army in the Civil War.* Washington D.C.: n.p., 191_.

Dwyer, John. *Address of John Dwyer.* New York: Herald Press, 1914.

Early, Jubal A. *Autobiographical Sketch and Narrative of the War between the States.* Philadelphia: J. B. Lippincott, 1912.

———. "Stonewall Jackson at Fredericksburg," *Historical Magazine* 8 (July 1870).

Evans, Clement A. *Intrepid Warrior.* Ed. Robert Grier Stephens, Jr. Dayton: Press of Morningside House, Inc., 1992.

Fairchild, Charles B. *History of the Twenty-seventh Regiment New York Volunteers.* Binghamton: Carl and Matthews, Printers, 1888.

Favill, Josiah M. *The Diary of a Young Officer.* Chicago: R. R. Donnelley and Sons, 1909.

The Fifth Reunion of the 155th Regiment Penna. Volunteers. Pittsburgh: Rawthorne Engraving and Printing Co., 1896.

Fitzpatrick, Marion H. *Letters to Amanda.* Culloden, Ga.: 1976.

Fletcher, William A. *Rebel Private Front and Rear.* Beaumont, Texas: Press of the Greer Print, 1908.

Ford, Andrew E. *The Story of the Fifteenth Regiment Massachusetts Volunteer Infantry.* Clinton: Press of W. J. Coulter, 1898.

Franklin, William B. *A Reply of Maj.-Gen. William B. Franklin to the Committee on the Conduct of the War.* New York: D. Van Nostrand, 1863.

Frederick, Gilbert. *The Story of a Regiment: Being a Record of the Military Services of the Fifty-seventh New York State Volunteer Infantry.* N.p., 1895.

Fuller, Charles A. *Personal Recollections of the War of 1861.* Sherburne, N.Y.: News Printing House, 1906.

Fuller, Richard F. *Chaplain Fuller.* Boston: Walker, Wise, 1863.

Fulton, William Frierson. *The Family Record and War Reminiscences of William Frierson Fulton.* N.p., 191_.

Galwey, Thomas F. *The Valiant Hours.* Harrisburg: Stackpole, 1961.

Gearhart, Edwin R. "Reminiscences of the Civil War." Parts 1, 2, and 3. *The Spur—Life in Virginia Past and Present* 6, no. 12 (March 1956); vol. 7, no. 1 (April 1956); vol. 7, no. 2 (May 1956).

Gerrish, Theodore. *Army Life: A Private's Reminiscences of the Civil War.* Portland, Maine: Hoyt, Fogg and Donham, 1882.

Gibbon, John. *Personal Recollections of the Civil War.* New York: G. P. Putnam's Sons, 1928.

Goddard, Henry P. *Regimental Reminiscences of the War of the Rebellion.* Middletown, Connecticut: C. W. Church, Printer, 1877.

Goldsborough, William W. *The Maryland Line in the Confederate Army.* Baltimore: Guggenheim, Weil, 1900.

Gould, Joseph. *The Story of the Forty-eighth.* Philadelphia: Alfred M. Slocum, 1908.

Graham, Matthew J. *The Ninth Regiment New York Volunteers (Hawkins' Zouaves).* New York, 1900.

Gregg, J. Chandler. *Life in the Army.* Philadelphia: Perkinpine and Higgins, 1868.

Grew, William. *Fredericksburg.* N.p., 1899 (copy at Civil War Library and Museum, Philadelphia, Pa.).

Grimes, Bryan. *Extracts of Letters of Major-General Bryan Grimes*. Raleigh: Alfred Williams, 1884.

Groene, Bertram H., ed. "Civil War Letters of Colonel David Lang." *Florida Historical Quarterly* 54 (January 1976).

Haggard, Horatio C. "Cavalry Fight at Fredericksburg." *Confederate Veteran* 21, no. 6 (June 1913).

Haines, Alanson A. *History of the Fifteenth Regiment New Jersey Volunteers*. New York: Jenkins and Thomas, 1883.

Haley, John W. *The Rebel Yell and Yankee Hurrah: The Civil War Journal of a Maine Volunteer*. Ed. Ruth L. Silliker. Camden, Maine: Down East Books, 1985.

Hall, Henry S. *Personal Experience under Generals Burnside and Hooker, in the Battles of Fredericksburg and Chancellorsville, December 11, 12, 13, and 14, 1862, and May 1, 2, 3, and 4, 1863* Kansas City: Franklin Hudson, 1889.

Handerson, Henry E. *Yankee in Gray*. Cleveland: Press of Western Reserve University, 1962.

Hanifen, Michael. *History of Battery B, First New Jersey Artillery*. Ottowa, Ill.: Republican-Times, Printers, 1905.

Haskell, John C. *The Haskell Memoirs*. Ed. Gilbert E. Govan and James W. Livingood. New York: G. P. Putnam's Sons, 1960.

Haupt, Herman. *Reminiscences of General Herman Haupt*. Milwaukee: Wright and Joys, 1901.

Hill, Edward. "The Last Charge at Fredericksburg." In *Proceedings of the Third Brigade Association, First Division, Fifth Army Corps*. New York: Rider and Driver, 1892.

A Historical Sketch of the Quitman Guards, Company E, Harris' Brigade. New Orleans: Isaac T. Hinton, Printer, 1866.

History of the First Regiment Minnesota Volunteer Infantry. Stillwater: Easton and Masterman, 1916.

History of the Nineteenth Massachusetts Volunteer Infantry. Salem: Salem Press, 1906.

History of the 118th Pennsylvania Volunteers (Corn Exchange Regiment). Philadelphia: J. L. Smith, 1888.

History of the 121st Regiment Pennsylvania Volunteers. Philadelphia: Burk and McFetridge, 1893.

History of the 127th Regiment Pennsylvania Volunteers. Lebanon: Report Publishing Co., 1902.

Hitchcock, Frederick L. *War from the Inside*. Philadelphia: J. B. Lippincott, 1904.

Hodgkins, Joseph E. *The Civil War Diary of Lieut. J. E. Hodgkins*. Ed. Kenneth C. Turino. Camden, N.J.: Picton Press, 1994.

Holmes, Oliver W., Jr. *"Touched by Fire": Civil War Letters and Diary of Oliver Wendell Holmes, Jr*. Ed. Mark De Wolfe. Cambridge: Harvard University Press, 1947.

Holsinger, Frank. "How Does One Feel under Fire?" In *War Talks in Kansas: A Series of Papers Read before the Kansas Commandery* [etc.], ed. Military Order of the Loyal Legion of the United States, Kansas Commandery. Kansas City: Franklin Hudson, 1906.

Hood, John Bell. *Advance and Retreat*. Philadelphia: Press of Burk and McFetridge, 1880.

Hopkins, William P. *The Seventh Rhode Island Volunteers*. Providence: Providence Press, 1903.

Houghton, Edwin B. *The Campaigns of the Seventeenth Maine*. Portland: Short and Loring, 1866.

Howard, Oliver O. *Autobiography of Oliver Otis Howard*. 2 vols. New York: Baker and Taylor, 1907.

Humphreys, Henry H. *Andrew Atkinson Humphreys: A Biography.* Philadelphia: John C. Winston, 1924.

———. *Major General Andrew Atkinson Humphreys United States Volunteers at Fredericksburg and Farmville.* Chicago: Press of R. R. McCabe, n.d.

Hussey, George A. *History of the Ninth N.Y.S.M.* New York: J. S. Ogilvie, 1889.

Hutchison, J. G. "Fredericksburg." In *War Sketches and Incidents*, ed. Military Order of the Loyal Legion of the United States, Commandery of Iowa. Des Moines: N.p., 1898.

Jackman, Lymann. *History of the Sixth New Hampshire Regiment.* Concord: Republican Press, 1891.

Jackson, Edgar A., ed. *Three Rebels Write Home.* Franklin, Va.: News Publishing Company, 1955.

Jackson, Mary Anna. *Memoirs of "Stonewall" Jackson.* Louisville, Ky.: Courier Journal Job Printing Co., 1895.

James, Henry B. *Memories of the Civil War.* New Bedford, Mass.: Franklin E. James, 1898.

Jaques, John W. *Three Years' Campaign of the Ninth N.Y.S.M., during the Southern Rebellion* New York: Hilton, 1895.

Jones, J. William. *Life and Letters of Robert Edward Lee, Soldier and Man.* New York: Neale, 1906.

Judd, David W. *The Story of the Thirty-third N.Y.S.V.* Rochester: Benton and Andrews, 1864.

Judson, Amos M. *History of the Eighty-third Pennsylvania Volunteers.* Erie: B. F. H. Lynn, 1865.

Keely, John W. "Reminiscences." *Atlanta Constitutional Magazine*, March 15, 1931.

Kepler, William. *History of the Fourth Regiment Ohio Volunteer Infantry in the War for the Union.* Cleveland: Leader Print Co., 1886.

Kerbey, Joseph O. *On the Warpath.* Chicago: Donohue, Henneberry, 1890.

Kerr, John H. *Oration Delivered at the First Reunion of the 155th Regiment Pennsylvania Veteran Volunteers.* Pittsburgh: Samuel F. Kerr, Printer, 1875.

Kimball, Orville S. *History and Personal Sketches of Company I, 103rd N.Y.S.V.* Elmira: Facts Printing Co., 1900.

Lapham, Oscar. "Recollections of Service in the Twelfth Regiment, R.I. Volunteers." In *Personal Narratives of Events in the War of the Rebellion: Rhode Island Soldiers and Sailors Historical Society.* Providence: Rhode Island Soldiers and Sailors Historical Society, 1885.

Leach, J. Granville. "History of the Twenty-fifth New Jersey Volunteer Regiment, Company F." *Cape May County Magazine of History and Genealogy*, June 1974.

Lee, Robert E., Jr. *Recollections and Letters of General Robert E. Lee.* New York: Doubleday, Page, 1904.

Lewis, George. *The History of Battery E, First Regiment Rhode Island Light Artillery.* Providence: Snow and Farnham, 1892.

Lewis, Richard. *Camp Life of a Boy of Bratton's Brigade.* Charleston, S.C.: News and Courier Presses, 1883.

Lindsley, John B., ed. *The Military Annals of Tennessee.* 2 vols. Nashville: J. M. Lindsley, 1886.

Lloyd, J. C. "The Battles of Fredericksburg." *Confederate Veteran* 23 (1915).

Lloyd, William P. *History of the First Regiment Pennsylvania Reserve Cavalry.* Philadelphia: King and Baird, 1864.

Locke, William Henry. *The Story of a Regiment*. Philadelphia: J. B. Lippincott, 1868.

Loehr, Charles T. *War History of the Old First Virginia Infantry Regiment*. Richmond: William Ellis Jones, Printer, 1884.

Longstreet, James. "The Battle of Fredericksburg." In vol. 3 of *Battles and Leaders of the Civil War*, ed. Clarence C. Buel and Robert U. Johnson. New York: Century Publishing, 1887.

———. *From Manassas to Appomattox*. Philadelphia: J. B. Lippincott, 1896.

———. "'The Ruling Ideas' of the Pennsylvania Campaign." Ed. Richard Rollins. *Gettysburg Magazine*, no. 17 (1997).

MacNamara, Michael H. *History of the Ninth Regiment Massachusetts Volunteers*. Boston: E. B. Stillings, 1899.

———. *The Irish Ninth*. Boston: Lee and Shepard, 1867.

Malone, Bartlett Yancey. *Whipt 'Em Everytime*. Jackson, Tenn.: McCowat-Mercer Press, 1960.

Maxfield, Albert, and Robert Brady, Jr. *Roster and Statistical Record of Company D, of the Eleventh Maine Infantry Volunteers*. New York: Press of Thomas Humphrey, 1890.

McClellan, Carswell. *General Andrew A. Humphreys at Malvern Hill and Fredericksburg*. St. Paul: privately printed, 1888.

McClellan, Henry B. *The Life and Campaigns of Maj.-General J. E. B. Stuart*. Boston: Houghton, Mifflin, 1885.

McClendon, William A. *Recollections of War Times*. Montgomery, Ala.: Paragon Press, 1909.

McClenthen, Charles S. *Narrative of the Fall and Winter Campaign*. Syracuse: Masters and Lee, 1863.

McCrea, Tully. *Dear Belle*. Middletown, Conn.: Wesleyan University Press, 1965.

McDaniel, Henry D. *With Unabated Trust*. Monroe, Ga.: Historical Society of Walton County, 1977.

McLaws, Lafayette. "The Battle of Fredericksburg." In *Addresses Delivered before the Confederate Veterans of Savannah, Georgia*. Savannah, 1895.

———. "The Confederate Left at Fredericksburg." In vol. 3 of *Battles and Leaders of the Civil War*, ed. Clarence C. Buel and Robert U. Johnson. New York: Century Publishing, 1887.

Meade, George Gordon. *Life and Letters of George Gordon Meade*. 2 vols. New York: Charles Scribner's Sons, 1913.

Mehen, J. R. "An Incident of Fredericksburg." *Confederate Veteran* 23 (Sept. 1915).

Melcher, Holman S. *With a Flash of His Sword: the Writings of Major Holman S. Melcher*. Ed. William B. Styple. Kearny, N.J.: Belle Grove, 1994.

Merchant, Thomas E. *Eighty-fourth Regiment, Pennsylvania Volunteers Address*. N.p., 1889.

Merrill, Samuel H. *The Campaigns of the First Maine and First District of Columbia Cavalry*. Portland: Bailey and Noyes, 1866.

Milans, Henry G. "Eyewitness to Fredericksburg." Ed. Doug Land. *North-South Trader's Civil War* 19 no. 6 (Christmas 1992).

Moore, David S. *I Will Try to Send You All the Particulars of the Fight*. Albany: Friends of the New York State Newspaper Project, 1995.

Morrow, William H. *Under the Red Patch: The Story of the Sixty-third Regiment Pennsylvania Volunteers*. Pittsburgh: Press of Market Review Publishing Co., 1908.

Mulholland, St. Clair A. *Military Order Congress Medal of Honor Legion of the United States*. Philadelphia: Town Printing Co., 1905.

———. *The Story of the 116th Regiment Pennsylvania Volunteers.* Philadelphia: F. McManus, Jr., 1903.

Murphey, Josiah F. *The Nantucket Experience Including the Memoirs of Josiah Fitch Murphey.* Ed. by Richard F. Miller and Robert E. Mooney. Nantucket, Mass.: Wesco, 1994.

Nash, Eugene A. *A History of the Forty-fourth Regiment New York Volunteer Infantry.* Chicago: R. R. Donnelley and Sons, 1911.

Nisbet, James C. *Four Years on the Firing Line.* Chattanooga: Imperial Press, 1915.

Norman, William M. *A Portion of My Life.* Winston-Salem: John F. Blair, 1959.

Norton, Oliver Willcox. *Army Letters, 1861–1865.* Chicago: O. L. Deming, 1903.

Nugent, Robert. "The Sixty-ninth Regiment at Fredericksburg," In *Third Annual Report of the State Historian of the State of New York.* Albany, 1898.

Oates, William C. *The War between the Union and the Confederacy.* New York: Neale, 1905.

Official Records of the Union and Confederate Navies in the War of the Rebellion. 31 vols. Washington, D.C.: Government Printing Office, 1895–1929.

Orwig, Joseph R. *History of the 131st Pennsylvania Volunteers.* Williamsport: Sun Book and Job Printing House, 1902.

Owen, William M. *In Camp and Battle with the Washington Artillery of New Orleans.* Boston: Ticknor, 1885.

———. "A Hot Day on Marye's Heights." In vol. 3 of *Battles and Leaders of the Civil War,* ed. Clarence C. Buel and Robert U. Johnson. New York: Century Publishing, 1887.

Page, Charles. *History of the Fourteenth Regiment Connecticut Volunteer Infantry.* Meridian, Conn.: Horton Printing Co., 1906.

Palfrey, Francis W. *The Antietam and Fredericksburg.* New York: Charles Scribner's Sons, 1882.

Paris, Louis-Phillipe-Albert d'Orléans, comte de. *History of the Civil War in America.* 2 vols. Philadelphia: Joseph H. Coates, 1876.

Parker, Francis J. *History of the Thirty-second Regiment Massachusetts Volunteers.* Boston: C. W. Calkins, 1880.

Parker, John L. *History of the Twenty-second Massachusetts Infantry.* Boston: Rand Avery, 1887.

Parker, Thomas H. *History of the Fifty-first Regiment of Pennsylvania Volunteers.* Philadelphia: King and Baird, Printers, 1869.

Patrick, Marsena R. *Inside Lincoln's Army.* Ed. David S. Sparks. New York: Thomas Yoseloff, 1964.

Paxton, Elisha F. *The Civil War Letters of Frank "Bull" Paxton.* Ed. John G. Paxton. New York: Neale, 1907.

Pender, William D. *The General to His Lady: The Civil War Letters of William Dorsey Pender.* Ed. William W. Hassler. Chapel Hill: University of North Carolina Press, 1965.

Pendleton, William N. *Memoirs of William Nelson Pendleton.* Ed. Susan P. Lee. Philadelphia: J. B. Lippincott, 1893.

Personal Narratives of Events in the War of the Rebellion: Rhode Island Soldiers and Sailors Historical Society. 7 vols. Providence: Rhode Island Soldiers and Sailors Historical Society, 1884.

Pettit, William B. "The Boys Who Wore the Gray." *Bulletin of the Fluvanna County Historical Society,* no. 42 (October 1986).

Pleasants, Reuben B. *Contributions to a History of the Richmond Howitzers Battalion.* Pamphlet no. 3. Richmond: Carlton McCarthy, 1884.

Plum, William R. *The Military Telegraph during the Civil War in the United States.* Chicago: Jansen, McClurg, 1882.

Poague, William T. *Gunner with Stonewall.* Jackson, Tenn.: McCowat-Mercer Press, 1957.

Polley, Joseph B. *Hood's Texas Brigade.* New York: Neale, 1910.

Powell, William H. *The Fifth Army Corps.* New York: G. P. Putnam's Sons, 1896.

Pryor, Shepherd G. *A Post of Honor: The Pryor Letters.* Ed. Charles R. Adams, Jr. Fort Valley, Georgia: Garrett Publications, 1989.

Pyne, Henry R. *The History of the First New Jersey Cavalry.* Trenton: J. A. Beecher, 1871.

Rauscher, Frank. *Music on the March, 1862–1865.* Philadelphia: William F. Fell, 1892.

Rawlings, Benjamin C. *Benjamin Carson Rawlings, First Virginia Volunteer for the South.* Ed. Byrd Tribble. Baltimore: Butternut and Blue, 1996.

Reeves, James J. *History of the Twenty-fourth Regiment, New Jersey Volunteers.* Woodbury, N.J.: S. Chew, Printer, 1889.

Reunions of the Nineteenth Maine Regiment Association. Augusta, Maine: Sprague, Owen and Nash, 1878.

Rhodes, Elisha H. *All for the Union: The Civil War Diary and Letters of Elisha Hunt Rhodes.* Ed. Robert H. Rhodes. New York: Orion Books, 1985.

Rhodes, John H. *The History of Battery B, 1st Regiment Rhode Island Light Artillery.* Providence: Snow and Farnham, 1894.

Roemer, Jacob. *Reminiscences of the War of the Rebellion.* Flushing, N.Y.: Estate of Jacob Roemer, 1897.

Rutter, Samuel H. "The Civil War Correspondence of Samuel Hockley Rutter." *Bulletin of the Historical Society of Montgomery County, Pennsylvania.* 1975.

Sanford, George B. *Fighting Rebels and Redskins: Experience in Army Life of Colonel George B. Sanford, 1861–1892.* Ed. by E. R. Hageman. Norman: University of Oklahoma Press, 1969.

Sawyer, Franklin. *A Military History of the Eighth Regiment Ohio Volunteer Infantry.* Cleveland: Fairbanks, 1881.

Scales, Alfred M. *The Battle of Fredericksburg: An Address.* Washington, D.C.: R. O. Polkinhorn and Son, Printer, 1884.

Scott, Kate M. *History of the One Hundred and Fifth Regiment of Pennsylvania Volunteers.* Philadelphia: New-World Publishing Co., 1877.

Sheldon, Winthrop D. *The Twenty-seventh: A Regimental History.* New Haven: Morris and Benham, 1866.

Sloan, John A. *Reminiscences of the Guilford Grays.* Washington, D.C.: R. O. Polkinhorn, Printer, 1883.

Small, Abner R. *The Road to Richmond.* Berkeley: University of California Press, 1939.

———. *The Sixteenth Maine Regiment in the War of the Rebellion.* Portland: B.Thurston, 1886.

Smith, Abram P. *History of the Seventy-sixth Regiment New York Volunteers.* Syracuse: Truair, Smith and Miles, Printers, 1867.

Smith, James Power. *With Stonewall Jackson in the Army of Northern Virginia.* Gaithersburg, Md.: Zullo and Van Sickle Books, 1982.

Smith, John Day. *History of the Nineteenth Maine Volunteers.* Minneapolis: Great Western, 1909.

Smith, Weston A. *The Anson Guards*. Charlotte, N.C.: Stone, 1914.

Smith, William F. *Autobiography of Major General William F. Smith*. Ed. by Herbert M. Schiller. Dayton: Press of Morningside, 1990.

———. "Burnside Relieved." *Magazine of American History* 15 (1885).

———. "The Military Situation in Northern Virginia from the 1st to the 14th of November, 1862." In vol. 3 of *Papers of the Military Historical Society of Massachusetts*. Boston: Military Historical Society of Massachusetts, 1899.

Sorrel, Gilbert Moxley. *Recollections of a Confederate Staff Officer*. New York: Neale, 1905.

Spangler, Edward W. *My Little War Experience*. York, Pa., 1904.

Spear, Ellis. *The Civil War Recollections of General Ellis Spear*. Ed. Abbott Spear. Orono: University of Maine Press, 1997.

Sprenger, George F. *Concise History of the Camp and Field Life of the 122d Regiment, Pennsylvania Volunteers*. Lancaster: New Era Steam Book Print, 1885.

Stevens, Charles A. *Berdan's Sharpshooters in the Army of the Potomac*. St. Paul: Price McGill, 1892.

Stevens, George T. *Three Years in the Sixth Corps*. Albany: S. R. Gray, 1866.

Stevens, Henry S. *Souvenir of Excursion to Battlefields by the Society of the Fourteenth Connecticut Regiment*. Washington, D.C.: Gibson Brothers, 1893.

Stevens, John W. *Reminiscences of the Civil War*. Hillsboro, Texas: Hillsboro Mirror Print, 1902.

Stewart, William H. *A Pair of Blankets*. New York: Broadway, 1911.

Stiles, Robert. *Four Years under Marse Robert*. New York: Neale, 1903.

Stine, James H. *History of the Army of the Potomac*. Philadelphia: J. B. Rodgers Printing Co., 1892.

Stone, James M. *Personal Recollections of the Civil War*. Boston: published by the author, 1917.

The Story of the Twenty-first Regiment Connecticut Volunteers. Middletown: Press of the Stewart Printing Co., 1900.

Stuckenberg, John H. W. *I'm Surrounded by Methodists: Diary of John H.W. Stuckenberg*. Ed. by David T. Hedrick and Gordon Barry Davis, Jr. Gettysburg, Pa.: Thomas Publications, 1995.

Supplement to the Official Records of the Union and Confederate Armies. 70 vols. Wilmington, N.C.: Broadfoot, 1994–2000.

Sutton, E. H. *Civil War Stories*. Demorist, Ga.: Banner Printing Co., 1910.

Swinton, William. *Campaigns of the Army of the Potomac*. New York: Charles Scribner's Sons, 1882.

Sypher, Josiah R. *History of the Pennsylvania Reserve Corps*. Lancaster: Elias Barr, 1865.

Taylor, Walter H. *Four Years with General Lee*. New York: D. Appleton, 1877.

———. *Lee's Adjutant: The Wartime Letters of Colonel Walter Herron Taylor*. Ed. R. Lockwood Tower. Columbia: University of South Carolina Press, 1995.

Thompson, Gilbert. *The Engineer Battalion in the Civil War*. Washington, D.C.: Press of the Engineer School, Washington Barracks, 1910.

Thompson, James B. *The Civil War Letters of Lieutenant James B. Thompson*. Ed. Richard Sauers. Baltimore: Butternut and Blue, 1995.

Thompson, S. Millett. *Thirteenth Regiment of New Hampshire Volunteer Infantry*. Boston and New York: Houghton, Mifflin, 1888.

Thomson, O. R. Howard, and William H. Rauch. *History of the "Bucktails": Kane's Rifle Regiment of the Pennsylvania Reserve Corps.* Philadelphia: Electric Print Co., 1906.

Thorpe, Sheldon B. *The History of the Fifteenth Connecticut Volunteers.* New Haven: Price, Lee and Adkins, 1893.

Tobie, Edward P. *History of the First Maine Cavalry, 1861–1865.* Boston: Press of Emery and Hughs, 1887.

Truxell, Ada Craig, ed. *Respects to All: Letters of Two Pennsylvania Boys in the War of the Rebellion.* Pittsburgh: University of Pittsburgh, 1962.

Under the Maltese Cross. Pittsburgh: 155th Regimental Association, 1910.

U.S. Congress. *Report of the Joint Committee on the Conduct of the War.* 37th Cong., 3rd sess., no. 108. 3 vols. Washington, D.C.: Government Printing Office, 1863.

Wainwright, Charles S. *Diary of Battle: The Personal Journals of Colonel Charles S. Wainwright.* Ed. Allan Nevins. New York: Harcourt, Brace and World, 1962.

Walcott, Charles F. *History of the Twenty-first Regiment Massachusetts Volunteers.* Boston: Houghton, Mifflin, 1882.

Walker, Francis A. *History of the Second Army Corps.* New York: Charles Scribner's Sons, 1891.

———. "Reams Station." In vol. 5 of *Papers of the Military Historical Society of Massachusetts.* Boston: Military Historical Society of Massachusetts, 1905.

The War of the Rebellion: A Compilation of the Official Records of the Union and Confederate Armies. 128 vols. Washington, D.C.: U.S. Government Printing Office, 1880–1901.

Ward, Joseph R. C. *One Hundred and Sixth Regiment Pennsylvania Volunteers.* Philadelphia: F. McManus, Jr., 1906.

Warfield, Edgar A. *A Confederate Soldier's Memoirs.* Richmond: Mason Home Press, 1936.

Warren, Horatio N. *Two Reunions of the 142d Regiment Pa. Vols.* Buffalo, N.Y.: Courier Co., Printers, 1890.

Warren, Kittrell J. *History of the Eleventh Georgia Volunteers.* Richmond: Smith, Bailey, 1863.

Watson, William. *Letters of a Civil War Surgeon.* Lafayette: Purdue University Studies, 1961.

Weygant, Charles H. *History of the 124th Regiment N.Y.S.V.* Newburgh, N.Y.: Journal Printing House, 1877.

Weymouth, Albert B. *A Memorial Sketch of Lieut. Edgar N. Newcomb.* Malden, Mass.: Alvin G. Brown, 1883.

Weymouth, Harrison G. O. "The Crossing of the Rappahannock by the Nineteenth Massachusetts." In vol. 3 of *Battles and Leaders of the Civil War*, ed. Clarence C. Buel and Robert U. Johnson. New York: Century Publishing, 1887.

White, Wyman S. *The Civil War Diary of Wyman S. White.* Ed. Russell C. White. Baltimore: Butternut and Blue, 1991.

Whitman, George W. *Civil War Letters of George Washington Whitman.* Ed. Jerome M. Loving. Durham: Duke University Press, 1975.

Whitney, John H. E. *The Hawkins Zouaves.* New York: published by the author, 1866.

Wightman, Edward K. *From Antietam to Fort Fisher.* Ed. by Edward G. Longacre. Rutherford: Fairleigh Dickinson University Press, 1985.

Williams, Frank B. *Reminiscences of the Fiftieth New York Regiment Engineers.* Washington, D.C.: Chronicle Print, n.d.

Wingfield, Henry W. "Diary of Capt. Henry W. Wingfield 58th Va. Reg." *Bulletin of the Virginia State Library* 16, nos. 2–3 (July 1927).

Wood, James H. *The War, Stonewall Jackson, His Campaigns and Battles, the Regiment, as I Saw Them.* Cumberland, Md.: Eddy Press, 1910.

Woodbury, Augustus. *General Halleck and General Burnside.* Boston: John Wilson and Son, 1864.

Woodward, Evan M. *History of the Third Pennsylvania Reserve.* Trenton, N.J.: MacCrellish and Quigley, Printers, 1883.

———. *Our Campaigns.* Philadelphia: John E. Potter, 1865.

Wren, James. *From New Berne to Fredericksburg.* Ed. John M. Priest. Shippensburg, Pa.: White Mane, 1990.

Young, Jesse B. *What a Boy Saw in the Army.* New York: Hunt and Eaton, 1894.

PUBLISHED SECONDARY SOURCES

Alexander, Ted. *The 126th Pennsylvania.* Shippensburg: Beidel Printing House, 1984.

Angle, Paul M. and Earl Schenck Miers. *The Living Lincoln The Man, His Mind, His Times, and the War He Fought, Reconstructed from His Own Writings.* New Brunswick, N.J.: Rutgers University Press, 1955.

Austin, Aurelia. *Georgia Boys with Stonewall Jackson.* Athens: University of Georgia Press, 1967.

Bache, Richard M. *Life of General George Gordon Meade.* Philadelphia: Henry T. Coates, 1897.

Bigelow, John. *The Chancellorsville Campaign.* New Haven: Yale University Press, 1910.

Blair, William A. "Barbarians at Fredericksburg's Gate: The Impact of the Union Army on Civilians," In *The Fredericksburg Campaign: Decision on the Rappahannock*, ed. Gary W. Gallagher. Chapel Hill: University of North Carolina Press, 1995.

Brogan, Hugh, ed. *The Times Reports the American Civil War.* London: Times Books, 1975.

Case, Lynn M., and Warren F. Spencer. *The United States and France: Civil War Diplomacy.* Philadelphia: University of Pennsylvania Press, 1970.

Catton, Bruce. *Mr. Lincoln's Army.* Garden City, N.Y.: Doubleday, 1951.

Cavanagh, Michael. *Memoirs of General Thomas Francis Meagher.* Worcester, Mass.: Messenger Press, 1892.

Chambers, Lenoir. *"Stonewall" Jackson.* 2 vols. New York: William Morrow, 1959.

Cleaves, Freeman. *Meade of Gettysburg.* Norman: University of Oklahoma Press, 1960.

Conyngham, David P. *The Irish Brigade and Its Campaigns.* New York: William McSorley, 1867.

Cook, Roy Bird. *The Family and Early Life of "Stonewall" Jackson.* Charleston, W.Va.: Jarrett Printing Co., 1924.

Coughlin, R. E. *Engineer Operations in Past Wars.* Fort Humphreys, Va.: The Engineer School, 1926.

Dabney, Robert L. *Life and Campaigns of Lieut.-Gen. Thomas J. Jackson ("Stonewall" Jackson).* New York: Blelock, 1866.

Dalton, Cyndi. *The Blanket Brigade.* Union, Maine: Union Publishing Co., 1995.

Davis, William C., ed. *The Confederate General.* 6 vols. N.p.: National Historical Society, c. 1991.

Driver, Robert J., Jr. *The First and Second Rockbridge Artillery*. Lynchburg, Va.: H. E. Howard, 1987.

Dyer, John P. *The Gallant Hood*. Indianapolis: Bobbs-Merrill, 1955.

Ellison, B. M., and B. F. Emanuel. *The Humane Hero of Fredericksburg: The Story of Richard Kirkland*. Lancaster, S.C.: Carolina Museum, 1962.

Forney, John W. *Life and Military Career of Winfield Scott Hancock*. Philadelphia: Hubbard Brothers, 1880.

Fox, William F., ed. *New York at Gettysburg*. 3 vols. Albany: J. B. Lyon, 1900.

Freeman, Douglas Southall. *R. E. Lee*. 4 vols. New York: Charles Scribner's Sons, 1934–1936.

———. *Lee's Lieutenants*. 3 vols. New York: Charles Scribner's Sons, 1942–1944.

Gallagher, Gary W. "The Yanks Have Had a Terrible Whipping: Confederates Evaluate the Battle of Fredericksburg." In *The Fredericksburg Campaign: Decision on the Rappahannock*, ed. Gary W. Gallagher. Chapel Hill: University of North Carolina Press, 1995.

Gambone, Al M. *The Life of General Samuel K. Zook*. Baltimore: Butternut and Blue, 1996.

Greene, A. Wilson. "Morale, Maneuver, and Mud: The Army of the Potomac, December 16, 1862–January 26, 1863." In *The Fredericksburg Campaign: Decision on the Rappahannock*, ed. Gary W. Gallagher. Chapel Hill: University of North Carolina Press, 1995.

———. "Opportunity to the South: Meade versus Jackson at Fredericksburg." *Civil War History* 33, no. 4 (1987).

Greene, Jacob L. Gen. *William B. Franklin and the Operations of the Left Wing at the Battle of Fredericksburg*. New York: Belknap and Warfield, 1900.

Hagerty, Edward. *Collis' Zouaves*. Baton Rouge: Louisiana State University Press, 1997.

Harrison, Noel G. *Fredericksburg Civil War Sites*. 2 vols. Lynchburg, Va.: H. E. Howard, 1995.

———. *Gazetteer of Historic Sites Related to the Fredericksburg and Spotsylvania National Military Park,* 2 vols. Fredericksburg: National Park Service, 1989.

Harper, Douglas R. *"If Thee Must Fight": A Civil War History of Chester County, Pennsylvania*. West Chester, Pa.: Chester County Historical Society, 1990.

Hassler, William W. *Colonel John Pelham: Lee's Boy Artillerist*. Richmond: Garrett and Massie, 1960.

Hawley, Steven C. "Barksdale's Mississippi Brigade at Fredericksburg," *Civil War History* 40, no. 1 (1994).

Henderson, George F. R. *The Campaign of Fredericksburg*. London: Gale and Polden, 1891.

———. *"Stonewall" Jackson and the American Civil War*. 2 vols. New York: Longmans, Green, 1904.

Hickerson, Thomas F. *Echoes of Happy Valley*. Chapel Hill: published by the author, n.d.

Hubbell, Raynor. *Confederate Stamps, Old Letters and History*. N.p., 1959.

Imholte, John Quinn. *The First Volunteers: History of the First Minnesota*. Minneapolis: Ross and Haines, 1963.

Jones, Kenneth D. "The Fourth Alabama Infantry: A Fighting Legion." *Alabama Historical Quarterly* 38 no. 3 (fall 1976).

Jordan, Donaldson, and Edwin J. Pratt. *Europe and the American Civil War*. Boston: Houghton Mifflin, 1931.

Krick, Robert E. L. *Fortieth Virginia*. Lynchburg, Va.: H. E. Howard, 1985.

Krick, Robert K. *The Fredericksburg Artillery*. Lynchburg, Va.: H. E. Howard, 1986.

———. *Lee's Colonels: A Biographical Register of the Field Officers of the Army of Northern Virginia.* Dayton: Press of Morningside House, 1991.

———. "Maxcy Gregg: Political Extremist and Confederate General." *Civil War History* 19, no. 4 (1973).

Lambert, Darwin. *Undying Past of Shenandoah National Park.* Niwot, Colo.: Roberts Rinehart, 1989.

Lightsey, Ada Christine. *The Veteran's Story.* Meridian, Miss.: Meridian News, Printers, 1899.

Long, E. B. *The Civil War Day by Day: An Almanac.* Garden City, N.Y.: Doubleday, 1971.

Longacre, Edward G. *The Man behind the Guns: A Biography of General Henry J. Hunt.* South Brunswick, N.J.: A. S. Barnes, 1977.

Lord, Francis A. *Lincoln's Railroad Man: Herman Haupt.* Rutherford: Fairleigh Dickinson University Press, 1969.

Marvel, William. *Burnside.* Chapel Hill: University of North Carolina Press, 1991.

———. "The Making of a Myth: Ambrose E. Burnside and the Union High Command at Fredericksburg." In *The Fredericksburg Campaign: Decision on the Rappahannock*, ed. Gary W. Gallagher. Chapel Hill: University of North Carolina Press, 1995.

———. *Race of the Soil: The Ninth New Hampshire.* Wilmington, N.C.: Broadfoot, 1988.

McCabe, James D. *Life and Campaigns of General Robert E. Lee.* New York: Blelock, 1867.

McMurry, Richard M. *John Bell Hood and the War for Southern Independence.* Lexington: University Press of Kentucky, 1982.

The Medal of Honor of the United States Army. Washington, D.C.: Government Printing Office, 1948.

Mercer, Philip. *The Life of the Gallant Pelham.* Macon, Ga.: J. W. Burke, 1929.

Michigan Adjutant-General's Department. *Record of Service of Michigan Volunteers in the Civil War.* 46 vols. Kalamazoo: Ihling Brothers and Everard, Printers, 1905.

Mills, William H. "From Burnside to Hooker: The Transfer of the Army of the Potomac," *Magazine of American History* 15 (1885).

Moe, Richard. *The Last Full Measure: The Life and Death of the First Minnesota Volunteers.* New York: Henry Holt, 1993.

Moore, Albert B. *Conscription and Conflict in the Confederacy.* New York: Macmillan, 1924.

Mundy, James H. *Second to None: The Story of the Second Maine Volunteer Infantry.* Scarborough, Maine: Harp Publications, 1992.

Murray, Alton J. *South Georgia Rebels.* St. Mary's, Ga.: published by the author, 1976.

Naisawald, L. VanLoan. *Grape and Canister.* New York: Oxford University Press, 1960.

Nevins, Allan. *The War for the Union.* 4 vols. New York: Charles Scribner's Sons, 1960.

Nichols, James L. *General Fitzhugh Lee: A Biography.* Lynchburg, Va.: H. E. Howard, 1989.

Nichols, Edward J. *Toward Gettysburg: A Biography of General John F. Reynolds.* State College: Pennsylvania State University Press, 1958,

Nolan, Alan T. "Confederate Leadership at Fredericksburg." In *The Fredericksburg Campaign: Decision on the Rappahannock*, ed. Gary W. Gallagher. Chapel Hill: University of North Carolina Press, 1995.

Ogden, James H., III. "Prelude to Battle: Burnside and Fredericksburg, November 1862." *Morningside Notes* (1988).

O'Reilly, Frank A. "One of the Greatest Military Feats of the War." *Journal of Fredericksburg History* 2 (1997).

————. "The Pennsylvania Reserves at Fredericksburg." *Civil War Regiments* 4, no. 4 (1995).

————. *"Stonewall" Jackson at Fredericksburg: The Battle of Prospect Hill.* Lynchburg, Va.: H. E. Howard, 1993.

Pearson, Henry G. *James S. Wadsworth of Geneseo.* New York: Charles Scribner's Sons, 1913.

Pennsylvania at Gettysburg. 2 vols. Harrisburg: William Stanley Ray, 1904.

Pennypacker, Isaac R. *General Meade.* New York: D. Appleton, 1901.

Pfisterer, Frederick. *New York in the War of the Rebellion.* 5 vols. Albany: J. B. Lyon, 1912.

Poore, Benjamin P. *The Life and Public Services of Ambrose E. Burnside: Soldier, Citizen, Statesman.* Providence: J. A. and R. A. Reid, 1882.

Preston, David L. "The Glorious Light Went Out Forever: The Death of Brig. Gen. Thomas R. R. Cobb." *Civil War Regiments* 4, no. 4 (1995).

Rable, George C. "It Is Well That War Is So Terrible: The Carnage at Fredericksburg." In *The Fredericksburg Campaign: Decision on the Rappahannock,* ed. Gary W. Gallagher. Chapel Hill: University of North Carolina Press, 1995.

Ray, Frederic E. *"Our Special Artist": Alfred R. Waud's Civil War.* Mechanicsburg: Stackpole Books, 1994.

Reardon, Carol. "The Forlorn Hope: Brig. Gen. Andrew A. Humphreys's Pennsylvania Division at Fredericksburg." In *The Fredericksburg Campaign: Decision on the Rappahannock,* ed. Gary W. Gallagher. Chapel Hill: University of North Carolina Press, 1995.

Reese, Timothy J. *Sykes' Regular Infantry Division, 1861–1864.* Jefferson, N.C.: McFarland, 1990.

Richardson, Albert D. *The Secret Service: The Field, the Dungeon, and the Escape.* Hartford: American Publishing Co., 1865.

Ripley, Warren. *Artillery and Ammunition of the Civil War.* Charleston, S.C.: Battery Press, 1984.

Robertson, James I., Jr. *General A. P. Hill: the Story of a Confederate Warrior.* New York: Random House, 1987.

————. *"Stonewall" Jackson: The Man, the Soldier, the Legend.* New York: Macmillan, 1997.

Ropes, John C. *The Story of the Civil War.* 2 vols. New York: G. P. Putnam's Sons, 1894–1898.

Sears, Stephen W. *George B. McClellan: The Young Napoleon.* New York: Ticknor and Fields, 1988.

————. *Landscape Turned Red: The Battle of Antietam.* New Haven: Ticknor and Fields, 1983.

Simpson, Harold B. *Hood's Texas Brigade: Lee's Grenadier Guard.* Waco: Texian Press, 1970.

————. *Gaines' Mill to Appomattox.* Waco: Texian Press, 1963.

Slocum, Charles Elihu. *Life and Services of General Major-General Henry Warner Slocum.* Toledo: Slocum, 1913.

Stackhouse, William R. and Walter F. Stackhouse. *The Stackhouse Family.* Morehead City, N.C.: Stackhouse Foundation, 1993.

Stegeman, John F. *These Men She Gave: Civil War Diary of Athens, Georgia.* Athens: University of Georgia Press, 1964.

Thomas, Emory. *Bold Dragoon: the Life of J. E. B. Stuart.* New York: Harper and Row, 1986.

Thomason, John W. *J. E. B. Stuart.* New York: Charles Scribner's Sons, 1930.

Tucker, Glenn. *Hancock the Superb.* Indianapolis: Bobbs-Merrill, 1960.

Warner, Ezra. *Generals in Blue*. Baton Rouge: Louisiana State University Press, 1964.

———. *Generals in Gray*. Baton Rouge: Louisiana State University Press, 1959.

Whan, Vorin E. *Fiasco at Fredericksburg*. State College: Pennsylvania State University Press, 1961.

White, Henry A. *Robert E. Lee and the Southern Confederacy*. New York: G. P. Putnam's Sons, 1898.

Whitman, William E. S., and Charles H. True. *Maine in the War for the Union*. Lewiston: Nelson Dingley Jr., 1865.

Wiley, Bell I. *The Life of Johnny Reb*. Baton Rouge: Louisiana State University Press, 1943.

Wise, Jennings Cropper. *The Long Arm of Lee*. 2 vols. Lynchburg, Va.: J. P. Bell, 1915.

Wyckoff, Mac. *History of the Second South Carolina Infantry*. Fredericksburg, Va.: Sgt. Kirkland's Museum and Historical Society, 1994.

Wynne, Elizabeth M. A. *Geneologies and Traditions*. Indiana, Pa., 1931.

Young, William A., Jr., and Patricia C. Young. *Fifty-sixth Virginia Infantry*. Lynchburg, Va.: H. E. Howard, 1990.

INDEX